The Ultimate Book Of

QUILTING

CROSS STITCH & NEEDLECRAFT

The Ultimate Book Of QUILTING CROSS STITCH & NEEDLECRAFT

A complete practical and inspirational guide to traditional and contemporary handiwork techniques with over 200 step-by-step projects and 1500 photographs

Lucinda Ganderton
and
Dorothy Wood

HERMES HOUSE

This edition is published by Hermes House

Hermes House is an imprint of Anness Publishing Ltd
Hermes House, 88–89 Blackfriars Road, London SE1 8HA
tel. 020 7401 2077; fax 020 7633 9499; info@anness.com

A CIP catalogue record for this book is available from the British Library.

Publisher: Joanna Lorenz
Project Editors: Judith Simons and Belinda Wilkinson
Photographers: James Duncan and Gloria Nicol
Step Photographers: Madeleine Brehaut and Lucy Tizard
Designers: Martin Lovelock and Louise Morley
Illustrator: Lucinda Ganderton

Previously published in three separate volumes,
A Stitch in Time, *Cross Stitch: Techniques & Designs*
and *The Practical Encyclopedia of Quilting & Quilt Design*

1 3 5 7 9 10 8 6 4 2

CONTENTS

Introduction

Traditional needlecrafts form an essential part of our lives and have been carried on throughout the world since ancient times in their many forms. For hundreds of years, sewing skills were a necessary part of running a household: making and mending the family linen. Today needlecrafts offer an escape from the uniformity of shop-bought products. A basic grasp of handiwork skills enables us to personalize clothing, create original gifts for friends and family, or stitch soft furnishings to make our homes more distinctive and individual. The recent development of materials such as water-soluble fabrics, metallic threads and iron-on fusible bondings means that many tasks have been simplified, and exciting new effects can be achieved. This book shows you how to exploit modern techniques while remaining true to tradition, and serves as a comprehensive introduction to a wide range of fascinating crafts.

Embroidery

Embroidery, or the use of decorative stitchery, is an ancient craft which can be reinterpreted in a highly personal style today. The possibilities for combining threads and stitches are endless, and almost any fabric or garment can be embroidered either by hand or machine. This section introduces the basic techniques, and the exciting projects include original accessories for the home and items to wear, to keep or to give as presents.

Embroidery
Tools and Materials

An inspiring selection of fabrics and threads is available which, with imagination, can be combined to produce individual and exciting embroideries. The basic equipment needed is minimal: every sewing box should contain the tools listed, along with pins and sewing thread. A steam iron is necessary for all needlecrafts, to finish work professionally.

From top to bottom, three types of even-weave linen, and one non even-weave linen.

THREADS

Threads come in a broad spectrum of colours. Silk and metallic threads give texture, but the most popular threads are 6-stranded cottons which can be separated for fine stitching. Perlé cotton is a single thread with a shiny finish. Wool threads, including finely spun crewel yarn and 3-stranded Persian yarn, are used singly for embroidery. Machine threads can be glossy or metallic, and some are even space-dyed with stripes.

From left to right, woven Aida bands with decorative edging in blue and red, and natural linen.

FABRIC

Ordinary linens are used for free stitchery but single-thread even-weave linens have a regular mesh so that the stitches are even. They are designed for counted thread and pulled or drawn work. There are several types of double-thread even-weaves. The finest is Hardanger fabric which has a count of 22, i.e., there are 22 threads to 2.5cm (1in). 14-count Aida cloth is suitable for cross stitch and 6-count Binca is ideal for beginners. Narrow bands of fabric with woven edges are also available.

FRAMES

Adjustable tapestry or scroll frames are best for large pieces, while hoops suit most other work. They can be bought with stands so that the user's hands are left free to work the piece. Round plastic frames with metal inner rings are especially good for machine embroidery.

From top to bottom, Hardanger fabric, Aida cloth in white and green, Binca.

TOOLS AND ACCESSORIES

Needles come in different widths and lengths, the most useful being large-eyed crewel needles. Tapestry needles are thick and blunt, while chenille needles are larger but pointed.

Long-bladed dressmaker's shears are essential for cutting fabric and a small pair of sharp embroidery scissors is needed for threads. An unpicker is always very useful for correcting mistakes and a thimble protects the finger.

Water-soluble or fading dressmaker's felt-tip pens are used to mark directly on to fabric. Carbon pencils and dressmaker's carbon will transfer designs from paper to cloth.

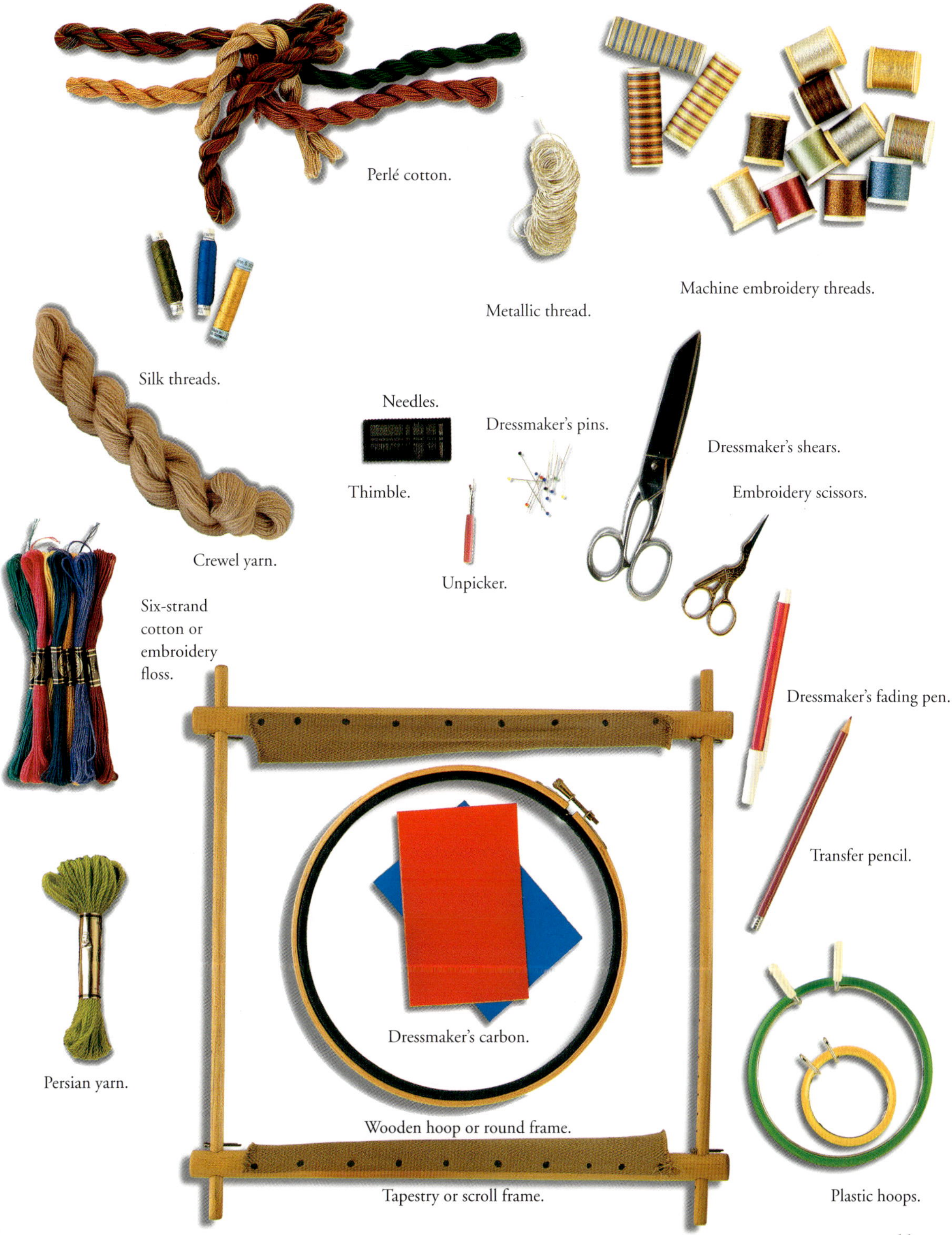

Perlé cotton.

Metallic thread.

Machine embroidery threads.

Silk threads.

Crewel yarn.

Needles.

Thimble.

Dressmaker's pins.

Unpicker.

Dressmaker's shears.

Embroidery scissors.

Six-strand cotton or embroidery floss.

Dressmaker's fading pen.

Transfer pencil.

Persian yarn.

Dressmaker's carbon.

Wooden hoop or round frame.

Tapestry or scroll frame.

Plastic hoops.

Starting Off

Most embroidery should be worked in a frame to allow an even stitch tension and to prevent the fabric becoming distorted. A tapestry frame is suitable for larger pieces of work but for small hand-stitched projects and all machine embroidery, a two-part hoop frame is used. To keep delicate fabrics taut, the inner ring can be bound with bias binding.

Right: Hoop frames are easy to manage and portable, and can be used for working larger pieces by changing the position when each area is completed, although this may cause distortion to finer embroidery.

1 USING A FRAME To mount the cloth in the hoop, loosen the screw on the outer ring and separate the two parts. Place the fabric over the inner ring and press the outer ring down in place.

2 Stretch the fabric so that it is taut. Be sure that the weave lies squarely as shown. Tighten the screw. For machine embroidery the fabric should be right side up with the stitching area at the bottom of the hoop.

1 BEGINNING TO STITCH Working threads should not be longer than 45cm (18in) or they will fray and become tangled. The needle selected should always be the right size for the thread and fabric; a small eye can harm the thread, while a thick needle will leave large holes. Threads have a natural tendency to twist back on themselves; if this happens, let the needle and thread hang down and untwist. It is not advisable to anchor the thread with a knot at the back as it may distort the surface. Instead, when starting the first stitches of a piece, make a knot and insert the needle from the front, a short distance away from the area to be worked, so that the thread will be held fast at the back by the stitching. The knot can then be snipped off.

2 Subsequent threads can be started off by slipping the needle under the back of the existing stitches and working a back stitch. Finish off in the same way, and trim the loose ends.

Transferring and Charting

Patterns can be transferred on to a background in several ways; the choice depends on the nature of the design itself as well as the fabric and thread to be used. It is important that any lines marked should not show through the stitches; dressmaker's pens are now available which are either water-soluble or which fade completely over time. These are particularly suitable for fine freehand drawing or tracing directly on to the fabric via a light box. A chalk pencil can be used for bolder designs. Dressmaker's carbon paper is also used for indirect tracing and is best for smooth fabrics.

Right: The strawberry motif makes a perfect decoration for this ready-made lacy jam-pot cover.

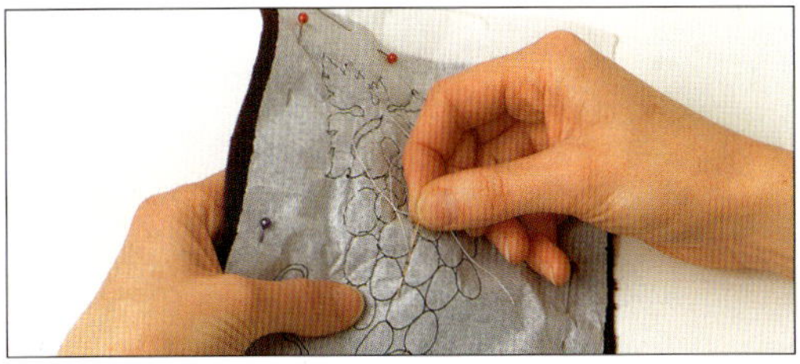

1 TISSUE TACKING (BASTING) This is used for textured materials such as velvet, where a drawn line would not show. Trace the design on to tissue paper then pin to the right side of the fabric. With a contrasting thread, work over the design using a small running stitch.

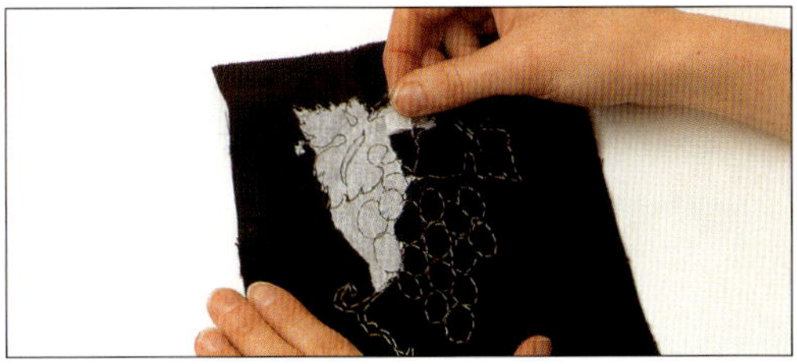

2 When complete, carefully tear away the tissue paper without pulling the thread. The embroidery is then worked over this guideline and any tacking (basting) which remains can be cut away.

TRANSFER PENCIL Using an embroidery transfer pencil and thin paper, trace the design. If the pattern is symmetrical or needs to be reversed, place the paper, with the pencil side down, on to the fabric, pin in place and press with a cool iron. For an outline which is the same as the original, trace it with a pencil, turn the paper and draw over the lines with the transfer pencil.

CROSS STITCH CHARTS The regular format of cross stitch makes it ideal for charting designs on to graph paper, where one square represents one stitch. Trace the design on to special tracing paper printed with a grid, as shown, or transfer it on to squared paper. Fill in the outline with coloured pens or pencils, to match the colours to be used.

Straight Stitches

There is an enormous variety of traditional stitches which provide the foundation for hand embroidery and sewing throughout the world. Some may be intricately textured or interwoven with precious gold thread; others use a simple row of stranded cotton to outline a design, or form twisted knots to make a single point of colour. All of them, however, are derived from three basic ways of working: straight, looped or knotted stitches. A wide range of textures and effects can be achieved just by using simple variations of flat, straight stitches. They can be worked in rows, at different angles and in varying sizes or combined to produce geometric shapes.

Right: These satin stitch butterflies were stitched with shiny silk thread on this piece of antique Chinese embroidery.

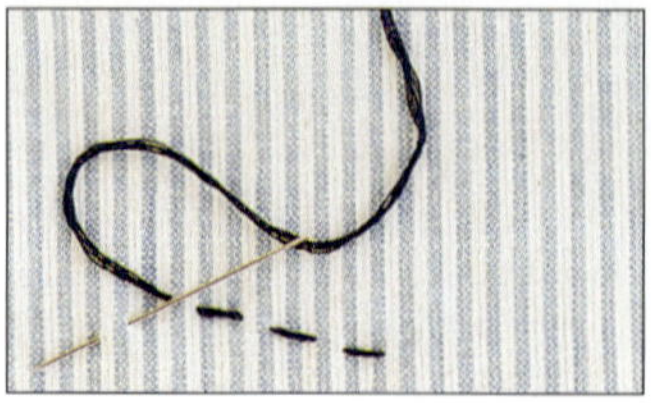

RUNNING STITCH This is the most basic of stitches, and is used to join pieces of fabric, outline motifs and for quilting. The stitches should all be equal in length and evenly spaced. A long running stitch is used for tacking (basting).

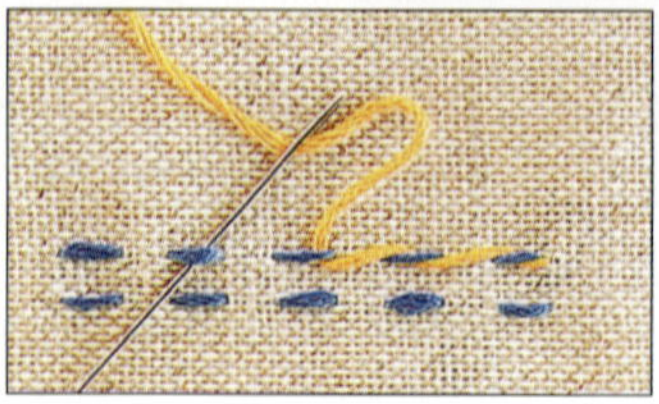

WHIP STITCH A contrasting thread is woven through a basic line of running stitch to give a twisted effect to this stitch. Be careful not to pick up any of the background fabric.

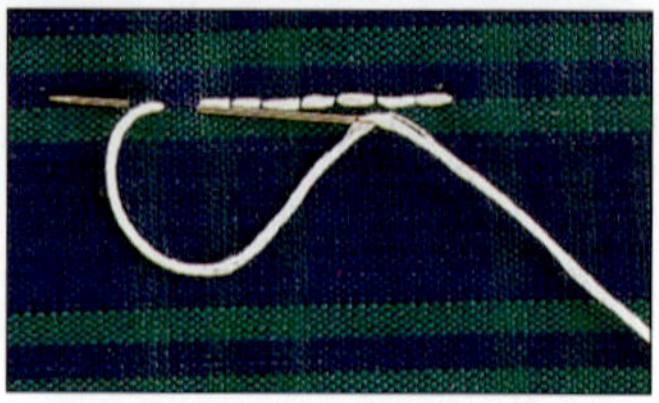

BACK STITCH This consists of a continuous line of even stitches. The needle is carried behind the work for twice the length of the finished stitch. It is used for outlines, especially in Assisi or blackwork.

STEM STITCH Also known as crewel stitch, this is similar to back stitch. The thread should always lie to one side of the needle. The width can be altered by varying the stitch angle.

SEED STITCH Short detached stitches, all measuring the same length, are worked at random to produce a powdered filling, or to add pattern to a plain area. As a variation, two parallel stitches can be worked to give a more raised surface.

SATIN STITCH It may take some practice to achieve the distinctive smooth finish and tidy edge of this versatile stitch. The individual stitches, which should not be too long, are all worked in the same direction.

The main shape of this "naive" fish is outlined in back stitch, with an irregular running stitch infill. Its strong graphic impact comes from the use of white thread on a dark fabric.

ARROWHEAD STITCH Two equal straight stitches at right angles form the arrow points, which can be evenly spaced in regular rows or worked as random individual stitches to give a scattered filling over a larger area.

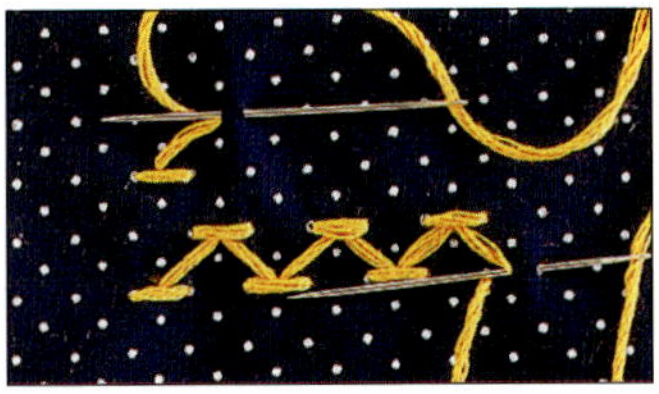

CHEVRON STITCH This looks particularly effective when worked on striped or spotted fabric. It is made up of a line of straight stitches worked at right angles to each other with a short back stitch at the intersection point.

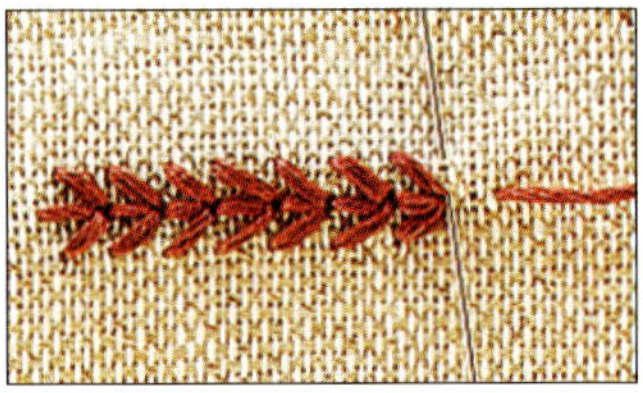

FERN STITCH This gives a leafy effect, which is ideal for plant designs. It is made up of three small stitches radiating from a point, and can be worked in straight or curved lines, or detached as a filling stitch.

This Indian bird is worked entirely in straight stitches and uses coloured cottons on a natural linen background. It is framed by a triple row of interlaced running stitch.

Cross Stitches

A basic cross stitch is formed by working one straight stitch across another. There are several variations where the angle of the cross is altered or the stitches overlap, and all can be worked in rows or singly. The regular pattern produced by all these stitches is ideally suited for embroidering on ginghams, striped fabrics or even-weave linen. Cross stitch is the foundation for the traditional embroidery of many cultures, from ancient Egyptian textiles to the geometric designs of modern Scandinavian work.

In the past, children learnt to sew by practising cross stitch samplers, and today a wide range of charted designs is available.

Narrow strips of even-weave fabric with decorative borders can be bought by length and are ideal for making small gift items such as bookmarks, decorative cake-ribbons or these monogrammed napkin rings.

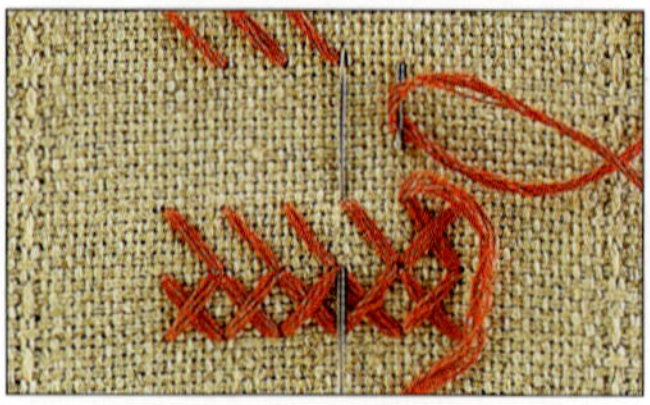

CROSS STITCH This stitch can be worked individually for outlines and letters, but is usually made in two separate rows, as shown, when a larger area has to be covered. The second line of stitches should always lie in the same direction for an even appearance.

HERRINGBONE STITCH This is often used to form a border around work and is particularly effective when stitched between two lines on a striped fabric. It is worked from left to right with an even space between the overlapping arms.

LACED HERRINGBONE STITCH Extra interest can be added to plain herringbone stitch by interlacing it with a contrasting colour. A blunt needle is used to prevent any of the foundation fabric getting caught up, and the thread should not be pulled too tightly.

CLOSED HERRINGBONE STITCH This is worked as for herringbone but the space between the stitches is closed up. It is sometimes sewn on the reverse of a fine fabric so that the front gives the appearance of two lines of back stitch and the diagonal stitches are visible through the cloth. This technique is known as "shadow work".

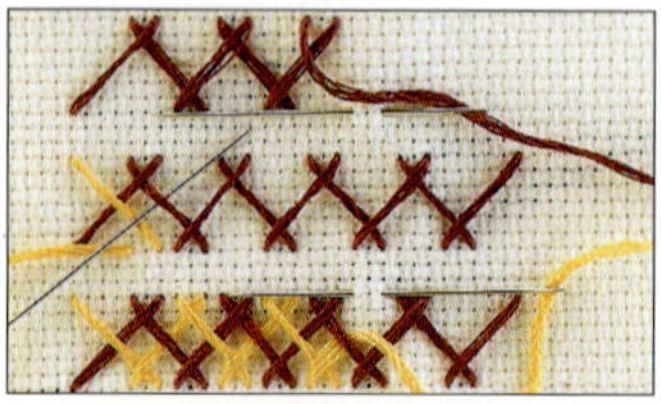

DOUBLE HERRINGBONE STITCH To produce an interlaced effect, the needle is passed down and below the upward stitches on the first row, so that they all lie above the downward stitches. The second row uses a contrasting colour, and is worked in the same way, with the upward stitches threaded under the downward stitches of the first row.

LONGARM CROSS STITCH This overlapping stitch produces a dense, braided finish and is useful for heavy outlines. It is worked from left to right, with a longer and more slanted second arm and the diagonals meet at the top and bottom.

DOUBLE CROSS STITCH This star-shaped stitch can be worked individually or in lines. It is made up of two simple cross stitches worked one over the other.

ERMINE FILLING An upright straight stitch is overlapped with a single cross stitch to produce a six-pointed star, which can be repeated at random or in regular rows for a more formal effect.

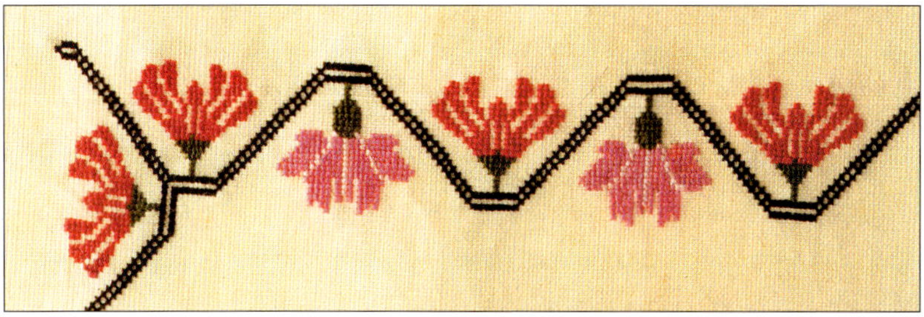

Left: The cross stitch samplers of the nineteenth century were embroidered with alphabets, mottoes and pictorial motifs. This typical carnation border is a combination of both geometric and floral elements.

Right: This lavender sachet is made from Aida cloth, a woven fabric which is produced especially for cross stitch work. It is easy to use, as there is no need for complicated thread counting, and is available in a range of sizes and colours.

Assisi Work

This historic variation originated in the Italian town of Assisi. It reverses the usual method of working cross stitch patterns – with striking results. The main motifs are first outlined with a single line and the background filled in with solid rows of cross stitch. The stylized imagery is based on birds, fish and animals – both real and mythical – along with geometric and floral motifs. It underwent a revival in the early 1900s, when the old patterns were redrawn. It is traditionally worked on cream or white even-weave linen, using a combination of red, blue and black embroidery threads.

Right: This heraldic dragon is worked in black against red and edged with a Greek key pattern. Single stitches emphasize the claws and the eye is marked with a detached cross stitch.

On a much smaller scale, these two ducks (above) were adapted from a pattern card, published in the early twentieth century when there was a great renewal of interest in Assisi work.

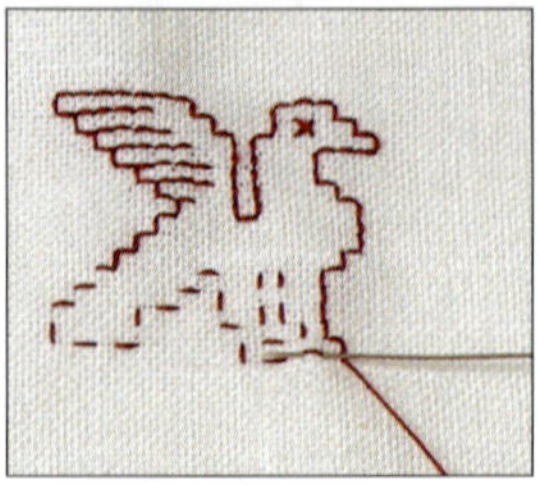

1 Work the motif and border with Holbein stitch, which resembles back stitch. This is sewn as two rounds of running stitch, the second row filling the spaces left between the first.

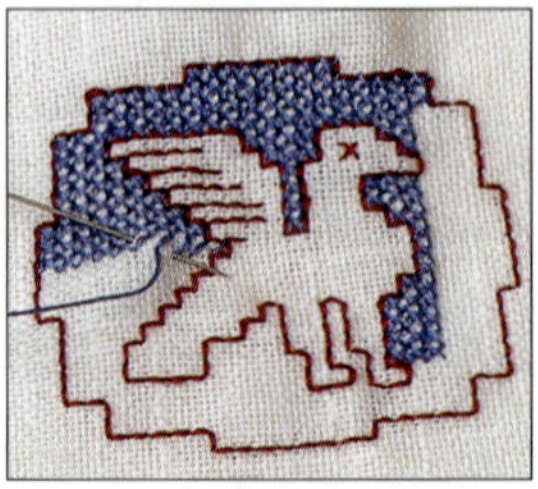

2 The background is completely filled with cross stitch, in a bright primary colour. The stitches can be worked singly, or, as is usual with this technique, back and forth in rows.

3 The elaborate linear border is worked in Holbein stitch, using the main colour again.

Blackwork

Blackwork uses straight and back stitches to create small-scale all-over patterns. This distinctive embroidery became popular in sixteenth-century England, when it was used to decorate caps, gloves, sleeves and bodices. Design at that time was naturalistic; the geometric repeats of blackwork were worked to fill in the flowing outlines of flower petals, leaves and fruit. It is traditionally done using stranded cotton on even-weave linen, but Aida cloth provides a quicker alternative.

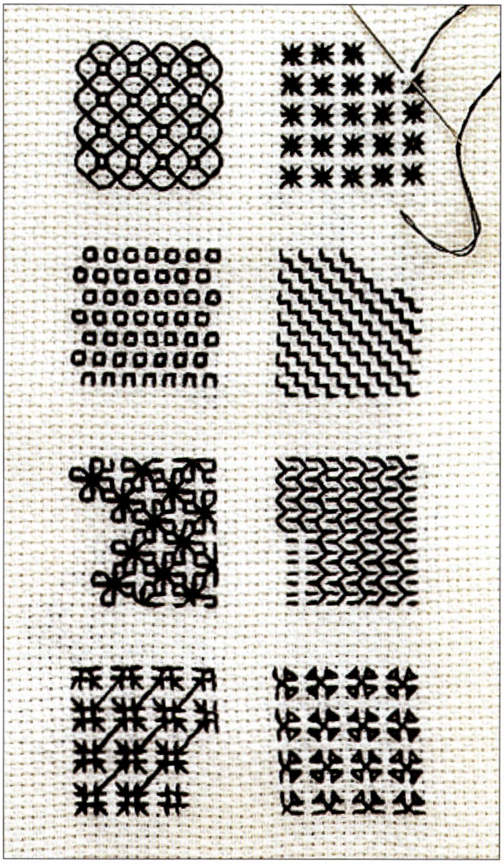

Right: Different patterns all have their own tonal value, ranging from dark to light, depending on how the stitches are arranged. This sampler features some old and new variations (clockwise from top right): *Algerian eye stitch* consists of eight straight stitches radiating from a central point; *Zigzag stitch* is worked in diagonal rows of stepped back stitch; *Fishscale stitch* is built up in rows of short straight stitches, linked with a zigzag; *Shoofly stitch* consists of four triangles arranged at the points of a cross stitch; *Grid stitch* consists of separate motifs, which may be joined with diagonal back stitches; *Pinwheel stitch* is worked in back stitch as a series of individual shapes; *Square stitch*, a half-drop repeat, can be made singly or by working rows of running stitch; and *Lattice stitch* is a deceptively simple pattern of interlocking diamonds and squares.

There is an infinite array of geometric patterns that can be used for blackwork (above). Any tiny shape can be adapted by charting it on to graph paper and working out a repeat. The border of a fragment of broken pottery was the inspiration for this series of single motifs and all-over fillings.

The symmetry of blackwork means that the most basic computer graphics package can be used to produce suitable patterns. This computer-designed example (left) has the appearance of a piece of very traditional work, but is, in fact, a marriage of old and new.

Looped and Knotted Stitches

Instead of simply sewing in and out of the background as for the previous stitches, the stitches in this group are all formed by looping the thread and holding it down on the surface, either with further stitches, or by passing the needle through the thread to form a knot. Variations range from functional blanket stitch to the raised textures of bullion and French knots. Chain and feather stitches can be worked quickly and produce a decorative effect, which is popular for "crazy" patchwork. It is important that all of these stitches are worked with an even tension and that the loops are not pulled tightly.

Above: This Indian marriage cloth is embroidered with a variety of stitches, which includes rows of closely worked chain stitch to define squares and chevrons.

CHAIN STITCHES

Chain stitch Pass the needle down and under the fabric for the correct length and pull through, keeping the thread tucked below the point. Work the next stitch through the loop, into the hole where the thread emerged.

Threaded chain stitch A row of evenly spaced detached chain stitches forms the foundation for this double link chain. Each one is secured below the loop with a small stitch. A contrasting thread is threaded under the loops in each direction.

Lazy daisy stitch Single chain stitches are sewn in the round to form this popular flower shape. Each flower should be arranged evenly in a circle and worked from the centre out. Further single stitches can be used to make leaves.

Blanket stitch This can be worked as an edging or surface stitch, or closely together for buttonholes. It is worked from left to right, in a row of regular upright stitches, with the thread always passing under the needle.

Feather stitch This is worked from top to bottom as a series of alternate slanting stitches. Again, the thread always lies under the needle to form the characteristic loops. It is often used in conjunction with smocking.

Double feather stitch This border stitch is an elaboration of the basic feather stitch. Two stitches, instead of one, are made to one side and then to the other. It can be varied by changing the angle.

Knotted stitches *French knot* Bring the needle out and hold the thread taut. Wrap it twice round the needle and tighten the thread. Push the needle back through the fabric, close to the point from which it emerged.

Bullion knot The method is similar to the French knot. Start off with a back stitch of the required length. Wrap the thread round several times and hold it down as the needle is pulled carefully through the loops and inserted back at the start.

Coral stitch This attractive outline can be worked regularly or so that the knots are spaced at random. Pass the needle through a small amount of fabric at an angle, looping the thread over the needle and pulling through to form a knot.

Whitework

1 With a dressmaker's pen or soft pencil, draw round the leaf on to the background fabric.

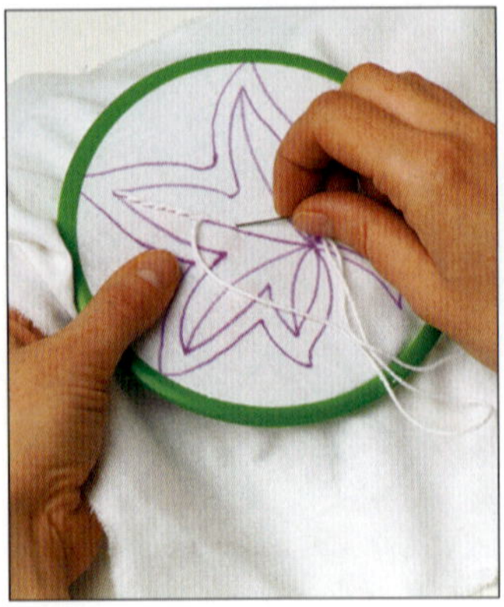

2 Thread a large-eyed needle with crochet cotton and work the veins in stem or back stitch.

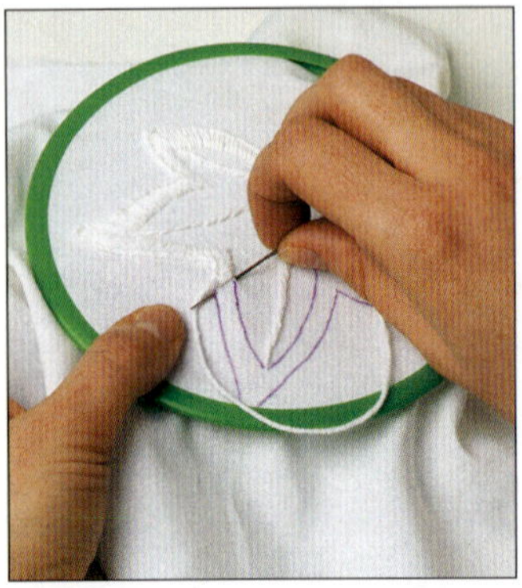

3 Work a closely stitched border of satin or blanket stitch around the outline, and pick out the stalk in stem stitch.

Whitework is a generic term for the many types of white-on-white embroidery, unlike blackwork which describes a single, specialized technique. It is most often used on household linens: tray or tablecloths, pillow covers, nightdress cases, lingerie and handkerchiefs. Variations include the delicate floral Scottish Ayrshire Work, the traditional decoration for christening gowns, Norwegian Hardanger stitchery and the open lace work of *broderie anglaise* (eyelet lace). Mountmellick work is the Irish version of whitework, named after the town in which it was first developed. It is worked in a variety of raised and textured stitches, using a matt (non-shiny) crochet-type thread on a cotton drill (twill) background. Like much other whitework, it draws on the natural imagery of plants, fruit and flowers, but interprets it in a bold, graphic style. It was used to make articles that varied in scale from babies' bibs and collars to bedspreads. Special pattern books and transfers were also produced. A contemporary and personal interpretation is to collect interestingly shaped leaves – from the garden or from a country walk – to use as templates.

This *broderie anglaise* (eyelet lace) sprig was worked by outlining the petals with a narrow satin stitch, then cutting away the surplus fabric to form the distinctive eyelets.

Right: A delicate handkerchief was once an essential accessory; this lace-edged antique example is densely embroidered with the owner's initials and a deep border. It is stitched in cotton on a fine lawn ground.

Pulled and Drawn Thread Work

These two techniques are used to create delicate lace-like effects on fine, even-weave fabrics. They have long been classified as whitework, but they can look very dramatic if done in coloured threads or on a patterned fabric. In pulled work the stitches are worked tightly so that the threads of the fabric are forced apart to create a pattern, whereas in drawn thread work threads are removed from the foundation fabric for a more open look.

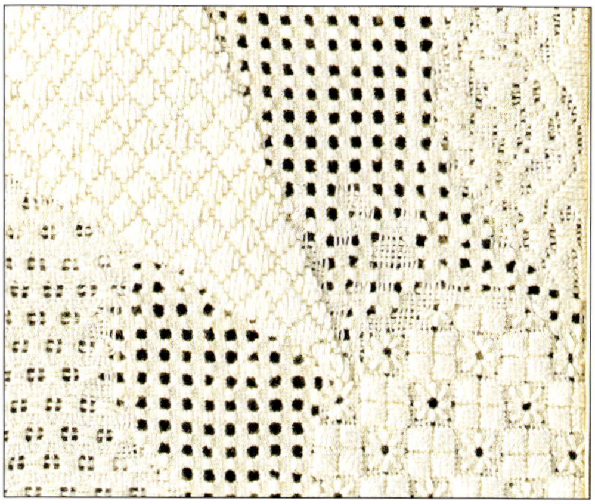

Right: Interesting areas of texture can be produced by experimenting with the many pulled thread stitches, as in this abstract sampler.

1 PULLED THREAD STITCHES
Algerian eye stitch This open eyelet is formed by working 16 straight stitches, radiating from a central point. It can be worked singly or in rows.

2 *Honeycomb darning* This regular open background stitch is worked over three threads, in rows from right to left, then left to right.

3 *Single faggot stitch* This filling stitch is worked in stepped diagonal rows, which build up to form a grid.

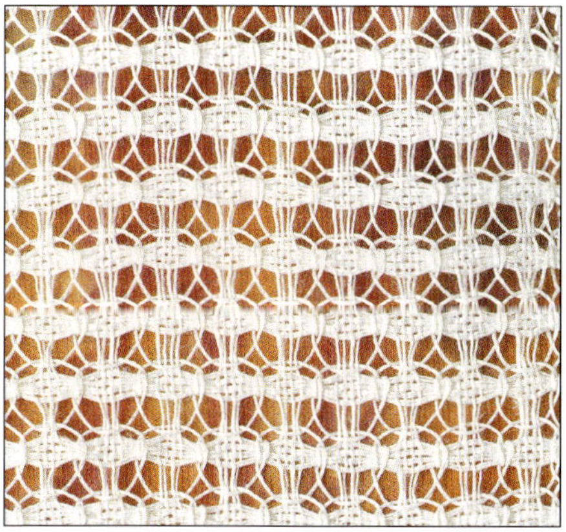

Above: Beautiful all-over patterns can be produced by working in white thread on white linen. The intricacy of this design is emphasized by a backing of hand-dyed silk.

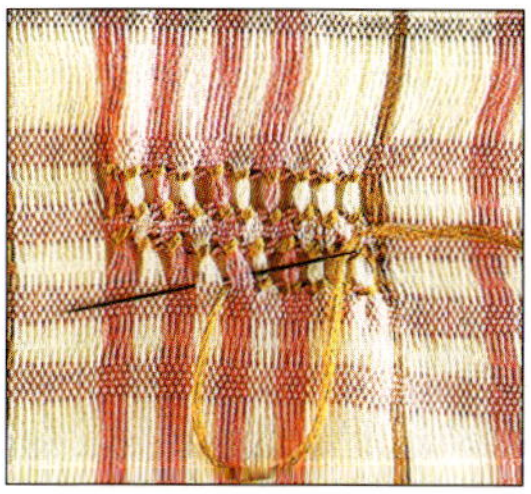

1 DRAWN THREAD STITCHES
Ladder stitch These simple examples are worked on loosely woven checked linen, from which bands of thread were removed. Back stitch is used to pull the remaining threads into clusters.

2 *Corded clusters* Solid clusters are made by binding the embroidery thread tightly around groups of foundation threads.

Couching and Laid Thread Work

Couching and laid thread work are two closely related techniques which have been used for centuries when embroidering with textured, silk floss and metallic threads, or narrow cords and ribbons that cannot be drawn through the background fabric. Instead, these threads are attached to the surface with tiny straight or ornamental stitches worked in a finer thread. Couching is a fast and effective way to define curves, outlines and decorative spirals, while laid thread work is generally used to fill motifs and to cover backgrounds. An embroidery frame should always be used for these techniques, to prevent the stitches from puckering. Neither thread should be pulled too tightly or the shapes will distort.

Above: The motifs of this panel are worked in several filling stitches, and show the depth and texture that can be created.

COUCHING *Plain couching* Place the thread to be couched in the position required on the fabric. Make small detached stitches at regular intervals to anchor it down, in a contrasting thread. Tidy the piece by drawing the loose ends to the back of the fabric.

Decorative couching Embroidery stitches such as cross stitch or blanket stitch can be used to secure the laid thread for a more decorative effect. Here square chain stitch is worked through the fabric, across several strands of cotton.

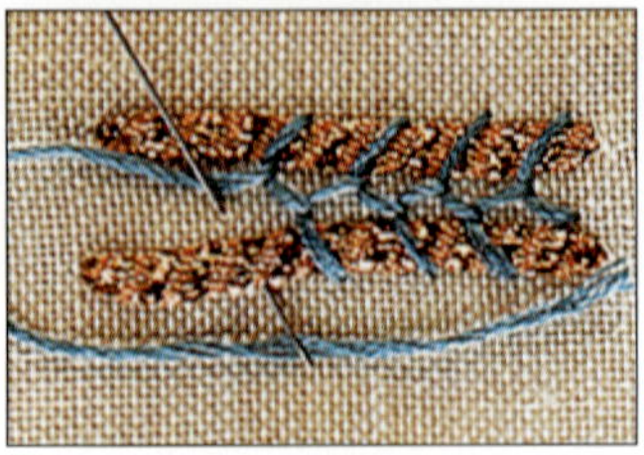

Double couching Two parallel lines of broad metallic thread are held down by a row of feather stitch, with half of the feather stitch being worked over each line of metallic thread.

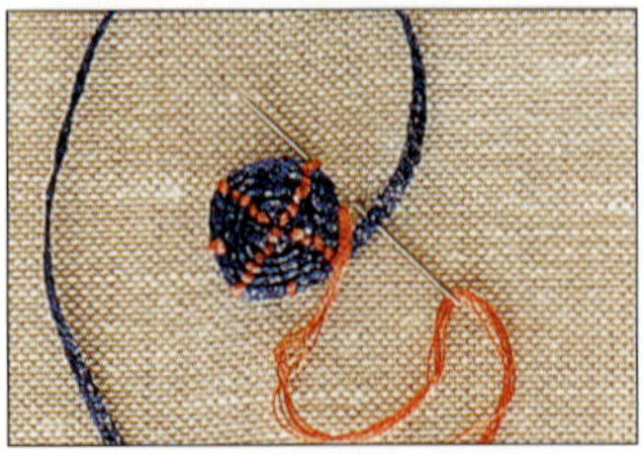

Spiral couching To fill a circle, bring both threads up in the centre of the circle. Coil the thread to be couched in a spiral, and couch down with the other thread at regular intervals to form a spoked pattern.

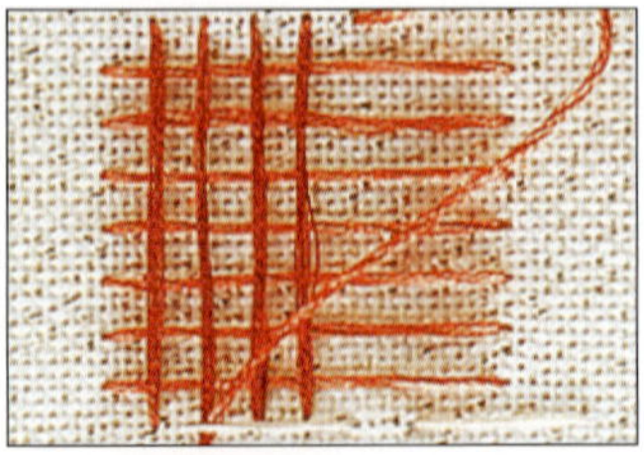

1 LAID WORK *Lattice work* Large areas or individual shapes can be covered with this filling stitch. The basic lattice is made by working rows of long parallel stitches, both horizontally and vertically, to form a regular grid.

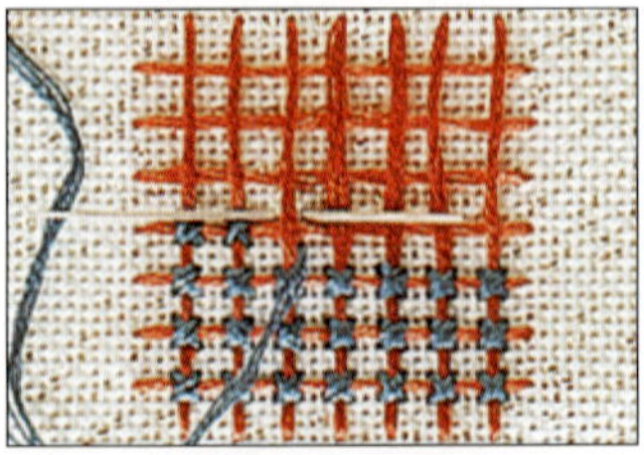

2 Small contrasting stitches are worked over each thread intersection to secure the long threads to the background and to decorate the grid. Further patterning can be added by working extra stitches within the squares.

Left: This jewel-like patchwork has been assembled from fragments of antique gold and mirror work from northern India. A variety of couching techniques has been used to create the geometric patterns.

Right: Contrasting couched threads have been used to emphasize the outline of these simple animal figures, and to disguise the edges of the appliquéd shapes.

Above: These luxurious and innovative samples use a range of couched techniques, including a spiral of silver wire which is held in place with almost invisible stitches.

Machine Embroidery

Machine embroidery is innovative, quick to work and growing in popularity. Sewing machines have always been used to produce decorative effects, as well as for plain stitching, but the swing-needle machine has great potential as a creative tool. The latest generation of electronic machines is increasingly sophisticated and comes complete with pre-programmed patterns, alphabets and even the capability of scanning in designs. Despite this, exciting effects can still be achieved with the simple straight and zigzag stitches of the standard domestic machine. The instruction manual will have details of any special embroidery feet or attachments which have been supplied and it should be consulted for information about basic stitching methods. Starting to work in this unfamiliar way may seem a little daunting at first, so take time to become familiar with how the machine works and don't be afraid to experiment. Always stitch at the slowest speed and do not race the machine.

The background and main blocks of plain colour in these amusing illustrations have been filled in with multi-directional satin stitch in varying widths, with the fine details worked in straight stitch.

FREE STITCHING

For normal use the machine stitch is controlled by the "feed dog" which produces an even stitch by regulating the pace at which the fabric goes under the presser foot. If this is lowered or covered (depending on the machine model – check the manual for details of how to do this) the stitch can be controlled by moving the fabric in the desired direction.

SATIN STITCH The fabric should be kept taut in a frame, and held lightly with both hands. Thread the machine as normal and set the controls to zigzag. Apply gentle pressure to the pedal and move the frame slowly forwards so that a close satin stitch is built up. The width can be varied by adjusting the controls.

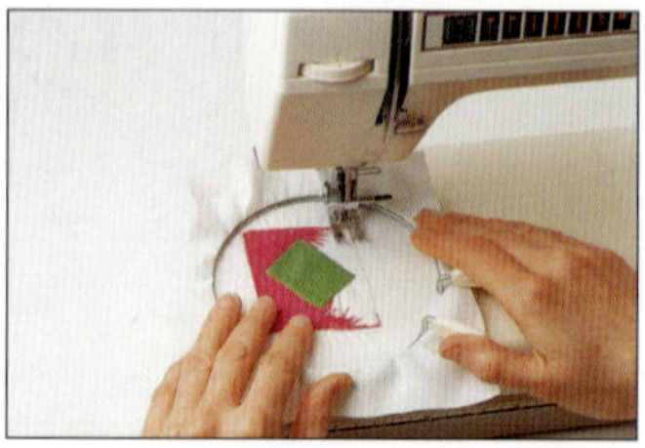

1 STRAIGHT STITCH Lines of straight stitch can be worked in exactly the same way as satin stitch, and if they are made in different directions, interesting textures can be created. The frame can be moved from side to side or back and forth.

2 With practice and experiment, curved and wavy lines can be easily achieved. These are best sewn at a gentle speed so that the background can be manipulated below the presser foot.

Machine embroidery need not be limited to the usual fabrics; the baroque picture frames which surround these batik figures are made from dyed heavyweight interfacing.

Layers of straight stitch can be built up to create a great depth of colour and interest within a piece of work, as in these dynamic portraits of African women.

Once the basic methods have been mastered, machine embroidery can become a very flexible way of "drawing"; this notebook contains a series of experimental images which include more advanced techniques such as changing the tension of either the top or bobbin threads to produce irregular, looped stitches.

Working on a Painted Background

Machine embroidery can be used to produce a free outline, which is as flexible as a hand-drawn line. Straight stitch is particularly useful for adding detail to and defining a design, which may be painted on material with fabric paints or with watercolours, gouache or acrylics on to paper.

Right: The colours and shapes of a pineapple inspired this lively tropical design. The yellow stars are given an added dynamism by the diamond shapes that surround them.

1 Choose a design which has clear areas of colour and a strong outline and paint it on to heavy paper; watercolour paper is ideal. Mount the design onto a second, slightly larger, piece of paper for extra support.

2 Thread the machine with black cotton and stitch slowly around the outlines. These can be emphasized by working twice over some areas.

3 Fill in various blocks of colour with a free zigzag stitch, using a thread that is a shade darker than the painted background to give a feeling of depth.

Left: This linen placemat was made in the 1950s, at the time when machine embroidery was first being explored as an art form. It is worked in straight stitch on a screen-printed background.

Working with Paper

Paper can be used like fabric as a background for machine embroidery, but it can also be put to many other uses. It can be painted, torn or cut into shapes and interwoven with ribbons to create interesting multi-layered and collage effects. Be sure that the stitch tension is not too tight when working on paper as it can easily tear.

Above: For this colourful example, bright lines of straight stitch have been sewn to run parallel with the weave. These contrast with the floral motifs sewn on to the surface.

Above: This illustration was made by gluing torn paper shapes on to a plain background, then "drawing" on the black lines in free straight stitch.

1 Woven paper with ribbons Find some gift ribbons and paint cartridge paper with bands of colour to match. Cut into narrow strips and arrange horizontally with the ribbons on the backing paper. Fix with masking tape along one side and interweave the vertical pieces.

2 When the work is the desired size, tape the edges to hold the paper and ribbons in place for stitching.

3 Stitch through the backing, the woven strips and ribbon around the outer edge, then free stitch over the surface in a variety of colours.

Machine Lace

Machine lace fabrics are constructed by building up a network of interlocking stitches on a specially produced background material, which is then removed to leave an open web of thread. This is done by applying heat or by dissolving it in water. There are three different fabrics available, each with special qualities. The working method is the same for all three, however: the rows of stitching must always intersect and cross each other so that the finished piece retains its shape. For extra flexibility in stitching, the presser foot can be taken off. This means that the fabric can be moved in a freer way. It is worth taking time to become familiar with this way of working, by practising on a frame stretched with fine cotton. The hoop must always be held at the outer rim to avoid accidents.

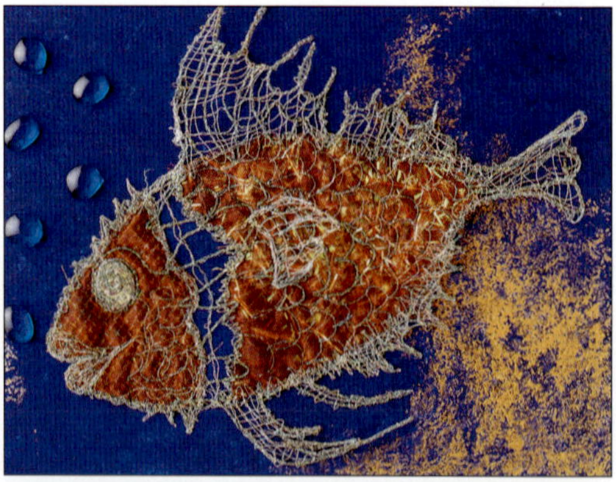

Above: The fins and tail of this exotic fish are worked in a mesh of metallic threads and the glittering body is formed from tiny scraps of shiny fabric and glitter which have been trapped between two layers of bronze organza (organdy).

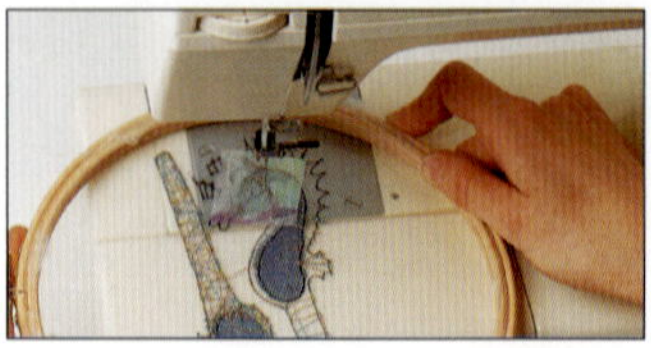

1 MULTILAYERED WATER-SOLUBLE METHOD Stretch the fabric tautly in a hoop and trace the outline with a felt-tip pen. Use a size 9 needle and thread the machine with metallic machine embroidery thread. Drop or cover the feed dog, set the stitch length to zero, then sew over and within the shape to form a tracery of thread. To create extra colour, add small cuttings of thread and net between two pieces of organza (organdy) and stitch over.

2 Rinse the finished piece in a bowl of water or directly under the cold tap. The backing fabric will simply disappear and all traces can be washed away.

3 Blot the work between layers of paper towel and ease into shape. Leave to dry away from any direct heat.

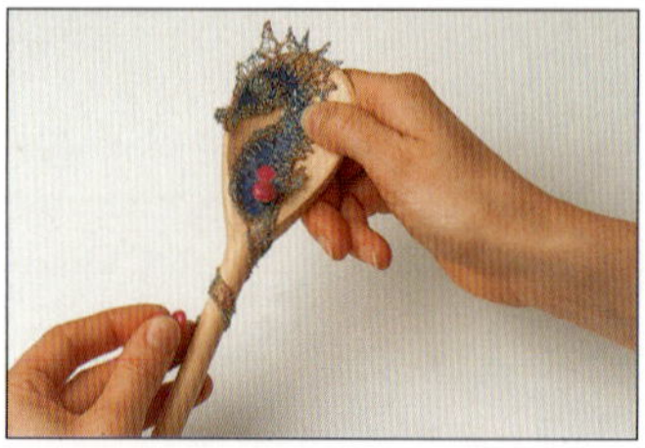

4 An extra dimension can be added by stiffening the piece with spray varnish. It can then be moulded or shaped and left to dry.

VANISHING MUSLIN is a stiffened loose-weave material which is worked in a frame then pressed under a cloth with a hot iron or put in a pre-warmed oven at 300°F/150°C for five minutes. The heat causes the fibres to discolour and disintegrate.

COLD-WATER-SOLUBLE FABRIC is made from a natural fibre which is a derivative of seaweed. It is delicate and must be worked in a hoop. It is not suitable for very dense sewing – although a double layer can be used if stitching closely – but it is ideal for creating fine multilayered textures, incorporating fragments of decorative cloth and fibre.

HOT-WATER-SOLUBLE FABRIC is stronger and stiffer than the cold-water version. It is used for heavier stitching and can be worked without a frame. The finished piece is then boiled for five minutes in a saucepan of water to dissolve the backing, and then stretched back into shape as it dries.

Above: Tiny pearls and fine lace have been used to decorate the golden machine lace garments worn by this ethereal fairy.

Below: These dramatic large-scale figures each measure 45cm (18in) high. The embroidery has been worked directly over the wire frames which support them, on a backing of water-soluble fabric, to create a wide range of intricate patterns and textures.

Right: The jewel-like effect of metallic machine lace makes it particularly suitable for use in small projects such as earrings. Special jewellery findings are available from most craft stores.

Alphabet Sampler

In the 1800s, schoolteachers and private governesses would combine the teaching of literacy and needlecraft by giving their pupils – both boys and girls – the painstaking task of embroidering a cross stitch sampler. Surviving antique examples, by children as young as six, sometimes exhibit remarkably accomplished sewing skills. Specially printed pattern books were used as a guide and this lower-case alphabet first appeared in a French publication at the turn of the nineteenth century.

MATERIALS

25cm (10in) square of 14-count white Aida cloth
Stranded embroidery threads in burgundy, scarlet, burnt orange, yellow gold and olive green
Embroidery scissors
20cm (8in) square wooden picture frame with glass
Fabric marker pen

1 The layout of the alphabet used here is for a 15cm (6in) square, but it could easily be adapted to fit a rectangular shape. Allowing a 5cm (2in) margin, work the first A in the top left corner, using three strands of burgundy thread. Be sure that all the cross stitches lie in the same direction. Finish off the first colour and, with scarlet thread, work the B. Use burnt orange, yellow gold, then olive green for the next letters and continue working the alphabet, keeping the same sequence of colours in each row.

2 Press the finished embroidery lightly from the back. Place the glass from the frame on to the right side and centre the design. Cut a piece of card to fit the frame, fold the edges of the fabric around the card and lace tightly at the back.

Potpourri Bag

Simple checked fabric has long been produced in many parts of the world and is a favourite choice for household textiles. This homespun cotton potpourri bag is inspired by the functional hand-woven cloth made by the American Shaker community. Its square weave forms a good basis for the counted threads of cross stitch and the contrasting heart motif fits neatly into the blue and white squared pattern. The natural texture of the raffia tie gives the finished bag a country-style appeal.

MATERIALS

23 x 33cm (9 x 13in) piece of checked fabric
Stranded embroidery thread in dark pink
Matching cotton sewing thread
Dressmaker's pins
Potpourri, lavender flowers or sweet-scented dried herbs
Length of garden raffia

1 Following the chart given, embroider three cross stitch hearts, spaced evenly along one half of one long edge of the fabric. Use three strands of the thread and work over three or four threads of fabric, depending on the size of the weave. Make sure that the stitches are all worked in the same direction.

2 Fold the short edges together, with the embroidery on the inside. Pin together the short edges, and the bottom (with embroidery). Hand or machine stitch, leaving a 12mm (½in) seam allowance. Fold the open top edge over and hem on the wrong side.

3 Clip the corners, then turn the bag right side out and press lightly. Fill the bag with potpourri, lavender flowers or sweet-scented dried herbs. Tie a length of raffia around the top of the bag to make a decorative bow. Make a hanging loop from another, shorter length of raffia.

Fabric Book

This fabric-covered book could be put to many uses: as a photo album containing pictures of a special event, as a sketchbook or as a notebook in which to write down favourite quotations and memories. The direct naive style of the birds and the tree is reminiscent of the Pennsylvania Dutch folk tradition, but the interpretation is fresh and contemporary.

Cotton fabrics with small-scale floral designs, sometimes known as "charm" prints and sold specifically for making patchwork, are best suited to this project.

MATERIALS

2 pieces of mounting board 23 x 28cm (9 x 11in)
Masking tape
2 sheets of watercolour paper
56 x 33cm (22 x 13in) piece of floral fabric
Strong (heavy-duty) white thread
Double-sided sticky tape
28 x 75cm (11 x 30in) piece of gingham
Pinking shears
Stranded embroidery thread in yellow, dark green, dark pink, light pink, brown, light green, blue and violet;
Small pieces of hessian (burlap)
Iron-on fusible bonding;
2 other floral fabrics
Small red and blue glass beads
Gold lurex thread
25cm (10in) length of narrow ribbon

1 Join the two pieces of mounting board along both sides of one long edge with masking tape. Check they can close easily. Cut the watercolour paper to size for the inside pages, fold in half and sew into the spine with strong (heavy-duty) thread. Cover the outside of the book with floral fabric, securing with double-sided tape. Line the inside with gingham. Cut a square of gingham to fit on to the front cover, pink the edges and embroider the border with yellow cross stitch. Stick on to the front of the book with double-sided tape.

2 Cut the hessian (burlap) to fit inside the gingham and fray the edge. Enlarging as necessary, trace the tree, hill and bird from the template on to separate pieces of fusible bonding. Iron on to the back of the floral fabrics and cut out; cut two birds. Remove the backing paper and iron the hill and tree on to the hessian (burlap).

3 Secure the hill and tree with small, dark green stitches. Embroider the leaves in light green by making four small back-stitches and winding the thread around them, or making detached chain stitches. Work lines of brown chain-stitch along the tree trunk and branches.

4 Iron the birds into position. Sew on blue beads for the eyes and stitch the wings in pink, as for leaves. The tail is worked with three detached chain stitches in yellow and blue.

5 Embroider each flower by making a French knot in yellow and surrounding it with five detached chain stitches in blue or violet. Make a stem with a straight stitch in light green and work a leaf. Couch three stars in the sky with gold lurex and sew a few red beads on to the tree as berries.

6 Finish off by working blanket stitch in light pink around the edge of the hessian (burlap) and sticking it on to the front of the book using double-sided tape. Cut the ribbon in half and attach a length to the inside of the front and back covers to make a tie.

Rocket Bag

This small bag uses straight stitch to bold graphic effect, with its futuristic design of space rockets, shooting stars and asteroids. It is worked in a selection of brightly coloured perlé threads on to utilitarian denim. Either side of the background fabric can be used. Each gives a different effect; the steps show the right side and the finished project shows the lighter-coloured reverse.

MATERIALS

Two 20cm (8in) squares of denim
Dressmaker's chalk or carbon
Embroidery hoop
Perlé cotton embroidery thread in a selection of colours
Dressmaker's pins
5 x 25cm (2 x 10in) strip of denim
Pearl button
Blue cotton sewing thread

1 Enlarge the template pattern and transfer the design on to one of the denim pieces, using dressmaker's chalk or carbon. Stretch the fabric in the embroidery hoop and fill in the main shapes of the design with satin stitch.

2 Use the outlines of the design to indicate the stitch direction. Sew parallel lines of simple running stitch to represent the trails left by the flying objects. Refer to the finished picture as a colour guide.

3 With right sides facing, pin and stitch the squares together on three sides. Press under 12mm (½in) around the open edge and hem. For the strap, fold the strip in half lengthways and stitch along the raw edge. Turn through.

4 Slip stitch the strap firmly in place on to the bag. Press the finished bag lightly. Sew the pearl button to the centre front edge of the bag. Make a buttonhole loop on the opposite side using blue cotton sewing thread.

Tea Towel

This cheerful tea towel, with its border of jaunty tea cups, may not stand up to the rigours of drying crockery. It would, however, make a lovely table cover, or would be certain to brighten a small kitchen window if used as a curtain. The cups are cut out of cotton which has been specially coloured with fabric paint and the details are added with back, cross and running stitches.

MATERIALS

Fabric paints and plain cotton fabric or scraps of coloured fabric
Tracing paper
Dressmaker's chalk or carbon
Stranded embroidery thread in contrasting colours
Anti-fraying solution or diluted pva adhesive
Striped tea towel

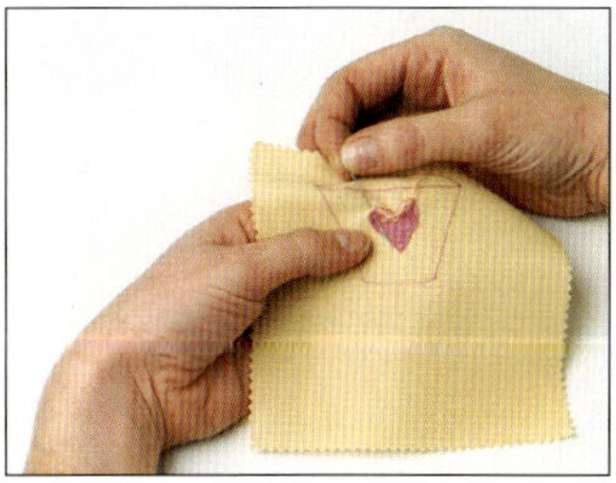

1 The tea cup shapes are cut from cotton fabric. Scraps of coloured cloth would be suitable, or white fabric could be painted specially, using fabric paints. Trace the outlines from the template on to separate pieces of fabric (enlarging to fit), using dressmaker's chalk or carbon.

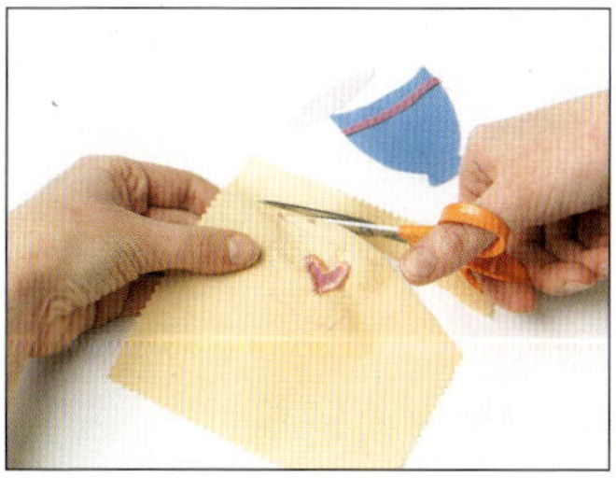

2 Embroider the pattern details on to the cups with three strands of embroidery thread, using straight or satin stitch. Cut out the cup shapes and tack (baste) them along the border of the tea towel in a pleasing pattern, using the main picture as a guide.

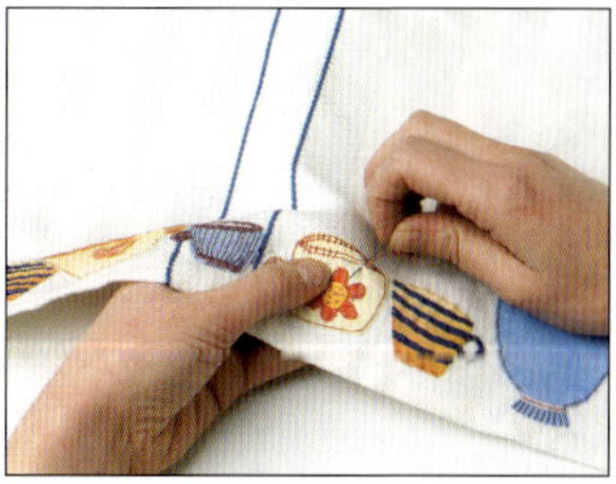

3 If the fabric has been painted, it should not unravel at the edges, but the reverse unpainted side can be coated with a specially manufactured anti-fraying solution or with diluted pva adhesive. Finally, sew the cups in place with back stitch and add extra stitched details.

House and Garden Picture

Gardeners always combined flowers and vegetables in their country plots, and this charming embroidered cottage has a flourishing garden full of both kinds of plants. Basic stitches are imaginatively used to give an added texture to the work. The feathery carrot tops and the cabbages are worked in a loose chain stitch, and the roof is stitched in irregular lines of satin stitch to suggest thatch. The house itself and the windows are outlined in back stitch and the garden is enclosed with a straight stitch picket fence.

MATERIALS

25 x 30cm (10 x 12in) piece of linen fabric
Transfer pencil or water-soluble marker pen
Tracing paper; cotton sewing thread
Stranded embroidery threads in dark and light green, pink, orange, red, yellow, rust and dark beige
Anti-fraying solution or diluted pva adhesive
Scraps of cotton fabric in dark and light green, pink, orange and red
20 x 25cm (8 x 10in) piece of cardboard
20 x 25cm (8 x 10in) picture frame

1 Transfer the house and garden outline on to the linen. This can be done by drawing freehand with a water-soluble marker pen, or by tracing the design (enlarged as required) on to tracing paper with a transfer pencil and ironing it on to the fabric. Remember to reverse the design first if using the latter method. Working with three strands of dark beige embroidery thread, back stitch over the outline of the house, garden, door and windows.

2 Using rust embroidery thread, work the roof and door in satin stitch. The door has three even rows of stitching, while the lines on the roof are less formal and more textured. Next, using dark beige embroidery thread, work a band of satin stitch across the chimney top.

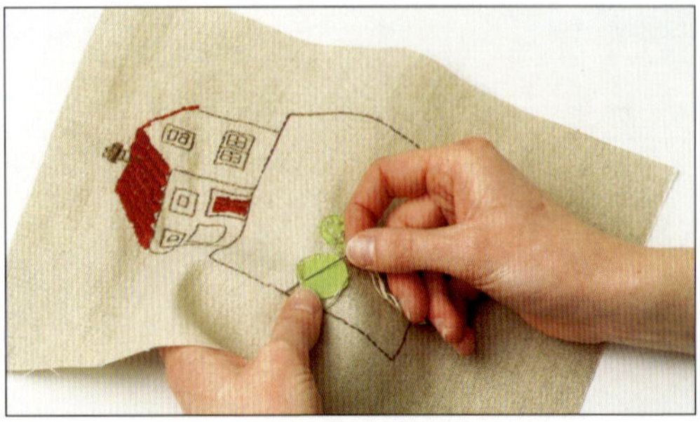

3 Coat the back of the fabric scraps with a proprietary (commercial) anti-fraying solution or with diluted pva adhesive. Cut out four rough circles measuring approximately 2.5cm (1in) in diameter, from light green cotton fabric for the cabbages. Tack (baste) in place, then work the leaf markings in loose chain stitch. Stitch around the outside edge in an uneven blanket stitch.

4 Cut sixteen small carrots from orange cotton fabric. Stitch down with running stitch and sew several straight stitches across each shape. The leafy tops are worked in loose chain stitch in dark green. Work the fencing around the border to complete the garden. The flowers, stalks and leaves are cut from cotton fabric and stitched down with running stitch. Embroider a few yellow satin stitches in the centre of the petals. Lightly press the finished work from the back and stretch over the cardboard, lacing firmly at the back with cotton thread, before framing.

Folk Art Gloves

The exuberant floral motif that decorates these gloves was inspired by the patterns on an antique tablecloth from Eastern Europe. The motif has been cleverly adapted to fit on to the back of the hand and along the fingers. The two variations, working on both white and black backgrounds, show how skilful use of colour can alter the appearance of a design. The basic outline is transferred on to the glove as a guide and the embroidery is worked freehand in tapestry wool.

MATERIALS

Pair of white or black woollen gloves
Ruler; pencil; thin cardboard
Tracing paper
Dressmaker's pins
Persian tapestry wool in pink, emerald green, royal blue, dark yellow, peach, kingfisher blue, bright pink, mint green, acid green, lime green and yellow
Tapestry needle

1 To support each glove while embroidering on to it, cut narrow strips from the card to insert in the fingers and a rectangle to fit the palm. Trace the template (enlarging as necessary) and cut out around the outer edge and inner circle. Pin to the glove, matching the top of the template with the finger tips and centring the flower on the back of the hand. Mark the inner circle with a row of small pink running stitches and the dotted lines with emerald green, then remove the template by cutting away between the stitches.

2 Using pink wool, work a circle of satin stitch in the centre of the flower, using the running stitches as a guide. With peach, work a ring of stem stitch close to the inside edge of the centre circle.

3 Embroider the three leaves around the sides and base of the circle in green satin and stem stitch. Unpick the original marker stitches if they still show.

4 Using dark yellow wool, blanket stitch the outer edge of the four petals. Inside this, back stitch a line in royal blue. Fill each with a detached chain stitch, then add a ring of small satin stitches in bright pink wool.

5 Work the stamens in chain stitch, beginning each one between the markers on the centre circle and working down to 2cm (¾in) from the finger tip. Use a different shade of green wool for each one. At the top of each stamen sew a different-coloured circle by making a detached chain stitch and working over it with small satin stitches. In the centre of each circle embroider a striped bullion stitch by threading the needle with one strand each of pink and yellow yarn.

6 Finish the flower by working six bullion stitches in kingfisher blue, arranged in a star pattern to fill the centre circle. To complete, sew a two-coloured bullion stitch in the middle of these stitches.

Hairslide (Barrette)

Decorative hair accessories have always been popular. In the past women needed many pins, combs and clips to keep their elaborate hairstyles in place. These were adorned with everything from feathers, lace and flowers to beads and jewels. This oval hairslide (barrette) is covered with black satin which has been embroidered with flowing lines of silver metallic thread and a contrasting pattern of cream satin stitch. The variation is less formal in design and, with the comb, should provide inspiration for further ideas.

MATERIALS

6.5 x 10cm (2½ x 4in) oval hairslide (barrette)
Tracing paper; tissue paper
Pencil
Remnant of black satin
Embroidery hoop
Cotton sewing thread in black and white
Dressmaker's chalk or carbon; dressmaker's pins
Perlé cotton in black and cream
Silver lurex yarn
Fine silver metallic thread
Remnant of black cotton fabric
Impact adhesive
Iron-on fusible bonding

1 Copy the template, adapting it to fit the slide (barrette). Trace the grid and oval outline on to a piece of tissue paper and the oval outline and spirals on to another. Stretch the satin in the hoop and tack (baste) through the tissue with white sewing thread to mark the grid and oval, then remove the paper. Mark the outside edge with chalk 12mm (½in) from the oval outline. Embroider the diamonds alternately in black and cream satin stitch, then take out the tacking.

2 Pin the second piece of tissue paper on to the hoop, lining up the design. Use silver lurex thread for the straight stitch spiral, stitching through the paper. Tear away the tissue and use the same thread to whip over the lines to define them.

3 Use fine silver metallic thread to sew squares on to the black diamonds and black sewing cotton to embroider star stitches on to the cream. Cut out the design around the chalk line.

4 Cut a paper pattern for the backing by drawing round the slide (barrette), marking the position of the clip. Sew a gathering thread around the outside edge of the embroidered fabric and draw up slightly. Place over the slide (barrette) and adjust to fit. Pull the thread tightly, knot the ends and glue down the surplus fabric. Iron the bonding on to the black cotton fabric, then pin the pattern for the backing to this fabric and cut out the backing. Cut a slit in the backing for the clip, then stick the backing on to the slide.

Drawstring Bag

This sophisticated drawstring bag is embroidered in dark grey, cream and silver threads on two contrasting black background fabrics.

MATERIALS

30 x 90cm (12 x 36in) piece of black satin
30 x 41cm (12 x 16in) piece of black velvet
Black cotton sewing thread; contrasting sewing thread
Embroidery hoop; dressmaker's carbon or chalk
Embroidery thread in dark grey
Silver lurex thread; cream perlé embroidery thread
Fine silver metallic thread; 1.37m (1½ yd) black cord
Safety pin; dressmaker's pins

1 Enlarge the pattern. Cut one piece A from satin and one piece B from velvet for the front. Reverse the templates and repeat for the back. Cut one C from satin and one from velvet. Mark the notches. Stitch the curved edges together to form two rectangles, trim and press the seam. With contrasting thread, tack (baste) from 'a' to 'a' across the centre of each piece to mark the fold line which will eventually be the top of the bag. Work the embroidery on the lower front. Following the main picture, mark three diamonds. Outline with whipped running stitch, with six strands of grey thread.

2 Sew the two inner diamonds with silver lurex thread, using whipped running stitch. With cream crochet thread work a second diamond in straight stitch 12mm (½in) outside each silver shape and stitch a large cross in the centre of each diamond. Outline crosses with dark grey and, with the same thread, stitch a diamond around each (one long stitch per side). With metallic thread work tiny silver crosses between cream straight stitches; couch down the long stitches around crosses. Add final centre crosses with cream perlé thread. Remove from hoop and press.

3 With right sides together, stitch front and back long edges; leave four spaces between notches 'b'. Press seams and top stitch around openings. Pin, tack, then stitch velvet base C to short velvet edges of main piece; right sides together, matching notches. Stitch satin base C to short satin edges of main piece, right sides together. Leave 5cm (2in) gap in seam.

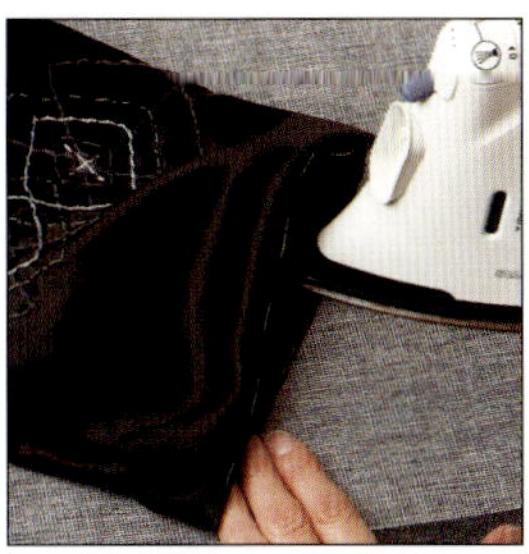

4 Turn bag right sides out through gap. Slipstitch the gap closed. Fold and press along tacked line a-a, and push satin end into velvet end to form a bag with a lining. Stitch lines at 12mm (½in) and 4cm (1½in) down from fold to make a channel for the cord, match with topstitched holes; unpick tacking. Thread cord twice through channel and stitch the two ends together.

Embroidered Hat

The embroidery on the satin brim of this elegant hat uses an interesting selection of textured threads and freestyle stitches. The spiral shapes are worked in whipped running stitch and couching, with sparkling details in metallic thread. The hat itself is made from velvet, and lined with heavy satin to match the turn-back. The coordinating scarf is made from two lengths of velvet with matching embroidery at one end.

MATERIALS

90cm (36 in) burgundy velvet
90cm (36 in) olive-green heavy satin
45cm (18 in) wide green cotton calico
Couching thread; tracing paper; pencil; tissue paper
Matching cotton sewing thread; embroidery hoop
Perlé embroidery thread in crimson and pink
Metallic thread in purple and bronze
Sewing machine; dressmaker's pins

1 Trace the pattern pieces, enlarging as necessary, then cut out in the fabrics indicated, on the bias. Cut a piece of satin 25 x 65cm (10 x 26in) for the embroidered turn-back. Trace the first part of the design on to tissue paper, including the notches in the seam allowance, and tack (baste) through on to the satin. Remove the tissue. Stretch the fabric in a hoop and, starting at the left edge, work the spirals in embroidery thread in a mixture of couched stitches and interlaced double running stitch.

2 Trace off the second part, up to the centre front. Then tack on to the satin, matching notches and marking the centre front notches. Remove the tissue. Embroider the four diamond shapes in straight and satin stitches, and the spirals in a mixture of threads.

3 Add detail to the diamonds with purple and bronze metallic thread in zigzag stitch or star shapes. Reversing the design, continue along the satin strip, moving it in the hoop, embroidering the right-hand side of the brim with the same stitches and colours as the left.

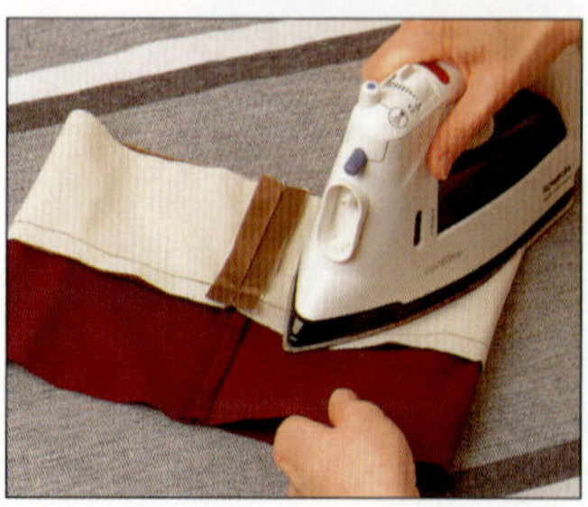

4 Press the completed embroidery. Pin calico piece C on to the back of the embroidered satin, matching notches. Cut the satin to the same shape as the calico and tack together. Join the centre back seam. Then join centre back seam of velvet piece C, pressing the seams flat. Trim the seam allowance on the velvet. Place the velvet and satin/calico with right sides together and sew along the top edge. Open out, press the seam towards the velvet, and edge-stitch through these layers, close to the seam.

5 Join the centre back seam of velvet piece B (side piece) and press open. Clip along the top edge. With right sides together, pin to velvet piece A (top of hat), matching notches. Tack, then sew together. Repeat with the two satin pieces A and B. Trim the seam allowance on the velvet and press open. Take piece C, turn the velvet over and press on the satin side. Pin together along the lower edge.

6 Pin together the lower edges of velvet pieces B and C, with pile sides together, matching the centre back seams and notches. Turn and sew together 12mm (½in) from the edge. Pin the satin lining in place with the right side facing right side of velvet (as above). Tack, then machine along 12mm (½in) seam allowance, leaving 10cm (4in) space. Pull the hat through this opening, then hand-stitch the space. Finally edge-stitch close to the seam all round to hold the satin lining in place.

Placemat

An ordinary placemat can be changed into a conversation piece for any meal time if it is embroidered with a fanciful trompe-l'oeil place setting. The knives, forks and spoons are worked with several rows of straight stitch in gold thread. This project is a good introduction to using the sewing machine for free stitching, as the firm fabric of the mat does not need to be held within a frame and the outline is easy to follow.

MATERIALS
Ready-made woven placemat
Tissue paper; pencil; dressmaker's pins
Sewing machine
Machine embroidery thread in gold; yellow cotton sewing thread

1 Trace the cutlery designs from the template on to tissue paper, enlarging as necessary. Cut out and arrange the designs on the placemat. Pin in place.

2 Lower the feed dog on the sewing machine and change to a darning foot, using gold thread. Wind the bobbin with yellow sewing thread. Sew a line of straight stitch over the outlines.

3 Having removed the tissue paper, work four closely parallel lines of straight stitch to emphasize the outlines and decoration of the cutlery pieces. Finish off any loose ends.

Cat Picture

Machine embroidery is particularly effective when worked in solid blocks of colour. This sleeping cat is sewn in three varieties of pink, which gives the stitched surface an illusion of light and shade. The background satin stitch has been cut to give a textured tufted finish, which shows to best advantage when the picture is mounted in a deep frame.

MATERIALS

25cm (10in) square of white cotton fabric
Tracing paper; pencil
Dressmaker's chalk or carbon
Embroidery hoop
Sewing machine
Machine embroidery or sewing thread in 3 shades of the main colour and 1 background colour
Embroidery scissors
Contrasting embroidery thread

1 Trace the full-size cat outline from the template on to tracing paper. Transfer the design on to the white cotton fabric using dressmaker's chalk or carbon. Stretch the fabric in an embroidery hoop.

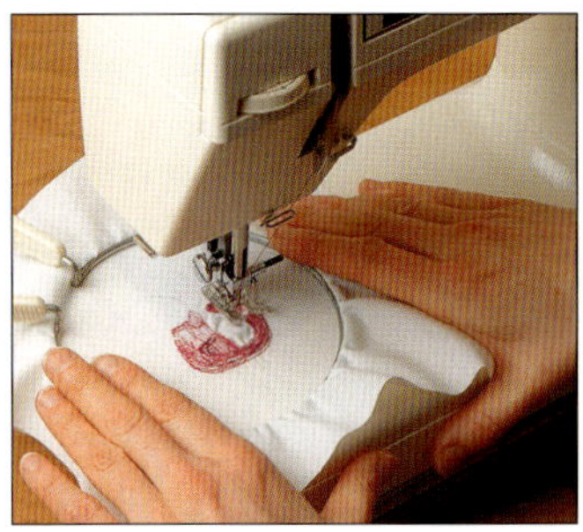

2 Lower the feed dog on the sewing machine and, with one shade of the main colour, fill in the outline with straight stitch. Work random lines of the other two shades of the main colour into the stitched surface, marking the paws and back leg.

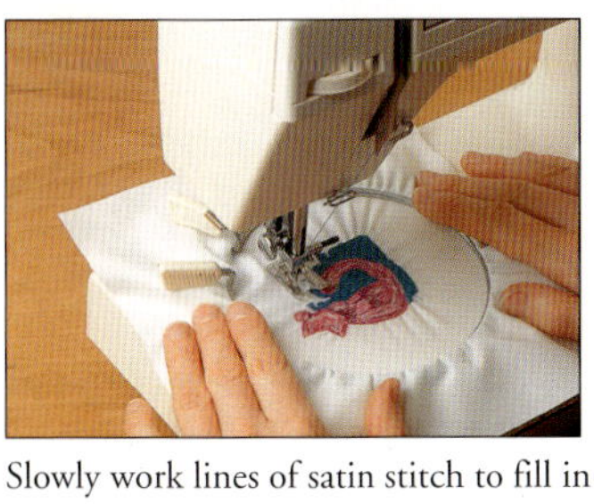

3 Change the top and bottom threads on the machine to the single background colour and adjust the machine to a close zigzag. Slowly work lines of satin stitch to fill in the background, being careful not to stitch over the cat. Remove from the hoop and press lightly.

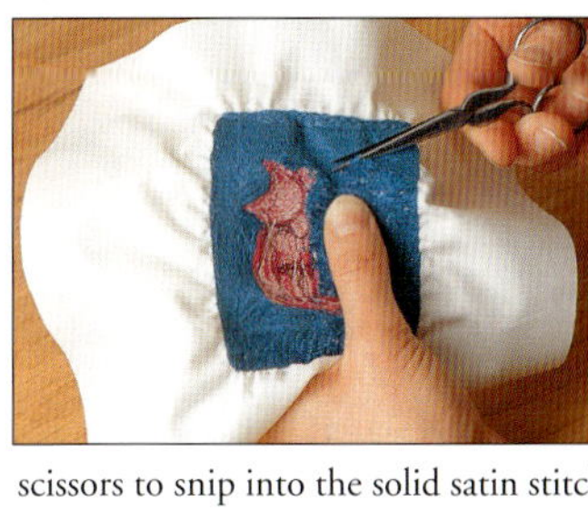

4 To obtain a textured, carpet-like background to the completed picture, use the sharp point of a pair of embroidery scissors to snip into the solid satin stitch to give a tufted surface. With three strands of contrasting embroidery thread, hand stitch the eyes, whiskers and claws.

Picture Frame

The paintings of Gustav Klimt, the Austrian symbolist artist, were the influence behind this decorative photograph frame. The jewel-like surfaces of his work are densely patterned with geometric shapes and sinuous lines, reminiscent of brocades, silks and other luxurious textiles. The embroidery is machine-worked in a free straight-stitch with a darning foot, and the fabric feed is lowered to allow a greater fluidity of movement.

MATERIALS

20 x 25cm (8 x 10in) piece of black velvet
20 x 25cm (8 x 10in) piece of metallic organza
Tissue paper; pencil; embroidery hoop
2 pieces of 15 x 20cm (6 x 8in) mounting (mat) board
Sewing machine
Machine embroidery thread in gold, cream, yellow and light blue
20 x 25cm (8 x 10in) piece of self-adhesive black felt
Black cotton sewing thread; pva adhesive
Short length of cord for the hanging loop

1 Trace the design from the template on to tissue paper, enlarging as required. Layer the tissue, organza and velvet and tack together across the centre and then around the edges. Stretch the fabric in a hoop.

2 Thread the machine with gold thread and use a darning foot. Lower the feed dog and set to straight stitch, then sew along the wavy lines and around the triangles, moving the frame as necessary.

3 Tear off the tissue paper and fill in the triangles with rows of straight stitch, using the various coloured threads. Thread all the loose ends of cotton to the back of the work.

4 Cut a rectangle from the centre of one of the pieces of mounting (mat) cardboard, to leave a 3.5cm (1½in) wide frame. Place on the reverse of the embroidery and cut out the middle section, leaving a 12mm (½in) seam allowance.

5 Mitre the corners of the frame, then fold the edges to the back and pull together with large stitches, making sure that the corners are tidy Take the second piece of board and cover with self-adhesive felt.

6 Glue the board to the frame along the two sides and bottom edge, so that the picture can be inserted from the top. Attach a short length of cord to the back of the frame to make a hanging loop, or make a simple stand from a triangle of cardboard which has been covered with black felt.

Fish Mobile

Shimmering gauzes and translucent organzas (organdy) give a wonderfully watery feel to this mobile, which would look equally at home in the bathroom or the nursery. The seahorses, fish and seaweed are worked in metallic machine embroidery threads on to water-soluble fabric. This special technique means that fine, net-like fabrics can be created, which are ideally suited to the seaside theme.

MATERIALS

Water-soluble fabric; indelible felt-tip pen; tracing paper; pen; embroidery hoop; sewing machine
Assortment of crystalline and metallic organzas (organdies), tinsel and other shiny fabrics; dressmaker's pins
Matching metallic machine embroidery threads
60cm (24in) length of 12mm (1/2in) dowelling
Blue and green diluted craft paints
Nylon fishing line; clear glass beads

1 Copy the templates for the fish, seaweed and seahorse, enlarging as necessary. Trace a fish and a frond of seaweed on to water-soluble fabric and put into the hoop. Cut two scraps of organza and sandwich small fragments of metallic fabrics between them for the body. Pin to the underside of hoop. Thread machine with metallic thread, lower feed dog and set to straight stitch. Sew around the main body and head.

2 Work the seaweed in the same way as step 1, using matching green thread and green organza. Extra freedom in stitching can be achieved by removing the presser foot on the sewing machine, but this way of working demands special care in handling the hoop, and is not absolutely necessary.

3 Turn the embroidery hoop over and trim back the excess fabric, then, to complete the fish, work the main fins and tail by outlining them with a zigzag stitch, filling in the space with interlacing lines of straight stitch. Work the two separate fins in the same way, then work a frilly zigzag stitch around the seaweed.

4 Dip the completed pieces of the mobile into water and allow the water-soluble backing fabric to dissolve. Rinse the pieces carefully to remove any traces of the backing fabric, then dry each on a towel, away from direct heat.

5 Following the same method, make eight extra lengths of seaweed, two seahorses and four more fish. Alter the shape and colour schemes so that the fish are all different. Attach each fish to a piece of fishing line, varying the lengths. Twist seaweed around the line and sew in place.

6 Cut the dowel into one 25cm (10in) and two 18cm (7in) lengths and stain with the craft paint. Stitch the seaweed to the dowel as shown. Hang the mobile and adjust so that it is evenly balanced. Sew glass beads to the fish and seaweed, to add both extra weight and decoration.

Table Cloth

Water-soluble fabric can be adapted to a variety of uses when embroidering with the sewing machine. It is usually used as a foundation for making net-like fabrics, but it also serves as an effective support when two materials of very different weights are being used. For this project, delicate openwork motifs in pearly white organza (organdy) are set into a heavy linen table cloth to make an attractive centrepiece.

MATERIALS
Dressmaker's chalk or carbon
Linen table cloth
Tissue paper
30 x 60cm (12 x 24in) piece of white organza (organdy)
30 x 60cm (12 x 24in) piece of water-soluble fabric
Dressmaker's pins
White cotton sewing thread; sewing machine
Embroidery hoop; sharp embroidery scissors

1 With dressmaker's chalk or carbon draw out a 20cm (8in) square centrally on the reverse side of the table cloth. Trace the cut-out design on to tissue paper and use the main picture as a guide to setting out the motifs. Cut a piece of organza (organdy) and water-soluble fabric to size and line up along one side of the square. Pin the tissue paper on top.

2 Thread the machine with white thread, lower the feed dog and put on a darning foot. Place the fabric in an embroidery hoop. Following the marked line, straight stitch around the motif, then remove the tissue paper.

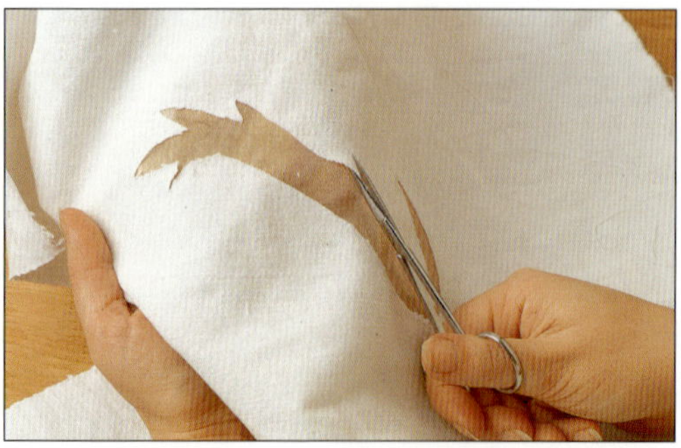

3 Turn the cloth over and, with sharp scissors, cut away the linen from inside the shape, taking care not to snip through either the outline stitches or the organza.

4 Set the machine to a wide close satin stitch and sew over the straight stitch line enclosing the raw edges. Work the other four sides of the square in the same way, then wash away the water-soluble fabric in cold water. Allow to dry, then press.

Needlepoint

Needlepoint involves working stitches on to a canvas to create geometric or illustrative designs. Its simplicity means that it is growing in popularity, and only a needle, some yarn and a piece of canvas are required to get started. Many ready-to-work kits are available, but, with some knowledge, it is easy to create individual pieces, from simple tent stitch pictures to elaborate textured cushions (pillows).

Needlepoint
Tools and Materials

Needlepoint, or canvas work, is the craft of stitching on to a firm open-weave square mesh or canvas, as opposed to the softer background fabrics used for embroidery. It is traditionally worked with wool, although many different yarns can be used to produce interesting effects.

Persian yarns.

THREADS

4-ply tapestry and 2-ply crewel yarns are both available in skeins or hanks, in a full range of colours. Vivid Persian yarn comes in three separate strands which can be divided.

CANVAS

Like embroidery linen, canvas is gauged by the number of threads that make up 2.5cm (1in): 10-count canvas is used for most tent stitch, rug canvas has just three squares to 2.5cm (1in) and fine 22-count fabric is used with single crewel yarns. Light-coloured canvas is suitable for working with pale colours, but antique or undyed canvas should be chosen for darker yarns so that it does not show through.

Mono, or single-thread canvas is available in a wide range of gauges for traditional needlepoint: for best results use interlock canvas which has a twisted warp and therefore does not pull out of shape easily. Double, or Penelope canvas is woven with pairs of thread, for tramming, which can also be sub-divided for areas of smaller stitching. Plastic canvas is sold by the sheet and can be cut to shape with scissors. It does not distort and is ideal for making three-dimensional shapes.

Crewel and tapestry yarns.

TOOLS AND ACCESSORIES

To avoid large pieces of work becoming distorted, a rectangular stretcher frame or an adjustable scroll frame must be used to mount the canvas. For smaller projects, the canvas can be simply bound with masking tape to prevent it unravelling and, if necessary, blocked into shape when complete.

A tapestry needle has a large eye for easy threading and a blunt point to pass between the canvas threads. Tapestry needles come in different sizes ranging from number 13 for coarse work, to the most common, number 20, down to the finest, number 25.

Both large and small scissors will be needed to cut canvas and yarns and a marker pen or acrylic paints are used to transfer designs directly on to the working canvas.

Embroidery scissors.

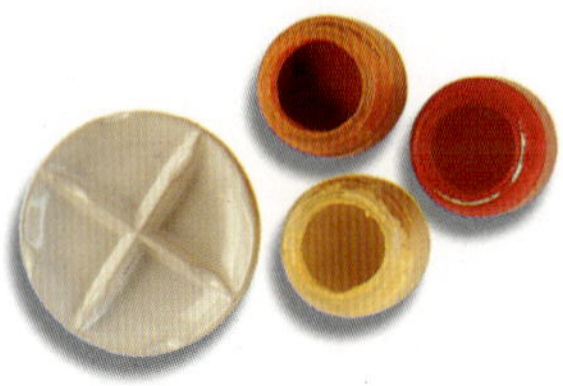

Acrylic paints with paint mixer.

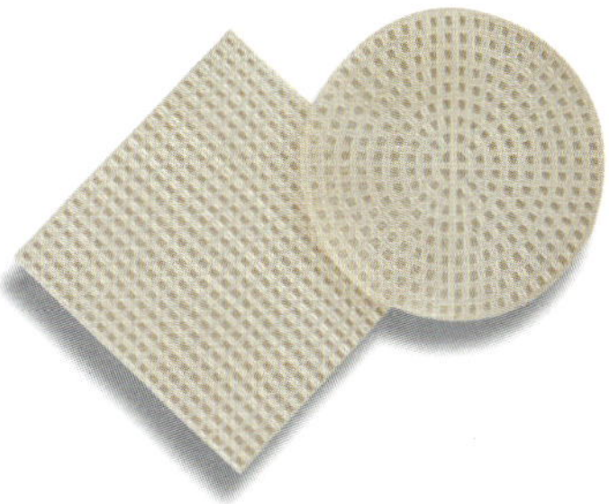

Plastic canvas.

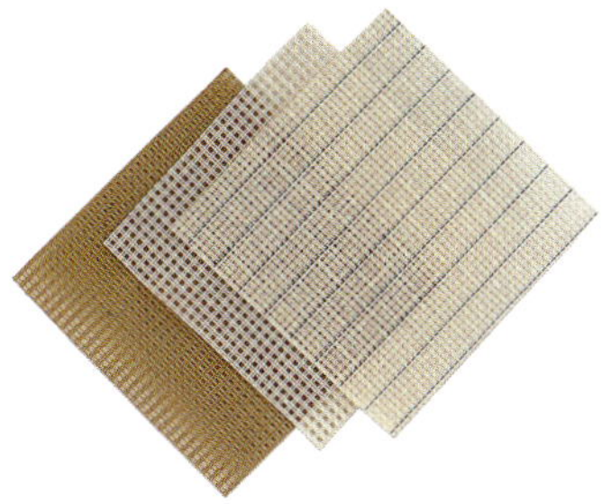

Double or Penelope canvas of different gauges.

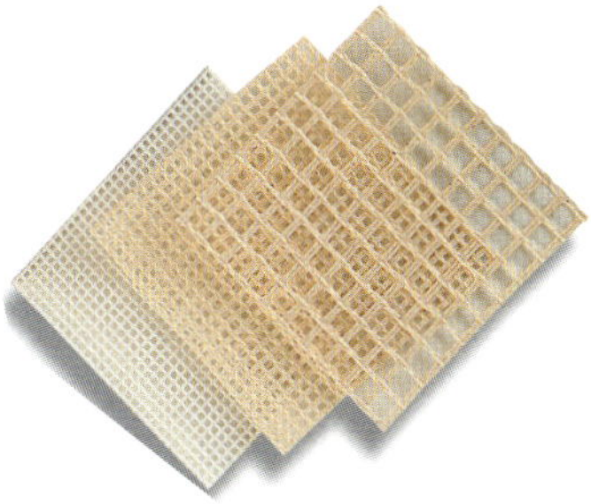

Interlock canvas of different gauges.

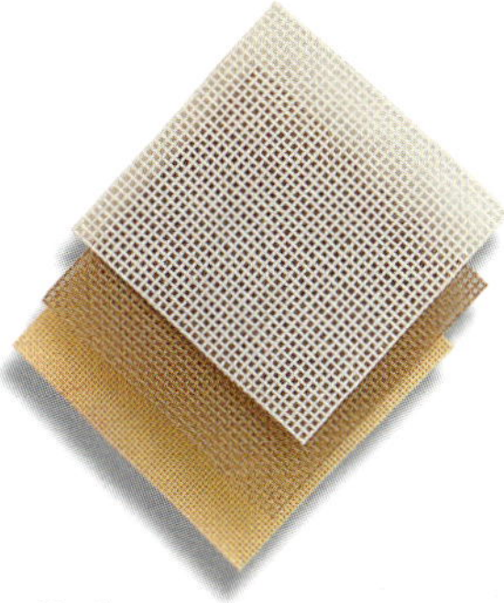

Single or mono canvas.

Dressmaker's shears.

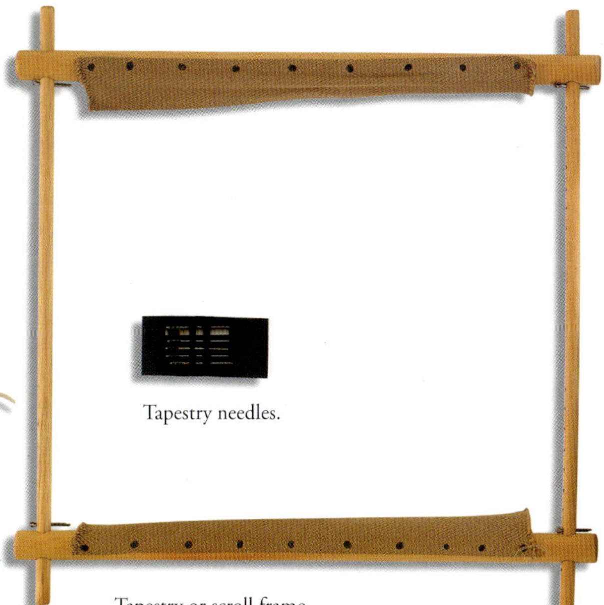

Tapestry needles.

Permanent marker pen.

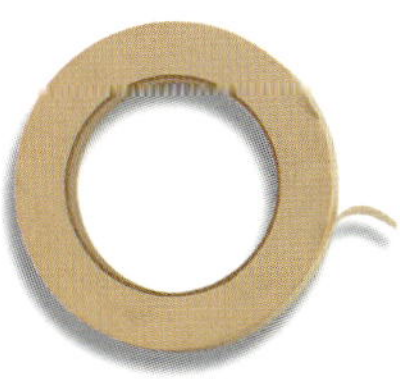

Masking tape.

Tapestry or scroll frame.

Creating the Design

The scope for creating new designs is unlimited. Visual inspiration is all around: a single motif from a furnishing fabric can be adapted to make a co-ordinating cushion (pillow), or used on a smaller scale as an all-over repeat; a photograph of an exotic flower may suggest a representational tent stitch picture or a more abstract colour pattern, worked in textured stitches. It is important to bear in mind the scale of the finished piece – for a fast result, bold shapes can be worked on 7-count canvas with three strands of Persian yarn, but for fine detail 12- or 14-count canvas should be used with crewel or tapestry wool. Try combining stitches: tent stitch is good for details and fine lines, while decorative stitches will cover background areas more quickly.

DRAWING ON TO CANVAS

This Gothic Revival pattern has been traced directly on to the canvas, using a waterproof felt-tip pen. The canvas should be placed directly over the drawing. Be sure that the design is squared up correctly. This can be done by ruling horizontal and vertical guides to indicate the centre of the canvas and matching them with similar lines marked on the design. Tape the canvas in place before starting to draw.

1 MAKING CHARTS
The regular grid of graph paper resembles the mesh of woven canvas, which makes charting an ideal way to produce accurate needlepoint designs. It is particularly good for tent stitch patterns, where one coloured square represents one stitch. Match the scale of the paper to the canvas for easier working, e.g., 12-count paper to 12-count canvas.

2 Choose a design that has a strong shape and solid blocks of colour. Trace the outline with a soft pencil and transfer on to graph paper.

3 Using the original picture as a guide, colour in the squares, simplifying the most complicated shapes.

PAINTING ON TO CANVAS

Highly detailed designs can be painted directly on to canvas using textile paints, which are then ironed to fix the colour. This technique works best on "antique" canvas which is made of unbleached fibres.

Working with Colour

Almost any type of thread can be used for needlepoint. Metallic yarns and silk floss provide highlights within a design; heavy-duty rug yarn is suitable for large-scale canvases, and perlé or stranded embroidery threads give a smooth lustrous texture. Woollen yarns are, however, the most popular choice, especially for items that will receive a lot of wear. A wide range of colours is available, from several specialist manufacturers. The yarn is spun from specially selected fibres, which make it more durable than knitting wool. Needlepoint wools come in three main types: tapestry yarn, crewel wool and Persian yarn. The first is a 4-ply single-strand yarn, supplied in skeins or larger hanks, which is used on medium canvases. Crewel wool is a 2-ply single strand yarn and can be worked singly on fine-mesh canvas for the most detailed work, or with several strands combined. Four strands are the equivalent of tapestry yarn. Persian yarn is also 2-ply and consists of three fine strands, which can easily be separated. The thread chosen for any work must cover the canvas threads completely without being so thick that it cannot be pulled through easily. Sew with a length of about 45cm (18in) to prevent the yarn becoming frayed or knotted.

1 By combining several separate strands of either crewel or Persian yarn, an infinite number of hues can be created. This can give depth to a representational image or, as here, be an excuse to work in bands of pure colour. The selection of yarns is based on the richly shaded landscape of the Channel Islands.

2 To blend the colours, cut equal lengths from the skeins and separate the strands.

3 Thread the needle with two contrasting or closely shaded yarns and work as usual. Up to four strands can be used on wider-mesh canvases; if all of these are different, some stunning results can be produced.

Left: The patterns on well-worn cotton print fabrics are the inspiration for this patchwork hand and heart. The subtle faded colours are reproduced by working with closely matched shades of Persian tapestry yarns.

This simple geometric design is based on the Saw-tooth Star quilt motif and worked in two strands of crewel yarn on a fine canvas. The changes in colour give a lively appearance to the pattern surface.

Starting and Finishing

Needlepoint's popularity comes from the fact that only the most basic equipment is needed, there are no special techniques to be learned and it is quick to work. The yarn must be started and ended correctly, and an even tension maintained. This will come with experience, so it is worth practising a few stitches on spare canvas.

1 Preparing the canvas The canvas should be bound with masking tape to prevent the edges unravelling and to stop the yarn from catching. If a frame is not being used, the sides of a large piece of work can be rolled up, so that only the area being stitched shows.

2 Getting started The end of the wool should not simply be knotted and pulled to the right side, as in embroidery, because it can easily become untied or work through the canvas. Instead the needle is passed through from the front, a short distance from the starting point, then brought up from the back. When the surplus yarn has been stitched over, the knot can be snipped off.

3 Finishing off The yarn is finished on the wrong side. Bring the needle through and weave it under the back of the finished stitches for about 2.5cm (1in). Trim the end. Try not to start and end the threads in the same place: this can make the work uneven.

Blocking

Most needlepoint stitches are diagonal, so the square weave of the canvas is bound to get pulled out of line during sewing. This is less likely to happen if the work has been supported on a frame, but some distortion is inevitable. The finished piece should be very lightly pressed from the wrong side with a steam iron, but may need to be "blocked" to restore its intended shape.

1 Dampen the work thoroughly on both sides, using a water spray.

2 Place a protective piece of plastic under the canvas, then pin down the first corner. Stretch the canvas and secure the opposite corner. Pull the work into shape and pin down the other two corners.

3 Push more drawing pins (thumb tacks) into the unstitched canvas, and use a ruler or set square to check the right angles at each corner. Leave to dry away from any direct source of heat.

Tent Stitch

Tent stitch, sometimes known as petit point, is the most flexible of all needlepoint stitches. It produces an even texture, and can be worked in large blocks of solid colour or used for shading effects and fine detail. It is worked diagonally, with all the stitches lying in the same direction. There are three different ways of forming the stitch: half cross stitch, continental stitch and basketweave stitch.

The reverse of these canvases shows the differences between the three methods of working tent stitch. Left to right: half cross stitch, continental stitch, basketweave stitch.

Half cross stitch

This must be worked on double or interlocked canvas to prevent the stitches slipping. Although it resembles continental stitch from the front, half cross stitch is worked quite differently, and using both stitches in one piece gives an irregular surface.

1 Start at the top left and work each row from left to right. Bring the needle through and take it up to the right over one intersection, then back down under one horizontal thread and out to start the next stitch.

2 Turn the canvas upside down, and work the next row in the same way.

Trammed tent stitch

Worked on double thread canvas, over a long foundation stitch, this method gives a slightly ridged and very resilient surface, which is traditionally used for stools or chair seats.

Left: Cushion (pillow) covers, which need to be hard-wearing, are usually worked in tent stitch.

Continental stitch

This second horizontal method can be used on single canvas, but uses slightly more thread than half cross stitch.

1 Starting at top right of the canvas, bring the needle out and up to the right, over one intersection. Insert it through the canvas, down under two horizontal threads and out to the front, and repeat to the end of the row.

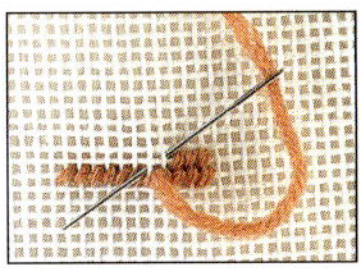

2 Next, turn the work upside down and work all subsequent rows in the same way.

Basketweave stitch

This diagonal way of working produces a stronger stitch which does not distort the canvas as much as the horizontal methods, but does tend to use more wool.

1 Work the first row from left to right. Pull the needle through and take it up to the right, over one intersection, then bring it back to the front, from under two horizontal threads.

2 Work the return row upwards from right to left, inserting the stitches in the spaces left from the first row.

Diagonal Stitches

Over the years many different needlepoint stitches have evolved and entire stitch dictionaries have been devoted to explaining them. They can be broken down, however, into just a few basic groups: diagonal stitches, straight stitches, square stitches, and variations on cross and star stitches. The diagonal stitches are useful background or filling stitches, ideal for covering large areas. They can be sewn in a single colour to give a smooth brocade-like surface, or in stripes for a more dramatic effect. The method of working means that there is a diagonal pull on the canvas, so the finished piece tends to become distorted.

From top to bottom: Moorish, Jacquard and Byzantine stitch.

BYZANTINE STITCH

This consists of diagonal zigzag rows, which can be worked over two, three or four intersections of the canvas. The size of each "step" can be varied, but should remain constant within the piece.

Work four diagonal stitches over two intersections, from left to right, then four stitches downwards. Repeat to form the zigzag, then work the subsequent rows in parallel. Fill in any space with graduated diagonal stitches.

MOORISH STITCH

Here the square elements of cushion (pillow) stitch are combined with zigzag lines. If Moorish stitch is worked in two colours, it produces a geometric checked pattern.

1 The first row consists of diagonal stitches worked over one, two, three, four, then three, two and one intersections.

2 Work a line of stepped stitches over two intersections to fit alongside the first row and repeat these two rows.

JACQUARD STITCH

This is made up of two repeated zigzags. The basic stepped row of Byzantine stitch is worked over two intersections and followed by a row of tent stitch.

Stitch the first stepped row as before, then work the second line in diagonal stitches over one intersection, across, and then down the canvas.

From left to right: small diagonal mosaic stitch, condensed Scottish stitch and Milanese stitch.

MILANESE STITCH

Diagonal rows of triangles facing in opposite directions make up this stitch, and it is particularly effective when worked in two colours.

1 Work diagonal stitches over one, two, three and four intersections to form a triangle, then repeat the unit.

2 The second row is reversed, so that the shortest stitch fits next to the longest stitch of the first row.

SMALL DIAGONAL MOSAIC STITCH

Also known as Parisian stitch, this is made by following a tent stitch over one intersection with a longer stitch over two intersections. Work the sequence along a diagonal of the canvas, and work the next row so that it fits beside the first. It can be worked from right to left or left to right.

CONDENSED SCOTTISH STITCH

This resembles parallel lines of interlocked diamond shapes and gives a strong diagonal appearance.

1 Work a unit of graduated stitches over two, three, four, and then three intersections. Repeat this along the diagonal.

2 Work the same sequence for the next row, interlocking the two lines so that the shortest stitch of one row fits against the longest. stitch of the adjacent row.

Square Stitches

This category includes diagonal, upright and horizontal elements, creating repeated square units, a chequerboard effect, and interesting variations when using more than one colour.

SMALL CUSHION (PILLOW) STITCH

Also known as mosaic stitch. When worked in a single colour, as in the finished sample, it gives an overall texture. Several colours produce a quite different effect.

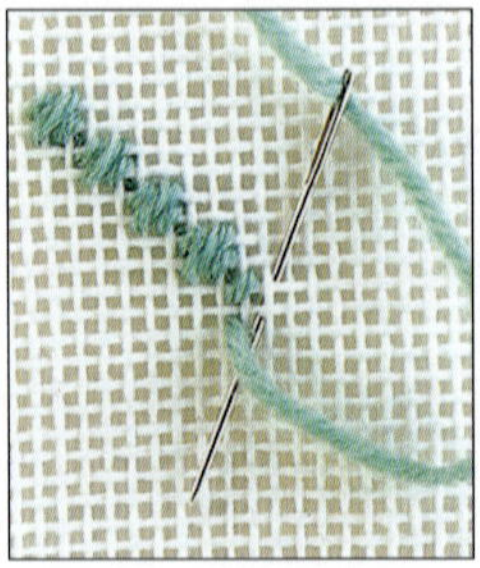

1 Start at the upper left and work diagonally downwards over first one, then two, intersections.

2 The following rows are worked up, then back down, so that each line fits into the previous stitches.

SCOTTISH STITCH

This gives a plaid effect, reminiscent of simple tartan patterns, which looks very effective when worked in contrasting yarns.

1 Work the grid first, using horizontal and vertical rows of tent stitch with a three- or four-thread space left between them.

2 Fill in the spaces with individual cushion (pillow) stitches.

From left to right: cushion (pillow) stitch, small cushion (pillow) stitch and Scottish stitch.

CUSHION (PILLOW) STITCH

This can be worked so that all the squares lie in the same direction, or at an angle to each other, which reduces the tension on the canvas.

1 This basic square is made up from seven stitches over one, two, three, four, three, two, then one intersections, worked in diagonal rows. For two-colour work, leave four thread spaces between rows.

2 Diagonal rows of the second colour are used to fill in the spaces.

CHEQUER (CHECKER) STITCH

This alternates small squares of tent stitch with lines of graduated diagonal stitch to produce an interesting texture, particularly when two colours are used.

1 Work diagonal lines of cushion (pillow) stitch squares over four threads.

2 With the second colour, work four rows of four tent stitches to fill in the spaces.

BRIGHTON STITCH

This is worked in alternate rows of diagonal stitches which form a diamond pattern. The small spaces are filled in with upright cross stitch.

1 Start with a block of five diagonal stitches worked from left to right, then a second block slanting the other way. Work the next row so that it is a mirror image of the first.

2 Work an upright cross stitch, in the same or in a contrasting colour, over the two threads which have been left unworked between the stitches.

WOVEN STITCH

This stitch produces an intriguing basketweave effect, which appears to have been interwoven. It can also be worked in just one colour.

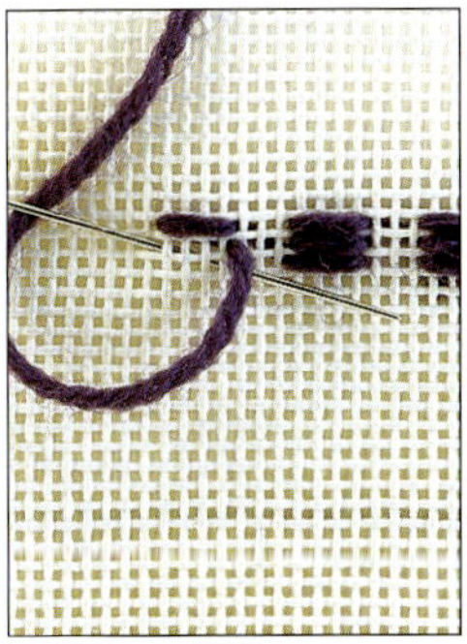

1 Working from right to left, make blocks of three parallel straight stitches over four threads, leaving a three- or four-thread space between. Work the next row so that the blocks lie immediately below the spaces above.

2 The second colour is used to fill in the spaces. Starting from the top right, work blocks of upright straight stitches over four threads, so that the first and last stitches of each block overlap the horizontal stitches from the first row.

From left to right: woven stitch, Brighton stitch and chequer (checker) stitch.

Crossed Stitches

The foundation of this group is the simple cross stitch, which is made from two diagonal stitches crossing in the centre. Other variations may combine upright and horizontal stitches, and consist of repeated units of two or four stitches. Crossed stitches should always be sewn in the same order, so that the upper stitches lie in the same direction.

From left to right: cross stitch, long arm cross stitch and herringbone stitch.

CROSS STITCH

This can be worked singly, or in rows when larger areas need to be covered. When small stitches, covering a single intersection, are required, they should be worked on a double or interlock canvas.

1 Individual cross stitches are worked from right to left, then from left to right. Bring out the needle and take it up to the left over two intersections. Push through the canvas, pass down behind two threads and bring it up. Work the second stitch over the first and bring the needle back to the starting point of the second stitch.

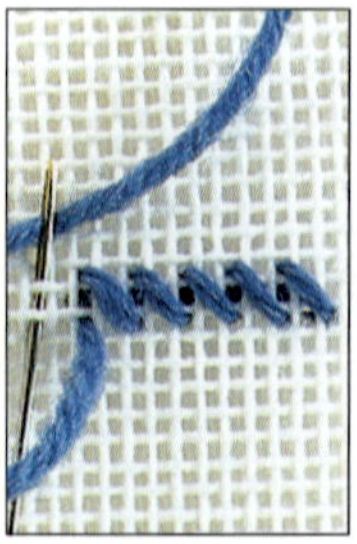

2 When working in rows, make the crosses in two passes. Form the lower stitches by sewing from right to left. Bring the needle out and up to the left over two intersections, and under two horizontal threads. Repeat to the end.

3 For the upper stitches, work a line of separate diagonal stitches in the same way, reversing the direction so that they cover the first line.

LONG ARM CROSS STITCH

Also known as Greek stitch, the long arm cross stitch forms a braid-like line, made by the stitches crossing off centre. It can be used singly as a border or in rows for a solid texture.

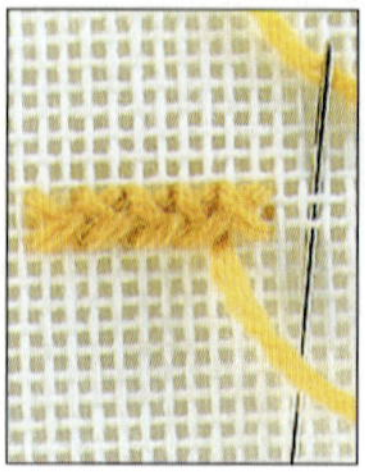

Work from left to right. Bring the needle up over two threads and four threads to the right to make a long diagonal stitch. Insert under two horizontal threads and bring up. Take up to the left, over two intersections, then insert under two horizontal threads and bring up. Repeat both stitches to the end of the row.

HERRINGBONE STITCH

This produces a dense woven look, particularly effective when worked in stripes of tonal colours.

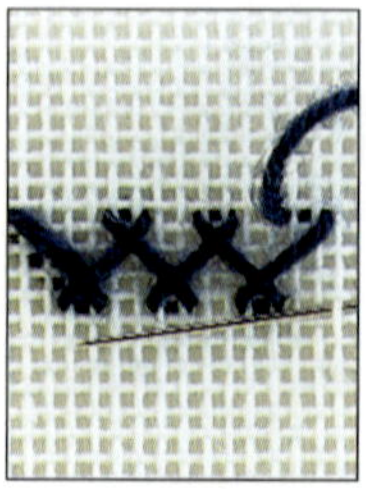

1 Starting at the upper left and working from left to right, bring the needle out and down diagonally to the right over four intersections. Pass left under two threads, then up diagonally right over four intersections. Pass the needle left under two vertical threads and bring out. Repeat to the end.

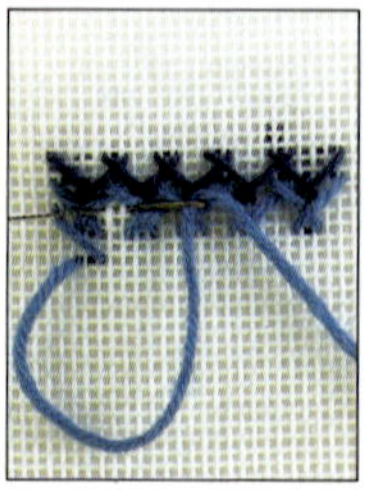

2 Start the next row and subsequent rows two thread spaces below the first stitch. Work the stitch as before, so that the rows interlock.

OBLONG STITCH VARIATION

This is made up of rows of longer stitches, which are held in place with small back stitches.

1 The base row is worked as for normal cross stitch, but the stitches are formed over four horizontal and two vertical threads.

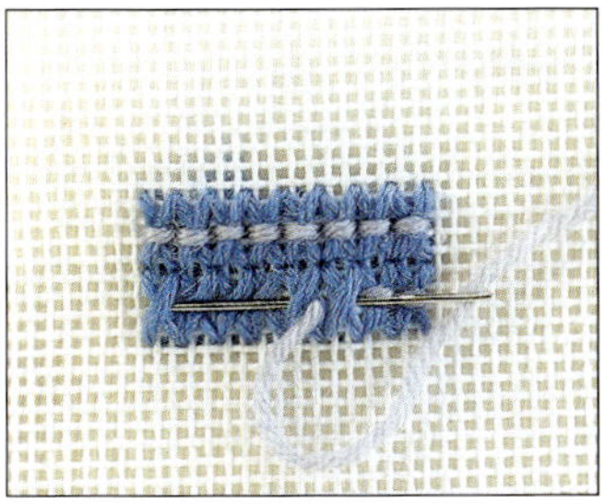

2 Using a matching or contrasting thread, make a row of back stitches over the two vertical threads in the centre of each stitch.

DOUBLE STRAIGHT CROSS STITCH

This forms a raised diamond consisting of four separate stitches (two crosses). Each unit is worked separately and the same order of construction must always be followed to give a regular appearance.

1 Bring the needle up and over four horizontal threads. Pass behind under two intersections, out and over four vertical threads to form a large cross. Bring up at the left, through the space that lies between the two arms.

2 Form a second cross by taking the needle down over two intersections, behind and to the left under two vertical threads, then up to the right over two intersections.

RICE STITCH

This very attractive stitch covers the canvas completely. Each stitch unit consists of a cross stitch which is held down at each corner with a grain-like back stitch.

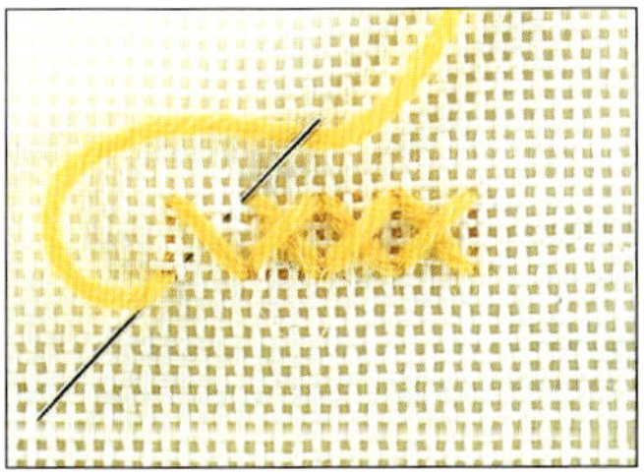

1 Work rows of large cross stitches over four intersections.

2 Using a contrasting colour, make four back stitches in a diamond shape over each cross.

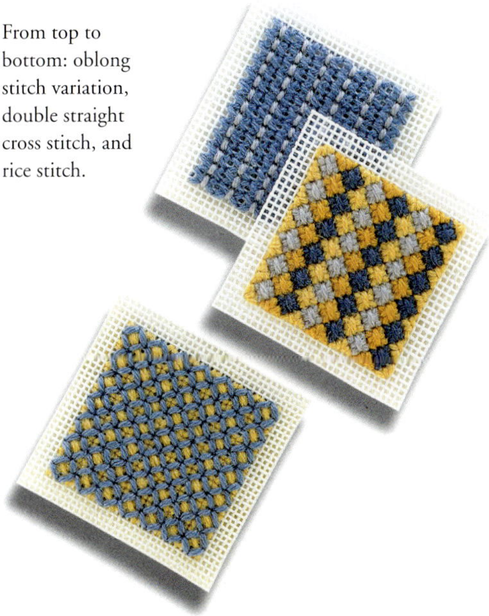

From top to bottom: oblong stitch variation, double straight cross stitch, and rice stitch.

Star Stitches

Stars combine diagonal and straight lines to produce bold dramatic shapes which look particularly effective when worked in rows of complementary colours. They are used to create definite shapes and patterns, rather than to fill in backgrounds or large areas.

From top to bottom: ray stitch, Algerian eye stitch and Rhodes stitch.

ALGERIAN EYE STITCH

Made up of 16 stitches radiating from a centre point, this should be worked in a thickish thread with a fairly loose tension, so that the canvas is covered.

1 Each stitch is worked over four threads. Bring the needle up at the centre, then insert it to the left over four threads, and pull back up through the original space. Count two threads down and four across for the second stitch. Make the third stitch over four intersections down to the left, the fourth over four horizontal threads and two vertical ones. Continue, working counter-clockwise, until the whole square has been covered.

2 Further stitches can be worked in horizontal or vertical rows. Lines of back stitch, over two threads, surround the finished stitches.

RAY STITCH

Also known as fan stitch, this consists of five stitches and resembles one corner of Algerian eye stitch. Its lively appearance comes from working each row in opposite directions.

Bring the needle through and take it down over four threads, then back to the starting point. Count down four threads and two threads to the left for the second stitch, then work the third stitch over four intersections to the left. Count up two for the fourth stitch, and work back over four threads, then work the final stitch at right angles to the first.

RHODES STITCH

This is usually worked on a single canvas to produce a raised, highly textured surface. All the stitches are worked in the same direction so that they match.

1 Bring the thread through, then count six threads to the right and four down. Insert the needle and bring back up one hole below the starting point and insert again, one hole above the end of the first stitch.

2 Continue working counter-clockwise in this way, until the whole six-thread square has been covered.

Straight Stitches

Straight stitches lie parallel with the weave and are usually worked on a single canvas so that the threads are covered completely. The most interesting variation is Florentine or flame stitch, used for Bargello work. This historic technique has long been popular, particularly in Italy. It is worked in repeated rows of an elaborate zigzag, and there are many variations on the basic pattern.

CHEVRON STITCH

This gives a strong horizontal zigzag pattern. Work over three to five threads to give wider or narrower bands.

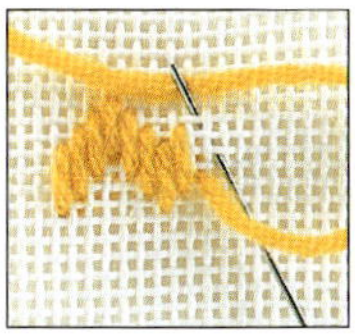

1 Over four threads, work four straight lines, starting each stitch one hole up to the right, then work three stitches sloping downwards. Continue to the end of the row.

2 Work the second row in the same way, so that the chevrons fit neatly together.

HUNGARIAN DIAMOND STITCH

A good filling stitch that can be worked in a single colour. The height of the stitches may be varied. Work a diamond shape of vertical stitches over two, four, six and four horizontal threads. Repeat to the end of the row. Work the next rows in the same way, with the longest stitch below the shortest stitch of the previous row.

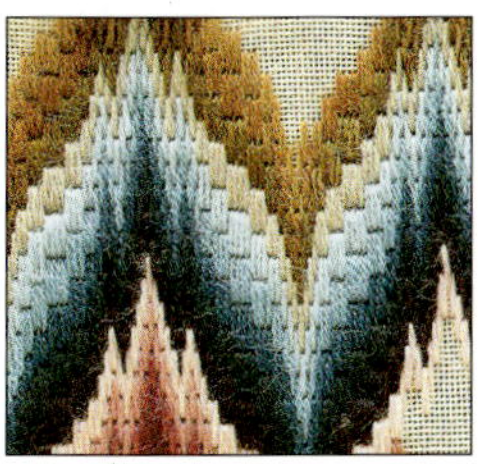

FLORENTINE STITCH

This is quick to work: once the first line has been stitched, the subsequent rows repeat the same series of peaks and valleys. Shades of the same colour can be used to give an antique feel to the work.

UPRIGHT GOBELIN STITCH

This resembles the ridged surface of hand-woven tapestries and is named after the work produced by the Gobelin family's factory in Paris.

Work from right to left, then from left to right. Bring the needle through, pass it down over two, three or four horizontal threads, then back up to form the next stitch.

GOBELIN FILLING STITCH

This can be used to produce subtle shaded effects, and can be worked in different lengths. The overlapping rows give a smooth surface.

Work a row of vertical stitches over six horizontal threads, leaving one row of holes between them. Work the next row between these stitches, starting three threads down from the top of the preceding row.

Clockwise from top: chevron stitch, Hungarian diamond stitch, Gobelin filling stitch and upright Gobelin stitch.

Jewellery Box

The soft, natural earth colours of this jewellery box echo the subtle, faded shades which are typical of old textiles. A simple outline for the pattern itself is given here, however, the actual yarns used can be chosen almost at random, and then blended together for an informal effect. The plastic canvas used for the lid is ideal for constructing three-dimensional objects; it is simple to cut to any size and strong enough to hold its shape.

MATERIALS

12.5 x 20cm (5 x 8in) piece of plastic canvas
Waterproof felt-tip pen
Tapestry yarn in a selection of toning colours
Tapestry needle
36 x 90cm (14 x 36in) piece of self-adhesive black felt
30cm (12in) square of sturdy cardboard
Metal ruler
Cutting board
Craft knife

1 Cut the box lid sections from the plastic canvas: one 12.5cm (5in) square, and four 2 x 12.5cm (¾ x 5in) rectangles to form the sides. Enlarge then trace the template on to the canvas with a waterproof pen. Work the design in tent stitch, blending the colours using two toning strands.

2 Sew the four side pieces of the fold in the same way as step 1, then overstitch the long edges to the square using two different colours of yarn in the needle. Join the short edges to complete the lid.

3 Overstitch the raw edges of the canvas to make a neat border. Cut an 18cm (7in) square of self-adhesive black felt to line the box lid. Clipping the corners to fit, peel off the backing paper and stick in place, trimming the lower edge as necessary.

4 To make the main box, mark a 11.5cm (4½in) square in the centre of the cardboard. Then on each side rule a 9 x 11.5cm (3½ x 4½in) rectangle. Cut out the cross shape and score along the folds.

5 Using this shape as a guide, cut out two pieces of black felt for the inside and outside of the box, each with tabs on the four sides and 12mm(½in) turn-over around the top edge on one piece.

6 Fold the cardboard along the scored lines and cover the outside with the felt, using the tabs to secure the corners and folding over at the top. Use the second piece of felt to line the inside of the box.

Lone-Star Cushion (Pillow)

This needlepoint cushion (pillow) is an adaptation of an Amish patchwork bedcover design from the 1930s and reflects their mastery of colour. Its strong graphic impact relies upon the interaction of light and dark shades in muted tones, which radiate from the centre in concentric rings. The design is worked in a diagonal stitch, which gives it an almost padded effect, suggesting the quilted patterns of the original cover.

MATERIALS

41cm (16in) square of 12-count single-thread canvas
Masking tape; tapestry needle; cotton sewing thread
Tapestry frame (optional)
Tapestry yarn:
- *1 skein each in pale lilac, dark peach, indigo, orange, crimson and dark gold*
- *2 skeins in light turquoise*
- *6 skeins in dark turquoise*
- *6 skeins in dark purple*

Matching velvet or needlecord fabric for the backing
30cm (12in) cushion (pillow) pad

1 Bind the edges of the canvas with masking tape to prevent them unravelling. Find the middle of the canvas by folding it in half each way and sew two rows of tacking stitch in contrasting thread to divide it into quarters. Mount the canvas on a frame if desired. Using the tacking lines as a guide, stitch the centre star in pale lilac yarn, working diagonally over four threads of canvas, Following the chart, sew the next round in dark purple.

2 Work the next four rounds in dark peach, indigo, dark turquoise, then light turquoise, and then continue with the dark purple round that starts to divide the points of the star, carrying the thread behind the work.

3 Using the picture as a guide, work the points, starting and finishing each colour separately. Fill the dark turquoise background in diagonal stitch.

4 Work a border of three lines of dark purple diagonal stitch, in the direction of the previous stitches. Stretch and block the work into shape, then cut a 33cm (13in) square of backing fabric. With right sides together, join to the canvas on three sides, turn right way out, insert the cushion (pillow) pad and slip stitch the final side closed.

Nine-Star Cushion (Pillow)

The nine-star is a variation of the distinctive lone-star quilt design. The basic unit is an eight-pointed star, which is repeated in three rows of three, to produce an interesting secondary pattern of squares and diamonds. The stars are worked in complementary faded tones of burgundy, rust and pinks, in diagonal stitch, and the cream background in textured cushion (pillow) stitch.

MATERIALS

41cm (16in) square of 12-count single-thread canvas
Masking tape; cotton sewing thread; tapestry needle
Tapestry frame (optional)
Tapestry yarn:
8 skeins in cream
1 skein each in pale lemon and light gold
2 skeins each in pale pink, rust and burgundy
3 skeins each in dark pink and dark gold
Toning fabric for the backing
30cm (12in) cushion (pillow) pad

1 Bind the outside edge of the canvas with masking tape to prevent it fraying. Mark the middle of the canvas with two lines of running stitch in contrasting thread, then mount on a frame if desired. Use the guides to position the centre star. Following the chart, work the first round with pale lemon yarn, using a diagonal stitch over three threads of canvas. Work the next two rounds in light gold and pale pink.

2 Stitch the next round in dark pink, then work the tapering diamond points following the main photograph. Find the position of the four stars around the centre star by stitching the diamonds at their tips, where they touch the outer points of the first star.

3 Work the four corner stars in the same way. Fill in the background with cushion (pillow) stitch squares using cream yarn. Work the other eight diamonds, then stitch a final row of cushion (pillow) stitch around the edge. Stretch and block the finished piece. Cut the backing fabric to the same size and sew together round three edges, with right sides facing. Turn the right way out, insert the cushion (pillow) pad and slip stitch the fourth side closed.

Heart Picture

The heart is the ultimate symbol of love and affection, and as such recurs throughout the applied arts of many cultures. For this dramatic tent stitch panel, one basic motif is repeated six times, in a format influenced by the Pop Art screen prints of Andy Warhol. The vibrant colour comes from blending individual strands of Persian yarn, which is dyed in particularly intense hues.

1 Plan the colour combinations before starting to sew. Choose complementary shades for subtle backgrounds, such as the pale blue and lilac square, and contrasting tones – lime and emerald green – for more impact.

2 Separate the yarn into strands and, working with two strands at a time, work the heart motifs in tent stitch. Follow the chart, on which one square represents one stitch.

3 Vary the colour within some individual shapes; two different pinks are used for the final heart. Plastic canvas has the great advantage that it does not need to be blocked into shape, so it is suited to work that will be framed. Trim the finished piece to fit the frame using sharp scissors.

MATERIALS

Persian yarn in a selection of pinks, reds, blues and greens
Tapestry needle
11.5 x 15cm (4½ x 6in) piece of 10-count plastic canvas
7.5 x 11.5cm (3 x 4½in) picture frame
Embroidery scissors

Circular Star

Plastic canvas is available in round shapes of various sizes, as well as in the more usual square grid pattern. This gives great scope for experimentation with designs based on the geometric division of a circle. Stars and snowflake motifs naturally lend themselves to this, and make unusual Christmas decorations. The scale of this project makes it a good way to use up small amounts of yarn. Use the photograph as a stitching guide.

MATERIALS

7.5cm (3in) diameter plastic canvas disc
Waterproof felt-tip pen (optional)
Tapestry needle
Tapestry wool yarn in a selection of toning colours
Small piece of self-adhesive felt
30cm (12in) length of satin ribbon

1 Copy the star design from the template. (The pattern could be traced directly on to the canvas with a waterproof felt-tip pen.) Thread the needle with two different coloured yarns to create a mottled effect. Stitch one-quarter of the design at a time, working from the centre outwards. To secure the ends of the yarn do not knot them, but leave a length and catch under the back when stitching.

2 Using the main picture as a guide to colour, finish off the outside edge by slip stitching.

3 Cut a 7.5cm (3in) circle of self-adhesive felt. Peel off the protective paper and stick the felt to the back of the work so that it conceals the ends.

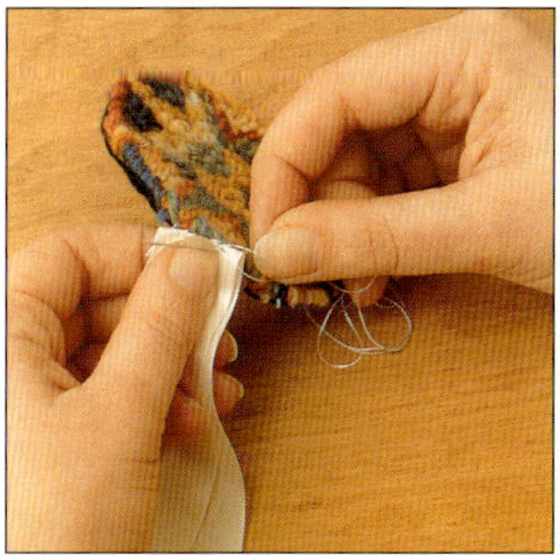

4 Fold the ribbon in half and stitch to the edge of the disc. Knot the ends together and trim.

Cup and Saucer

The familiar domestic image of a floral china tea cup and saucer is captured in this needlepoint design. The main part is worked in tent stitch with a border of cushion (pillow) stitch squares. The background is stitched in two shades of the same colour, graded from dark to light. The distinctive shape of the frame – known as an Oxford frame – gives the finished picture a rural aspect and charm.

MATERIALS
20 x 25cm (8 x 10in) piece of 12-count single-thread canvas
Waterproof felt-tip pen
Tapestry needle
1 skein Persian yarn each in dark and light olive, dark and light rust, dark and light pink, light gold, turquoise, dark blue and cream

1 Trace the cup and saucer template directly on to the canvas, using a waterproof felt-tip pen with a fine point. Work the main outline in dark blue tent stitch. Stitch a line of turquoise as a drop shadow.

2 Work the border around the rim and the flowers in pink, the leaves in olive and turquoise, the flower centres in gold and the cup in cream. With two shades of rust, fill in the background rectangle in tent stitch.

3 Next, work three rounds of cushion (pillow) stitch over four threads as a border, using olive for the final round. Stretch and block the finished piece, then fold under the surplus canvas and press.

Sun Pincushion

The sunburst is a universal image of life and energy. Like the heart, it appears as a decorative motif in various forms throughout the world. This interpretation is based on a drawing from a Renaissance manuscript and is worked in three rich golden shades of Persian yarn, with a contrasting cobalt blue background. Basic tent stitch is used throughout, and the finished design is framed with three bands of long-arm cross stitch.

MATERIALS

20cm (8in) square of 10-count double-thread canvas
Masking tape; tacking (basting) thread
Waterproof felt-tip pen; tapestry needle
1 skein Persian yarn each in pale yellow, dark golden yellow, warm gold, mid blue, chocolate brown and white
Matching cotton sewing thread
41 x 90cm (16 x 36in) piece of polyester wadding (batting)
Dressmaker's pins; matching fabric for the backing

1 Bind the edges of the canvas with masking tape to prevent them fraying and mark the centre with two lines of tacking stitch. Trace the design or draw it directly on to the canvas. Use two strands of yarn in the needle throughout. Outline the face first in brown, then pick out the cheeks, eyes, nose and mouth details using the photograph as a guide to colours.

2 Fill in the circle surrounding the face in blue, with rays of pale yellow and warm gold, then complete the square in white. Next, stitch three lines of long-arm cross stitch, using progressive shades of pale yellow, dark golden yellow, then warm gold, to frame the sun. Stretch and block the finished work.

3 Make a pad to fill the cushion (pillow): cut two 15cm (6in), four 12.5cm (5in) and three 10cm (4in) squares of wadding (batting) and stack them as shown. Pin, then stitch together.

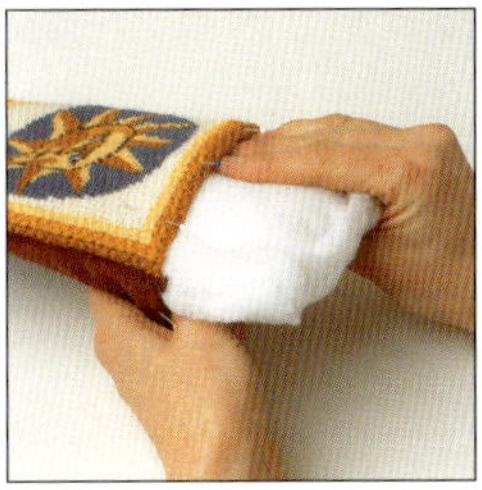

4 Cut an 18cm (7in) square of backing fabric and, right sides together, pin and stitch to the needlepoint on three sides. Turn under the 12mm (½in) seam allowance on the fourth side, insert the pad and slip stitch the side closed.

Brooch Cushion (Pillow)

A brooch cushion (pillow) can look very attractive, set among ornaments and cosmetic jars on the dressing table, and it is a good way to display a selection of favourite jewellery. The toning blues of this frilled version have been picked to match the fabric ruffle, but the colour scheme could easily be adapted to coordinate with the furnishings of a particular room.

MATERIALS

25cm (10in) square of 12-count single-thread canvas
Masking tape; tacking (basting) thread
Tapestry yarn:
2 skeins each in white, pale blue and mid blue
1 skein each in dark blue and indigo
50 x 75cm (20 x 30in) piece of polyester wadding (batting); tapestry needle; dressmaker's pins; matching cotton sewing thread
20cm (8in) square of printed fabric for the backing
20 x 122cm (4 x 48in) printed fabric for the frill
Sewing machine

1 Bind the edges of the canvas with masking tape and mark the centre with two lines of contrasting tacking stitch. The checked pattern is worked in diagonal stitch throughout. Start off in the middle of the canvas by working a small square over two threads, using indigo wool. Work a narrow line of mid blue on each side of the square and fill in the corners with white squares.

2 Following the chart, continue to work the checked pattern until the stitched area measures 14.5cm (5¾in). All the stitches should be worked so that they face the same direction, which will mean that the finished piece becomes distorted. Stretch and block it back into a square shape.

3 Make a cushion (pillow) pad by cutting four 16.5cm (6½in), four 14cm (5½in) and four 11.5cm (4in) squares of wadding (batting) and sandwiching them together as shown. Pin around the edge, sew, then trim away the excess. Cut a 16.5cm (6½in) square of backing fabric and, with right sides together, sew to the needlepoint around three sides, sewing close to the stitches. Turn through, clip the corners and press. Insert the cushion (pillow) pad and slip stitch the fourth side closed.

4 Join the short edges of the frill with a French seam, then make a narrow hem all around each long side, turning the fabric over twice to conceal the raw edges.

5 Run a strong gathering thread around one side. Fold the frill into four to mark it into quarters, then pin around the four sides of the cushion (pillow).

6 Draw up the thread and adjust the gathers so that they are even, allowing an extra fullness at the corners. Stitch on to the cushion (pillow) using small neat stitches, and working from the right side.

Needle Book and Scissor Case

A holder for needles is essential for everybody who sews, and this ivy-leaf needle book, with its matching scissor case, would make an appropriate gift for an embroiderer. Both are trimmed with cord, and the scissor case has a long loop so that it can be kept within easy reach when working. The symmetrical shape of the dark green leaves is offset by the trailing coils of couched gold thread. The informality of this naturalistic design means that there is no need to be too rigid in placing the leaves or copying the stem lines.

NEEDLE BOOK MATERIALS

Ruler; waterproof felt-tip pen
20 x 25cm (8 x 10in) piece of 12-count single thread canvas; tapestry needle
Gold metallic thread for the stems
1 skein of tapestry yarn in dark green and 6 skeins in light green; matching cotton sewing thread
12.5 x 18cm (5 x 7in) piece of green lining fabric
25cm (10in) square of felt; 70cm (28in) length of cord

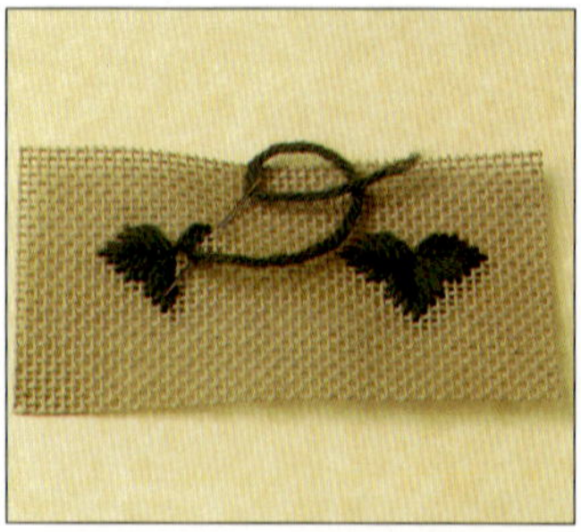

1 Using a waterproof felt-tip pen, rule a rectangle of 10 x 15cm (4 x 6in) on to the canvas. Trace the design. Stitch the leaves in dark green straight stitch. Fill in the background with light green tent stitch worked on the diagonal from the top right-hand corner. Couch a double strand of gold thread for the stems and tendrils.

2 Press the finished piece lightly, then cut out, adding 12mm (½in) canvas all round. Finger-press turnings to the wrong side. Cut the lining to the same size as the canvas. Press under the 12mm (½in) seam allowance, mitring the corners. Slip stitch to the back of the canvas and press from the wrong side on to a padded surface.

3 Cut four felt pages, slightly smaller than half the finished cover size, and stitch to the back cover.

4 Slip stitch cord around the outer edge of the cover, starting and finishing at the centre top. Knot the ends into a loop.

1 Following the diagram, draw the case outline on to the canvas. Work the four leaves in dark green straight stitch. Fill in the background in tent stitch in light green and couch a double strand of gold thread for the stems and tendrils. Make two pieces, reversing the design for the back.

SCISSOR CASE MATERIALS

Waterproof felt-tip pen
20 x 25cm (8 x10in) piece of 12-count single-thread canvas; tapestry needle
1 skein of tapestry yarn in dark green and 5 skeins in light green
Gold metallic thread for the stems
15 x 20cm (6 x 8in) piece of lining fabric
Sewing machine; matching cotton sewing thread; length of cord

2 Cut out one piece, leaving a margin around the stitching, and cut a piece of lining to the same size. With right sides of canvas and lining facing, stitch close to the worked area down one long side and up the other, leaving the top unstitched between points A and A.

3 Trim the surplus fabric around the stitched line as shown and clip the angles. Clip the canvas and trim the lining on the unstitched top edge. Press under the excess on both sides.

4 Gently turn through to the right side, making sure that the corners are crisp. Tidy the turn in around the top edge and stitch the lining and canvas together. Lay the work face downwards on a soft pad and press. Repeat the lining process for the second side.

5 With the wrong sides together, slip stitch the two sides, leaving the top open between points A. Trim with cord. Attach the cord to one point A, 35cm (14in) from one end. Slip stitch all around the top opening, then down one side and up the other. Join securely at second point A and cut the two long ends to equal lengths. Tie the two ends together in a knot.

Knitting

Hand knitting is a skill that can be enjoyed at many levels and most people remember with great affection making their first multi-coloured scarf. Only the most basic techniques are needed to make simple items but, once they have been mastered, there is great scope for creating beautiful knitted garments using the many patterns and yarns that are available.

Knitting
Tools and Materials

To the beginner, the tremendous array of yarns available may seem quite bewildering. Wools should be chosen with the end purpose in mind but all printed patterns give a recommended yarn, needle-size and tension (gauge).

KNITTING NEEDLES

There are three types of needle: single-pointed, double-pointed and circular. Single-pointed needles are used for most work and range from 2.00 to 10.00mm in diameter; the finest are made from metal and the thicker ones from plastic. Bamboo needles are more flexible and therefore easier on the hands. Large garment pieces and tubular knitting are worked on circular needles. Sets of four double-pointed needles are also used for small circular pieces such as socks or hats. Cable needles carry groups of stitches across the surface of the knitting.

TOOLS AND ACCESSORIES

Stitch counters record the number of rows worked and stitch markers can be slipped over the needles to indicate where a row begins in circular knitting. Use a gauge to check needle sizes – this is particularly useful as old needles were numbered to a different system. A crochet hook is useful for picking up dropped stitches and tapestry needles are used to stitch pieces together and for tidying up ends.

YARN

Knitting yarns come in many colours and textures, and are made from natural, synthetic and blended fibres. Wool and acrylic are warm and practical, and combinations of the two are specially formulated for easy washing. Constantly developing processes mean that new "novelty" yarns are always on the market.

Yarns are classified according to weight – light, medium or heavy – and by the number of threads or plys which are spun together to make the strand. Basic double knitting is a versatile 4-ply wool and 3-ply "fingering" is used for baby garments. Fine Shetland lace is knitted from 2-ply wool which comes in subtle natural colours. Cotton yarns are also made in several weights.

Thick bouclé.

Shetland single-ply.

Chenille.

Cotton yarn.

Space-dyed yarn.

Double knitting.

Chunky synthetics.

Textured and novelty yarns.

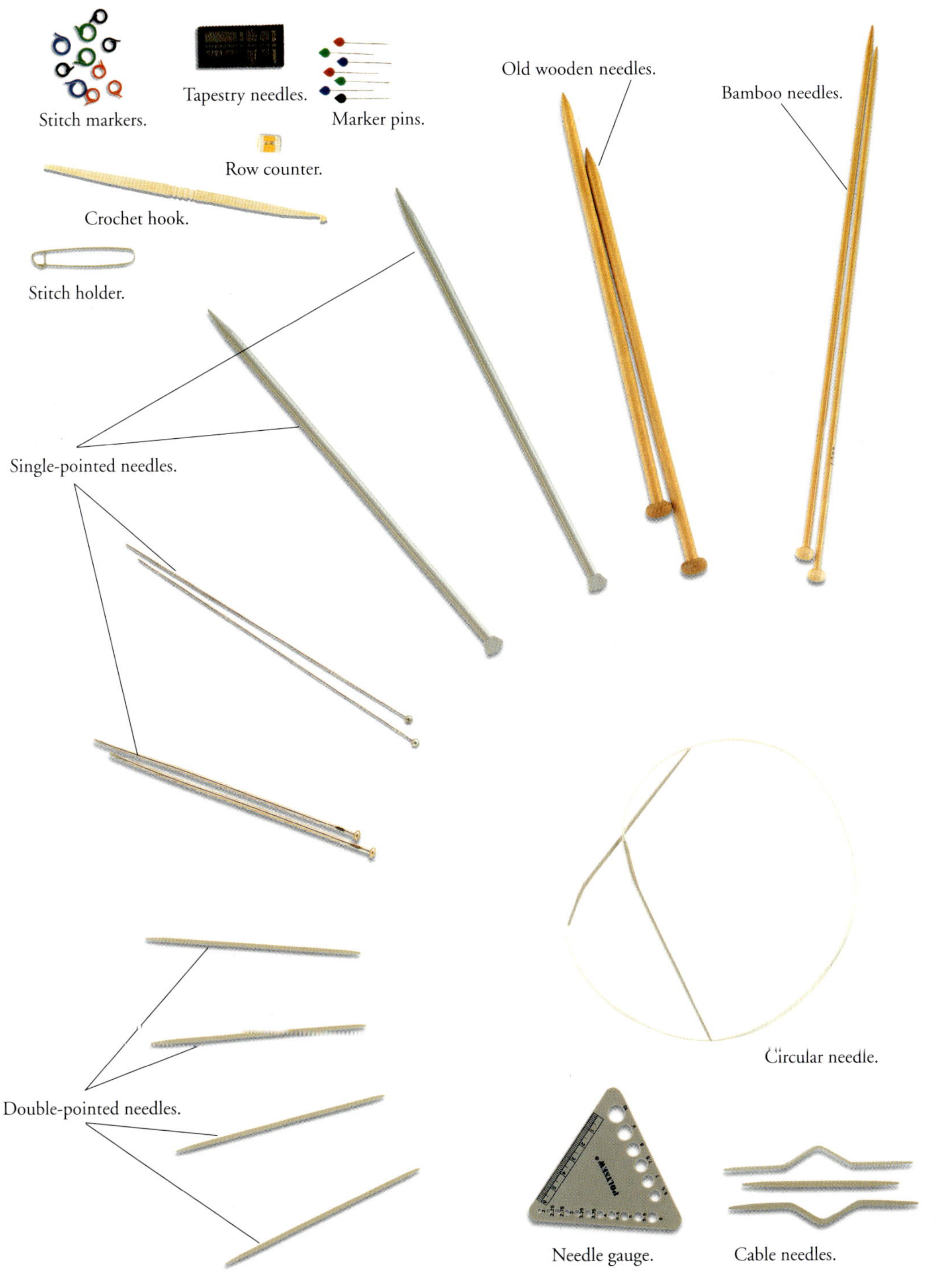
Stitch markers.
Tapestry needles.
Marker pins.
Row counter.
Old wooden needles.
Bamboo needles.
Crochet hook.
Stitch holder.
Single-pointed needles.
Circular needle.
Double-pointed needles.
Needle gauge.
Cable needles.

Casting On

Knitting is worked on two needles and the fabric grows as the stitches are passed from one to the other. There are no set rules about how to hold the yarn and needles – knitters in different parts of the world use them in entirely different ways – and, with practice, everybody finds their own personal method. Left-handed workers should use a mirror to reverse the technique pictures.

Plain stocking stitch is all that has been used here to create these exciting swatches, which are knitted from a selection of fashion yarns.

CASTING ON

The knitted stitches are built up on a foundation of loops. The two most common ways of making this initial row are the one-needle and the two-needle method. The first, sometimes called the thumb method, is perhaps the easiest for beginners and gives an elastic, hardwearing edge. Whichever technique is chosen, it is important to work with an even tension, or the stitches will be too tight to work.

Both methods of casting on begin with a slip loop, which forms the first stitch.

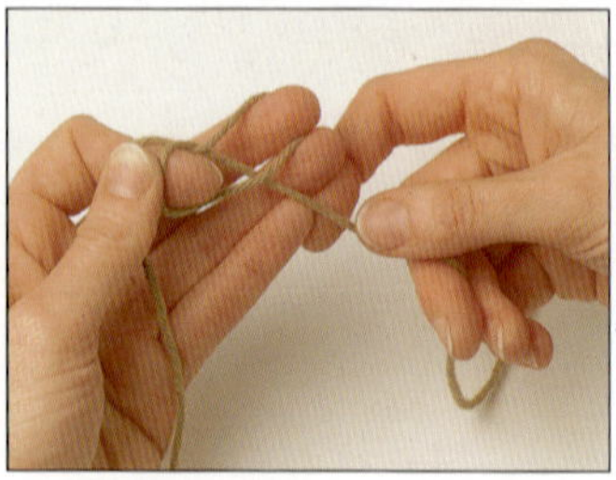

1 MAKING A SLIP LOOP Wrap the long end of the yarn around the short end.

2 Use the tip of the needle to lift the main strand through the loop.

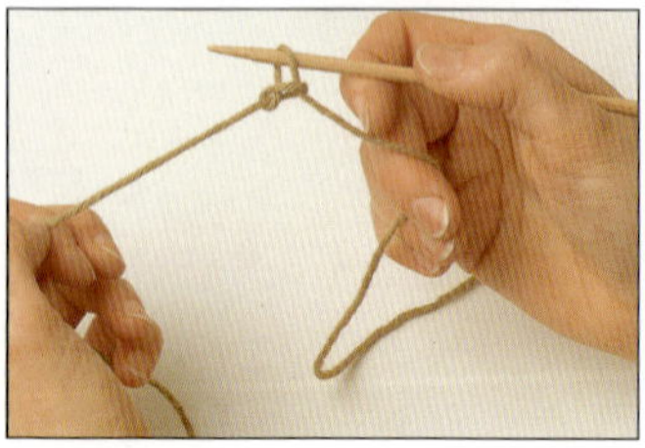

3 Pull on the short end to tighten the slip loop.

1 One-needle method
Make a slip loop at the end of the yarn, allowing at least 30cm (6in) plus an extra 2.5cm (1in) for each stitch. Place the loop on the needle and hold in the right hand. Wrap the short end under and over the left fingers and hold securely in place with the thumb.

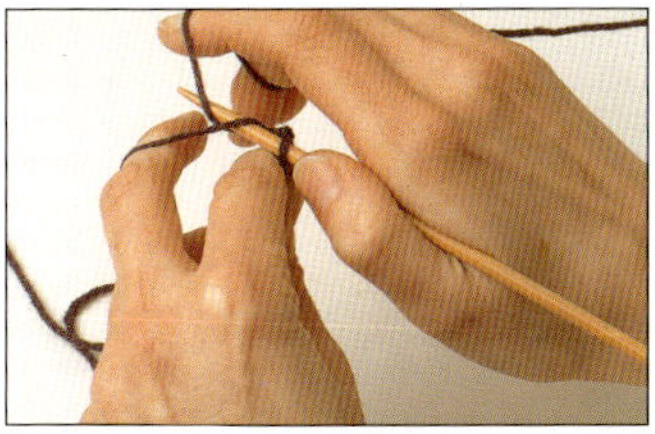

2 Insert the tip of the needle under the yarn between the first and second fingers, then with the right hand, wrap the long end of the yarn under and over the needle.

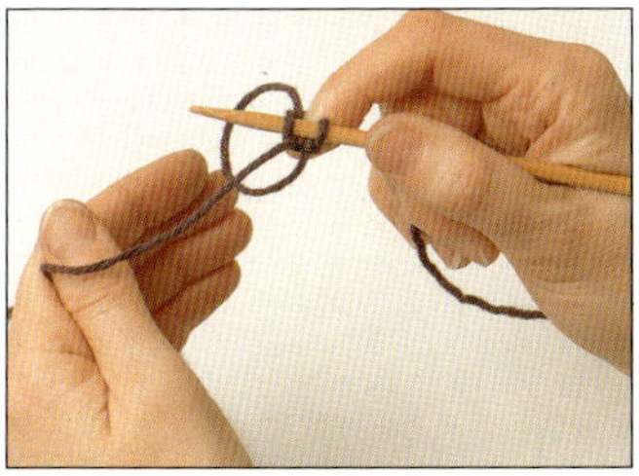

3 Bring the needle and yarn forward, under the taut thread, pulling with the left hand to tighten the new stitch that has been made.

4 Repeat the process for the next stitch and continue until the required number of stitches has been made.

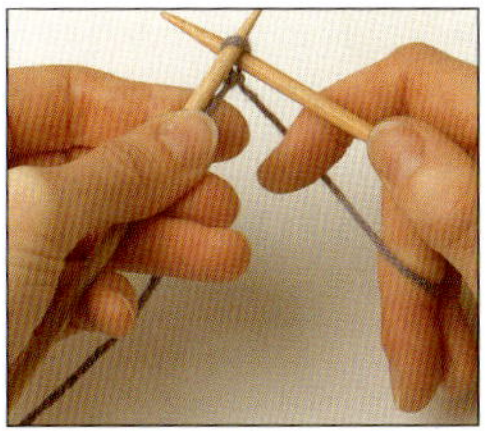

1 Two-needle method
Make a slip loop 30cm (6in) from the end of the yarn and place on the left needle. Insert the right needle through the loop from front to back. Hold the working yarn in the right hand, keeping the tension by passing it under the middle two fingers and around the little finger.

2 With the right hand, wrap the yarn forward, under and over the right needle.

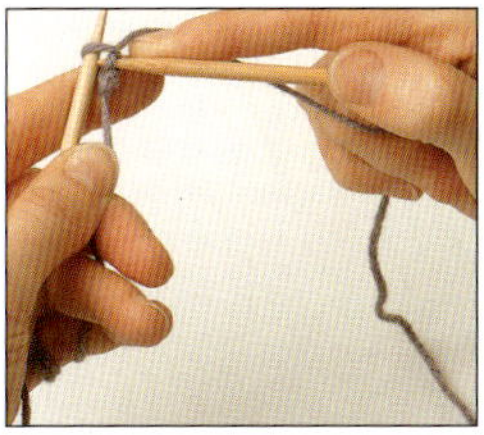

3 This forms the new loop: draw it through the slip loop with the tip of the right needle.

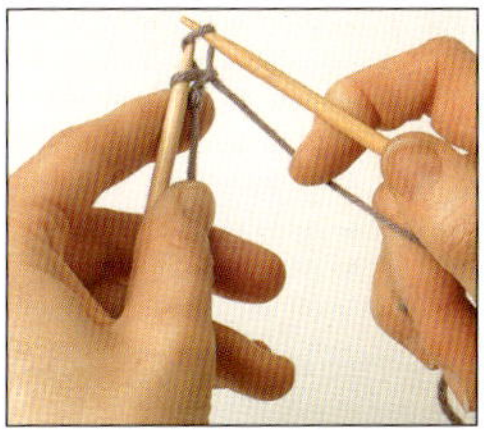

4 Pass the new loop on to the left-hand needle, next to the slip loop.

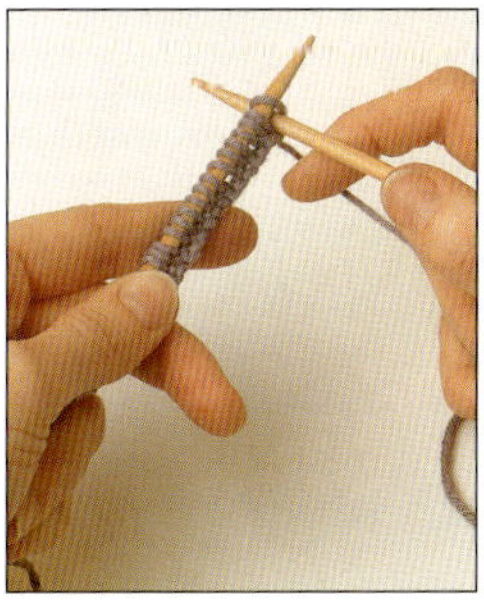

5 Insert the right needle through the front of the new stitch, wrap the yarn under and over the tip, then repeat the process to make another stitch. Continue until the required number of stitches has been made.

Knit and Purl

There are just two stitches – knit and purl – which form the basis of all knitting patterns. When a stitch is knitted, the loop lies at the back of the finished work so that the front of the stitch has a flat appearance; when a stitch is purled the loop lies to the front of the work, so that a small raised line is formed.

1 KNIT STITCH The working needle is held in the right hand, in the same way as a pencil. Maintain tension by passing the yarn over the first finger, under the two middle fingers and loosely around the little finger. It should pass through easily. Insert the right needle through the first loop on the left needle, from front to back.

2 The point of the right needle is now lying behind the left needle. Wrap the yarn forward, under and over the right needle.

3 Bring the point of the right needle forward, down and under the left needle, drawing the yarn through to make a new stitch.

Above: Garter stitch is the simplest of all stitches and is formed when every stitch of each row is knitted. The work is reversible and has an elastic texture, ideal for blankets, scarves or sweaters.

Above: Striped patterns can easily be created by changing the yarn colour between rows.

4 Slip the new stitch off the left needle and on to the right. Repeat until all the stitches have been knitted. Continue with the next row by turning the work and swapping the needles over.

STOCKING (STOCKINETTE) STITCH is most commonly used for garments and has a horizontal stretch. It is formed by knitting one row and purling the next, which produces its distinctively smooth "right" side.

REVERSE STOCKING (STOCKINETTE) STITCH is really the "wrong" side of stocking (stockinette) stitch, and has the appearance of a dense garter stitch. It is used as a contrast pattern, particularly in fisherman's sweater patterns.

1 PURL STITCH Bring the yarn to the front of the work and across the right needle.

2 Insert the tip of the right needle from right to left through the next stitch on the left needle.

3 Wrap the yarn back over the right needle, from right to left between the two points, and back under the right needle to the front.

4 Slide the point of the right needle down and back behind the tip of the left needle and slip the new stitch on to the right needle. Continue to the end of the row.

Following a Pattern

At first glance, any knitting pattern may appear to be just a string of complicated codes, but it is actually set out in a logical and concise form. A standard series of abbreviations and symbols is used to guide the worker through each row of the pattern: those used in this book are given here, although all printed patterns will include their own key.

Read the pattern carefully and be sure of the instructions before embarking on any new project. For the best results use the yarn specified, where possible. Different dye lots may vary in colour so read the label on each ball to make sure they match.

ABBREVIATIONS

beg	beginning
c	cable
cont	continue
dec	decrease
foll	following
inc	increase
K	knit
K2tog	knit 2 together
K2tog tbl	knit 2 together through back of loop
m1	make 1
patt (pat)	pattern
P	purl
P2tog	purl 2 together
psso	pass slip stitch over
RS	right side
rep	repeat
sl st	slip stitch
sts	stitches
tog	together
WS	wrong side
yrn (yo)	yarn round needle (yarn over needle)
yfwd (yf)	yarn forward
( )	repeat the instructions inside the brackets for the number of times indicated
*	repeat the instructions that follow the asterisk

Marker pins and a ruler are used to measure the number of stitches.

TENSION (GAUGE)

It is important to knit with the proper tension or gauge. This does not only mean working evenly, so that all the stitches are regular, but also ensuring that the work meets the measurements given in the pattern. Tension (gauge) determines the size of the stitch, and therefore the finished size of the knitted garment, so it is vital that it is correct.

Tension (gauge) is measured by knitting up a sample using the needle size and yarn specified by the designer and this should always be done before starting to make up any new project. Most patterns name a particular brand of yarn and the design will be sized with this in mind. If another yarn is substituted, it is even more necessary to check tension (gauge) first. The pattern will specify the amount of stitches which, when worked over a set number of rows, should reach a given measurement.

Work up the swatch, which should be at least 10cm (4in) square and pin it out on a flat surface without stretching it in any direction. Measure and mark out the given width and carefully count the number of whole stitches that lie within it. Count the number of rows in the same way. If there are not enough stitches, the tension (gauge) is too tight and needles one size larger should be used; if there are too many, the work is too loose and needles a size smaller should be used. Continue experimenting with different needles until the sample meets the correct tension (gauge). If it does not, the finished garment will be the wrong size and a lot of time and effort will have been wasted.

Knitting Gallery

There are many options open to the imaginative knitter. The selection of patterns available caters for every taste and level of skill. Specialist designers produce kits to make high-fashion garments, but even the plainest knitted sweater can be embellished with embroidery beads. The examples illustrated here should inspire some original ideas.

To create this delicate trellis pattern, pink and yellow crochet flower motifs have been appliquéd on to a hand-knitted background.

The raised texture of these bobble stitch grapes is emphasized by the choice of a velvety chenille yarn in a rich purple.

Traditional Fair Isle knitting draws on the imagery of nature; the geometric shapes on these gloves are reminiscent of snowflakes.

Woven carpets and other textiles from many cultures can be a great source of inspiration for intarsia knitting and the designs can be charted on to squared paper.

Small silver beads and subtle gold yarn provide delicate highlights on this floral pattern, which has a medieval simplicity.

Natural wooden beads have been applied to a textured background knitted from unbleached cotton in a mixture of stitches.

Correcting Mistakes

As with any new skill, all beginners are bound to make mistakes when starting to knit. It takes time to learn how to control the yarn and needles with confidence, and it may help to ask an experienced knitter for guidance. Dropped stitches, however, are easily corrected, or picked up, with the needles. They may slip off if the work is set aside in the middle of a row or if it has been knitted hastily. Sometimes a dropped stitch may go unnoticed and form a ladder, which will have to be picked up with a crochet hook.

1 PICKING UP A KNIT STITCH The dropped stitch will need to be brought back up to the same level as the rest of the row.

2 Insert the right needle through the front of the loose stitch from front to back, without twisting it, and under the strand of yarn behind it.

3 Use the tip of the left needle to lift the stitch over the yarn, keeping the new loop on the right needle.

4 Place the tip of the left needle through the front of the stitch from left to right and slide it back on to the needle, ready to be re-knitted.

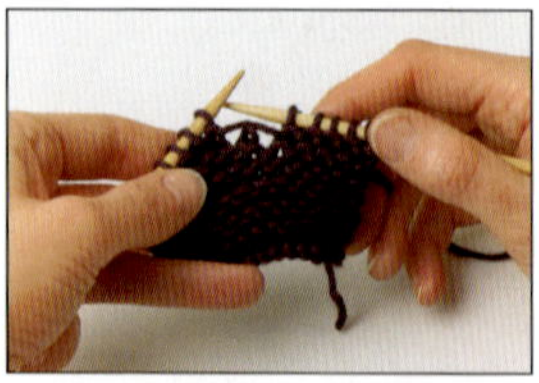

1 PICKING UP A PURL STITCH The dropped stitch is corrected by passing the loose yarn back through it.

2 Insert the right needle through the front of the loose stitch, from front to back and under the strand of the yarn.

3 Insert the left needle through the stitch from front to back and lift it over the strand, keeping the stitch on the right needle.

4 Slip the new stitch back on to the left needle, ready to continue with a purl row.

PICKING UP A LADDER
Knit stitch Insert a crochet hook through the front of the first dropped stitch and pull the loose strand from behind through the loop to form a new stitch. Repeat to the top of the ladder and slip the last stitch on to the left needle.

Purl stitch The method is the same as for knit stitch, but the hook is inserted from behind the work.

Casting Off

A piece of knitting is completed by casting off the stitches. This is usually done on the right side of the work and knit stitches should be cast off knitwise and purl stitches purlwise. This is especially important when casting off the ribbing at a cuff or neck edge. If the cast-off stitches are too tight they will distort the work, but using a larger size needle can help to make a looser finish. There are several specialized ways of casting off, but the method shown here is the most common and straightforward.

Above: The cast-off edge gives a neat selvage to the knitted piece. The loose yarn from the beginning and end should be sewn invisibly along the edge of the work.

1 CASTING OFF KNITWISE Knit the first two stitches as usual.

2 Insert the left needle under the first stitch made, from left to right.

3 Lift the stitch up and over the second stitch and over the point of the right needle. The first stitch has now been cast off.

4 Knit the next stitch from the left needle so that there are two stitches on the right needle. Lift the first stitch over the second and continue casting off to the end of the row. Cut the end of the yarn and draw it through the final stitch to finish off.

CASTING OFF PURLWISE The method is the same for casting off a purl row: purl two stitches and lift the first stitch over the second as before.

Knitted Pattern Stitches

Knitting has a rich heritage of pattern stitches which incorporates intricate cables, eyelets or raised bobbles, and knitwear designers are constantly developing new ideas. There are, however, many interesting textured patterns that can be created simply by combining knit and purl stitches to produce a textured surface. Moss stitch variations give a firm, reversible fabric while rib stitch gives a stretchy vertical stripe, used to finish the welts (bottom), cuffs and neck edges of sweaters. To ensure a snug fit, it is usually worked with needles a size smaller than those used for the main part of the garment. Horizontal furrows are formed by working alternate stripes of stocking and garter stitch.

Embossed textures show to best advantage when plain yarns, such as natural cottons, are used.

THREE BY THREE RIB This is worked over a multiple of six stitches, plus three.

Row 1 *K3, P3; rep from *, K3
Row 2 P3, *K3, P3p; rep from *
These two rows form the pattern.

RIDGED BANDS These are worked over any number of stitches.

Row 1 Knit
Row 2 Purl
Rows 3 and 4 Knit
Row 5 Purl
Row 6 Knit
Repeat these six rows to form the pattern.

MOSS STITCH This is worked over an uneven number of stitches.

Each row as follows: *K1, P1; rep from *, K1.

DOUBLE MOSS STITCH This is worked over a multiple of four stitches.

Rows 1 and 2 *K2, P2 rep from * to end
Rows 3 and 4 *P2, K2 rep from * to end
These rows form the pattern.

FISHERMAN'S SWEATER PATTERNS

Knit and purl patterns were traditionally used by the women of seafaring villages to ornament the sweaters worn by local fishermen. These garments were the main protection from the elements in the days before weatherproof clothing and had to stand up to hard physical wear. The various ports and fishing villages around the coasts of many countries evolved their own individual variations of diamond, zigzag or chevron panels, which are still design classics today.

BASKET WEAVE This is worked over a multiple of eight stitches, plus five.

Row 1 (RS) knit
Row 2 K5, *P3, K5; rep from *
Row 3 P5, *K3, P5; rep from *
Row 4 as row 2
Row 5 Knit
Row 6 K1, *P3, K5; rep from *, to last 4 sts, P3, K1
Row 7 P1, *K3, P5; rep from *, to last 4 sts, K3, P1
Row 8 as row 6
These eight rows form the pattern.

EMBOSSED LADDER PATTERN This is worked over a multiple of 14 stitches.

Row 1 *K1, P2, K1, P1, K2, P2, K2, P2, K1, rep from *
Row 2 *(P1, K2) twice, P2, (K2, P1) twice, rep from *
Row 3 *K1, P2, K2, P2, K2, P1, K1, P2, K1, rep from *
Row 4 *P1, K2, P3, K2, P3, K2, P1, rep from *
These four rows form the pattern.

WAVE STITCH This is worked over a multiple of eight stitches, plus six.

Row 1 (RS) K6, *P2, K6; rep from *
Row 2 K1, *P4, K4, rep from *, end P4, K1
Row 3 P2, *K2, P2; rep from *
Row 4 P1, *K4, P4; rep from *, end K4, P1
Row 5 K2, *P2, K6; rep from *, end P2, K2
Row 6 P6, *K2, P6; rep from *
Row 7 P1, *K4, P4, rep from *, end K4, P1
Row 8 K2, *P2, K2; rep from *
Row 9 K1, *P4, K4; rep from *, end P4, K1
Row 10 P2, *K2, P6, rep from *, end K2, P2
These ten rows form the pattern.

ZIGZAG This is worked over a multiple of six stitches.

Row 1 (WS) and all other odd rows, Purl
Row 2 *K3, P3, rep from *
Row 4 P1, *K3, P3, rep from *, end K3, P2
Row 6 P2, *K3, P3; rep from *, end K3, P1
Row 8 *P3, K3; rep from *
Row 10 P2, *K3, P3; rep from *, end K3, P1
Row 12 P1, *K3, P3; rep from *, end K3, P2
These 12 rows form the pattern.

Increasing and Decreasing

A piece of knitting is shaped as it is worked, by alternating the number of stitches on the needles. In effect, the width is increased by adding more stitches to the row and decreased by taking some away. There are several ways in which this can be done, depending on the type of fabric being knitted. The effect can be almost invisible, or give a decorative openwork effect.

Above: When lacy fabric, such as these delicate single-ply Shetland scarves, is being knitted, the number of stitches must remain constant, so for every one that is decreased, another is created.

1 DECREASING *Knit two together (K2tog)* The simplest way of decreasing is to work two stitches together, at either end, or in the middle of a row. The method for purling two stitches together is similar. At the start of the row, insert the needle from right to left through the first two stitches. Knit as usual. This gives a slant to the right.

2 Knit two together at the end of a row by inserting the needle from left to right through the last two stitches. This produces a slant to the left. It creates an invisible shaping and is used for sleeves as a paired decrease, one side sloping to the right and one to the left.

1 *Slipped stitch method (Sl1, K1, Psso)* At the beginning of a row, slip the first stitch on to the right needle without knitting it.

2 Knit the next stitch as usual.

3 Insert the left needle through the slipped stitch and lift it up, across the knitted stitch and off the end of the needle.

4 At the end of a row, slip the last but one stitch, knit the final stitch and pass the slip stitch over the knitted stitch.

INCREASING

Increasing between stitches (M1k) The extra stitch for this invisible method comes from working into the horizontal strand of yarn that lies between two stitches.

1 With the right needle, lift the horizontal strand between the last knitted stitch and the next and place it on to the left needle.

2 Knit into the back of the strand, to twist and tighten the loop.

3 Slip the new stitch on to the right needle.

Bar Method An additional stitch can also be made by knitting twice into the same loop. This does not give as smooth an appearance as the previous method, so it is used at seam edges.

1 Knit the stitch as usual, but keep it on the left needle.

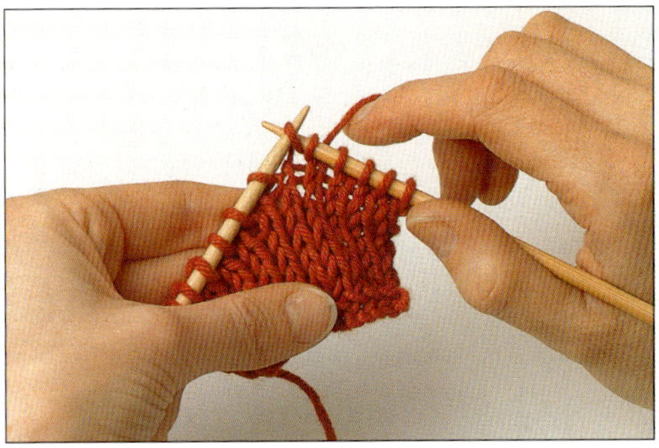

2 Insert the right needle into the back of the stitch just knitted and knit it again.

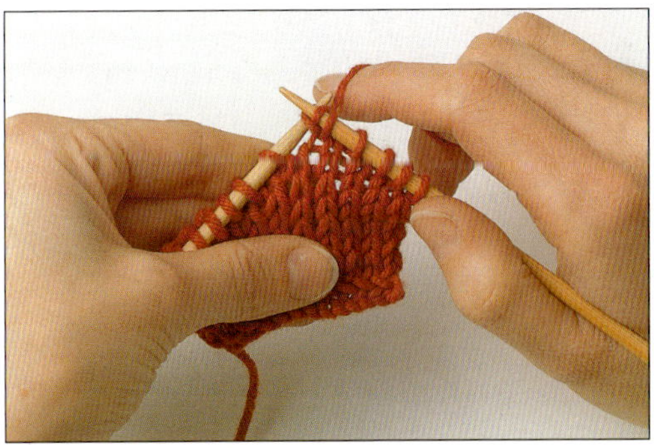

3 Slip the double stitch on to the right needle.

Working with Colour

A limitless range of multicoloured patterns, from traditional Fair Isle, to contemporary intarsia or Jacquard designs, can be created by combining different yarns. Stripes are the quickest and easiest way to introduce colour and can be boldly contrasting or subtly shaded. The Fair Isle way of working appears to be very complex, but, in fact, the intricate patterns are cleverly designed so that only two yarns are required in any one row.

Above: Multicoloured designs are usually worked from a chart on which one square corresponds to one stitch. These are straightforward to draw up, when designing original patterns, and can be filled in with coloured pencils. Many printed patterns are in black and white, and a series of symbols are used to represent the various colours.

JOINING COLOUR AT THE START OF A ROW

This is a quick method of working with two colours of yarn to create a horizontally striped fabric. Any loose ends can be sewn in when the piece is finished.

1 Insert the right needle as usual at the beginning of the yarn. Leaving an end of roughly 30cm (6in), loop the new colour over the needle with the old. Knit the stitch.

2 Let the first yarn drop to the side, knit the next two stitches with the double new yarn, then knit the rest of the row with the single strand of new yarn.

3 Carry the loose ends of the yarn along the outside edge as the stripes are knitted.

JOINING COLOUR WITHIN A ROW

Intarsia patterns may require yarn to be joined within a row to create new areas of colour. Sew in the short ends later.

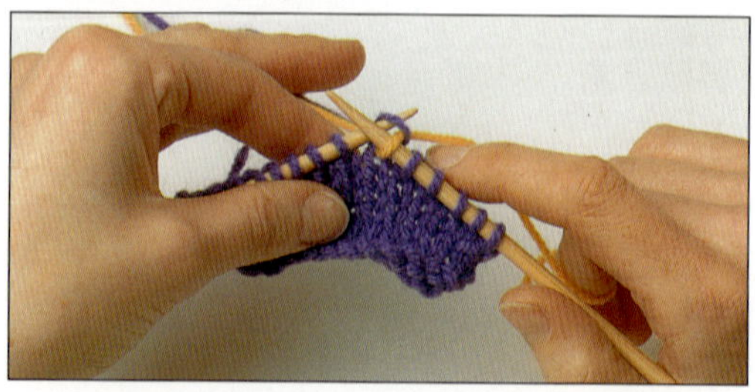

1 Leaving the first yarn at the back of the work, loop the new colour over the needle and knit the next stitch.

2 Working the next two stitches with the double yarn, let the short end drop and continue with the single yarn.

INTARSIA

When two blocks of colour meet within a row, the two yarns must be twisted together to give a smooth finish and to prevent holes appearing.

1 On knit rows, hold the first colour across the back of the work to the left and work the next stitch with the second colour so that the yarn passes over the taut strand.

2 On purl rows, hold the first colour across to the left and pass the second colour over it before purling the next stitch.

The different yarns in the traditional Fair Isle Symbister pattern are varied from dark to light by "shading in" the colour in interlocking rows of small diamonds.

CARRYING YARN ACROSS THE BACK

When two colours appear in the same row, only one is actually in use at any one time, so the second colour has to be carried across the back. This creates loose strands, or floats, which can pull and distort, so to maintain an even tension (gauge) they must be woven into the work every few stitches.

1 On a knit row, hold the floating colour out to the left so that the working yarn passes over it before knitting the next stitch.

2 On a purl row, hold the floating yarn up between the points of the two needles so that the working yarn goes across it before purling the next stitch.

3 Be sure that the float then drops clear of the working yarn, while it is being used.

The back of the sweater shows how the colours are carried across, so that no loop extends for more than three stitches.

Cable Cushion (Pillow)

The hand-knitted jerseys (sweaters) worn by fishing communities evolved a distinctive functional style over many years. They were made from heavy-duty wool, still impregnated with lanolin, to keep them waterproof and to stand up to hard wear. This attractive cushion (pillow) combines the newest indigo-dyed cotton yarns with long-established patterns; the moss stitch and cable pattern are reminiscent of Guernsey jumpers (sweaters) from the Channel Islands. The natural blue indigo dye is also used for denim; so, like jeans, this cushion (pillow) will fade with wear and use. The finished cushion (pillow) measures 30cm (12in) square.

(NOTE: Cotton yarn has very little "give". To ensure an even tension (gauge), knit as far towards the tips of the needles as you can.)

MATERIALS

100g (4oz) indigo cotton yarn in double knitting weight
Pair of 4.00mm knitting needles
Cable needle
33cm (13in) square of dark blue needlecord (pinwale corduroy)
33cm (13in) square of blue brushed cotton fabric
Matching cotton sewing thread
30cm (12in) square cushion (pillow) pad
Cardboard

1 The twisted cable pattern is worked by slipping three stitches on to a cable needle and holding it at the front of the work while knitting the next three stitches from the left-hand needle. The three stitches on the cable needle are then knitted. This is abbreviated as (C6f) for "cable six forward".

2 TO MAKE UP With right sides facing, sew the needlecord and brushed cotton fabric squares together around three sides, leaving a seam allowance of 12mm (½in). Press the seams and turn right side out. Slip stitch the knitted panel on to the cotton lining, using the indigo yarn.

3 Insert the cushion (pillow) pad and slip stitch the fourth side closed.

4 Make each looped tassel by winding a length of yarn round a 7.5cm (3in) wide piece of cardboard about 20 times. Slip off and sew the loop on to the corner as shown, binding the tassel head close to the stitching.

INSTRUCTIONS

Cast on 60 sts.
Row 1 K1, P1 to end.
Row 2 P1, K1 to end.
Row 3 as row 1;
Row 4 as row 2.
Row 5 K1, P1, K1, P1, P7, C6f, P7, (K1, P1) 6 times, P7, C6f, P7, K1,(P1, K1, P1
Row 6 P1, K1 P1, K1, K7, P6, K7 (P1, K1) 6 times, K7, P6, K7, P1, K1, P1, K1.
Row 7 K1, P1, K1, P1, P7, K6, P7, (K1, P1) 6 times, P7, K6, P7, K1, P1, K1, P1.
Row 8 P1, K1, P1, K1, P5, K2, P6, K2, P5 (K1, P1) 6 times, P5, K2, P6, K2, P5, P1, K1, P1, K1.
Row 9 K1, P1, K1, P1, K5, P2, K6, P2, K5, (K1, P1) 6 times, K5, P2, K6, P2, K5, K1, P1, K1, P1.
Row 10 P1, K1, P1, K1, P5, K2, P6, K2, P5 (P1, K1) 6 times, P5, K2, P6, K2, P5, P1, K1, P1, K1.
Repeat rows 5-10 twelve times. Repeat rows 1-4 (80rows). Cast off.

Basket Edging

Knitted lace is hard wearing, adaptable and can be worked in a variety of sizes and textures. The basket edging shown here is made on a large scale using unbleached craft cotton, but could easily be made on very fine needles with perlé crochet cotton or 2-ply Shetland wool to make a collar or cuff trimming for a garment. This traditional pattern is known as "ten stitch", as it is worked on a foundation of ten stitches.

MATERIALS

Cotton yarn in double knitting weight
Pair of 3.50mm knitting needles
Basket
Tapestry needle

1 The open lacy effect of the basket edging is created by repeating a simple stitch pattern: wind the yarn forward once around the needle to make an extra stitch, then knit the next two stitches together. This is abbreviated in the instructions as (yrn, K2 tog).

2 Cast off when the lace is long enough to fit around the basket, ending on row 14 so that the zigzag edge is complete. Join the two edges together neatly and fit the edging around the rim of the basket.

INSTRUCTIONS

Cast on 10 st. Rows 1-14 form the pattern.

Row 1 sl 1, K3 (yrn, K2 tog) twice, yrn, K2.
Row 2 and every even-numbered row, K to end.
Row 3 sl 1, K4 (yrn, K2 tog) twice, yrn, K2.
Row 5 sl 1, K5 (yrn, K2 tog) twice, yrn, K2.
Row 7 sl 1, K6 (yrn, K2 tog) twice, yrn, K2.
Row 9 sl 1, K7 (yrn, K2 tog) twice, yrn, K2.
Row 11 sl 1, K8 (yrn, K2 tog) twice, yrn, K2.
Row 13 sl 1, K to end.
Row 14 cast off 6 sts, K to end (10 sts).

3 Sew in place using a tapestry needle. Pass the needle right through the basket from one side to the other, using small tidy stitches and being careful not to pull the thread too tightly.

Shetland Lace Scarf

Shetland lies between Scotland and Scandinavia, and consists of some 100 islands, set at the crossroads of the North Sea and the North Atlantic. The hardy strain of Shetland sheep has long been bred on the islands, and for over 500 years their fleece has been spun and made into garments. The multicoloured Fair Isle pullovers are famous, but the finest of the single- and two-ply yarns are knitted into lace shawls and scarves. This pattern is inspired by the crashing waves of the seas that surround the islands. The finished scarf measures 90 x 25cm (36 x10in).

MATERIALS
2-ply Shetland wool:
25g (1oz) in white
15g ($^{1}/_{2}$oz) each in blue, pink and lilac
Pair of 3.00mm knitting needles
Tapestry needle

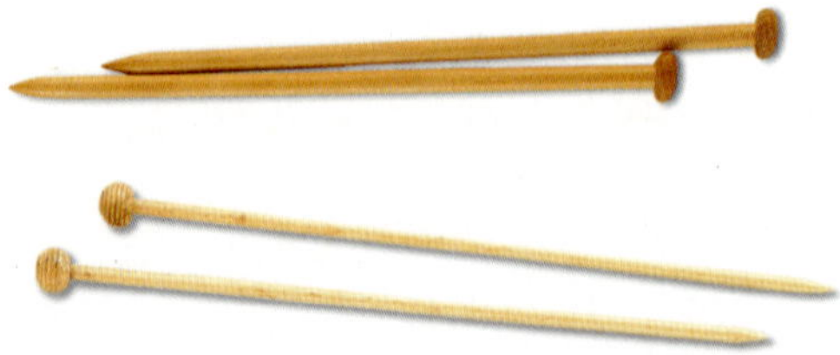

TENSION (GAUGE)
Using 3.00mm needles, 10 pattern rows measure 2.5cm (1in).
Cast on 75 st in white.
Row 1 K2, K2 tog (K3, yfwd, K1, yfwd, K3, K3 tog) to last 11 sts, K3, yfwd, K1, yfwd, K3, K2 tog, K2.
Row 2 K to end.
These two rows form the pattern: repeat five times more and then continue the pattern using the following colour sequence, breaking off the yarn at the end of each stripe.

*
**
2 rows blue
2 rows lilac
2 rows pink
2 rows white
2 rows pink
2 rows lilac
2 rows blue
**
8 rows white
Repeat from ** to ** once
8 rows white
Repeat from ** to ** to complete coloured wave
*
24 rows white
2 rows blue
24 rows white
Repeat coloured wave from * to * once
24 rows white
2 rows blue
24 rows white
Repeat coloured wave from * to * once
12 rows white to finish.

1 It is important not to work too tightly when knitting the three stitches together, so that the right-hand needle can pass easily through all the loops.

2 Cast off loosely and darn in all the loose ends.

3 Pin out both ends of the scarf so that the edges form peaks, then press lightly with a damp cloth. Allow to dry away from direct heat and sunlight.

Baby Wrap

This innovative baby wrap is warm and comfortable for winter outings. It is worked in double knitting yarn and lined with soft cotton. The pattern of geometric bands and child-like figures is knitted from an easy-to-follow chart. The front and back are made separately, then joined together, leaving the convenient zip (zipper) opening along the lower edge. The finished garment measures 51cm (20in) from collar to hem and 28cm (11in) across the chest.

MATERIALS

50g (2oz) double knitting yarn each in lilac, beige, purple, turquoise and dark green
Pair each of 3.25mm and 4.50mm knitting needles
3.25mm circular needle
Stitch holder
2 buttons
2 x 41cm (16in) zips (zippers)
60cm (24in) square of fabric for the lining
Matching cotton sewing thread

BACK

Using 4.50mm needles, cast on 68 sts in lilac.
Row 1 K to end
Row 2 P to end.
Row 3 inc 1, K to end, inc 1.
Work the pattern from the chart, increasing 1 st at each end of the 5th, 7th and 9th rows (76 sts). Carry the contrast yarn across the back of the knitting.
Row 54 dec 1 st at each end of this and following 4th rows until 60 sts remain. Work 12 rows from pattern.
Row 94 K to end of row and inc 20 sts.
Row 95 P to end of row and inc 20 sts. Continue to follow the chart, knitting on these 100 sts for the 17 remaining rows of the pattern. Knit 5 rows lilac. Cast off.

FRONT

Work as for the back until row 105, then decrease for the left shoulder and neck shaping, using the chart as a guide.
Row 106 K45, then put centre 10 sts on to st holder. Dec 1 at neck edge, K to end. Working on these 44 sts –
Row 107 dec 1 at end of row (neck edge).
Row 108 work row without decreasing.
Row 109 dec 1 st at end of row (neck edge).
Row 110 dec 1 st at beg of row.
Rows 111 – 115 work remainder of pattern, and knit 5 rows lilac.
Cast off. Reverse instructions for right shoulder and neck opening.

TO MAKE UP

Sew in the ends and press lightly. Set marks in contrasting yarn 27 sts from the cuff edge on the left-hand side of the front and back, at the centre front and back at the cast-on edge and 5 rows up from the cast-on edge back and front.

1 CUFFS Pick up 40 sts on size 3.25mm needles and work 8 rows K1, P1 rib. Cast off rib-wise.

2 SEAMS With right sides together, sew along the shoulder seams to the neck edge on the right-hand side and to the marker on the left-hand side.

3 NECK Pick up stitches round the neck with the circular needle, starting at the left-hand top: 4 sts along rib; 8 sts along neck edge; 10 sts from holder; 8 sts along neck edge; 20 sts along back neck; 4 sts along rib. Rib these sts for 4 rows and cast off. Sew buttons on to the shoulder fastening.

4 TO SEW IN THE ZIPS Pin the zip (zippers) in the opening at the bottom, then stitch in place to the markers on the lower edge of the front and back.

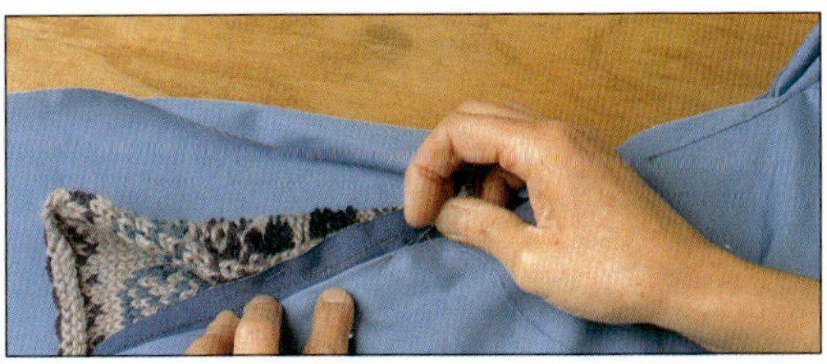

5 TO LINE Cut two shapes from the lining fabric 4cm (1½in) larger than the finished knitted wrap. Join at the shoulder, under the arm and along the side seams. With wrong sides together, sew the lining to the inside of the wrap at the cuffs, neck edges and along each open side.

TO FINISH THE NECK OPENING

Back Pick up 13 sts along from the marker to the neck edge. Rib 3 rows and cast off.

FRONT

Pick up 13 sts from the marker to the neck edge.
Rows 1 and 2 work in K1, P1 rib.
Row 3 K1, cast off 1, rib 4, cast off 1, rib 4.
Row 4 rib 4, cast on 1, rib 4, cast on 1, K1.
Cast off.

Baby Mittens and Baby Shoes

Knitted bootees or shoes are a popular present for a new baby, and a first pair is often kept as a souvenir. These brightly striped T-bar shoes will fit from newborn up to four months old and are worked in a practical, washable cotton yarn. The matching mittens are made in a basic design with minimal shaping and would be suitable for a baby of up to nine months.

BABY MITTENS MATERIALS

Small quantity of double knitting yarn in pink, orange and yellow
Pair each of 3.00mm and 3.50mm knitting needles
Tapestry needle

TENSION (GAUGE)

Using 3.50mm needles, 21 sts and 30 rows measure 10cm (4in) – st st.

Begin at the cuff. Using 3.00mm needles and pink yarn, cast on 34 sts.

Row 1 K2, P2 to end.

Row 2 P2, K2 to end.

Repeat 1st and 2nd rows 8 times more. Change to orange and yellow yarn and 3.50mm needles. Work in the stripe pattern throughout (2 rows orange, 2 rows yellow).

Eyelet row (K2, yfwd, K2 tog) to end.

Starting with a P row, work 19 rows st st.

Dec Row K1 (K2 tog tbl, K12, K2 tog) twice, K1.

Next row P to end.

Dec row K1 (K2 tog tbl, K10, K2 tog) twice, K1.
(30 sts) Cast off.

1 TO MAKE THE CORDS Cut six 45cm (18in) strands of yarn, two each in pink, orange and yellow. Knot together at one end, leaving 2.5cm (1in) of yarn to form a tassel. Secure the knot with a weight, or pin to a fixed object, then plait (braid) to the end. Make a knot 2.5cm (1in) from the end of the finished plait (braid). Brush and trim the tassels.

2 TO MAKE UP With wrong sides together, slip stitch the top seam using the end of the yellow yarn.

3 Turn right side out and stitch along the side seam.

4 Use pink yarn to join cuff. Thread cords through the eyelets.

Row 5 K1, inc 1, K13, inc 1, K1, inc 1, K13, inc 1, K1.
Row 7 K1, inc 1, K15, inc 1, K1, inc 1, K15, inc 1, K1.
Row 9 K1, inc 1, K17, inc 1, K1, inc 1, K17, inc 1, K1.
Row 11 K1, inc 1, K19, inc 1, K1, inc 1, K19, inc 1, K1.
Row 12 K to end.
Change to orange and yellow yarn and work the upper part of the shoe in the stripe pattern throughout (2 rows orange, 2 rows yellow).
Row 13 K17, sl 1, K1, psso, K11, K2 tog, K17.
Row 14 and every even-numbered row, P to end.
Row 15 K17, sl 1, K1, psso, K9, K2 tog, K17.
Row 17 K17, sl 1, K1, psso, K7, K2 tog, K17.
Row 19 K17, sl 1, K1, psso, K5, K2 tog, K17.
Row 20 P to end.
Row 21 K9.
Cast off 9, K5 (including st on needle after casting off) cast off 9, K9. Beginning with a P row, work 4 rows st st on these 9 sts. Cast off.

Baby Shoes Materials

Oddments of double knitting yarn in pink, orange and yellow
Pair of 3.00mm knitting needles
2 matching buttons or beads; tapestry needle

Tension (Gauge)

Using 3.00mm needles, 21sts and 30 rows measures 10cm (4in) – (st st).
Begin with the sole. Using pink, cast on 25 sts.
Row 1 K1, inc 1, K9, inc 1, K1, inc 1, K9, inc 1, K1.
Row 2 and every even-numbered row, P to end.
Row 3 K1, inc 1, K11, inc 1, K1, inc 1, K11, inc 1, K1.

To make the ankle strap

Return to the remaining 9 sts, cast on 12 sts (on to the same needle as 9 sts). P across these sts, then P across the group of 9 sts (21 sts).
Work 4 rows st st. Cast off.

To make the T-bar

Return to the centre 5 sts. Beginning with a P row, work 15 rows st st. Cast off.

Second shoe

Make as for the first shoe, reversing the shaping of the strap.

1 To make up Join the sole and upper seams along the centre back. With orange yarn make a small loop at the end of the ankle strap and work buttonhole stitch into the loop.

2 Fold the T-bar over the ankle strap and sew the end in place on the underside.

3 Sew the button or bead firmly on to the main part of the shoe.

Tasselled Hat

This child's hat is very straightforward to work, even for the beginner. It is made from the most basic of rectangular shapes and its appeal relies on the dynamic use of colour and the extravagant tassels that add a finishing decorative touch. The size given would fit a toddler, but, once the tension (gauge) has been worked out, it is easy to make the hat larger or smaller. The finished hat measures 35cm (14in) around the ribbed edge.

MATERIALS

Small quantities of double knitting yarn in:
(A) yellow (B) lime (C) pink (D) bright yellow
(E) orange (F) turquoise (G) red and (H) purple
Embroidery scissors
Pair each of 3.00mm and 3.50mm knitting needles
Tapestry needle
9cm (3½in) piece of cardboard

TENSION GAUGE

Using 3.50mm needles, 21sts and 30 rows measures 10cm (4in).
Using 3.00mm needles and yarn A, cast on 48 sts. Work 10 rows K1, P1 rib.
Change to 3.50mm needles and work the following striped pattern in st st:
6 rows B, 2 rows C
6 rows B, 2 rows D
6 rows B, 2 rows E
6 rows B, 2 rows F
6 rows B, 2 rows G
6 rows B, 2 rows H.
Work a further 2 rows for middle top of hat.
Continue in st st for back of hat:
6 rows F, 2 rows A
6 rows F, 2 rows C
6 rows F, 2 rows G
6 rows F, 2 rows E
6 rows F, 2 rows H
6 rows F, 2 rows B.
Break yarn. Using 3.00mm needles and yarn G, work 10 rows K1, P1 rib. Cast off.

1 TO MAKE THE TASSELS Wind a selection of the yarns used in the hat around the rectangle of cardboard to the required thickness – about eight times for each colour. Knot a length of yarn around the loop and tie tightly.

2 Slip the yarn off the card and, holding the loop firmly at one end, take a needle with yarn through the top of the loop twice and secure. Cut through the other end of the loop, then wind a length of yarn around the tassel 12mm (½in) from the top and tie tightly. Comb to separate the yarn strands. Trim level with sharp scissors.

3 TO MAKE UP Fold the hat in half with right sides facing inwards. Stitch the side seams together and turn to the right side.

4 Attach one tassel securely to each corner.

Fringed Scarf

Most novice knitters start out by making a striped scarf, either for themselves or for their teddy bears. It is still the best way to practise the rudiments of knitting. The yarns for this project are specially chosen in natural tweed-like colours, but knitting a multicoloured scarf can be the ideal way to use up odd balls of wool. A deep fringe gives an attractive finish and can be made to match or contrast with the scarf itself.

The finished scarf measures 25 x 140cm (10 x 55in), but could be made longer or narrower.

Materials

Double knitting yarn in various colours
Pair of 4.00mm knitting needles
20cm (8in) piece of cardboard
Large crochet hook

1 Cast on 50 sts and K each row to end. Work the scarf in random stripes of different widths, joining each new colour at the beginning of a row. The loose ends can be darned in afterwards, or worked in as shown simply by holding them behind the main yarn.

2 Trim the tidied ends close to the work.

3 Cast off loosely when the scarf has reached the desired length. Make the fringe by hooking small hanks of yarn through the finished edges. Wrap the wool about ten times round a rectangle of cardboard and slip off. Insert the crochet hook into the edge of the scarf and draw one end of the loop through the knitting. Pull the other end of the hank through the loop to form a knot. Repeat to the end – about 15 hanks.

4 Cut the looped end to form the fringe and trim carefully so that the edge is even.

Ski Hat

Making a simple garment such as this Nordic-style ski hat in the round, using a circular needle, is much easier than knitting it on two needles. The finished piece has no bulky seams to be joined and all the loose yarn is carried on the inside. The stocking-stitch appearance comes from working in knit stitch only, as the work does not have to be turned at the end of the row. The beginning of each round should be indicated with a stitch marker or a strand of contrasting yarn. The finished hat, which would fit an adult, has a circumference of 63cm (25in). Follow the charts for the Fair Isle stripes in the template section.

MATERIALS

50g (2oz) double knitting yarn each in brown, beige, light grey, cream and dark green

2 x 4.00mm circular needles 60cm (24in) and 40cm (16in) long tapestry needle

1 TO FINISH OFF Darn in the loose ends and pressing the hat lightly. Make the cord tie by twisting together three 60cm (24in) lengths of wool until they fold back on themselves. Knot the ends together to create a loop. Thread this cord through the eyelet holes in the top of the hat.

2 Make a small tassel by wrapping a 60cm (24in) length of yarn around a 5cm (2in) wide piece of card. Slip the hank through the loop at the end of the cord, stitch in place and trim the ends. Repeat for the other end of the cord.

Cast on 96 sts using brown yarn. Work 21 rows K2, P2 rib in stripes as follows, ensuring that the foundation row has not become twisted around the needle.

Rounds 1 and 2 brown.
Rounds 3 and 4 beige.
* **Round 5** brown.
Round 6 light grey.
Round 7 brown.*
Rounds 8 and 9 green.
Rounds 10-12 repeat from * to *.
Rounds 13 and 14 beige.
Rounds 15 and 16 brown.
Round 17 light grey.
Rounds 18 and 19 green.
Round 20 beige.
Round 21 brown.
Continue in st st:
Rounds 22-24 brown.
Round 25 (K3 brown; K1 beige) to end of round.
Round 26 K1 beige, *(K1 brown, K3 beige) rep from * to last 3sts, K1 brown, K2 beige.
Round 27 beige.
Rounds 28-32 follow charted pattern 1, reading from right to left.
Round 33 beige
Round 34-39 follow pattern 2, using beige background.
Round 40 beige.
Rounds 41 and 45 follow pattern 1.
Round 46 beige.
Round 47 (K1 brown, K1 beige) to end of round.
Round 48 brown.
Rounds 49-55 follow pattern 3.
Rounds 56 and 57 brown.
Rounds 58 and 59 beige.
Round 60 green.
Round 61 and 62 beige.
Round 63 with light grey, K10, K2 tog tbl, K2 tog, *(K20, K2 tog tbl, K2 tog), rep from * 3 times, K10 (88 sts).
Change to smaller needle.
Round 65 with brown, K9 K2 tog tbl, K2 tog *(K18, K2 tog tbl, K2 tog) rep from * 3 times, K9 80sts).
Round 66 beige.
Round 67 with beige, K8, K2 tog tbl, K2 tog, *(K14, K2 tog tbl, K2 tog), rep from * 3 times, K8 (72 sts).
Round 68 light grey.
Round 70 brown.
Round 71 with light grey, K6, K2 tog tbl, K2 tog, *(K1, K2 tog tbl, K2 tog) repeat from * 3 times, K6 (56 sts):
Round 72 with brown (K1, cast off 1) to end.
Round 73 with brown (K1, make 1) to end.
Round 74 brown.
Round 75 cast off.

Purse Bag

The favourite Scandinavian colour combination of red and white is used to dramatic effect for this attractive purse bag. Chenille yarn gives it a rich velvety texture which is complemented by mother-of-pearl buttons. The festive motifs of deer and snowflakes make it ideal for Christmas-time, either as a present in itself or as a special package for a tiny gift. The finished bag measures 16.5 x 12.5cm (6½ x 5in).

MATERIALS

50g (2oz) chenille yarn in red
50g (2oz) chenille yarn in white
Pair of 4.50mm knitting needles
Tapestry needle
2 mother-of -pearl buttons

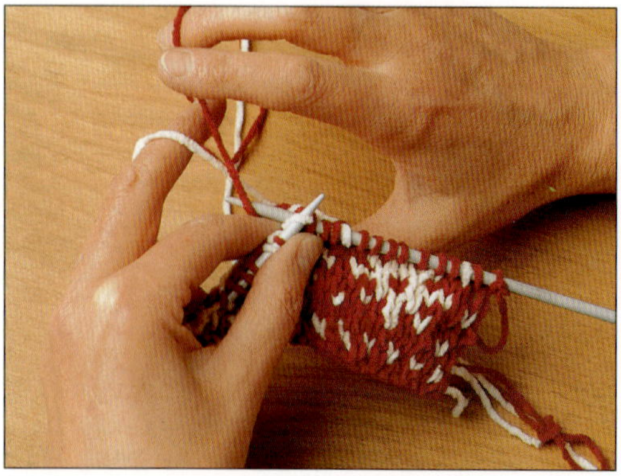

1 Cast on 33 sts and work in stocking stitch. Follow the charted pattern for 54 rows and cast off.

2 Make the button loops on the bottom edge of the finished piece. Using a tapestry needle threaded with red yarn, work blanket stitch into the first 11 stitches, then make a 2cm (¾in) loop, stitch into the next 9 stitches, make another loop, then work to the end. Fold the work in half, right sides facing, and join the two side seams. Turn the bag to the right side and blanket stitch down each side to tidy.

3 Make the cord from two 90cm (36in) lengths of red and one of white yarn. Hold together tightly at one end and twist until the cord folds in half. Make a knot at each end to secure, leaving enough to form a small tassel.

4 Stitch above the knot to fasten the cord to the bag, then sew the two buttons on to the front.

Baby Doll

Knitted toys have a great charm of their own and this engaging baby doll has a very special appeal. He is full of character and certain to delight both adults and children alike. This project is deceptively simple to make: nose, ears, toes, fingers, arms and legs are all knitted separately, using a minimum of shaping, then sewn on to the main body.

MATERIALS

Pair each of 3.00mm and 3.50mm knitting needles
50g (20g) dishcloth yarn (100% pearl cotton)
Oddment of double knitting yarn for the nappy (diaper)
Embroidery cotton in black
Washable polyester toy stuffing
Safety pin
Tapestry needle
Pink crayon

BODY AND HEAD

Begin at lower edge of body. Using dishcloth yarn (crochet cotton) and 3.00mm needles, cast on 16 sts.

Row 1 inc k-wise into every st (32 sts).

Starting with a P row, work 19 rows st st.

Shape for head

Next row K6, (K2 tog) 3 times, K8 (K2 tog) 3 times, K6 (26 sts).

Work 13 rows st st.

Dec row (K2 tog) to end – 13 sts.

Break yarn and thread end back through remaining sts.

ARMS

Begin at hand: cast on 5 sts.

Row 1 inc K-wise into every st (10 sts).

Beginning with a P row, work 13 rows st st.

Cast off.

FIRST LEG

Begin at toes: cast on 10 sts, work 6 rows st st.

Shape heel

K5, turn.
Sl 1, P3, turn.
Sl 1, K2, turn.
Sl 1, P1, turn.
Sl 1, K2, turn.
Sl 1, P3, turn.
Sl 1, K4 turn.
Sl 1, P5 turn.

Continuing in st st, work 14 rows. Cast off.

SECOND LEG

Work as given for first leg, but decrease for heel on last 5 sts on needle instead of first.

EARS

Cast on 3 sts, K1 row. Cast off P-wise. Tie ends of yarn together to form ear shape.

NOSE

Cast on 3 sts. Cast off. Tie ends together to form a small round shape.

BIG TOE

Work 2, as for nose.

LITTLE FINGER

Cast on 2 sts. Cast off.

THUMB AND TWO MEDIUM-SIZED FINGERS

Cast on 3 sts. Cast off.

MIDDLE FINGER

Cast on 4 sts. Cast off.

NAPPY (DIAPER)

Using textures DK yarn and 3.50mm needles, cast on 34 sts. K 1 row.

Dec row K2 tog at beg and end of row.

Next row K to end.

Rep last 2 rows until 2 sts remain.

Next row K2 tog, thread end through remaining st and secure.

1 TO MAKE UP BODY With right sides together, join the seam. Turn to the right side and stuff firmly. Gather up the stitches around the lower edge and close the gap. Tie a length of yarn firmly around the neck and thread the ends back through the work.

3 Sew the arms on to the body, with the body seam at the centre back.

5 Attach the big toe to the end of the foot and sew the legs to the body. Shape the bottom by stitching through the lower part of the body.

TUMMY BUTTON Work a vertical back stitch just below the centre of the tummy.

2 ARMS With right sides together, sew the seam lengthways. Turn to the right side and stuff. Tie a length of yarn around the wrist and thread the ends back through the work. Arrange the fingers and thumb and sew to the hand.

4 FEET AND LEGS With right sides together, sew the seam lengthways. Turn to the right side and stuff. Tie a length of yarn around the ankle and thread the ends back through the work. Using a length of dishcloth yarn (100% pearl cotton), sew back and forth through the work near the end of the foot to form toes.

6 FACE Attach the ears and nose. Work the eyes and mouth in straight stitch, using a single strand of black embroidery cotton. Lightly colour in the cheeks, the end of the nose, the knees and tummy button with a soft pink crayon.

HAIR Sew small loops of black cotton through the head and knot firmly, then clip to form tufts. With a pink crayon lightly colour in the cheeks, the end of the nose, the knees and the tummy button.

NAPPY (DIAPER) Fold on the nappy (diaper) and fasten with a safety pin. If the doll is intended for a child, the nappy (diaper) should be secured in place with a few stitches instead.

Crochet

An amazing range of crocheted items – from chunky hats to delicate lace – can be produced with just a hook and yarn. The versatility of crochet has been exploited by international fashion designers, and crocheted garments are included in many collections. The basic stitches can be adapted to many uses, and unconventional materials, such as raffia or strips of torn cloth, bring a new dimension to a well-known craft.

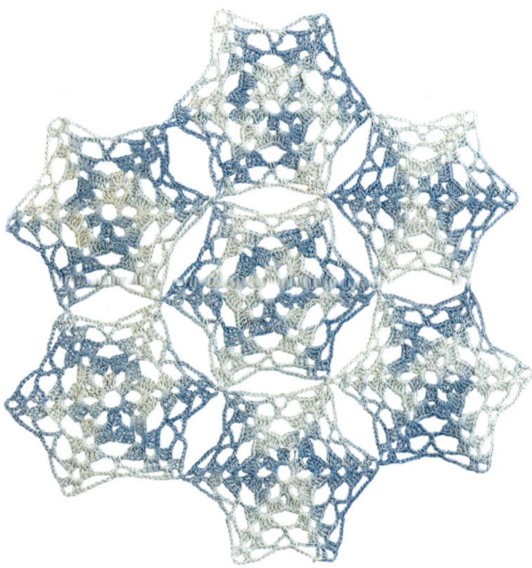

Crochet
Tools and Materials

A simple ball of yarn and a hook are all that is needed to begin to crochet. Any wool or cotton yarns can be used, as well as more unusual materials such as string or raffia, but in addition, there is a selection of special crochet cottons for creating more delicate fabrics.

YARNS

Crochet cottons come in balls and are sold by weight. They are numbered from No 3, which is the thickest 2-ply thread, known as craft cotton, up to No 60, which is a firmly twisted 6-ply, used for the finest lace. Space-dyed variations are available for interesting multicoloured effects. No 20 is a thicker 6-ply yarn used for most mats, edgings and traditional white work, but it is also available in other colours. Perlé thread, similar to embroidery thread, has a lustrous mercerized finish. Cotton double knitting yarns form hard wearing fabrics, suitable for bags and placemats or larger projects such as bedspreads. Novelty yarns work up into light and airy garments while metallic yarns come in different weights and colours, perfect for evening wear.

HOOKS

The finer the yarn used, the smaller the hook needed. Like knitting needles, crochet hooks are graded from a delicate 0.75mm up to 10.00mm, which is used for working strip rugs or for creating open, "loopy" textiles. The smallest are made from steel, the larger sizes from resilient plastic. Some workers find that wooden-handled or all-wood hooks are easier to hold. The best hooks have smooth edges that do not snag the wool. In the past, hooks were turned from bone and examples of these can still be found in antique shops. Basic sewing tools are also necessary: a selection of needles is useful for sewing in ends and for joining seams, and small sharp scissors will be needed to cut threads.

String.

Metallic yarns.

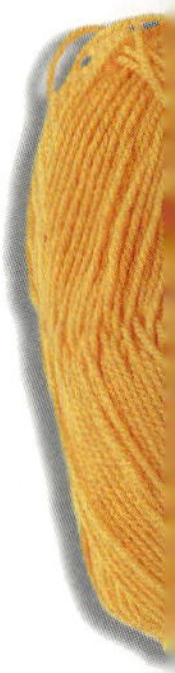

Raffia.

Fine cottons.

Textured yarns.

Crochet cottons.

Double knitting.

Cotton yarn.

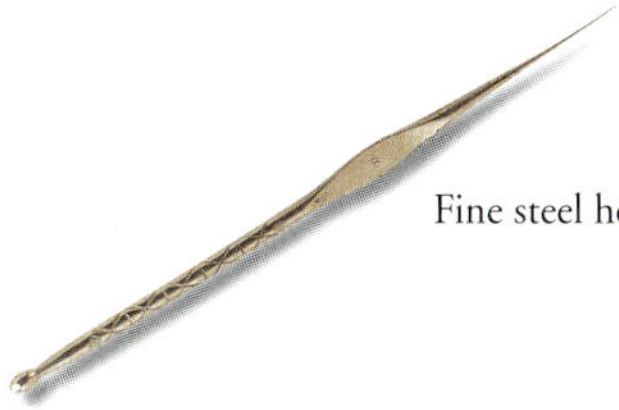

Fine steel hook.

Chunky knitting wool.

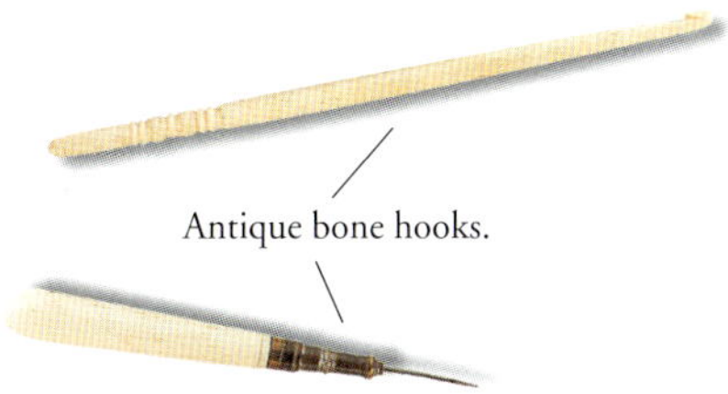

Antique bone hooks.

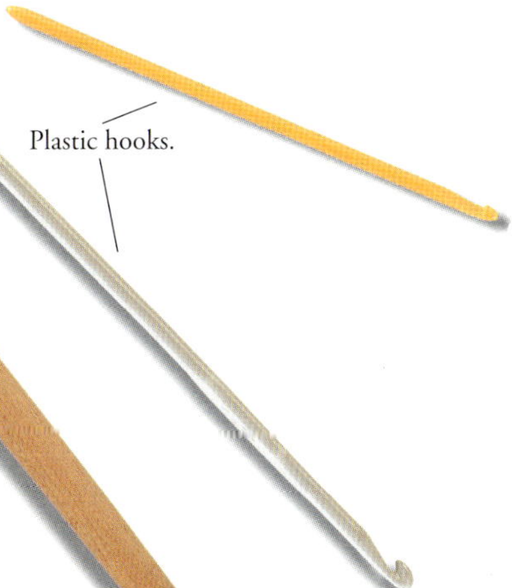

Plastic hooks.

Embroidery scissors.

Needles.

10.00mm hook.

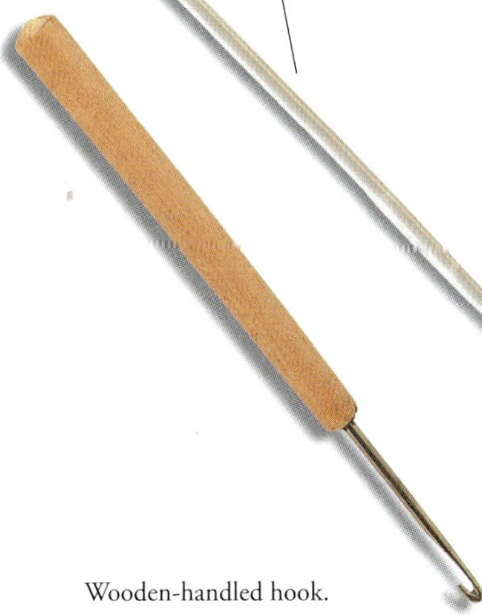

Wooden-handled hook.

Starting Off

A crochet stitch is formed simply by using a hook to pull one loop of yarn through another. Unlike knitting, where there can be many stitches on the needles, there is only ever one single stitch on the hook, which makes it easy to manage. The thread and work are held in one hand, the hook in the other. As with any new skill, it will take practice to learn how to crochet with an even tension (gauge), but all workers evolve their own way of holding the yarn and hook. Take time to find the most natural movement – and try using a larger or smaller size hook to alter the tension (gauge). The hand positions should be reversed for left-handed workers; it may help to reflect the pictures in a small mirror.

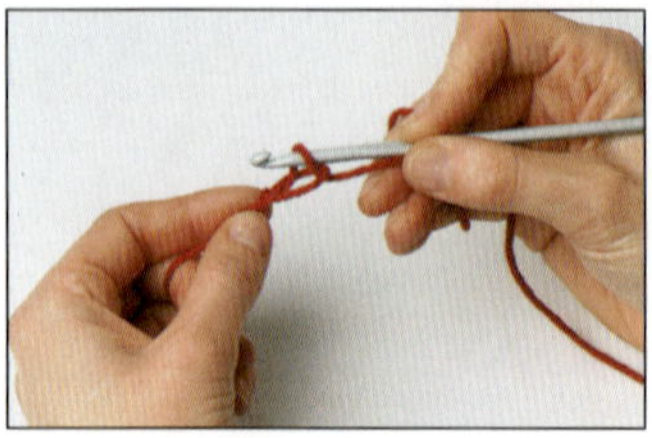

1 HOLDING THE HOOK AND MAKING THE LOOP Make a slip loop by wrapping the main yarn over the short end and using the hook to pull it through. Here the hook is held in the "pencil" position.

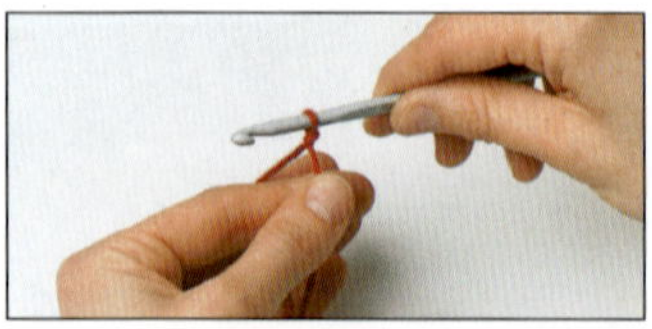

2 Tighten by pulling both ends of the yarn. Here the hook is in the "knife" position.

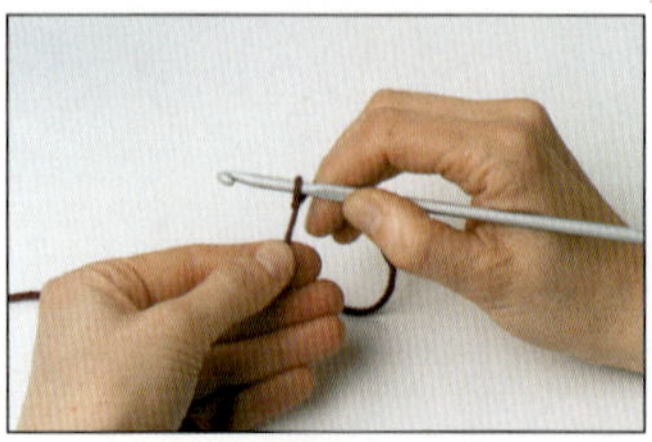

HOLDING THE YARN The work is held between the thumb and first finger of the left hand. To maintain a regular tension (gauge), the yarn is passed back over the two middle fingers, then under and round the little finger. This gives a taut length of thread between the first and second fingers, on which to work, while tension (gauge) is controlled with the tip of the second finger.

CHAIN STITCH (CH)

Chain is the basis for all crochet and the foundation on to which further stitches are worked.

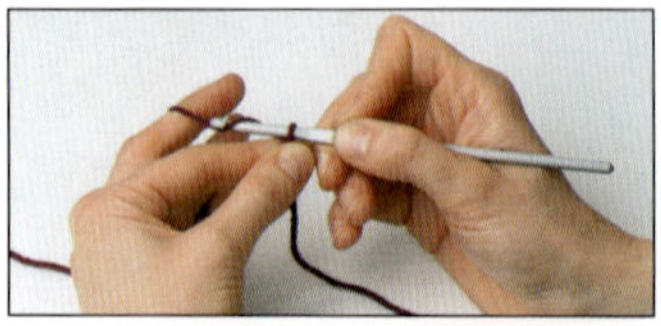

1 Hold the slip loop firmly, then wrap the hook under and over the yarn (yoh or yo).

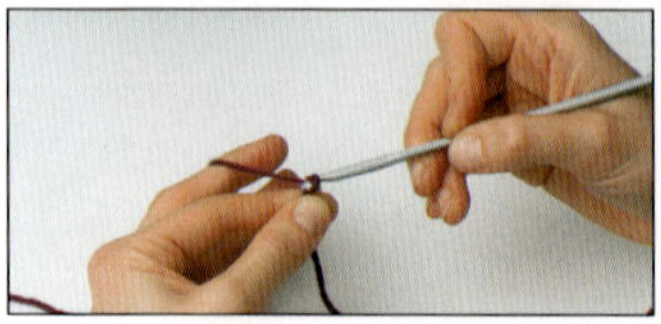

2 Carefully draw the yarn through the loop on the hook, to form a new loop.

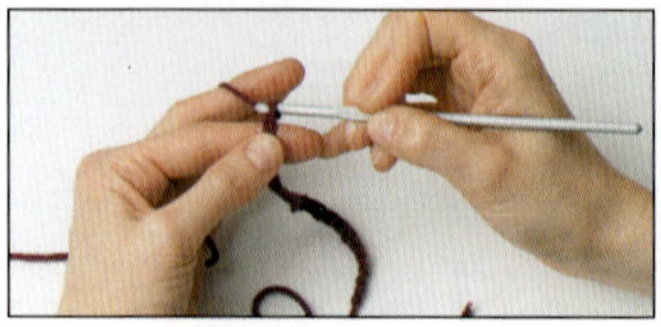

3 Repeat this process until the chain reaches the desired length.

FOLLOWING A PATTERN

All crochet instructions are written with special abbreviations and symbols to make them easy to understand. The most familiar are listed.

alt	alternate	inc	increase
beg	beginning	lp(s)	loop(s)
bet	between	patt (pat)	pattern
chs	chain (chain stitches)	rep	repeat
		rnd	round
cont	continue	sc	single crochet
dc	double crochet	sk	skip
dec	decrease	sp(s)	space(s)
hdc	half double crochet	t-chs	turning chain
dtr	double treble (triple)	tog	together
		tr	treble (triple)
htr	half treble (triple)	yoh (yo)	yarn over hook

* Instructions following an asterisk should be repeated as specified.

( ) Brackets either indicate a stitch combination which has to be repeated, or they enclose extra information such as the number of stitches made in a row.

CONVERSION CHART

UK	US
slip stitch (sl st)	slip stitch (sl st)
double crochet (dc)	single crochet (sc)
half treble (h tr)	half treble crochet (h dc)
treble (tr)	double crochet (dc)
double treble (d tr)	treble (tr)
triple treble (tr tr)	double treble (d tr)
work straight	work even
yarn over hook (yoh)	yarn over (yo)

Working in Stripes

Once the basic crochet stitches *(see pages 122–3)* have been learnt, they can be combined to produce many interesting textures, but, with the imaginative use of colour, even simple rows of trebles can be transformed into striped or squared pattern swatches.

Checks and stripes are just some of the effects that can be created by combining colours.

1 HORIZONTAL STRIPES Stripes are created by working in bands of different colours. Join in the new yarn at the end of the previous row by using it to complete the last stitch.

2 The ends of the yarn can be cut off at the end of each stripe and joined back in when needed. The loose ends should then be sewn invisibly into the work.

3 Wider stripes are made by working two or more rows the same colour. When a repeating sequence is being used, carry the yarn loosely up the side of the work.

WORKING WITH TWO COLOURS

Diagonal or vertical stripes are worked by crocheting with two or more colours in each row. The same technique is used for blocks of colour, such as squares, and for more complicated intarsia patterns.

1 The colours are changed within a single row by swapping yarns over on the final stitch of each block. Draw the second colour through with the hook to complete the stitch.

2 Continue working along the row, changing colours every few stitches. The method is the same, whichever stitch is used.

3 Loose (floating) yarn is concealed by crocheting the next row of stitches over it when making narrow stripes; for wider three-coloured stripes, the yarn is carried across the back of the work.

Basic Stitches

There are five main crochet stitches from which all variations have developed. They progress from slip stitch, a travelling stitch which does not make any height, to tall double trebles (triples), depending on the number of loops from which they are formed. When working in rows, extra chain, called turning chain (t-ch) must be worked at the beginning of each row so that the yarn is at the right level to begin the next stitch. It is important to complete each row by working the last stitch into the turning chain of the previous row. This keeps the number of stitches constant and the sides straight. The first row of any stitch is worked through the back loop of the foundation chain, but on subsequent rows the hook passes under both loops of the previous stitch, from front to back, to give a firm fabric.

Clockwise from top: treble; half treble; double and crochet; double treble.

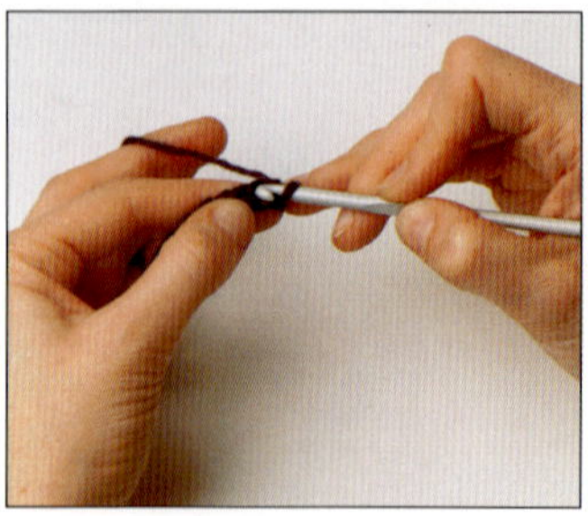

1 SLIP STITCH (SL ST) Skip 1ch, *insert hook under top lp of next ch.

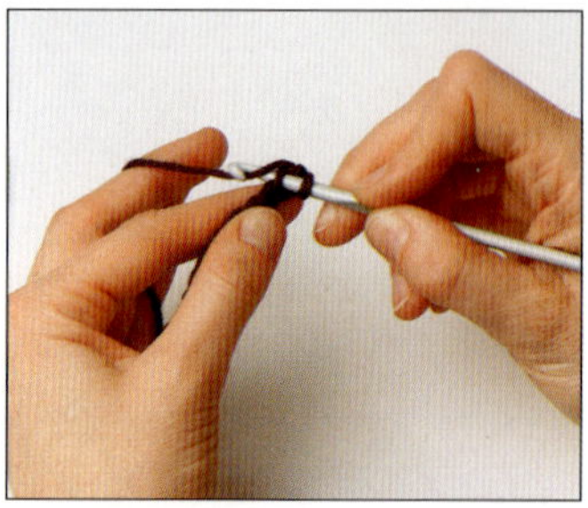

2 Yoh (yo), draw through ch and lp on hook. (1sl st formed).

3 Repeat from * to end of ch. Turn, make 1 t-ch and cont, working the next sl st under both lps of 2nd st from hook. Work the last sl st of the row into the t-ch.

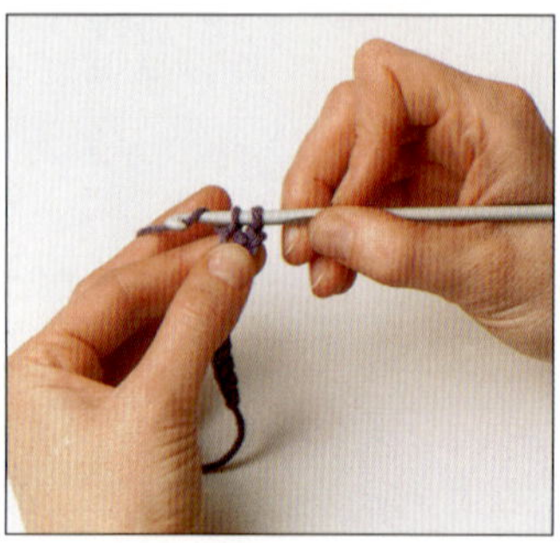

1 DOUBLE CROCHET (DC) Skip 1ch, * insert hook under top lp of next ch.

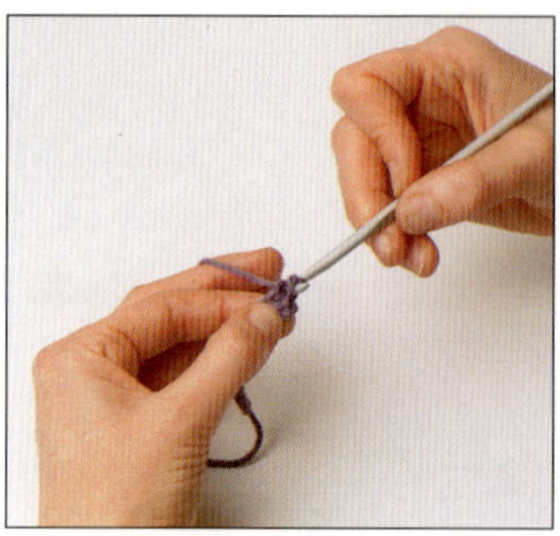

2 *Yoh, draw through ch only. Yoh and draw through both lps on hook (1dc formed). Repeat from * to end of ch. Turn.

3 Make 1t-ch and cont, working the next dc under both lps of 2nd st from hook. Work the last dc of the row into the t-ch.

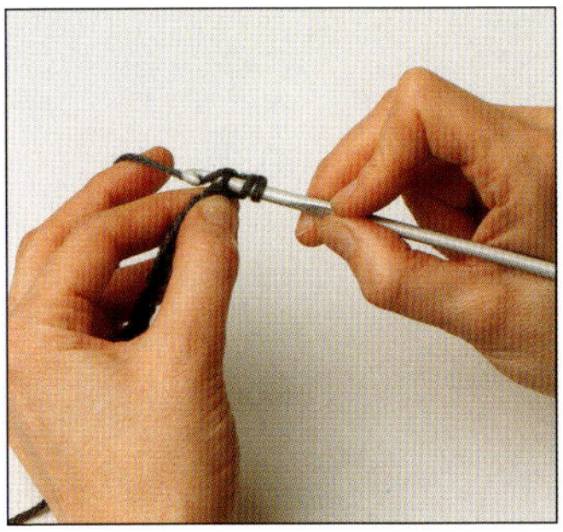

1 HALF TREBLE (HTR) Skip 2ch1 *yoh, insert hook under top lp of next ch.

2 Yoh, and draw through ch only (3lps on hook).

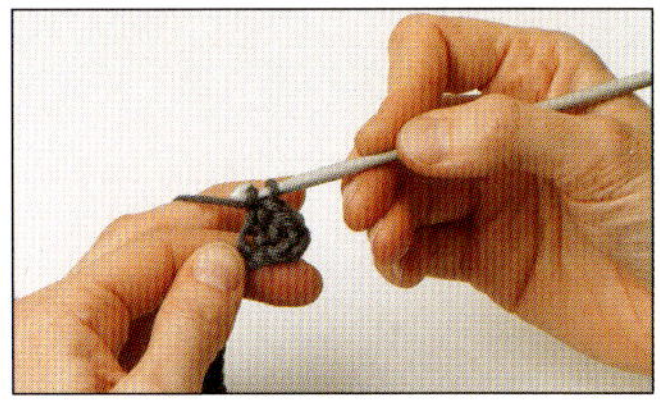

3 Yoh, draw through all 3lps on hook (1htr formed). Repeat from * to end of chain. Turn. Make 2t-ch and cont, working the next htr under both lps of the 2nd st from hook. Work the last htr of the row into the 2nd of 2t-ch of the previous row.

1 TREBLE (TR) Skip 3ch, *yoh, insert hook under top lp of next ch, yoh and draw yarn through ch only (3lps on hook).

2 Yoh, draw through next 2lps on hook (2lps on hook).

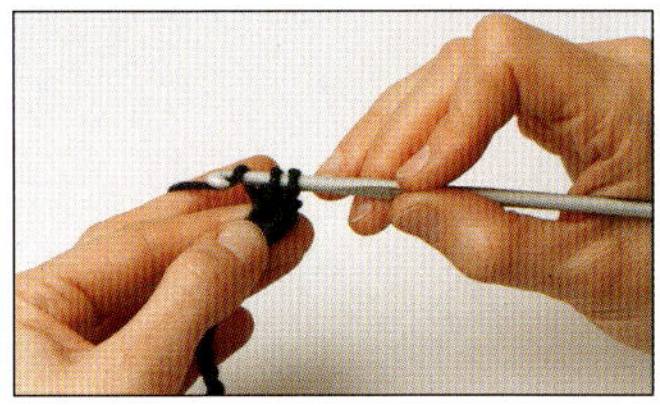

3 Yoh, draw through 2 remaining lps on hook (1tr formed). Repeat from * to end of ch. Turn. Make 3t-ch and cont, working the next tr under both lps of the 2nd st from hook. Work the last tr of the row into the 3rd of 3t-ch of the previous row.

1 DOUBLE TREBLE (DTR) Skip 3ch, *yoh twice, insert hook under top lp of next ch, yoh and draw through ch (4lps on hook).

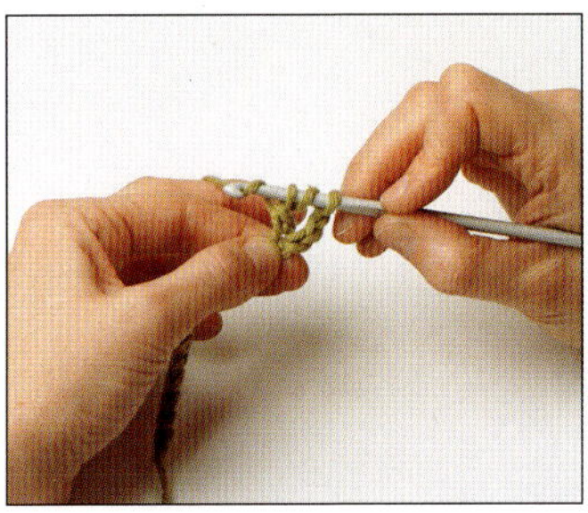

2 Yoh, draw through next 2lps on hook, (3lps on hook), yoh, draw through next 2lps on hook (2lps on hook).

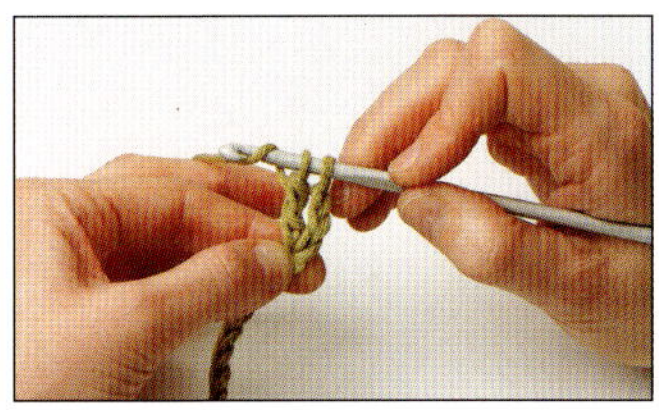

3 Yoh, draw through last 2lps (1dtr formed). Repeat from * to end. Turn. Make 4 t-ch and cont, working the next dtr under both lps of 2nd st from hook. Work the last dtr of the row into the 4th of 4t-ch of the previous row.

FINISHING OFF

All work should be finished off properly to prevent it unravelling. After the last stitch, pull the final loop out with the hook, and cut the yarn, leaving an end of about 13cm (5in). This loose end can then be sewn invisibly into the work using a tapestry needle.

Working in the Round

When crocheting in the round, the foundation chain is joined to make a loop. The stitches are then worked into this ring, in ever-increasing circles, without turning. This technique is used to make small medallions and motifs which can be joined together patchwork-style, as well as traditional lace doilies and larger accessories such as shawls or tablecloths. Hats and other three-dimensional items can be created by increasing and decreasing the number of stitches in each round.

Left: Small floral shapes are easy to crochet in the round. These flowers are joined together by the edges of their petals.

1 MAKING THE FOUNDATION RING
Make a short length of chain stitch and insert the hook under the top loop of the last stitch.

2 Join by pulling the yarn through the loop to form a slip stitch.

3 Work the first round into the ring, so that the hook actually passes through it to pick up the yarn.

TREBLE (TRIPLE) CIRCLES

Circles of crochet can be made by increasing the number of stitches in alternate rounds. New colours can be joined on each round and the ends concealed by working over them. Each round starts with one, two or three standing chain, which take the place of the first stitch, in the same way as turning chain.

1 **Round 1** Make 5ch and join with sl st into 1st ch. 3ch, then work 16tr into ring. Join with a sl st to 3rd ch st. **Round 2** 3ch, 1tr into same sp as tr, (2tr into 1tr) to end of round. Join with a sl st to 3rd ch st.

2 **Round 3** 3ch, (2tr into 1tr, 1tr into 1tr) to end of round. Join with a sl st to 3rd ch st. **Round 4** Work (2tr into 1tr, 2tr into 2tr). **Round 5** (2tr into 1tr, 3 tr into 3tr).

Right: This sunflower is an introduction to working with clusters of stitches, a way of shaping within a circle. Here they are formed from triple trebles (triples), abbreviated as tr tr.

INSTRUCTIONS FOR TWO OR THREE COLOURS

With first colour make 8ch and join with a sl st.

Round 1 3ch, 15tr into ring, join with sl st to 3rd ch. Join next colour, if using.

Round 2 2dc into sp between next 2tr. 2dc into sp. 2dc into each sp to end, sl to 1st dc (32dcs). Join next colour.

MAKING THE CLUSTER

Round 3 6ch, * yoh (yo) 3 times, insert hook into next dc. Yoh (yo) and draw through (5lps on hook), (yoh (yo) and draw through 2lps) three times (2lps on hook). Repeat from * twice, yoh (yo) and through all the loops to form cluster.

** 9ch (4tr tr into next 4dc to make cluster). Repeat from ** to end of round, sl st to top of 1st cluster.

Round 5 1ch (9dc over 9ch) to end of round. Join with a sl st to 1ch, finish off.

Right: These Irish crochet roses are worked in the round, using a thick Aran wool. They have been appliquéd on to a richly cabled knitted background.

Left: These hexagons are worked from remnants of bright yarn. The stained-glass window effect comes from edging each motif with black, which contrasts dramatically with the other colours.

Crochet Squares

The familiar afghan, or grannie squares, are long-established favourites. The first afghan rugs were made as a means of economizing; at one time yarn was precious and outgrown garments would be unravelled so that the yarn could be re-used. Crochet squares were a practical way of keeping warm, and as a planned colour scheme was then a luxury, colours were used at random. Today, afghan square rugs are still a good way of using up odd balls of yarn, for beginners and experienced workers alike.

Above: This sampler combines afghan square techniques with Irish crochet roses and clusters. It is worked in cotton yarn for a crisp texture.

THE BASIC SQUARE

The squares can be made to any size; small multicoloured arrangements have a jewel-like effect, particularly if edged with a single colour, or one single huge square can make a useful blanket.

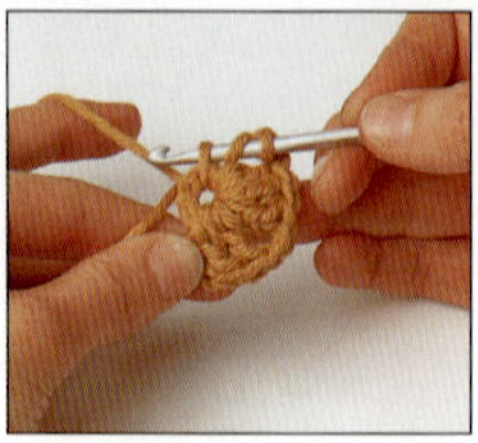

1 Make 6ch and join with sl st to form foundation ring.
Round 1 3ch (to stand as 1st tr), then 2tr into the ring, (* 2ch, 3tr) 3 times, 2ch, join with sl st to 3rd ch. Finish off 1st colour.

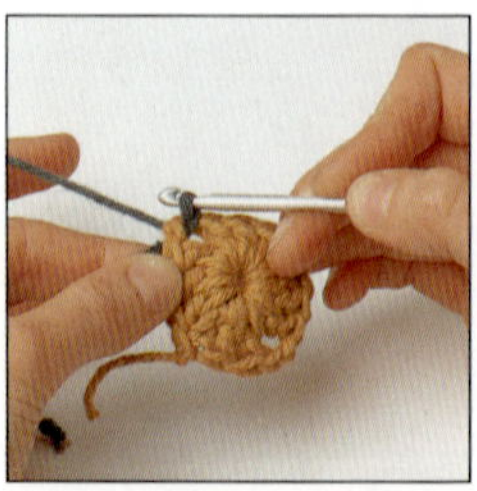

2 Join 2nd colour to one corner by holding the end of the yarn and pulling a loop under the chain. Work the first stitches over the loose ends of both colours.

3 **Round 2** 3ch, (2tr, 2ch, 3tr) into same space, (3tr, 2ch, 3tr into next sp) 3 times, join with sl st to top of 3ch. Continue the following rounds in the same way, working a 3-tr cluster into every space along the four sides, with two in each corner.

JOINING MOTIFS

Individual squares can be joined together in two ways, by sewing or with double crochet. Hand stitching gives a flat seam, which is invisible if worked in matching yarn, while crocheting produces a ridged effect. All the ends should be darned in securely.

1 Thread a tapestry needle with a 45cm (18in) length of yarn. Fasten on with a back stitch, concealing the end. Hold the squares, with wrong sides facing, and stitch firmly through both loops on each side.

2 Double crochet makes a strong, attractive join, worked through both loops on each side. Squares can be joined singly, or when all the motifs for one project have been completed. Lay them out in the final order, then work all the horizontal, then all the vertical joins.

Left: The centre of this afghan variation is made from eight raised clusters. The combination of chenille and woollen yarns gives an interesting effect.

Left: Hexagonal afghan motifs can be made by working 12 stitches into the first round, two to a side, and increasing in the usual way.

Left: Many variations on the basic square can be worked by mixing the colours within each round. A patchwork block effect can be created by choosing a predominant background colour such as cream, and keeping to a tight colour scheme.

SHELLS AND CLUSTERS

Shells are fan-shaped groups of stitches made by working several trebles into one space. Clusters appear as inverted fans, and are created by retaining the final loops of several adjacent trebles on the hook while they are worked, then drawing them together with one movement. By combining the two, many interesting patterns can be created.

Above: These coloured swatches illustrate just a few of the textured crochet fabrics that can be developed by working alternate rows of shells and clusters.

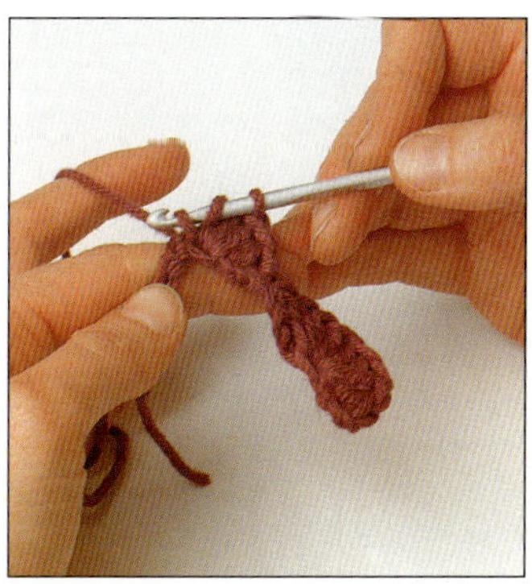

WORKING A SHELL

Insert the hook into the 3rd ch from hook, then work 7tr into this sp. Anchor final st with a sl st into 3rd ch from hook.

Filet Crochet

Filet crochet is an old technique, which reached elaborate heights in the late nineteenth century. It is still very popular today, particularly in Holland, France and Germany, where it is used to make curtains, tablecloths and figurative panels, as well as decorative edgings. It consists of a regular square mesh, made from trebles (triples) and chain stitches, and the design is created by filling in some of the spaces with blocks of stitches.

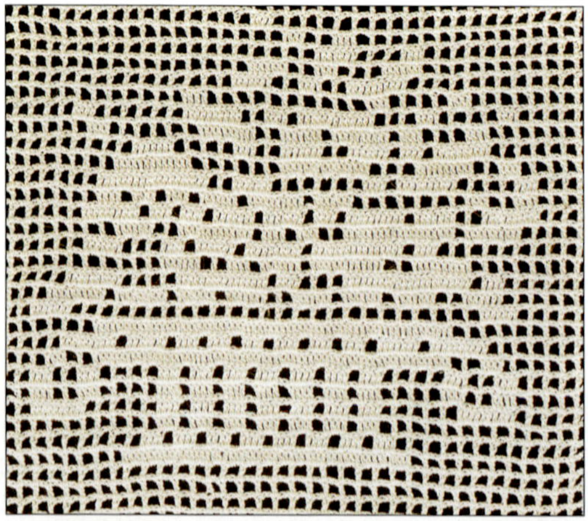

This flower basket design was adapted from a pattern that first appeared in the 1900s, when many women led a more leisurely life and had time to work exquisite crochet to show off their skills. It uses a fine thread worked with a steel hook.

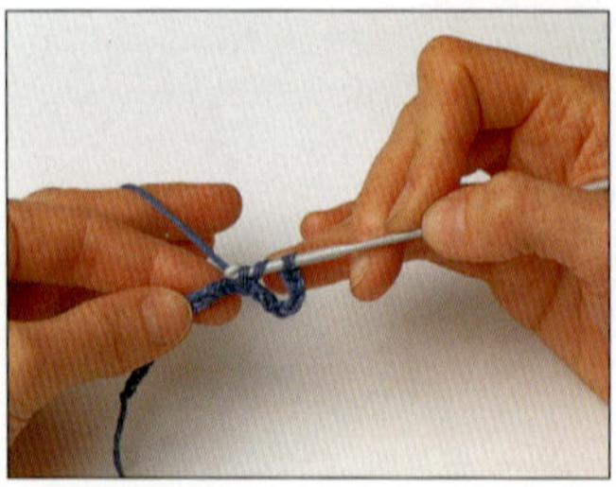

1 MAKING THE MESH Each charted square represents 3ch, so calculate the length of the foundation chain by multiplying the number of squares needed by 3 and adding 5t-ch. Work 1tr into the 8th ch from hook.

2 (Make 2ch, skip 2ch, 1tr into next ch) to end of row, ending with 1tr, 5t-ch.

3 For the next and following rows, * 1tr into 2nd tr from hook, skip 2ch, 1tr into next tr, to end, 5t-ch. Work the trs through both lps of the previous tr.

1 MAKING THE BLOCKS A block is made by working 2tr *under* the 2ch of the previous row. For a block at the beginning of a row, make 3t-ch then make 2tr into 2ch 5p, and 1tr into next tr.

2 A chequerboard (checkerboard) effect can be built up by working alternate blocks and spaces. Work the last tr into the t-ch of previous row.

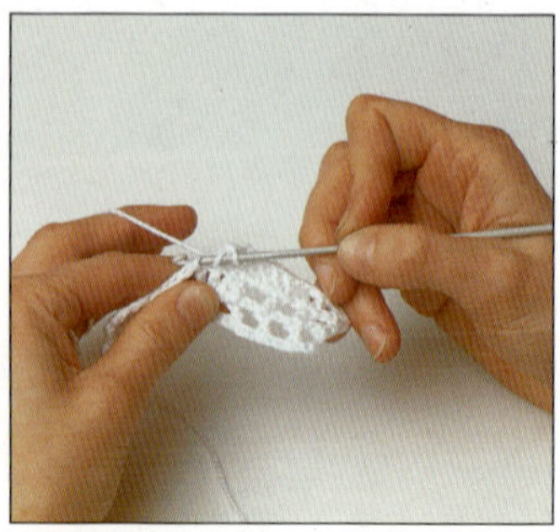

3 When working a block on top of another block, make the 4tr through both loops of the previous stitches.

FOLLOWING A PATTERN

There are many publications which include filet crochet patterns. They are printed on a square grid and are easy to follow. Each plain square represents a mesh and each filled-in square is a block. The first and following odd rows are worked from right to left, starting at the bottom right square, and the even rows read from left to right. For complicated designs, it is worth making an enlarged photocopy of the chart and marking off the lines as they are completed to keep track of how the work is progressing. Many cross stitch patterns can be adapted to filet crochet, and it is easy to draw up designs on to squared paper.

Filet crochet can be worked on a large or small scale, and in a variety of threads. Extra decoration has been added to this simple indigo cotton mesh by interweaving the trebles (triples) with striped braid. This technique would work well on lacy garments, which could be decorated with silk ribbons.

Although not strictly filet crochet, this chenille scarf is worked in a V-shaped mesh variation, which gives it an interesting texture.

Flower Box

Crochet is a very versatile textile medium. Its use need not be limited to wool and cotton yarns, nor only to two-dimensional objects. In fact, with a little imagination and the creative use of brightly coloured raffia, for example, an empty circular Camembert cheese box can be transformed into the cheerful flower-shaped container shown here.

MATERIALS

1 hank each 2 colours raffia for lid and sides
Small quantities of raffia in various colours for the petals
3.50mm crochet hook
Round cardboard box with lid, approximately 11.5cm (4½in) in diameter
Pencil; silver foil; tape measure; pva adhesive
Sharp large-eyed needle
Sticky tape

1 The box base and lid are both covered with silver foil, which has been crumpled and straightened out again for a textured effect. Draw around the lid on to the foil, add 5cm (2in) all round and cut out the circle. Snip from the outside edge to the inner circle every 10mm (⅜in), then glue to the top of the box lid, folding and sticking the tabs around both sides of the rim. Draw around the base twice, add a 4cm (1½in) allowance and cut out the two circles. Cut tabs as before, then stick one circle to the inside of the box and one to the outside, to cover entirely.

2 With one of the main colours of raffia, work the box lid:
Round 1 3ch, sl st into 1st ch to form ring. 1 ch, 6 dc into ring, sl st into 1st dc at beg of round.
Round 2 1 ch, 2 dc into each of next 6 sts, sl st into 1st dc at beg of round.
Round 3 1 ch, * (1 dc into 1st st, 2 dc into next st) rep from * to end, sl st into 1st dc at beg of round.
Round 4 1 ch, 1 dc, into each st to end of round, sl st into 1st dc at beg of round. Repeat rounds 3 and 4 three more times.
Round 11 1 ch, 1 dc into each of next 60 sts, sl st into 1st dc at beg of round.
Change to green raffia and work the sides as follows:
Round 12 working into the back loop of each st, work 1 ch, * (1 dc into each of next 14 sts, miss 1 st), rep from * 3 times. Sl st into 1st dc at beg of round.
Round 13 1 ch, 1 dc into each of next 56 sts, sl st in 1st dc at beg of round.
Repeat round 13 once more, or until the sides are the same depth as the box. Finish off, leaving a 90cm (36in) end for sewing.
Make the crochet base using the other main raffia colour and repeat rounds 1-10. Miss round 11 and continue with rounds 12 and 13. Finish off, leaving a long end of raffia.

3 Stretch the crochet raffia over the box lid. Using the raffia length, overstitch the cover to the rim. Attach the crochet base to the main box with running stitch. The crochet should reach only halfway up the sides so that the lid will fit.

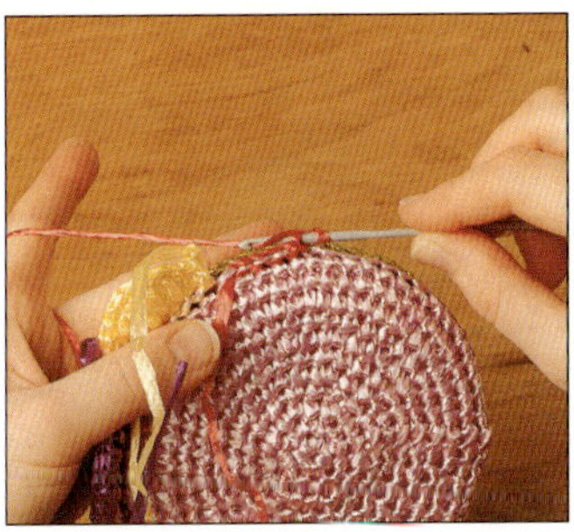

4 Crochet the petals around the box lid, using a different colour for each petal as follows: With the inside of box facing, join raffia on to last pink round and work 1 sl st into each of next 5 sts, 1 ch, turn box so that right side is facing. Working back over previous row, 1 dc and 1 htr into 1st st. 2 tr into 2nd st, 2 dtrs into 3rd and 4th sts, 2 trs into 5th st, 1 htr and 1 dc into last st. * ch, turn box around, 1 sl st into each of next 12 sts on previous row, finish off thread.

Working anti-clockwise, with inside of box facing, start the next petal in the stitch on the left of first. Repeat until ten petals have been made. Sew all the ends through to the inside of the box.

5 Make a centre pull for the box lid: 4 ch, sl st into 1st ch to form ring, 1 ch, 10 dc into ring, sl st into 1st dc at beg of round. Finish off, leaving a long end to stitch on to the centre of the lid. Sew the loose ends through to the inside of the lid. Work 8 straight stitches, each in a different colour, around the pull. Trim and tape down the ends inside the box lid and cover with a circle of foil-covered cardboard.

Fabric Bag

This country-style bag uses a technique adapted from rag-rug making, and is crocheted from torn strips of recycled fabric. It is a practical way to use up dressmaking remnants, or to give a second life to the material from an old garment. Cotton or cotton-mix materials provide the best textures. The fabric strips do not have much "give", unless they are cut on the bias, so it is essential to keep the tension loose when working.

MATERIALS
3m (3¼yd) assorted patterned cotton fabric
10.00mm crochet hook
Matching cotton sewing thread; needle

1 Tear the cloth into 12mm (½in) strips, join them together with a few machine or hand stitches and roll each colour into a ball. Make stripes by changing fabric colours as you would if using yarn.

Round 1 Make 4 ch. 1 standing ch, 1 dc in each of 3 ch, 4 dc into 4th ch. On other side of 4 ch make 2 dc, 3 dc in 4th ch. Sl st to 1st ch (12 st).

Round 2 1 ch, 1 dc in same place. 2 dc into each of next 11 dc, sl st to 1st ch (24 sts).

Round 3 1 ch, 8 dc, 2 dc into next dc, 1 dc, 2 dc into next dc, 8 dc, 2 dc, into next dc, 1 dc, 2 dc, into next dc, 1 dc, sl st to 1st ch (28 sts).

2 **Round 4** 1 ch, 8 dc, 2 dc into next dc, 1 dc, 2 dc into next dc, 11 dc, 2dc into next dc, 1 dc, 2dc into next dc, 1 dc, sl st to 1st ch (32 sts).
Round 5 1 ch, 9 dc, 2 dc into next dc, 1 dc, 2 dc into next dc, 13 dc, 2 dc into next dc, 1 dc, 2dc into next dc, 2 dc, sl st to 1st ch (36 sts).
Round 6 1 ch, 1 dc into each dc to end, sl st to 1st ch (36 sts).
Round 7 1 ch, 9 dc, 2 dc into next dc, 1 dc, 2 dc, 15 dc, 2 dc into next dc, 1 dc, 2 dc into next dc, 4 dc, sl st to 1st ch (40 sts).
Round 8 1 ch, 1 dc into each dc to end, sl st to 1st ch (40 sts).
Round 9 1 ch, 9 dc, 2 dc into next dc, 1 dc, 2 dc into next dc, 17 dc, 2 dc into next dc, 1 dc 2 dc into next dc, 7 dc, sl st to 1st ch (44 sts).
Round 10 1 ch, 1 dc into each dc to end, sl st to 1st ch (44 sts).
Round 11 1 ch, 9 dc into next dc, 1 dc, 2 dc into next dc, 19 dc, 2 dc into next dc, 1 dc, 2 dc into next dc, 9 dc, sl st to 1st ch (48 sts).
Round 12 1 ch, 1 dc into each dc to end, sl st to 1st ch (48 sts).
Round 13 as round 12.
Round 14 1 ch, 9 dc, 2 dc into next dc, 1 dc, 2 dc into next dc, 21 dc, 2 dc into next dc, 1 dc, 2 dc into next dc, 11 dc, sl st to 1st ch (52 sts).
Round 15 1 ch, 1 dc into each dc to end, sl st to 1st ch (52 sts).
Round 16 as round 15.
Round 17 1 ch, 1 dc into next 9 dc, 2 dc into next dc, 1 dc, 2 dc into next dc, 23 dc, 2 dc into next dc, 1 dc, 2 dc into next dc, 13 dc, sl st to 1st ch (56 sts).
Round 18 1 ch, 1 dc into each dc to end, sl st to 1st ch (56 sts).
Round 19 as round 18.
Round 20 1 ch, 9 dc, 2 dc into next dc, 1 dc, 2 dc into next dc, 25 dc, 2 dc into next dc, 1 dc, 2 dc into next dc, 15 dc, sl st to 1st ch (60 sts).
Round 21 1 ch, 1 dc into each dc to end, sl st to 1st ch (60 sts).
Round 22 as round 21.
Round 23 1 ch, 9 dc, 2 dc into next dc, 1 dc, 2 dc into next dc, 27 dc, 2 dc into next dc, 1 dc, 2 dc into next dc, 17 dc, sl st to 1st ch (64 sts).
Round 24 1 ch, 1 dc into each dc, sl st to 1st ch (64 sts).
Round 25 as round 24.
Finish off.

3 To make the handles, join the fabric to the top edge of the bag, one-third of the way along from the right-hand side. Make 37 chains and join on to the top edge one-third away from the left-hand side. Turn, and work 1 dc into each chain. Cut off the short end and, with a needle and thread, stitch the fabric securely to the inside of the bag. Repeat on the other side for the second handle.

Baby Blanket and Woollen Balls

This blanket would brighten any nursery and the rainbow colours make it a perfect present for a baby girl or boy. The dramatic chevron pattern is a variation of basic treble stitch, and is quick and easy to work. The matching balls are a good way to use up leftover wool, and can be made in any combination of stripes. They are stuffed with washable polyester fibre, but could be filled with dried beans to make juggling balls for an older child – or adult – to play with. The finished blanket measures about 90cm (36in) square.

BABY BLANKET MATERIALS

50g (2oz) baby double knitting yarn each in red, salmon pink, yellow, green, light blue, dark blue and purple
3.50mm crochet hook
Tapestry needle

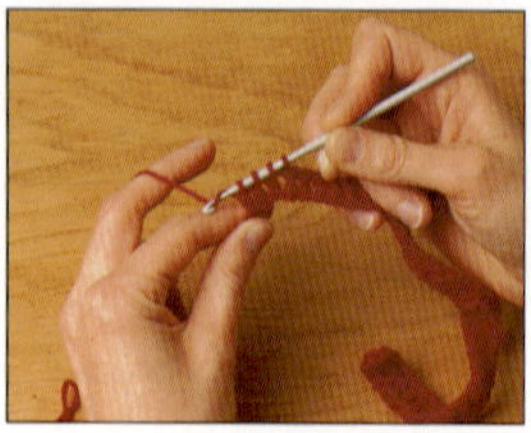

1 With red yarn, make a foundation row of 153 ch.
Row 1 Make 1 tr into 4th ch from hook. Make 7 tr into next 7 ch. Into next 3 sts *(yoh [yo], insert hook into ch, draw yarn through, yoh [yo], draw through 2 loops leaving last loop on hook). Repeat from * twice more (4 loops on hook) yoh [yo] and draw through all 4 loops. 13-treble cluster (3 tr cluster) made. 9 tr, 3 tr into next ch, 9 tr*.

2 Repeat from * to * 7 times to end of row. On final repeat work last 2 tr into same ch, turn.
Row 2 3 ch, 1 tr into 1st of 3 ch made, i.e. 2 sts in same place. Work 7 tr. *(1 tr cluster, 9 tr, 3 tr into next tr, 9 tr). Repeat from * to end of row, working last 2 tr into same tr, turn. Repeat row 2 to form the pattern.
Break off the red wool and join the salmon pink wool to the beginning of row for the second stripe.

3 Work two rows of each colour in the spectrum sequence: yellow, green, light blue, dark blue, purple, and repeat the seven-stripe pattern four times, finishing off with an extra two rows of red.

4 Darn in the loose ends of wool. Press the blanket lightly into shape using a damp cloth and cool iron.

WOOLLEN BALL

MATERIALS

Remnants of double knitting yarn
3.50mm crochet hook
Washable polyester toy filling (batting)
Tapestry needle

1 Make a foundation row of 16 ch.
Row 1 1 ch, skip 1 ch, 4 dc, 8 tr, 4 dc, turn.
Row 2 1 ch, 4 dc into next 4 dc, 8 tr into 8 tr, 4 dc into 4 dc turn.

2 These two rows form the basic pattern and are repeated nine times to form the ball shape. A plain ball can be worked just in one colour, but changing yarn at the beginning of each or every alternate row will create interesting patterns. The top of the tomato variation is worked in double crochet.

3 Use a tapestry needle to gather the two edges together, making sure that all the loose ends of yarn are pushed to the inside of the ball.

4 Sew the edges together with a neat overstitch, to halfway down the seam. Stuff firmly with polyester filling (batting), then complete the seam and finish off the end of the yarn. Roll the ball into shape between your hands.

Strawberry and Tomato Hats

These charming fruit-inspired baby hats could not fail to delight both youngsters and their parents. Stem, calyx and the main part are worked all in one piece, in the round, and the strawberry seeds are embroidered in thick cotton thread. The same pattern is followed for the tomato variation, which is made in a warmer shade of red. The finished hat measures 35cm (14in) around the outer edge and will fit a child of up to one year old.

MATERIALS

Cotton double knitting yarn:

50g (2oz) in red

20g (3/4oz) in green

10g (1/4oz) in black

10g (1/4oz) in yellow

3.50mm and 4.50mm crochet hooks

Large-eyed needle

1 Using green yarn and a 4.50mm hook, make 5 ch.1 sl st in 2nd ch from hook. * sl st in each of 3 remaining ch to form the stem.

Round 1 3 ch, sl st into 1st ch to form a ring. 1 ch, 5 dc into ring, sl st into 1st dc at beg of round.

Round 2 1 ch, 2 dc into each of next 5 sts. Sl st into 1st dc.

Round 3 1 ch, (1 dc in 1st st, 2 dc in next st) 4 times, sl st into 1st dc.

Round 4 1 ch, (1 dc in each of next 2 sts, 2 dc in next st) 4 times, sl st into 1st dc.

Round 5 1 ch, (1 dc in each of next 3 sts, 2 dc in next st) 4 times, sl st into 1st dc.

Round 6 1 ch, (1 dc into each of next 4 sts, 2 dc into next st) 4 times, sl st into 1st dc (30 sts).

2 Work the leaves as follows:
Round 7 *(12 ch, 1 sl st into 2nd ch from hook, 1 sl st into next ch, 1 dc into each of next 2 ch, 1 htr into each next 2 ch, 1 tr into each of next 2 ch, 1 dtr into each of next 3 ch. Join leaf to hat with a sl st into the front loop only of 4th st from beg of 12 ch, 1 sl st into the front loop of next st). Repeat from * 5 times.

3 Change to red and, working into the back loop of each st in the previous row, make 1 ch (1 dc into each of the next 5 sts, 2 dc into next st) 4 times, sl st into 1st dc at beg of round.

Round 8 1 ch (1 dc into each of next 6 sts, 2 dc in next st) 4 times, sl st into 1st dc

Round 9 1 ch, (1 dc in each of next 7 sts, 2 dc into next st) 4 times, sl st into 1st dc.

Round 10 1 ch, (1 dc into each of next 8 sts, 2 dc into next st) 4 times, sl st into 1st dc.

Round 11 1 ch, (1 dc into each of next 9 sts, 2 dc into next st) 4 times, sl st into 1st dc.

Round 12 1 ch, (1 dc into each of 1st 10 sts, 2 dc into next st) 4 times, sl st into 1st dc.

Round 13 1 ch, 1 dc into each of 60 sts, sl st into 1st dc. Repeat round 13, 13 more times to row 27.

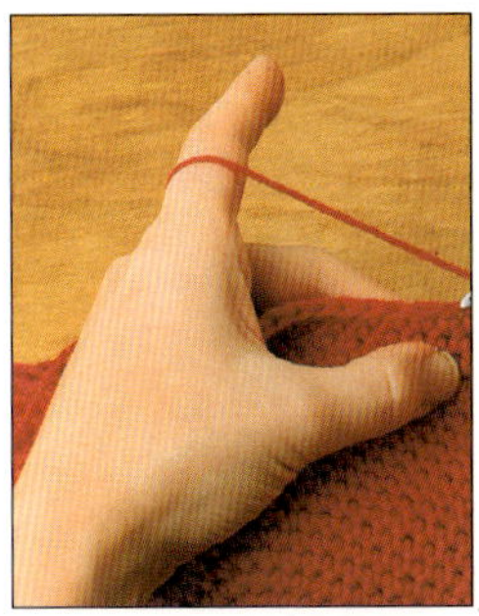

4 **Round 27** Change to 3.50mm hook and work 2 ch, 1 tr into same st, 1 tr into each of next 59 sts, sl st into 1st tr. Fasten off and sew in all ends of yarn.

5 If making the strawberry hat, embroider the seeds with black yarn. Work each one with a daisy stitch, keeping the floating threads between each stitch on the inside of the work as short as possible. Complete by making a small straight stitch in yellow in the centre of each black seed.

Cotton Duffle Bag

This lightweight duffle bag is made in natural unbleached crochet cotton. It can easily be packed away and would make an ideal beach bag for a summer holiday. Two different-sized hooks are used: a 3.50mm to make compact stitches for a firm base and a 4.50mm to achieve a bulkier crunchy effect for the openwork V-stitch sides. The two pieces are crocheted together to make a strong seam which will stand up to hard wear.

The finished bag measures 35cm (14in) deep and 51cm (20in) around the top.

MATERIALS
150g (5oz) craft cotton
3.50mm and 4.50mm crochet hooks
Tapestry needle

1 BASE With a 3.50mm hook, make 5 ch and join into a ring with a sl st into 1st ch.

Round 1 1 ch, 11 dc into ring, join with sl st to top of 1st ch (12 sts).

Round 2 3 ch (to stand as 1 tr), 1 tr into same place, (1 tr into next dc, 2 tr into next dc) to end of round, sl st to top of 3rd ch at beg of round (18 sts).

Round 3 3 ch, 1 tr into same place, 2 tr into each tr to end of round, sl st to top of 3rd ch (26 sts).

Round 4 3 ch, 1 tr into each tr to end of round, sl st to top of 3rd ch (54 sts).

Round 5 3 ch, (1 tr in each of next 2 tr, 2 tr in next tr), to end of round, sl st to top of 3rd ch (70 sts).

Round 6 3 ch, 1 tr into each tr, to end of round, sl st to top of 3rd ch (70 sts).

Round 7 3 ch, (1tr into next tr, 2 tr into next tr) to end of round, sl st to top of 3rd ch (106 sts).

Round 8 3 ch, 1 tr in each tr to end of round, st st to top of 3 ch, finish off yarn (106 sts).

2 SIDES Using a 3.50mm hook, make 103 ch.

Row 1 1 tr into 4th ch from hook, 1 tr into each ch to end (100 tr), turn.

Row 2 3 ch (to stand as 1 tr), 1 tr into each tr to end (100 tr), turn.

Row 3 repeat row 2.

Row 4 Change to a 4.50mm hook.
4 ch, skip 2 tr (1 dtr, 1 ch, 1 dtr [= 1 V st] into next tr. miss 2 tr, 1 V st into next tr) to end of row, 1 dtr into last st, turn.

Row 5 4 ch (1 V st into 1 V st), repeat to end, 1 dtr into last st, (31 V sts), turn.

Rows 6–21 Repeat row 5, 16 times.

EYELET ROW Change to a 3.50mm hook.

Row 22 1 ch, 1 dc into each st of previous row (95 dc).

Row 23 1 ch, 1 dc into each dc to end (95 dc).

Row 24 3 ch, (1 tr into 1 dc) twice, (2 ch, skip 2 dc, 3 tr into next 3 dc) repeat to end of row, ending with 3 tr.

Row 25 1 ch, 1 dc into each st to end of row.

Row 26 1 ch, 1 dc into each dc to end of row. Finish off.

3 MAKING UP Press all the pieces lightly into shape and darn in any loose ends with a tapestry needle. Join the two short sides of the main bag together with double crochet, then attach the base in the same way to the lower edge of the bag.

SHOULDER STRAPS Using a 3.50mm hook, make 10 ch.

Row 1 make 1 tr in 4th ch from hook, 1 tr in each ch to end (7sts), turn.

Row 2 1 ch, 1 dc into each tr to end (7sts), turn.

Row 3 3 ch, 1 tr into each dc to end (7sts), turn.

Repeat rows 2 and 3 until the strap measures 51cm (20in).

4 Fold the strap in half and stitch securely to the top edge of the bag across the seam. Sew the two ends to the base of the bag as shown. Make a cord from a length of chain stitch or by twisting a long length of yarn back on itself, and thread through the eyelets.

Coasters and Placemat

Thick cotton in a subtle range of colours is used to crochet this placemat and coaster set, which makes it both attractive and practical; the yarn is heat-resistant, absorbent and keeps its shape when washed. The rectangular mat is in basketweave pattern. This raised-effect stitch is usually worked in a single colour, but the introduction of stripes gives it an added depth and texture. Making the coasters is a good way to practise crocheting circles; each is made in a different combination of three colours.

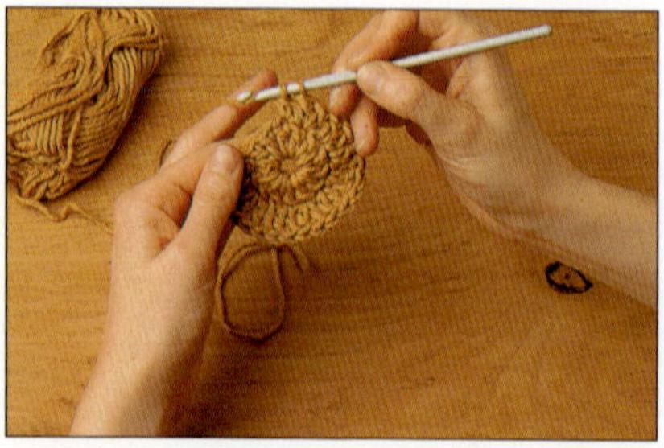

1 COASTERS With colour 1, make 7 ch and join with sl st to form a circle. **Round 1** 3 ch, 14 tr into circle, join with sl st into top of 3 ch. **Round 2** 3 ch, 1 tr in same sp, (2 tr into 1 st) to end of round, join with sl st to top of 3 ch, break yarn (28 sts).

2 **Round 3** join colour 2. 3 ch, 1 tr (2 tr into next st, 1 tr) to end of round, join with sl st to top of 3 ch, break yarn (42 sts). **Round 4** join colour 3. 2 ch, 1 htr into each st to end of round, join with sl st to top of 2 ch (42 sts).

3 Finish off, darn in the end and press lightly.

COASTER MATERIALS

50g (2oz) balls of thick cotton yarn each in dark purple, claret, mustard, sage green and sap green

4.50mm crochet hook; large-eyed needle

PLACEMAT MATERIALS

50g (2oz) balls of thick cotton yarn each in dark purple, claret, mustard, sage green and sap green

4.00mm crochet hook; large-eyed needle

1 PLACEMAT **Row 1** Using dark purple yarn, make 42 ch. Work 1 tr into 4th ch from hook, then 1 tr into each ch to end of row, turn.

Row 2 3 ch, yoh. Instead of working through loops at top of next tr, insert hook from right to left under the stitch itself, draw yarn through, then complete tr as usual (= 1 raised front treble, rftr). 1 rftr in next tr.

2 The next 3 raised sts are worked in the same way, but the hook is inserted from the back of the work and from right to left under the stitch (= raised back treble, rbtr). Work (3 rftr, 3 rbtr) 5 times to last 3 sts, 3 rftr, turn.

Row 3 3 ch, 2 rftr, (3 rbtr, 3 rftr) 6 times. Break yarn, turn.
Row 4 Join claret yarn and work 3 ch, 2 rftr (3 rbtr, 3 frtr) 6 times to end, turn.
Row 5 (3 rftr, 3 rbtr) 6 times to last 3 sts, 3 rftr, break yarn, turn.
These 2 rows form the basketweave pattern.
Continue working in the following stripes:
Rows 6 and 7 mustard
Rows 8 and 9 sage green
Rows 10 and 11 sap green
Rows 12 and 13 sage green
Rows 14 and 15 mustard
Rows 16 and 17 claret
Rows 18 to 20 dark purple.

3 Work the border in sage green. Join the yarn to the edge of the mat at the top right edge and work 1 tr in each st and 3 tr into each corner st. Along the sides, make 3 tr, evenly spaced, into the side of each tr, so that the stitches cover the loose ends of the yarn. Alternatively you can darn these in. Darn in the green yarn and press the mat lightly into shape.

Curtain Heading

Filet crochet is traditionally worked with a fine hook and white cotton thread and has always been a favourite trimming for net (lace) curtains and soft furnishings. This curtain heading is based on an Edwardian idea. It could be made with a full-length net or organza (organdy) curtain or as a shorter cafe-style curtain for a kitchen.

The lace could also be used as an insertion on linen and the lacets threaded with narrow ribbon. The border is 7.5cm (3in) deep and the repeat pattern measures 6.5cm (2½in).

MATERIALS

50g (2oz) ball of 20 crochet thread in white
1.25mm crochet hook
Sheer fabric measuring one and a half times the width of the window
Dressmaker's pins
White cotton sewing thread; needle
Brass curtain loops

1 Make 57 ch. **Row 1** 1 tr into 4th ch from hook, 1 tr into next tr, 2 ch, skip 2 ch, 1 dc into next ch, 2 ch, skip 2 ch, 1 tr into next ch, (2 ch, skip 2 ch, 1 tr into next ch) 6 times, 1 tr into each of next 3 ch (2 ch, skip 2 ch, 1 tr into next ch) 2 ch skip 2 ch, 1 dc into next ch, 2 ch, skip 2 ch, 1 tr into each of next 2 ch, turn.

Row 2 3 ch, 1 tr into 1 tr, 5 ch, 1 tr into next tr (2 ch, skip 2 ch, 1 tr into next tr) 5 times, 2 tr into sp, 1 tr into next tr, 11 ch, skip 2 tr, 1 tr into next tr, 2 tr into sp, (2 ch, skip 2 ch, 1 tr into next tr) 5 times, 5 ch, 1 tr into each of next 2 tr, turn.
Row 3 3 ch, tr into 1 tr, 2 ch, skip 2 ch, 1 dc into next ch, 2 ch, skip 2 ch, 1 tr into next tr (lacet st made) (2 ch, skip 2 ch, 1 tr into next tr) 4 times, 2 tr into sp, 1 tr into next tr, 6 ch, 3 dc into 11 ch loop, 6 ch, skip 3 tr, 1 tr into next tr, 2 tr into sp, 1 tr into next tr (2 ch, skip 2 ch, 1 tr into next tr) 4 times, 2 ch, skip 2 ch, 1 dc into next ch, 2 ch, skip 2 ch, 1 tr into each of next 2 tr, turn.
Row 4 3 ch, 1 tr into next tr, 5 ch, 1 tr into next tr (2 ch, skip 2 ch, 1 tr into next tr) 3 times, 2 tr into next sp, 1 tr into next tr, 6 ch, 1 dc into sp, 1 dc into each of next 3 dc, 1 dc into sp, 6 ch, skip next 3 tr, 1 tr into 4th tr, 2 tr into next sp, 1 tr into next tr (2 ch, skip 2 ch, 1 tr into next tr) 3 times, 5 ch, 1 tr into each of next 2 tr, turn.
Row 5 3 ch, 1 tr into next tr, 2 ch, skip 2 ch, 1 dc into next ch, 2 ch, skip 2 ch, 1 tr into next tr, (2 ch, skip 2 ch, 1 tr) twice, 2 tr into next sp, 1 tr into next tr, 6 ch, 1 dc into sp, 1 dc into each of next 5 dc, 1 dc into sp, 6 ch, skip 3 tr, 1 tr into next tr, 2 tr into sp, 1 tr into next tr, (2 ch, skip 2 ch, 1 tr into next tr) twice, 2 ch, skip 2 ch, 1 dc into next ch, 2 ch, skip 2 ch, 1 tr into each of next 2 tr, turn.
Row 6 3 ch, 1 tr into next tr, 5 ch, 1 tr into next tr, 2 ch, skip 2 ch, 1 tr into next tr, 2 tr into sp, 1 tr into next tr, 6 ch, 1 dc into sp, 1 dc into each of next 7 dc, 1 dc into sp, 6 ch, skip 3 tr, 1 tr into next tr, 2 tr into next sp, 1 tr into 1 tr, 2 ch, skip 2 ch, 1 tr into next tr, 5 ch, 1 tr into each of next 2 tr, turn.
Row 7 3 ch, 1 tr into next tr, 2 ch, skip 2 ch, 1 dc into next ch, 2 ch, skip 2 ch, 1 tr into next tr, 2 ch, skip 2 ch, 1 tr into next tr, 2 ch, skip 2 tr, 1 tr into next tr, 3 tr into sp, 6 ch, skip 1 dc, 1 dc into each of next 7 dc, 6 ch, 3 tr into sp, 1 tr into next tr, skip 2 tr, 1 tr into next tr, 2 ch skip 2 ch, 1 tr into next tr, 2 ch, skip 2 ch, 1 dc into next ch, 2 ch, skip 2 ch, 1 tr into each of next 2 tr, turn.
Row 8 3 ch, 1 tr into next tr, 5 ch, 1 tr into next tr, (2ch, skip 2 ch, 1 tr into next tr) twice, 2 ch, skip 2 tr, 1 tr into next tr, 3 tr into sp, 6 ch, skip 1 dc, 1 dc into each of next 5 dc, 6 ch, 3 tr into sp, 1 tr into next tr, 2 ch, skip 2 tr, 1 tr into next tr (2 ch, skip 2 ch, 1 tr into next tr) twice, 5 ch, 1 tr into each of next 2 tr, turn.
Row 9 3 ch, 1 tr into next tr, 2 ch, skip 2 ch, 1 dc into next ch, 2 ch, skip 2 ch, 1 tr into next tr (2ch, skip 2 ch, 1 tr into next tr) 3 times, 2 ch, skip 2 tr, 1 tr into next tr, 3 tr into sp, 5 ch, skip 1 dc, 1 dc into each of next 3 dc, 5 ch, 3 tr into sp, 1 tr into next tr, 2 ch, skip 2 tr, 1 tr into next tr, (2 ch, skip 2 ch, 1 tr into next tr) 3 times, 2 ch, skip 2 ch, 1 ch into next ch, skip 2 ch, 1 tr into each of next 2 tr, turn.

2 **Row 10** 3 ch, 1 tr into next tr, 5 ch, 1 tr into next tr, (2 ch, skip 2 ch, 1 tr into next tr) 4 times, 2 ch, skip 2 tr, 1 tr into next tr, 3 tr into sp, 2 ch, 3 tr into sp, 1 tr into next tr, 2 ch, skip 2 tr, 1 tr into next tr, (2 ch, skip 2 ch, 1 tr into next tr) 4 times, 5 ch, 1 tr into each of next 2 tr, turn.

Row 11 3 ch, 1 tr into next tr, 2 ch, skip 2 ch, 1 dc into next ch, 2 ch, skip 2 ch, 1 tr into next tr, (2 ch, skip 2 ch, 1 tr into next tr) 5 times, 2 ch, skip 2 tr, 1 tr into next tr, 2 tr into next 2 ch sp, 1 tr into next tr (2 ch, skip 2ch, 1 tr into next tr) 6 times, 2 ch, skip 2 ch, 1 dc into next ch, 2 ch, 1 tr into each of next 2 tr.

These 11 rows form the pattern: work the length to fit the window where the curtain is to be hung. Sew the ends and press lightly.

3 TO MAKE UP Hem the fabric around all four sides and sew a line of loose running stitch along the top edge. Draw up the thread.

4 Pin the fabric to the lace and adjust the gathers to fit. Stitch the two edges together tidily.

5 Sew the loops to the top of the curtain, spacing them evenly.

Jug (Pitcher) Cover

Lacy beaded jug (pitcher) covers were popular in Victorian times, both indoors, where they were used to protect the milk in the pantry or on the tea table, and outside, where they were a vital summer picnic accessory, keeping insects away from lemonade. This pretty modern version is crocheted in fine blue and white thread and edged with brightly coloured, clear glass beads.

MATERIALS

20g (3/4oz) ball of 20 crochet thread in white and a small quantity in blue

1.25mm crochet hook; 28 glass beads

INSTRUCTIONS

Using blue thread, make 10 ch, sl st to form a circle.

Round 1 into circle make: 4 ch, 4 dtr. Remove hook, insert into top of 4 ch and then into top of 4th dtr. yoh (yo) and draw through to form popcorn st, 6 ch *(5dtr into circle, remove hook, insert into top of 1st dtr, then into top of 5th dtr, yoh, draw through to form popcorn st, 6 ch). Repeat from * 5 times, 6 popcorn sts made, sl st to top of 1st popcorn st. Finish off blue thread.

Round 2 join white thread to centre of any 6 ch loop. 7 ch, *into next loop make 3 dtr leaving last loop of each st on hook, yoh, draw through all loops on hook – 1 dtr cluster made – 7 ch. Into same loop make (1 dtr cluster, 7 ch) twice. Repeat from * twice, 1 dc into next 6 ch loop, sl st to 1st ch made.

Round 3 sl st along 1st 4 ch of next 7 ch loop *9 ch, 1 dc into next 7 ch loop. Repeat from * to end of round, sl st to 1st ch.

Round 4 sl st along 5 ch of next 9 ch loop *11 ch, 1 dc into next 9 ch loop. Repeat from * to end of round, sl st to 1st ch made.

Round 5 sl st along next 6 ch *13 ch. 1 dc into next 11 ch loop. Repeat from * to end of round, sl st to 1st ch made.

Round 6 sl st along 7 ch. 9 ch, *(1 dtr cluster, 7 ch) three times, 1 dtr cluster, 9 ch, 1 dc into next loop. Repeat from * five times, sl st to 1st ch made.

Round 7 sl st along 5 ch *(7 ch, 1 dc into next loop). Repeat from * to end of round, sl st to 1st ch. Fasten off white thread.

Round 8 join blue thread to 4th ch of any 7 ch loop. *(3 ch, 1 tr, 2 ch, 2 tr) all into same ch sp, 1 ch (2 tr, 2 ch, 2 tr) into centre ch of next loop, 1 ch. Repeat from * to end of round, sl st to 1st ch.

Round 9 1 sl st into next tr, sl st into next 2 ch sp (3 ch, 2 tr, 3 ch, 3 tr) all into 2 ch sp. 1 dc into next 1 ch sp. Into next 2 ch sp make *(3 tr, 3 ch, 3 tr, 1 dc into 1 ch sp). Repeat from * to end of round, sl st to top of 1st 3 ch. Finish off blue thread.

Round 10 rejoin white thread to a 4 ch sp behind blue shell, working into the last white row. (7 ch, 1 dc into next 4th ch) to end, sl st to 1st ch.

Round 11 sl st to 4th ch of loop. (9 ch, 1 dc into next loop) to end, sl st to 1st ch.

Round 12 sl st along 5 ch (11 ch, 1 dc into next loop) to end, sl st to 1st ch.

Round 13 repeat round 12.

Round 14 repeat round 12.

Round 15 sl st to 6th ch (12 ch, 1 dc into next loop) to end, sl st to 1st ch.

Round 16 repeat row 15.

Round 17 sl st to 6th ch (13 ch, 1 dc into next loop) to end, sl st to 1st ch.

Round 18 sl st to 7th ch (14 ch, 1 dc into next loop) to end, sl st to 1st ch.

Round 19 from the ball in use measure a length of yarn about 4.5m (5yd) long and cut. Thread the beads on to the yarn.

ATTACHING THE BEADS

*(14 ch, remove hook from loop. Slip one bead over chain, put hook back into loop, 1 dc into next loop). Repeat from * to end, sl st to 1st ch. Fasten off and tidy ends. Press lightly.

Snowflake Motif

Crochet motifs can be used in a great variety of ways. The appearance of one basic shape can be changed if it is worked in different colours and various weights of thread. This six-sided pattern can be made singly or several can either be joined together to make a mat or, for the ambitious, a table cloth.

MATERIALS

Small quantity of 20 crochet thread
1.25mm crochet hook
Pearl beads (optional)

Make 12 ch and join into a ring with sl st into 1st ch.
Round 1 3 ch, into ring make 2 tr, 5 ch, (3 tr, 5 ch) 5 times, sl st to top of 3rd ch at beg of round (6 sp).

1 **Round 2** sl st to 5 ch sp. 4 ch, 4 tr, 4 ch, 5 tr *into next sp make (5 tr, 4 ch, 5 tr). Repeat from * 5 times, sl st to 4th ch.

2 **Round 3** sl st to next 4 ch sp, 3 ch, 3 tr, 3 ch, 4 tr, 3 ch * into next sp make (4 tr, 3 ch, 4 tr, 3 ch). Repeat from * 5 times, sl st to 4th ch.

Round 4 sl st to next sp. (3 ch, 2 tr, 3 ch, 3 tr) into sp, 6 ch, 1 dc into next 3 ch sp, 6 ch, *(3 tr, 3 ch, 3 tr into next 4 ch sp, 6 ch,1 dc into 3 ch sp, 6 ch). Repeat from * 5 times, sl st to 3rd ch.
Round 5 sl st to 3 ch loop, (3 ch, 1 tr, 3 ch, 2 tr) into 3 ch sp. 6 ch, 1 dc into 6 ch sp, 3 ch, 1 dc into 6 ch sp, 6 ch *(2 tr, 3 ch, 2 tr all into 3 ch sp, 6 ch, 1 dc into 6 ch sp, 3 ch, 1 dc into 6 ch sp). Repeat from * 5 times, sl st to 2nd ch.

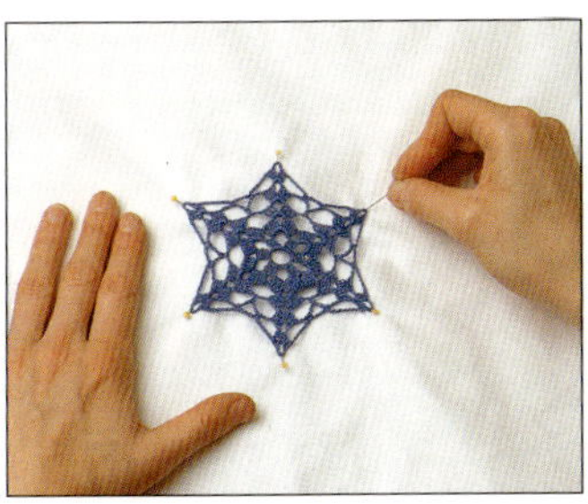

3 Finish off and darn in the loose ends. Pin out to shape on a cloth, pulling out the six points of the star, and press lightly with a damp cloth.

4 Just the first two rounds can be crocheted to make a tiny motif, which fits perfectly into a brooch mount.

Special Techniques

This section is an introduction to the many needlework techniques which fall outside the usual categories. Some, like smocking and rug-making, are crafts in themselves, whilst others will provide innovative ideas to add an individual touch to your projects. Familiar items such as beads, sequins, tassels, ribbons and buttons can all be used in creative and sometimes unexpected ways – all that is needed is a little ingenuity!

Dyeing

Using dyes to bring original colours to yarn and cloth can add a whole new dimension to many textile crafts. Traditional vegetable dyeing techniques give subtle and sometimes unexpected hues, and using them is an art in itself. Chemical dyes, however, are straightforward and quick to use, and are available in both hot- and cold-water versions for synthetic and natural fibres. Special compounds that can be used safely in the washing machine are suitable for larger quantities of material.

SPACE-DYED YARNS

Hanks of cotton thread or pure wool can be dyed as easily as fabrics, with exciting results. The random colour bands that are formed by space-dyeing yarn will create interesting patterns when the threads are worked up. Finer threads can be dyed for free-form embroidery stitches, in specially chosen co-ordinating colours.

1 Wind the yarn into hanks and secure at intervals. Loose ties will allow the colours to blend gently; tight ties will leave a resist band of white yarn. Soak well, then wring out excess water.

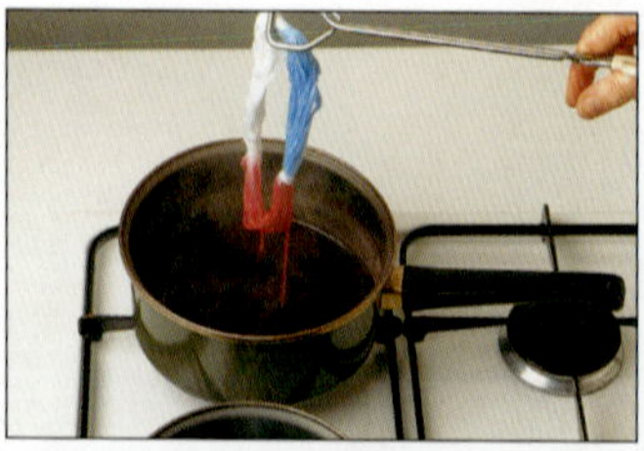

2 Following the manufacturer's instructions, prepare the hot-water dye solution in an old saucepan and maintain it at simmering point. When working with several dyes, only a small amount of each powder need be used. Holding the yarn with a pair of tongs, dip the parts of the skein in between the ties into the dye for a minute. Repeat with the second and third colours.

3 Wash the skeins in a hand-wash liquid to remove any surplus dye, rinse well and allow to dry thoroughly. Carefully snip away the ties without cutting through the yarn, then wind into balls.

It is fascinating to knit or crochet with space-dyed yarns and watch the haphazard colours fall into orderly diamonds and stripes.

Carefully planned space-dyeing is used to produce the figurative and geometric design that patterns the warp of this decorative Ikat fabric.

Tie-Dye Scarf

Tie-dyeing is a well-known way of producing surface patterns on fabric or garments, and, perhaps because of this overfamiliarity, it is often underestimated. Simply knotting, gathering, folding or pleating the material and tying it with string, or binding it with elastic bands, will create varied and unpredictable shapes. Several colours can be used on one piece for a vivid multicoloured effect.

MATERIALS

Large scarf in plain white silk or cotton
String
Hot- or cold-water dye
Salt

VARIATION 1

Circular designs are created by placing a bead or button in the centre of the fabric and holding it in place with an elastic band. Bunch the rest of the material together and tie it at intervals with string.

VARIATION 2

Roll or fold the fabric into a roll and bind at random for a striped effect.

1 If the scarf is new, wash it to remove any dressing (finishing). Rinse well, then wring out. Lay it out on a flat surface and place a long piece of string over one corner. Carefully roll the fabric over the string.

2 Pull the two ends of the string together, gently easing the fabric into a circular shape and making sure that it does not unravel. Knot the string securely.

3 Dye the scarf, following the manufacturer's instructions, and using an old saucepan as a dyebath. Cut the string and unroll the fabric. Wash again to remove any surplus dye.

Fabric-Strip Rugs

A hand-made hearth rug in front of the fireplace has long been a feature of family life. Scraps of wool and fabric can be stitched or tufted on to a backing cloth or canvas to form elaborate pictorial designs, but the quickest rugmaking methods are those in which the rug itself is constructed from strips of braided fabric.

BRAIDED RUGS

Braided rugs, which are made from a coiled stitched braid of material, are among some of the oldest surviving antique examples. This technique was often used in combination with knitting, particularly by the Amish people of Lancaster County, Pennsylvania. A central medallion, made from fabric knitted into squares or six-pointed stars, would be surrounded by braided bands. If possible, cut the fabric strips on the diagonal so they will be less rigid. Cloth salvaged from women's and girls' dresses was cut into long strips, then joined and wound into a ball for working. Knitting with fabric strips can be hard work since they have no elasticity. It is important to keep the tension quite loose and to work on extra-large needles – size 10.00mm upwards.

1 MAKING A KNITTED RUG Collect together scraps and remnants of patterned dress-weight fabrics and tear into 4cm (1 ½in) strips. Sew together and wind into a ball.

2 The rug is knitted in strips of approximately 7.5cm (3in) wide, as anything else would be too unwieldy. Cast on 10 stitches and work in garter stitch as usual. This will make the rug reversible.

3 The finished strips can be sewn together with strong thread. By working in strips of even length, you can produce a chequered (checkered) pattern.

This crochet rug has been worked in basic double crochet stitch with a 12.00mm hook. Each round is worked in a separate colour to give a pattern of concentric circles and the soft colours come from using old fabric.

Braided Rug

The first fabric-strip floorcoverings were made at a time when new cloth was in short supply. Their distinctive muted appearance came from the use of mixed fabrics, recycled from clothing and domestic textiles, as few of the early makers could afford the luxury of planning a special colour scheme for their work. The striking effect of this round rug shows how a traditional technique can be updated to create an unquestionably modern effect. It is made from a vivid selection of bright acetate fabrics, overdyed ginghams and sari fabric.

Materials

Selection of coloured fabrics
Button-hole thread
Sewing needle
Safety pin
Kitchen weights (optional)
Heavy-duty fabric for the backing (optional)

1 Tear the fabric, along the grain, into strips that measure about 6.5m (2½in) wide. Three strips of the same shade braided together will give a broad strip of colour, whereas mixing the colours will produce a "speckled" effect.

2 Stitch three strips together at one end, then secure to a firm surface: fasten to the arm of an upholstered chair with a safety pin, hold down with large kitchen weights, or attach to a wall hook.

3 Plait (braid) the three strips together, turning the raw edges to the inside. Further lengths can either be stitched on, end to end, as the plait progresses, or folded around the end of the preceding strip as shown, to save time sewing.

4 When the braid is a few metres (yards) long, the sewing process can begin. Tidy the stitched end, then, working on a flat surface, coil the braid around it. Sew together with ladder stitch or a flat stitch, catching together a small amount of fabric from each side, and turning to maintain a round shape. A strip of about 18m (20yd) will make a circle of 60cm (24in) diameter, and the rug can be enlarged to any size. A heavy-duty backing fabric can be sewn on if the rug is to receive a lot of wear.

Smocking

Smocking has been used in garment making, as an ornamental method of gathering surplus material, since medieval times. In the English countryside, smock frocks were worn by male agricultural workers for centuries and the tradition survived in rural Essex among the older generation until the 1930s. The smock was a practical, protective, outer garment made from tough linen that could stand up to heavy wear and repel water. It was made from large rectangles of fabric with the fullness gathered into narrow pleats at the yoke, shoulders and cuffs and held together with rows of smocking stitches.

HOW TO WORK SMOCKING

Before being embroidered, the fabric must be drawn into narrow tubes. Rows of dots, in a grid formation, are marked on the reverse of the fabric. Iron-on transfers are the quickest way to prepare plain or patterned fabric.

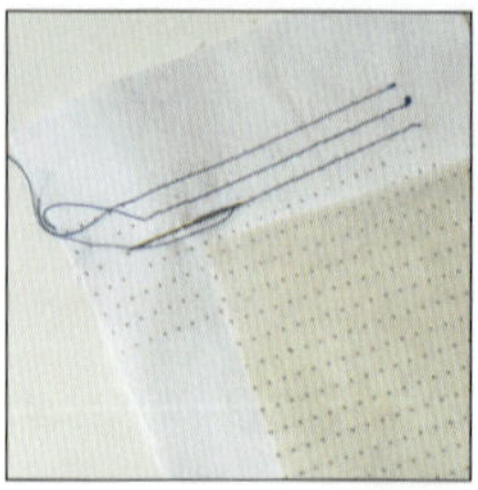

1 Place the transfer face down and press carefully. Work a row of gathering stitches from right to left, along each horizontal line, picking up a few threads at each dot.

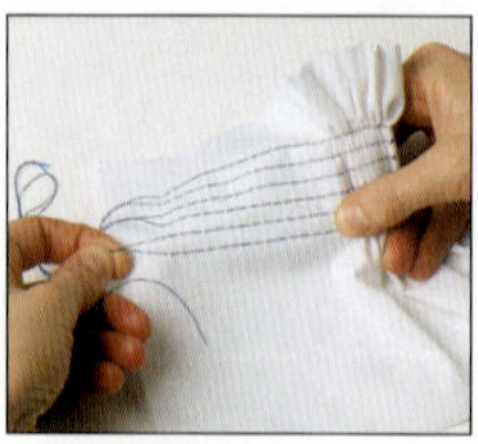

2 Pull all the lengths of cotton up evenly, so that the fabric falls into a series of tubes. Secure the ends by tying them.

3 You can gather fabrics printed with regular dots or checks by simply following the lines of the pattern.

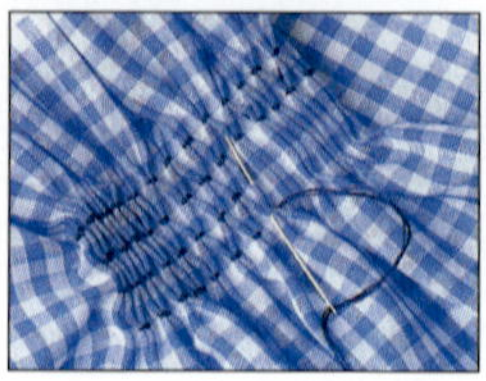

HONEYCOMB STITCH

This is worked along two rows of dots. Bring the needle out to the left of the first fold and work two back stitches over the first two folds. Bring the needle down and out on the next row of dots, between the next two folds. Work two back stitches over these and bring the needle back up to the top line of stitches. Continue to the end of the row, then work the next line of stitches on the third and fourth rows of dots. Surface honeycomb stitch is worked in the same way, but the needle is passed over the surface of the fabric, rather than through the tube.

CABLE STITCH

This stitch is also worked from left to right. Start at the left of the first fold. Be sure that the thread lies below the needle. Make a stitch over the second fold and bring the needle out between the first two folds. Hold the thread above the needle and make a stitch over the third fold, bringing the needle out between the second and third fold. Continue to the end.

Child's Sun Dress

The appealing charm of smocking has made it a favourite for children's clothes, and generations of young girls have worn floral print frocks with smocked yokes. This pretty sun dress would fit a toddler of up to eighteen months, and requires only the most basic of dressmaking skills. The bodice is worked in honeycomb stitch, which produces a very elastic fabric that eliminates the need for a back opening or any fastening.

MATERIALS

35 x 154cm (14 x 60in) piece of dotted cotton fabric
Matching cotton sewing thread; sewing machine
Cotton tacking (basting) thread; needle; dressmaker's pins
Stranded embroidery thread in blue, blue-green, green, pale blue-green, white, pale lime green, yellow and bright yellow

1 Cut a strip of fabric measuring 30 x 154cm (12 x 60in). Turn in a narrow hem at the top and bottom edges, machine stitch and trim back. Turn over and machine again.

2 On the wrong side of the fabric, work six long rows of contrasting gathering thread, starting about 2cm (¾in) in from one hemmed edge. Use the printed dots as a guide, but if they are too far apart, pick up a few threads of cloth between each one.

3 Draw up the gathers and secure by wrapping thread round pins. On the right side of the fabric, beginning at the outside edge of the gathers, work eight rows of surface honey-comb stitch in colours as follows: blue, blue-green, green, pale blue-green, white, pale lime green, yellow and bright yellow. Remove the gathering stitches and machine stitch the back seam. Tidy with zigzag stitch and trim.

4 Cut four strips of fabric each measuring 5 x 30cm (2 x 12in) to make the straps. Fold with right sides together and machine stitch, tapering off at one end. Trim and turn through. Press, top stitch and tidy the raw end. Sew the straps securely to the inside of the yoke at the top of the stitching. Finish off by knotting together at the shoulders.

Ribbons and Bows

There are many craft applications for ribbons, which are available in an ever-increasing choice of weights, patterns and widths. Manufacturers are constantly developing new ideas, such as sheer rainbow gauzes, metallic gold and silver braids (which are ideal for Christmas decorations) and reversible printed satin ribbons. More traditional types – moiré taffeta, country-style ginghams, luxurious velvets and grosgrain – can be found in a wide range of colours in craft shops and department stores.

RIBBON ROSES, ROSETTES, BOWS AND FAVOURS

These can be used to add a personal touch to all kinds of gifts and accessories. Special Valentine ribbons printed with hearts, Christmas designs or wedding ribbons with a pattern of bells and lucky horseshoes can all be used to decorate special presents. Look out for pastel baby ribbons to decorate tiny garments or blankets. Lengths of ribbon can also be appliquéd on to a fabric background.

Ribbon roses are suprisingly straightforward to make and can be used to decorate many different sewing projects. Satin ribbons give a luxurious effect, especially if several harmonizing colours are used together.

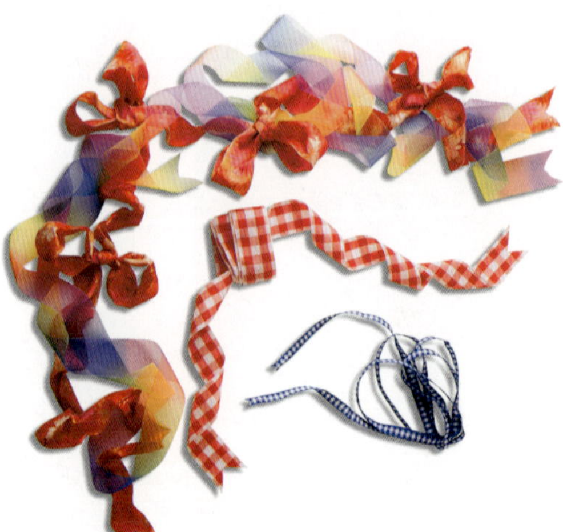

1 RIBBON ROSE
Fold the ribbon under at a right angle, two-thirds along its length, and then pass the long end under the triangular fold and hold in place. Pass the short end under, then continue to make accordion folds to the end of the ribbon.

2 Hold the two ends together and grip with the thumb and forefinger of one hand while drawing up the long end. This action ruffles the ribbon and forms the rose.

3 Still holding the rose, so that it does not come undone, stitch through the base to hold the petals in place.

WIRE-EDGED RIBBONS
These make spectacular bows, which will retain their shape. The loops and ends can be gently bent into flowing curves.

Ribbon-Weave Cushion (Pillow)

Authentic tartan (plaid) and textured grosgrain ribbons are woven together to make this eye-catching cushion (pillow). The basic technique used is called a square (or tabby) weave. The foundation ribbons are laid down to form the warp,then further lengths of ribbon, known as the weft, are passed alternately under and over them. Endless variations can be produced, by using different colours and widths of ribbon in various combinations.

MATERIALS

A: 122cm (48in) length of red tartan (plaid) ribbon 4cm (1½in) wide
B: 244cm (96in) length of blue tartan (plaid) ribbon 2.5cm (1in) wide
C: 122cm (48in) length of green ribbon 2.5cm (1in) wide
D: 122cm (48in) length of red ribbon 1cm (3/8in) wide
E: 122cm (48in) length of blue ribbon 1cm (3/8in) wide
F: 61cm (24in) length of yellow ribbon 2.5cm (1in) wide
Masking tape
30.5cm (12in) square, at least, of fusible bonding web
Two x 30.5cm (12in) squares of backing fabric
28cm (11in) square cushion (pillow) pad
Sewing machine; machine sewing thread to match the ribbon and/or backing fabric; iron; pins; and baking parchment

1 Place the bonding web shiny side down on a clean, flat surface. Cut the ribbon into 30.5cm (12in) lengths. There should be 26 lengths altogether. Arrange single lengths of ribbon across the web in the order: B, E, A, C, D, B, F, B, D, C, A, E, B. Pin each end of the ribbons to the web.

2 Weave the remaining ribbons vertically through the horizontal lengths in the same order. Pin them at each end in the same way to hold them in place. You should end up with an exact 30.5cm (12in) square.

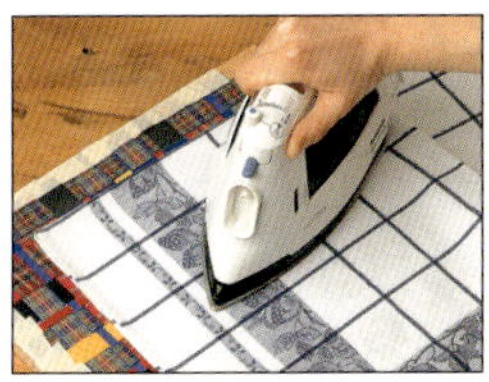

3 To adhere the ribbon to the fusible bonding web, place a sheet of baking parchment over the ribbons (to protect the iron plate), and use the heat of the iron to bond the layers together. Press from the centre out and remove the pins as you come to them, rather than ironing over them. Follow the manufacturer's instructions as a guide to pressing time.

4 Remove the parchment and check that the ribbon is firmly adhered. Trim away any excess web. Remove the shiny backing paper from the other side of the fusible web and place the ribbon panel web side down on to a backing square. This layer won't be seen, but will provide stability to the ribbon weave, so it can be quite a thin fabric. Fuse the fabrics together as before, protecting the ironing board and iron from the glue. Stitch around the edge of the panel to secure the layers together.

5 To make up the cushion, place the cushion backing and the ribbon panel right sides together. Pin, then machine stitch around the cushion leaving a large gap in one side. Turn the cushion through to the right side, push out the corners and press. Insert the cushion pad, then slip stitch the gap closed.

Tassels and Pompoms

A whole art surrounds the making of furnishing trimmings, which is correctly known as *passementerie*, and the most elaborate tassels and fringes can be very expensive. The basic shapes are not difficult to make, however, and a special tassel can add a distinctive finishing touch to many projects. Virtually any yarn or thread can be used: raffia gives a natural feel to bedroom and bathroom accessories, gold machine embroidery thread is extravagant enough for the most special gifts, chenille yarn is luxurious, while bright wools or cotton yarns create a less sophisticated effect. Tassels can be made to coordinate with any interior design scheme and to adorn most soft furnishings.

HOW TO MAKE A TASSEL

Different weights of yarn will produce different results, but the basic method does not vary. The top of the tassel can be further ornamented with a binding of contrasting threads or by the addition of beads.

1 Cut a piece of cardboard slightly wider than the finished tassel and wind the thread around it. Tie a length of thread around the loop when it has reached the required thickness.

2 Slip the loop from the cardboard, hold the tied end firmly and cut through the threads at the opposite end.

3 Keep the tassel in shape by binding the top with matching thread and finishing off the ends securely.

BLACK VELVET AND CHENILLE YARN

Opulent velvet and chenille yarn have been combined to make this spectacular cushion (pillow) above. The blue tassels are sewn by hand at regular intervals and contrast with the smooth texture of the velvet cover.

Pompom Necklace

Like tassels, pompoms are easy and fun to make, especially for children. They can be used to decorate hats, scarves and sweaters, strung together to make soft toys – caterpillars or snakes – or threaded with beads to make this colourful play necklace. These pompoms are all made from a single colour of cotton yarn, which has a rich velvety finish, but interesting multicoloured effects can be produced by mixing yarns.

Materials

Pair of compasses; pencil
Cardboard
Darning needle
Remnants of cotton yarn in various colours
Round cord elastic
Multicoloured wooden beads

1 Using the compasses, draw two 4cm (1½in) circles on the cardboard and mark 2cm (¾in) circles within them. Cut out round the outer card and inner circles to form the two cardboard rings. Thread the darning needle with yarn and, holding the two cardboard rings together, begin to wrap the yarn around the cardboard as shown.

2 Continue until the cardboard is completely covered and the centre space filled, adding extra yarn as necessary. Cut carefully around the outside edge, inserting the scissor blades between the discs.

3 Wrap a length of yarn several times around the cut strands, and between the cardboard discs. Tie loosely in a knot, then remove the cardboard discs. Trim the pompom to make a tidy round ball. Make seven more pompoms in the same way, using different colours.

4 Thread the needle with elastic and string on three wooden beads. Push the needle through the centre of the first pompom, then add another three beads. Continue until all the elements have been threaded together, then tie the elastic tightly in a knot and hide the ends by threading them back through the beads.

Beads and Sequins

Embroidery with beads and sequins has always been associated with glamorous fashion garments – from the fantasy wedding dresses that provide the finale to Paris fashion shows, to the eleborate confections worn by ballroom dancers. A more restrained use of beading can bring interest to many textile techniques, by highlighting detail and adding colour.

WORKING WITH BEADS AND SEQUINS

Sequins can be bought from many craft suppliers. Some of the most exciting varieties are imported from India and come in exotic shapes and colours. They can be sewn on in three ways: in overlapping rows so that the thread is hidden; with decorative contrasting stitches; or anchored in place with a small bead.

FLOWER SEQUINS

Tiny white rocaille beads will make attractive ornamental centres for these flower-shaped sequins.

SEWING A ROW OF SEQUINS

Bring the needle through a sequin's centre hole and make a straight stitch over the edge. Place the edge of the next sequin over the hole in the first. Bring the needle up through its centre and sew down, over the edge.

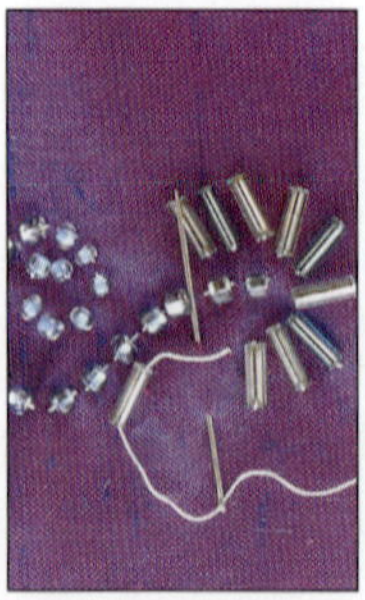

SEWING ON BEADS

Individual beads can be sewn into elaborate patterns: stitch each one down with a fine needle.

CONTINUOUS THREAD

Using decorative back stitches, so that the thread can be seen through the fabric, gold sequins have been sewn on to metallic organza (organdy).

FLAT SEQUINS

Using a fine needle, thread through both the sequin and a bead, then take the thread back through the hole so that the sequin is held in place by the bead.

CUP SEQUINS

This star-shaped Indian Christmas decoration is covered in glittering muticoloured cup sequins, held down by small iridescent beads.

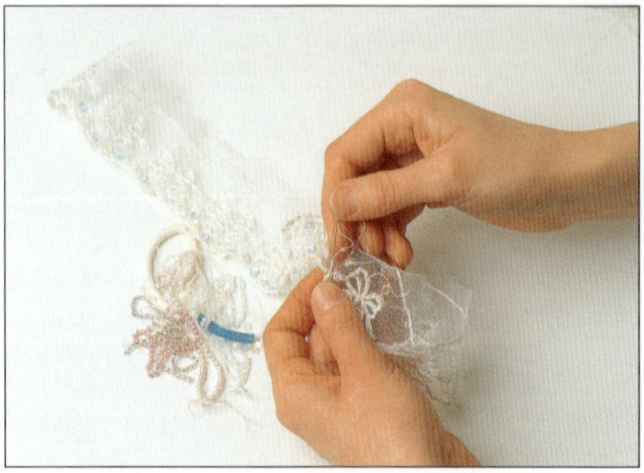

Lace edgings can be decorated with beads and sequins to emphasize aspects of the woven design.

Once part of a chair seat cover, this hydrangea-like flower is made up entirely of beads that have been stitched on to double-thread canvas.

Beaded Heart

Silk flowers and fine satin ribbons combine with beads and sequins to lend an Edwardian appearance to this romantic heart. It is based on a piece of antique lace that has been given a new lease of life: the damaged areas have been disguised with cut-out motifs and beading, and the fragile fabric tacked (basted) on to a heart-shaped padded cushion (pillow) as support. The finished heart would look lovely on a dressing-table, but could also be hung in a wardrobe to perfume clothes.

MATERIALS
Satin fabric
Matching sewing thread
Polyester toy stuffing
Potpourri (optional)
Fragment of old lace
Tiny glass beads
Translucent sequins
Dressmaker's pins
Silk flowers and leaves
Narrow ribbon

1 Cut out two heart shapes from the satin and, with right sides facing, stitch together, leaving a small space in one side. Clip the curves and corners and turn through. Fill with toy stuffing and slip stitch the opening together. Potpourri could be added to give a sweet scent.

2 Mark out the heart shape on the lace, then sew it with beads and sequins, picking out the shapes within the lace pattern. Cut out small motifs from the spare pieces of lace to cover any holes.

3 Pin the lace on to the heart cushion (pillow), stretching it over the upper part and folding over the surplus fabric. Stitch in place, then sew on a posy of silk flowers and ribbons.

Buttons

Buttons are essentially a utilitarian part of everyday life, used by everybody to do up their clothing. Over the years they have been made from every imaginable material: horn, seashell, coconut, plastic, glass, pottery and metal. Elaborate buttons have always been a fashion accessory in themselves. Eighteenth-century dandies sported buttons of gold set with semi-precious stones or even painted with miniature portraits. Today the interlocking Cs on a Chanel suit are instantly recognizable and say as much about the wearer as monogrammed blazer buttons.

This fascinating set of buttons was made as showcase for various specialized stitches and includes blackwork, drawn threadwork, needleweaving, laid threadwork and inlay appliqué.

SELF-COVER BUTTONS

Fabric-covered buttons are used by dressmakers as an unobtrusive yet decorative fastening. Larger version are used for soft furnishings to match or contrast with upholstery fabric, but can also be covered with small circles of embroidery or needlepoint.

1 Following the manufacturer's guide, which is supplied with self-cover button kit, cut out a circle of fabric to fit the button top.

2 Run a gathering thread around the edge of the fabric, draw up and slip over the button top. Pull tightly and secure, then press the backing firmly into place.

Buttons can be combined with many embroidery and applique techniques. Mother-of-pearl shirt buttons have been stitched to the centres of these cotton flowers and are well suited to the naive graphic style of the piece.

Button Mirror

In addition to their obvious function, buttons can be put to many decorative uses. This mirror frame is ornamented with simple embroidery stitches, tiny discs of Indian shisha glass and round mother-of-pearl buttons. Raid the button box to find a selection of buttons in various shapes, colours and sizes; this monochrome colour scheme is just one interpretation of the idea.

MATERIALS
Dressmaker's chalk or carbon
Piece of black cotton twill 5cm (2in) larger all round than the frame
Wooden frame 5cm (2in) wide
Mother-of-pearl buttons
Embroidery thread in red and silver
Shisha glass
Pva adhesive
Buttonhole thread
Mirror to fit inside the frame
Panel pins

1 Draw the outline on to the fabric, using the frame as a template. Mark on the positions of the two rows of shisha glass, buttons and crosses. Sew on the buttons, using red or silver thread, and glue on the shisha glass with pva adhesive.

2 Embroider the crosses in silver thread. The arrangement of shisha, buttons and crosses should not be too orderly or regular. Cut out the centre rectangle of fabric, leaving an allowance of at least 2.5cm (1in).

3 Stretch the fabric over the frame and fold over the edges. Draw together with large stitches in buttonhole thread. Mitre the outside corners and neatly finish the inside corners. Fix the mirror securely in place with panel pins.

Cross Stitch

Embroidery, like many other traditional pastimes, is currently enjoying a revival. Cross stitch is a particularly easy and satisfying skill to learn, relying only on neatness and accuracy to produce simple as well as more complicated designs.

The majority of cross stitch projects are worked on evenweave fabric which allows accurate counting and spacing of stitches. The easiest fabric to use is Aida, where threads are woven in blocks to facilitate sewing the cross stitches. Aida is a very popular fabric both for beginners and more experienced stitchers, however in recent years linen-type fabrics have also made a comeback. Although these fabrics look more difficult to use, stitchers quickly get used to counting the threads and the professional finish is well worth the extra effort.

Many of the projects in this book use the traditional stranded cotton but other threads such as coton perlé and flower thread can also be used to great effect. Whatever your level of expertise, each project has been designed to provide clear instructions and the useful techniques section gives guidance on all aspects of cross stitch.

Clear step-by-step photographs illustrate the more complicated projects. You are also encouraged to try other craft skills such as sewing, painting and basic woodwork to complete the designs and display the finished cross stitch to its best advantage.

THREADS

Although stranded cotton is probably the most popular and versatile thread for cross stitch embroidery, there is an amazing range of different threads available.

Coton perlé produces attractive raised stitches and tapestry wool makes big, chunky cross stitches on a seven or eight count canvas. Some of the projects in this book use other familiar threads such as coton à broder or soft cotton but many are worked in new threads such as silky Marlitt or the more rustic flower thread which is ideal for stitching on linen. New threads are appearing on the market all the time. Look out for unusual flower threads which have been dyed in shaded natural colours and metallic threads which have been specially made for cross stitching.

TAPESTRY WOOL

Although traditionally associated with needlepoint, tapestry wool is also suitable for some cross stitch. It is usually worked on a chunky seven count canvas and makes a warm, hard-wearing cover for cushions, stools and chairs.

COTON PERLÉ

This twisted thread has a distinct pearly sheen and is available in over 300 different colours. It comes in several different thicknesses and is generally used to produce a slightly raised effect on a variety of fabrics.

FLOWER THREAD OR NORDIN

This rustic cotton thread is ideal for working on evenweave linen fabrics. In thickness it is equivalent to two or three strands of stranded cotton. It is available in solid colours, but look out for the space-dyed skeins.

STRANDED COTTON

This is the most popular embroidery thread and is available in over 400 different colours. It is a versatile thread which can be divided into six separate strands. The separated strands of several colours can be intermingled to create a mottled effect when stitched.

MARLITT

A lustrous rayon thread, Marlitt has been introduced to provide the sheen and beauty of silk at an economical price. Although only available in solid colours, it has four strands, allowing the colours to be mixed "in the needle".

METALLIC THREADS

Although traditionally unsuitable for cross stitch embroidery, some metallic threads are now specially made to sew through fabric. They are available in a range of colours as well as gold and silver. Finer metallic threads known as blending filaments can be worked together with strands of embroidery thread to add an attractive sparkle or sheen.

FABRICS

Evenweave fabrics have the same number of threads running in each direction. The number of threads in each 2½ cm (1 in) of fabric determines the gauge or "count". The larger the number of threads, the finer the fabric. Aida and Hardanger are woven and measured in blocks of threads. However, cross stitches worked on 28 count linen are the same size as those on 14 count Aida because the stitches are worked over two threads of linen.

LINEN

Traditionally pure linen was used, but there are now several different mixed fibre evenweave fabrics in a wide range of colours.

AIDA AND HARDANGER

These popular fabrics have groups of threads woven together to produce distinctive blocks over which the embroidery is worked.

Aida comes in 8–18 count whereas Hardanger is a 22 count fabric. It can be used for fine stitching or worked as an 11 count fabric.

EVENWEAVE BANDS

Aida or evenweave bands come in a variety of widths. Some are plain and others have decorative edges. Once stitched, these bands can be applied to a background fabric or made up into bows, tie-backs or bags.

FANCY WEAVES

Fabrics specially woven with distinct areas for cross stitching are suitable for making into napkins, tablecloths and cot covers. There are also some unusual evenweaves which have linen or Lurex threads interwoven into the fabric for special effects.

CANVAS

Double and single thread canvas is usually associated with needlepoint but can be used successfully for cross stitch embroidery. Wool and coton perlé are particularly suitable threads for using when stitching on canvas.

WASTE CANVAS

A non-interlocked canvas is used to work cross stitch on non-evenweave fabric or ready-made items. It is specially made so that it can be frayed and removed after the cross stitch is worked.

NON-FRAY FABRICS

Plastic canvas, vinyl weave and stitching paper are all used for cross stitch projects where it is important that the fabric should not fray.

ADDITIONAL FABRICS

Iron-on interfacing is sometimes used to provide a backing for the cross stitch design.

Fusible bonding web is generally used for appliqué.

1: linens; 2: plastic canvas, stitching paper, fusible bonding web, iron-on interfacing; 3: aida and linen bands; 4: 14 and 10 count waste canvas; 5: Aida and white Hardanger; 6: canvases; 7: fancy weaves.

TOOLS AND EQUIPMENT

ALL-PURPOSE GLUE

This type of glue is suitable for gluing paper and card (cardboard). Follow the manufacturer's instructions for sticking fabric.

BODKIN/SAFETY PIN

Use either to turn rouleaux or to thread lengths of cord and tape through casings.

COLOURED PENS/PENCILS

Cross stitch charts are much easier to follow if they are coloured in with pencils or pens rather than being drafted in black and white.

COMPASS CUTTER

This specialist tool is ideal for cutting small round shapes from card (cardboard). Protect the work surface with a cutting mat or board.

CRAFT KNIFE

Always use a craft knife with a sharp blade and a safety ruler to cut card safely. Protect the work surface with a cutting mat or board.

DOUBLE-SIDED TAPE

Double-sided tape can be used to stick fabric on to card and mount board (backing board). It is less messy than glue and quicker than using thread.

EASY GRID

These clear acetate sheets with grids printed on them come in different count sizes. They are easy to use and are very useful for creating a cross stitch design from a drawing, photograph or picture.

EASY TURN

This tool makes it easier to turn rouleaux through, but a bodkin or safety pin can be used instead.

EMBROIDERY HOOP (FRAME)

These round frames come in several sizes. A fairly small hoop is ideal for most designs stitched on linen-type fabrics as the frame can be moved as you work. Always release the fabric from the hoop at the end of each sewing session. Embroidery hoops are unsuitable for canvas work as the tight rings damage the canvas.

FRAME

Cross stitch projects are usually worked in a frame. The frame holds the material firm so the stitches remain even and accurately spaced. Each project has a recommended frame, but there are many different frames available for cross stitching and you may have a personal preference for one type.

GRAPH PAPER

This paper is used to draft cross stitch charts and is generally marked out in blocks of 10 squares for easy counting. It is available in other counts to work out a design to the actual size it appears on the fabric.

HOLE PUNCH

This type of hole punch cuts one hole at a time and is more versatile for craft projects.

INTERLOCKING BAR FRAME

These bars are sold in pairs and can be made to fit any size of project but are especially useful for working small square or rectangular projects. The fabric is stretched and temporarily pinned or stapled to the frame until the work is complete.

MASKING TAPE

This tape is useful for temporary sticking. It can be used to prevent evenweave fabric fraying or used to hold wood or card (cardboard) together while the glue dries.

NEEDLES

Tapestry needles have a large eye to accommodate the thicker embroidery thread and a blunt point to prevent the fabric threads being damaged. They come in various graded sizes from fine (14) to coarse (26).

Embroidery (crewel) needles are similar to tapestry needles but have a sharp point.

PAINTBRUSHES

Use good quality brushes for painting, matching the type and size of the brush to the project. Sponge or poly brushes are ideal for applying emulsion-type paints. They do not leave brush marks and make it fairly easy to paint a straight edge.

PROJECT CARD

Thread sorters can be made from plastic or card (cardboard). They hold cut lengths of thread, in each colour, ready to use in the project.

QUILTER'S PENCIL

Use this special pencil to make fine marks or guidelines on fabric which can be washed. Silver shows up well on dark fabrics and yellow is ideal for lighter colours.

ROTARY FRAME

This frame is used mainly for canvas work or long pieces of work such as band samplers and bell pulls. Each end of the evenweave fabric is stitched securely to the webbing of the frame and then rolled up until the fabric is taut.

SCISSORS

Keep separate scissors for cutting paper and for fabric, and choose different scissors depending on the size of the work involved. Small embroidery scissors are ideal for snipping threads while larger scissors should be used to cut pieces of fabric. Pinking shears are used to cut a serrated, decorative edge on fabric making it less likely to fray.

TAILOR'S CHALK

This is used to make a temporary rough mark or line on fabric before cutting or stitching.

TAPE MEASURE/RULER

Use a tape to measure fabric and a ruler for paper and card (cardboard). Always remember that special safety rulers are recommended when cutting card with a craft knife.

THREADS

Although tacking (basting) thread is generally white and breaks more easily than sewing thread, use any contrasting colour thread for tacking and marking guidelines on evenweave fabrics. When stitching and making up the projects use a matching sewing thread.

TOP ROW: rotary frame, embroidery hoop (frame), interlocking bar frame, graph paper, Easy grid, easy turn, hole punch, craft knife, project card, tape measure, double-sided tape, masking tape, coloured pencils. SECOND ROW: compass cutter, tailor's chalk, ruler. THIRD ROW: safety pins, pins, needles, bodkin, tapestry needles. BOTTOM ROW: dressmaking scissors, pinking shears, paper scissors, embroidery scissors, all-purpose glue, white tacking (basting) thread, sewing thread, vanishing ink pen, pencil, quilting pencil, poly brush, paintbrushes.

VANISHING INK PEN

The ink from this pen vanishes completely after several days and is ideal to use if the project will not be washed after making up.

BASIC STITCHES

Cross stitch can either be worked as a single stitch or in a row which is completed in two journeys. Irrespective of which method is used, the top stitch should always face in the same direction. If working a border or a detailed piece of cross stitch, it is helpful to put a pin in the work showing the direction in which the top stitch should face.

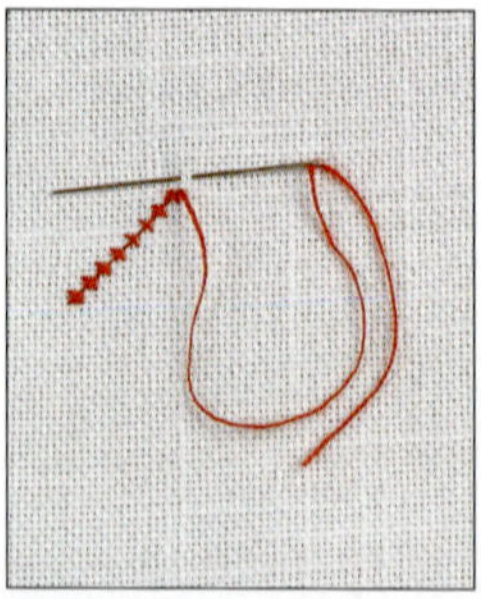

SINGLE CROSS STITCH

This produces a slightly raised cross and should be used for individual stitches and small details. It is also ideal when stitching with tapestry wool.

SMYRNA CROSS STITCH

This decorative stitch is made up of a single cross stitch with an upright cross worked on top. It can be worked in one colour or two colours.

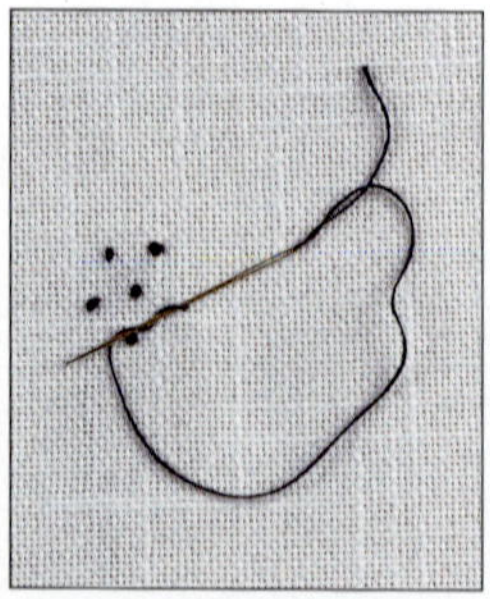

FRENCH KNOT

The French knot is a raised stitch used to add tiny details, such as eyes, flower centres and berries or to add texture to large areas of cross stitch.

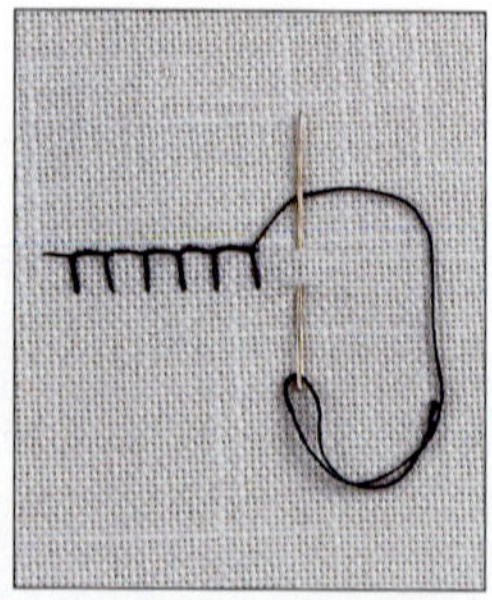

BLANKET STITCH

Use this stitch to neaten the edges of evenweave fabric before working the cross stitch design or decorative edging on mats, waistcoats and bags.

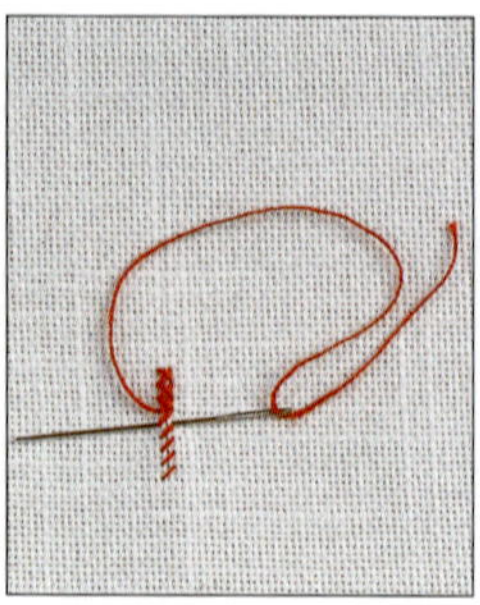

ROW OF CROSS STITCH

First work a row of half cross stitches either diagonally or in a straight line. Complete the cross stitches by stitching the other half on the way back.

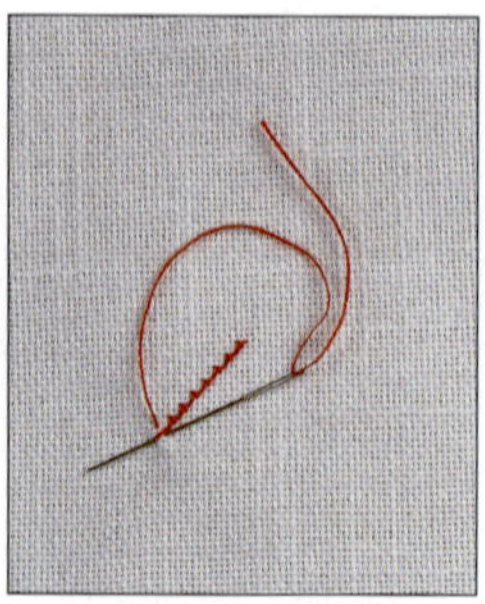

THREE-QUARTER CROSS STITCH

This stitch is used when more detail and precise colour changes are required. It is made up of a half and quarter cross stitch.

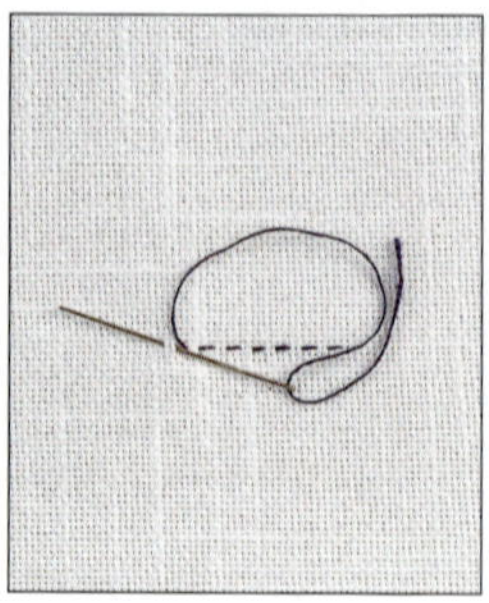

RUNNING STITCH

This is used for tacking (basting) guidelines and stitching decorative details. Holbein stitch is similar but the spaces are filled in with a second row.

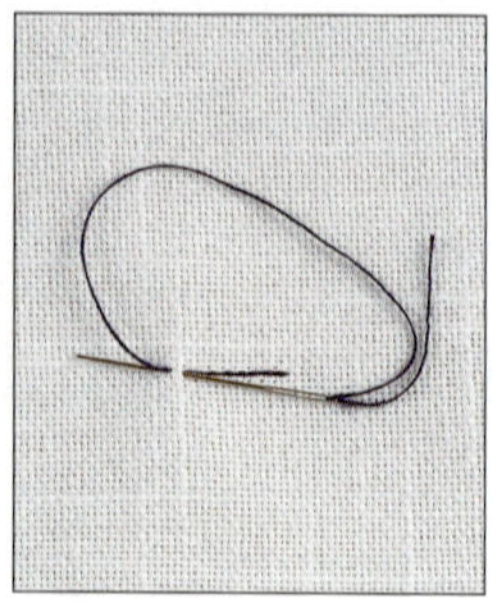

BACKSTITCH

This produces a slightly raised linear stitch. It is used to work lines and to outline areas of cross stitch. The surface stitches are the same length.

WORKING FROM A CHART

The cross stitch charts in this book are made up of coloured blocks with symbols and straight lines. The symbols allow you to photocopy the chart and enlarge it if required. Each coloured square represents one cross stitch and the straight lines are backstitch.

Every project has detailed instructions telling you how to mark the exact position of the cross stitch and where to begin. Usually there are two guidelines running across the middle of the fabric in both directions. It may help, especially on larger projects, to tack (baste) the guidelines carefully, going over and under ten threads at a time. The cross stitch is then worked from the centre outwards.

The size of the stitch is determined by the type of fabric and threads used in the project. Some fabrics, like Aida and Hardanger, are woven in fabric blocks to make counting and stitching fairly straightforward. Evenweave fabrics, such as linen and Jobelan, on the other hand, are worked over a number of threads. Do not be daunted by the prospect of working on linen-type fabrics. They may appear more difficult to work on but, in fact, they are much easier than they look and the results are worth the extra effort.

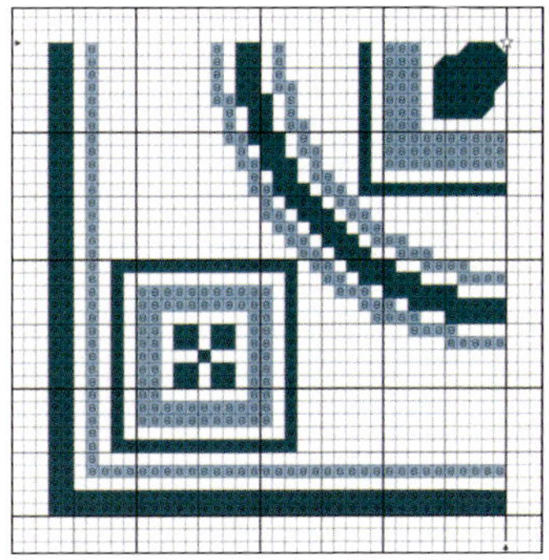

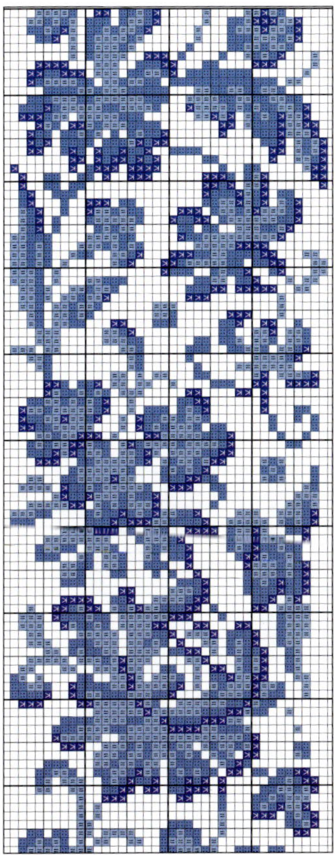

WORKING A REPEAT

Sometimes, because of restrictions in space, only part of the chart is shown. Shelf or curtain border charts, for example, show a single motif or a block which can be repeated. The project instructions explain exactly where to stitch the next motif. If it is a repeat pattern, continue the design, block by block as far as required.

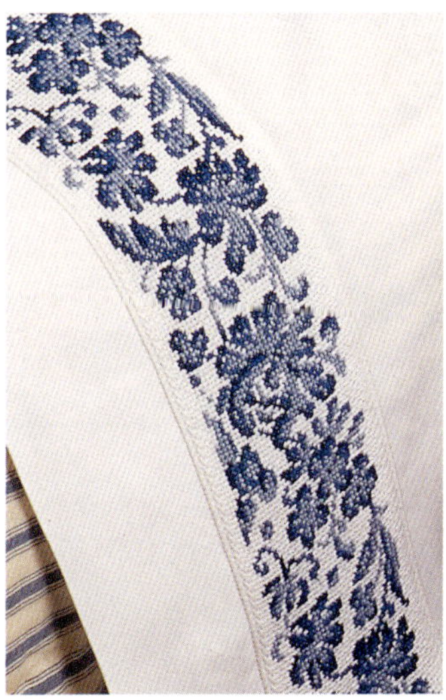

WORKING A QUARTER CHART

Read the instructions carefully and look at the finished project before completing a quarter chart. The final appearance of the cross stitch will depend on how you repeat the design. The work can be done in any one of the three following ways:

1. Stitch one quarter, work the mirror image of this first quarter in the next space and complete the design by working the mirror image of the completed first half. (Work out the mirror image by holding a mirror along one edge of the chart and transferring the reversed image to a piece of graph paper.)

2. Mark the evenweave into four equal squares and stitch the same motif in each area.

3. Stitch one quarter, turn the fabric through 90 degrees and work the same design again. Repeat another two times to complete the embroidery.

TECHNIQUES: BEGINNING

PREPARING THE FABRIC

Many of the projects in this book use evenweave fabrics which tend to fray easily, therefore it is advisable to finish the edges before starting the embroidery. An allowance has been made for neatening the edges in calculating the materials needed.

MASKING TAPE

A quick method for projects worked on interlocking bar frames. The tape can be stapled or pinned to a frame.

ZIGZAG

Machine-stitched zigzag is used when embroidering parts of a garment since the seams will be neatened ready to stitch together.

BLANKET STITCH

This is the best all round method of neatening evenweave fabric. Either turn a small hem or stitch round the raw edge.

LEFT TO RIGHT: masking tape, zigzag and blanket stitch.

COVERING A HOOP

Embroidery hoops (frames) have two rings, one is solid and the other has a screw-fastening. The fabric is sandwiched between the two rings and the screw-fastening adjusted to keep the fabric taut. In order to protect the fabric and stitches from damage, the inner ring is wrapped with narrow cotton tape. Remember that some delicate fabrics can be damaged in an embroidery hoop (frame). In these cases it is advisable to use a large hoop which extends beyond the cross stitch area. Interlocking bar frames are ideal for small projects and a rotating frame is best for large pieces of work.

STARTING & FINISHING THREADS

There are several ways to begin a piece of cross stitch. Finish by sliding the needle under several stitches and trimming the end.

1 Fold a length of cotton in half and thread into the needle. Work the first half of the cross stitch, then thread the needle through the loop on the reverse side.

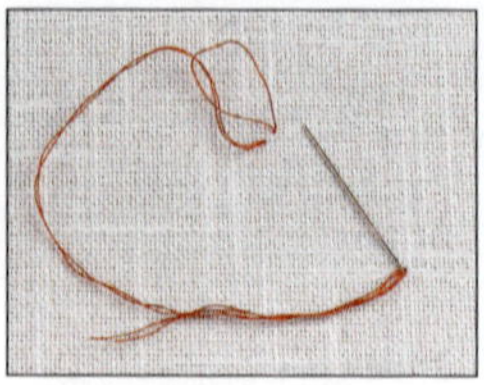

2 Leave a length of 5cm (2in) thread at the back of the fabric and weave this in when you have worked a block of stitches.

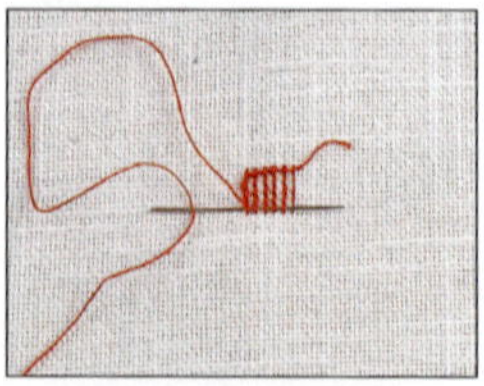

WASTE CANVAS

This technique allows charted cross stitch to be worked on non-evenweave fabric or ready-made items such as towels and cushions. Waste canvas is specially made so that the threads can be easily removed. It is only available in 10 and 14 count but you could use ordinary canvas provided that the threads are not interlocked.

1 Tack (baste) a piece of canvas on to the area to be stitched. Make sure there will be plenty of canvas round the design once it is complete.

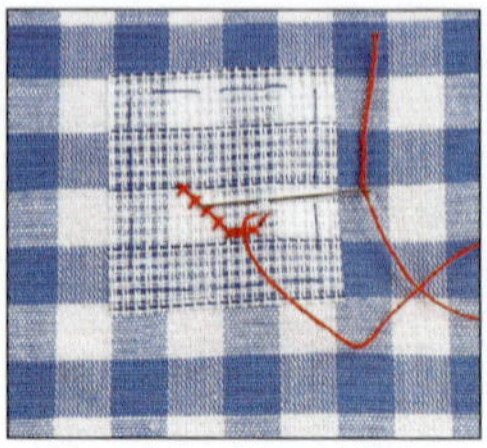

2 Work the cross stitch design over the canvas and through the fabric. Take care to make all the stitches as even as you possibly can.

3 Once complete, fray the canvas and pull the threads out one at a time. It will be easier if you tug the canvas gently to loosen the threads.

TECHNIQUES: FINISHING

MITRED CORNER

Tablecloths and mats can be finished neatly with mitred corners. These reduce bulk and make a secure hem which can be laundered safely.

1 Fold the hem, run your fingers along and open out. Cut across the corner from crease to crease and refold the hem.

2 Turn under a further 0.5 cm (¼ in) and pin the hem in place. Slip stitch the mitred corner and machine or hand stitch the hem.

STRETCHING

As a general rule embroidery should always be stretched using thread so that it can be easily removed and cleaned in the future. However, small projects which may be kept for only a limited time can be quickly and successfully mounted using double-sided tape.

1 Cut the card (cardboard) to the required size and stick double-sided tape along all the edges. Trim across the corners and remove the paper backing. Stretch the fabric on to the tape and mitre the corners neatly.

MOUNTING

If a project such as a sampler or picture is likely to be kept for a long time, great care should be taken in mounting the finished work. Acid-free mount board (backing board) or paper should be used under the embroidery and glue or tape which leave an acid residue on the fabric should be avoided.

The following easy method of mounting ensures that the embroidery will be absolutely straight and exactly where you want it.

1 Cut the mount board to size and mark the mid point across the top and bottom of the board. Allow for a wider border at the bottom if required. Mark the mid point of the embroidery at each side of the board and draw in the lines. Lay the embroidery face down on a flat surface and place the mount board on top of it.

2 Line up the guide-lines on the embroidery with the lines on the board. Fold the top edge over and put a pin into the mount board at the centre line. Stretch the fabric slightly and put another pin at the bottom. Repeat the process at the sides. Work your way along each edge from the centre out putting in pins every 2.5 cm (1 in) keeping the grain of the fabric straight.

3 Using a long length of double thread, sew from side to side spacing the stitches about 12 mm (½ in) apart. Join in more thread using an overhand knot. Once complete lift the threads up one at a time to pull them tight and secure. Mitre or fold the corners and repeat along the remaining sides.

ADDITIONS

Most embroidery is embellished by the addition of trimmings, and cross stitch is no exception. Whether it is an Asian design with shisha mirrors and tassels or a traditional English lavender bag edged with Victorian lace, the "additions" always enhance the cross stitch design and add the finishing touch to an attractive piece.

BEADS

Beads are attached using a double thread and in contrast to all other forms of embroidery, begun with a securely tied knot. Sew the beads on individually, as if you were stitching the first half of a cross stitch.

BUTTONS

Buttons with four holes can be stitched on with a large cross stitch to make a very attractive addition to a design.

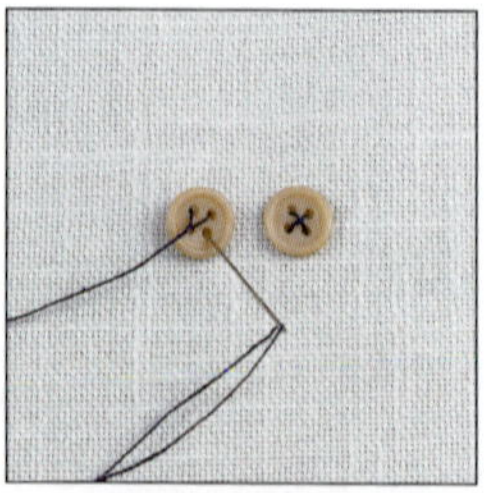

RIBBON

Ribbon looks very effective when used to create a grid for a repeat design of small cross stitch motifs. The ribbon is laid straight along the grain before the cross stitch has been worked. Choose a ribbon which is the same width as one cross stitch. If the ribbon is to be applied diagonally it is easier to work the cross stitch motifs first.

1 Pin the strips of ribbon in position in one direction and pin the rest across the top. Check that the spacing is correct, then tack the ends.

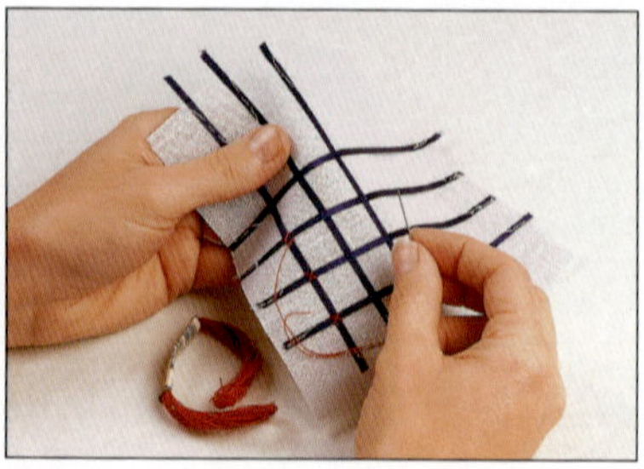

2 Sew a cross stitch at each junction where the ribbons overlap. Remember that if the ribbons are applied diagonally, the cross stitch will be upright.

MAKING A CORD

Embroidery threads are ideal for making into fine cord. The threads can be all one colour or mixed colours to match each particular project.

The amount of thread you need depends on the final thickness of the cord required. As a rough guide, a 1m (39in) length of threads ready to twist will make a cord about 40cm (16in) long.

1 Cut several lengths of thread, two and a half times the final cord length. Fix one end to a secure point. Slip a pencil through the threads at the other end and twist the pencil like a propeller.

2 Keep turning until the cord begins to twist together. Hold the middle of the cord and bring the ends together. Smooth any kinks with your fingers and tie the ends with an overhand knot.

SHISHA MIRROR

These irregular pieces of mirror are stitched on to garments and hangings as a protection against evil. If spirits see themselves reflected in the mirror then, it is believed, they will flee.

Traditional shisha mirrors can be bought from ethnic suppliers, but large modern sequins are a suitable alternative. As extra security, stick the mirror or sequins in position using a small piece of double-sided tape or a dab of glue.

1 Sew two threads across the shisha from top to bottom. Sew across the shisha in the other direction looping the thread round each laid thread to create a framework.

2 Bring the needle up close to the shisha, make a loop through the framework, cross over the loop and pull the thread gently towards you. Take the needle back to the reverse side.

3 Continue round the shisha beginning each stitch between the ends of the previous loop. Finish the thread off on the reverse side.

MAKING TASSELS

One of the prettiest ways to complete a project is to make your own tassels from threads which were used in the embroidery. There are many different ways to make tassels, but most use the same basic technique.

The two following methods are both easy to make. The first tassel is ideal for stitching on to the corners of cushions, mats or bookmarks whereas the second is worked over the end of a cord or rouleau and produces a very professional result. Make the tassels more ornate by adding beads or stitching rows of interlocking blanket stitch round the head until it is completely covered.

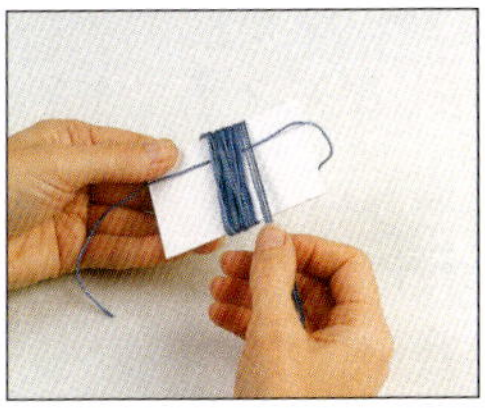

1 Cut a piece of card (cardboard) slightly deeper than the finished length of the tassel. Wind threads round the card as required and slip a length of thread underneath.

2 Cut along the bottom of the threads and tie the bundle together using a sailor's knot. This is like a reef knot, but the thread is twisted round twice before pulling it tight.

3 Wrap another length of thread round the tassel to form a neck and tie off as before. Trim the ends neatly.

1 Wind threads round the card (cardboard) and cut along one side. Tie a knot near the end of the cord or rouleau and place it in the middle of the bundle of threads.

2 Enclose the knot with the threads and tie a separate length of thread around just above the knot.

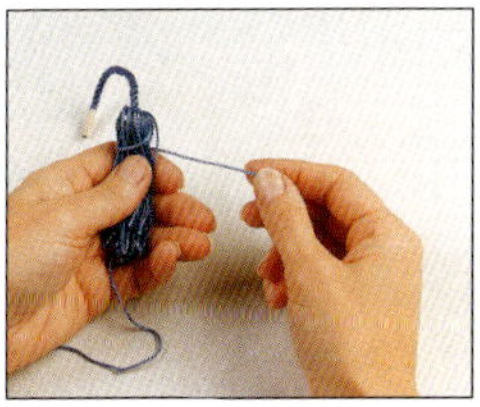

3 Hold the cord and bring all the threads down together. Wrap a length of cord round underneath the knot and tie off securely as before. Trim the tassel ends neatly.

MAKING BIAS STRIPS

Bias strips, cut across the diagonal grain of fabric, are useful for binding edges, making piping and making into rouleaux. The strips stretch lengthways and widthways, making it easy to fit the piping or binding round corners.

1 Fold one corner of the fabric over till the selvedge meets the straight grain and press down the fold. Using tailor's chalk, draw lines across the fabric parallel to the fold line. The width of the strips will depend on the project, but they are usually 5–8cm (2–3in) wide.

2 Bias strips are joined together by stitching along the straight grain. Pin two pieces together as shown and stitch. If there is an obvious right and wrong side to the fabric, one end of the strip may have to be trimmed. Press the seam flat and trim the points of fabric which are sticking out.

MAKING ROULEAUX

A rouleau is literally "a roll of fabric". It is made from a strip of bias fabric which has been folded lengthways and stitched. The seam allowance forms the padding when the strip is turned through. Rouleaux can be used as a drawstring instead of cord, they can be stitched on to cross stitch designs in the same way as ribbon to create texture or plaited together to make a bag strap.

1 Press a 5cm (2in) bias strip to remove some of the stretch. Fold the strip lengthways and stitch 8mm (5⁄16in) from the folded edge. Trim the raw edge and feed the tube on to an easy turn rouleau maker.

ABOVE: Rouleaux can be used to add an attractive three-dimensional element to ethnic and contemporary cross stitch designs.

2 Hook the wire on to the end of the fabric tube and pull gently to turn the rouleau through.

This is by far the easiest way to make rouleaux but you can use a large needle or bodkin instead. For a more padded effect, pull strands of wool through the rouleau as it is being turned or thread through later with a large needle.

FINISHING A CUSHION

Cushions come in all shapes and sizes. Small cushions filled with pot pourri or herbs look most attractive with a lace or wide ribbon frill whereas larger cushions can be given a professional finish with a piped edge.

TO EDGE WITH LACE

1 Measure the perimeter of the cushion and cut a piece of lace twice that length. Sew two rows of gathering threads along the straight edge of the lace. Gather the lace up to fit the perimeter of the cushion and pin it in place. Adjust the gathers and tack (baste). To join the ends of the lace, trim round a motif, overlap the ends and hand stitch securely.

TO PIPE THE EDGES

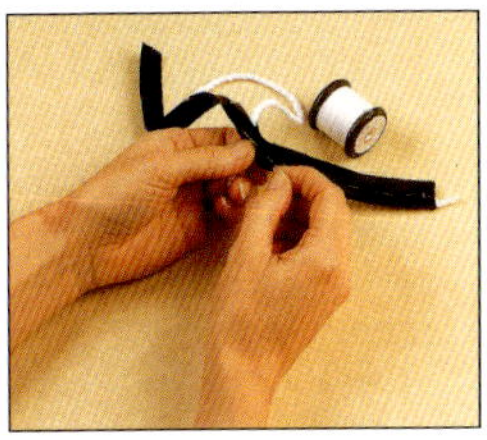

1 Cut and join enough bias strips to fit round the outside of the cushion. Fold the bias strip over the piping cord with the right side facing out, and then tack (baste) close to the cord.

2 Pin and tack the piping along the seam line. Either overlap the ends or mark the length of piping required and sew the bias strip together before tacking (basting) the last edge.

One of the embroidery thread colours has been picked out and used for the contrasting piped edge on this pretty cushion.

COVERING A FRAME

Picture frames, photo mounts and mirror frames are all begun in the same way. The technique of covering card (cardboard) mounts with fabric has become much easier with the introduction of double-sided tape.

1 Cut the mount board (backing board) to size and draw the position of the opening. It is usual for the borders to be equal at the top and sides and slightly deeper along the bottom. Cut out the middle of the mount.

2 Lay the embroidered panel face down and place the mount on top. Cut into the corners and trim the fabric to about 1.5cm (⅝in). Stick double-sided tape along the inner edge of the mount then stick the fabric flaps on to the tape. Keep the fabric straight along the edge of the mount. Mitre the outside corners and stick the remaining fabric on to the board. The mount can be stitched on to backing card and made into a frame.

TRACING & TRANSFERRING

Nowadays, with the right computer equipment, it is possible to scan pictures directly into a cross stitch or graphics program and produce your own charts. The design can be simplified on screen by merging colours to reduce the number of different colours needed. Colours can be changed readily and interesting details, borders or motifs can be copied and used to create new attractive designs.

Most of us though, still need to transfer a design on to graph paper to create a chart for cross stitch. You can draw directly on to graph paper, but the finished design can look "boxy". It is possible to trace and transfer a simple motif but the simplest method is to use an "Easy grid." This is a sheet of clear acetate which has been printed with grid lines. The grids come in different sizes to match the various counts of fabric. You can also use a colour photocopier to enlarge or reduce the design before using the correct count grid to make the chart.

1 Choose a picture which is the same size as the finished cross stitch. Lay the selected grid on top of the picture and tape down. Either work the cross stitch directly from the grid or transfer the design on to graph paper. If a square is mainly one colour then stitch it that colour. If the square is half and half, work two three-quarter cross stitches, one in each colour to fill the square.

NEEDLEWORK TIP

If the picture you want to use is larger or smaller than the proposed size of cross stitch, you can use a different count Easy grid to scale the chart up or down. For example, you might want a 40cm (16in) square cross stitch design for a cushion using tapestry wool on 7 count canvas, but the picture you have is only 20cm (8in) square. In this case use a 14 count Easy grid to make a chart from the picture and the design will work out the correct size.

TO TRACE THE DESIGN

If the picture you wish to use is much smaller than the finished size of the proposed cross stitch, it is often quicker to trace and enlarge the design using squared paper. Remember that the final result you achieve will depend upon how accurately you trace the initial picture. When tracing, always use a very sharp hard pencil and take care to draw the details exactly.

1 Lay the tracing paper over the picture area and secure with masking tape. Draw round the edges of the design motif carefully with a sharp pencil. Try to include as many of the tiny details as possible to make the enlarged design more accurate and interesting.

2 Turn the tracing paper over on to the graph paper and position the design . Draw along the lines carefully. In this way the design will be inverted. To reproduce the original motif, scribble over the reverse side of the tracing and then draw over the lines.

TO ENLARGE THE DESIGN

1 Draw a line round the design area and adapt the motif to suit. In this case, a stem has been added to the flower head.

Draw a similarly shaped large rectangle the exact size of the proposed cross stitch design. Count the squares across and down the side of the small motif and then mark out the same number on the larger grid. Working from left to right, square by square transfer the lines from the small to the larger grid.

2 Refer to the original picture and mark the shaded areas on the petals and flower centre. Use pens or pencils to colour the design. The design can be worked directly from the graph paper using 10 count waste canvas or use the appropriate sheet of Easy grid to stitch on other counts of evenweave fabric.

Above: Once you have transferred a design you can use it as a small detail, or a large, bold, single motif, as on this cushion.

TO ROTATE THE DESIGN

At this stage, the design could be transferred on to computer. There are many cross stitch design packages now available which allow you greater flexibility and speed when trying out different colourways of the same design. Cross stitch computer programs also enable you to flip motifs vertically and horizontally as well as rotating them through 45 or 90 degrees. This feature is invaluable when designing borders and turning corners. If you do not have access to a computer the traditional method of rotating, using a mirror is quite satisfactory.

1 Stand a mirror tile upright on the cross stitch chart at an angle of 45 degrees. On a separate piece of graph paper draw out the corner design you can see reflected in the mirror. To get a mirror image, hold the mirror straight along the edge of the cross stitch motif and draw the reversed image.

ANTIQUE
AND
MEDIEVAL

MEDIEVAL TIEBACKS

These beautiful chunky tiebacks are the ideal size to hold back a big heavy curtain for the front door.

YOU WILL NEED

70cm (3/4yd) natural hessian fabric
scissors
pins
tacking (basting) thread
needle
tapestry wool Anchor two 10m skeins of 8400, four of 8592 and five of 8630
tapestry needle
embroidery hoop (frame)
70cm (3/4yd) lining fabric
70cm (3/4yd) wadding (batting)
sewing thread
two large brass curtain rings

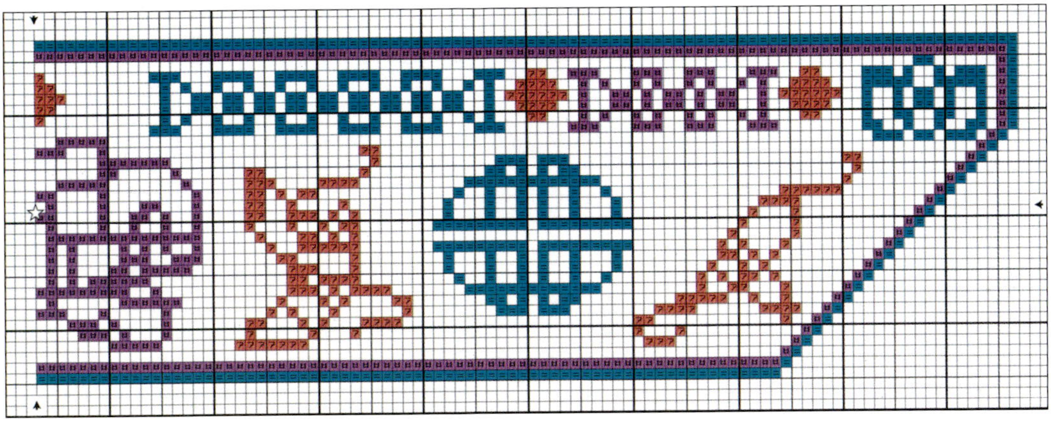

WORKING THE CROSS STITCH

The size of these tiebacks will depend very much on the type of hessian you buy. You can adjust the size to match the curtains. Mark off 20 threads in each direction with pins and measure. This will be equivalent to 10 squares on the chart. Work out the length and depth required and add extra for fringing. Cut a piece of hessian the required size. Tack (baste) guidelines in both directions across the hessian and work the cross stitch over two threads. Once complete, press on the wrong side and trim to 12mm (½in).

Anchor
7 7 8400
= = 8630
H H 8592

☆ Middle point

1 To make up: cut the lining fabric the same size and fold under a 12mm (½in) seam allowance. Cut a piece of wadding (batting) slightly smaller than the pressed lining. Lay the tieback face down and put the wadding on top. Pin the lining through all the layers and hem close to the cross stitch.

2 Sew a curtain ring on the inside at each end of the tieback. Make a fringe by carefully fraying the hessian with a blunt needle as far up as the stitching. Make a second tieback in the same way, if required.

MEDIEVAL CUSHION

Young teenagers will love the bright colours and bold heraldic patterns in this design. The cushion is the ideal size for lounging on a bed.

YOU WILL NEED

46cm (18in) square of 7 count Sudan canvas

needle

tacking (basting) thread

tapestry wool Anchor 8004, 8016, 8114, 8140, 8218, 8414, 8588, 8714, 8788, 8784, 9078, 9096, 9768

tapestry needle

rotating frame

pins

scissors

180cm (2yd) natural cord piping

sewing thread

sewing machine

46 x 56cm (18 x 22in) cream backing fabric

40cm (16in) cushion pad

WORKING THE CROSS STITCH

Tack (baste) guidelines across the centre of the canvas in both directions. Work the cross stitch and once it is completed, block to even out the stitches and square up the design.

1 To make up: tack (baste) the piping round the edge of the cross stitch and machine in place. Stitch a 1cm (3/8in) hem on both short ends of the backing fabric. Cut crossways down the centre and overlap the hems to make a 30cm (12in) square.

2 Tack the backing pieces together and pin on top of the cross stitch with right sides facing. Tack and machine round the sides.

3 Trim the seams and cut across the corners before turning through. Press lightly and insert the cushion pad.

Anchor	Anchor	Anchor
8588	9078	8114
8414	8016	8140
8004	9768	8788
8714	9096	☆ Middle point
8784	8218	

Celtic Cushion

ANTIQUE AND MEDIEVAL

This cushion will look most effective teamed with several others in different shades of blue and yellow and scattered on a couch.

YOU WILL NEED

35cm (14in) square of 7 count Sudan canvas

tacking (basting) thread

needle

tapestry wool Anchor 8 skeins of 8704, 4 skeins of 8896, 2 skeins each of 8020 & 8836

tapestry needle

rotating frame

pins

scissors

125cm (1⅓yd) blue cord piping

sewing thread

sewing machine

30 x 38cm (12 x 15in) deep blue backing fabric

30cm (12in) cushion pad

WORKING THE CROSS STITCH

Tack (baste) guidelines across the centre of the canvas in both directions. Work the cross stitch and block once completed to even out the stitches and square up the design.

1 To make up: tack (baste) the piping round the edge of the cross stitch and machine in place. Stitch a 1cm (⅜in) hem on both short ends of the backing fabric. Cut crossways down the centre and overlap the hems to make a 30cm (12in) square. Tack (baste) the backing pieces together and pin on top of the cross stitch with right sides facing.

2 Tack round all the sides and machine. Trim the seams and cut across the corners before turning through. Press lightly and insert the cushion pad.

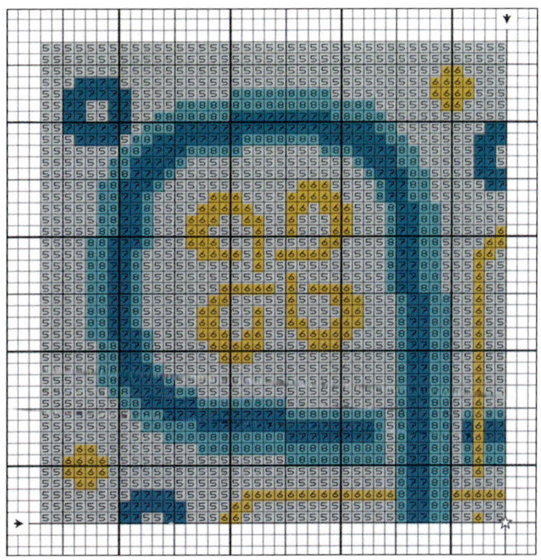

Anchor		Anchor		
5 5	8704	7 7	8836	☆ Middle point
6 6	8020	8 8	8896	

FIRESCREEN

Fitted into a firescreen, this fantastic dragon design makes a wonderful focal point in front of an empty fireplace.

YOU WILL NEED

tacking (basting) thread

needle

51 x 61cm (20 x 24in) grey/blue 28 count Quaker evenweave linen

stranded cotton Anchor two skeins of 1014 and 891

one skein of 273, 274, 357, 403, 779, 830, 831, 849, 853, 855, 856, 868, 875, 877, 898, 900, 943, 945, 5975, 8581

tapestry needle

embroidery hoop (frame)

mount board (backing board)

craft knife

safety ruler

strong thread

firescreen

WORKING THE CROSS STITCH

Although this is a large project, it is sewn on evenweave linen and it can be worked a small area at a time, in a small round embroidery frame to make it easier to handle.

1 Tack (baste) guidelines across middle of the linen in both directions and work the cross stitch over two threads using two strands of cotton. Work the backstitch on the wings using a single strand of 900 and all other backstitch using two strands of 403.

2 To make up: press on the reverse side. Cut the mount board (backing board) to fit the firescreen. Stretch the embroidery over the mount board and fit into the firescreen.

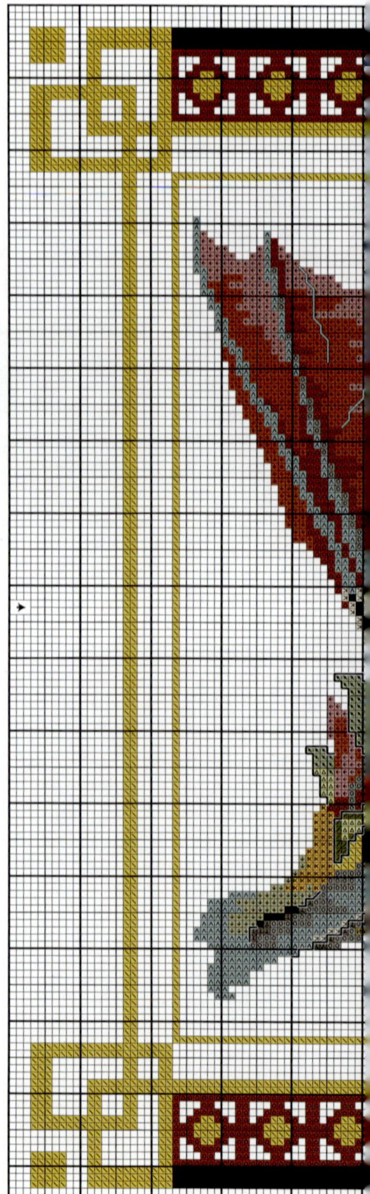

Anchor	Anchor	Anchor	Anchor	Anchor	
357	856	945	403	868/5975	
830	891	1014	274/875	849/877	
831	898	5975	779/877	853/855	
853	900	8581	830/943	831/898	
855	943	273	830/831	898/945	☆ Middle point

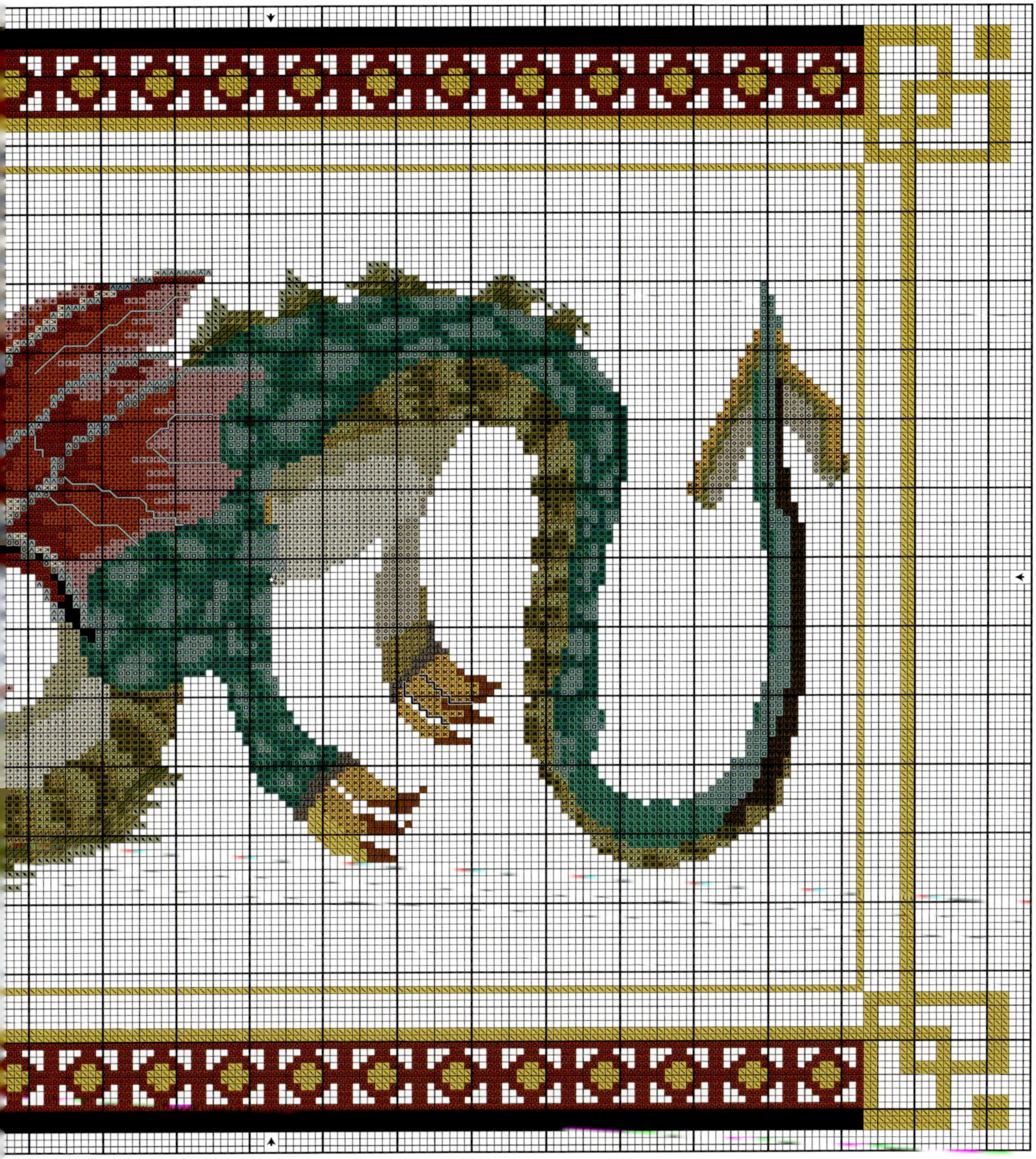

ANTIQUE AND MEDIEVAL

NAPKIN RING

These unusual napkin rings will look very elegant slipped around plain linen napkins.

YOU WILL NEED

5 x 15cm (2 x 6in) 10 count single canvas
tapestry needle
stranded cotton Anchor 70, 276
scissors
5 x 15cm (2 x 6in) cream felt
needle

WORKING THE CROSS STITCH

Work the design using all six strands of cotton. The stitches will lie better if you separate the strands and put them together again before sewing. Press the embroidery on the wrong side once completed.

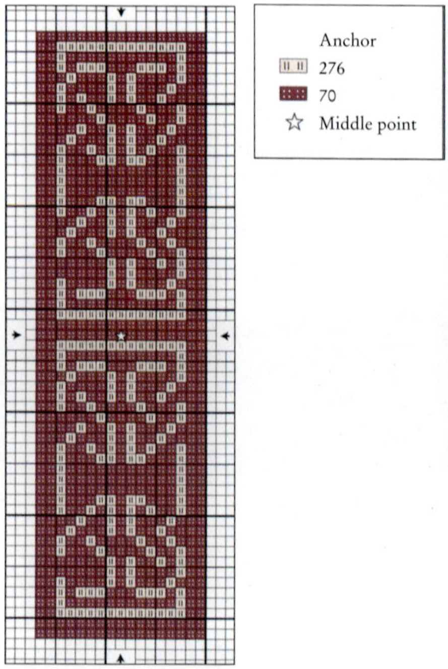

1 To make up: trim across the corners and fold the excess canvas over to the wrong side.

2 Cut the felt to size and sew in place using buttonhole stitch. Bring the ends together and buttonhole stitch through the previous stitching to complete.

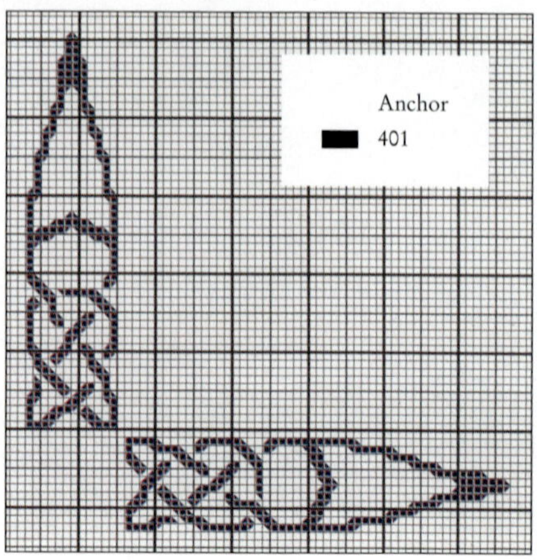

NAPKIN

This Celtic knot design is quick and easy to sew. Finish the napkins with a simple frayed edge.

WORKING THE CROSS STITCH

Tack (baste) guidelines 5cm (2in) in from the edge along two sides of the linen. Work the design in the corner as shown using two strands of cotton over two threads. Press gently on the reverse side when complete.

1 To make up: cut along the grain about 4cm (1½in) from the stitch-ing to give a straight edge to the napkin. Withdraw the linen threads to make a 2½cm (1in) deep fringe all round.

YOU WILL NEED

40cm (16in) square of pale grey 28 count evenweave linen

tacking (basting) thread

needle

tapestry needle

stranded cotton Anchor 401

small embroidery hoop (flexihoop)

scissors

CHAIR COVER

Renovate a worn mahogany chair cover with this warm and comfortable wool cross stitch design. This cover fits a standard-sized dining room chair with a drop-in seat.

YOU WILL NEED

56cm (22in) square of 7 count Sudan canvas

tacking (basting) thread

rotating frame

tapestry needle

tapestry wool DMC 5 skeins of 7406, 4 skeins of 7472, 4 skeins of 7544, 7 skeins of 7590, 9 skeins of 7591

scissors

upholsterer's tacks

hammer

56cm (22in) square of calico

padded seat frame

WORKING THE CROSS STITCH

Tack (baste) guidelines across the centre of the canvas in both directions. Fit the canvas on to a rotating frame and work the cross stitch, beginning in the centre. Once the cross stitch is complete, block the embroidered panel to even out the stitches and square up the canvas. Press on the reverse side.

1 To make up: beginning in the middle of the front edge, stretch the canvas over the padded seat frame and secure on the underside with a tack. Working out from the centre, hammer tacks in every 5cm (2in). Repeat the process on the rear of the seat and then stretch the sides. Trim away any excess canvas on the corners to reduce the bulk.

2 Tack a square of calico to the underside to finish.

DMC	DMC
7472	7590
7406	7544
7591	☆ Middle point

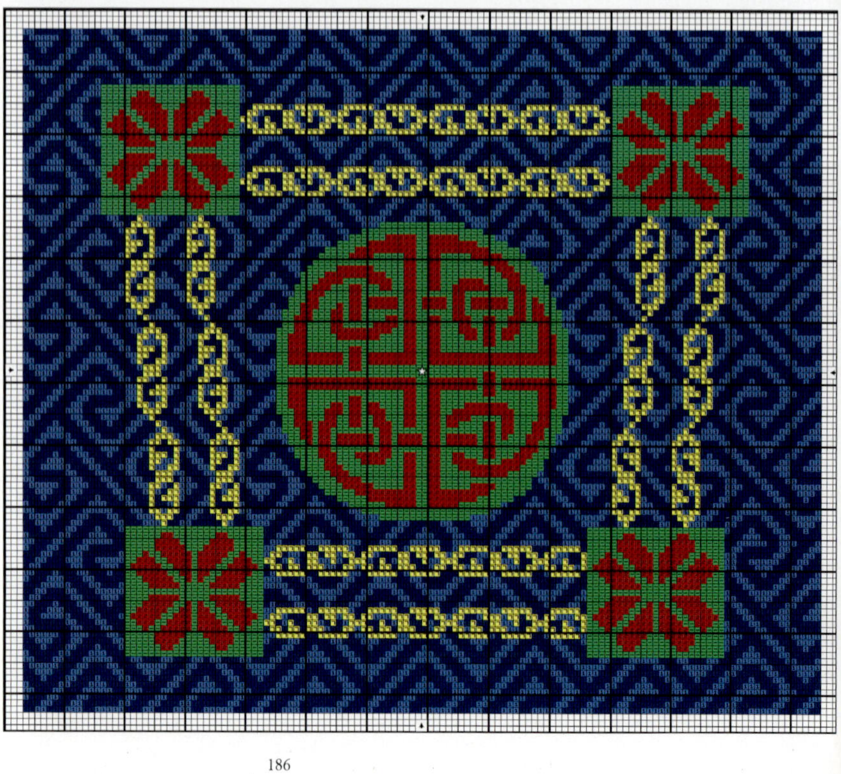

CELTIC BAG

This versatile bag looks attractive, but it is also very practical, and strong enough to carry the vegetables and even a bag of potatoes home.

YOU WILL NEED

scissors

50cm (½yd) Antique Aida 27 count Linda, Zweigart E1235

tacking (basting) thread

needle

stranded cotton DMC 335, 400, 772, 783, 800, 890, 931, 938, 988, 3750

tapestry needle

embroidery hoop (frame)

18cm (7in) square of lightweight iron-on interfacing

sewing thread

150cm (1½yds) calico lining

sewing machine

WORKING THE CROSS STITCH

Cut two 41 x 45cm (16 x 18in) pieces of linen for the bag. Tack (baste) a guideline lengthways down the centre of one piece. Mark the top edge of the bag by tacking a line crossways 4½cm (1¾in) down from the top. Tack a guideline crossways in the centre of the marked panel. Beginning in the centre, work the cross stitches over two threads using two strands of thread. The backstitches are worked in several different colours – body 938, tail 3750 and tongue 355. When the embroidery is complete, press on the wrong side. Ensure the design is square on before ironing the interfacing on to the reverse side. This will help to stabilize the embroidery.

Anchor

- 335
- 400
- 772
- 783
- 800
- 890
- 931
- 938
- 988
- 3750

Backstitch

- 335
- 3750
- 938

☆ Middle point

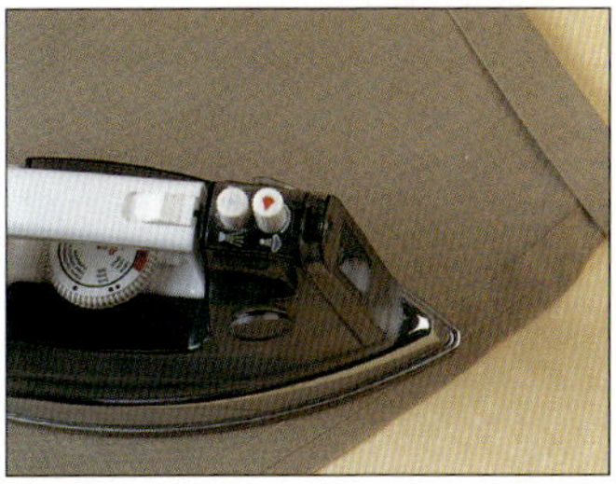

1 To make up: with right sides together, sew down both sides and across the bottom. Trim across the corners and press the seams flat. Make a lining in the same way using two 41cm (16in) squares of calico, then stitch again just outside the first row of stitches for extra strength.

2 Fold over 12mm (½in) at the top edge of the bag, fold over again along the tacked line and press. Turn the bag through to the right side and insert the calico lining, tucking it under the folded edge. Pin, tack and top stitch along both edges of the hem.

3 Cut two 10 x 45cm (4 x 18in) pieces of linen for the straps. Fold them in half lengthways and stitch 12mm (½in) from the cut edge, leaving the ends open. Press the seam open and turn through. Press again making sure that that the seam lies down the centre. Zig-zag across the ends. Pin the handles 10cm (4in) in from each edge and stitch securely.

COVERED BUTTONS

Add a touch of elegance to a plain black coat or cardigan with these sparkly medieval buttons. This design will cover 3cm (1¼in) buttons, but could be adapted for other sizes.

YOU WILL NEED

black 27 count Linda, Zweigart E1235
tapestry needle
stranded cotton Anchor white
fine antique gold braid Kreinik 221
small embroidery hoop (flexihoop)
scissors
thin card (cardboard)
quilter's pencil
needle
sewing thread
3cm (*1¼in*) *self-cover buttons*

WORKING THE CROSS STITCH

Work each button design within a 5cm (2in) area and press on the reverse side when completed.

Anchor
· · White

Backstitch
— Kreinik Antique Gold 221 fine braid

☆ Middle point

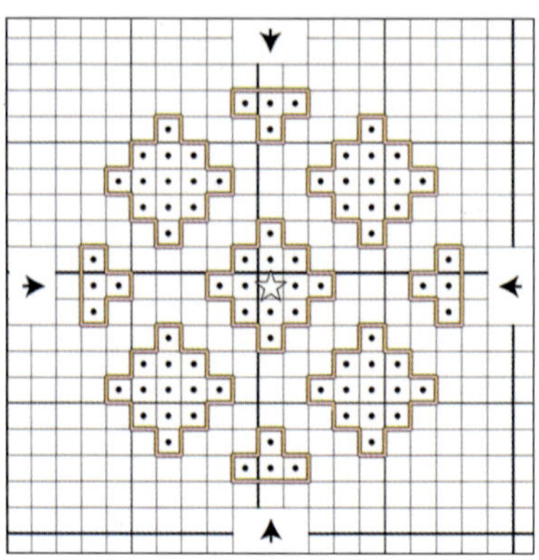

1 To make up: cut out a 4cm (1½in) card (cardboard) circle and then cut out a smaller circle in the centre to make a card ring. (This lets you see the centre of the stitches.) Position the card ring over the embroidery and draw round the outside of it with a pencil.

2 Cut out the button cover and work a row of tiny running stitches round the edge. Lay the button on the reverse side of the cover, pull up the stitches tightly and secure. Press the back on to the button to complete.

STOOL COVER

ANTIQUE AND MEDIEVAL

Add a soft, warm cover to a simple wooden stool or use the finished design to upholster a footstool.

YOU WILL NEED

40cm (16in) square of 7 count Sudan canvas

rotating frame

tacking (basting) thread

needle

scissors

tapestry needle

tapestry wool Anchor 6 skeins of 8024, 2 skeins each of 8016, 8106 and 8138, 1 skein of 8136

28cm (11in) square of thick wadding (batting)

double-sided tape

28cm (11in) diameter stool

1m (1yd) of 3cm (1¼in) wide dark brown braid

sewing thread

WORKING THE CROSS STITCH

Tack (baste) guidelines across the centre of the canvas in both directions and work the cross stitch in wool.

Once the cross stitch is complete, block the design to even out the stitches and trim to 4cm (1½in).

1 To make up: cut the wadding (batting) to fit the top of the stool. Put double-sided tape round the side rim of the stool. Stretch the cover over the wadding and stick down, keeping the stitching just over the edge.

2 Stitch the braid invisibly along the top edge and then sew the ends securely.

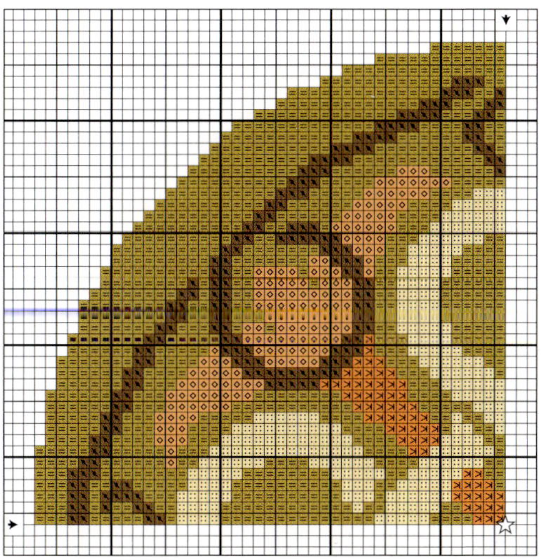

Anchor
- 8024
- 8136
- 8106
- 8016
- 8138

☆ Middle point

ALPHABET BLOCK

Babies and toddlers will love this big, chunky brick. It's easy to catch and so soft it won't hurt anyone.

YOU WILL NEED

18 x 109cm (7 x 43in) navy 14 count Aida, Zweigart E3246
scissors
tacking (basting) thread
needle
embroidery hoop (frame)
coton perlé no.5 DMC 554, 718, 725, 995, 996
stranded cotton DMC 823
tapestry needle
spray starch
sewing thread
polyester stuffing

WORKING THE CROSS STITCH

Cut the Aida into 18cm (7in) squares and bind the edges to prevent fraying. Tack (baste) guidelines in the centre of each panel and work the cross stitch in coton perlé. Once complete, work the backstitch with two strands of stranded cotton. Press and spray starch on to the reverse side.

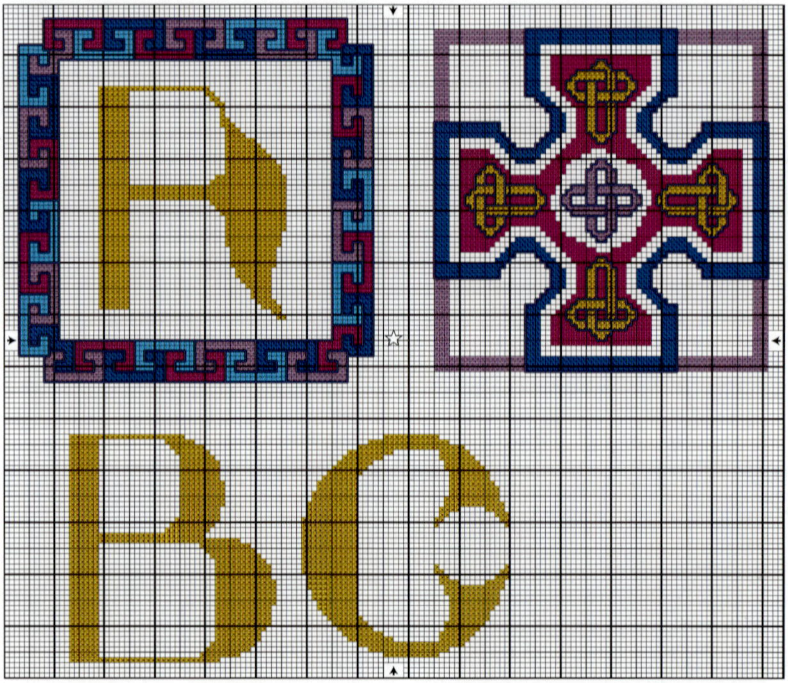

DMC
554
996
725
718
995

Backstitch
823

☆ Middle point

1 To make up: trim round each panel leaving four squares of Aida showing. Stitch the squares together as illustrated in the template section and turn the cube through to the right side. Ease out the corners and fill with stuffing.

2 Slip stitch the last two edges together and pat into shape.

ANTIQUE
AND
MEDIEVAL

GIFT TAG

Using the waste canvas technique, this handsome medieval bird could also be used to decorate a man's tie.

YOU WILL NEED

15cm (6in) square of grey/blue 28 count Jobelan

needle

stranded cotton DMC 739, 740, 817, 3808

tapestry needle

scissors

small embroidery hoop (flexihoop)

tacking (basting) thread

stiff card (cardboard)

all-purpose glue

red gift tag

DMC
739
740
3808
817

French knot
739

☆ Middle point

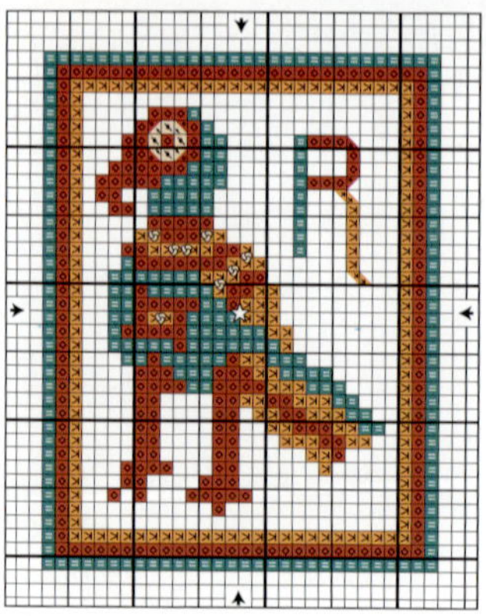

WORKING THE CROSS STITCH

Mark guidelines across the centre of the linen in both directions. Work the cross stitch over two threads using two strands of cotton. Once the cross stitch is complete, press on the wrong side before working the French knots.

1 To make up: measure the embroidered panel and cut a piece of stiff card (cardboard) the same size. Trim the fabric round the embroidery to 2cm (¾in) and stretch over the card, mitring the corners carefully. Stick the covered card on to the gift tag.

BOOKMARK

ANTIQUE AND MEDIEVAL

Any book-lover would be delighted to receive this beautiful, tasselled medieval bookmark which will bring a distinguished academic air to any paperback.

YOU WILL NEED

8 x 20cm (3 x 8in) stitching paper

soft pencil

tapestry needle

stranded cotton DMC 311, 312, 367, 918, 3046, 3722

scissors

5cm (2in) square of card (cardboard)

WORKING THE CROSS STITCH

Mark the centre of the stitching paper with a soft pencil and work the cross stitch design using three strands of cotton.

NEEDLEWORK TIP

Be careful when using stitching paper since it tends to rip easily if you have to unpick stitches. The paper can be repaired if necessary with sticky tape and the holes repunched using a sharp needle.

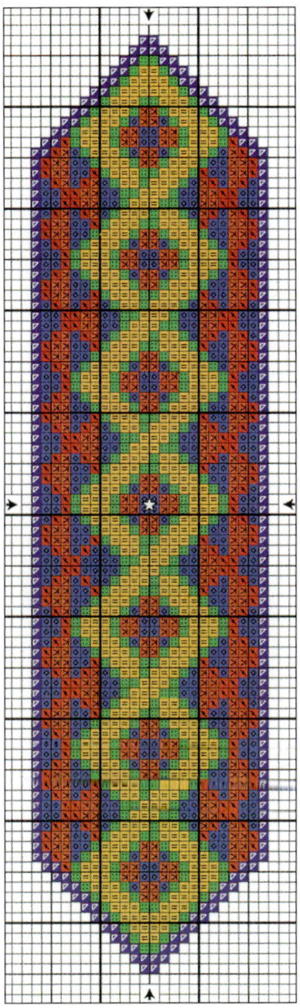

1 To make up: once the design has been completed trim away the excess paper. Any paper remaining visible can be coloured using a felt pen.

2 Cut a 50cm (20in) length of each embroidery thread colour and separate out the strands. Wind the threads round the card (cardboard) and make a tassel to sew on to one end of the bookmark to complete.

DMC
- 918
- 311
- 312
- 3722
- 367
- 3046

☆ Middle point

SEWING KIT

Be prepared for any small repair jobs with this handy sewing kit which keeps everything you need together in one place.

YOU WILL NEED

18 x 38cm (7 x 15in) black 14 count Aida

embroidery hoop (frame)

tapestry needle

sewing thread

stranded cotton DMC 3 skeins 972, 1 skein each of 321, 796, 909, 995

scissors

28 x 69cm (11 x 27in) black iron-on interfacing

40cm (16in) square of black felt

5 x 13cm (2 x 5in) piece of wadding (batting)

5 x 13cm (2 x 5in) piece of stiff card (cardboard)

all-purpose glue

2m ($2^{1}/_{4}$yd) of 25mm (1in) wide black bias binding

sewing machine

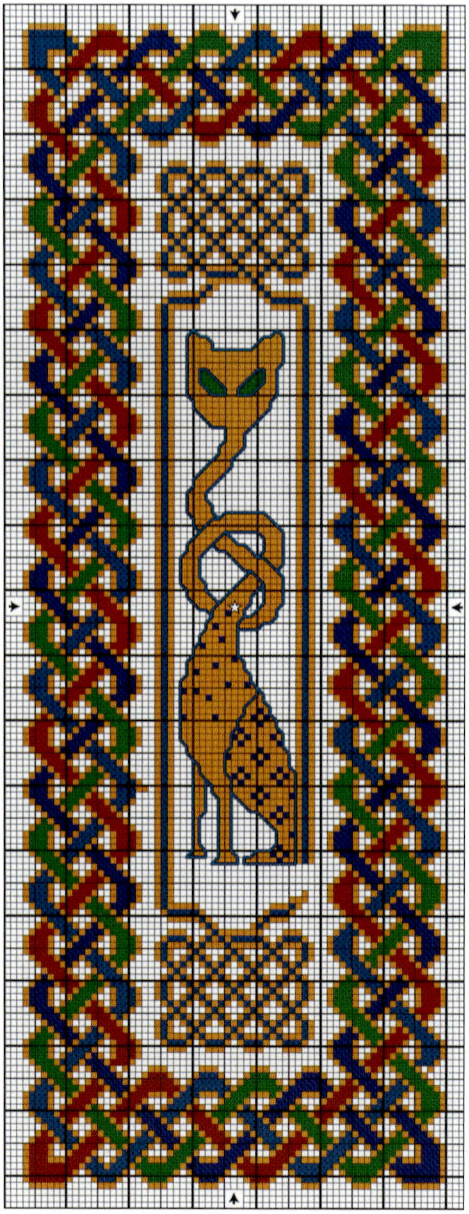

DMC
321
995
796
972
909

Backstitch
995

☆ Middle point

WORKING THE CROSS STITCH

Mark guidelines across the centre of the Aida in both directions and work the cross stitch using two strands of cotton. Work the backstitch with two strands of turquoise (995). Press on the reverse side.

1 To make up: cut a piece of interfacing the same size as the Aida and iron on to the wrong side. Cut one piece of felt the same size, one 10 x 30cm (4 x 12in), another 10 x 18cm (4 x 7in) and the last piece 10 x 13cm (4 x 5in). Stick the wadding (batting) to the card (cardboard) and lay on top of the small piece of felt. Trim across the corners, stretch the felt and stick the flaps down.

2 Iron interfacing on to one side of the 10 x 30cm (4 x 12in) piece of felt for added strength and stitch in place on the backing felt. Pin the needle flap in position, lay the pin cushion pad along one edge and stitch securely.

3 Tack (baste) the completed felt backing on to the wrong side of the Aida. Stitch 3mm (1/4in) all round, then remove the tacking (basting) thread. Fold a 76cm (30in) length of bias binding in half lengthways. Tuck in the ends and stitch close to the edge to make the ties. Fold the binding in half and tack in the middle of one end of the Aida. Pin and tack the rest of the bias binding round the edge of the sewing kit, mitring the corners neatly. Machine close to the edge of the binding to complete.

CELTIC KNOT SAMPLER

This unusual design features nine different Celtic knots. You could stitch them individually to make a set of greetings cards.

YOU WILL NEED

25cm (10in) square of beige 28 count evenweave linen

tacking (basting) thread

needle

stranded cotton Anchor 187, 229

tapestry needle

embroidery hoop (frame)

20cm (8in) square of mount board (backing board)

strong thread

picture frame

WORKING THE CROSS STITCH

Tack (baste) guidelines across the centre of the linen in both directions and work the cross stitch over two threads using two strands of cotton. Press the embroidery on the reverse side when complete.

1 To make up: stretch the piece of embroidery over the mount board (backing board).

2 Fit the sampler into a frame which complements the design.

Anchor
229
187
☆ Middle point

Celtic Cross

ANTIQUE AND MEDIEVAL

The Highlands of Scotland, with their wild landscapes and beautiful sunsets, are the backdrop for this quintessential Celtic cross.

Anchor	
	393
	905
	129
	279
	923
	48
	342
	862
☆	Middle point

YOU WILL NEED

25 x 30cm (10 x 12in) pale blue 14 count Aida

tacking (basting) thread

needle

stranded cotton Anchor 48, 129, 279, 342, 393, 862, 923, 905

tapestry needle

embroidery hoop (frame)

18 x 23cm (7 x 9in) mount board (backing board)

strong thread

picture frame

WORKING THE CROSS STITCH

Tack (baste) guidelines across the centre of the Aida in both directions and work the cross stitch using two strands of cotton. Press the embroidery on the wrong side.

1. To make up: stretch the embroidery over the mount board (backing board).

2. Fit the design into a frame which complements it to complete.

ANTIQUE
AND
MEDIEVAL

BYZANTINE GIFT BAG

This little bag is the ideal size to hold a brooch or earrings. The design was adapted from a Byzantine Gospel book.

YOU WILL NEED

40cm (16in) of 8cm (3in) natural linen band, Inglestone Collection 983/80

tacking (basting) thread

needle

stranded cotton Anchor 44, 306, 861

sewing thread

tapestry needle

pins

scissors

50cm (20in) ochre yellow cord

WORKING THE CROSS STITCH

Tack (baste) a guideline across the linen 15cm (6in) from one end and mark the centre line lengthways. This is the front of the bag and the motif faces towards the short end. Work the cross stitch and backstitch over two threads using two strands of thread. Once this is complete, press the embroidery on the wrong side and work the French knots as shown.

Anchor	French knots
306	
44	306
861	861

☆ Middle point

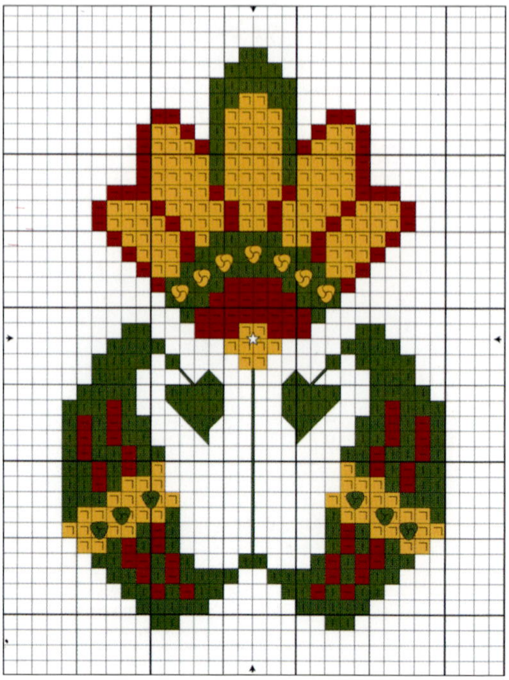

1 To make up: fold over 5cm (2in) to the wrong side at both ends. Turn under 1cm ($^3/_8$in) and pin in place. Stitch across the hem close to the turned edge and again 1cm ($^3/_8$in) away to make a casing for the cord.

2 Fold the band in half crossways, with right side facing out. Stitch down both sides as far as the casing line.

3 Cut the cord in two. Thread one piece through one way and then thread the other in the opposite direction. Tie the ends together with an overhand knot and unravel the ends to form simple tassels.

BLACKWORK FRAME

Display a treasured old photograph in this tiny little frame. For a richer effect, work the embroidery over the whole of the frame area.

YOU WILL NEED

30 x 60cm (12 x 24in) cream 27 count Linda, Zweigart E1235
scissors
needle
sewing thread
stranded cotton Anchor 403
fine gold braid Kreinik 002
tapestry needle
20cm (8in) square of mount board (backing board)
craft knife
safety ruler
30 x 60cm (12 x 24in) calico

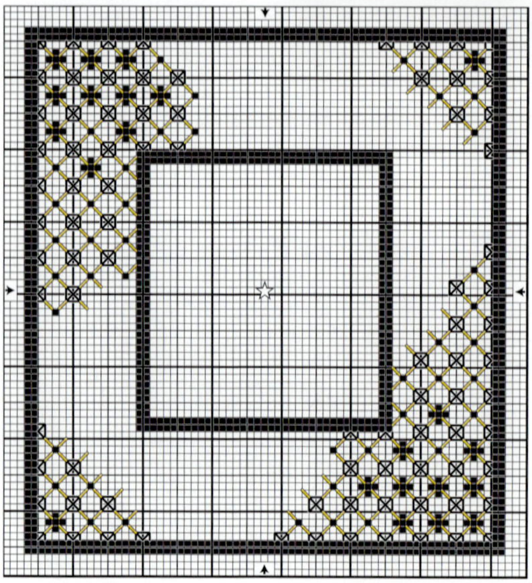

Anchor		Backstitch	
■	403	—	Anchor 403
☆	Middle point	—	Kreinik 002

WORKING THE CROSS STITCH

Cut a 15 x 30cm (6 x 12in) piece of linen. Tack (baste) guidelines across the centre in both directions. Work the cross stitch using two strands of cotton and the backstitch using one strand of black or gold thread. Press on the reverse side.

1 To make up: measure the outside edge of the embroidered panel and cut two pieces of mount board (backing board) that size. Measure the size of the centre panel and the distance from each edge. Use these measurements to cut a window in one piece of card (cardboard).

2 Trim the embroidered panel about 2½cm (1in) from the stitching. Cut into the corners of the window and stretch over the mount board frame. Stretch linen over the other piece of mount board.

3 Cut two pieces of calico 12mm (½in) larger than the frame and press over the turnings. Pin in place on the back of each part of the frame and hem. Oversew the two sections of the frame together along three sides.

4 Make a stand by scoring a piece of card 2½cm (1in) from the end and covering it in calico. Oversew the stand on to the back of the frame to complete.

LABYRINTH PAPERWEIGHT

This labyrinth design was inspired by a 300BC coin from Knossos in Crete, home of the mythical Minotaur.

YOU WILL NEED

10cm (4in) square of 18 count single canvas
tacking (basting) thread
needle
coton perlé no.3 DMC 307, 796
tapestry needle
scissors
all-purpose glue
7cm (2½in) clear glass paperweight
8cm (3in) square of blue felt

NEEDLEWORK TIP

The perlé thread is quite thick for this gauge of canvas, but it produces an attractive raised stitch.

WORKING THE CROSS STITCH

Tack (baste) guidelines across the centre of the canvas in both directions and work the cross stitch using a single strand of coton perlé.

1 To make up: trim the canvas to fit the bottom of the paperweight and stick in place around the outer edge. Cut the felt to size and glue over the canvas to complete.

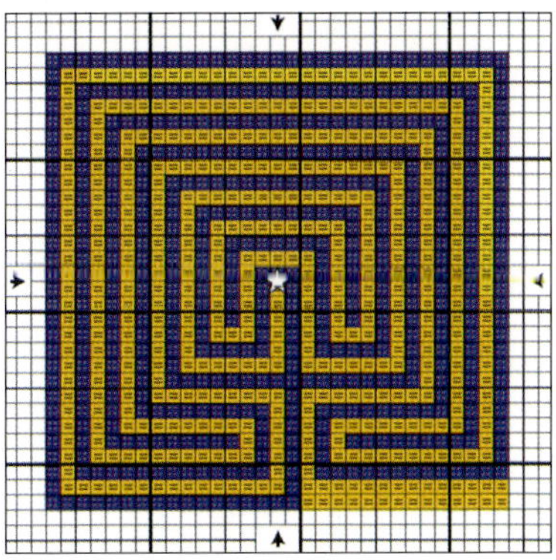

DMC
307
796
☆ Middle point

ANTIQUE AND MEDIEVAL

TRINKET BOWL

This pretty frosted glass bowl is decorated with a Celtic motif adapted from a design on an ornate Saxon dagger.

YOU WILL NEED

15cm (6in) square of antique white 28 count Cashel linen, Zweigart E3281

tacking (basting) thread

needle

tapestry needle

small embroidery frame (flexihoop)

stranded cotton DMC 926, 3808

fine antique gold braid Kreinik 221

9cm (3½in) frosted glass bowl, Framecraft GT4

Kreinik fine braid
Antique gold 221

DMC
3808
926

French knot
926

☆ Middle point

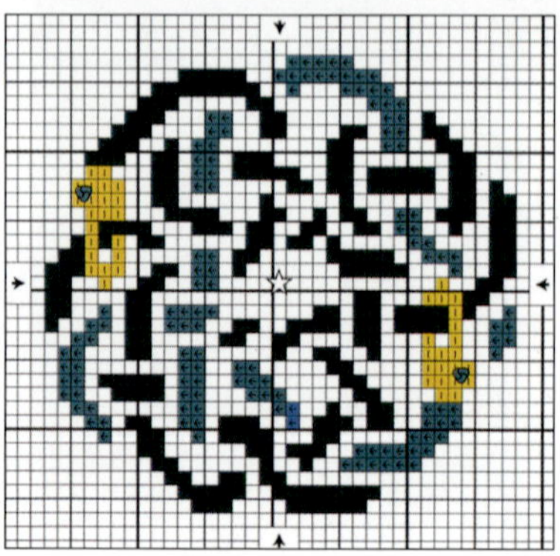

WORKING THE CROSS STITCH

Tack (baste) guidelines across the centre of the linen in both directions. Work the cross stitch using two strands of cotton and a single strand of gold thread. Press on the reverse side and then work the French knots to complete the design.

1 To make up: fit the piece of embroidery into the lid of the glass bowl following the manufacturer's instructions.

EMBROIDERED BLOUSE

These medieval motifs were inspired by the Book of Hours and will match the waistcoat on the following page.

YOU WILL NEED

white medieval-style blouse
scissors
14 count graph paper
pencil
double-sided tape
needle
tacking (basting) thread
tapestry needle
sewing thread
stranded cotton Anchor white, 133, 246, 290, 335, 369, 380, 397, 398, 400, 403
embroidery hoop (frame)
30cm (1/3yd) black 27 count Linda, Zweigart E1235
pins

WORKING THE CROSS STITCH

Make the blouse using a similar pattern or adapt a bought one to suit the design. Trim the seam allowance off the cuff and neck facing pattern pieces. Lay the pieces on 14 count graph paper and draw an outline, then transfer any pattern markings. Draw one red flower in the centre of the cuff and space both small flowers on either side. Draw out the motifs for the neck facing on separate graph paper. Cut carefully round the motifs and arrange them on the pattern outline, keeping them at least two squares from the edge, and stick them in place.

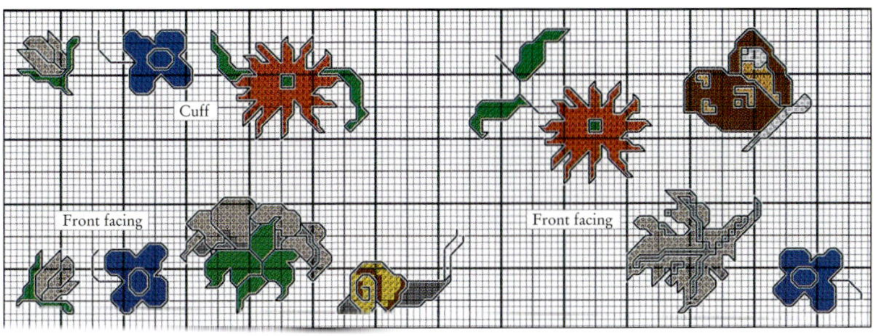

Anchor	
403	
400	
398	
397	
white	
290	
246	
133	
380	
369	
335	
Backstitch	
403	
246	

1 Draw an outline of the pattern pieces on the linen and tack (baste) a central guideline. Work the cross stitch and the backstitch using two strands of cotton over two threads of linen.

2 To make up: once complete, press on the wrong side and cut out adding 1½cm (⅝in) seam allowances all round. Turn under the seam allowance, snipping the curves and tack close to the edge.

3 Pin and tack on to the blouse and slip stitch in place. Make a small loop from a bias strip to fasten the cuffs and neck opening and sew on the buttons to complete the fastenings.

ANTIQUE AND MEDIEVAL

WAISTCOAT

This stunning design could also be added to an existing waistcoat using the waste canvas technique.

YOU WILL NEED

75cm (7/8yd) black 27 count Linda, Zweigart E1235

75cm (7/8yd) lining fabric

scissors

needle

sewing thread

sewing machine

14 count graph paper

pencil

double-sided tape

pins

tacking (basting) thread

stranded cotton Anchor 3 skeins each of white and 397, 2 skeins of 398 and one each of 133, 246, 290, 335, 369, 380, 400, 403

WORKING THE CROSS STITCH

Enlarge the pattern pieces or use a simple bought pattern and cut out the waistcoat front in linen. Sew the darts and press towards the centre. Trim the seam allowance from the pattern piece, then draw an outline on 14 count graph paper and transfer any pattern markings. Draw out the motifs on separate graph paper. Cut carefully round them and arrange on the pattern outline keeping them at least two squares from the edge. Once you are satisfied with the arrangement, stick them in place. Mark the outline of the unicorn and work the cross stitch from the chart. Sew the backstitch to finish the embroidery. Work the other side of the waistcoat as a mirror image of the first side and press both front panels on the reverse side.

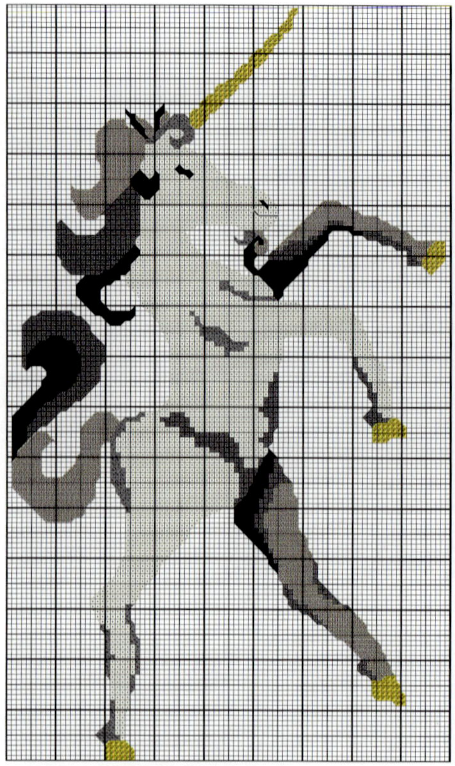

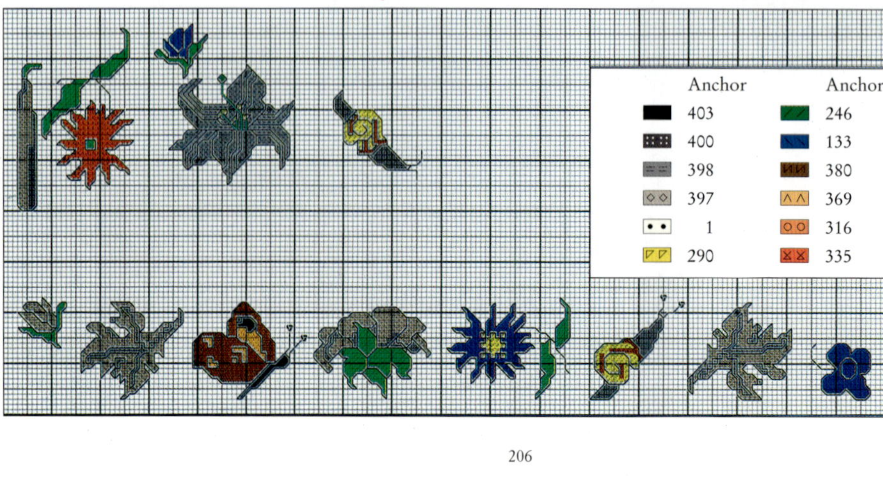

Anchor	Anchor	Backstitch
403	246	403
400	133	246
398	380	
397	369	French knot
1	316	403
290	335	

1 To make up: cut out the front lining and two backs in lining fabric. Sew all the darts and press. With right sides together, stitch the front lining to the linen leaving the shoulder and side seams free. Stitch the back pieces together along the armhole edge, the neck edge and the bottom. Trim the seam allowances and snip across the corners before turning through.

Pin and sew the back and front together at the shoulder and side seams, leaving the lining free. Trim the seams and press flat.

2 Turn under the lining seam allowance and slip stitch. Press the waistcoat on the reverse side and add a fastening if required.

ANTIQUE AND MEDIEVAL

Ringbearer's Cushion

This delightful Celtic design could be stitched in two complementary colours to match the bridesmaids' dresses or the wedding flowers.

YOU WILL NEED

30cm (12in) square of antique white 28 count linen
tacking (basting) thread
needle
stranded cotton DMC 224, 3685
tapestry needle
embroidery hoop (frame)
1m (1¼yd) of 2cm (¾in) wine coloured ribbon
1m (1¼yd) piping cord
sewing thread
sewing machine
scissors
30cm (12in) square of antique white backing fabric
polyester stuffing
1m (1¼yd) 3mm (¼in) wine-coloured ribbon

WORKING THE CROSS STITCH

Tack (baste) guidelines across the centre of the linen in both directions. Work the centre motif using two strands of cotton. Count out the threads carefully and stitch the border. Press on the reverse side.

1 To make up: fold the wide ribbon over the piping cord and tack in position round the edge of the cushion 2cm (¾in) away from the cross stitch. Stitch the piping in place along one side. With right sides facing, sew the cushion cover together along the remaining three sides. Trim across the corners and turn through. Give the cushion a final press and fill with stuffing.

2 Slip stitch the opening. Cut the narrow ribbon in half, find the middle of each half and sew securely in the centre of the cross. Stitch a decorative cross stitch on top to finish.

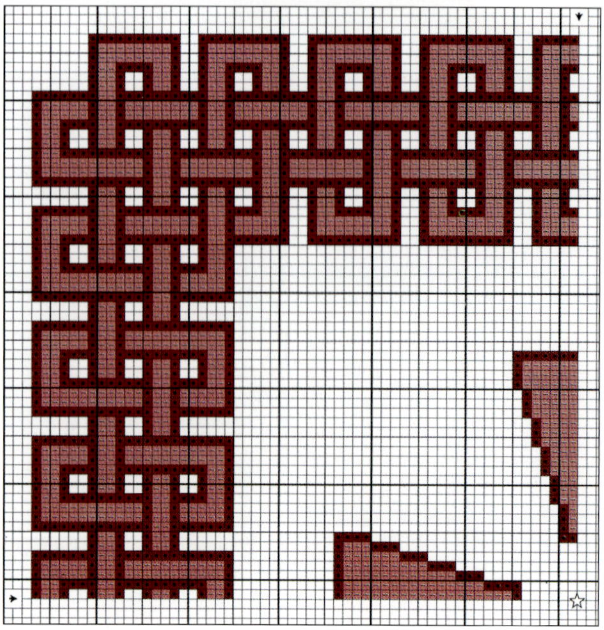

DMC	
224	
3685	

☆ Middle point

CHESSBOARD

The black squares are stitched in Assisi embroidery, a variation of cross stitch where the design areas are left blank and the background is filled with cross stitch.

YOU WILL NEED

38cm (15in) square of white 14 count Aida

tacking (basting) thread

needle

scissors

embroidery hoop (frame)

stranded cotton Anchor 403

tapestry needle

safety ruler

30 x 60cm (12 x 24in) mount board (backing board)

craft knife

strong thread

all-purpose glue

125cm (1⅓yd) black cord

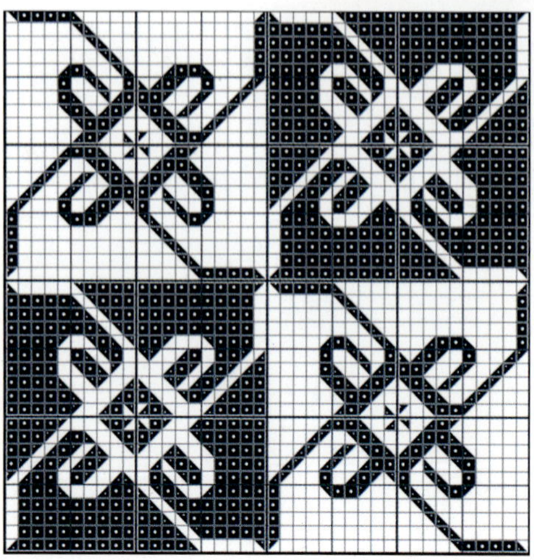

WORKING THE CROSS STITCH

Tack (baste) guidelines across the centre of the Aida in both directions and work the cross stitch using two strands of cotton. Press the embroidery on the wrong side.

1 To make up: measure the length of two adjacent sides of the embroidery. Cut two pieces of mount board (backing board) that size and stretch the embroidery over one of them.

2 Oversew the cord to the edge of the chessboard. Unravel the ends and stitch them flat underneath the board. Stick the second piece of mount board (backing board) to the bottom of the chessboard to cover the raw edges.

Anchor
403

BEDSIDE TABLECLOTH

ANTIQUE AND MEDIEVAL

This unusual Celtic design could be repeated on the border of a much larger tablecloth.

YOU WILL NEED

51cm (20in) square of cream 28 count evenweave linen

tacking (basting) thread

needle

tapestry needle

scissors

embroidery hoop (frame)

Anchor Marlitt 831, 1140

gold thread DMC Art.284

sewing thread

Anchor Marlitt
831
1140

Backstitch
DMC Art.284

☆ Middle point

WORKING THE CROSS STITCH

Tack (baste) guidelines across the centre of the linen in both directions. Count the threads out to the border on all four guidelines and double-check the spacing before beginning to sew.

1 To make up: first, sew the cross stitch on to the centre motif using a single strand of Marlitt thread over two threads of linen, then work the backstitch in gold thread. Once the design is complete, press the embroidery on the wrong side.

2 Trim away the excess fabric, leaving 2½cm (1in) all round for the hem i.e. a 46cm (18in) square. Mitre the corners and make a 12mm (½in) hem all round. Tack in position, then hem. Slip stitch the mitred corners and press on the wrong side to finish.

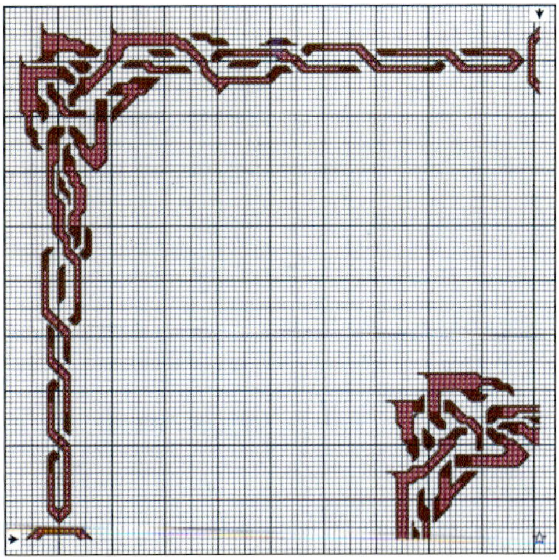

BLACKWORK DECORATIONS

Although traditionally black on white or cream fabric, these "Blackwork" Christmas decorations look equally good worked in red on black fabric.

YOU WILL NEED

pencil
craft knife
thin card (cardboard)
scissors
15 x 30cm (6 x 12in) cream or black 27 count Linda, Zweigart E1235
vanishing marker pen
flexihoop (small embroidery frame)
tapestry needle
stranded cotton Anchor 47, 275, 403
fine gold braid Kreinik 002
needle
sewing thread

WORKING THE CROSS STITCH

Trace the template and cut out three card (cardboard) shapes for each decoration. Place the shape on the linen and draw three outlines using the vanishing marker pen. Stitch the blackwork design inside the lines and press on the wrong side.

Anchor	Backstitch
47	403
	275
	Kreinik gold

Anchor
403
Kreinik gold

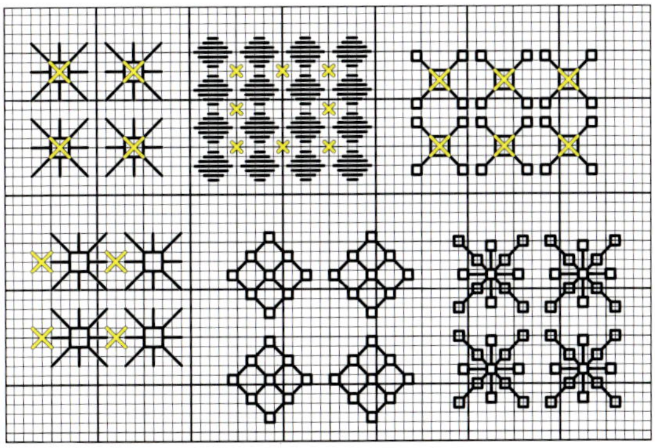

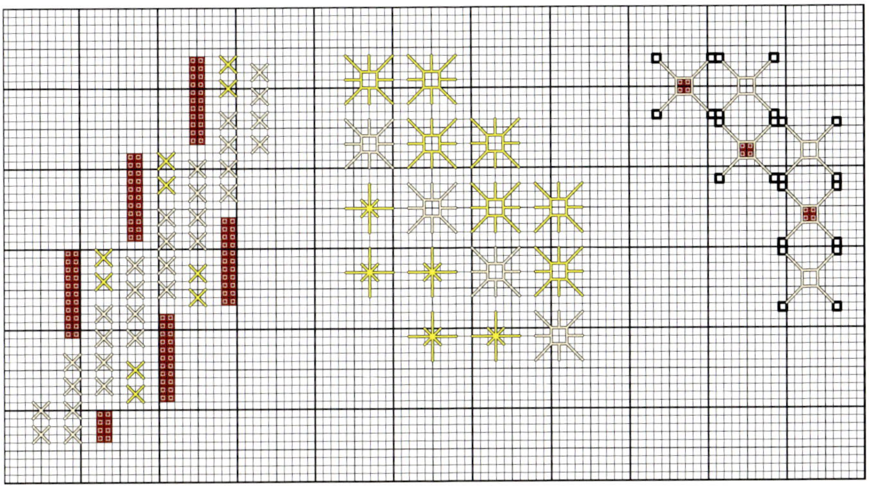

1 To make up: stretch the pieces of linen over each of the card shapes using a double length of sewing thread.

2 Make a 10cm (4in) loop of gold braid and sew it to the top of one panel on the wrong side. Hold two of the shapes together and oversew the edges together. Stitch the third panel in place to make a three-dimensional decoration.

3 Cut a 5cm (2in) square of card. Mix some black and gold thread and wrap them round the card several times. Tie a loop of gold at the top and cut the threads at the bottom. Wrap a length of gold thread round the tassel to make the waist and tie off. Trim the ends and sew on to the bottom of the decoration.

NIGHTDRESS CASE

TRADITIONAL

Match the ribbon in the white crocheted lace edging to the brilliant blue of these pretty cornflowers and bow.

YOU WILL NEED

1.5m (1²⁄₃yd) white cotton fabric

10 x 13cm (4 x 5in) 12 count waste canvas

tacking (basting) thread

needle

embroidery hoop (frame)

stranded cotton DMC 798, 799, 3347

embroidery needle

tailor's chalk

sewing machine

sewing thread

scissors

60cm (24in) white crocheted lace with ribbon insert

pins

WORKING THE CROSS STITCH

Tack (baste) the waste canvas in the centre of the cotton fabric 10cm (4in) from one end. Work the cross stitch through the waste canvas using two strands of cotton. The bow should be at the end of the fabric. Manipulate the canvas to loosen the threads and pull them out one by one. Press the embroidery on the reverse side.

DMC
798
799
3347

☆ Middle point

1 To make up: fold the fabric in half crossways and mark the triangular flap with tailor's chalk. With right sides together, stitch round the edge, leaving a gap on one side. Trim the seams and cut across the corners before turning through.

2 Ease out the corners and point of the flap and press on the reverse side. Pin and tack the lace along the edge of the flap and stitch it in place. Fold in the ends of the lace and hand sew. Slip stitch the side seams to finish.

TRADITIONAL

TABLECLOTH AND NAPKIN

This pretty table linen set with its colourful border will make Sunday lunch a very elegant affair.

YOU WILL NEED

115cm (45in) square of white 28 count Jobelan for the tablecloth

50cm (20in) square of white 28 count Jobelan for the napkin

tacking (basting) thread

scissors

needle

embroidery hoop (frame)

stranded cotton Anchor 3 skeins each of 131 and 133, 1 skein each of 35, 47, 110, 112, 211, 297

tapestry needle

pins

sewing thread

sewing machine

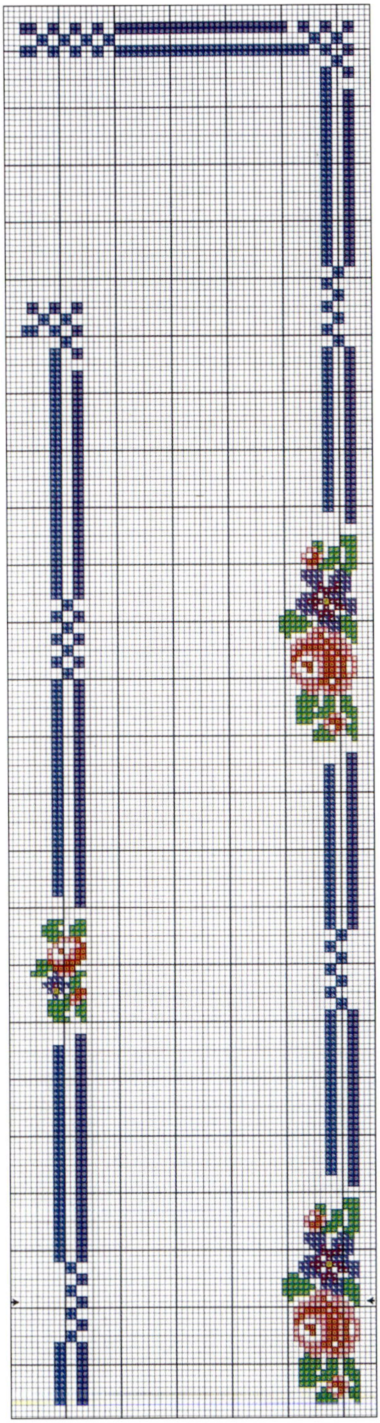

TABLECLOTH

WORKING THE CROSS STITCH

Fold the fabric in half and tack (baste) a guideline about 20cm (8in) along one fold to mark the centre on each side. Tack a line across one of these sides, 16cm (6¼in) from the edge, as a starting-point. Work the cross stitch using two strands of cotton over two threads.

1 To make up: the chart shows one half of one side. Repeat the design on the other side, keeping the floral motifs facing in the same direction. Continue the cross stitch round the other sides of the tablecloth.

2 Press on the wrong side of the fabric when finished. Trim the fabric to a 95cm (37½in) square, mitre the corners and fold over a 2.5cm (1in) hem. Stitch close to the turned edge and slip stitch the mitred corners.

NAPKIN

WORKING THE CROSS STITCH

Tack (baste) the centre line as before and mark the starting point 8cm (3in) in from the side. Work the cross stitch using two strands of cotton over two threads, repeating the design on all sides.

1 To make up: press the fabric on the reverse side when complete and trim to 45cm (18in). Mitre the corners and fold over a 2cm (¾in) hem. Finish in the same way as the tablecloth.

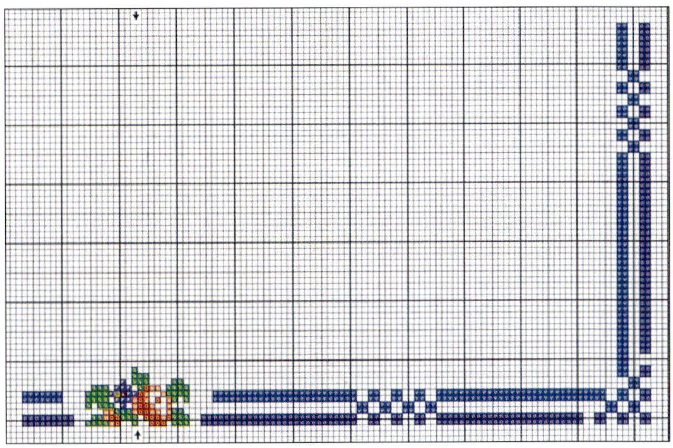

Anchor	
297	211
133	112
131	110
47	
35	

FLORAL TIEBACKS

TRADITIONAL

These tiebacks are quick and easy to make and are ideal for the kitchen or utility room.

YOU WILL NEED

1.5m ($1\frac{2}{3}$yd) of 8cm (3in) raw linen band, Zweigart E7272

scissors

tacking (basting) thread

needle

tapestry needle

stranded cotton DMC 517, 518, 553, 554, 561, 562, 563, 741

pins

four 2.5cm (1in) brass rings

WORKING THE CROSS STITCH

Cut the linen band into four equal pieces. Tack (baste) guidelines across one of the bands to mark the centre and work the cross stitch using two strands of cotton over two threads. Turn the band round and repeat the design at the other end.

DMC
517
518
553
554
562
563
741

Backstitch
561
553
517

☆ Middle point

1 To make up: press the band on the reverse side and fold over 5mm (¼in) at each end. Fold in the corners to make a point, then pin and tack. Finish a plain piece of linen band in the same way: this will form the backing.

2 Pin the tieback and its facing together, with the raw edges to the inside. Sew a decorative cross stitch every 1cm (½in) along the border to join the two pieces together. Slip a brass ring between the layers at each point and sew cross stitches on the point and at either side to secure. Make a second matching tieback in exactly the same way.

TRADITIONAL

HERB BOX AND POT STAND

Keep the herb box on the windowsill filled with fresh herbs. The special heatproof glass inside the pot stand frame will protect the design.

YOU WILL NEED

60cm (24in) of 10cm (4in) wide plain bleached linen, Inglestone collection 900/100

tacking (basting) thread

needle

stranded cotton DMC white, 210, 211, 300, 310, 311, 318, 340, 349, 445, 472, 500, 562, 704, 726, 741, 742, 809, 966, 3607, 3746

tapestry needle

scissors

30cm (12in) pinewood box

staple gun

HERB BOX

WORKING THE CROSS STITCH

Tack (baste) guidelines across the centre of the linen band in both directions then work the cross stitch design using two strands of cotton over two threads of the linen.

1 To make up: once complete, press the linen on the wrong side and then fit round the box. Turn under the ends and staple them to the back of the box.

POT STAND

YOU WILL NEED

23cm (9in) square of white 18 count Aida

tacking (basting) thread

needle

scissors

tapestry needle

embroidery hoop (frame)

stranded cotton Anchor 120, 122

hexagonal frame, Framecraft WTS

DMC		DMC	
	210		809
	211		966
	311		3607
	340		3746
	349		white
	310		3607 +211 (1 strand each)
	300		
	318	Backstitch	
	445		500
	472		300
	500		472
	562		966
	726		318
	704		310
	741		
	742	☆	Middle point

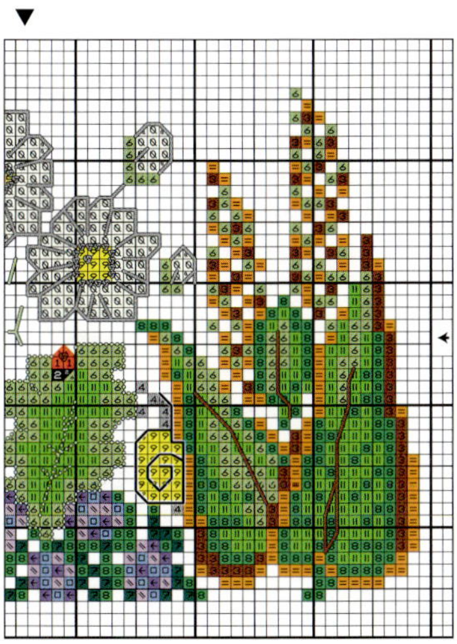

WORKING THE CROSS STITCH

Tack (baste) guidelines across the centre of the Aida in both directions. Work the cross stitch using two strands of cotton. Sew the backstitch outlines and press the work on the wrong side. Follow the manufacturer's instructions to fit the embroidery inside the frame. The pot stand has a felt base to protect tables.

Anchor (in two strands)	Backstitch (in one strand)	Backstitch (in two strands)
122	122	120
120		☆ Middle point

TRADITIONAL

EMBROIDERED SHEET AND PILLOW CASE

This classic bed linen would look superb with a Victorian blue and white wash bowl and jug set on a marble washstand.

YOU WILL NEED

8cm (3in) wide Aida band, Fabric Flair BA7349

scissors

sheet and pillow case

stranded cotton Anchor pillow case – two skeins of 130, 132 and one of 134
single sheet – six skeins of 130, five of 132 and three of 134

tapestry needle

pins

sewing thread

sewing machine

Anchor
- 130
- 132
- 134

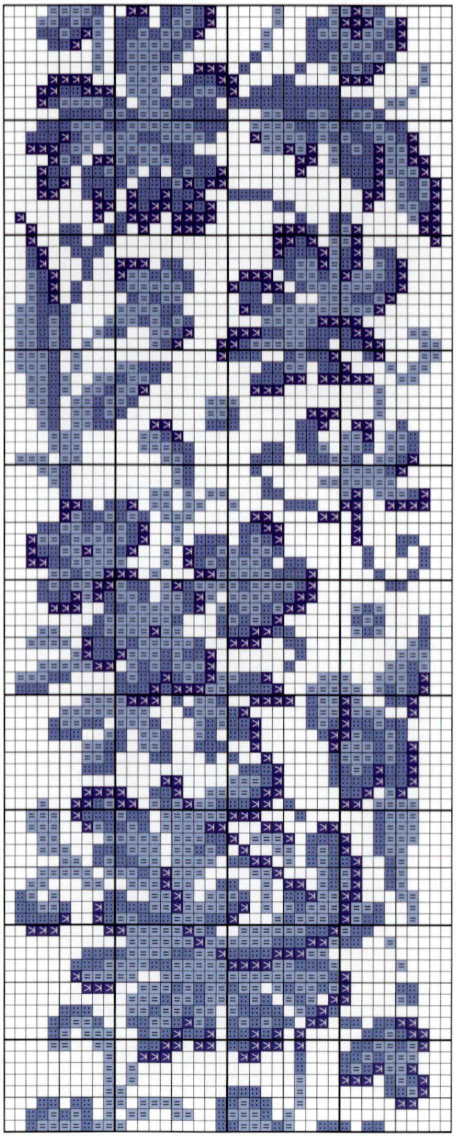

WORKING THE CROSS STITCH

Measure the widths of the sheet and pillow case and cut the Aida band 10cm (4in) longer. Work the cross stitch design using two strands of cotton, beginning 5cm (2in) from one end.

1 To make up: once complete, press on the wrong side and pin to the sheet or pillow case 6cm (2½in) in from the edge. Turn under the ends and stitch the band in place.

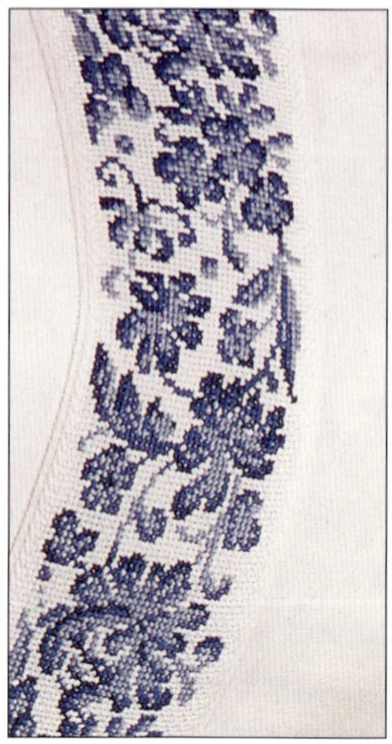

TRADITIONAL

SPOT MOTIF SAMPLER

Birds, butterflies and flowers were very popular motifs in the nineteenth century, but the pillars make this sampler quite unusual.

YOU WILL NEED

25cm (10in) square of Antique Aida 27 count Linda, Zweigart E1235

tacking (basting) thread

needle

embroidery hoop (frame)

stranded cotton Anchor 10, 303, 337, 352, 681, 844, 848, 884

tapestry needle

27 x 30cm (10½ x 12in) mount board (backing board)

strong thread

picture frame

WORKING THE CROSS STITCH

Tack (baste) guidelines across the centre of the linen in both directions. Work the cross stitch design using two strands of cotton over two threads.

1 To make up: press the embroidery on the reverse side when complete. Stretch the embroidery over the mount board (backing board) and fit into a picture frame of your choice.

Anchor
- 848
- 681
- 337
- 303
- 884
- 844
- 10
- 352

Backstitch
- 681
- 848
- 352

☆ Middle point

TRADITIONAL

EMBROIDERED COATHANGER

Protect delicate silk negligées and soft woollen sweaters with this pretty padded coathanger.

YOU WILL NEED

30 x 60cm (12 x 24in) fabric for the cover

scissors

5 x 25cm (2 x 10in) 10 count waste canvas

pins

tacking (basting) thread

needle

stranded cotton Anchor 19, 35, 118, 218, 302, 304

embroidery needle

30cm (12in) polyester wadding (batting)

wooden coathanger

sewing thread

double-sided tape

50cm (20in) fine cord

WORKING THE CROSS STITCH

Cut the fabric for the cover in half lengthways and the waste canvas into five equal pieces. Pin and tack (baste) a square of waste canvas in the middle of the fabric. Position the other pieces of canvas on either side, leaving a gap of 4cm (1½in) between them, and tack securely. Work the cross stitch using two strands of cotton. Once complete, loosen the threads of the waste canvas and pull them out one at a time. Press on reverse side.

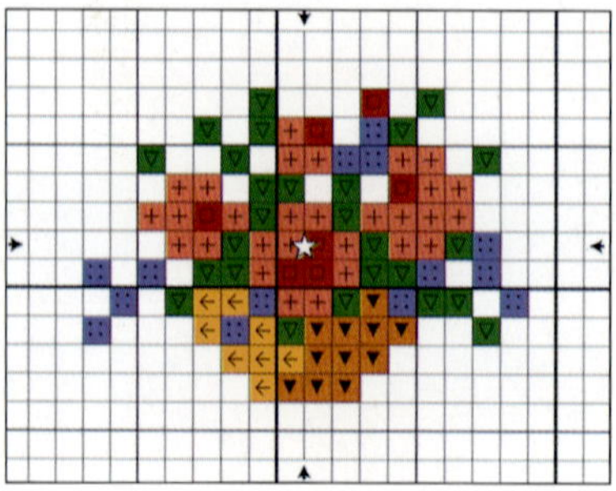

Anchor	Anchor
118	302
35	218
19	
304	☆ Middle point

1 To make up: cut the wadding (batting) into four 5cm (2in) strips and one of 10cm (4in). Wrap the narrow bands round the coathanger and finish with the wider band. Oversew the ends.

2 Trim both pieces of fabric to a width of 11cm (4½in), making sure that the cross stitch motifs are along the centre line. With right sides facing and a seam allowance of 1.5cm (⅝in), stitch the pieces together, leaving a small gap in the middle for the hook. Press the seam flat and place over the coathanger, feeding the hook through the gap. Turn under the front edge of the fabric, overlap at the bottom of the coathanger and slip stitch.

3 Fold in the fabric at the end of the coathanger and sew tiny running stitches close to the edge. Gather up the stitches and sew in to secure. Cover the hook with double-sided tape. Starting at the curved end, wrap the cord tightly round the hook and sew the end into the wadding of the coathanger to finish.

SILK TOILET BAG

TRADITIONAL

The design on this luxurious bag was inspired by the African violet, a flower much loved by the Victorians.

YOU WILL NEED

40cm (16in) of eyelet edge natural linen band, Inglestone Collection 979/50

stranded cotton DMC 341, 550, 744, 3746

tapestry needle

pins

35 x 40cm (14 x 16in) burgundy silk dupion (mid-weight silk)

sewing thread

sewing machine

25 x 40cm (10 x 16in) lining fabric

scissors

needle

six 12mm (½in) brass rings

1m (1yd) cream cord

WORKING THE CROSS STITCH

Fold the linen band in half lengthways and count the threads to find the centre of the band. Work the cross stitch using two strands of cotton over two threads of linen and repeat the design working out to each end.

1 To make up: press on the reverse side, pin the band to the silk 10cm (4in) from the bottom edge and stitch close to the edges. With right sides together, stitch the lining to the silk along the top edge. Press the seam open and stitch the other edges together so that they make a tube shape.

2 Position the seam at the centre back and press open. Stitch along the bottom of the silk, trim and turn through. Turn in the seam allowance of the lining and slip stitch before tucking inside.

3 Cover the rings with buttonhole stitch. Stitch round the top of the bag along the seam line and space the rings evenly before stitching securely in place. Cut the cord in half. Thread the two pieces through in opposite directions and tie the ends together with overhand knots. Unravel the ends of the cord to make pretty tassels.

DMC	French knot
3746	
341	3746
550	
744	

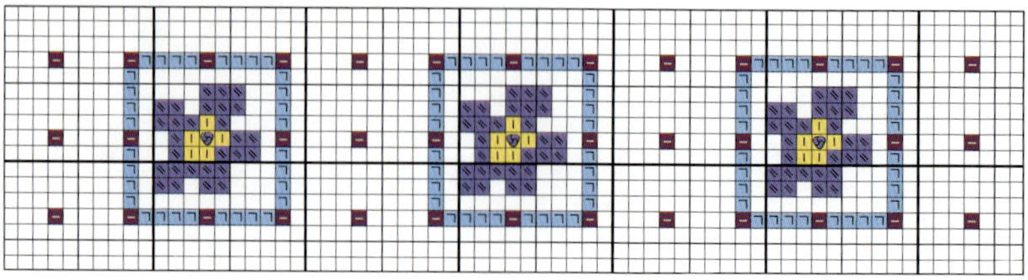

VICTORIAN CUSHION

TRADITIONAL

This design is adapted from some blue and white tiles which were very popular in Victorian times.

YOU WILL NEED

20cm (8in) square of Antique white 32 count Belfast linen, Zweigart E3609
tacking (basting) thread
needle
embroidery hoop (frame)
stranded cotton Anchor 1031, 1036
tapestry needle
scissors
50cm (1/2yd) of 90cm (36in) navy chintz
tailor's chalk
ruler
sewing machine
sewing thread
1.5m (1 2/3yd) piping cord
36cm (14in) cushion pad
pins

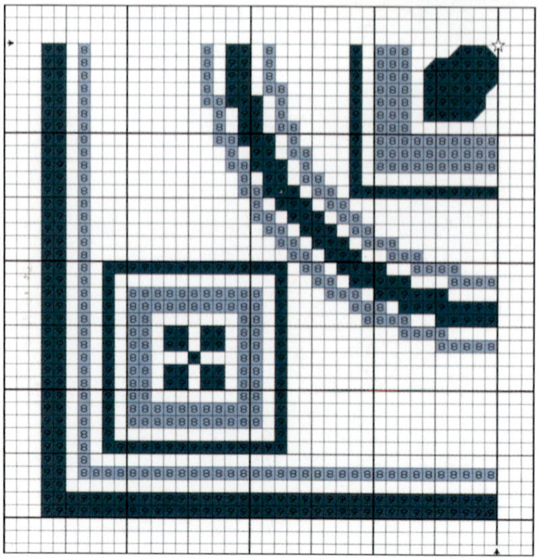

Anchor
88 1032 99 1036 ☆ Middle point

WORKING THE CROSS STITCH

Tack (baste) guidelines across the centre of the linen in both directions and work the cross stitch using two strands of cotton over two threads. Turning the linen through 90 degrees each time, repeat the design in the other three quarters.

1 To make up: trim the linen to within 1.5cm (5/8in) of the cross stitch. Turn under 1cm (3/8in), mitre the corners and press on the reverse side. Cut two 38cm (15in) squares of chintz. Pin and tack the panel in the centre of one piece and slip stitch securely. Draw out suf-ficient 5cm (2in) bias strips on the rest of the fabric to fit round the cushion. Join the bias strips, trim the seams and press open. Cover the piping cord with the strips and tack in place round the edge of the embroidered cushion panel. Stitch. Lay the other panel on top with right sides together and stitch around three sides. Insert the cushion pad and slip stitch the fourth side to complete.

TOWEL BORDER

TRADITIONAL

These embroidered Arum lilies, commonly known as cuckoo pint, look most attractive on a set of pale yellow towels.

WORKING THE CROSS STITCH

Tack (baste) guidelines in both directions across the centre of the cross stitch panel. Work the cross stitch using two strands of cotton and gold thread. Once complete work the leaf veins using a single strand and the outlines using two strands.

1 To finish: remove the tacking (basting) thread and press on the reverse side.

YOU WILL NEED

white terry hand towel with cross stitch border

tacking (basting) thread

needle

embroidery hoop (frame)

scissors

stranded cotton DMC 310, 680, 725, 727, 783, 895, 3346, 3362

tapestry needle

gold thread DMC Art.284

DMC

- 3 3 727
- 4 4 Art.284
- ⊥ ⊥ 783
- □ □ 725
- 895
- 3362
- 3346

Backstitch

- 680
- 310
- 895

☆ Middle point

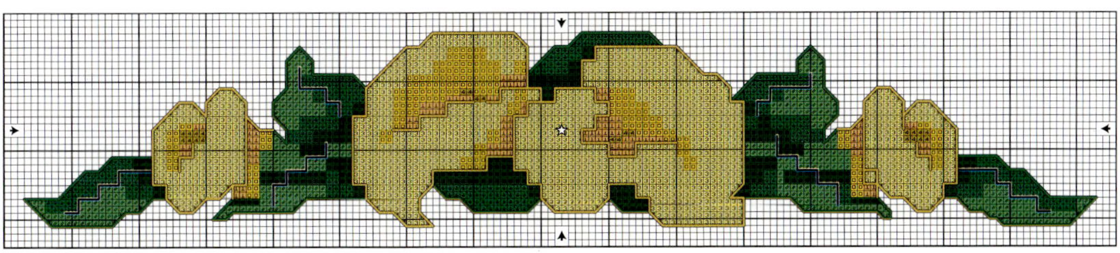

LAVENDER BAG

TRADITIONAL

Tuck this little bag into a drawer to keep your clothes fresh and to remind you of late summer evenings and sweet-smelling flowers.

YOU WILL NEED

30cm (12in) of 7.5cm (3in) raw linen band with blue scalloped edges, Zweigart E7272

tacking (basting) thread

needle

coton perlé no. 8 DMC 208, 550, 780, 783, 907

tapestry needle

scissors

blue stranded cotton (thread) to match the scalloped edge

sewing thread

dried lavender flowers

WORKING THE CROSS STITCH

Tack (baste) a guideline lengthways down the centre of the band. Tack a second line crossways 6cm (2½in) from the top edge. Work the cross stitch over two threads and press on the reverse side.

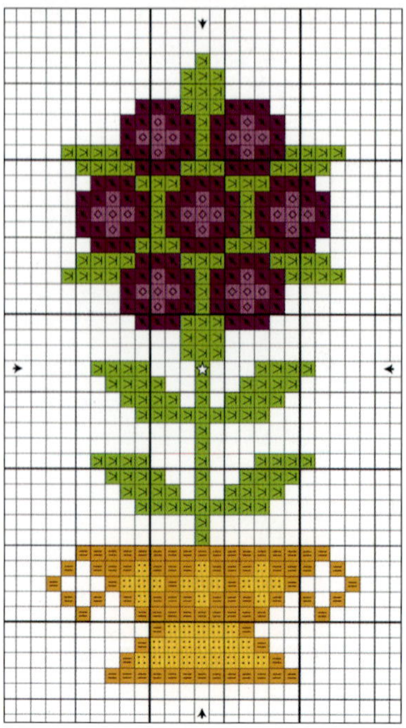

1 To make up: press under 12mm (½in) on each raw edge of the band and sew two rows of running stitch using two strands of blue embroidery thread to secure.

2 Fold the band in half crossways and slip stitch the side seams. Fill with dried lavender flowers or pot pourri and slip stitch the top edges together.

DMC			
	780		208
	783		550
	907	☆	Middle point

TABLE RUNNER

TRADITIONAL

The linen for the runner is very fine, but the design is fairly quick to sew.

YOU WILL NEED

50 x 100cm (20 x 40in) 36 count white evenweave linen

tacking (basting) thread

needle

embroidery hoop (frame)

stranded cotton Anchor six skeins of 391

tapestry needle

scissors

sewing machine

sewing thread

WORKING THE CROSS STITCH

Tack (baste) a guideline in one corner, 12cm (4¾in) in from each side. This marks the outside edge of the design. Work the cross stitch using two strands of cotton over three threads of the fabric. The second quarter of the design is a mirror image of the first and the second half of the design is a mirror image of the first half.

1 To make up: on completion of the stitching, press on the wrong side. Keeping an equal border all round the embroidery, trim the fabric to 40 x 88cm (16 x 35in). Mitre the corners and fold over a 2.5cm (1in) hem. Sew close to the fold and slip stitch the corners.

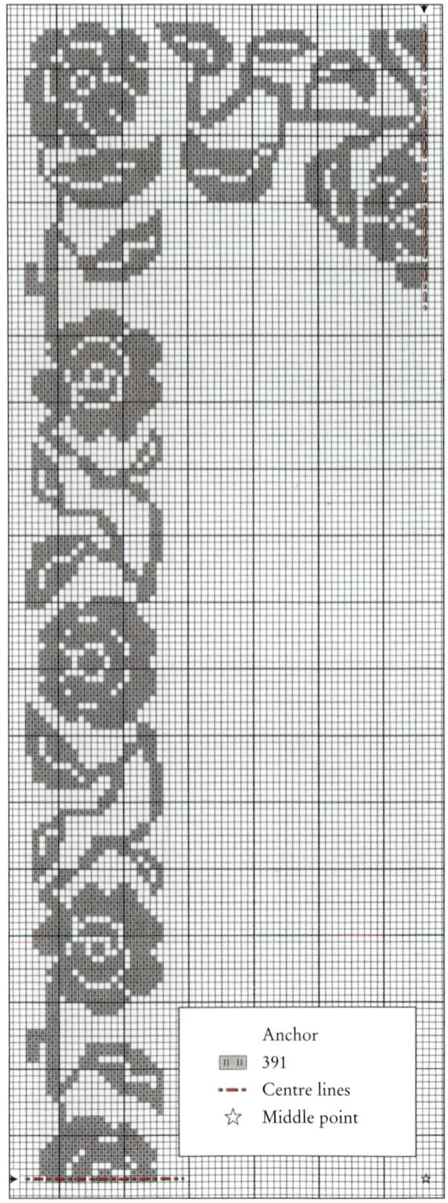

PICTURE MOUNT

TRADITIONAL

Personalize the design by adding a name in the panel below the photograph.

WORKING THE CROSS STITCH

Mark a 25cm (10in) square in the middle of the canvas and a second 10cm (4in) square in the centre of that one. Tack (baste) guidelines in the centre of each side of the "mount" and begin by stitching the bow. The second side is a mirror image of the first. Press the embroidery on the reverse side once complete.

1 To make up: cut out a 10cm (4in) square from the centre of the mount board (backing board) and stick double-sided tape round this edge. Cut into each corner of the centre square on the fabric and trim. Position the fabric under the mount and stretch gently on to the tape. Put more tape round the outside edge. Mitre the corners and stretch the fabric on to the tape, checking that the design is square. Fit into a frame of your choice.

YOU WILL NEED

35cm (14in) square 32 count natural evenweave linen

safety ruler

tailor's chalk

tacking (basting) thread

needle

embroidery hoop (frame)

white stranded cotton

tapestry needle

scissors

25cm (10in) square of mount board (backing board)

craft knife

double-sided tape

picture frame

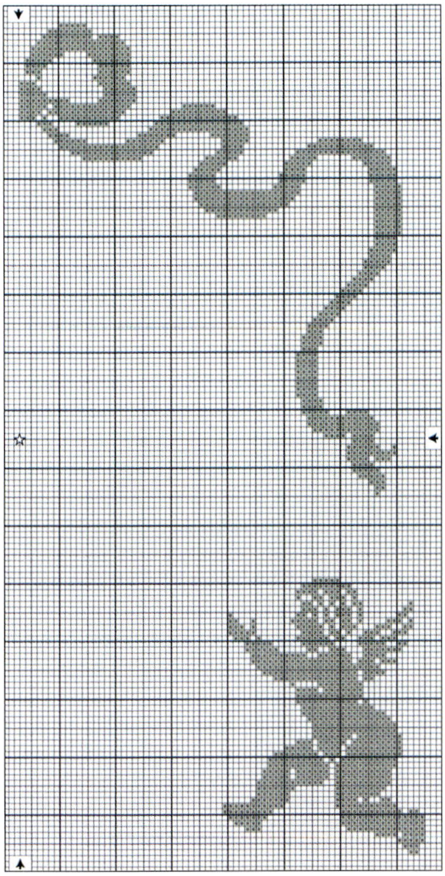

Anchor
white
☆ Middle point

JEWELLERY BOX

TRADITIONAL

This Charles Rennie Mackintosh design could be adapted to fit any square or rectangular box you may have.

YOU WILL NEED

25cm (10in) square gold 32 count evenweave linen

tacking (basting) thread

needle

interlocking bar frame

tapestry needle

stranded cotton DMC ecru, 310, 645, 648

Anchor Marlitt 872

light gold thread DMC Art.282

gold thread Glissen gloss luster numbers 02 and 03

balger cord Kreinik 105C and 225C

scissors

double-sided tape

polyester wadding (batting)

wooden box

1m (1yd) of 15mm (5/8in) corded ribbon

WORKING THE CROSS STITCH

Tack (baste) guidelines in both directions across the centre of the linen. Work the cross stitch using two strands of cotton and single lengths of cable. Press the design on the reverse side when complete and trim to 3cm (1¼in) larger than the box.

DMC
310
Ecru
645
648
Art 282

Anchor Marlitt
872

Glissen Gloss
Gold #02
Gold #03

Kreinik Balger
105C
225C

☆ Middle point

1 To make up: cut a square of wadding (batting) and stick it to the lid of the box. Put double-sided tape round the side of the lid and stretch the linen on to it, folding in the corners neatly.

2 Put more double-sided tape round the side of the lid and stick the ribbon down to cover the raw edges. Fold over the end and stick down.

FLORAL TRAY

TRADITIONAL

This delightful tray has a glass inset to protect the embroidery.

YOU WILL NEED

30cm (12in) square of cream 28 count Cashel linen, Zweigart E3281

tacking (basting) thread

needle

embroidery hoop (frame)

stranded cotton DMC 347, 500, 646, 648, 918, 919, 948, 3047, 3768, 3815

tapestry needle

24cm (9½in) wooden tray, Framecraft WSST

strong thread

WORKING THE CROSS STITCH

Tack (baste) guidelines in both directions across the centre of the linen. Work the cross stitch using two strands of cotton and press on the reverse side when the design is complete.

1 To make up: stretch the embroidery over the supplied mount board (backing board) and assemble the tray according to the manufacturer's instructions.

DMC
648
729
924
754
948
918
919
347
500
3768
3815
3047

Backstitch
500

French knots
646

☆ Middle point

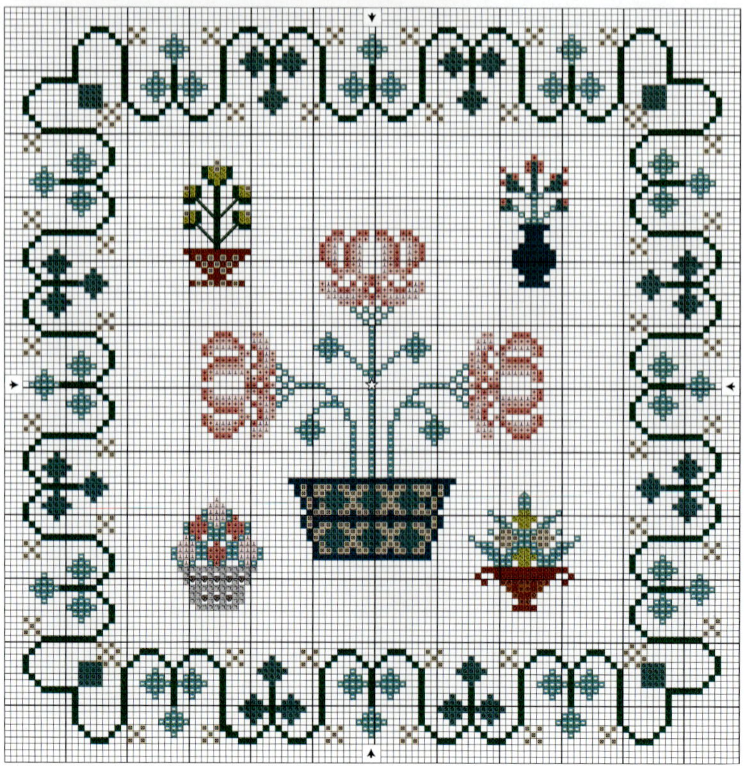

EMBROIDERED SLIPPERS

TRADITIONAL

A plain pair of slippers can be made special with this pretty rose motif.

YOU WILL NEED

pair of black velvet slippers
two 9cm (3½in) squares of 14 count waste canvas
Anchor Nordin 22, 35, 47, 244, 246, 306, 365, 9046
tapestry needle
thimble
steam iron

WORKING THE CROSS STITCH

Position the waste canvas on the front of the first slipper and tack (baste) in place. Find the centre point of the canvas and begin stitching the design. The stitches are worked through the velvet only, using a thimble for ease.

1 To make up: the second slipper design is a mirror image of the first. When both are complete, pull the canvas threads out one at a time. Steam the front of the slippers to even out the stitches.

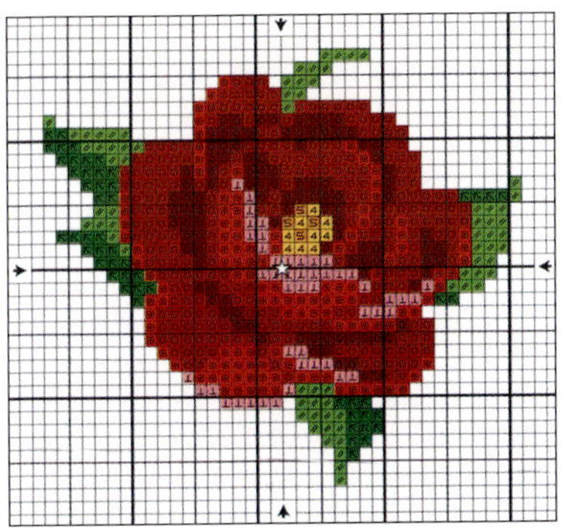

Anchor Nordin

4 4	306
5 5	365
	22
	35
	47
	9046
	244
	246

☆ Middle point

PRAM QUILT

TRADITIONAL

Children can learn basic colours and numbers using this cleverly designed bright and cheerful quilt.

YOU WILL NEED

61cm x 76cm (24in x 30in) Anne fabric, Zweigart E7563

embroidery hoop (frame)

stranded cotton DMC 310, 349, 550, 608,700, 702, 741, 781, 783, 791, 793, 898, 972

tapestry needle

51 x 64cm (20 x 25in) medium weight iron-on interfacing

61 x 76cm (24 x 30in) cotton lining fabric

61 x 71cm (24 x 28in) 4oz wadding (batting)

pins

sewing machine

sewing thread

scissors

needle

3m (3¼yd) of 7mm (¼in) ribbon

DMC	DMC	DMC	Backstitch	French knots
898	791	702	898	310
310	793	781	791	898
349	550	783	741	
608	741		781	
972	700			

WORKING THE CROSS STITCH

Cross stitch the border design inside each square, then find the centre and work the numbers and motifs as shown.

1 To make up: iron the interfacing to the wrong side. Lay the Anne fabric and lining down with right sides together. Lay the wadding (batting) on top and pin through all the layers.

2 Stitch round the sides close to the cross stitch, leaving a small gap for turning. Trim the excess fabric, turn the quilt through and ease out the corners. Slip stitch the gap and press the seams gently. Attach a 15cm (6in) piece of ribbon at the corners of each square, sewing through all the layers to give a quilted effect. Sew or tie the ribbon into a small bow to finish.

BROOCH CUSHION

TRADITIONAL

Keep your brooches safe by pinning them to this delicate cushion.

YOU WILL NEED

two 20cm (8in) squares of white 36 count evenweave linen
tacking (basting) thread
needle
embroidery hoop (frame)
stranded cotton DMC 221, 223, 224, 225, 501, 502, 503, 832, 834, 839, 3032, 3782
tapestry needle
80cm (32in) wine piping
pins
sewing machine
sewing thread
scissors
20cm (8in) cushion pad

WORKING THE CROSS STITCH

Tack (baste) guidelines in both directions across the centre of the cross stitch panel. Work the cross stitch using a single strand of cotton over two threads of linen.

1 To make up: tack the piping round the edge of the embroidered panel, overlapping the ends of the piping at one corner. With right sides together, stitch round three sides of the cushion, close to the piping. Trim the seams and corners, then turn through. Press the cushion cover and insert the pad. Slip stitch the gap to finish.

DMC
- 501
- 502
- 503
- 221
- 223
- 224
- 225
- 839
- 832
- 834
- 3032
- 3782

☆ Middle point

GREETINGS CARD

TRADITIONAL

The card makes a present in itself for someone special.

WORKING THE CROSS STITCH

Tack (baste) the fine calico to the back of the silk and fit into a hoop. Tack the waste canvas on to the middle of the fabric, keeping the canvas in line with the grain of the fabric. Mark the centre of the canvas. Stitch the design using two strands of cotton. When complete, fray and pull out the canvas threads one at a time. Press on the reverse side and trim to fit behind the opening.

1 To make up: stick tape round the inside edge of the opening and position the embroidery on top. Stick the backing card in position. Use double-sided tape to assemble because glue tends to buckle the card.

YOU WILL NEED

20cm (8in) square of fine calico

20cm (8in) square of cream silk dupion (mid-weight silk)

tacking (basting) thread

needle

embroidery hoop (frame)

13 x 15cm (5 x 6in) 14 count waste canvas

stranded cotton DMC 221, 223, 224, 744, 3362, 3363

embroidery needle

scissors

craft card with an 8 x 12cm (3 x 4¾in) aperture (opening)

double-sided tape

DMC

224	3363
223	3362
221	
744	☆ Middle point

TRADITIONAL

HANDKERCHIEF CASE

No more scrabbling in the drawer, this pretty and practical pouch will keep all your hankies tidy.

YOU WILL NEED

two 53 x 20cm (21 x 8in) pieces of white 36 count evenweave linen

tacking (basting) thread

needle

embroidery hoop (frame)

stranded cotton DMC 221, 223, 224, 225, 501, 502, 503, 832, 834, 839, 3032, 3782

tapestry needle

pins

sewing machine

sewing thread

scissors

1m (1yd) wine coloured piping

WORKING THE CROSS STITCH

Tack (baste) a guideline crossways 10cm (4in) from one end of the linen. Mark the centre of this line and begin the cross stitch. The bottom of the design is the side nearest the raw edge.

Work the design using a single strand of cotton over two threads of linen. A magnifying glass might help. When the embroidery is complete, press on the reverse side.

DMC	DMC
501	225
502	839
503	832
221	834
223	3032
224	3782

☆ Middle point

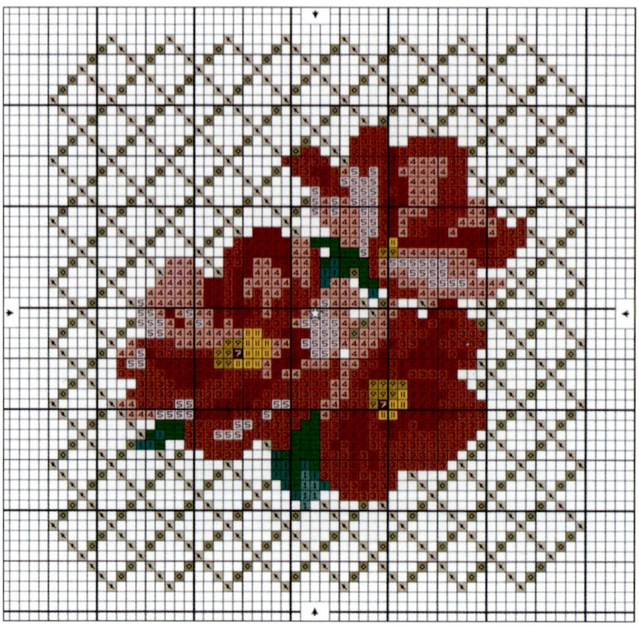

1 To make up: pin the two linen panels together with the embroidery to the inside. With a 2cm (¾in) seam allowance, sew all round leaving a gap on one side for turning. Trim the seams and across the corners, then turn through.

2 Fold the panel in three and tack along the fold lines. Pin the piping to the inside of the front flap and down both sides as far as the second fold line. Turn under the ends and slip stitch the piping in place. Slip stitch the side seams to complete the case.

TRADITIONAL

CHRISTMAS DECORATIONS

These Victorian toys are quick and easy to sew on this special vinyl canvas which has a similar weave to Hardanger.

YOU WILL NEED

20cm (8in) square of 14 count vinyl weave canvas

stranded cotton Anchor white, 46, 134, 399, 778

fine gold braid Kreinik 002

tapestry needle

scissors

20cm (8in) square of thin gold card (cardboard)

all-purpose glue

WORKING THE CROSS STITCH

Stitch the designs on to the canvas using three strands of cotton or the fine gold braid as it comes.

1 To make up: cut round the edge, leaving one row of canvas showing. Oversew the edges with gold braid, except for the rocker on the horse which is oversewn with three strands of blue stranded cotton.

2 Sew a loop of braid on to the saddle, one on to the helmet and one in the middle of the top edge of the drum.

3 Draw round each decoration on to the card (cardboard). Cut out inside the lines and stick the card on to the back of the decoration. Trim away any excess card which is visible on the right side.

Anchor		Kreinik
	134	
399	778	fine braid gold 002
white	46	

CHRISTMAS CARDS

TRADITIONAL

These snowflakes could be mounted back to back in a card ring to make an unusual tree decoration.

WORKING THE CROSS STITCH

Tack (baste) the calico on to the back of the fabric and fit into a small embroidery hoop (frame). Tack guidelines across the fabric to divide it into six equal segments. Mark the centre of one strip of canvas and tack on to the fabric, matching the centres and the guidelines.

Anchor white — Kreinik fine silver braid 001

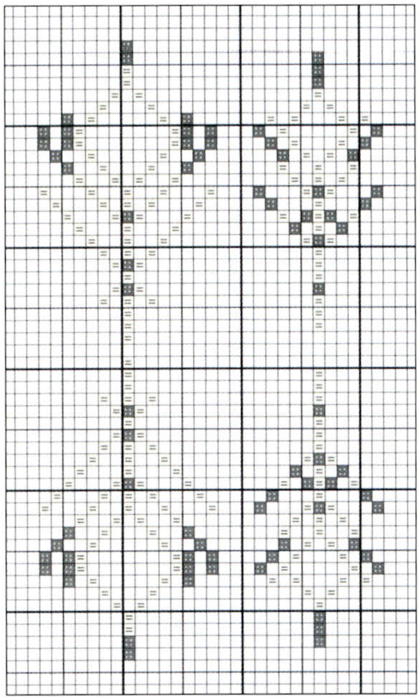

YOU WILL NEED

15cm (6in) square of silk dupion (mid-weight silk) or panné velvet

15cm (6in) square of fine calico

tacking (basting) thread

needle

flexihoop (small embroidery frame)

three 5 x 13cm (2 x 5in) strips of 14 count waste canvas

vanishing marker pen

tapestry needle

white stranded cotton

fine silver braid Kreinik 001

silver blending filament Kreinik 001 (optional)

scissors

greetings card with a 9.5cm (3¾in) diameter aperture (opening)

double-sided tape

1 To make up: work one of the cross stitch designs using two strands of cotton or the fine braid as it comes. Note that the centre stitch is omitted at this stage and sewn later. Once complete, remove the waste canvas carefully, one thread at a time.

2 Repeat the same design on each of the other guidelines to complete the snowflake. Once all the waste canvas is carefully removed, stitch the centre cross.

3 Remove from the frame, trim to size and stick behind the opening of the card. Stick the flap down to finish. Make another card stitching the other snowflake design on to a different fabric.

TRADITIONAL CHRISTMAS STOCKING

Hang this beautiful brocade stocking on the fireplace and who knows what Santa might bring?

YOU WILL NEED

50cm (20in) of 10cm (4in) wide bleached linen band, Inglestone collection 900/100
tacking (basting) thread
needle
tapestry needle
fine gold braid Kreinik 102
stranded cotton DMC 99, 3052, 3802
blending filament Kreinik 045, 093
scissors
45 x 60cm (18 x 24in) pink and cream floral brocade
38 x 60cm (15 x 24in) lining
pins
sewing machine
sewing thread

WORKING THE CROSS STITCH

Tack (baste) guidelines across the linen band and stitch a motif in each space, staggering them diagonally. Work the cross stitch using three strands of cotton over two threads of linen. Add a strand of blending filament with the green and pink threads before stitching.

DMC
- Kreinik fine braid gold 102
- 3052 + Blending filament 045
- 99 + Blending filament 093
- 3802

☆ Middle point

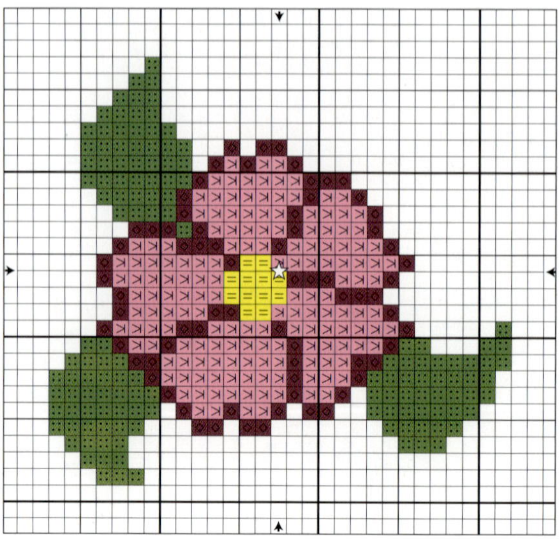

1 To make up: draw out seven threads near the top and bottom edge of the linen band. Using three strands of 3802, twist groups of three threads as shown to make a decorative border.

2 Scale up the template and cut two pieces each out of brocade and lining. With 2cm (¾in) seam allowances, stitch the lining pieces together with right sides facing. Trim the seams and snip into the curves. Make the stocking in the same way but with a 1.5cm (⅝in) seam allowance. Turn through and fold the top edge over 5cm (2in).

3 Make a tab using a piece of brocade 8 x 20cm (3 x 8in). Fold lengthways and stitch, then turn through and press with the seam in the middle of the reverse side. Fold the tab in half and pin on to the back seam of the stocking and sew securely. Fold over 1cm (3/8in) at the top of the lining and tuck inside the stocking. Pin and tack in position 5cm (2in) down from the top and slip stitch. Pin the cuff round the top of the stocking. Slip stitch the back seam and use running stitch to secure the cuff to the stocking.

NEEDLEWORK TIP

Make a small version of the stocking in evenweave linen with a single motif stitched on the front.

Nine Star Picture

A simple design inspired by early American patchwork heart and star pictures.

YOU WILL NEED

46cm (18in) square of antique white 28 count Cashel linen, Zweigart E3281

vanishing marker pen

tracing paper

pencil

paper scissors

tacking (basting) thread

needle

stranded cotton Anchor 39, 150, 169, 246, 305

tapestry needle

30cm (12in) square of mount board (backing board)

strong thread

frame

WORKING THE CROSS STITCH

Mark a 25cm (10in) square in the middle of the linen and stitch the border design, sewing 20 hearts across and 24 down. Fold the fabric in half both ways to find the centre and mark with the vanishing marker pen. Work the heart cross stitch pattern within the lines beginning with a heart on the centre mark.

1 To make up: trace and cut out the star template. Place in the centre of the border and draw round it carefully with the pen.

2 Following the grain of the fabric make a second mark on the left 8cm (3in) from the centre. Draw round the star template and fill with another cross stitch pattern. Continue in this way, spacing the centres 8cm (3in) apart, until all nine stars are complete. Finish the design by stitching a grid of blue running stitch mid way between the stars to make nine equal 8cm (3in) boxes.

3 Stretch the linen over the mount board (backing board) and put in a simple frame.

Anchor	Backstitch
4 4 246	39
5 5 305	305
6 6 169	246
7 7 39	French knots
8 8 150	150

Curtain Pelmet

FOLK ART

These delightful geese would be ideal for a child's bedroom. Simply wrap the fabric round a curtain pole or finish with heading tape.

WORKING THE CROSS STITCH

Measure the width of the window and cut a piece of gingham twice as wide and about 50cm (20in) deep. Tack (baste) the squares of waste canvas about 15cm (6in) apart along the bottom of the fabric, allowing for the hem and side turnings. Try to position the centre lines of the canvas on the same check each time. Work the cross stitch using three strands of cotton.

1 To make up: once the embroidery is complete, carefully remove the canvas threads one at a time and press the fabric on the reverse side.

2 Finish the raw edges at the side of the pelmet and turn under 5cm (2in). Turn up the hem of the pelmet and stitch. Add curtain tape along the top edge or simply wrap the fabric round a curtain pole and adjust the gathers.

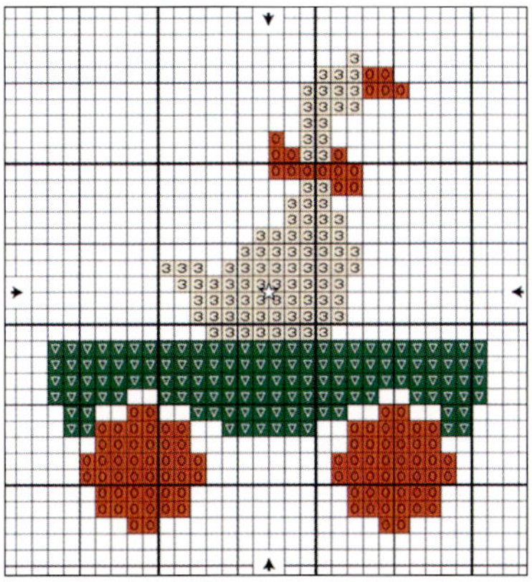

YOU WILL NEED

tape measure

red, green and cream gingham

scissors

10 count waste canvas, 10cm (4in) square for each motif

tacking (basting) thread

needle

stranded cotton Anchor 386, 879, 1006

embroidery needle

sewing thread

curtain tape (optional)

Anchor

3 3 386

0 0 1006

▽ ▽ 879

☆ Middle point

HEART VINE WREATH

Make the wreath with fresh Virginia creeper or clematis stems and let it dry out under a weight to hold the heart shape.

YOU WILL NEED

20 x 30cm (8 x 12in) antique white 28 count Cashel linen, Zweigart E3281
flexihoop (small embroidery frame)
red Anchor Nordin 47
embroidery needle
15 x 23cm (6 x 9in) lightweight iron-on interfacing
scissors
pencil
pins
scraps of different red gingham fabrics
sewing thread
polyester stuffing
Virginia creeper or clematis stems
string

WORKING THE CROSS STITCH

Embroider the six hearts on to the linen using one strand of Nordin over two threads of linen, leaving about 2.5cm (1in) round each design.

1 To make up: iron on 8cm (3in) squares of interfacing to the reverse side and cut out. Draw a heart on each piece, pin to a square of gingham and stitch. Trim the seams, turn through and stuff then slip stitch the gap.

2 Cut eight 60cm (24in) lengths of vine. Split the bundle in two and make into a heart shape securing the ends with vine. Wind some more vine round and round the rest of the wreath to hold it together.

3 Sew a 13cm (5in) length of embroidery thread through the back of each heart and use it to tie the hearts round the wreath. Add a loop for hanging or fit over a nail.

Anchor Nordin
47
Backstitch
47

GAME BOARD

FOLK ART

This game board is quite easy to make with only basic woodworking skills. It is antiqued using crackle varnish and oil paint.

YOU WILL NEED

30 x 36 cm (12 x 14 in) gold 32 count evenweave linen
scissors
tacking (basting) thread
needle
embroidery hoop (frame)
stranded cotton Anchor white, 44, 170, 211, 403
tapestry needle
28 x 51 cm (11 x 20 in) of 5 mm (¼ in) medium density fibreboard (MDF)
off-white acrylic or emulsion paint
paintbrush
ruler
pencil
blackboard paint
1.6 m (1¾ yd) of 2.5 cm (1 in) wood edging
56 cm (22 in) of 2 cm (¾ in) wood edging
fretsaw
wood glue
masking tape
Craquelure, Steps 1 & 2 varnish
raw umber oil paint
soft cloth
antique brown wax
23 x 28 cm (9 x 11 in) mount board (backing board)
safety ruler
craft knife
double-sided tape

WORKING THE CROSS STITCH

Cut the linen in half lengthways. Tack (baste) guidelines down the centre in both directions and work the cross stitch using two strands of cotton over two threads. Stitch the second piece to match and press on the reverse side.

1 To make up: paint a 28cm (11in) square in off-white in the middle of the MDF and allow to dry. Beginning in the middle of one side, mark every 33mm (1¼in). Repeat on the other edges and draw out the squares. (There should be an 8mm (½in) border all round). Paint the left hand square black, then paint every second square black in alternate rows. When these are dry, paint the remaining black squares.

2 Cut two 51cm (20in) pieces and two 28cm (11in) pieces from the 2.5cm (1in) wood edging. Glue these to the side of the board and hold in place with masking tape. Cut the narrower strip to fit inside and stick down across the board. Paint the completed board with an even coat of the first varnish and allow to dry according to the manufacturer's instructions. Brush on the second varnish which takes a little longer to dry. Cracks will appear but may not be obvious as the varnish is transparent.

3 Next day rub some raw umber oil paint into the cracks with a soft cloth and leave to dry. Rub the entire board with antique brown wax. Measure the end sections and cut the mount board (backing board) slightly smaller. Stretch the embroidery over the mount board and stick securely inside the end sections using double-sided tape to complete.

	Anchor		French knots
7 7	170	♥	403
– –	211		
+ +	403	☆	Middle point
1 1	1		
2 2	44		

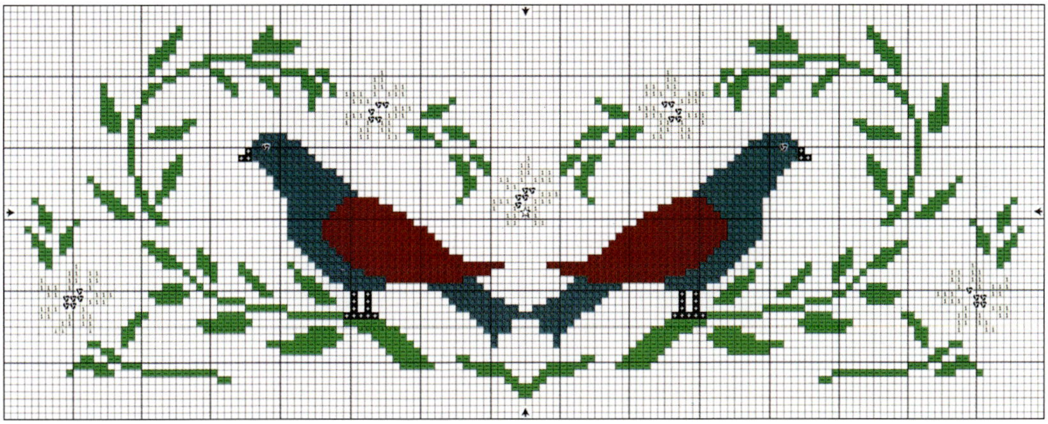

Napkin

The edge of this napkin has been finished with a pretty two-colour border to match the heart design.

YOU WILL NEED

40cm (16in) square of grey/blue 28 count Jobelan

sewing machine

sewing thread

scissors

Anchor Nordin 127, 150, 326, 341

embroidery needle

tacking (basting) thread

needle

embroidery hoop (frame)

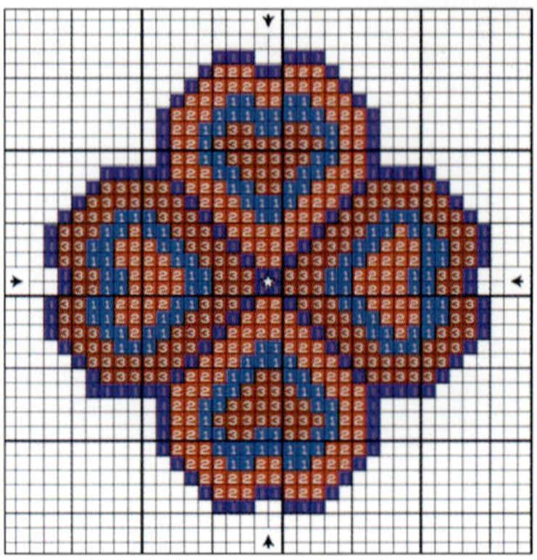

WORKING THE CROSS STITCH

Turn under 5mm (¼in) round all sides and machine stitch. Mitre the corners and turn over a further 5mm (¼in). Hold the hem in place with running stitch in dark blue going over and under four threads at a time. Complete the border with rust. Tack (baste) a guideline round one corner of the napkin, 3cm (1¼in) in from the edge. Work the cross stitch over two threads and press.

Anchor

- 1 1 — 127
- 1 1 — 150
- 2 2 — 326
- 3 3 — 341
- ☆ Middle point

HERB DECORATION

FOLK ART

This delightful little gingerbread man will cheer up any kitchen and could be filled with a sachet of herbs or potpourri.

WORKING THE CROSS STITCH

Tack (baste) guidelines across the centre of one square of the linen in both directions and work the cross stitch using two strands of cotton over two threads. When complete press on the reverse side.

1 To make up: cut the ribbon in half and pin to the top edge of one square 4cm (1½in) apart. Pin the two pieces of linen together with right sides facing, tucking the ribbon inside. Stitch round the sides leaving a 5cm (2in) gap at the bottom. Trim the seams and across the corners then turn through.

2 Cut two squares of wadding (batting) the size of the cushion and tuck inside together with a sachet of herbs. Slip stitch the gap closed. Tie a bow for hanging.

YOU WILL NEED

two 16cm (6¼in) squares of evergreen 28 count Belfast linen, Zweigart E3609

tacking (basting) thread

needle

interlocking bar frame

stranded cotton DMC 221, 310, 676, 729, 825, 3823

tapestry needle

1m (1yd) of 2cm (¾in) gingham ribbon

scissors

pins

sewing machine

sewing thread

polyester wadding (batting)

dried herbs or pot pourri

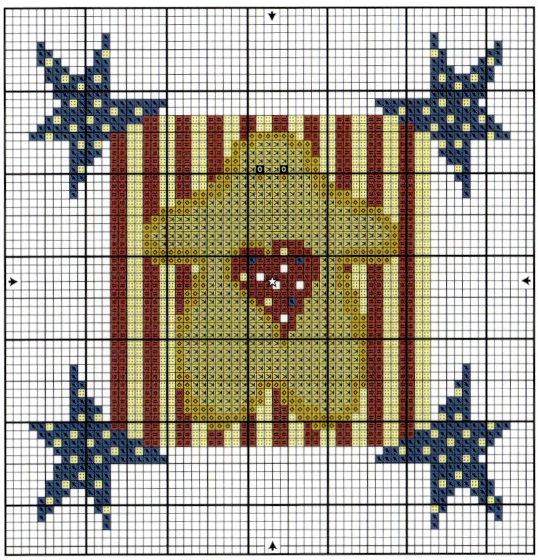

DMC			
221	676	825	☆ Middle point
3823	729	310	

PATCHWORK CUSHION

The motifs on this homespun patchwork cushion are based on nineteenth-century North American samplers.

YOU WILL NEED

nine 13cm (5in) squares of different gingham fabrics with approximately 10 squares to 2.5cm (1in)

embroidery hoop (frame)

stranded cotton DMC 304, 444, 801, 924, 3821, 3830

embroidery needle

pins

sewing machine

sewing thread

four small pearl buttons

scissors

needle

40 x 60cm (15 x 24in) contrast backing fabric

30cm (12in) cushion pad

WORKING THE CROSS STITCH

Work the cross stitch using three strands of cotton over each small square. Stitch one orange basket and two of each of the other designs. Once complete, press on the reverse side and lay out the squares on a flat surface to check their positions.

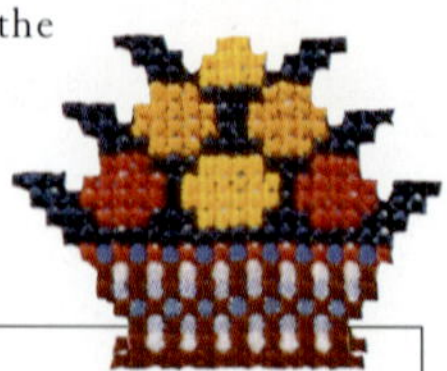

DMC	
444	304
3821	801
3830	924

1 To make up: stitch three lots of three squares together with 12mm (½in) seam allowances and press the seams open. Pin the rows together matching the seams, stitch and press again. Sew a button at each corner of the centre square.

2 Cut the contrast backing fabric in half to make two 30 x 40cm (12 x 15in) rectangles and sew a narrow hem lengthways along one side of each. With right sides together, pin one piece to the left side of the patchwork square and the second piece to the right side. Overlap the hems and sew round all four sides. Trim across the corners and turn through. Tuck the cushion pad inside to complete.

KITCHEN APRON

FOLK ART

Everyone will be happy to wear this big, bright apron with its three cheery gingerbread men.

YOU WILL NEED

large cook's apron
15 x 30cm (6 x 12in) 10 count waste canvas
tacking (basting) thread
needle
coton perlé no.5 DMC 543
embroidery needle

WORKING THE CROSS STITCH

Tack (baste) the waste canvas on to the bib of the apron, positioning it about 8cm (3in) down from the top edge. Work the cross stitch as shown through the waste canvas. Once complete remove the tacking thread.

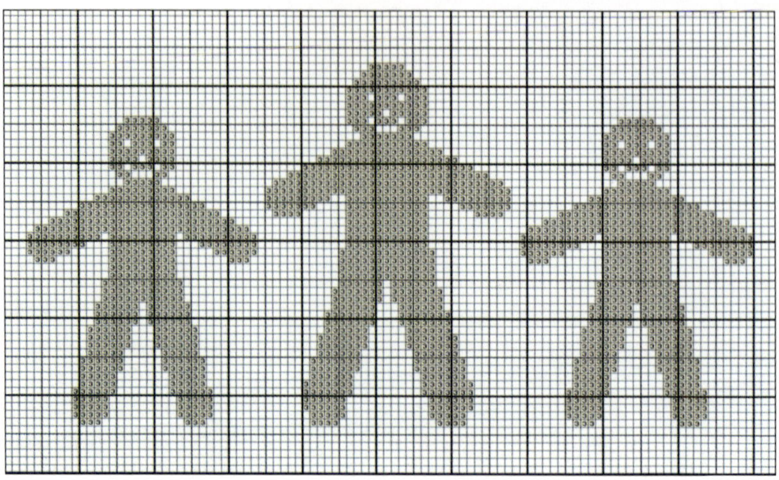

1 To make up: once complete, remove the canvas threads one at a time. You may find it easier to take out the shorter threads first. Press the embroidery on the reverse side.

DMC coton perlé no.5
33 543

HAND TOWEL

Make this pretty border to sew on to a plain waffle towel and add your own initials.

YOU WILL NEED

white waffle hand towel

20 x 90cm (8 x 36in) homespun cotton gingham with approximately 10 squares to 2.5cm (1in)

scissors

tacking (basting) thread

needle

stranded cotton DMC 321, 815, 3808

embroidery needle

pins

sewing machine (optional)

sewing thread

DMC
- 3808
- 321
- Your choice
- 815

WORKING THE CROSS STITCH

Wash both the towel and the gingham to check for shrinkage. Cut the gingham so that it measures 5cm (2in) wider than the towel. Tack (baste) guidelines across the centre of the gingham in both directions and work the cross stitch using three strands of cotton over each square. Stitch your choice of initials first, then work the hearts on either side.

1 To make up: press the embroidery on the reverse side. Trim the long edges so that there is 4cm (1½in) on either side of the cross stitch. Press under 12mm (½in) on all sides and pin to the end of the towel. Fold the short ends to the back and tack. Hand or machine stitch the gingham close to the edge using matching thread.

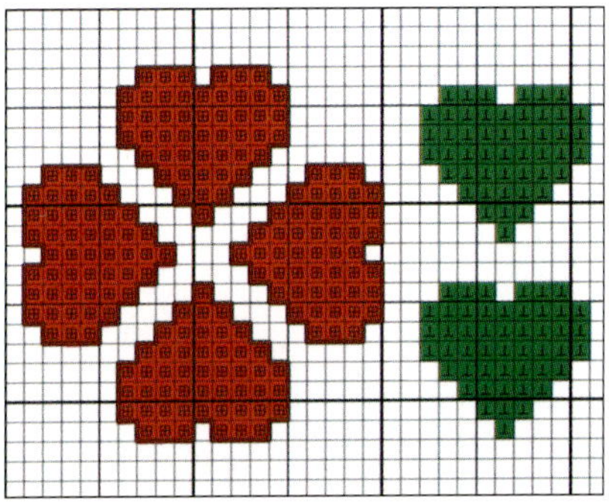

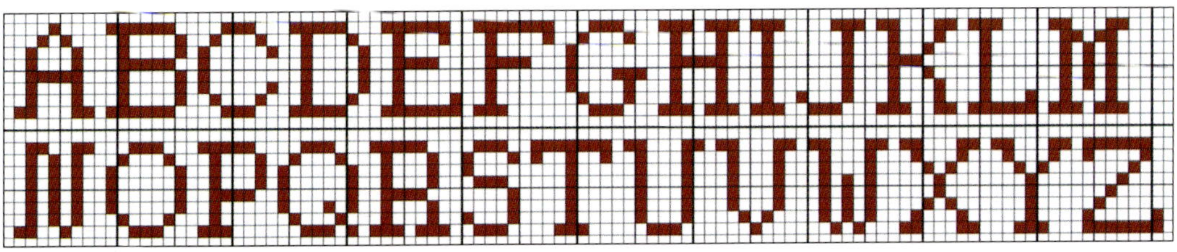

WOODEN SPOON MOBILE

Paint an old wooden spoon and make a charming kitchen decoration with some oddments of gingham and embroidery cotton.

YOU WILL NEED

three 8cm (3in) squares of different gingham fabric
three 5cm (2in) squares of 14 count waste canvas
tacking (basting) thread
needle
six 10cm (4in) squares of contrast gingham
8 x 25cm (3 x 10in) fusible bonding web
scissors
Anchor Nordin 13, 134, 281
embroidery needle
sewing machine
sewing thread
polyester stuffing
wooden spoon
pencil
hand drill
yellow paint, Colourman 122
paintbrush
adhesive tape
large eye needle

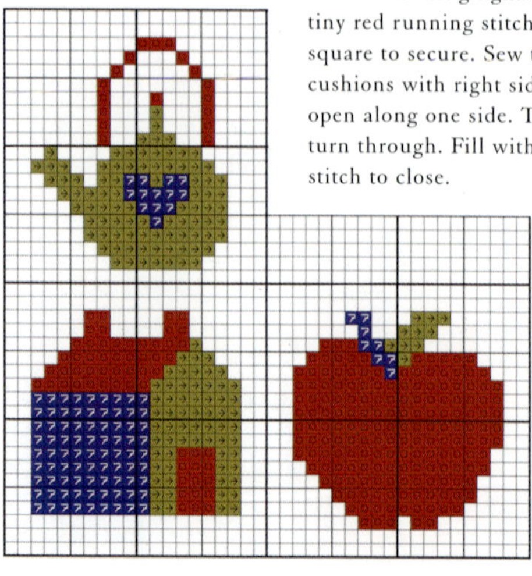

Anchor
- 134
- 13
- 281

WORKING THE CROSS STITCH

Tack (baste) the waste canvas on to the small gingham squares and work one motif in the centre of each. Remove the waste canvas one thread at a time once the embroidery is finished and press lightly on the reverse side.

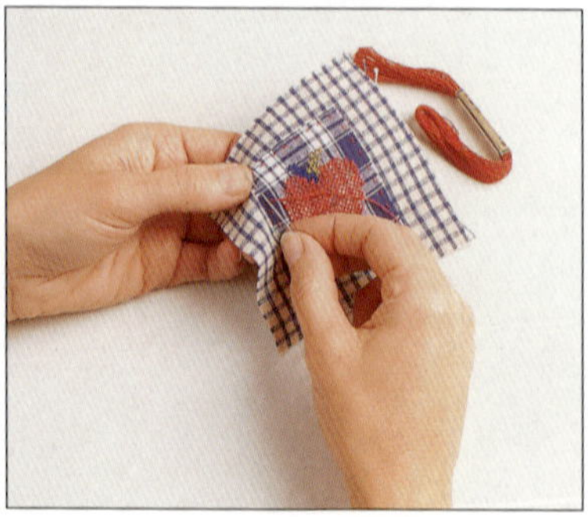

1 To make up: iron fusible bonding web on to the reverse side of the squares and trim them to 5.5cm (2¼in). Remove the backing paper and iron the embroidered squares on to three squares of the contrast gingham. Work a row of tiny red running stitches round each small square to secure. Sew the backs on to the cushions with right sides facing, leaving open along one side. Trim the corners and turn through. Fill with stuffing and slip stitch to close.

2 Lay the cushions under the spoon and mark the position of the holes. Drill small holes through the spoon and paint with two coats of yellow paint.

3 Make a 60cm (24in) cord with Anchor Nordin 281. Cut it in three equal pieces and tape the ends to prevent them unravelling. Thread a cord through each hole and sew the ends into one corner of each cushion.

Gifts

PARTY HORSE

FOLK ART

Children love to role-play with this traditional folk art doll who is dressed in her Sunday best and ready for a tea-party.

YOU WILL NEED

20 x 30cm (8 x 12in) white cotton fabric
tracing paper
pencil
5cm (2in) square of 14 count waste canvas
tacking (basting) thread
needle
stranded cotton DMC 799, 3347
embroidery needle
30cm (12in) broderie anglaise
pins
scissors
sewing machine
sewing thread
30cm (12in) of 5mm (¼in) white ribbon
40cm (½yd) of 90cm (36in) wide natural linen or fine wool
polyester stuffing
two 5mm (¼in) black beads
0.25m (¼yd) of 115cm (45in) wide blue cotton print

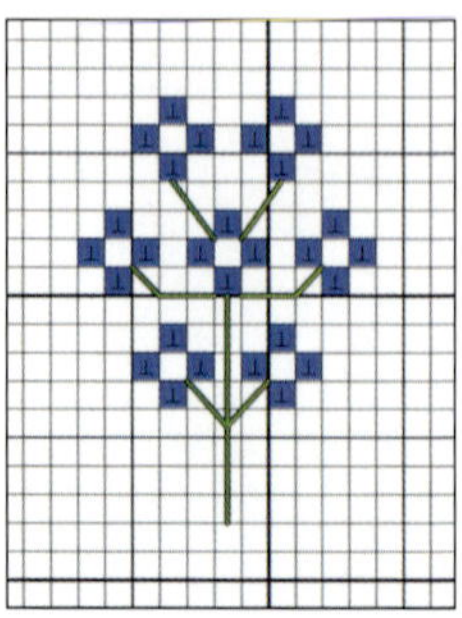

DMC
799
Backstitch
3347

WORKING THE CROSS STITCH

Trace the apron template on to the white cotton. Tack (baste) the waste canvas in the middle of the lower half and work the cross stitch using three strands of cotton. Remove the waste canvas thread by thread and complete the backstitch as shown. Press the embroidery on the reverse side. Pin the broderie anglaise round the embroidered section of the apron. Fold the apron in half with right sides together and stitch, leaving a gap on one side. Turn through and press. Pin the ribbon across the top of the apron and stitch all round close to the edge.

1 To make up: enlarge the templates and cut out the pattern pieces for the horse. Using 5mm (¼in) seam allowance, stitch the heads, ears, arms and legs together in pairs leaving the short straight edges unstitched. Stuff all the pieces except for the ears. Turn the raw edges inside, pinch the bottom of each ear and hand sew on either side of the head seam.

2 For the eyes, stitch on one bead and take the thread through to the other side. Pull it taut to sink the eye slightly and sew on the second bead. Stitch the torso leaving open between the dots and at the top and bottom. Tuck the head inside and slip stitch securely. Attach the arms in the same way, then stuff the body firmly.

3 Pin the legs in place and backstitch through all layers along the bottom of the torso. Cut out the dress bodice and a 20 x 61cm (8 x 24in) rectangle for the skirt. Stitch the outer sleeve seam and the underarm seam. Sew a small piece of lace to the neck edge and hem the sleeve ends. Stitch the short ends of the skirt together to form a tube and gather round one end. Pin to the bodice and stitch. Fold under a narrow hem and stitch to complete.

GUEST TOWEL

FOLK ART

Screw two brass hooks to the back of a door or hang this unusual guest towel from a row of wooden pegs.

YOU WILL NEED

white waffle hand towel

30 cm (12in) homespun check fabric with approximately 10 squares to 2.5cm (1in)

scissors

tacking (basting) thread

needle

embroidery hoop (frame)

coton perlé no.5 DMC 311, 400, 469, 726, 814

embroidery needle

pins

sewing machine

sewing thread

40cm (16in) woven tape

two pearl buttons

WORKING THE CROSS STITCH

Wash the towel and gingham before beginning to check for colour fastness and shrinkage. Cut the gingham 2.5cm (1in) wider than the towel. Fold the fabric in half crossways and mark this with a line of tacking (basting). Beginning with the red flower, embroider the motifs 5cm (2in) up from the bottom of the fabric. Reverse the motifs for the other side.

1 To make up: with right sides together, stitch the bottom edge of the embroidered panel to the top of the hand towel. Fold and press under a 12mm (½in) seam allowance along the top edge. Fold the gingham in half with right sides together, stitch the side seams, then trim and turn through.

2 Slip stitch the folded edge to the back of the towel. Cut the tape in half. Fold into loops and pin the raw edges to each corner of the embroidered panel. Stitch across the bottom of the loop, fold it over on itself and stitch securely. Sew a button to the front of each corner as a trimming.

DMC	Backstitch
726	726
400	311
814	
311	☆ Middle point
469	

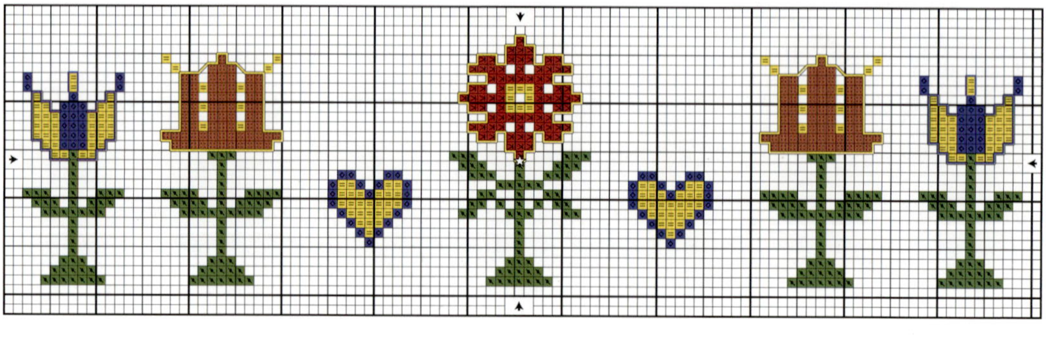

FOLK ART COW

Children will love this traditional folk art style cow and the bright colourful border.

WORKING THE CROSS STITCH

Tack (baste) guidelines across the middle of the Aida in both directions. Begin in the middle and work the cow picture. Leave two rows of Aida clear all round for the green ribbon. Next, work the patchwork border.

1. To make up: pin the ribbon round the edge of the cross stitch and in the space left round the cow. Stitch the ribbon to the Aida with tiny hem stitches.

2. Cut the mount board (backing board) slightly larger than the outside ribbon edge. Stretch the embroidery over the board and put into a frame of your choice.

YOU WILL NEED

36 x 40cm (14 x 16in) white 14 count Aida

tacking (basting) thread

needle

interlocking bar frame

coton à broder DMC ecru, 10, 444, 553, 603, 605, 702, 799, 827, 898, 954, Anchor 254

tapestry needle

1.5m (1⅝yd) of 3mm (⅛in) green satin ribbon

scissors

pins

sewing thread

30 x 36cm (12 x 14in) mount board (backing board)

craft knife

safety ruler

strong thread

frame

DMC
ribbon
954
702
444
Ecru
10
898
605
603
553
799
827
254 Anchor
Backstitch
898
☆ Middle point

FOLK ART

HERBS ON A ROPE

Fill these five lovely bags with cinnamon sticks, chilli peppers or dried herbs and hang on the kitchen wall.

YOU WILL NEED

10 x 15cm (4 x 6in) white 16 count Aida

scissors

stranded cotton DMC 311, 815

tapestry needle

12 x 20cm (4¾ x 8in) dark blue denim

pins

embroidery needle

pinking shears

five 15 x 20cm (6 x 8in) rectangles in different red and blue checks

all-purpose glue

sewing machine

sewing thread

cinnamon, chilli peppers and other dried herbs

1m (1yd) heavyweight cotton cord

2.5cm (1in) brass curtain ring

coarse string

WORKING THE CROSS STITCH

Cut five 4.5cm (1¾in) squares out of the Aida. Work a cross stitch heart in the middle of each piece using three strands of cotton and then complete the red cross stitch.

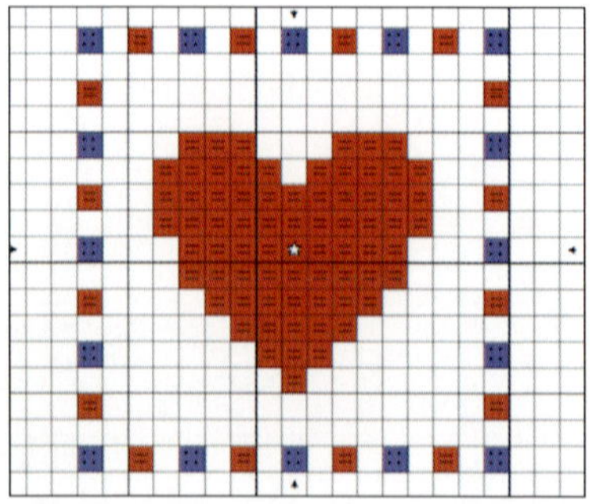

Anchor

815

311

Middle point

1 To make up: cut five 7cm (2¾in) denim squares and pin the embroidered pieces to them. Work the blue cross stitch through both layers. Fray the edge of the Aida squares and trim the edges of the denim with pinking shears. Glue each heart motif to the centre of a check rectangle, 4cm (1½in) from the lower edge. Fold in half so that the heart is on the inside and stitch the short edges together. Position the seam at the centre back and press flat. Stitch along the bottom edge, trim the corners and turn through. Trim the tops of the bags with pinking shears and work a row of running stitches 4cm (1½in) from the top.

2 Fill with different herbs, pull up the running stitches and fasten securely. Thread the brass ring on to the cord, fold it in half and bind the top with string to secure. Tie the bags on to the double string at intervals using short lengths of string.

FOLK ART

EMBROIDERED LAUNDRY BAG

Embroider your own choice of initials in a similar style and make one of these big, useful laundry bags for each member of the family.

YOU WILL NEED

50cm (20in) of 6cm (2½in) Aida band with red border, Zweigart E7315

stranded cotton DMC 815

tapestry needle

80 x 100cm (31 x 39in) white linen or a textured woven cotton

scissors

pins

sewing machine

sewing thread

quilting pencil

needle

2m (2¼yds) medium white piping cord

safety pin

comb

WORKING THE CROSS STITCH

Fold the Aida band in half crossways to find the centre and work the cross stitch using three strands of cotton.

1 To make up: cut the white fabric into two 50 x 80cm (20 x 31in) rectangles. Pin, then stitch the band to one piece, 20cm (8in) from the lower edge.

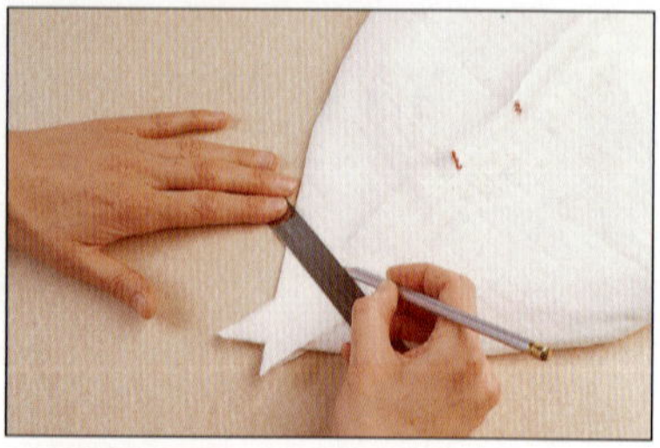

2 With the embroidered band on the inside, pin the two pieces together. Starting and finishing 20cm (8in) from the top, stitch round the sides and along the bottom. Press the seams open and flatten the corners to make a right angled point at each end of the bottom seam. Measure 5cm (2½in) in from each point and mark a diagonal line across each corner. Pin and stitch across the corners to form a flat base.

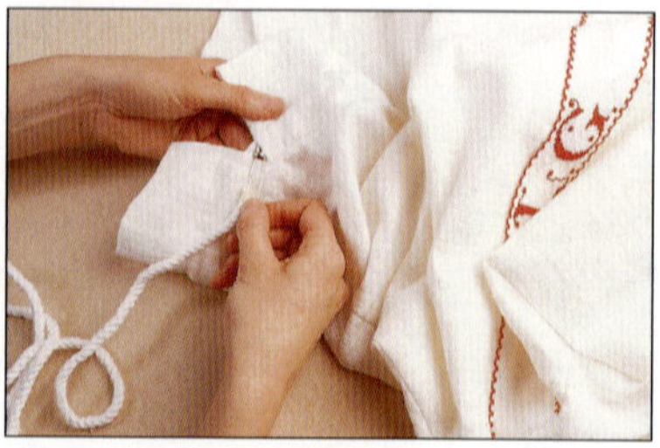

3 Fold over and stitch the seam allowance round both top flaps. Fold in half to the inside and stitch along the edge of the hem. Make a second row of stitching 4cm (1½in) up from this to form a drawstring channel. Cut the cord in two and thread through opposite ends of the channel using a safety pin. Knot the two ends of each cord together 8cm (3in) from the end. Unravel the ends to form a tassel, comb the ends out and trim neatly.

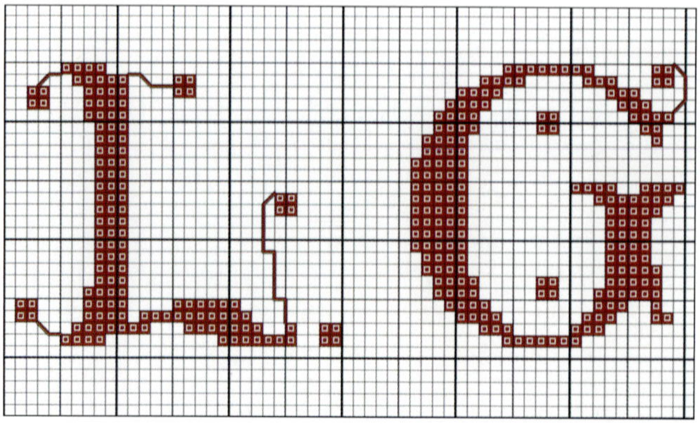

DMC	Backstitch
815	815

L.G.

SWISS ALPHABET SAMPLER

Samplers worked in a single colour were particularly popular in Europe in the nineteenth century.

YOU WILL NEED

30 x 36cm (12 x 14in) white 14 count Aida

tacking (basting) thread

interlocking bar frame

needle

stranded cotton DMC 3 skeins of 304

tapestry needle

23 x 28cm (9 x 11in) mount board (backing board)

strong thread

picture frame

DMC
304

☆ Middle point

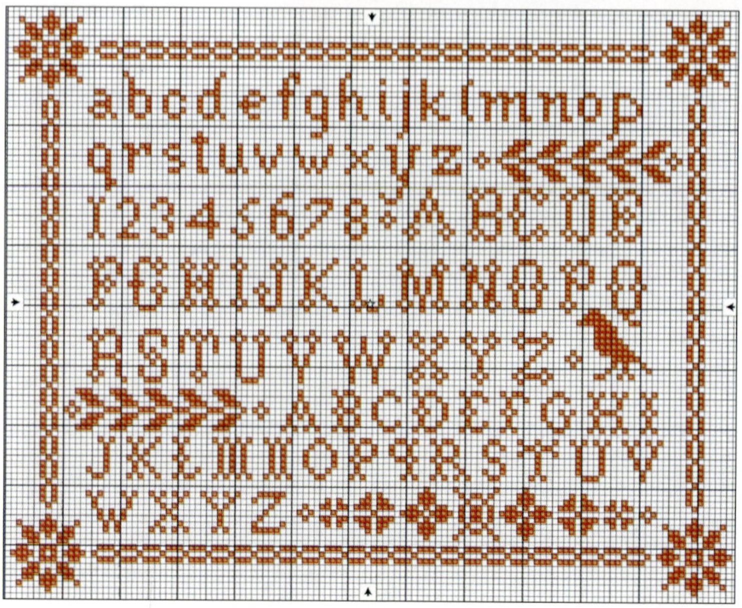

WORKING THE CROSS STITCH

Tack (baste) guidelines across the middle of the Aida in both directions and work the cross stitch using three strands of cotton. Work the middle row of letters, then those above and below. Finally stitch the border and corner motifs.

1 To make up: once complete, press on the reverse side and trim any ends of thread so that they do not show through on the right side. Stretch the embroidery over the mount board (backing board) and put into a frame of your choice.

Swiss Pillowcase

FOLK ART

European countries each have their own particular style of cross stitch. Plain red on white or cream is typical of Switzerland.

YOU WILL NEED

white Oxford pillowcase

25cm (10in) 14 count waste canvas

scissors

tacking (basting) thread

needle

stranded cotton Anchor 47

embroidery needle

NEEDLEWORK TIP

The corner design on this pillowcase will depend very much on the length of the border. Adapt the chart to suit, if necessary.

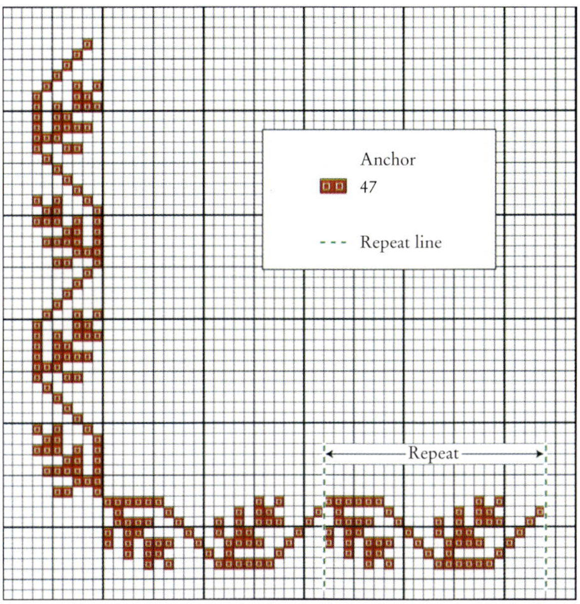

1 Cut 2.5cm (1in) strips of waste canvas and tack (baste) in position round the border of the pillow-case, 12mm (½in) from the stitching. Beginning in the centre of one long side, work the cross stitch using two strands of cotton.

2 Stop when you are near the corner and plan the design to fit the corner based on the cross stitch chart. Complete the other half of the side to match and then finish the rest of the stitching. Press the pillowcase on the reverse side.

SHELF BORDER

FOLK ART

Red and blue cross stitch is very popular in Eastern Europe where the carnation is a traditional motif.

YOU WILL NEED

7cm (2¾in) bleached linen blue-edged band, Inglestone collection 950/70

stranded cotton Anchor 161, 1006

tapestry needle

sewing thread

needle

Anchor
1006
161

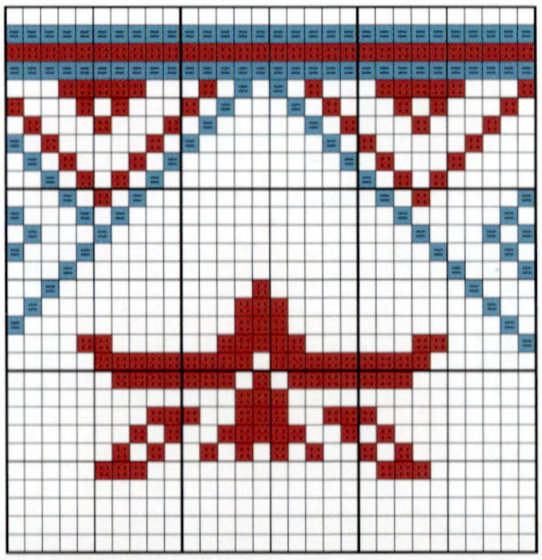

WORKING THE CROSS STITCH

The amount of band and stranded cotton required will depend on the length of your shelf.

1 To make up: fold the band in half crossways and begin stitching the design in the centre six threads down from the border. Continue, then repeat out to both ends of the linen band.

2 Press on the reverse side and stitch a narrow hem at each end to finish the raw edges.

BEDSIDE TABLECLOTH

This versatile design could be stitched on to napkins or on each corner of a much larger tablecloth.

YOU WILL NEED

46cm (18in) square of antique white 28 count Cashel linen, Zweigart E3281

tacking (basting) thread

needle

stranded cotton DMC three skeins of 311, one of 3350

tapestry needle

embroidery hoop (frame)

scissors

sewing thread

8cm (3in) square of card (cardboard)

WORKING THE CROSS STITCH

Tack (baste) a guideline round a corner of the linen 2.5cm (1in) in from the edge. The design begins 90 threads from the corner of the guideline. Work the cross stitch and backstitch over two threads using two strands of cotton.

1 To make up: trim the square to leave a 1.5cm (5/8in) seam allowance outside the cross stitch. Mitre the corners and turn a narrow hem. Slip stitch the corners and along the hem.

2 Work the same design in the corner diagonally opposite and press on the reverse side when complete.

3 Wrap blue thread round the card (cardboard) and make four tassels. Stitch these securely to each corner of the mat.

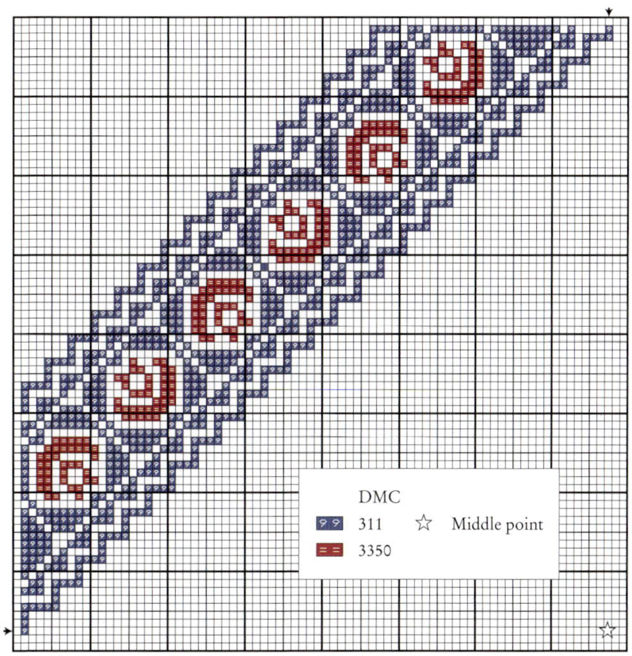

CHINESE BOX

FOLK ART

The tiger design on this box is adapted from a cylindrical Chinese seal from Hong Kong.

YOU WILL NEED

30 x 50cm (12 x 20in) white 25 count Lugana, Zweigart E3835

scissors

tacking (basting) thread

needle

stranded cotton Anchor 132, 403

tapestry needle

sewing thread

20 x 40cm (8 x 16in) thin card (cardboard)

adhesive tape

30cm (12in) square of blue lining fabric

all-purpose glue

WORKING THE CROSS STITCH

Cut a 13 x 25cm (5 x 10in) rectangle of evenweave and tack (baste) guidelines across the middle in both directions. Using two strands of cotton over two threads, outline the tigers in Holbein stitch (two rows of running stitch making a solid line). Fill in the cross stitch and work the Holbein stitch borders. Press the embroidered panel on the reverse side. Fold in half and stitch the short sides together close to the cross stitch to form a tube.

1 To make up: from thin card (cardboard) cut one 9 x 38cm ($3\frac{1}{2}$ x 15in) and one 10 x 19cm (4 x $7\frac{1}{2}$in) rectangle. Curl the long piece round till the two ends meet and secure with tape. Tuck the tube inside the embroidered tube. Stick the raw edges to the inside. Cut a 15 x 22cm (6 x $8\frac{1}{2}$in) piece of lining on the bias. Stitch the two short sides together. Curl the second piece of card round until it fits inside the embroidered tube and tape.

2 Put the lining inside the tube and stretch the fabric to the outside. Glue a turning of 12mm ($\frac{1}{2}$in) at the bottom and the larger area at the top. Cut two circles out of card to fit the bottoms of the tubes. Cover the smaller one with lining fabric and the larger with evenweave. Oversew the lining circle with the raw edges facing out and the evenweave with them facing in.

3 Cut a 2 x 38cm ($\frac{3}{4}$ x 15in) strip of card. Curl it to fit loosely round the lip of the box. Make a fabric tube from a 6 x 22cm ($2\frac{3}{8}$ x $8\frac{1}{2}$in) piece of evenweave. Fold it in half and tuck the tube inside. Stitch round the edge of the card through both layers. Cover a disc with linen as before and stitch round the ring, tucking the raw edges inside. Cut a disc to fit inside the lid and cover with lining fabric. Stick the disk on the inside to complete.

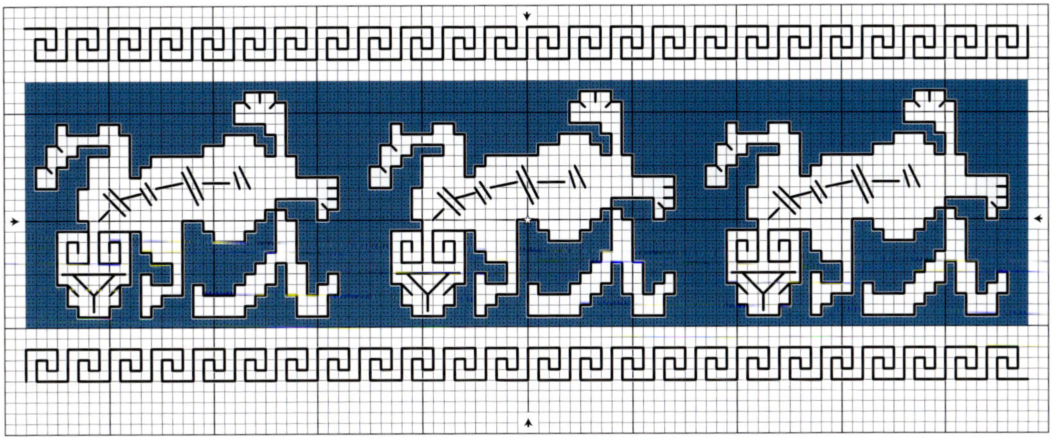

Anchor		Backstitch
132	—	403
	☆	Middle point

FOLK ART

INDIAN NECK PURSE

This little bag is typical of those made by the nomadic Banjara people. The design layout was inspired by the wooden architecture in Gujarat.

YOU WILL NEED

two 15 x 18cm (6 x 7in) pieces of red 20 count evenweave linen

tacking (basting) thread

needle

interlocking bar frame

coton à broder no.16 DMC 321, 444, 552, 700, 796, 907, 943, 947

flower thread DMC 2333, 2531, 2797, 2907, 2917, 2947, 2956

tapestry needle

scissors

50cm (20in) of 90cm (36in) wide fine navy cotton

sewing machine

sewing thread

easy-turn rouleau maker or bodkin

pins

red wool

8cm (3in) square of card (cardboard)

WORKING THE CROSS STITCH

Experiment by mixing the different colours before working this exciting embroidery project. Subtle changes will occur depending on whether the dark or light thread is on top.

Tack (baste) vertical guidelines corresponding to the panels of the chart on both pieces of linen. The centre panel is worked in coton à broder and the borders in flower threads with each stitch worked over four threads.

Cut several 5cm (2in) wide bias strips of the navy cotton and stitch 8mm (3/8in) from the fold, then turn through to make rouleaux. Place the rouleaux in the spaces between the stitching and couch down with groups of two red cross stitches. Leave a border of eight threads round the cross stitch and trim the linen.

DMC
- light areas
- dark areas

1 To make up: pin and tack each piece on to a 20 x 23cm (8 x 9in) rectangle of navy cotton. Machine stitch close to the edge. Mitre the corners of the backing fabric and turn a narrow hem on to the right side of the embroidery. Slip stitch in place.

2 With right sides facing out, oversew the two panels together down the sides and along the bottom.

3 Make three 1m (39in) lengths of rouleaux. Thread several strands of red wool through the centre of each to pad. Plait the rouleaux and knot the ends separately. Stitch the rouleaux together 8cm (3in) from the end by winding the cottons around the card (cardboard) and making a tassel over each knot. Sew the straps to the bag with cross stitches on the front and the back.

BUCKET BAG

The shape of this bag is based on a shigra basket from Ecuador. The people there use it to carry fruit and vegetables.

YOU WILL NEED

60 x 84cm (24 x 33in) sand canvas fabric
scissors
tailor's chalk
Anchor Nordin 326, 341, 365
embroidery needle
pins
tacking (basting) thread
needle
sewing thread
sewing machine
160cm (1¾yd) thick cord

Anchor Nordin
326
341
365

WORKING THE CROSS STITCH

This project is unusual because the cross stitch is worked on ordinary canvas. The weave on canvas is quite prominent and it is quite easy to follow the grain. With a little practice you will be able to make evenly sized and spaced stitches.

Cut two 30 x 63cm (12 x 25in) rectangles. Fold one piece in half lengthways and mark the fold line with chalk. Work a row of spaced cross stitches in 326, 2cm (¾in) either side of the chalk line. Work the single cross stitches and fish motifs between the lines. Work parallel rows of cross stitch 8cm (3in) from the raw edge, then finish the other six stitches of the vertical lines to complete the design.

1 To make up: with right sides together stitch the short seams of both panels to form a tube. Cut two 20cm (8in) circles from the canvas. Pin one circle to the bottom of each tube, easing the fabric as you go. Tack (baste) and stitch round the base. Snip into the curves and turn the embroidered piece through to the right side.

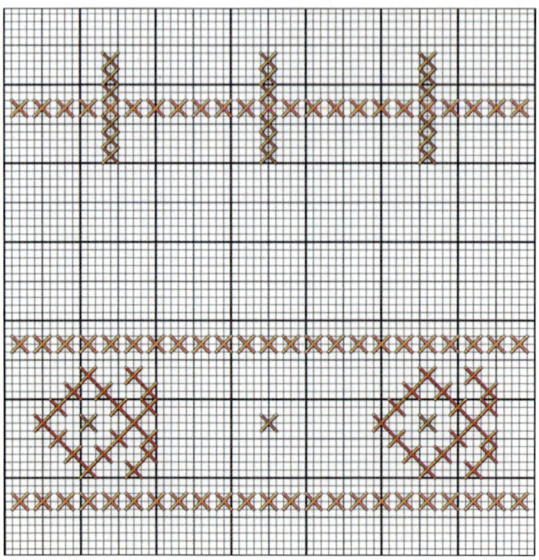

2 Cut the cord in two and pin one piece 6cm (2½in) to either side of the centre back seam, with the loop facing towards the bag. Pin the other strap on the opposite side and stitch securely inside the seam allowance.

3 Tuck the lining inside the bag and fold over the top edge of both pieces by about 1.5cm (⅝in). Pin and tack the layers together and stitch close to the top edge. Stitch again 5mm (¼in) away to finish.

MEXICAN TOY BAG

FOLK ART

Toddlers will be delighted to help tidy their bricks into this big strong bag.

YOU WILL NEED

18 x 46cm (7 x 18in) antique white 20 count Bellana, Zweigart E3256

tacking (basting) thread

needle

stranded cotton DMC 300, 310, 349, 603, 704, 806, 972

tapestry needle

80 x 60cm (32 x 24in) navy heavyweight twill fabric

scissors

pins

sewing machine

sewing thread

160cm (1¾yd) thick white cord

safety pin

comb

DMC			
972		310	
704		603	
300		806	
349		Backstitch	
		— 310	

WORKING THE CROSS STITCH

Tack (baste) guidelines across the middle of the evenweave. Work the cross stitch design using two strands of cotton over single threads, then work the backstitch. Press gently on the reverse side when complete.

1 To make up: cut the navy fabric in two, crossways. Turn in the long edges of the embroidered panel and pin it 15cm (6in) from the bottom of one piece of fabric. Tack (baste) and stitch the two long sides. With right sides facing, pin the pieces together down the sides and bottom. Stitch, leaving a 4cm (1½in) gap on both sides 7cm (2¾in) from the top. Zig-zag close to the stitching, then trim and turn through.

2 Fold over the top edge and make a 5cm (2in) hem. Pin and sew the hem in place and then top stitch 1cm (½in) down from the top fold line. Cut the cord in half. Using a large safety pin, thread the pieces of cord through the casing in opposite directions. Tie the ends together 8cm (3in) from the end to form a tassel. Unravel the threads, comb them out and trim neatly to finish.

SHOE BAG

FOLK ART

Geometric weaving designs can be adapted quite easily into cross stitch. These stylized animals come from a hammock made in Ghana.

YOU WILL NEED

28 x 66cm (11 x 26in) golden tan 28 count Quaker evenweave linen

scissors

tacking (basting) thread

needle

stranded cotton DMC 300, 498, 676, 919, 976

tapestry needle

pins

sewing machine

sewing thread

safety pin

WORKING THE CROSS STITCH

Cut a 5 x 66cm (2 x 26in) strip from the fabric for the cord. Fold the larger piece in half both ways and tack (baste) along the folds. Work the cross stitch using two strands of cotton over two threads. Begin at the bottom of the chart, working the cockerel above the crossways tacking. Press on the wrong side when complete.

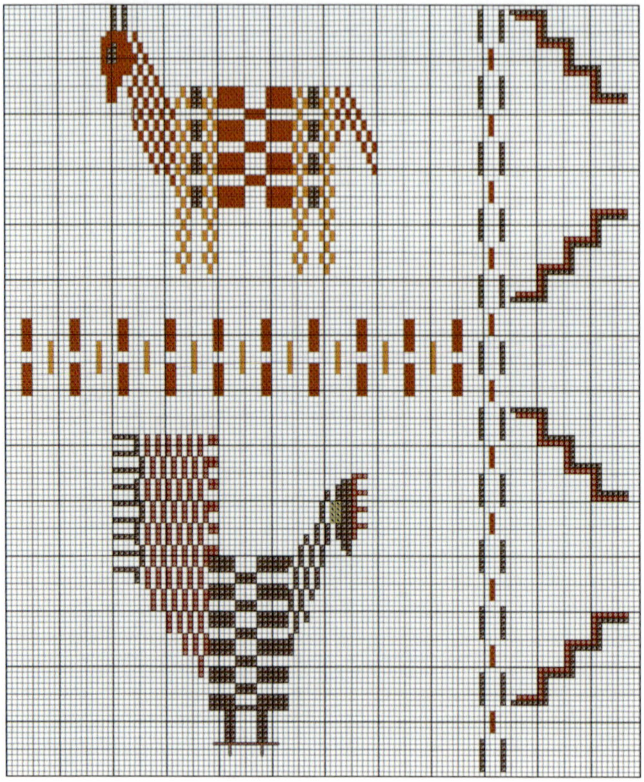

1 To make up: fold the fabric in half with the embroidery facing in. Pin and stitch the two side seams, leaving a 5cm (2in) gap on one side 2.5cm (1in) from the top. Press the seams open.

2 To make the casing, fold over 5cm (2in) at the top. Turn under 12mm (½in), then pin and stitch in place. Stitch again close to the top edge.

3 Press the long edges of the reversed fabric strip into the centre. Turn the ends in 12mm (½in) and then fold the strip lengthways again. Pin and stitch round all sides. Thread the strap through the casing with a safety pin and stitch the ends together securely. Pull the joined ends through to the other side of the bag to complete the project.

DMC	Backstitch
919	300
976	919
300	
498	
676	

MEXICAN WALLHANGING

FOLK ART

This little hanging was inspired by traditional Mexican god's eyes. Why not make one or two more to hang alongside it?

WORKING THE CROSS STITCH

Cut two 18 x 25cm (7 x 10in) rectangles of linen. Tack (baste) a guideline lengthways down the middle of one piece. Tack a second line across the linen, 10cm (4in) from the top. Work the cross stitch and backstitch using two strands of cotton over two threads of linen. Press on the reverse side when complete.

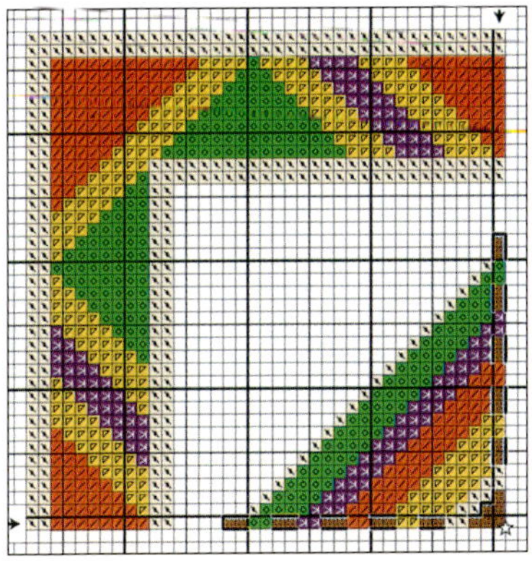

YOU WILL NEED

36cm (14in) square of 32 count natural evenweave linen

scissors

tacking (basting) thread

needle

small embroidery frame (flexihoop)

stranded cotton DMC 310, 435, 550, 701, 712, 743, 900

tapestry needle

sewing machine

sewing thread

pins

15cm (6in) twig

30cm (12in) fine cord

1. To make up: cut two 5 x 13cm (2 x 5in) rectangles of linen. Fold each in half lengthways and stitch a 12mm (½in) seam allowance. Press the seams open and turn through. Position the seams at the centre back and press again.

2. Fold the tabs in half with the seam to the inside and pin along the top edge, on either side of the embroidered panel. Pin the two pieces of linen together, with the embroidery and tabs to the inside, and stitch along the top and down both sides. Trim the seams and corners and turn through.

3. Fray the bottom edge of the hanging and press on the reverse side. Slip the twig through the tabs and tie the cord at each end to hang.

DMC	
435	900
550	
701	Backstitch
712	— 310
743	☆ Middle point

INDIAN MOBILE

FOLK ART

Shisha mirrors are traditionally hung to protect against evil, in the belief that any spirit seeing its reflection will be terrified and flee.

YOU WILL NEED

two sheets of dark green stitching paper, Jane Greenoff's Inglestone collection

stranded cotton DMC 3 skeins of 783 and 796, 4 skeins of 911 and 1 skein of 815 and 3765

tapestry needle

scissors

1.5cm (⅝in) square of thin card (cardboard)

30cm (12in) piano wire

WORKING THE CROSS STITCH

Stitching paper is prone to tear but it can be repaired with sticky tape and the holes repunched with a large needle. Work the different motifs and their mirror images on to the stitching paper using three strands of cotton, and leaving spaces for the shisha mirrors. Apply the mirrors as shown in the techniques section and then fill in any spaces with cross stitch.

1 To make up: cut out the different motifs taking care not to snip the stitches. Oversew the two halves together using a single strand of cotton. Separate strands of cotton and make some 1.5 cm (5/8in) mini-tassels for the elephants. Sew three on each side of the larger elephants and two on the smaller ones. Sew a tassel on one corner of the diamond motif.

2 Lay out the pieces on a flat surface, leaving gaps of about 4cm (1½in). Use all six strands of yellow cotton to hold the mobile together. Loop a 20cm (8in) length on to the wire. Sew one end to the bottom of the peacock and the other end to the back of the largest elephant. Stitch the other large elephant and the diamond under-neath. Loop three strands of cotton over the ends of the wire and stitch the little elephants in place. Complete the mobile with some tassels and stitch a loop for hanging to the back of the peacock.

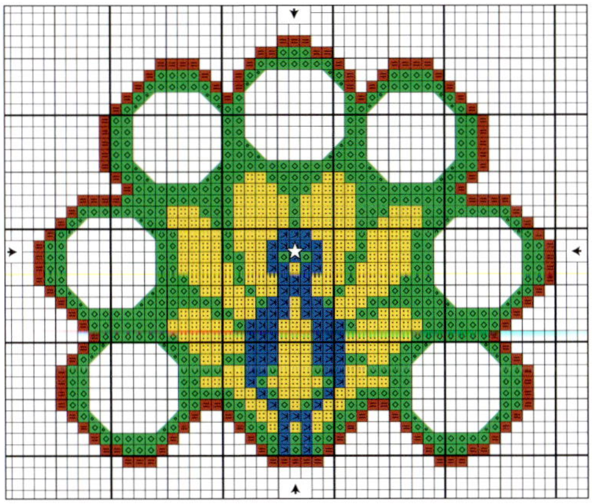

Peacock motif

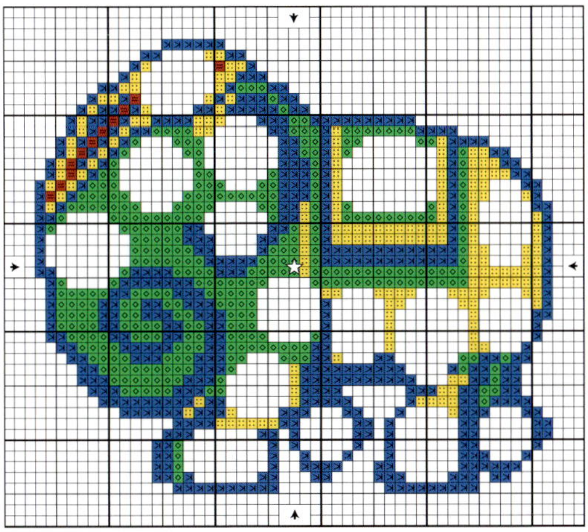

Large elephant motif

DMC

815	911
783	3765
796	☆ Middle point

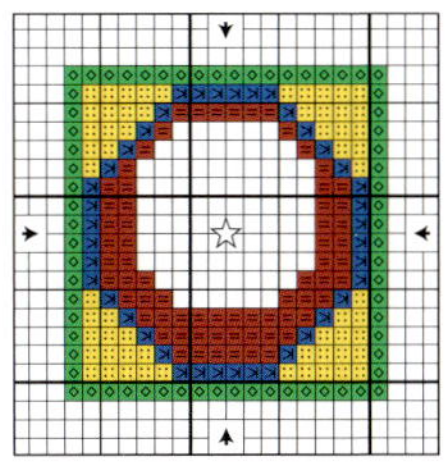

Diamond motif

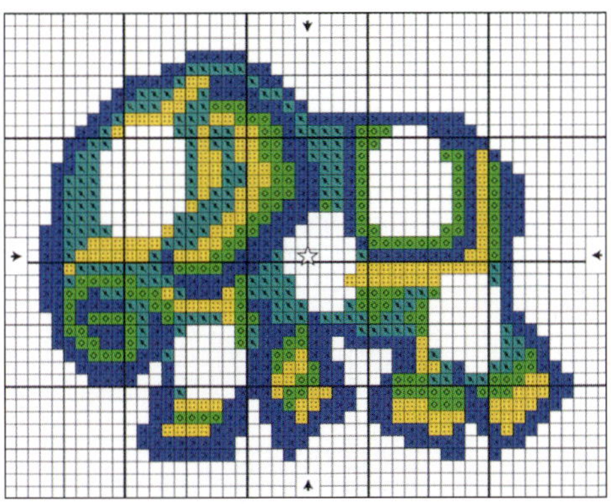

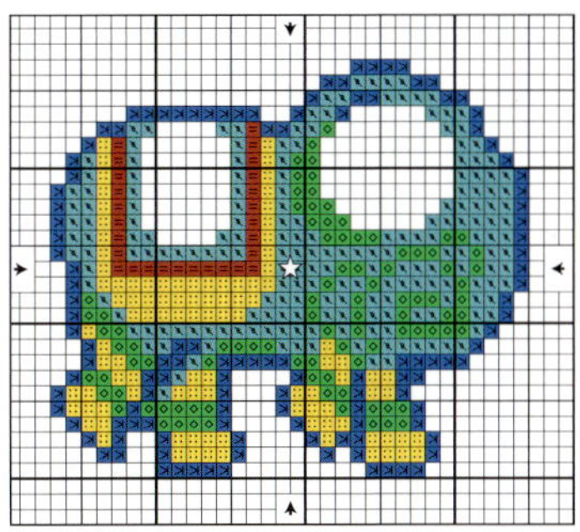

Left: medium elephant *Above: small elephant*

CONTEMPORARY

EMBROIDERED DUNGAREES AND HAT BAND

YOU WILL NEED

denim dungarees with a plain bib

10 x 15cm (4 x 6in) 14 count waste canvas

pins

tacking (basting) thread

needle

pencil

stranded cotton Anchor 6, 9, 46, 238, 291, 896

embroidery needle

straw hat

60cm (24in) of 2.5cm (1in) wide cream Aida band, Zweigart E7002

scissors

sewing thread

These projects match perfectly and make a lovely design for a child's dungarees and straw hat.

TO MAKE THE DUNGAREES

WORKING THE CROSS STITCH

The design area for this pig measures 7 x 13cm (2¾ x 5in) and is suitable to stitch on age 5–6 dungarees. If you want to embroider a larger area, use 10 count canvas which gives a design size of 10 x 18cm (4 x 7in).

Pin and tack (baste) the waste canvas in the middle of the bib. Mark the centre of the canvas with a pencil and work the cross stitch using two strands of cotton (three for 10 count). Once complete, remove the canvas threads one at a time and then press.

Anchor		Backstitch
6	291	896
9	46	
896	238	☆ Middle point

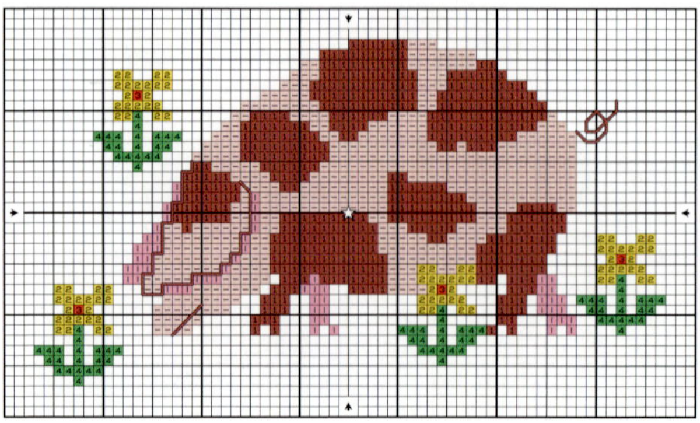

TO MAKE THE HAT BAND

WORKING THE CROSS STITCH

Measure the hat and cut the Aida band 5cm (2in) longer. Fold the band in half and put in a pin to mark the centre. Work a flower on the centre line and continue the design out towards each end. Try to finish with a flower or the border pattern.

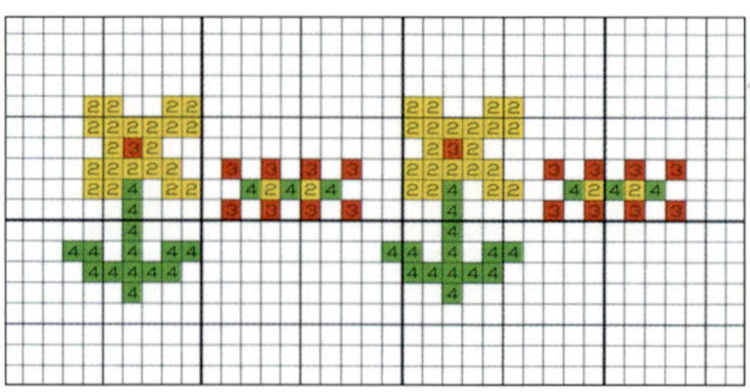

Anchor
291
46
238

1 To make up: fit the band round the hat. Turn one end in and pin on top of the other end. Slip stitch the ends together. If necessary, secure the band on to the hat by stitching it with prick stitch (tiny running stitches on the front and long stitches on the back).

CONTEMPORARY

EMBROIDERED BOOK

This little book is made from off-cuts of card (cardboard) and fabrics and contains some small sheets of handmade paper.

YOU WILL NEED

11 x 13cm (4⅜ x 5in) gingham
stranded cotton Anchor 352, 890
embroidery needle
25cm (10in) square of blue moleskin or denim
scissors
15cm (6in) square of floral cotton fabric
15cm (6in) square of brown cotton fabric
15 x 30cm (6 x 12in) fusible bonding web
all-purpose glue
two pieces of 15 x 18cm (6 x 7in) card (cardboard)
masking tape
23 x 38cm (9 x 15in) striped cotton
double-sided tape
18 x 33cm (7 x 13in) check cotton
pinking shears
5 sheets of hand-made paper 18 x 33cm (7 x 13in)

WORKING THE CROSS STITCH

Cross stitch a border round the edge of the piece of gingham. Cut a piece of moleskin to fit inside the border and sew on to the gingham with larger, cruder cross stitches. Iron the fusible bonding web on to the reverse sides of the brown and floral cotton fabrics. Cut out the tree shape and eight petal templates. Remove the backing paper and iron the pieces in place on the moleskin. Sew tiny cross stitches round the shapes. Stitch three crosses along the bottom of the tree and one in the centre of each flower and press on the reverse side. Cut a 12 x 14cm (4¾ x 5½in) piece of moleskin and stick to the back of the embroidered gingham with bonding web or glue.

1 To make up: tape the two pieces of card together leaving a 1cm (⅜in) gap so that they will fold up like a book. Lay the card in the middle of the reverse side of the striped cotton. Put double-sided tape along the outside edges of the card and stretch the fabric on to the tape, mitring the corners neatly.

2 Cut round the edges of the check fabric with pinking shears to fit on to the inside cover and stick in place. Fold the paper in half crossways and position in the middle of the book. Stitch the pages into the book down the centre fold. Stick the embroidered panel on to the front of the cover to finish.

TIEBACKS

CONTEMPORARY

These big sunflowers stand out beautifully against the dark blue and white gingham fabric.

YOU WILL NEED

1m (1yd) of 90cm (36in) wide blue and white gingham

scissors

18 x 50cm (7 x 20in) 14 count waste canvas

pins

tacking (basting) thread

needle

stranded cotton DMC 300, 301, 400, 433, 742, 743, 904, 906, 938, 977, 986

embroidery needle

tracing paper

pencil

36 x 66cm (14 x 26in) medium weight iron-on interfacing

sewing machine

sewing thread

four white "D" rings

WORKING THE CROSS STITCH

If you can buy evenweave gingham, which is produced but is not readily available, work the design directly on to the fabric. Cut the gingham into four 23 x 68cm (9 x 27in) pieces. Fold one piece in four to find the centre and open out. Pin and tack (baste) half the waste canvas in the centre of the right hand side. Mark the centre of the waste canvas and work the cross stitch using two strands of cotton. Once complete, remove the canvas one thread at a time and press the embroidery on the reverse side.

DMC		
300	742	938
301	743	977
400	904	986
433	906	☆ Middle point

1 To make up: trace and enlarge the template on to tracing paper. Cut out a back and front from the tieback pattern, making sure that the sunflower is positioned correctly. Iron interfacing to the back pattern piece. With right sides together, sew the front and back together along both long sides. Trim the seams and snip into the curves.

2 Turn the tieback through, roll the edges between your thumb and first finger to centre the seams and press on the reverse side. Turn each end over the straight edge of a "D" ring, folding the excess fabric into tucks. Turn under a small hem and stitch securely. Make a second tieback in exactly the same way, stitching a mirror image of the sunflower on the left hand side of the gingham.

TOWEL

CONTEMPORARY

This towel is designed to match the sunflower tiebacks. They would make a co-ordinating set for a plain white bathroom.

YOU WILL NEED

navy blue towel

25cm (10in) square of 14 count waste canvas

pins

tacking (basting) thread

needle

stranded cotton DMC 300, 301, 400, 433, 742, 743, 938, 977

embroidery needle

scissors

WORKING THE CROSS STITCH

Pin and tack (baste) the canvas at one end of the towel where you wish to stitch the motif. Work the cross stitch over two pairs of threads using six strands of cotton. You will get a better result if the strands are separated and recombined before stitching. Once complete, fray and remove the canvas threads one at a time. Press lightly with a steam iron on the reverse side, taking care not to damage the towel.

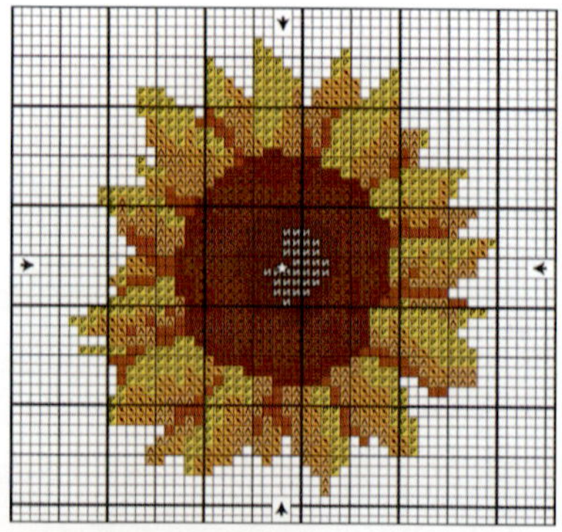

DMC
300
301
400
433
742
743
938
977
☆ Middle point

Daisy Cushion

CONTEMPORARY

The petal colour on this huge daisy could be changed to match a different check cushion. Choose a dark and light shade of the same colour.

Anchor	
22	45
33	896
44	306
55	305
66	891
▽▽	212

1 To make up: once the cover is complete, fray and remove the canvas threads one at a time. Press the embroidery on the reverse side, then turn the cover through and insert the cushion pad to finish.

Working the Cross Stitch

Pin and tack (baste) the waste canvas in the middle of the cushion cover with the opening to the bottom. Fit a large embroidery hoop (frame) on the front of the cushion cover. Mark the centre of the canvas and work the cross stitch using three strands of cotton.

You Will Need

30cm (12in) check cushion cover

15 x 30cm (6 x 12in) 10 count waste canvas

pins

tacking (basting) thread

needle

large embroidery hoop (frame)

pencil

stranded cotton Anchor 45, 212, 305, 306, 891, 896

embroidery needle

30cm (12in) cushion pad

GARDEN APRON

CONTEMPORARY

This big apron, with its large pocket, is ideal for holding small tools and protecting your clothes while working in the garden.

YOU WILL NEED

paper
pencil
90cm (1yd) of 115cm (45in) wide sand canvas
tailor's chalk
scissors
pins
sewing machine
sewing thread
tacking (basting) thread
needle
safety pin
20cm (8in) square of 10 count waste canvas
stranded cotton Anchor 46, 212, 226, 238, 316, 926
embroidery needle

WORKING THE CROSS STITCH

You may find it easier to work the cross stitch after you have made up the apron. Pin and tack (baste) the waste canvas in the middle of the bib. Work the cross stitch and the backstitch details on the plants using three strands of cotton. Then stitch the French knots. Remove the waste canvas before working the rest of the backstitch. Mark the position of the squares and stitch along the grain of the canvas to complete the design.

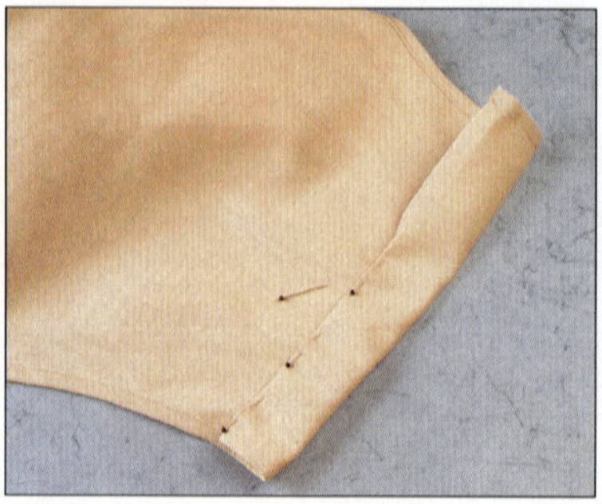

1 To make up: enlarge the pattern pieces and draw round them on to the canvas. Cut out two pockets, one front pattern piece and three 5 x 50cm (2 x 20in) strips. Turn over and stitch a small hem along the curved edges, the sides and bottom of the apron. Fold over 12mm (½in) along the top edge and then a further 2.5 cm (1 in). Pin, tack (baste) and stitch round all sides of the turning.

2 Fold the strips in half lengthways. Sew 12mm (½in) from the raw edge, leaving the straps open at one end, and turn through with a safety pin. Tuck the raw edges inside and press the straps. Pin and tack one strap to either side of the apron and the other one to the top of the bib. Machine stitch in a rectangle to secure the straps. Stitch again for extra strength.

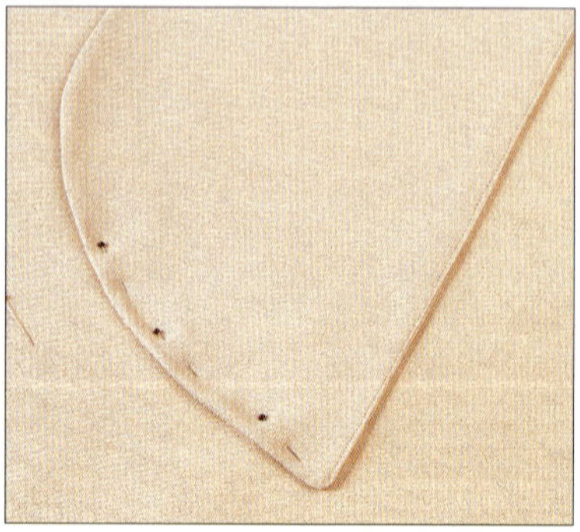

3 Sew the pocket pieces together, with right sides facing, leaving an 8cm (3in) gap along the straight edge. Trim and snip the curves, then turn through. Roll the edges between your fingers to make a good curved edge and press. Top stitch the straight edge, pin and tack to the apron and stitch in place. Stitch round the curved edge again for extra strength and sew straight down the centre of the pocket in the same way. Once complete, pin and tack the waste canvas in the middle of the bib.

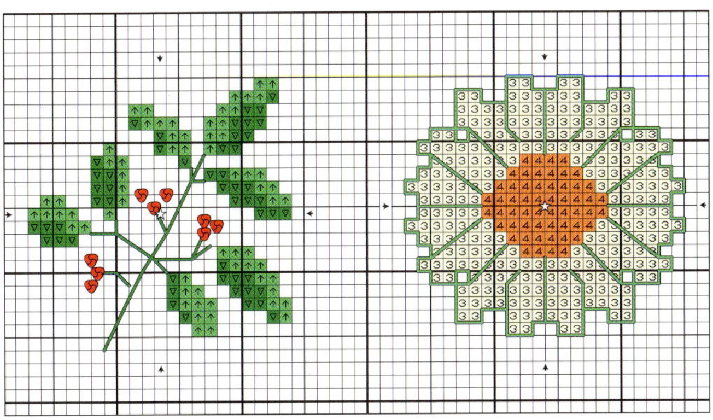

Anchor	Backstitch	
926	238	☆ Middle point
316	212	
212	French knots	
226	46	

DECORATIVE BATH MAT

CONTEMPORARY

This plain cotton bath mat has been stitched with large swirls and cross stitches to co-ordinate with the bathroom accessories.

YOU WILL NEED

natural cotton bath mat
tacking (basting) thread
needle
soft cotton Anchor 11, 13, 228, 242, 305, 307
large sharp needle
scissors

1 Stitching the lines about 2.5cm (1in) apart, tack (baste) twelve large swirls spaced evenly over the bath mat. Leave a 5cm (2in) end of soft cotton on the reverse side and stitch the spirals using 2.5cm (1in) running stitches. When you reach the end of the spiral, work back along the stitching line to fill in the spaces.

2 Work two spirals in each colour, tying the ends of the cotton together with a secure knot.

3 Work the cross stitches in between the spirals, beginning and finishing the thread in the same way. Finish the mat with a row of different coloured cross stitches along each end.

Clock

CONTEMPORARY

Navy and cream paint has been cracked with crackle varnish to make an unusual frame for this beautiful Assisi work.

YOU WILL NEED

20cm (8in) square of 18 count navy Aida, Zweigart E3793
tacking (basting) thread
needle
Anchor stranded cotton 1223
tapestry needle
scissors
22cm (9in) square of 6mm (¼in) thick MDF
hand drill with 10mm (⅜in) drill bit
1.2m (1⅓yd) wood architrave
hand saw
wood glue
masking tape
sandpaper
acrylic paint in dark blue and cream
crackle varnish
paint brushes
clock mechanism with plastic hands
14cm (5½in) square of mount board (backing board)
pencil
strong thread
double-sided tape

WORKING THE CROSS STITCH

Tack (baste) guidelines across the middle of the Aida in both directions. Work the backstitch using a single strand of cotton. Fill in the background with rows of cross stitch. Press on the reverse side when complete.

Anchor
1223

Backstitch
1223

☆ Middle point

1 To make up: drill a 10mm (⅜in) hole in the centre of the MDF. Mitre one end of the wood trim, measure 14cm (5½in) along the inside edge and mitre the other end. Saw another three pieces the same size. Spread glue on the underside and mitred edges of the wood trim and stick to the MDF. Tape the frame together and allow to dry, then sand the edges.

2 Paint the frame with dark blue paint. Let each layer dry before applying the next. Paint with a coat of crackle varnish, then with a coat of cream paint. The last coat can be dried with a hair dryer which will help the cracks to form. Trim the clock hands if necessary and paint in the same way.

3 Check that the mount board (backing board) fits inside the frame. Mark the position of the hole and cut one in the mount board. Stretch the embroidery over the board, mitring the corners neatly, and trim away any excess fabric. Cut into the fabric carefully and insert the front of the clock mechanism into the hole. Stick the mount board on to the frame and screw on the rest of the clock fitments.

ROMAN BLIND

This stunning blind is made all the more dramatic by the choice of bold striped fabric shaded from dark to light blue.

YOU WILL NEED

measuring tape
striped cotton fabric
25cm (10in) wide 10 count waste canvas
tacking (basting) thread
needle
stranded cotton DMC four skeins of 700, two skeins of 307 and one skein each of 105, 743, 995 (approximate quantities)
embroidery needle
pencil
ruler
binding tape
pins
sewing machine
sewing thread
scissors
fusible bonding web to fit size of blind
brass rings
2.5 x 5cm (1 x 2in) wood strip the width of the window
hand saw
tacks
hammer
screw eyes
fine non-stretch cord
2.5cm (1in) wooden batten the width of the window
cleat (for winding the cord round)

WORKING THE CROSS STITCH

Measure the height and width of your window and add 8 cm (3 in) to the width and 15 cm (6 in) to the length. You will need two pieces of fabric this size for the blind. Tack (baste) the waste canvas 15 cm (6 in) from the bottom of one piece of fabric. Mark the centre and work the cross stitch using three strands of cotton. Continue the design out towards each side, stopping after a complete tree. Fray the canvas and pull out the threads one at a time. Press on the reverse side when complete.

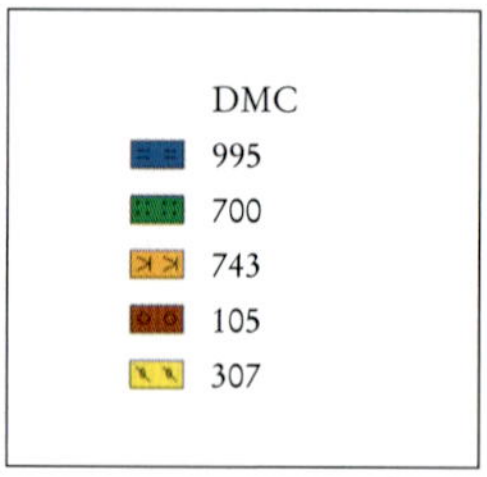

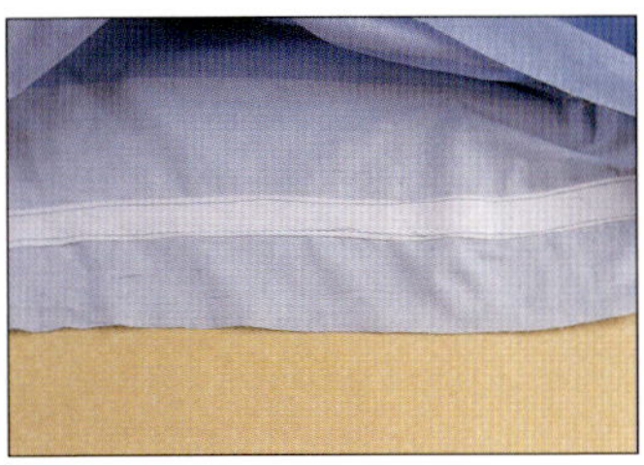

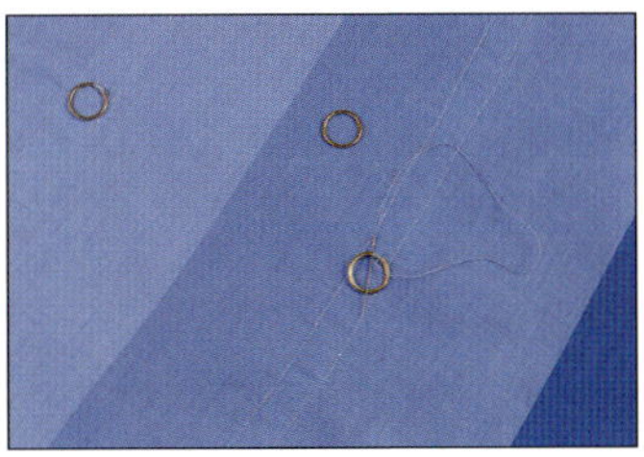

1 To make up: draw vertical lines down the right side of the lining fabric about 30cm (12in) apart with the outside lines about 8cm (3in) in from the edge. Pin and tack tape down all these lines and machine stitch down both sides. Iron fusible bonding web to the reverse side of the embroidered fabric. Remove the backing paper and lay the lining on top. Making sure the fabric is flat, press the layers together.

2 Turn in a 2.5cm (1in) hem down both sides of the blind and stitch. Turn up and stitch a 4cm (1½in) hem along the bottom edge. Making sure they are quite level, sew rings to the tapes every 15cm (6in) starting just above the hem.

3 Cut a headboard to fit the width of the window. Hammer in tacks to fix the top of the blind to the edge of the board. Fix screw eyes to the underside of the board so that they line up with the rings on the blind. The last ring on the right hand side should be large enough to take all the cords.

TO FINISH

Thread a length of cord through the large screw eye and down through the first line of rings. Knot it to the bottom ring. Thread cords through the other lines of rings in the same way, bring the cords together, and then tie a knot just below the large screw eye and plait the excess cord. Tie a knot at the end and trim. Slip the batten into the bottom hem and slip stitch both ends. Fit the heading board above the window and screw the cleat in at a comfortable height.

CHAMBRAY PILLOWCASE

Monograms give bed linen a touch of class. Choose your own initials to stitch in the corner of a classic Oxford pillowcase.

YOU WILL NEED

chambray Oxford pillowcase
small embroidery frame (flexihoop)
10cm (4in) square of 10 count waste canvas
stranded cotton Anchor 2
tacking (basting) thread
embroidery needle
white stranded cotton

Anchor
■■ 342

WORKING THE CROSS STITCH

Fit the embroidery hoop (frame) inside the pillow case and tack (baste) the canvas in the corner. Work the cross stitch design using three strands of cotton.

1 Once complete, fray and remove the canvas threads one at a time. Press on the reverse side. Stitch the same monogram on the corner of a matching sheet or duvet cover.

Miniature Picture

CONTEMPORARY

These tiny frames are very popular and this design would make a delightful gift for a partner or friend.

YOU WILL NEED

15cm (6in) square of 36 count linen

small embroidery frame (flexihoop)

stranded cotton Anchor 133, 152, 226, 289

tapestry needle

ready-made frame with a 5cm (2in) window

6cm (2½in) square of wadding (batting)

double-sided tape

scissors

WORKING THE CROSS STITCH

Fit the linen into the frame (flexihoop) and work the cross stitch border using a single strand of cotton over two threads. Complete the heart and work the backstitch to finish the design and press on the reverse side.

1 To make up: remove the back from the frame and use the card insert to mount the embroidery. Stick the wadding (batting) to the card, trim the embroidery to an 8cm (3in) square and stretch the fabric over the wadding, sticking it down on the reverse side.

2 Fit the embroidery into the frame. Add another layer of card (cardboard) if required and fit the back.

Anchor	Backstitch
289	226
152	
133	☆ Middle point
226	

CAFETIÈRE COVER

CONTEMPORARY

Keep fresh coffee warm with this stylish cover, designed to fit a standard one-litre (two-pint) cafetière.

YOU WILL NEED

20 x 36cm (8 x 14in) white 14 count Aida

tacking (basting) thread

needle

interlocking bar frame

stranded cotton Anchor 148, 360, 370, 373, 398, 846

tapestry needle

scissors

30cm (12in) blue and white patterned fabric

15 x 28cm (6 x 11in) wadding (batting)

pins

sewing machine

sewing thread

bodkin

WORKING THE CROSS STITCH

Tack (baste) guidelines across the middle of the Aida in both directions and work the cross stitch using two strands of cotton. Once complete, work the backstitch and press the embroidery on the reverse side.

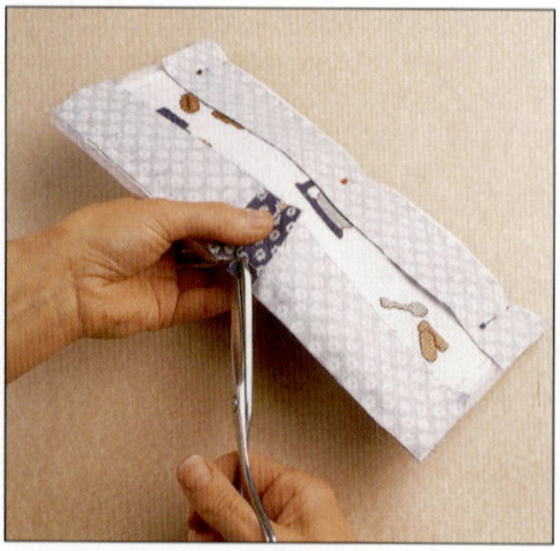

1 To make up: cut the embroidered panel and a piece of patterned fabric the same size as the wadding (batting). Tack the layers together with the wadding in between the fabrics. Cut three 6 x 38cm (2½ x 15in) strips of patterned fabric. With right sides facing, pin one piece along the bottom edge of the cover. Cut the other two strips in half. Cut a "v" in the centre of the top seam allowance. Fold over a 5mm (¼in) turning at one end of two of the short strips and butt the folds in the centre. Pin and tack along the top edge, and stitch using a 12mm (½in) seam allowance.

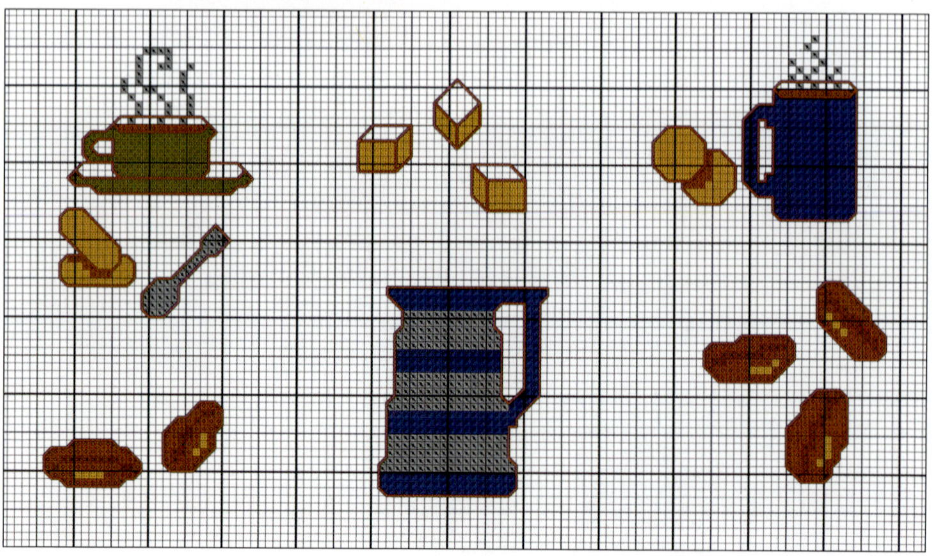

Anchor			Backstitch
846	360	398	360
373	370	148	

2 Turn under 12mm (½in) and fold the bindings to the reverse side. Pin and tack in position. Snip the top fold of the binding and tuck the end inside. Slip stitch along each side of the "v" and along the edges of the binding.

3 Cut two bias strips of patterned fabric about 30cm (12in) long and make them into rouleaux. Tack one to the middle of each side with the long end facing on to the cover. Pin and tack (baste) the remaining binding strips to the sides. Stitch to the edge of the top and bottom bindings. Trim the ends, turn in and fold the binding to the reverse side. Slip stitch the binding to complete the cafetière cover.

SHELF BORDER

CONTEMPORARY

Stitch this smart teddy bear border, sewing a different coloured bow tie on each bear, and make a matching cushion.

YOU WILL NEED

10cm (4in) wide Aida band with red edges, Zweigart E7195

measuring tape

scissors

pins

tacking (basting) thread

needle

stranded cotton Anchor 369, 370, 403

for bow ties 4, 6; 38, 42; 108, 111; 217, 208; 293, 297

tapestry needle

sewing thread

double-sided tape or coloured drawing pins

WORKING THE CROSS STITCH

Measure the length of the shelf and cut a piece of Aida band the same length plus 5cm (2in) for turnings. Each bear is about 8cm (3in) wide. Decide on the spacing of the bears and mark the centre line of each with a pin. Tack (baste) guidelines across the band at each pin and again along the middle of the band to mark the centre of each bear. Work the cross stitch using two strands of cotton, changing the colours in the bow ties on each bear. Once complete, work the backstitch using two strands of cotton and press on the reverse side.

1 To make up: trim and turn under a narrow hem at each end of the band. You could either use coloured drawing pins or double-sided tape to fix the border in position on the shelf.

NEEDLECRAFT TIP

To make a matching cushion panel, divide a 40cm (16in) square of 7 count canvas in four. Allowing a 5cm (2in) margin round the outside edge, cross stitch a bear in the middle of each square using tapestry wool, and fill in the background to match the decor of the room.

Anchor

370

403

369

38

42

Backstitch

— 403

☆ Middle point

CHILD'S WAISTCOAT

CONTEMPORARY

Denim can be given a much softer appearance with the addition of some simple appliqué flowers and big bold cross stitches.

WORKING THE CROSS STITCH

Using the vanishing marker pen, measure and mark dots every 1.5cm (5/8in) round the front and bottom edges of the waistcoat. Sew large pink cross stitches using all six strands of cotton, slipping the needle between the layer of denim to get to the next mark. Sew two tiny back stitches on the reverse side to secure the thread, and trim neatly.

YOU WILL NEED

child's denim waistcoat

vanishing marker pen

ruler

stranded cotton Anchor 254, 894, 939

embroidery needle

scraps of cotton fabric

15cm (6in) square of fusible bonding web

scissors

four small 4-hole buttons

1 To make up: iron fusible bonding web on to the reverse side of the fabric scraps and cut out 16 petals. Remove the paper backing and iron the petals in position on the pockets and on the back of the waistcoat. Sew the petals in place with cross stitches.

2 Sew a button in the middle of each flower with blue stranded cotton. Sew a small green cross stitch in the corners of the top pocket and a row along the top of the lower pockets. Thread blue stranded cotton underneath the cross stitches on the pockets to finish.

CHILD'S BAG

CONTEMPORARY

This bag will appeal to all ages and will become a firm favourite with children and young teenagers to hold their bits and pieces.

YOU WILL NEED

28 x 100cm (11 x 39in) blue gingham
scissors
stranded cotton Anchor 225, 311, 894, 1028
embroidery needle
5 x 25cm (2 x 10in) pink denim
fusible bonding web
18 x 46cm (7 x 18in) blue denim
pins
sewing machine
sewing thread
tacking (basting) thread
1.5cm (5/8in) button

WORKING THE CROSS STITCH

Cut a piece of gingham 10 x 14cm (4 x 5½in) and press under a small 1cm (3/8in) turning all round. Using three strands of cotton, sew the cross stitch border. Iron fusible bonding web on to the reverse side of a 5cm (2in) square of pink denim. Cut out three small hearts, remove the backing paper and iron on to the gingham. Sew in place with tiny stitches and stitch a blue cross in the middle of each heart to complete. Press on the reverse side.

1 To make up: fold the blue denim in half crossways and open out. Pin the gingham patch on the top half and stitch. With the embroidery to the inside, fold the denim in half again and stitch both sides. Make a slightly narrower gingham lining in the same way and insert into the bag. Turn over a 2.5cm (1in) hem. With right sides facing, fold the pink denim strip in half lengthways and stitch the long edge. Trim and press the seam open, then turn through and press again with the seam at the centre back. Fold the strip to make a loop and pin under the hem at the centre back. Tack in position then stitch round the lower edge of the hem. Fold the loop back on itself and stitch.

2 Cut an 8 x 100cm (3 x 40in) strip of gingham and sew large cross stitches up the middle. Fold lengthways with the embroidery to the inside and stitch the long seam. Trim and press the seam open, then turn through and press again with the seam down the centre back. Turn under 12mm (½in) at each end of the strap and pin over the side seams. Tack (baste) and stitch securely. Sew the button on the front of the bag and sew a large cross stitch to hold the loop flat.

KITCHEN HANGING

CONTEMPORARY

Kitchens are busy places and often neglected, but you could change things by making this delightful decoration to hang on the wall.

YOU WILL NEED

15 x 30cm (6 x 12in) cream 28 count evenweave linen

scissors

tacking (basting) thread

needle

interlocking bar frame

stranded cotton DMC 312, 316, 435, 743, 3802, 3815, 3823

tapestry needle

sewing machine

sewing thread

two 11cm (4⅜in) squares of wadding (batting)

5cm (2in) of 15mm (⅝in) ribbon or tape

pins

40cm (16in) plant support or 46cm (18in) wire with the ends bent over

bay leaves and dried apple slices

WORKING THE CROSS STITCH

Cut the linen in half crossways. Tack (baste) guidelines across the middle of one piece in both directions and work the cross stitch using two strands of cotton over two threads. Once complete, work the backstitch using one strand of cotton and then press on the reverse side.

DMC			
	3802		3815
	312		3823
	316		Backstitch
	435		3823
	3827	☆	Middle point

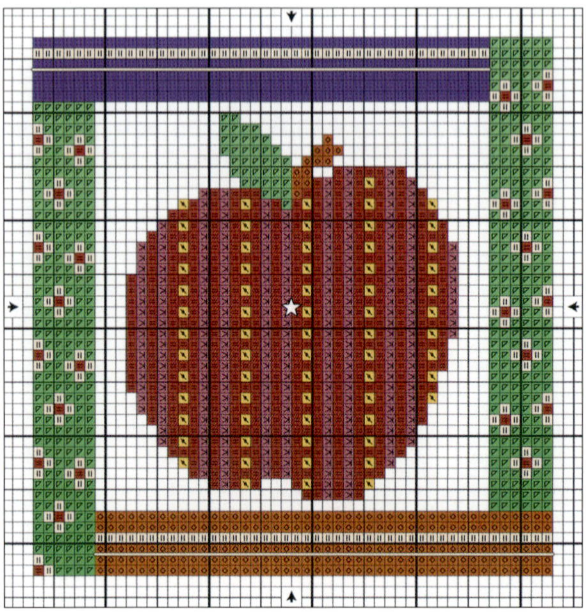

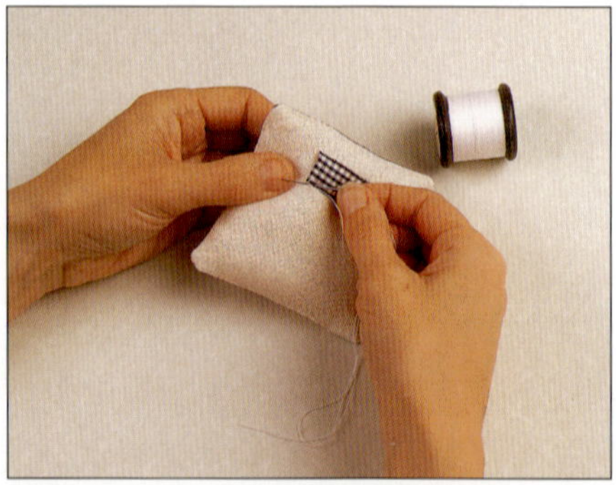

1 To make up: with the embroidery facing in, sew the two pieces of linen together. Stitch two threads away from the cross stitch and leave a 5cm (2in) gap at the bottom. Trim the seams and corners and turn through. Tuck the wadding inside and slip stitch the gap. Fold over the ends of the ribbon and pin to the back of the cushion, 2cm (¾in) down from the top. Oversew on both long sides.

2 Thread the cushion on to the wire loop. Make small holes in the bay leaves and thread on to the wire with slices of dried apple in between. Some of the larger bay leaves are bent over and threaded through again to create a looser effect. Oversew the corners of the cushion to hold them secure, loop over the ends of the wire and hang in the kitchen.

Pot Holder

CONTEMPORARY

This colourful and stylish tile design was inspired by the lemon trees and deep blue sea of the Mediterranean.

YOU WILL NEED

15cm (6in) square of white 14 count Aida

tacking (basting) thread

needle

interlocking bar frame

stranded cotton DMC 307, 322, 336

tapestry needle

scissors

pins

two 23cm (9in) squares of dark blue chintz (glazed cotton)

sewing machine

sewing thread

10cm (4in) navy cord

10cm (4in) cushion pad

WORKING THE CROSS STITCH

Tack (baste) guidelines across the middle of the Aida in both directions and work the cross stitch using two strands of cotton. Press on the reverse side once complete.

1 To make up: trim the Aida to a 13cm (5in) square, mitre the corners and turn under 12mm (½in) on all sides. Pin, tack and stitch in the centre of one piece of chintz (glazed cotton). Fold the cord in half and sew it, loop facing in, to one of the corners.

2 With right sides facing, sew the pieces of chintz together, with a gap on one side. Trim the seams and across the corners and turn through.

3 Insert the cushion pad and pin in the middle of the cover. Tack round the edges of the cushion pad and stitch. Slip stitch the gap closed to finish.

DMC

307

322

336

☆ Middle point

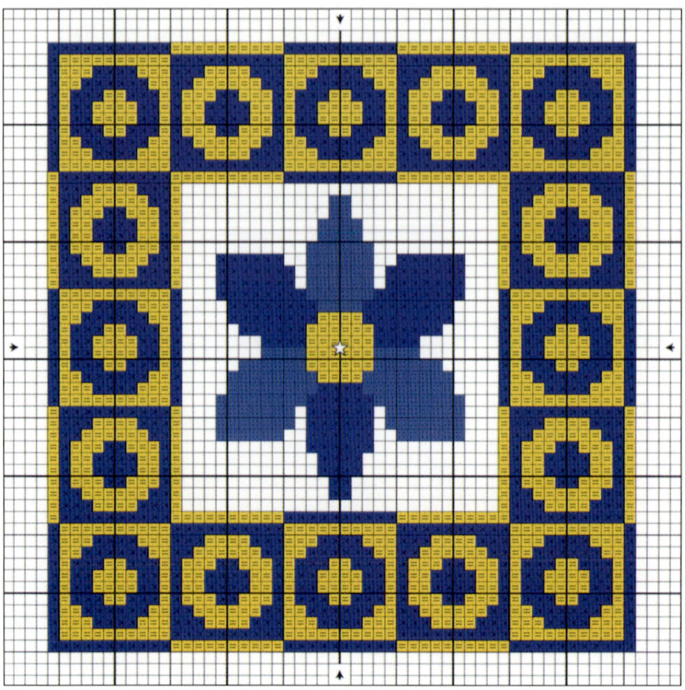

RUCKSACK

Rucksacks are extremely useful bags for all kinds of activities. Sew the zebra panel to your own bag or make this one following the easy instructions.

YOU WILL NEED

20 x 25cm (8 x 10in) white 18 count Aida

tacking (basting) thread

needle

interlocking bar frame

stranded cotton Anchor white, 22, 189, 297, 399, 403, 410

tapestry needle

paper

pencil

scissors

pins

From 1.50m (1⅝yd) of 115cm (45in) wide berry canvas, cut the following pieces: a 31 x 77cm (12 x 30in) back panel; a 56 x 77cm (22 x 30in) front panel; a 31 x 13cm (12 x 5in) base; two 28 x 19cm (11 x 7in) flap pieces; and two 8 x 69cm (3 x 27in) straps

sewing machine

sewing thread

four large "D" rings

10 large eyelets and tool

white cotton cord

button

14 x 18cm (5½ x 7in) fusible bonding web

WORKING THE CROSS STITCH

Tack (baste) guidelines across the middle of the Aida in both directions and work the cross stitch border using two strands of cotton. Next, work the zebra design and press on the reverse side once complete.

1 To make up the rucksack: pin the front and back panels together down both long sides and stitch together. Press the seams flat and fold in half with the seams to the inside. Tack the raw edges together, matching the seams. Top stitch round the folded edge and again 5cm (2in) away. Cut two 5 x 15cm (2 x 6in) pieces from the remaining canvas. Turn under 12mm (½in) on the long sides, fold in half and top stitch down both sides. Slide two "D" rings on to each strap, fold the straps in half and pin, with the rings facing on to the bag.

2 Pin and tack the base to the bottom of the bag. Snip the corners and stitch. Pin the flap pieces together and cut a half circle at one of the shorter sides to form a curved edge. Sew around the curved edge, trim the seam and snip the curves. Turn through. Roll the seam between your fingers then press and top stitch. For the straps, fold under a short end, then make as before. Pin and tack the raw edge between the seams and just below the second top stitching line. Pin the bag flap on top. Stitch across the flap, fold it over the raw edges and stitch a rectangle to secure.

3 Mark the position of the eyelets round the top of the rucksack and fit them following the manufacturer's directions. Thread a cord through the eyelets and tie 5cm (2in) from each end. Unravel the cord at the ends to make tassels. Make a buttonhole on the bag flap and sew a button in place.

Anchor			
▪	403	▪	22
▪	399	▪	189
▪	white		
▪	297	☆	Middle point
▪	410		

TO FINISH

Iron fusible bonding web on to the back of the cross stitch. Peel off the backing and pin the panel to the front of the bag. Press on the reverse side and back-stitch with 22 round the panel, one row out from the last stitching. Once the panel is complete, trim to about 1.5cm (5/8in) and fray the Aida.

EGG CABINET

CONTEMPORARY

Eggs keep much better at room temperature than in the fridge. This little cabinet with a broody hen on the front is ideal.

YOU WILL NEED

25cm (10in) square of pinky beige 28 count Jobelan

tacking (basting) thread

needle

embroidery hoop (frame)

wildflower cotton one skein each of terracotta/dark blue and spice

stranded cotton DMC white, 816, 841, 842, 3031

tapestry needle

egg cabinet with a 15cm (6in) door opening

paint, Colourman 104, 109, 114 (optional)

paintbrush

rubber gloves

medium steel wool

15cm (6in) square of mount board (backing board)

strong thread

15cm (6in) square of hardboard

panel pins

hammer

WORKING THE CROSS STITCH

Wildflower cotton is a variegated colour thread, not unlike flower thread or Nordin in weight and appearance. Open out the terracotta yarn and cut out the darkest blue sections. Work the main body of the hen in the variegated wildflower cotton and the shadows and head details in the blue.

Tack (baste) guidelines across the middle of the linen in both directions and work the cross stitch using one strand of wildflower cotton. Using two strands of stranded cotton, work the rest of the cross stitch. Once complete, work the backstitch and then press on the reverse side.

DMC
- white
- 3031
- 841+842
- 841
- 816

Wildflower
- Terracotta/dark blue
- Spice
- Terracotta/dark blue (removed)

Backstitch ~ DMC
- 841

☆ Middle point

1 To make up: paint the egg cabinet with blue paint and allow it to dry completely. Paint on top with the cream paint. You may need to add a touch of terracotta paint to tone the final look in with the linen.

2 Wearing rubber gloves to protect your hands, rub down the cabinet to reveal some of the blue paint and give the cabinet a "distressed" look. Brush out all the loose dust and wipe down with a barely damp cloth.

TO FINISH

Stretch the embroidery over the mount board (backing board) and fit inside the door frame. Fit a square of hardboard at the back and fix in place with panel pins.

GIFT BAG

CONTEMPORARY

This luxurious bag with its hand-stitched monogram makes a very personal and beautiful wrapping for a special gift.

YOU WILL NEED

two 15 x 25cm (6 x 10in) pieces of metallic organza
sewing machine
sewing thread
two 15 x 25cm (6 x 10in) pieces of burgundy silk dupion (mid-weight silk)
scissors
pins
tacking (basting) thread
needle
5cm (2in) square of 14 count waste canvas
Anchor Marlitt 1034
stranded cotton Anchor 150
embroidery needle
46cm (18in) navy cord
bodkin
two navy tassels

1 To make up: fold over a 5cm (2in) hem on the short sides of the organza pieces and stitch down 4cm (1½in) on both sides. Repeat with the silk but turn up 1cm (¼in) of the hem before stitching. Trim across the corners, snip into the bottom of the stitching and turn through. With both hems facing the reverse side, layer the silk and organza together. Stitch across the hem twice, 1cm (⅜in) apart, to form a casing. Pin and tack (baste) the waste canvas in the bottom right corner, 6cm (2⅜in) from the raw edges.

2 Work the cross stitch using two strands of Marlitt and the backstitch using two strands of cotton. Once the embroidery is complete, remove the canvas threads one at a time. Press on the reverse side. Pin both sections together with right sides facing, and stitch round the three sides. Zigzag close to the stitching to neaten and trim the seam.

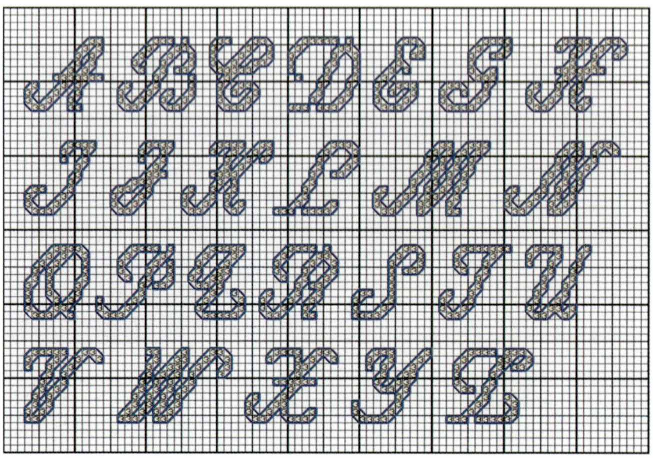

Anchor Marlitt	Backstitch ~ Anchor
1034	150

3 Turn the bag through and thread the cord through the casing with a bodkin. Slip one tassel over both cords to use as a fastening. Thread the other tassel on to one end of the cord. Overlap the ends of the cord and sew them together. Pull the cord gently until the join is inside the casing.

Quilting and Patchwork

Patchwork, appliqué and quilting have a fascinating past which reflects the social history of their makers. The cotton patchwork quilts made by the early American settlers are quite different to the richly decorated crazy patchwork loved by the Victorians. Recreate the historical style by stitching one of these beautiful traditional designs, perhaps to commemorate a wedding or birth, and create your own family heirloom.

Tools and Equipment

Many needleworkers will already have most of the equipment listed here. However, the more specialist items are readily available from craft shops and department stores.

Scissors and Cutting Tools

Dressmaker's scissors or shears Use for cutting out fabric only, so as not to dull the blades.
Paper scissors Sharpen these regularly and only use for paper.
Embroidery scissors These small, sharp and sometimes decorative scissors are used in patchwork, quilting and appliqué to cut thread and trim fabric.
Pinking shears These scissors have serrated blades and are used to prevent fraying on cut edges and also for cutting decorative edges.
Rotary cutter This tool should always be used in conjunction with a cutting mat. Use to cut out patch pieces accurately. Check blades for any nicks and replace when necessary.
Craft knife Useful for cutting out cardboard or plastic (acetate) templates. Always cut away from the body.

Measuring Tools

Metal-edged ruler Use when drafting templates and also when cutting cardboard and fabric with a rotary cutter or knife.
Metre rule Use together with a set square to cut lengths of fabric.
Set square Use to measure accurate right angles and use with a metre rule to cut lengths of fabric.
Tape measure A flexible measuring tool, useful for measuring lengths of fabric.
Pair of compasses Use for drawing circles.

Markers

Adjustable marker and gauge A useful tool for checking measurements.
Vanishing marker Marks made with this special marker will fade on contact with water or air and therefore can be used to mark designs on to fabric. A soft lead pencil can also be used, but only on the reverse of the fabric.
Dressmaker's wheel and chalk A piece of tailor's chalk can be used directly on fabric as it will brush off later. It can also be used in conjunction with a dressmaker's wheel for pouncing (see Basic Techniques).

Sewing Equipment

Needles "Sharps" are used for hand-sewing appliqué and patchwork and "betweens" for making smaller stitches.
Crewel needles These are used for working embroidery stitches and come in sizes 1 to 10. Use size 7 for cotton and sailcloth fabrics.
Pins Discard any blunt or rusty pins. Quilting pins are longer than dressmaker's pins and pass through several layers of fabric easily.
Safety pins These are sometimes used in place of pins to hold together several layers of a quilt.
Beeswax Run the wax along quilting thread before stitching so that the thread passes smoothly though the fabric.
Thimble These are essential, especially for hand quilting where the needle has to be pushed through several layers at once.
Unpicker An essential tool used to rip out machine stitches.
Iron Essential for pressing patchwork seams. If possible, use a steam iron to press seams and remove wrinkles. Otherwise use a dry iron with a damp pressing cloth.

Hoops and Frames

Embroidery hoop Two tightly fitting rings hold the fabric taut. Plastic hoops with a metal spring closure are recommended for use under the sewing machine. Use a large wooden hoop.
Embroidery frame These four-sided frames can be either freestanding or hand-held. Fabric is tightened by adjusting the side rollers.

Miscellaneous

Fabric glue This may be used in place of fusible bonding web to secure appliqué to the ground fabric.
Paper glue Spray glue is recommended for making templates.
Fabric paints and dyes Painted fabrics may be quilted and water-based non-toxic paints which are fixed by ironing are recommended. Use fabric dyes to create unusual colours, or to unify fabrics. Both hot and cold water dyes are available, although cold dyes need to be fixed. Follow the manufacturer's instructions.

Key:
1 Dressmaker's scissors or shears
2 Embroidery scissors
3 Pinking shears
4 Rotary cutter
5 Craft knife
6 Metal-edged ruler
7 Metre rule
8 Tape measure
9 Set square
10 Pair of compasses
11 Adjustable marker and gauge
12 Vanishing marker
13 Dressmaker's chalk
14 Needles
15 Beeswax
16 Quilting pins
17 Safety pins
18 Thimble
19 Unpicker
20 Embroidery hoop
21 Large hoop for quilting
22 Fabric glue
23 Fabric paints and dyes

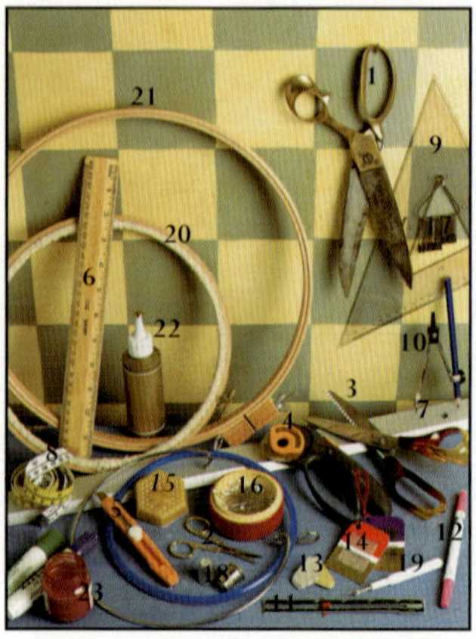

JAKAR 3011

MATERIALS

Most of the following materials are standard items used regularly in needlework. More specialist items are available from craft shops or department stores.

Acid-free paper Use to wrap textiles for safe storage.

Beads and sequins Choose from a wide selection of materials, including glass, wood, plastic and bone.

Bias binding This is a narrow strip of fabric used to cover raw edges. It can be purchased ready-made or hand-made (see Basic Techniques).

Buttons Choose from a wide variety of materials, including plastic, mother-of-pearl, wood or fabric-covered. Used as fastenings for clothing, buttons can also be used for decoration or to fasten quilts and cushions.

Dressmaker's carbon paper This is used to transfer designs to fabric.

Embroidery threads Choose from pearl cotton, a high sheen 2-ply thread; stranded embroidery thread, a 5-ply thread (separate the strands for fine work); machine embroidery thread, available in various weights and a full range of colours including metallic.

Eyelets (grommets) Available in kit form, these are used to thread cord or ribbon through for a tie fastening.

Iron-on fusible bonding web This bonds two layers of fabric together and is often used to bond an appliqué motif to the ground fabric. Templates can be traced on to the backing paper.

Iron-on interfacing Lightweight interfacing can be used on the wrong side of patch pieces to mark out the seam line for machine stitching. It can also be used to back fabric.

Isometric, graph or squared dressmaker's paper Use to accurately draw a motif or template.

Lace Strips of lace or patches of lace can be used to embellish appliqué.

Press studs (snap fasteners) These metallic fasteners can be used to secure two pieces of fabric together, such as a cushion cover opening.

Ribbon This can be used to embellish appliqué or crazy patchwork or to edge a border. Choose from a variety of materials, including velvet, satin or man-made fabric.

Stuffing This is used to fill cushions and soft toys and is made from cotton, wool and synthetic fibres.

Thread For hand-sewing, use 100% cotton thread, and for machine-sewing use 100% cotton or a polyester blend. Tacking (basting) thread is stronger than sewing thread and is used for temporarily securing layers of fabric. Quilting thread is also much stronger.

Tissue paper This is used for transferring designs and also for holding appliqué shapes together.

Tracing paper Use to trace off a design.

Trimmings These are used to make unusual edgings or to embellish a quilt or patchwork piece. Examples include fringing, pompon tape, tassels and flat ribbon tape.

Wadding (batting) This soft fabric is used as a middle layer for quilts and for filling trapunto designs. It is usually made from cotton, but is also available in silk, wool and synthetics.

Yarn Used in quilting to fill a corded quilt. It is also used for embroidery stitches and knitting.

Zip (zipper) Used to close together two open edges.

KEY:
1 Acid-free paper
2 Wadding (batting)
3 Beads and sequins
4 Bias binding
5 Buttons
6 Dressmaker's carbon paper
7 Eyelets (grommets)
8 Embroidery threads
9 Machine embroidery thread
10 Graph paper
11 Iron-on fusible bonding web
12 Iron-on interfacing
13 Lace
14 Stuffing
15 Press studs (snap fasteners)
16 Ribbon
17 Stencil card
18 Sewing thread
19 Tacking (basting) thread
20 Trimmings
21 Yarn

Fabrics

Many different types of fabric can be employed in patchwork, quilting and appliqué work. Detailed information on choosing fabric designs for your work is given in the following pages.

Calico A strong, plain-weave fabric, usually white or natural with darker flecks; available in a variety of weights.

Corduroy/needlecord (fine-wale corduroy) A plain-weave fabric with vertical pile-effect ribbing. Although it frays easily, it is suitable for appliqué and large-scale patch pieces.

Cotton Woven from the raw material, cotton is hard-wearing, and launders and presses well. Available in a wide range of plain and patterned print colours, this is the best choice for patchwork.

Felt This non-woven fabric is made from wool by compressing the fibres with moisture and heat. Felt shrinks, so is not suitable for articles that need regular washing. However, it is ideal for appliqué work as it does not fray.

Gingham Alternating stripes of coloured and white threads in the warp and weft produce this checked pattern in cotton or cotton blend fabric.

Lawn A fine crisp cotton, or cotton blend fabric, this is available in printed designs and plain colours.

Linen Woven from a natural fibre produced by the flax plant, the variable thickness of the yarn produces an uneven and attractive appearance to the fabric. Linen frays and creases easily, but is suitable as a ground fabric.

Muslin A white or natural open-weave cotton or cotton blend fabric, this is suitable for backing trapunto or corded quilts, shadow quilting and appliqué.

Organdy This fine cotton fabric is starched and is suitable for shadow work.

Organza A gauzy, crisp fabric woven from silk or synthetic fibres or a silk and synthetic blend. Available in plain colours, and with metallic and iridescent effects, it is suitable for appliqué and shadow work. It can also be used for delicate patchwork.

PVC/poly vinyl chloride (acetate) This plastic, cotton-backed cloth is not flexible like ordinary fabrics so is difficult to work with. However, it can be used for patchwork and appliqué if you lubricate your sewing machine and the machine foot before stitching.

Sateen This soft fabric has surface sheen and is more subtle than cotton or cotton blend fabrics. It is used in patchwork and is a popular choice for quilting.

Satin This shiny fabric can be woven from cotton, silk or synthetics. It frays and creases easily, but can be used to good effect in patchwork and appliqué.

Silk The queen of fabrics, silk works well for almost any project. Woven from the natural fibre produced by the silk worm, silk fabrics are lustrous and available in a wide variety of textures, colours, patterns and weights.

Shantung Woven with yarns of irregular thickness, giving an uneven surface, shantung fabric frays easily but can be used for patchwork and quilting.

Taffeta This is a plain-weave fabric with a two-tone effect. Produced in both natural and synthetic silk fibres, it is suitable for appliqué and especially effective in small patchwork.

Velvet Produced in cotton, cotton blend and synthetics, this fabric has a closely woven backing and a dense cut-pile surface. Dress velvet is lighter and more lustrous but frays easily and is difficult to handle. The fabric nap must always lie in the same direction for patchwork.

Voile This fine woven fabric is translucent and often used for shadow work. Cotton voile is finer and easier to work with than synthetic varieties.

Wool Made from woven fleece, the natural fibre has a springy texture and insulating properties. Synthetic blends mimic these properties well. However, wool does not launder easily because it is prone to shrinkage. Suitable for inlaid appliqué, light weights can also be used for patchwork.

KEY:
1 Corduroy/needlecord (fine-wale corduroy)
2 Cotton
3 Felt
4 Gingham
5 Linen
6 Organdy
7 Organza
8 PVC/poly vinyl chloride (acetate)
9 Satin
10 Silk
11 Taffeta
12 Velvet
13 Wool

Basic Techniques

The many varied projects in this book feature a wealth of design ideas employing a wide range of techniques, both old and modern, and from all four corners of the world. You will discover the secrets of San Blas appliqué, Seminole patchwork and sashiko quilting, along with shadow work, broderie perse and much more. However, there are many standard quilting, patchwork and appliqué techniques that need to be grasped before you begin a project – you will be coming across the same methods again and again.

Patchwork Techniques

Pieced patchwork is made from fabric scraps which are cut into regular shapes and then sewn together in geometric patterns to form a mosaic of cloth. The patches can be pieced or joined together by one of two basic methods: by machine or by hand. Machining is quickest, but hand sewing gives a traditional look to a finished piece with slightly irregular seams. For the beginner, working over backing papers is the best way to make precise angled shapes when piecing by hand. Whichever method is chosen, accurate templates, meticulous measuring and cutting, careful stitching and thorough pressing are all vital for a professional finish.

Templates

Accurate templates will allow you to make patches identical in size and shape that will fit perfectly together. There are several different types of template you can make or buy. You can cut them yourself from card (cardboard) or from firm, clear plastic (acetate). Alternatively, you can make window templates, which allow you to view the fabric. Always make a new template for each shape required in a project – old templates eventually become a little distorted round the edges. Templates can also be purchased ready-made in various shapes and sizes.

Patchwork templates should always include a seam allowance; in this book the seam allowance is usually 5mm (¼in). If you are using backing papers, you will need to cut two templates if using card or plastic – one with the seam allowance included for marking the fabric and one without the seam allowance for the backing paper. If using a window template, the outside edge of the frame is used to mark the fabric and the inside edge of the frame the backing paper.

Making card (cardboard) templates

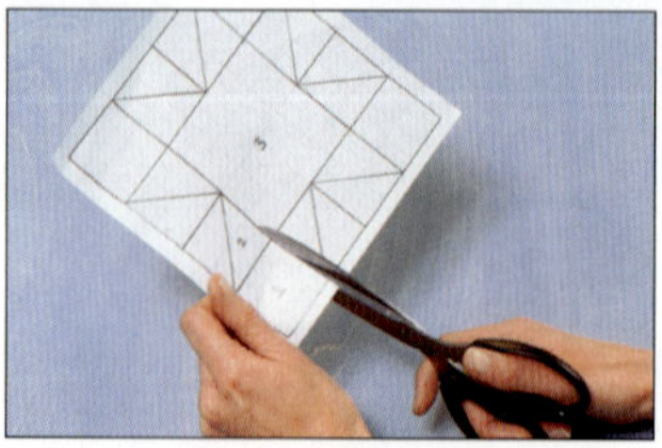

1

Transfer the design on to squared paper and cut round each shape with a sharp pair of scissors.

2

Glue the shapes to a piece of thin card (cardboard), and draw a seam allowance round each. Cut out the card.

3

Protect the seam allowance area with a thin coat of clear nail varnish.

MAKING PLASTIC (ACETATE) TEMPLATES

Place the clear plastic (acetate) over the design and draw round each shape. Then draw a seam allowance round each and cut out. Being transparent, the template can be accurately positioned on the fabric.

MAKING WINDOW TEMPLATES

Trace the shape on to card (cardboard), then draw a 5mm (¼in) seam allowance round it. Cut out the outer and inner parts, leaving a card frame the exact width of the seam allowance.

MAKING CURVED TEMPLATES

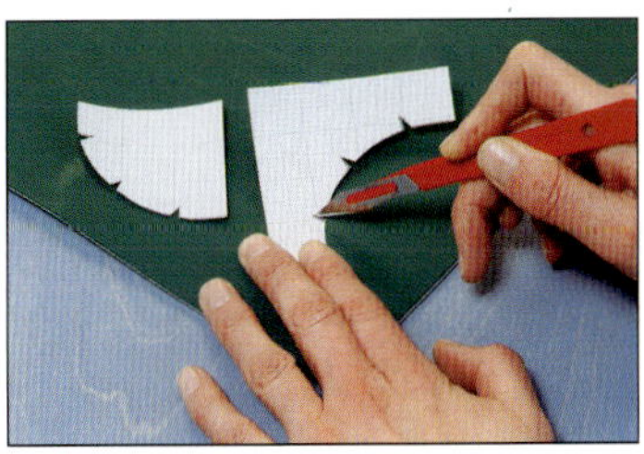

For curved blocks, mark notches on the seam lines of the pattern before cutting it into sections. Cut out each template and then carefully cut out the notches with a craft knife.

PREPARING PATCHES

Position the template on the fabric, lining up one straight edge with the grain of the fabric. Draw round it on to the reverse of the fabric using a vanishing marker, tailor's chalk or a soft pencil. Butt the shapes together to ensure a good fit.

CUTTING OUT PATCHES IN GROUPS

1

Several patches can be cut at once using this method. Fold the fabric like a concertina and then staple the card (cardboard) template to the layers.

2

Use a sharp rotary cutter or a craft knife and press hard into the cutting mat.

3

Organize the cut pieces by stringing them on a length of thread. You can store them like this and remove them one at a time.

ATTACHING BACKING PAPERS

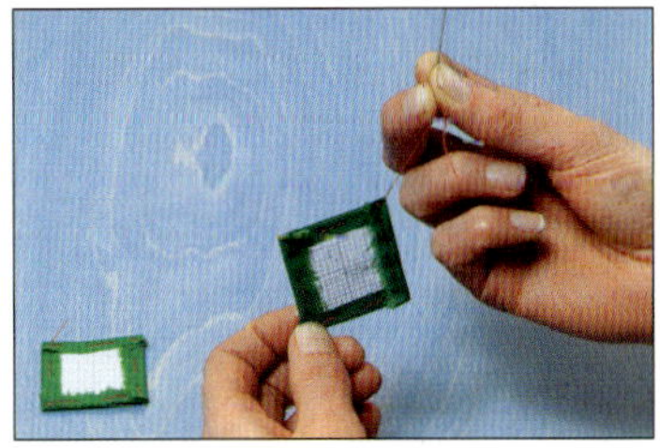

Pin the backing papers to the reverse of the fabric patches. Fold over or press the seam allowance. Leaving a short free end of thread, tack (baste) along the middle of the seam allowance to the end of the side and trim the corners. Fold over the adjacent seam allowance and continue to tack. Repeat on all sides, leaving the thread ends free so that the threads and the backing papers can be removed easily once the work has been pieced.

BACKING WITH INTERFACING

Iron-on interfacing can be used instead of backing papers. It is especially useful when machine piecing. Mark the patches on the interfacing adjacent to one another. Cut along the main lines first and then cut out the individual blocks. Iron these on to the reverse of the fabric, then mark a seam allowance round the interfacing on the fabric. Cut out the patches individually with scissors or as a group with a rotary cutter.

PIECING OR JOINING PATCHES

Lay out the cut patches to work out the final arrangement. When you are happy with the design, you can begin piecing the patches. There are several different methods of doing this, depending on whether you are piecing by hand or using a sewing machine.

HAND PIECING

Right sides facing, pin the prepared patches together. First pin each corner, and then pin at equidistant points along the side. Join the patches with a small, neat whip stitch – or overstitch – as shown. Insert the needle in one corner and work across to the other, removing the pins as you go.

MACHINE PIECING PATCHES BY THE FLAG METHOD

The flag method enables you to join several pairs of patches in one go. Right sides facing, pin the patches in pairs. Stitch along the seam line using the presser foot as a guide, removing the pins as you go. Leave a short uncut thread between each pair. Remove the flags and cut into units. Join enough pairs to make up the patched piece. To avoid bulk, always press the patch seams flat to one side and not open as in dressmaking.

JOINING PATCHES INTO ROWS

For both hand and machine piecing, make sure that the seam allowances match up perfectly before you pin and stitch the rows together. Press the seams in opposite directions to reduce bulk.

SETTING-IN – BOX PATCHWORK

Setting-in is the term used when a patch is sewn into an angle. To make the angled piece, stitch two pieces together along the seam line, stop stitching 5mm (¼in) from the end of the seam, and secure with back stitch. Right sides facing, pin one angled piece to the edge of the patch. Stitch from the corner out to the edge, then swing the adjacent angled piece to the other side of the patch, again stitching from the corner out. Press the two seam allowances of the set-in patch toward the angled piece.

SASHING AND BORDERS

These are two very different things although they are cut and sewn in the same way. Sashings are fabric strips used within a design to separate individual patches, or blocks of patches. Borders go round the edges of the work to cover and hide any raw edges.

BLOCKED BORDERS

For the long sides of a border, cut the strips the same length as the quilt. For the short sides, cut the strips the width of the quilt plus the double width of the border. Right sides facing, sew the long strips to the piece first, and then the short strips. Press the seam allowance away from the direction of quilting.

BORDERS WITH MITRED CORNERS

Cut the border strips as above, adding an extra 5cm (2in) to all four for mitring, and stitch to the quilt in the usual way. To mitre a corner by hand, press a border strip down at a 45 degree angle, pin and slip stitch on the right side to secure in place. To mitre by machine, work from the wrong side, pressing all the corners back at a 45 degree angle. Pin together and stitch along the fold. Trim the seam allowance and press flat.

LOG CABIN PATCHWORK

Always work from the middle out. Starting with a central square, pin and stitch strips to the square one by one, trimming each strip to the centre as you go. Work round the block anti-clockwise – each new strip will be slightly longer than the previous one. Continue adding strips until you reach the required size. Edge with mitred borders. Often several Log Cabin blocks are made and then stitched together to make a quilt.

QUILTING TECHNIQUES

Quilts are made from three layers: a top piece which is decorated, a layer of wadding (batting) for warmth and a backing piece. These layers are held together with lines of stitching which can be worked in a grid, straight rows or elaborate patterns. Quilted borders, medallions, knots and detailed corners are all possible. Originally, lines of tiny running stitches were worked to offer more warmth. Modern technology and new fibres have made this unnecessary, although the stitches still need to be of equal length.

TACKING (BASTING) QUILTS

Sandwich the wadding (batting) between the top piece and the backing, with the fabrics right side out. Tack (baste) together securely. Knot a long length of thread in a contrasting colour. Work from the middle out, tacking the layers together horizontally, vertically and diagonally. If quilting by machine or with a hoop, add extra lines round the edges.

HAND QUILTING

Place the inner hoop on a flat surface, lay the tacked fabric on top. Place the outer hoop over both and screw the nut to tighten the hoop. Stitch from the top, using your free hand to guide the needle up and down through the layers below.

MACHINE QUILTING

For quilting grids and straight lines, a quilting foot will allow the machine to move more easily over thick fabrics. For free-form quilting, remove the foot and lower the foot lever. Stretch the fabric taut either with a hoop or your hands, and stitch slowly so that you can accurately guide the stitches.

Appliqué Techniques

Appliqué can be worked in a variety of fabrics, including silk, wool and cotton, and strong, closely woven fabric is possibly the best choice. Felt is popular for appliqué designs because it does not fray. Design ideas are limitless and virtually any shape can be used. Broderie perse, Hawaiian appliqué and stained glass appliqué, together with cut and sew, inlaid and reverse appliqué methods, are just a few of the techniques featured in the book.

Iron-on fusible bonding web

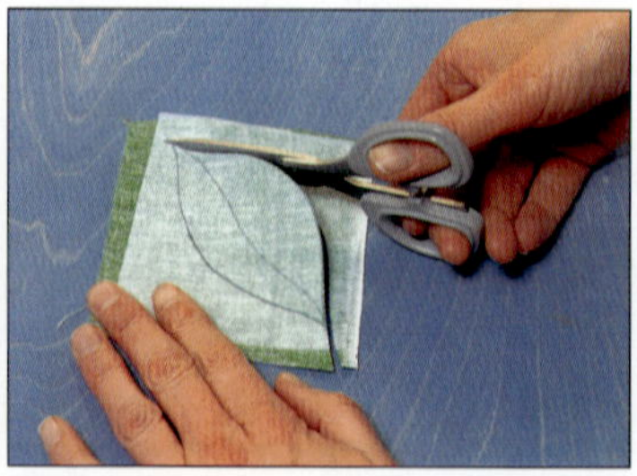

1

A quick and easy way to attach appliqué to the fabric. Because the appliqué fabric is fused to the web, it won't fray. Trace the outline on to the fusible web.

2

Roughly cut out the design and iron this on to the fabric. Cut round the outline with a sharp pair of scissors, a rotary cutter or craft knife.

3

Peel off the backing paper and iron, fusing the motif to the main fabric. Set the machine to a zig zag and stitch round the raw edge of the motif.

Pin tacking (basting)

Tack (baste) the seam allowance round the appliqué design. Mark the placement lines on the right side of the fabric. Arrange the appliqué shapes on the fabric following these lines. First position the background pieces, and then layer any extra pieces on top. Alternatively, attach the pieces with double-sided tape.

Below: This simple appliqué sunflower has been stitched on by hand.

STITCHES

Straight stitch is the standard machine sewing stitch, worked in straight lines and secured by back stitch at the end of each seam. Machine tacking stitches are worked by setting the machine to the longest stitch. To attach appliqué and crazy patchwork, set the machine to a close zig zag stitch and work a row of satin stitches. The following hand stitches are used throughout the book.

RUNNING STITCH

This is the main stitch used for hand quilting. It is also used for sewing seams in patchwork and quilting. Stitches should be of an even length, no bigger than 3mm (⅛in), and can be run a few at a time. Running stitch is also used in sashiko and kantha work.

HOLBEIN STITCH

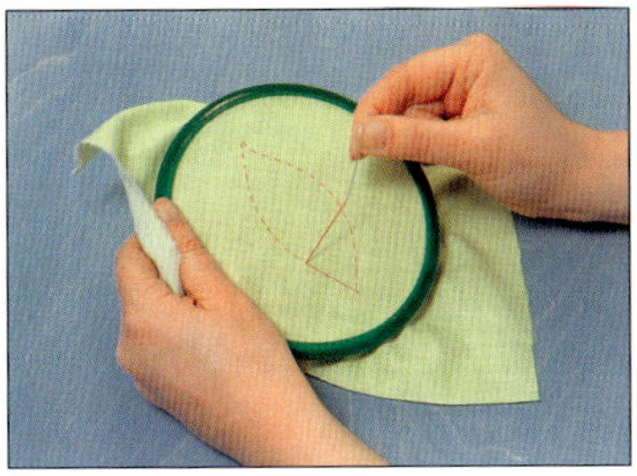

Work a row of running stitch in one direction and then fill in the spaces on the return journey.

SLIP-STITCH

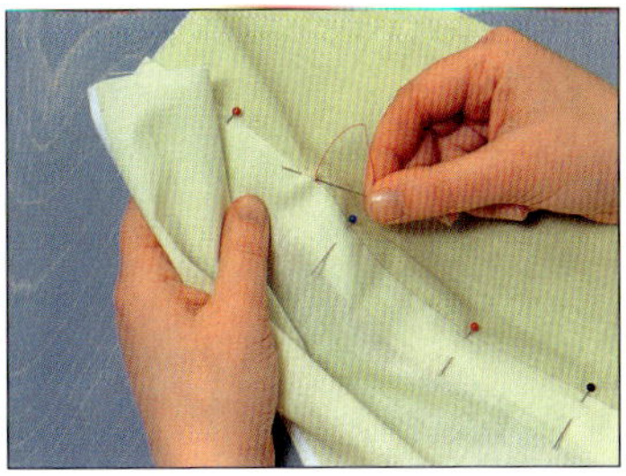

This stitch is used to secure a finished edge to another surface, like an appliqué or a binding. With the needle, catch a thread under the fabric together with a single thread on the fold of the fabric, spacing these small stitches evenly apart.

WHIP STITCH

Also known as oversewing and overcasting, this small straight stitch is used to hold together two edges. Work from back to front, inserting the needle at an angle and picking up a thread from each piece at the same time.

STAB STITCH

This stitch replaces running stitch when quilting thick fabric. Hold the needle perpendicular to the fabric, and work one stitch at a time. It is also used to outline individual shapes on quilted fabric.

BLANKET STITCH

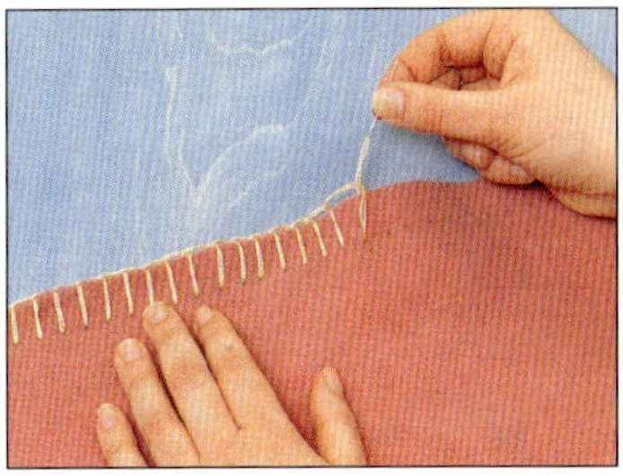

Blanket, or buttonhole, stitch is ideal for finishing off raw or scalloped edges on fabrics that don't fray, such as felt or blanket. It can also be worked over a fold. Insert the needle into the back so that it points up to the raw edge, wind the loose thread over the needle and pull through the loop. Make a decorative feature of large blanket stitches by sewing them in a contrasting colour.

General Techniques

Finding the grain of the fabric

It is necessary to find the grain to straighten raw edges. Nick the fabric just below the raw edge, pull a thread gently across the fabric and cut along the line made. You can pull threads to fringe a piece of fabric and also to mark a grid. Sometimes you will need to find the straight grain in order to centre a motif.

Enlarging a design

Trace the motif on to squared paper. On another sheet of paper, mark out the same number of squares to the required size of the finished design. Copy the motif on to the new grid so that the lines of the design correspond exactly with the original.

BELOW: This drawstring bag shows designs transferred on to the patchwork squares.

Transferring a design on to fabric

1

Copy the design on to dressmaker's carbon paper. Place the carbon on the reverse of the fabric and then trace over the outline with a pen, pressing heavily.

2

Pouncing is used to transfer a design on to the right side of the fabric for an appliqué or quilting design. Trace over the design on to paper with a dressmaker's wheel or an unthreaded sewing machine, so that the design appears as a broken line. Push tailor's chalk through the pierced paper with a brush or sponge to mark the fabric.

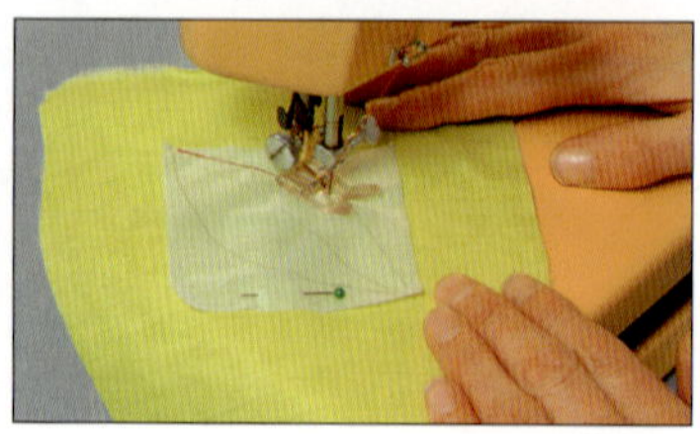

3

Trace the design on to tissue paper, pin to the wrong side of the fabric then machine round the outline. Rip away the tissue paper to reveal the outline. This method is good for fine or fragile fabric.

MAKING AND USING BIAS STRIPS

Bias strips are used for binding, piping and also in the stained glass appliqué method. Cut a square on the straight grain, fold it in half diagonally and stitch together the open edges. Press the seam allowance flat and trim. Mark parallel lines on to the fabric and then roll it into a tube so that the top edge aligns with the first marked line. Pin and stitch along this line. Press the seam flat and trim. Cut along the marked lines into one long continuous strip of bias binding. Alternatively, cut several strips on the diagonal and then join them together, pressing the seam allowance flat.

BINDING A MITRED CORNER

1

Stitch along one edge, reducing the size of the stitches near the corner. Stop stitching 5mm (¼in) from the corner, lift the presser foot and swivel the quilt to stitch the next edge. A tuck will form in the binding at the corner. Lower the presser foot, and carry on stitching the next side.

2

Fold over the binding, pin and sew close to the previous stitching line. Fold the tuck diagonally to mitre the corners and slip-stitch in place.

ENVELOPE CUSHION COVER

For the front, cut a square to fit the cushion pad, adding 1cm (½in) seam allowance on all sides. Cut a back piece 2.5cm (1in) bigger on one side, and then cut in half lengthways. Press, and sew a 1cm (½in) hem along the cut edge of both back pieces. Right sides facing, pin the front to the back pieces so that one hem lies slightly over the other. Sew round all four seams and, if directed, stitch in piping or fringing now. Clip the corners, press and turn right side out.

STRETCHING AND MOUNTING A PICTURE

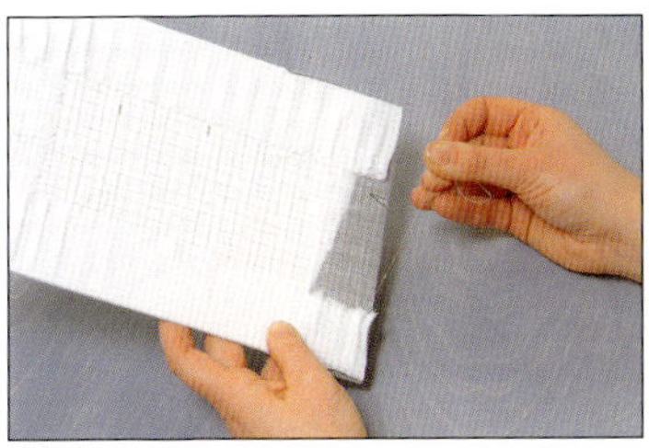

Stretch the finished piece taut over the backing. Using a strong thread, stitch back and forth, joining the raw edges in a criss cross pattern and pulling the thread tightly as you go. Work the long sides first, then repeat with the short sides. Secure to the backing board with tape.

DRAWSTRING BAG

1

Pin together two rectangles in main fabric and sew round three sides, leaving the top short side open. Cut two rectangles the same size in lining and stitch the two long sides. Stitch part way across the short end, break off for 5cm (2in), then stitch to the end. Right sides facing, pin the two bags together and stitch a continuous line round the top edge. Trim and clip the seam. Pull the bag through the lining. Press and slip-stitch to close the gap.

2

Push the lining into the bag and press flat. For the channel, machine stitch two parallel lines, 1cm (½in) from the top edge and 1cm (½in) apart. Make a hole in the seam between the two rows of stitching with a stitch unpicker and thread the drawstring through.

Velvet Scarf

Squares arranged on the diagonal form the serrated edge to the patchwork borders on this wide scarf. The patches are cut from both silk and velvet to create an interesting texture.

You Will Need

thin card (cardboard) and pencil

craft knife

dressmaker's scissors

scraps of silk and velvet in pink, rust and brown

1m x 90cm (40in x 36in) velvet

sewing machine and matching thread

iron

dressmaker's pins

1.8m x 40cm (72in x 16in) silk lining

Preparation

Follow the plan below. Each border uses 26 squares. Make the templates 9cm (3½in) square. Cut out 24 rust squares, 14 pink squares, 14 brown (velvet and silk) squares. Halve three of the pink squares and cut one diagonally into quarters. Halve six of the brown squares. Follow the plan and arrange the patches in two borders. Cut the velvet widthways and sew into a piece 2 m (2yd) long.

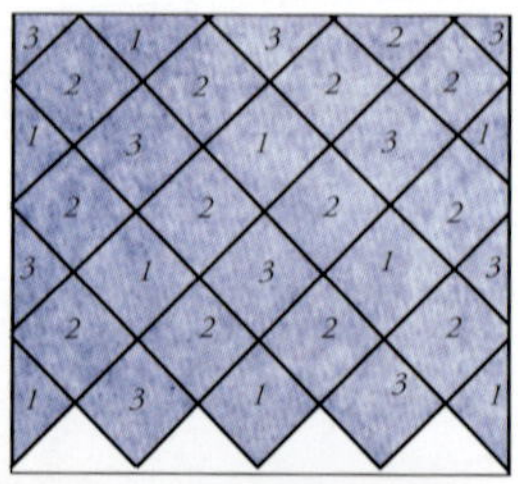

Key: 1 = brown
2 = rust
3 = pink

1

Sew the squares into strips and then join the strips into one piece (see Basic Techniques). Insert the triangles in the sides and top to make three straight edges. Press the seams. Make the second border.

2

Measure the borders and trim the velvet to fit. Pin the straight edge of each border to the velvet. Machine stitch close to the edge and then appliqué with a zig zag stitch. Trim and press.

3

Right sides facing, pin the velvet piece to the silk lining. Stitch round the seams leaving a gap on one long edge. Trim and clip the corners. Turn right side out and press. Slipstitch the opening.

Velvet Slippers

These children's slippers are made from velvet and silk scraps. The tops have been quilted with tiny kantha stitches. These repetitive filling stitches can run in any direction and are commonly worked on Indian kantha quilts.

You Will Need

dressmaker's paper and pencil
dressmaker's scissors
30cm x 90cm (12in x 36in) velvet
30cm x 90cm (12in x 36in) silk
15cm x 90cm (6in x 36in) calico
needle and tacking (basting) thread
craft knife
pair of insoles
fabric marker
fabric glue
metallic thread
sewing machine and matching thread
dressmaker's pins
pair of soles
4 small tassels

Preparation

Enlarge and draw the templates on to paper and cut out four slipper tops in both velvet and silk. Cut out four calico lining pieces and tack (baste) these to the reverse of the velvet. Cut a pair of insoles to size. Trace round the insoles on to a piece of velvet, adding a seam allowance and cut out.

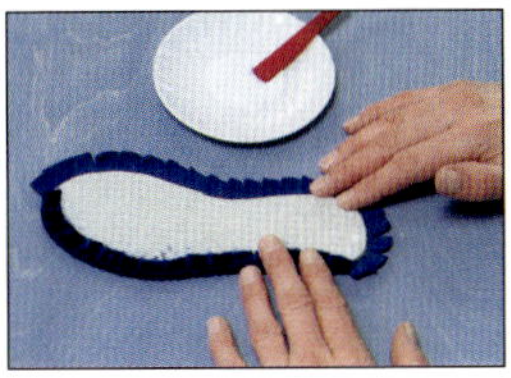

1

Place the insoles on the reverse of the velvet. Clip the seam allowance and turn under. Glue the edges, pressing firmly in place.

2

Decorate the velvet tops with metallic thread using tiny running stitches (see Basic Techniques). Join the tops along the centre seam. Right sides facing, stitch the velvet to the silk lining along the front edge. Turn right side out and tack (baste) the raw edges.

3

Pin the tops to the insoles and secure with slip-stitch.

To Finish

Glue the soles to the base of the slippers, hiding the turnings. Leave to dry. Sew the tassels to the slipper tops.

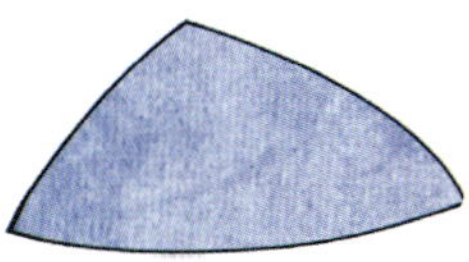

Calico Backing 50%

Top 50%

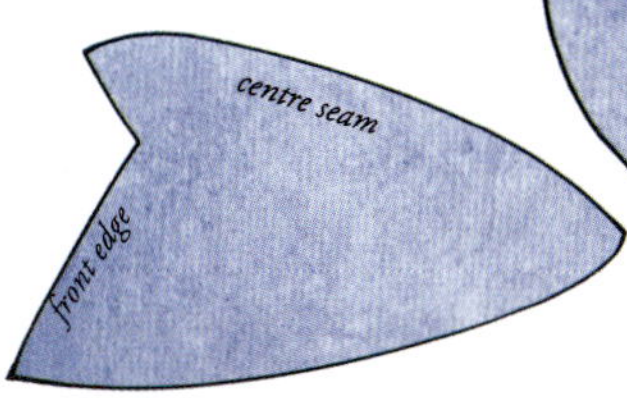

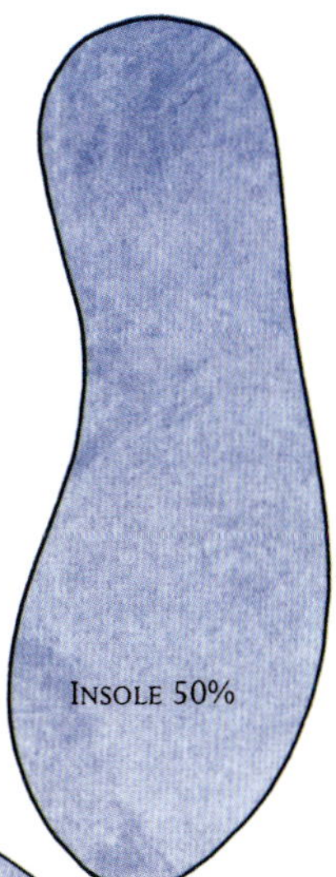

Crazy Patchwork Cushion

The appliqué on this cushion looks like crazy paving. The irregularly shaped patches are arranged at random. Choose fabrics of a similar texture and with varying tonal values for a professional look.

You Will Need

dressmaker's scissors

60cm x 90cm (24in x 36in) cotton fabric

thin card (cardboard) and pencil

scraps of fabric in six contrasting patterns

dressmaker's pins

needle and tacking (basting) thread

matching thread

iron

1.8m (72in) cotton furnishing (upholstery) fringe

sewing machine

38cm (15in) zip (zipper)

46cm (18in) square cushion pad

Preparation

Cut the cotton fabric into two 46cm (18in) squares. Enlarge the diagram and cut card (cardboard) templates to cover one square. A rough, open-textured cotton was used for the base, complemented with patches cut from scraps of furnishing fabrics with interesting, open weaves.

To Finish

Press the squares flat and, right sides facing, pin the fringe to one square. Stitch into the seams as you make up the cover. Insert the zip (zipper). Insert the cushion pad.

1

Cut out the crazy patches from the scraps of fabric, adding a 5mm (¼in) turning all round.

2

Tack (baste) the templates to the scraps. Pin and tack to the cushion fabric.

3

Slip-stitch round each shape in matching thread, to secure to the base.

Diagram of Whole Cover 33⅓%

Hatpin Cushion

An appliqué of crazy patchwork, in velvet, satin and silk, has been stitched into an extra large pin cushion for storing decorative hatpins.

You Will Need

dressmaker's scissors
dressmaker's paper
pair of compasses and pencil
scraps of silk, velvet and satin
50cm x 90cm (20in x 36in) calico
dressmaker's pins
sewing machine and matching threads
iron
wadding (batting)
needle

Preparation

Cut out the templates in paper. You will need a circular template with a diameter of 18cm (7in) for the base/top, and a rectangular one measuring 52cm x 10cm (20½in x 4in) for the band. Cut a silk base, and one top and one band in calico. Cut a strip on the bias in both velvet and silk measuring 52cm x 5cm (20½in x 2in).

1

Join the short ends of the calico band together and stitch the band to the silk base. Pin and stitch the calico top to the calico band leaving a small gap to turn through. Trim, press and fill with wadding (batting). Stitch the gap closed.

2

Cut out lots of random patches from the scraps. Turn under the raw edges and machine stitch the patches together, laying them over each other to make a piece of crazy patchwork. Cut out a top, using the template. Make a narrow patched strip from silk and velvet squares 52cm (20½in) long. Position the velvet and silk bias strips side by side and place the patched strip over the join. Pin, turn the raw edges under and machine stitch.

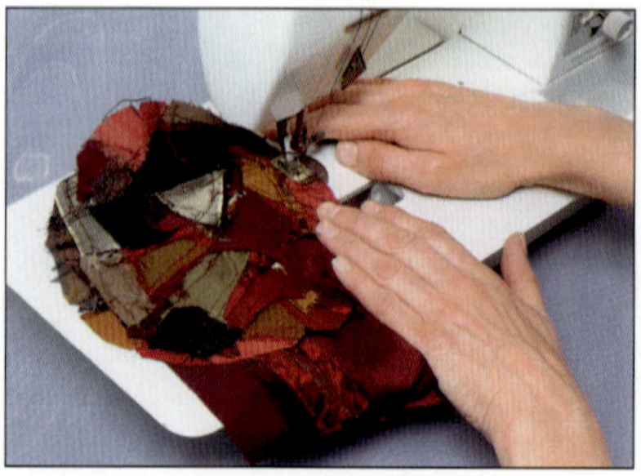

3

With right sides together, stitch the patched band to the patched top. Press and turn right side out.

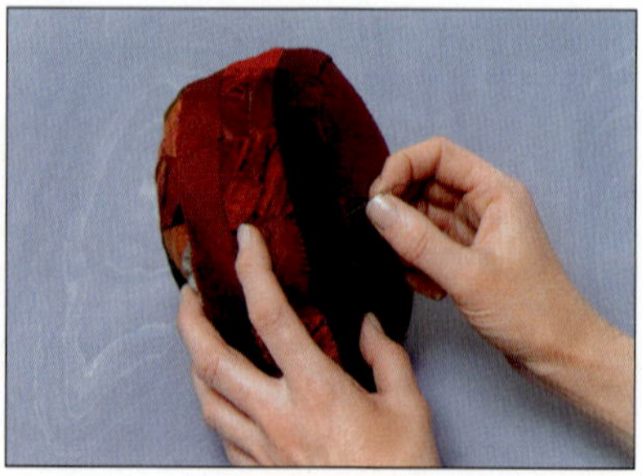

4

Pull the outer patched cover over the inner pad, turn a hem and slip-stitch along the edge.

Square Linen Quilt

This *faux* antique, square quilt is made up in white linen. The quilt is knotted in perlé thread in an even grid pattern, and stitches run round the borders in three lines to complement the look.

You Will Need

vanishing marker
90cm (36in) square white linen
ruler
dressmaker's pins
needle and tacking (basting) thread
90cm (36in) square wadding (batting)
2 skeins navy perlé thread
crewel needle
90cm (36in) square calico
matching thread
dressmaker's scissors

1

Using the vanishing marker, mark the linen with a dot at intervals of 5cm (2in) down the length. Centre the positioning so that the first dot at top, bottom and side are an equal distance away from the edges of the fabric. Draw out a single thread the width of the fabric at each point (see Basic Techniques).

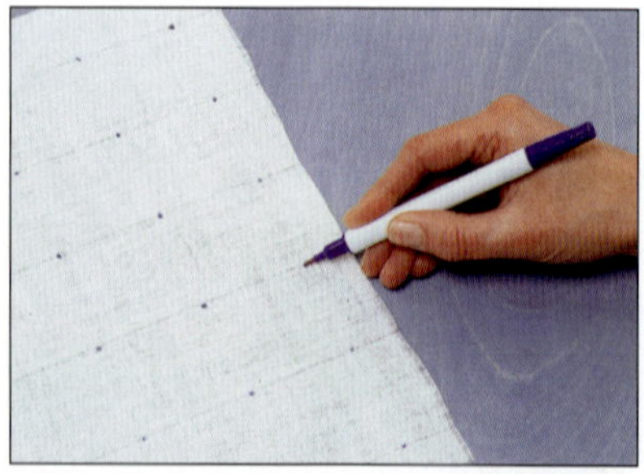

2

Turn the fabric to the wrong side and measure along the pulled lines every 5cm (2in) and mark a dot with the vanishing marker. Turn over again.

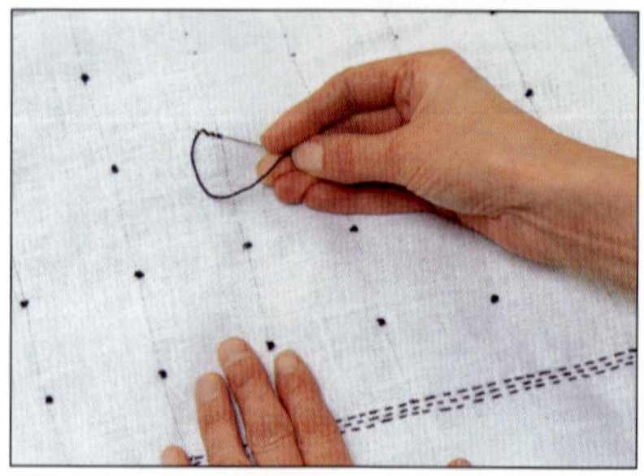

3

Tack (baste) the linen to the wadding (batting). Using the perlé thread, make a French knot over each dot, starting in the centre and working out. Run three parallel lines of running stitch, just outside the first dots marked, to edge the quilt.

To Finish

Pin the calico backing to the linen, with right sides facing. Machine stitch round the edges, leaving a gap. Turn the quilt right sides out, slip-stitch the opening closed and press. Top stitch round the edges, just inside the decorative border, to hold the wadding (batting) in place.

BATHROOM CURTAINS

These floaty curtains have a shell design appliquéd in delicate shades of pink on to fine voile. The raw edges of the shell are closely covered with buttonhole stitch to prevent them from fraying.

YOU WILL NEED

pair of voile curtains
tracing paper and pen
25cm x 90cm (10in x 36in) cream voile
dressmaker's carbon paper
dressmaker's pins
needle and tacking (basting) thread
embroidery hoop
pale pink perlé thread
crewel needle
embroidery scissors

PREPARATION

Make or buy a pair of voile curtains to fit your windows. Draw a curtain plan to work out where to position the shells and how many you will need. The amount of voile specified is sufficient for six appliqué shells.

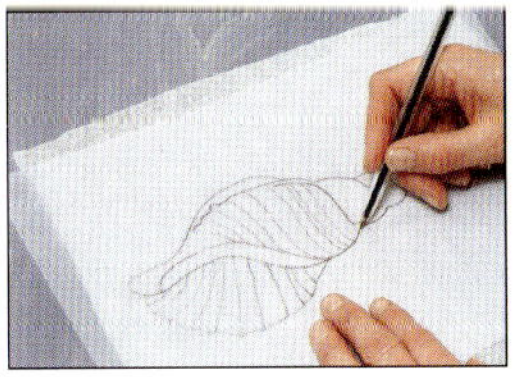

1

Trace the template on to tracing paper. Place over a piece of voile with dressmaker's carbon paper sandwiched in between. Draw over the outlines in pen to transfer the design.

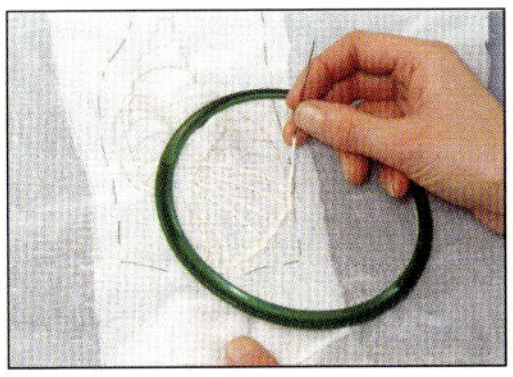

2

Aligning the fabric grain, position and tack (baste) the voile to the right side of the curtain. Place in the hoop and, using perlé thread, work the outlines in tiny buttonhole stitch and the interior lines in a mixture of stem stitch and running stitch (see Basic Techniques).

TO FINISH

Make as many appliqué shells as you need. Using embroidery scissors, carefully trim the excess voile round each shell's outline as close to the stitching as possible.

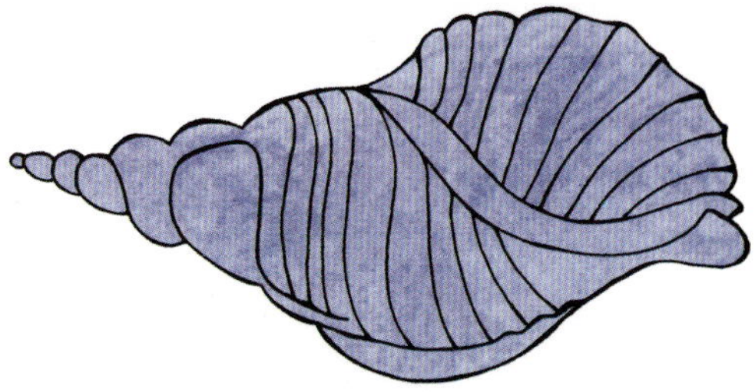

TEAPOT COVER

Stab stitches are worked around the outline of the printed floral motifs to raise and emphasize them on this quilted teapot cover. The teapot sits snugly inside the closed fabric "box".

YOU WILL NEED

dressmaker's paper and pencil

dressmaker's scissors

50cm x 90cm (20in x 36in) floral fabric

50cm x 90cm (20in x 36in) wadding (batting)

dressmaker's pins

needle and tacking (basting) thread

matching thread

small piece of Velcro

PREPARATION

Enlarge the templates. Cut four side pieces and two bases in fabric, and two side pieces and one base in wadding (batting), adding 5mm (¼in) seam allowances all round.

SIDE

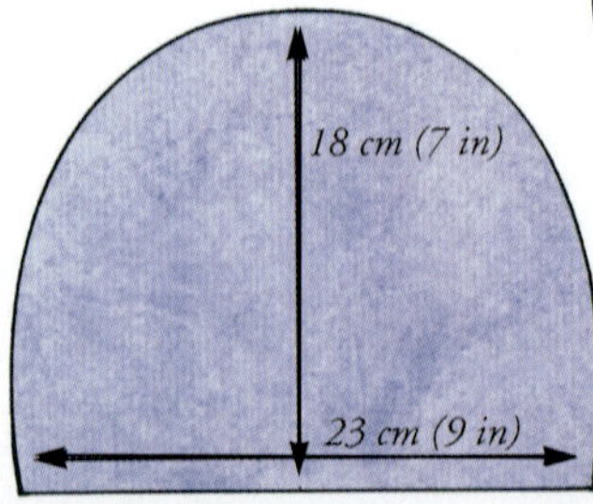

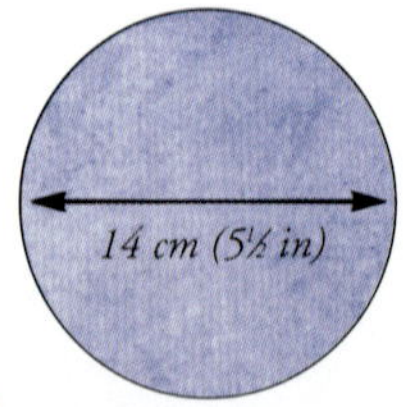

BASE

1

Place two fabric side pieces right sides together and tack (baste) to the wadding (batting). Stitch along the curved edge. Repeat for the other side and for the base. Clip the seams. Press and turn right side out. Top stitch 1cm (½in) from the curved edge.

2

Work in stab stitch round the flower shapes so that they stand out in high relief (see Basic Techniques). Outlining the individual motifs in this way quilts the fabric. Turn inside out again.

3

Pin and stitch the sides to the base. Trim and clip the base seam close to the stitching.

TO FINISH

Turn right side out, then tack (baste) and top stitch round the base 1cm (½in) from the edge, to enclose the raw edges. Sew on a small piece of Velcro to fasten the top.

Pot Holder

This pot holder has been inspired by a Charles Rennie Mackintosh design, which can be found on some of the walls of Glasgow School of Art.

You Will Need

dressmaker's scissors

30cm (12in) square mustard fabric

20cm x 26cm (8in x 10in) pink cotton fabric

22cm x 24cm (8½in x 9½in) polyester wadding (batting)

26cm x 28cm (10 x 11in) blue and white checked fabric

dressmaker's pins

needle and tacking (basting) thread

iron

matching threads

Preparation

Cut four mustard and eight pink 6cm (2¼in) squares. Cut a mustard rectangle the same size as the wadding (batting). Centre the wadding on the reverse side of the checked fabric and tack (baste) in position.

1

Press under a small turning on each side of the squares. Pin the small mustard squares to the centre front of the checked fabric. Pin a pink square to each corner and then centre a pink square on each side.

2

Slip-stitch the squares in place. Tack (baste) the mustard rectangle to the back, covering the wadding (batting). Press under a small turning on each side of the checked fabric, then turn again to cover the edges of the wadding and backing fabric. Slip-stitch in place and mitre the corners (see Basic Techniques). Sew a pink fabric loop to the centre of one edge, for hanging.

CATHEDRAL WINDOW NEEDLECASE

Don't be frightened if this piece of patchwork looks complicated. It is in fact easy to construct. This is not really a quilting method, but because the patches are layered the resulting fabric is very warm and so the idea could be translated into a quilt.

YOU WILL NEED

scrap of taffeta
dressmaker's scissors
iron
dressmaker's pins
needle and matching thread
scrap of silk organza
scrap of lining fabric
sewing machine and matching thread
4 pieces of felt
pinking shears
button

PREPARATION

Cut eight squares of taffeta on the straight grain, twice the intended size of the patch. Press under the raw edges.

1

Find the centre point of each square by matching opposite corners and press on the fold.

2

Fold each corner to the centre point. Press and pin in place.

3

Fold each corner to the centre point once more, then press and pin. Secure the corners at the centre with one small stitch.

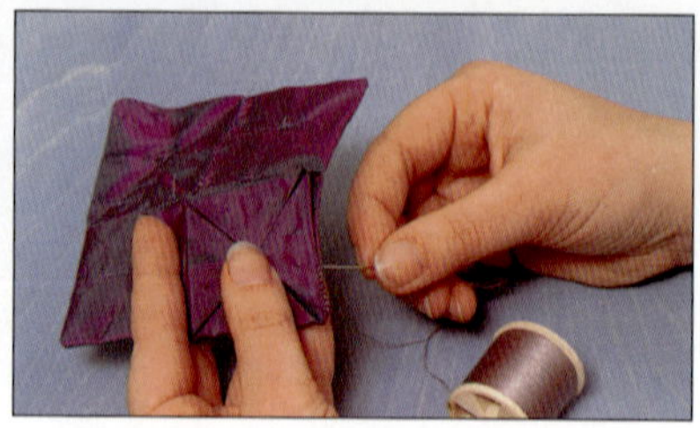

4

Place two patches wrong sides facing and whip stitch across the top. Sew two rows of four blocks in this way, and then join the rows.

5

Measure the fold from one corner to the centre point of one patch. Cut ten squares to this size in silk organza. Pin each piece diagonally over the seam. To cover the raw edge of the organza, roll the fold over and slip-stitch in place. Do the same on all the folds to create the cathedral window effect.

6

Cut the lining fabric to fit the case, adding a 5mm (¼in) seam allowance. Press under the seam allowance. Wrong sides facing, slip-stitch the lining to the needlecase. Sew a button on one side and a fabric loop on the other. Cut the felt to size and pink the edges. Stack the felt pieces, place in the needlecase and stitch down the centre line.

FOLDED-STAR PIN CUSHION

Although deceptively intricate, this pin cushion is easy to make. Squares are folded into triangles and then arranged on the base to make the star. Because the patches are unfitted and without seams, this technique is not classed as a true patchwork.

YOU WILL NEED

scraps of taffeta in two colours
dressmaker's scissors
iron
scrap of cotton fabric
dressmaker's pins
needle and matching threads
pair of compasses and pencil
scrap of velvet
sewing machine
stuffing

PREPARATION

Cut 12 taffeta rectangles 5cm x 9cm (2in x 3½in) in colour one, and eight the same size in colour two. Press a 5mm (¼in) turning along one long side of each rectangle. Cut a cotton base, 20cm (8in) square. Fold the opposite corners, first lengthways and then widthways into the centre of the square. Press along the fold lines.

1

On each rectangular patch, fold the two corners on the turned side down to the centre to form a triangle, and press.

2

Arrange four triangles in colour one on the centre of the base fabric, with folded sides facing, to form a square. Pin and slip-stitch the folded edges to the base.

3

For the second layer, arrange eight triangles in colour two round the centre point. First, pin four triangles to the base 2cm (¾in) from the centre, with the folded sides running parallel to the square. Then pin four diagonally so that they overlap these. Slip-stitch the outer edges.

4

Arrange eight triangles in colour one. Pin each triangle to the base, overlapping the previous layer, positioned 4cm (1½in) from the centre. Slip-stitch the triangle points to the base and tack (baste) round the outer edges.

TO FINISH

With the compass point centred, draw a circle round the star close to the outside edge. Cut a matching circle in velvet. Right sides facing, stitch the star to the velvet. Leave a small gap to turn through. Clip and press. Turn right side out. Fill with stuffing and slip-stitch the gap.

Patchwork Bear

Soft toys, like this delightful satin bear, were often made from patchwork in days gone by. Colourful satin patches are pieced together in box patchwork and then cut into a bear shape.

You Will Need

thin card (cardboard) and pencil

craft knife

50cm x 90cm (20in x 36in) iron-on interfacing

dressmaker's scissors

iron

scraps of satin fabric in assorted colours

dressmaker's pins

sewing machine and matching thread

needle and tacking (basting) thread

rotary cutter

stuffing

Preparation

Enlarge and make the teddy template and cut out in card (cardboard). Enlarge and make templates 1 and 2in card and transfer to the interfacing. Cut enough for two patched pieces for the bear, cutting twice as many patches from 2. Make all of piece 1 in one fabric. Make piece 2 in assorted colours, so that there is an equal number of light and dark shades. Iron the interfacing to the fabric scraps, then cut out the patches with a 5mm (¼in) seam allowance. When making up each box, join one light and one dark piece so that the dark piece is always on the same side in order to create the illusion of depth.

1

Right sides facing, join one light and one dark piece 2 to form an angle. Press the seam to one side. Pin piece 1 to the angled patch matching the corners. Stitch from one corner in the middle of the angle to the end of the seam and cut the threads. Swivel the adjacent angled piece to the other edge of piece 1 and pin. Stitch from the centre point to the end of the seam (for setting-in see Basic Techniques).

2

Make lots of boxes and stitch them together in horizontal rows. Press the seams in one direction only. Carefully tack (baste) the horizontal rows of box patchwork together and stitch. Press the seams in opposite directions (see Basic Techniques).

Piece 1 90%

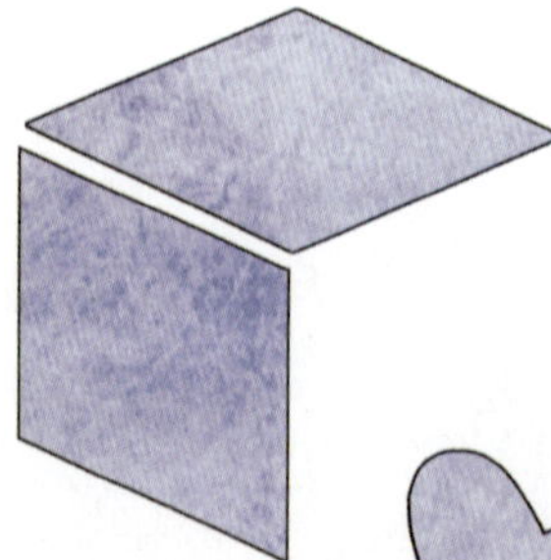

Piece 2 90%

Teddy 50%

To Finish

Make two patched pieces large enough for the bear. Cut out two bears without a seam allowance in interfacing. Iron to the wrong side of each patch. Fold the patch in half and pin the template along the fold line, adding a seam allowance. Cut out two pieces the same in box patchwork with a rotary cutter. Right sides facing, starting on an inside leg, stitch round the shape leaving 5cm (2in) open. Clip into the corners, trim and press. Turn right side out, fill with stuffing and slip-stitch the gap.

VELVET THROW

This project shows how to make a patched piece of velvet. Pairs of triangles are sewn into diamonds and then grouped into stars. The patchwork could easily be made into a quilt or a cushion.

YOU WILL NEED

thin card (cardboard) and pencil
iron-on interfacing
craft knife
iron
assorted velvet scraps
rotary cutter
dressmaker's pins
sewing machine and matching thread
silk lining fabric
needle and matching thread

PREPARATION

Measure the size required for the patch. Draw a triangle, with a base half the length of the other sides, and transfer on to card (cardboard). Work out how many templates will be needed and cut out in interfacing using a craft knife. Iron to the wrong side of the velvet and cut out the pieces with a 5mm (¼in) seam allowance. Arrange the cut triangles and manipulate into diamonds with the best design possibility. Combine the diamonds to make stars, using colour carefully. Draw a plan for reference.

1

Pin and stitch pairs of triangles together along the short edge to form a diamond, using the flag method (see Basic Techniques). Cut joining threads and press the seams flat.

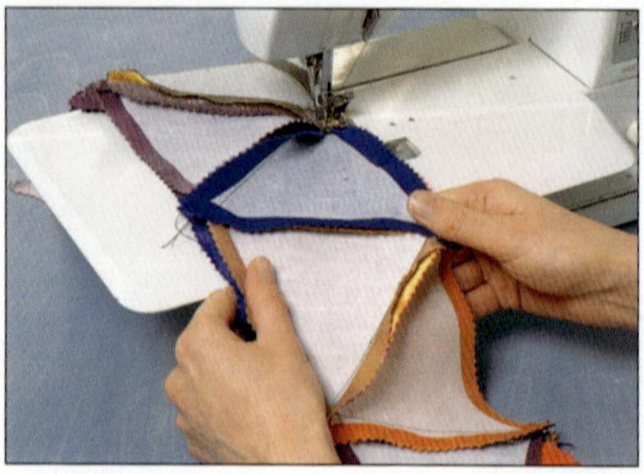

2

Stitch the pairs together in horizontal strips following your own colour scheme, and then join the strips together to make up the finished piece. Press the seams in opposite directions to reduce bulk (see Basic Techniques).

TO FINISH

To make the patched piece into a throw, cut a piece of silk lining to fit. Right sides facing, stitch round the seam line, leaving a 10cm (4in) gap. Clip the corners and press. Turn right side out and slip-stitch the opening. To make a quilt or cushion cover, see Basic Techniques for instructions.

SUITING THROW

This gentleman's throw is made out of scraps of suiting fabrics bought from a tailor. The scraps are cut into rectangles so that the stripes and patterns run in as many directions as possible.

YOU WILL NEED

thin card (cardboard) and pencil
craft knife
scraps of suiting
dressmaker's pencil
dressmaker's scissors
dressmaker's pins
sewing machine and matching thread
silk lining in a contrasting colour
needle and matching thread
iron
tacking (basting) thread
shirt buttons

PREPARATION

Cut a rectangular template in card (cardboard) and calculate the number of patches required. Transfer the template to the suiting using a dressmaker's pencil. Cut out the patches with a 5mm (¼in) seam allowance. Pin and stitch together in pairs using the flag method (see Basic Techniques). Stitch the pairs in horizontal rows and press the seams.

1

Join the horizontal strips of suiting together to make a large patched piece. Trim the seams and press in opposite directions to reduce bulk (see Basic Techniques).

2

Measure the patch and add 13cm (5in) all round for a loose border. Cut the lining to this measurement. Right sides facing, pin the lining to the patched piece and stitch 1cm (½in) from the edge. Leave a 10cm (4in) opening on one side and the corners free. Press the seam and pull through. Slip-stitch the gap.

3

Iron a loose and even fold of silk around the border. Pin and tack (baste) in place.

TO FINISH

Top stitch in matching thread close to the seam line between the suiting and the silk. Mitre the corners and slip-stitch (see Basic Techniques). Sew the shirt buttons round the border, as shown.

LAVENDER BAG

Stars are frequently found in patchwork and the LeMoyne Star is a popular choice. To achieve this tricky eight-seam join that meets in the centre of the star, work slowly and carefully.

YOU WILL NEED

tracing paper and pencil
thin (card) cardboard
craft knife
scraps of silk organza in three colours
rotary cutter
scrap of lining silk
dressmaker's pins
sewing machine and matching thread
needle and matching thread
dried lavender
ribbon

PREPARATION

Trace the star and make the templates. For each star (you will need two), cut out eight pieces from template 1 in two colours and four pieces each from templates 2 and 3 in the third colour. Use a rotary cutter, if wished.

1

To make the star, with right sides facing, pin together two of piece 1, in two colours, and stitch. Make another pair to match. Press flat.

2

Join the two pairs together, carefully matching the centre seams, pin and stitch. Press the seam flat to one side. Make the other half of the star in the same way.

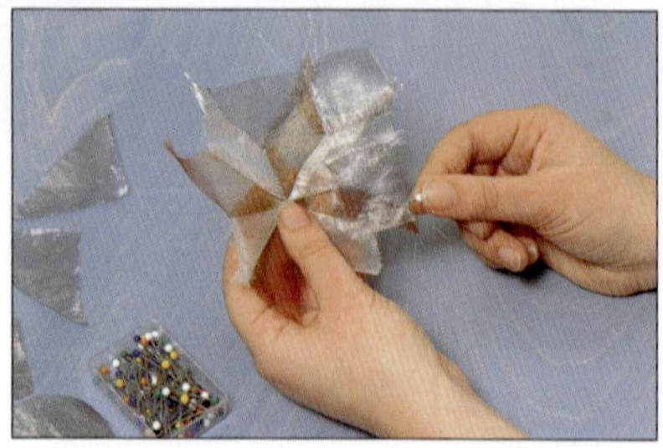

3

To set in the square 3, swivel the square to match the corner points and pin to the angled edge (see Basic Techniques). To set in the triangle 2, match the corner points and pin to the angled edge. Stitch and press.

LEMOYNE STAR

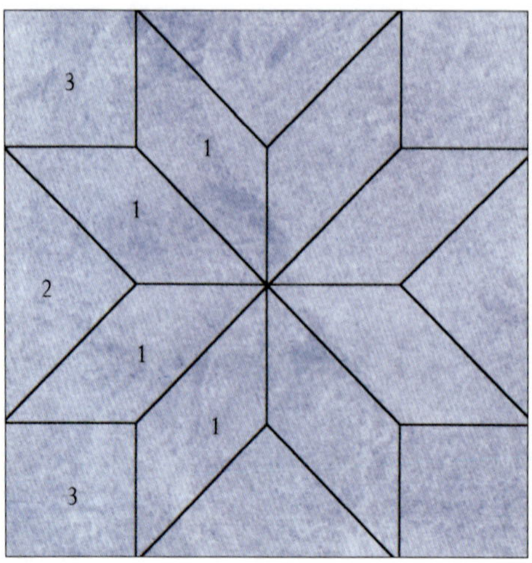

TO FINISH

Set in three more squares, and three more triangles to make the patch. Make a second patch the same. Measure one side and cut two pieces of organza this length plus 5cm (2in) wide. Stitch one to the top of each patch and press. Right sides facing, stitch round the base and sides of the bag and turn through. Fold a 1cm (½in) hem round the top of the bag, press and top stitch. Fill the bag with dried lavender and tie with a ribbon bow.

Nightdress Case

This patchwork design is traditionally used on quilts to celebrate a marriage. The curved lines meet and overlap at regular intervals, giving the overall impression of two interlocking rings.

You Will Need

thin card (cardboard)
craft knife
dressmaker's scissors
scraps of organza in five colours
dressmaker's pins
sewing machine and matching thread
iron
needle and matching thread
press studs (snap fasteners)

Preparation

Make the templates from the back of the book. Each wedding ring design is made up of eight arcs, four patches 4 and one centre 5, and you will need six wedding rings in total. For each arc, cut four of section 1 in the first colour. Cut 32 of 1. For each arc, cut two of section 2 in the second colour. Cut 16 of 2. For four arcs only, cut one of section 3 in colour four, and cut one of section 3 in colour five. Cut eight of 3. Cut two of 4 in the second, and two of 4 in the third colour. Cut two of 5 in the fourth, and two of 5 in the fifth colour.

1

To make an arc, pin together and stitch four pieces of section 1. Press seams to one side. Pin and stitch one piece of section 2 at each end of the arc.

2

Take section 4 and match the notch to the centre seam of one arc, and align the end pieces to the points of 2. Pin and stitch. Make three more patches the same.

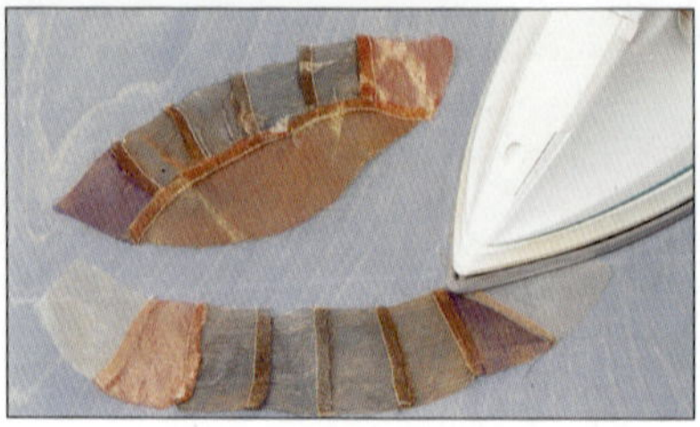

3

For the four remaining arcs, pin and stitch section 3 at each end of the arc, in two contrasting colours. Press seams to one side.

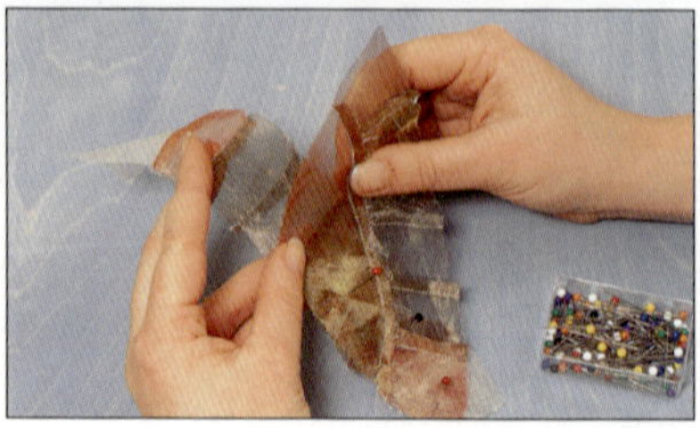

4

Match the centre seam of one patched arc to the notch on 4. Pin and stitch. Press the seam to the arc. Make four patches in the same way.

5

Take section 5 and match the notch to the centre seam on one of the oval patches, align the corners and stitch. Press the seam towards the oval. Pin the second oval piece to the other curved edge of 5, matching the centre points and alternating the colours of the patches. Stitch and press towards the oval.

To Finish

Join a second piece 5 to the curved edge of the second oval as before and continue to make a square. Measure the square, add a 1cm (½in) seam allowance on three sides and a 2cm (¾in) seam allowance on the other. Cut a piece of organza to fit. Halve the long edge and cut. Press under a double hem on both pieces and stitch. Overlap the two pieces, right sides to the patched piece and make an envelope cover (see Basic Techniques). Make a silk lining in the same way, if wished. Stitch pairs of press studs (snap fasteners) to the opening.

Corded Purse

Corded quilting is a very old technique that was popular in Italy and so became known as Italian quilting. The fabric is quilted in parallel lines to make channels, which are then threaded with cord or yarn to form raised lines. This method is often used with trapunto quilting.

You Will Need

tissue paper and marker pen
30cm x 90cm (12in x 36in) muslin
fabric marker
needle and tacking (basting) thread
30cm x 90cm (12in x 36in) bronze satin
sewing machine and matching thread
cord or yarn
flat blunt needle
dressmaker's pins
30cm x 90cm (12in x 36in) blue satin
dressmaker's scissors
press stud (snap fastener)

Preparation

Trace the design on to tissue paper. Tack (baste) the muslin to the wrong side of the bronze satin and stitch round the edge. Pin the template to the muslin and stitch the design. Cut and secure the ends and remove the template.

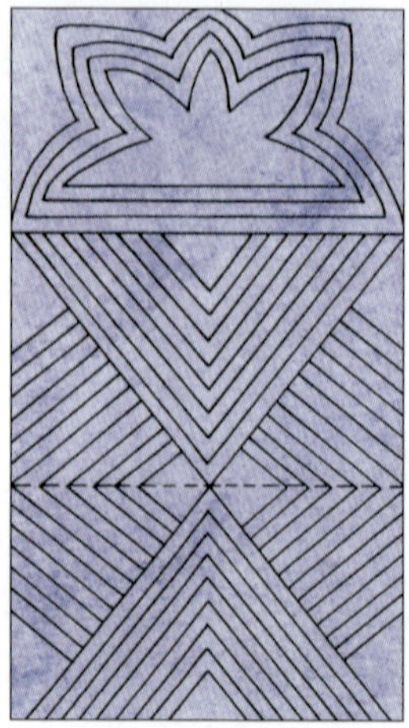

Corded Design 25%

1

Use the flat blunt needle to thread the cord or yarn through the channels. Pull the yarn out at the corners and leave a loop so as not to tighten and distort the fabric.

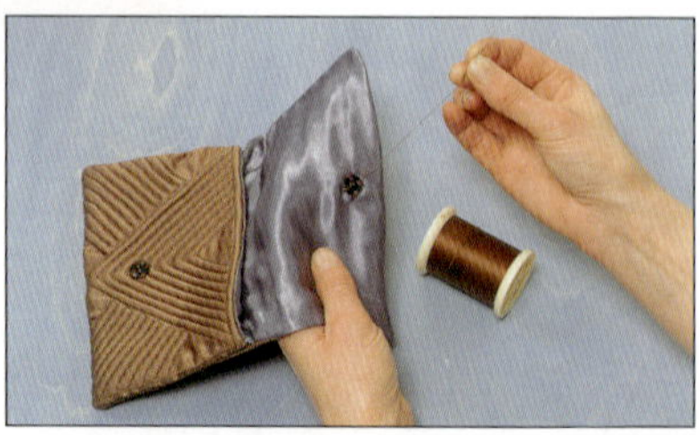

2

Right sides facing, pin to the blue satin. Stitch round the flap and across the opposite end. Clip and press to the right side. Slip-stitch the sides. Sew on the press stud (snap fastener).

CORDED QUILT

This method of quilting is worked by stitching the outline of a design in two parallel lines on to two layers of cloth. This creates channels which are then filled. This method can be worked all over for a whole cloth, or it can simply be used to make decorative borders.

YOU WILL NEED

dressmaker's scissors
satin fabric
muslin
tissue paper and pencil
dressmaker's pins
needle and tacking (basting) thread
sewing machine and matching thread
flat blunt needle
woollen yarn
calico for lining

PREPARATION

Decide on the size of your quilt and cut the satin and muslin to fit. Trace the design on to tissue paper several times until you have enough to make a complete border. Tack (baste) the muslin to the wrong side of the satin fabric and stitch round the quilt, close to the edge.

1

Pin the template to the muslin. Stitch the design in even parallel lines either side of the outline. Cut and secure the ends and remove the template.

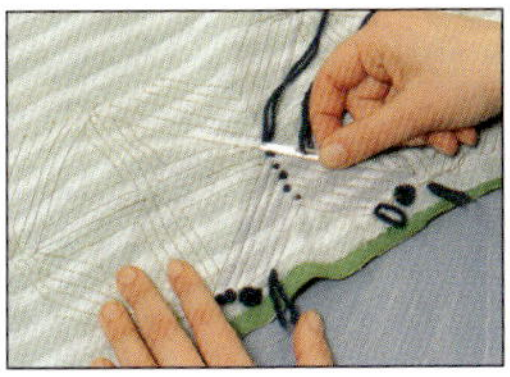

2

Thread the flat needle with yarn and insert it into a channel working the yarn between both layers of fabric. To turn a corner, bring out the needle to the wrong side, make a loop and then push back into the channel. Where two channels cross, cut the yarn and then continue on the other side. Fill the border of the quilt in this way.

TO FINISH

Trim the satin and muslin and cut the lining to fit. Right sides facing, stitch together, leaving a 10cm (4in) opening. Turn right sides out and slip-stitch the opening.

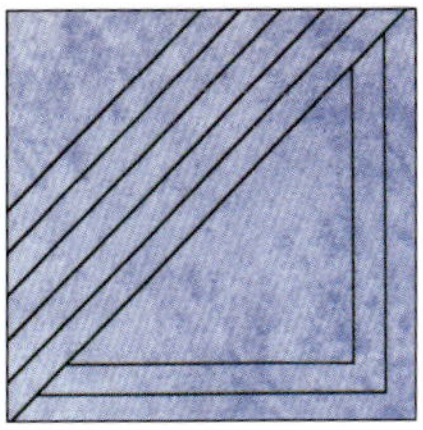

ONE-QUARTER OF DESIGN SHOWN. ENLARGE TO SIZE REQUIRED FOR QUILT.

MEDIEVAL QUILT

This medieval-inspired quilt makes use of a harmonious colour scheme of frosty blues, soft golds and antique creams in glazed cotton, satin, brocade and moiré. The patches can be quilted individually, which is especially useful on a large-scale project such as this.

YOU WILL NEED

paper and pencil
dressmaker's scissors
fabric scraps in glazed cotton, brocade, satin and moiré
iron
dressmaker's pins
sewing machine and matching thread
calico
wadding (batting)
needle and tacking (basting) thread
thin card (cardboard)
craft knife
iron-on fusible bonding web
fabric scraps in metallic tissue and iridescent organza
crewel needle and thick metallic thread
beads and sequins

PREPARATION

This quilt is made up of 36cm (14in) square panels. Half of the panels have a large central diamond design and the other half are divided into four with either four diamond designs or two diamond and two square. Make a plan of the quilt and plan the colour fall. Enlarge the diagram and cut out a diamond template in both sizes, a triangular template in both sizes and a square template from paper. Cut out as many fabric patches as you need, adding a turning all round. Press under the turnings. Pin the patches together to form panels and machine together using zig zag stitch. Cut out the same number of panels in calico and wadding (batting). Sandwich the wadding between the patched fabric and the calico and tack (baste). Machine quilt the panels using zig zag stitch.

1

Enlarge and transfer the animal motifs from the back of the book to thin card (cardboard) and cut out. Iron the bonding web to the wrong side of the iridescent and metallic scraps. Cut out an animal motif for each panel with a large diamond design.

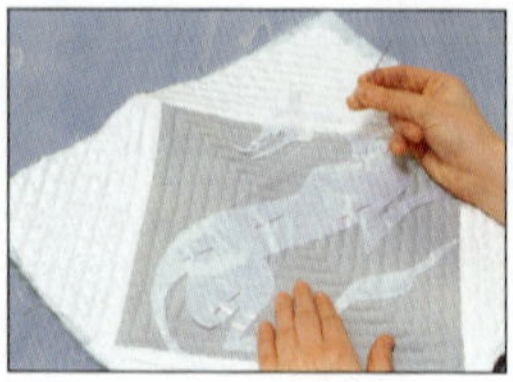

2

Peel off the backing paper and iron the motifs to the panels, then embellish with metallic thread, beads and sequins.

3

Hand quilt details on some of the panels using the thick metallic thread. On other panels, wrong side facing, machine quilt using thick metallic thread in the bobbin and regular thread on top.

PLAN AND TEMPLATES 25%

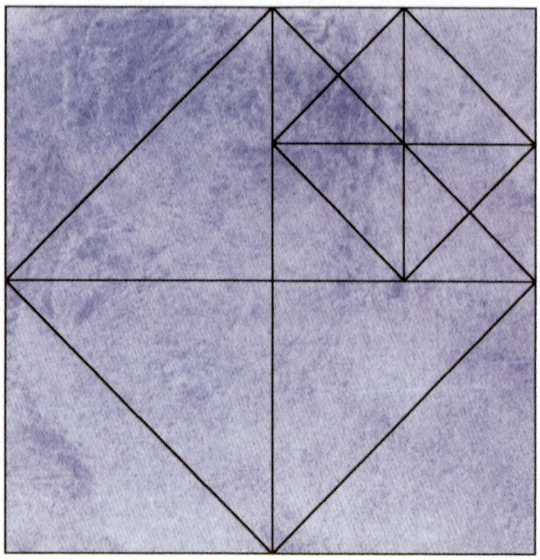

TO FINISH

To join the panels together, turn under the raw edges on the front and back and pin together. Zig zag the panels together from the back. Cut strips of calico about 5cm (2in) wide and as wide and as long as the quilt. Press under a turning along the long edges. Position the strips over the panel joins and top stitch to the front of the quilt using zig zag stitch. Make a border using calico and top stitch to the quilt in the same way.

QUILTED WAISTCOAT

The paisley motif originated in India and was brought to Europe by the East India Company in the 18th century. A paisley design has been painted on to the waistcoat fronts and then each shape is hand quilted in stab stitch.

YOU WILL NEED

commercial waistcoat pattern
dressmaker's scissors
calico
black lining fabric
vanishing marker
gold gutta outliner
black, green and purple silk paint
paintbrush
wadding (batting)
needle and tacking (basting) thread
sewing machine and matching thread

PREPARATION

Cut out the waistcoat back and fronts in both calico and lining material. Enlarge the template from the back of the book and transfer the paisley design on to the calico fronts with the vanishing marker.

1

Outline the paisley design with the gold gutta outliner. Leave to dry overnight.

2

Fill in the pattern using the silk paints. Work one colour at a time and leave it to dry before starting the next colour. Then fill in the background colour.

3

Sandwich the wadding (batting) between the calico and the lining and tack (baste) in place. Work stab stitch round each motif to make it stand out (see Basic Techniques).

TO FINISH

Make up the waistcoat following the instructions with the commercial pattern.

Cameo Picture

This popular appliqué idea is fun to make. Copy a silhouette from a book or a piece of china and for unashamed plagiarism use a Wedgwood blue backing. A photograph of someone you know can also be used, so long as it is in profile. Mount the finished cameo in a frame or, alternatively, make a brooch following the instructions for the Gothic Jewels project.

You Will Need

marker pen
fine white or black iron-on interfacing
dressmaker's scissors
iron
blue backing material
embroidery hoop
sewing machine and matching thread
small frame

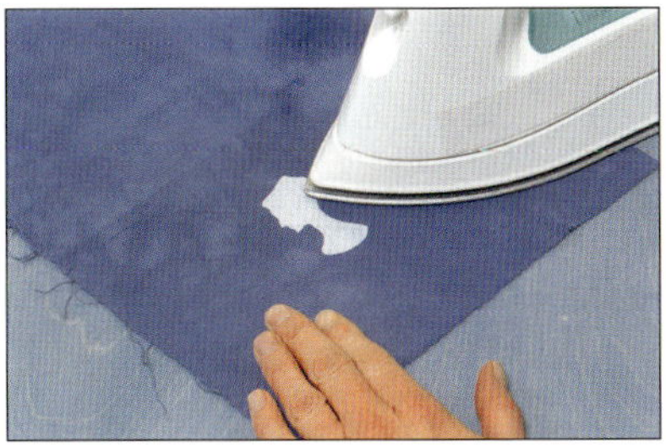

1

Trace the silhouette on to the interfacing. Cut out and iron on to the backing fabric.

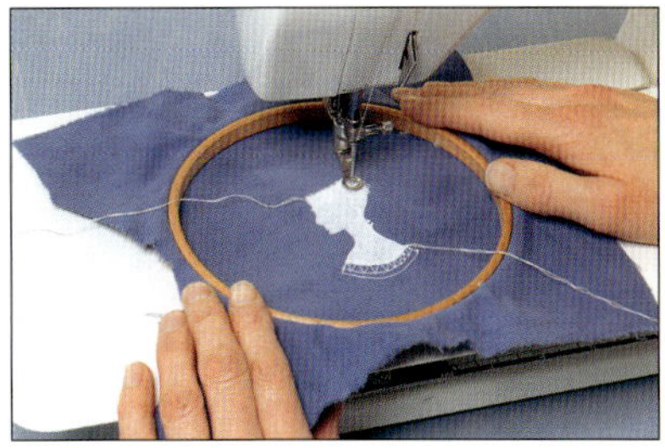

2

Stretch the backing material on an embroidery hoop. Remove the presser foot from your sewing machine and stitch round the outline. Add decorative details to the collar and hair to complete the design.

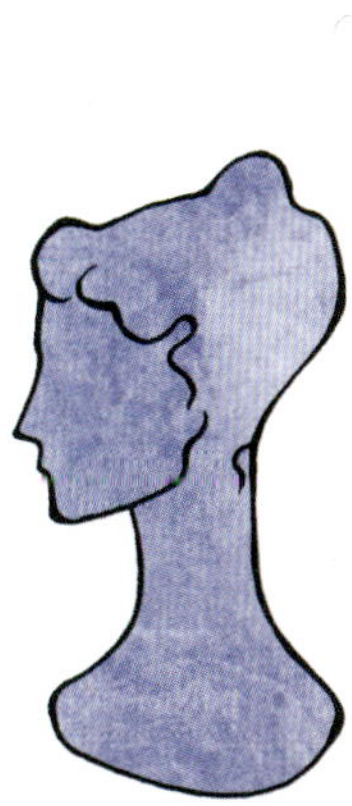

To Finish

Mount the finished cameo picture in a small frame (see Basic Techniques).

TRAPUNTO BOX

Trapunto, a very old art form, is by far the most admired form of quilting. Outlines are stitched to the fabric and then filled from the back. Quilt a Tudor rose in this way to cover a box lid.

YOU WILL NEED

dressmaker's scissors

40m x 90cm (16in x 36in) blue satin

30cm x 90cm (12in x 36in) calico

18cm (7in) hexagonal box

dressmaker's pins

needle and tacking (basting) thread

vanishing marker

sticky back felt

sewing machine and gold thread

wadding (batting)

fabric glue

50cm (20in) braid

PREPARATION

Cut the satin 40cm (16in) square. Cut a piece of calico the same size as the lid, and centre on the reverse side of the satin. Tack (baste) to secure in place. Enlarge and trace the template and draw the centred outline on to the satin with the vanishing marker. Draw round the base and sides of the box and round the base of the lid on to the sticky back felt. Cut out.

1

Machine stitch the outline of the Tudor rose in gold thread.

2

Slash the calico back of one petal and fill with wadding (batting). Stitch up the slit. Repeat on all shapes until the rose is full.

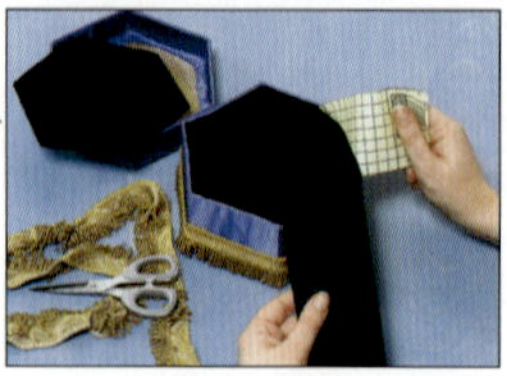

3

Centre the quilted design on the lid and glue. Stretch the satin over the lid and sides and stick the edges to the inside of the lid. Trim any excess. Cover the box in satin. Line the box with the sticky back felt. Glue the braid round the base of the box and round the lid.

50%

QUILTED BOX

The method used for the box lid illustrates simple machine quilting. Wadding (batting) is sandwiched between two layers and held together by the stitched outline of the diamond and fleur-de-lys motif.

YOU WILL NEED

vanishing marker
50cm x 90cm (20in x 36in) gold satin
small rectangular box
wadding (batting)
dressmaker's scissors
needle and tacking (basting) thread
sticky back felt
sewing machine and matching thread
fabric glue

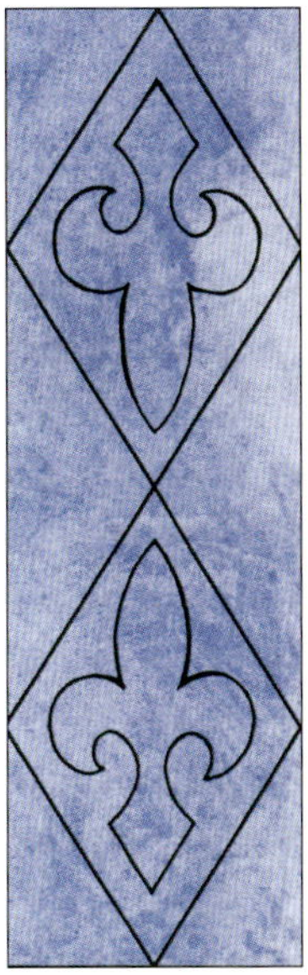

50%

PREPARATION

Enlarge the template and transfer the design with the vanishing marker on to a piece of gold satin, cut slightly larger than the lid. Cut the wadding (batting) to fit the lid. Centre and tack (baste) to the satin. Draw round the base of the box and lid on to the sticky back felt. Cut out.

1

Machine stitch the outline of the design.

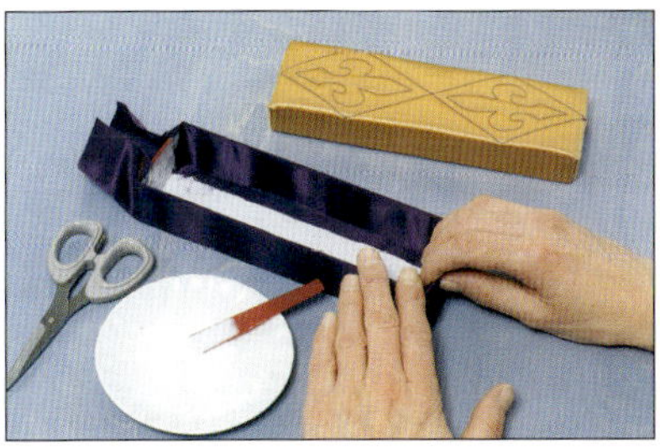

2

Glue the wadding (batting) to the lid. Fold the satin over the edge and inside the lid. Mitre the corners and glue. Cover the box in satin.

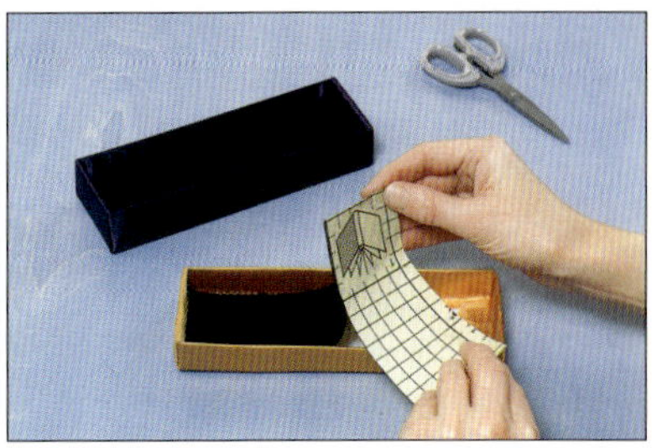

3

Attach the sticky back felt to the lid and the base of the box.

QUILTED HAT

This pull-on hat is made from wool and silk. The raised trapunto quilting on the hat band, in the form of diamonds, is embellished with bronze thread.

YOU WILL NEED

thin card (cardboard) and pencil
craft knife
dressmaker's paper
dressmaker's scissors
50cm x 90cm (20in x 36in) calico
50cm x 90cm (20in x 36in) pink wool
50cm x 90cm (20in x 36in) pink silk
sewing machine and matching thread
iron
dressmaker's pins
wadding (batting)
crewel needle and bronze thread
1m x 90cm (40in x 36in) silk lining
needle and tacking (basting) thread
50cm x 2.5cm (20in x 1in) petersham

PREPARATION

Enlarge and cut out the motif templates in card (cardboard). Enlarge the hat templates from the back of the book and cut out piece 1in calico and wool. Cut piece 2in calico and silk. Cut crown piece 3in wool and calico. Stitch pieces 1 and 2 together to make the hat band, first in calico, and then in wool and silk, taking a 1.5cm (½in) seam allowance. Clip and press the seams.

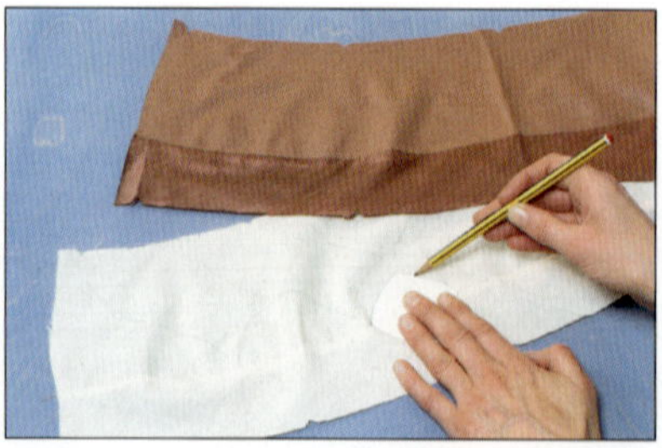

1

Draw round the templates on to the calico hat band, alternating the motif templates and spacing them evenly.

2

Stitch the ends of the hat band together and press. Wrong sides facing, pin the bands together and stitch round the motifs through both layers of fabric.

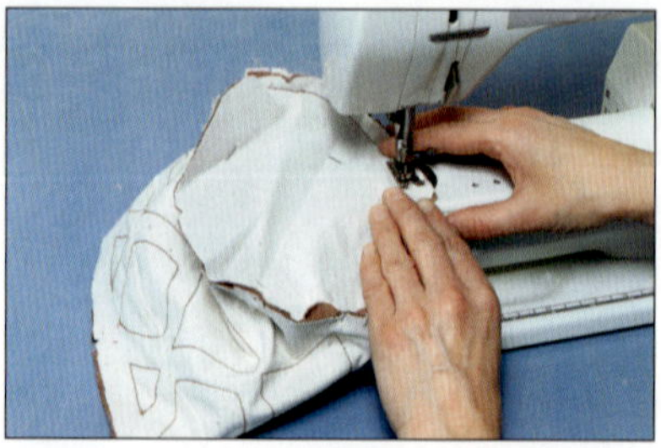

3

Wrong sides facing, pin together the two crown pieces. Pin and stitch to the quilted hat band. Turn right side out and top stitch close to the crown seam.

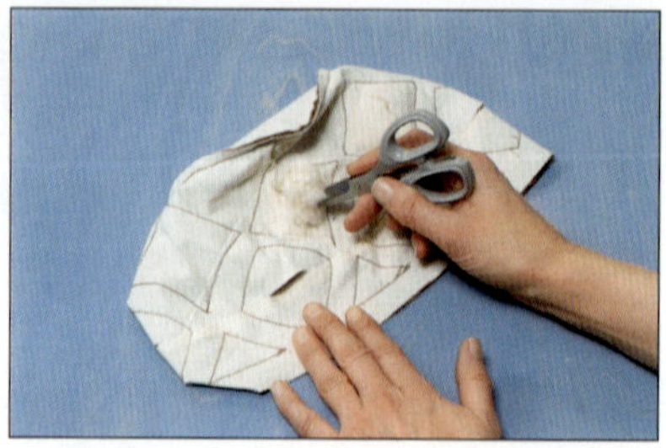

4

Turn inside out and carefully slash the calico behind each motif. Fill each motif with wadding (batting) then stitch closed. Embroider the diamonds with bronze stars. Make up a lining using the same pattern pieces and slip stitch in position.

5

Tack (baste) the petersham band to the lower inside edge of the hat. Stitch and press under.

DIAMOND MOTIFS
50%

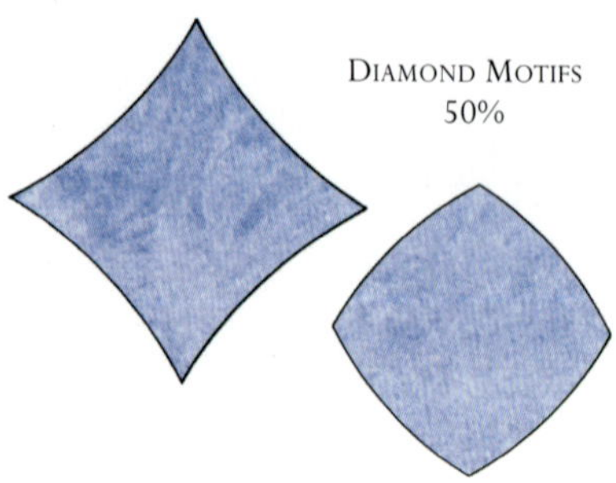

CRIB QUILT

Quilts like this were first made in the 19th century. Use washed out fabrics to achieve an old look. Pieces that look too bright can be sewn wrong side out. Beg or borrow scraps from friends and neighbours to make a family heirloom.

YOU WILL NEED

thin card (cardboard) and pencil
craft knife
assortment of cotton and calico scraps
dressmaker's scissors
needle and tacking (basting) thread
iron
matching thread
75cm x 64cm (30in x 25in) wadding (batting)
75cm x 64cm (30in x 25in) calico
dressmaker's pins
crewel needle and ecru embroidery thread
sewing thread in three contrasting colours

PREPARATION

Make two templates, one 8cm (3in) square and one 4cm (1½in) square. Cut 31 large and 128 small card (cardboard) squares. Cut the small patches from fabric scraps and the large patches from calico scraps, allowing for a 1cm (½in) turning on all sides. Tack (baste) the card squares to the patches. For the borders, cut two fabric strips 5cm x 80cm (2in x 32in) in three different colours, and two strips 5cm x 65cm (2in x 26in) in the same colours. Press a turning on the long sides of each strip.

1

Oversew the small squares into blocks of four. Alternate these blocks with the larger squares and oversew to make a quilt the equivalent of seven large squares wide and nine large squares deep. Remove tacking (basting) threads and the card (cardboard). Press the quilt seams open.

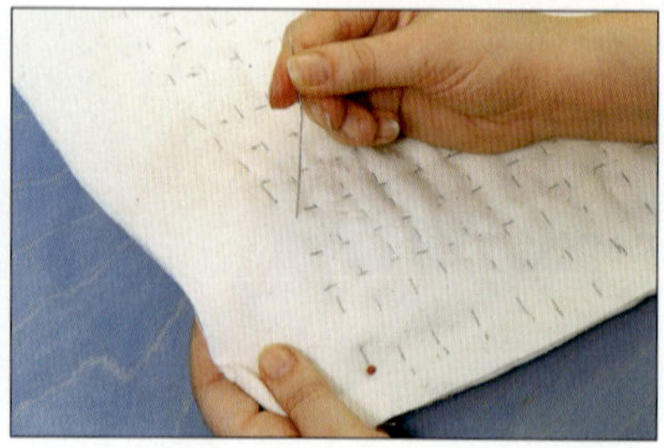

2

Place the patchwork face down and cover with wadding (batting) and calico. Pin the layers together, starting at the middle and gradually moving out. Tack the layers in lines of running stitches, removing the pins as you go.

3

To tuft the quilt, use embroidery thread to make a small stitch at the corners of each block and in the middle of the four square patches. Cut the threads to 4cm (1½in), securely knot and fluff out the ends with a needle.

4

Attach the borders to the front of the quilt with lines of running stitch in sewing thread using the Log Cabin method (see Basic Techniques). Mitre the corners (see Basic Techniques). Trim the raw edges, fold over and slip-stitch to the lining. Take the fabric over at the corners to show the Log Cabin effect.

STRING PATCHWORK FRAME

String patchwork is created by sewing similiar lengths of fabric of different widths into one piece. Interesting effects are made by adjusting the angle of the strips and by making chevron shapes.

YOU WILL NEED

black and white satin
dressmaker's scissors
sewing machine and matching thread
two squares of thin card (cardboard)
craft knife
double-sided tape
masking tape
self-adhesive felt
needle

1

Cut the satin into narrow strips, varying the widths slightly. Right sides facing, machine stitch the strips together. Adjust the angles of the strips to make interesting effects.

2

Cut a window from one square of card (cardboard). Cut the patch into four sections to fit each side of the frame, allowing for a turning. Mitre the corners (see Basic Techniques).

TO FINISH

Stick the fabric to the frame with double-sided tape. Fold the raw ends to the inside and secure with masking tape. Cover the backing square with self-adhesive felt cut to size. Slip-stitch the front and back of the frame together round three sides.

STAINED GLASS APPLIQUÉ CUSHION

This cushion has been worked using the overlay method of appliqué. Keep design ideas bold and simple. It is also important that each shape within the design is not too small.

YOU WILL NEED

thin card (cardboard) and marker pen

48cm (19in) square red silk

dressmaker's pins

dressmaker's scissors

scraps of yellow and green silk

iron

iron-on interfacing

sewing machine and matching threads

tracing paper

transfer pencil

two 48cm (19in) squares black silk

craft knife

45cm (18in) square cushion pad

needle and matching thread

PREPARATION

Enlarge and transfer the template to the card (cardboard). Place the template over the red silk square and transfer the star outline, following the dotted lines, using pin prick marks. Cut along the pin pricks, without cutting the outer red frame. Make a template for each diamond shape and the centre piece, following the dotted lines. Draw round the templates on to the silk scraps. Cut four yellow and four green diamonds, and one red centre piece. Iron one piece of interfacing to the red frame.

1

Arrange the yellow and green diamonds and the red centre piece on the interfacing. Pin and iron in place. Machine stitch in place.

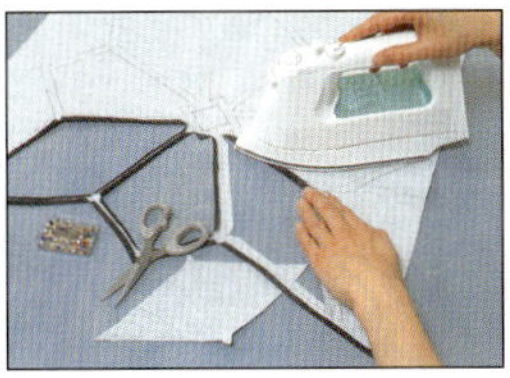

2

Following the continuous lines, trace the black frame on to tracing paper with a transfer pencil. Turn over and iron on to the second piece of interfacing. Iron the interfacing to the wrong side of one of the black silk squares. Cut out each diamond with a craft knife, leaving a small turning on all sides. Pin and press the turnings.

3

Pin the black frame on top of the appliqué star and machine along all the edges.

TO FINISH

Right sides facing, place the appliqué patch to the second black silk square and stitch a seam 1cm (½in) from the edges. Leave an opening. Clip the corners, press and turn right side out. Insert the cushion pad and slip-stitch the opening.

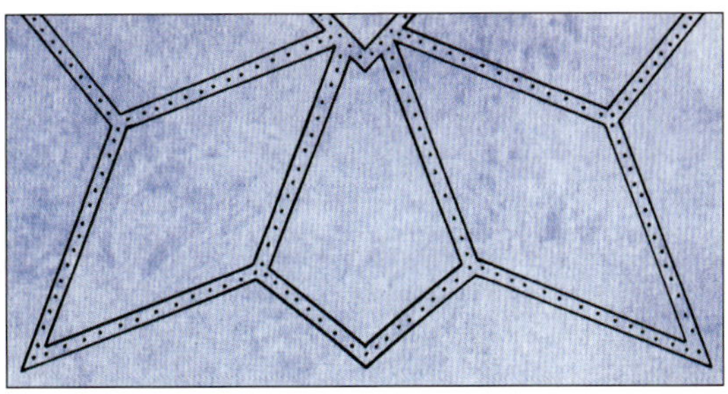

HALF OF PLAN SHOWN 25%

SILKEN BAG

This delicate piece of quilted silk sports a design of hearts, vine leaves and a bow surrounded by small running stitches. The finished quilt is sewn into a tiny drawstring bag.

YOU WILL NEED

dressmaker's scissors

40cm x 90cm (16in x 36in) lining silk

40cm x 90cm (16in x 36in) calico

tracing paper and pencil

8cm x 30cm (3in x 12in) wadding (batting)

needle and tacking (basting) thread

crewel needle and white perlé thread

sewing machine and matching thread

50cm (20in) cream silk ribbon

PREPARATION

Cut two pieces of lining silk and calico measuring 23cm x 30cm (9in x 12in). Enlarge and trace the design and transfer to one piece of silk. Sandwich the wadding (batting) between the two pieces of calico, positioning the wadding where you want the quited design. Place the marked silk on top and tack (baste) the layers together.

1

Outline the heart, vine and bow design in stab stitch (see Basic Techniques).

2

Work tiny running stitches round the design until the whole area has been covered.

TO FINISH

Cut 10cm (4in) diameter circle from lining silk and calico for the base of the bag. Make a lined drawstring bag using the remaining piece of lining silk and the base pieces (see Basic Techniques). For the channel, stitch two parallel lines 1cm (½in) apart with the top one 1cm (½in) from the edge. Thread and knot the silk ribbon.

BRODERIE PERSE APPLIQUÉ NAPKINS

This once popular craft was thought to closely resemble Persian embroidery. As it developed, more and more images were incorporated into the designs. A rose has been combined with a gardening fork to create these charming napkins.

YOU WILL NEED

tracing paper and pencil

scraps of plain grey, and pink and green floral chintz fabric

dressmaker's scissors

4 linen napkins

dressmaker's pins

needle and tacking (basting) thread

sewing machine and matching thread

iron

PREPARATION

Transfer the fork template from the back of the book to the grey fabric. Add a small seam allowance and cut out. Cut out a flower shape, such as a rose, with a stem from chintz fabric, adding a small seam allowance.

1

Position the flower on a napkin with the stem entwined the prongs of the fork. Pin and tack (baste) through the middle of the motifs. Turn under and tack a small turning and clip the edges as you work round the motifs.

2

Hand or machine stitch round the edges of the motifs to secure.

TO FINISH

Embellish all four napkins in the same way. Remove the tacking (basting) threads and press carefully. Embroider thorns on the rose stem in tiny stitches if you wish.

Broderie Perse Appliqué Tablecloth

The technique of cutting out a design in printed cloth to appliqué to a fabric base grew out of both necessity and the desire to preserve old favourites. Appliqué chintz fabric with a large, floral motif to a linen cloth for an antique appearance.

You Will Need

dressmaker's scissors

Irish linen

dressmaker's pins

needle and tacking (basting) thread

sewing machine and matching thread

scraps of pink and green floral chintz fabric

iron

needle and matching thread

Preparation

Cut the linen to the shape and size you require. Turn under a small hem and stitch.

1

Draw a vase shape on to a scrap of chintz and cut out. Press under a small hem. Pin and tack (baste) to the corner of the cloth.

2

Cut a border in contrasting chintz. Press under a hem, pin and tack to the vase.

3

Cut out several flower shapes and leaves. Arrange in the vase, pin and tack in place.

4

Clip and turn the edges as you sew the motif to the cloth. When the shapes overlap each other, be sure to sew the base one first.

Silk Dress

This technique uses up scraps of patterned silk. The silk patches are randomly joined into panels with French seams. The idea is to make enough patched squares to sew into a large piece of fabric, which is then made into a dress. Dye the dress a strong colour to unify the design.

You Will Need

dressmaker's paper and pencil

dressmaker's scissors

scraps of fine silk or silk scarves

dressmaker's pins

sewing machine and matching thread

iron

commercial dress pattern

cold water dye

Preparation

The panels measure 26cm (10in) square and they can be made up of patches following either or both diagrams. Enlarge the two diagrams and make templates for each shape and size of patch. Cut out patches from scraps of silk, allowing for a 1cm (½in) seam allowance on sides.

Dress Panels

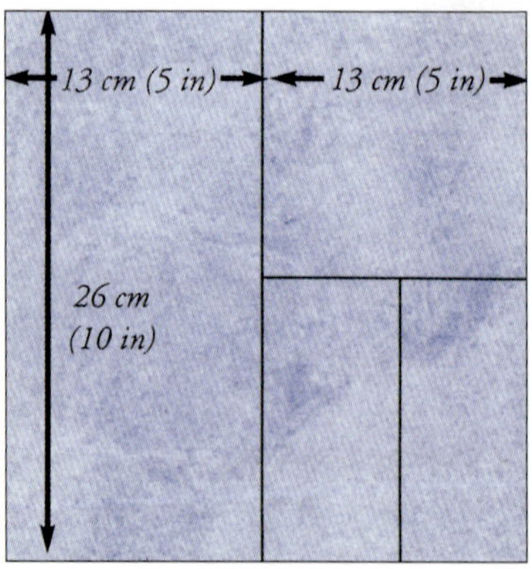

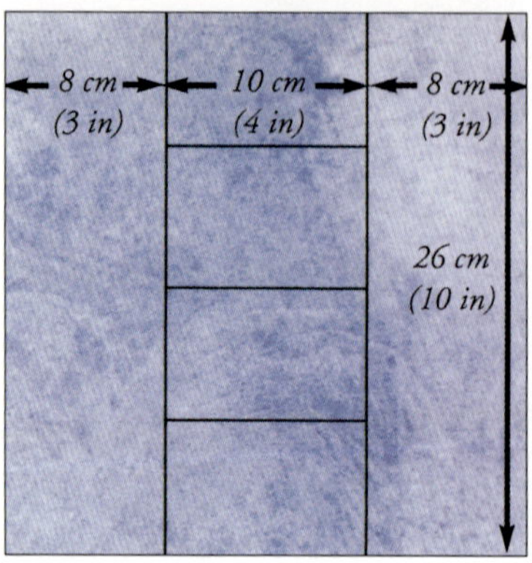

1

Using the flag method (see Basic Techniques), pin the patches in pairs with wrong sides facing. Machine and press the seams to one side. To make French seams, trim one edge back close to the stitching line. Press a small turning on the uncut edges, fold over again to cover the stitch line and press. Pin and stitch along the new fold.

2

Join the patches into panels, and the panels together in the same way to make a large piece of patched fabric.

To Finish

Cut out and make the dress following the instructions with the commercial dress pattern. Make up the cold dye solution, following the manufacturer's instructions. Then scrunch the dress up and dye.

Child's Skirt

Patches and strips of contrasting silk fabrics are sewn together in a creative mix to make this skirt. The appliqué silk patches sewn round the hemline add to the historic feel.

You Will Need

thin perspex and marker
craft knife
dressmaker's scissors
1.2m x 115cm (47in x 45in) floral silk
scraps of contrasting silks
iron
dressmaker's pins
sewing machine and matching thread
needle and tacking (basting) thread
six buttons

Preparation

Enlarge and make the templates in perspex. Cut the floral fabric in half lengthwise. Cut two strips of contrasting silk 7cm x 1.2m (2½in x 47in), and press a 1cm (½in) seam allowance along the long edge. Cut four side strips in the same fabric, each 5cm x 55cm (2in x 22in).

To Finish

Halve the waist measurement and make two waistbands. Check the length of the skirt and trim if necessary. Gather the skirt on to the waistbands and top stitch. Make buttonholes and sew on the buttons.

1

Pin the templates to the silk scraps and cut out. Press under the seam allowances on patches.

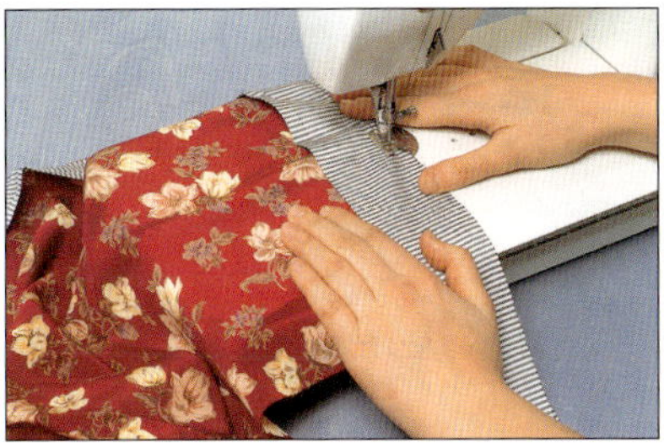

2

Machine stitch one long strip to the wrong side of one piece of floral silk. Press over to the right side and top stitch. Repeat for the second piece. Attach the side strips in the same way.

3

Arrange the patches on the lower edge of the skirt, pin and tack (baste) in place. Machine stitch close to the edge.

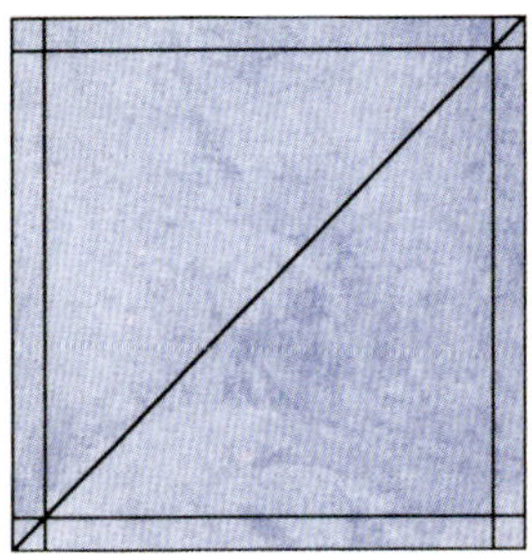

50%

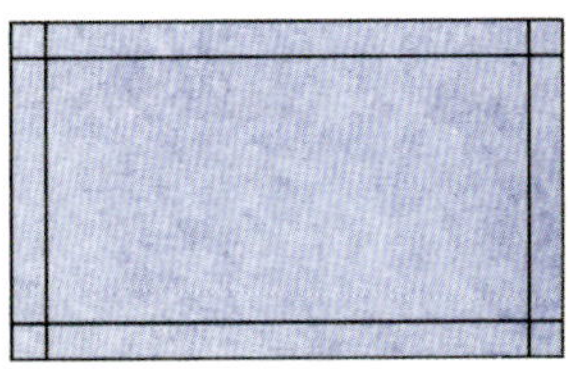

Satin Handbag

This classic handbag is made from a piece of quilted satin. It has self-made handles and a quilted base for extra strength. Chose an unusual brass button to fasten the bag.

You Will Need

40cm x 60cm (16in x 24in) heavy interfacing

vanishing marker

dressmaker's scissors

40cm x 60cm (16in x 24in) wadding (batting)

40cm x 60cm (16in x 24in) satin

46cm x 30cm (18in x 12in) lining fabric

dressmaker's pins

sewing machine and matching thread

needle and tacking (basting) thread

iron

brass button

Preparation

Transfer the bag design from the back of the book to the interfacing. Cut out a piece of wadding (batting) to fit, and cut out the satin and a lining piece, adding a seam allowance on all sides. Sandwich the wadding between the marked interfacing and the satin, then pin and stitch round the edge. Machine quilt the grid. Cut out two satin and two lining side pieces and two satin handles, all with a seam allowance. Cut out an interfacing base 16cm x 7cm (6½in x 2¾in).

1

Position and tack (baste) the interfacing base to the bag. Trim the raw edges.

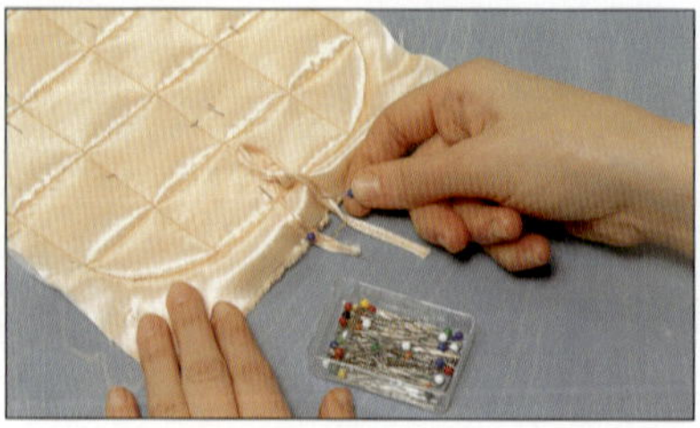

2

Make a narrow silk rouleau 5cm x 20cm (2in x 8in). Pin to the right side of the flap, with the loop pointing outwards. Make it big enough to fit the button. Right sides facing, pin the lining to the bag and stitch just inside the machine line, leaving an opening to turn through. Turn and slip-stitch closed.

3

Right sides facing, place satin and lining side pieces together in pairs. Machine round three sides, then turn through one long edge. Fold in half lengthwise and press. Machine stitch along fold to within 4cm (1½in) of the lower edge.

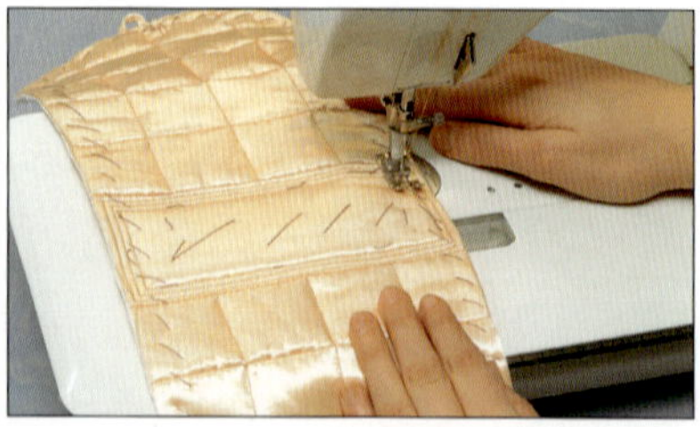

4

Top stitch round the base, the flap fold and the front edge of the bag.

5

Fold the handles in half lengthwise and press under a 1cm (½in) turning on both long sides and top stitch to 2.5cm (1in) of both ends. Open out the ends and top stitch to the bag.

To Finish

Slip-stitch the side pieces into the bag. Sew on a decorative button.

Country Throw

This delightful cotton throw is made from checked patches alternating with plain ones. This appliqué project lends itself to a country image with bold designs colouring plain squares.

You Will Need

60cm x 90cm (24in x 36in) calico

60cm x 90cm (24in x 36in) checked cotton fabric

dressmaker's scissors

tracing paper and pencil

20cm x 90cm (8in x 36in) iron-on fusible bonding web

iron

assortment of fabric scraps

dressmaker's pencil

crewel needle and assortment of embroidery threads

small glass beads

sewing machine and matching thread

1m x 115cm (40in x 45in) cotton drill

dressmaker's or safety pins

needle and tacking (basting) thread

shirt buttons

Preparation

Cut 13 calico and 12 checked cotton rectangles 17cm x 19cm (6½in x 7½in). Enlarge the motifs from the back of the book and trace on to the bonding web. Cut four hearts, three birds, two hands, and one pear, strawberry, grape and flower motif.

1

Roughly cut round the shapes on the bonding web and iron them on to the scraps. Cut out, peel off the backing paper and fuse to the calico squares.

2

Mark design details with a dressmaker's pencil and embroider round each shape. Use a variety of stitches and coloured threads. Sew on beads for the birds' eyes and holly berries.

3

Alternate checked with appliquéd squares in five rows, each row with five blocks. Use the flag method to join the blocks (see Basic Techniques), then join the rows.

4

Centre the patched piece on the cotton drill. Pin and tack (baste) through all the layers and round the outside edge. Stitch a small glass bead to each corner.

5

Press a 1cm (½in) hem round the outside edge, then fold in half to make a border. Pin, slip-stitch in place and mitre the corners (see Basic Techniques). Decorate the border with the shirt buttons.

Patchwork Frame

Patchwork squares are sewn into strips to make the cover for this pretty picture frame. Designed in checked fabric, it has its own naive style.

You Will Need

two pieces of thick A4-size card (cardboard)
craft knife
fabric marker
scraps of wadding (batting)
dressmaker's scissors
double-sided tape
20cm x 90cm (8in x 36in) calico
fabric glue
scraps of gingham
dressmaker's pins
sewing machine and matching thread
iron
needle and matching thread

Preparation

Cut a window in one piece of card (cardboard), with a 5cm (2in) frame. The second piece is for the backing board. Trace the frame on to the wadding (batting), cut out and stick together with double sided tape. Draw round the backing board on to the calico, and cut out with a seam allowance. Fold over the seam allowance and glue to the back. Cut a calico facing for the inner and outer frame. Cut the gingham scraps into 3.5cm (1½in) squares.

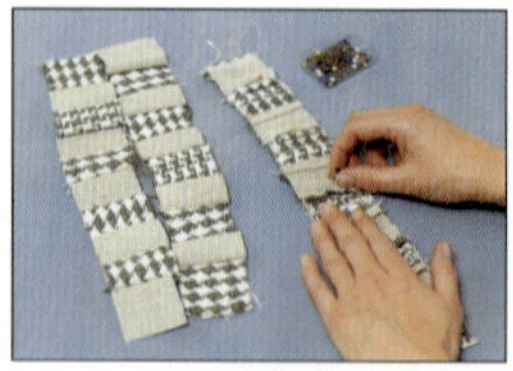

1

Pin the squares in pairs and stitch with a 5mm (¼in) seam allowance, using the flag method (see Basic Techniques). Make four strips of 10 patches, and four strips of three. Sew pairs of strips together. Press and then join the short strips to the long ones to make a frame.

2

Right sides together, stitch the facings round the inner and outer frame. Clip the corners, trim and press.

To Finish

Lay the fabric frame on the card (cardboard), fold over the facings and secure them with double-sided tape. Put the front and back of the frame together and slip-stitch round three sides.

APPLIQUÉ WOOL SCARF

A plain woollen scarf is appliquéd with unusual fabrics – suede, wool and corduroy. Earthy colours complement this organic motif.

YOU WILL NEED

tracing paper and pencil
thin card (cardboard)
craft knife
dressmaker's pencil
scraps of suede, corduroy and wool
dressmaker's scissors
rotary cutter
needle and tacking (basting) thread
30cm x 150cm (12in x 60in) wool fabric
sewing machine and matching thread
crewel needle and contrasting embroidery threads

PREPARATION

Enlarge and transfer the four motifs to the card (cardboard) and cut out.

MOTIFS 25%

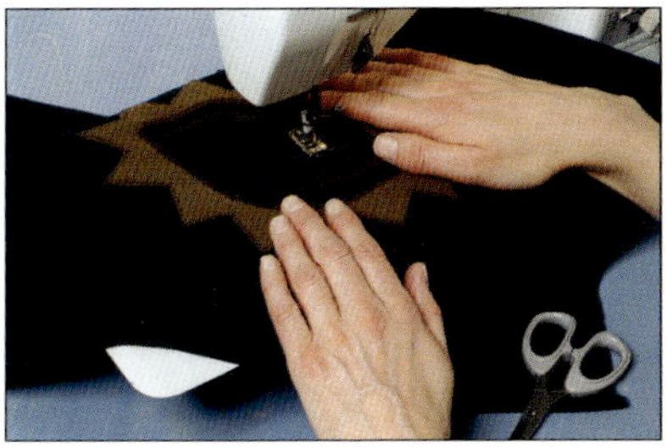

1

Draw round the templates on to the fabric scraps with a dressmaker's pencil. Cut out the shapes using scissors, a rotary cutter or sharp craft knife. Tack (baste) the motifs to the scarf edge. Machine zig zag round the motifs.

2

Turn a hem on the long sides of the scarf and top stitch. Work large buttonhole stitch along the other two sides in a contrasting colour (see Basic Techniques). Embroider a few stitches on to the motifs.

SUNFLOWER SHELF EDGING

Shelf edgings decorating kitchen mantels were a common feature in country cottages in past times. This shaped edging is appliquéd with cheerful sunflowers.

YOU WILL NEED

thin card (cardboard) and pencil
craft knife
16cm x 90cm (6½in x 36in) calico
dressmaker's pencil
iron-on fusible bonding web
dressmaker's scissors
iron
yellow, green and brown gingham fabric scraps
needle and cream thread
spray starch
pinking shears

PREPARATION

Enlarge and trace the template on to card (cardboard) and cut out with a craft knife.

1

Place the template at one end of the calico strip. Trace round the outline and repeat along the length of fabric.

2

Trace five flowers, five centres, and ten leaves on to the fusible bonding web. Iron on to the fabric scraps and cut round the outlines.

3

Peel off the backing paper and place two leaves above the first point on the calico. Place the sunflower on top, overlapping the leaves and iron in place. Work along the strip in this way using the points as guides.

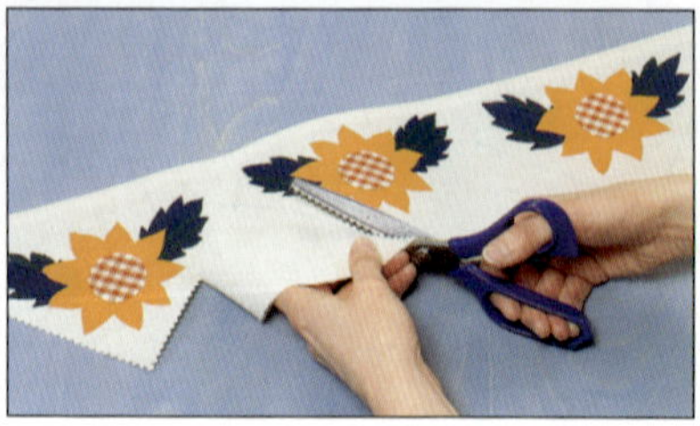

4

Turn under the top edge and press a 1cm (½in) hem. Slip-stitch in place. Spray the piece with starch and then pink the marked line.

50%

Bolster Cushion

A patchwork bolster will make a stylish feature in any room as well as providing luxurious comfort. The cover is fastened with buttons for easy removal on wash day.

You Will Need

dressmaker's paper and pencil
dressmaker's scissors
iron-on fusible bonding web
iron
50cm x 90cm (20in x 36in) cotton fabric
assorted fabric scraps
sewing machine and matching thread
2 buttons
45cm x 18cm (18in x 7in) bolster pad

Preparation

Enlarge the end piece and copy on to paper. Cut a rectangle 47cm x 70cm (18½in x 27½in) and two end pieces in the main fabric. Draw eight patch templates on to the fusible bonding web. Iron to the fabric scraps and cut out. Press under a hem on both short sides of the main fabric piece and machine stitch. Make two buttonholes along one of these hemmed edges and iron the rectangular patches to one of the long edges. To make the patchwork base, cut the scraps into 7cm x 4.5cm (3in x 2in) rectangles and sew into short strips.

Patch Template 50%

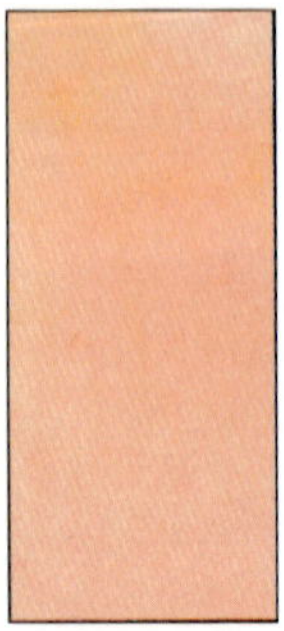

End Piece 25%

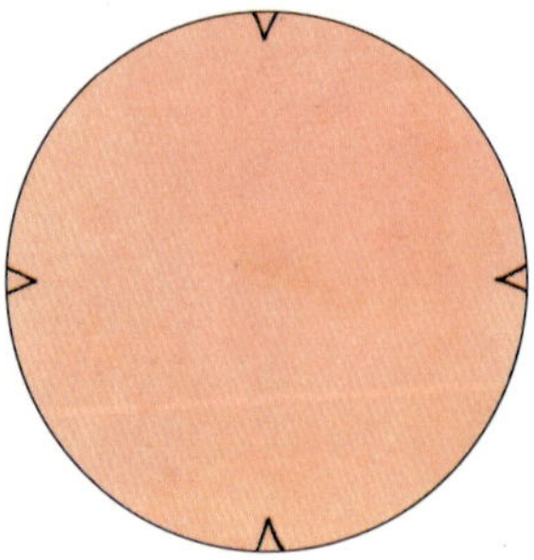

1

Set the machine to zig zag and outline each rectangular patch in satin stitch.

2

Pin and stitch the strips together to make a patch to fit the end piece. Lay the patch on one end piece, stitch round the edge and trim to fit.

To Finish

Pin the main piece into a tube. Insert the end pieces, sew, clip the curves and press. Turn right side out, and sew on the buttons. Insert pad.

COUNTRY WREATH CUSHION

"Ring a ring o' roses ..." This ticking cushion cover is decorated with posies arranged in a wreath. The flowers are cut from an array of cotton fabrics and appliquéd to the cover in a ring.

YOU WILL NEED

tracing paper and pencil
iron-on fusible bonding web
iron
assortment of fabric scraps
dressmaker's scissors
45cm x 95cm (18in x 38in) striped ticking
dinner plate
dressmaker's pencil
assortment of embroidery threads
crewel needle
sewing machine and matching thread
45cm (18in) square cushion pad

PREPARATION

Enlarge the templates and trace eight flowers, 18 flower centres and 24 leaves on to the fusible bonding web. Cut out roughly and iron on to the fabric scraps then cut round the outline. Fold the ticking into quarters to find the middle, centre a dinner plate on top and draw round it with the dressmaker's pencil.

1

Position the flowers on the ticking in an even circle and trace round them with the dressmaker's pencil. Peel off the backing paper.

2

Slip the leaves under the flowers – mix the colours, vary the angles and iron in place. Fix a centre on each flower and arrange the extra circles round the wreath to fill the gaps.

3

Using three strands of embroidery thread, work round the edges of the shapes with bold blanket stitches (see Basic Techniques).

TO FINISH

Press under a 1cm (½in) hem on both short ends and stitch. Mark 25cm (10in) from one edge, fold over the appliquéd front and pin in place. Repeat on the other side. Sew both edges, clip the corners and turn right side out. Insert the cushion pad.

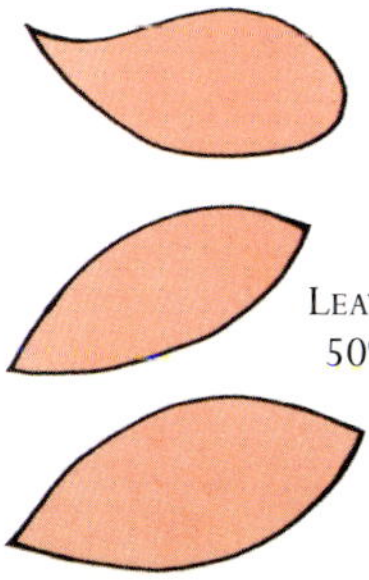

LEAVES 50%

FLOWER AND FLOWER CENTRE 50%

RAG BOOK

Over the years, rag books have retained their popularity as a safe and practical toy for small babies. This colourful book has ten leaves, filled with delightful appliqué motifs.

YOU WILL NEED

tracing paper and pencil
iron
iron-on fusible bonding web
assorted fabric scraps
dressmaker's scissors
60cm x 90cm (24in x 36in) calico
20cm x 90cm (8in x 36in) floral cotton fabric
sewing machine and matching thread
dressmaker's pins

PREPARATION

Select a range of simple and easy-to-identify images, together with letters and numbers. Trace on to the fusible bonding web. Iron to the reverse of the fabric scraps and cut out the shapes. Cut ten 20cm (8in) squares and a rectangle 14cm x 17cm (5½in x 6½in) in calico. Cut out two 20cm (8in) squares in floral fabric.

1

Remove the backing paper and iron the cut shapes to the calico squares.

2

Set the machine to zig zag and secure with satin stitch. Make the picture for the front cover on the small calico rectangle, centre and stitch to one of the floral squares.

3

Pin and stitch the squares, right sides facing, to form pages. Back pages one and ten with the floral squares. Turn right side out and collate.

4

Cut a wide bias strip from the floral fabric to bind the spine. Pin and stitch the strip to the centre seam.

5
6

APPLIQUÉ T SHIRT

The flowerpot motif is easy to make. Brightly coloured fabric scraps in various prints are appliquéd to the front of a child's T shirt.

YOU WILL NEED

tracing paper and pencil
iron-on fusible bonding web
iron
assorted fabric scraps
dressmaker's scissors
needle and tacking (basting) thread
dressmaker's pins
plain T shirt
matching thread

1

Trace the templates on to the bonding web and iron to the fabric scraps. Cut out with a small seam allowance. Clip and tack (baste) under the seam allowance round all of the shapes.

2

Arrange the flowerpot motif on the T shirt, pin and slip-stitch in place.

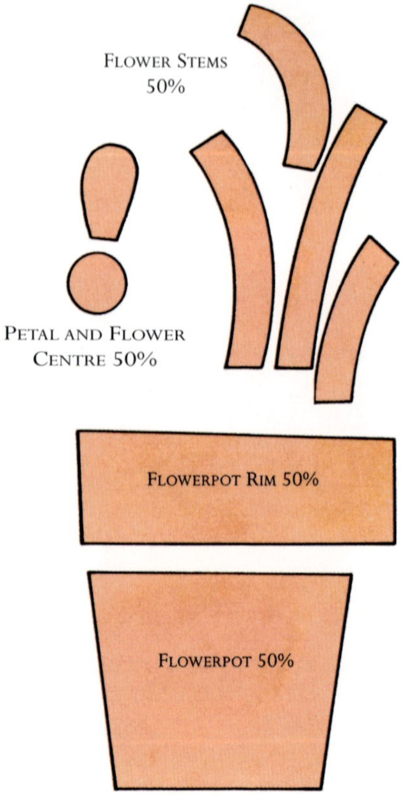

AUTUMN LEAF SHOE BAG

Brightly coloured leaves, in autumnal shades, have been appliquéd in satin stitch to a calico drawstring bag. This bag is so charming that you could hang it on the back of a door in full view.

YOU WILL NEED

tracing paper and pencil
20cm x 50cm (8in x 20in) iron-on fusible bonding web
dressmaker's scissors
iron
assorted fabric scraps
50cm x 56cm (20in x 22in) cotton waffle fabric
sewing machine
red and cream thread
1m (1yd) narrow tape
safety pin

PREPARATION

Enlarge the templates and trace on to the fusible bonding web. Roughly cut out the shapes and then iron to the fabric scraps.

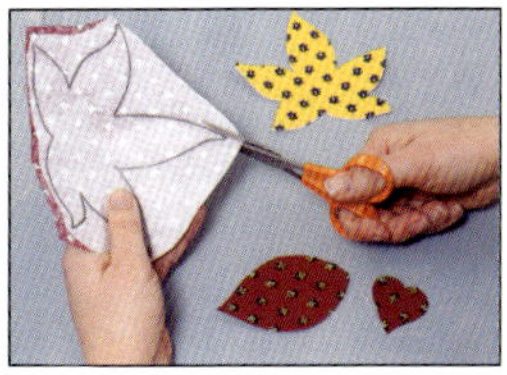

1

Carefully cut round the outline of each leaf and flower. Peel off the backing paper, arrange the shapes on the waffle fabric and iron on.

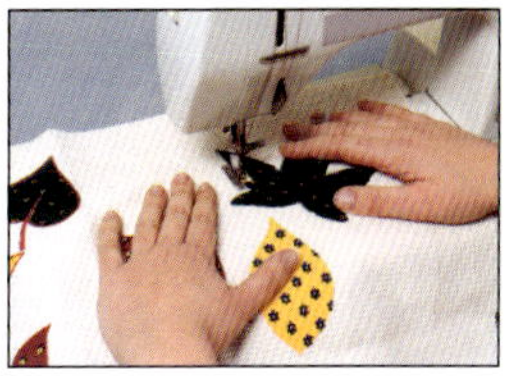

2

Set the machine to zig zag, and outline each shape in red satin stitch. Work a straight red line for the stems.

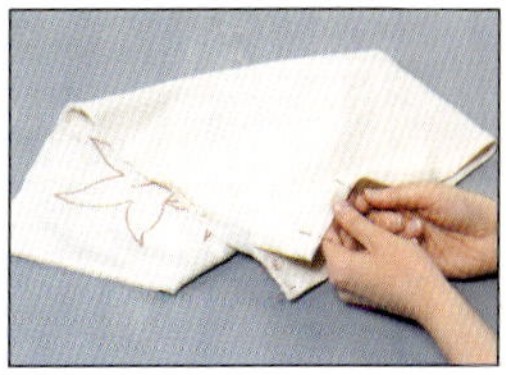

3

Right sides facing, make up the bag (see Basic Techniques), finishing the side seam 7cm (2¾in) from the top edge. Fold the top edge down 3cm (1¼in) and stitch.

LEAF TEMPLATES 50%

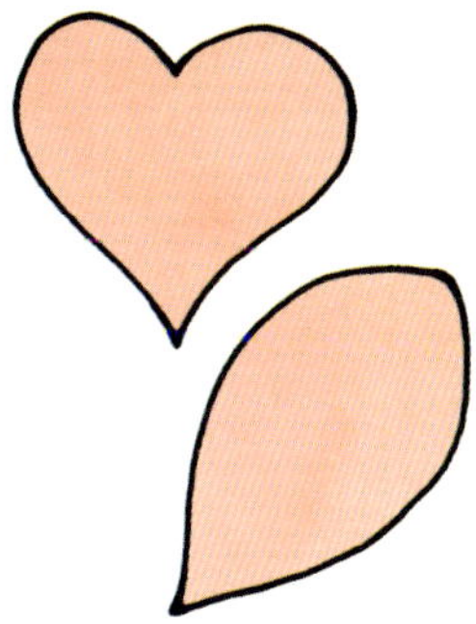

TO FINISH

Thread the tape through the channel using a safety pin. Tie the two ends together and trim the excess tape.

LITTLE HOUSE KEY RING

Keep your keys safe on this pretty key ring. The little house is made from tiny patched pieces which are appliquéd on to the fob.

YOU WILL NEED

tracing paper, paper and pencil
dressmaker's scissors
red and blue gingham and red fabric scraps
needle and tacking (basting) thread
iron
10cm x 32cm (4in x 13in) cream cotton fabric
10cm x 15cm (4in x 6in) wadding (batting)
red, cream and blue sewing thread
key ring

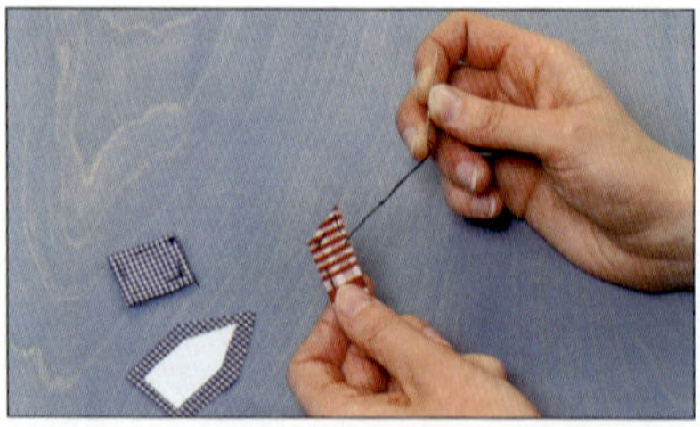

1

Trace the design on to paper and cut out two windows, two walls, two chimneys, a roof and a door. Cut out in scraps of fabric with a 5mm (¼in) seam allowance. Tack (baste) to the backing papers and press.

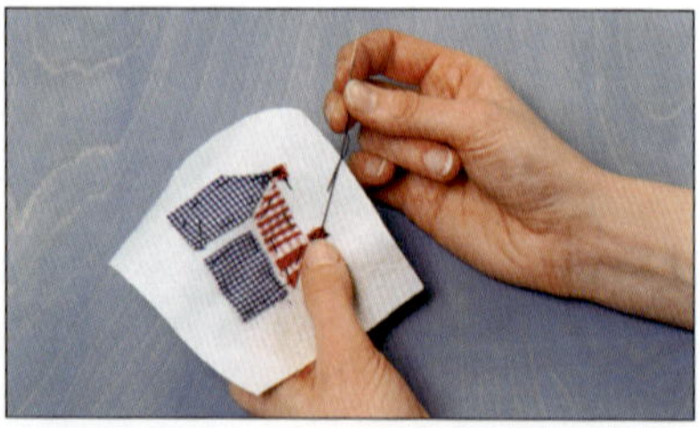

2

Cut two main pieces from cream cotton fabric and two from wadding (batting). Tack (baste) the house in sections to one piece of cotton fabric, removing the paper as you go. Slip-stitch with matching thread.

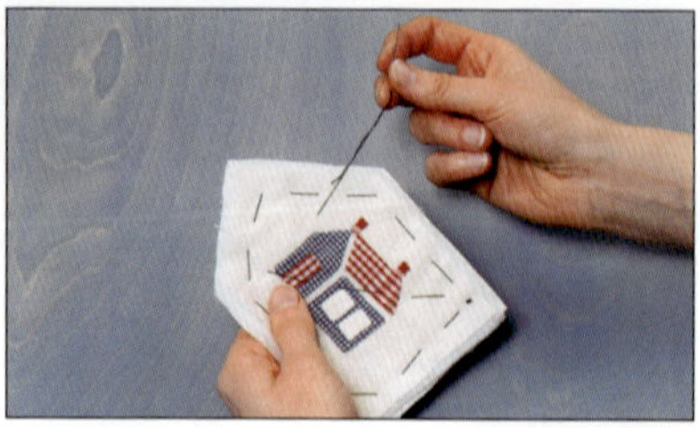

3

Sandwich the wadding between the appliquéd and plain fabrics, and tack through all the layers to secure.

4

Cut three bias strips in gingham (see Basic Techniques). Press under 5mm (¼in) turnings and bind the raw edges leaving 2.5cm (1in) free either side of the point. Thread the ends through the key ring and slip-stitch together.

KEY FOB AND MOTIF TEMPLATE

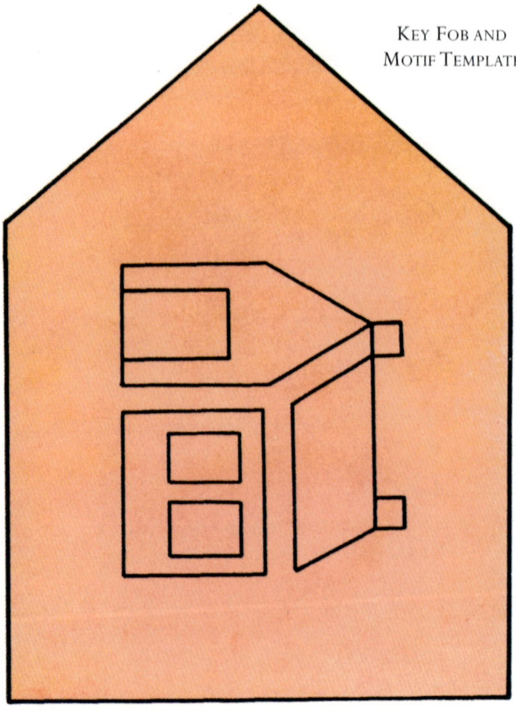

Hanging Heart Sachet

Ever popular, lavender sachets are an ideal way to sweeten cupboards and drawers, leaving a freshness reminiscent of long, hot summer days.

You Will Need

dressmaker's paper and pencil
scraps of cotton fabric
dressmaker's scissors
dressmaker's pins
needle and matching thread
iron
dried lavender
50 coloured glass beads
50 coloured headed pins
scrap of ribbon

Preparation

Enlarge the templates and make paper patterns. Cut out one of each shape from the fabric scraps.

50%

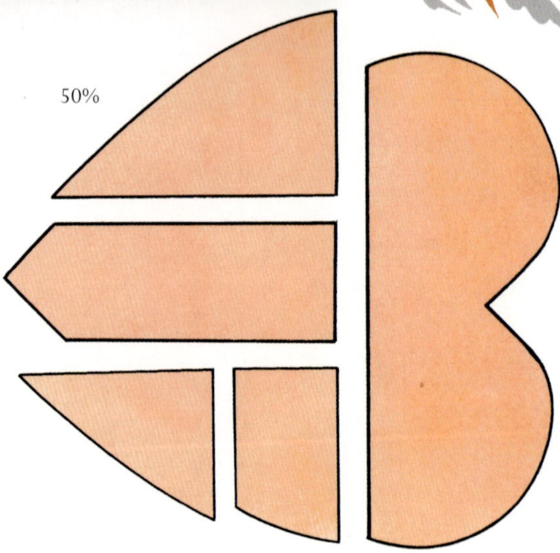

1

Right sides facing, pin and stitch the pieces to make a heart shape, taking a small seam allowance. Trim the raw edges. Use the patched piece as a template to cut out another heart in plain fabric.

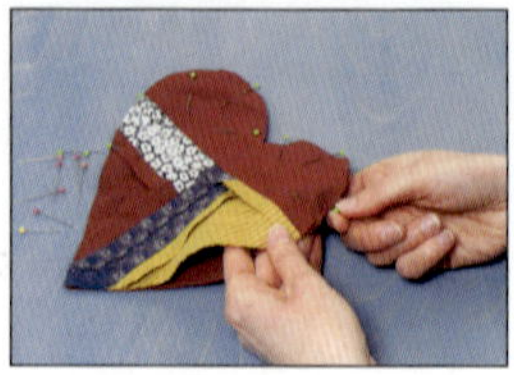

2

Right sides facing, pin and stitch round the heart, leaving a 5cm (2in) gap on one side. Clip the curves, press and turn right side out. Fill with lavender and slip-stitch the gap closed.

3

Thread the beads on to the coloured pins and space evenly round the edge. Sew a ribbon loop to the top.

Heart Appliqué Pillowslip

Customize plain bed linen, to give it country appeal, by stitching appliqué hearts to a pillowslip. Emphasize the hearts and raise the design with a halo of multi-coloured running stitches.

You Will Need

pencil and paper
25cm (10in) square iron-on interfacing
dressmaker's scissors
iron
assorted scraps of brightly coloured cotton
needle and tacking (basting) thread
pillowslip
dressmaker's pins
matching thread
assortment of embroidery threads
crewel needle

1

Draw 17 hearts, varying the sizes, on the interfacing and cut out. Iron the interfacing to the fabric scraps and cut out the shapes with a 5mm (¼in) seam allowance.

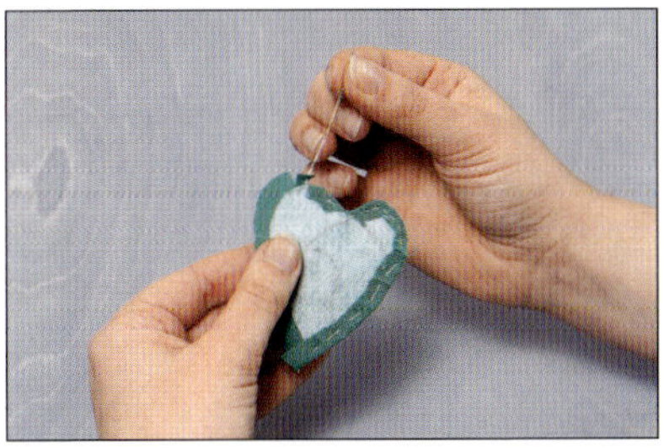

2

Clip the seam allowance round the curves, fold over and tack (baste) in place.

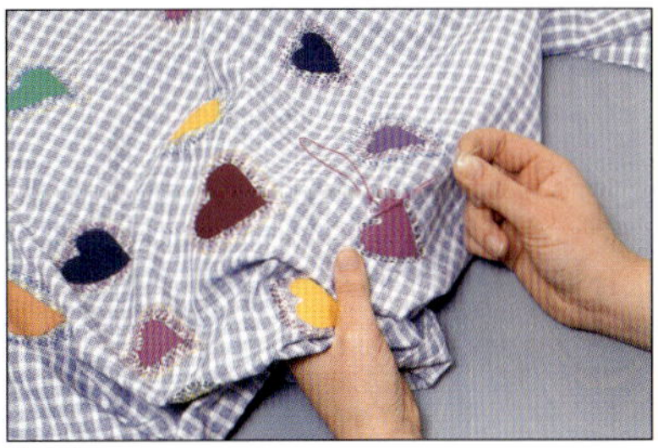

3

Arrange the hearts randomly on the pillowslip. Pin, tack and then slip-stitch in place. Using an assortment of coloured threads in one strand, work lines of tiny stitches around each heart in halos. Press to complete.

CHILD'S STRIP PATCHWORK RUCKSACK

Small children will love to carry their lunch to school in this practical rucksack. Floral and gingham fabrics are sewn into a patched piece, which is then quilted along the seams.

YOU WILL NEED

dressmaker's paper and pencil
dressmaker's scissors
60cm x 1m (24in x 40in) wadding (batting)
1m x 90cm (40in x 36in) gingham fabric
assorted floral and gingham cotton scraps
sewing machine and matching thread
needle and tacking (basting) thread
dressmaker's pins
1m (1yd) rope
wooden toggle

PREPARATION

Enlarge and trace the templates for a base and a flap on to paper. Make a paper template for the straps measuring 50cm x 4cm (20in x 1½in). Cut a rectangle 36cm x 85cm (14in x 34in) and a base, a flap and two straps in both the wadding (batting) and gingham. Cut a gingham casing for the rope tie 1m x 10cm (1yd x 4in), and a gingham bias strip 1.5m x 4cm (1½yd x 1½in). Cut the scraps into strips 6cm x 36cm (2½in x 14in). Taking a 5mm (¼in) seam allowance, sew the strips into a patched piece. From this cut a rectangle, a base, a flap and two straps. Lay the patchwork on top of the matching wadding and gingham pieces, tack (baste) through all layers and then quilt along the seam lines. Join the two short ends to make a tube. Centre the wadding along the gingham straps and fold the fabric round it. Turn under the raw edge, and stitch along the centre. Layer the patchwork, wadding and gingham base and flap pieces and quilt diagonally.

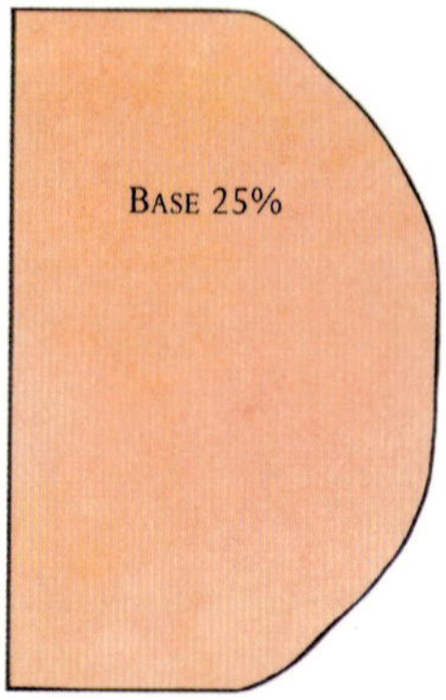

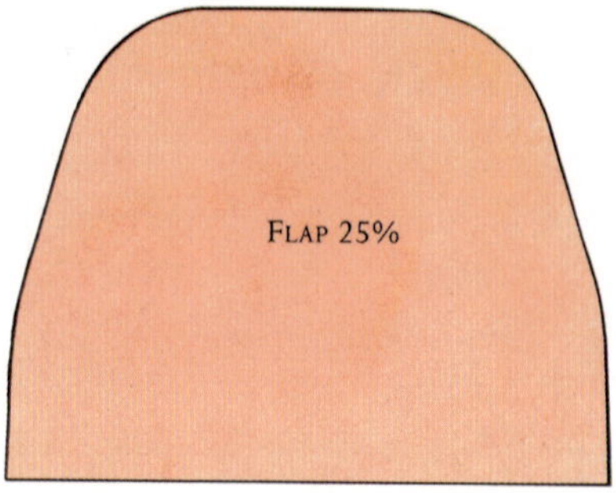

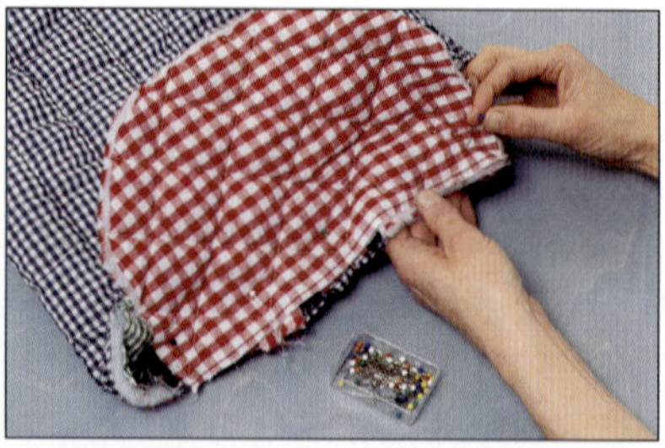

1

Wrong sides facing, pin the base to the tube. Insert the straps at either end, centred 5cm (2in) apart and pin to the bag. Bind the raw edges with the gingham bias strip.

2

Bind the top edge with the casing strip so that the ends meet at the centre front of the bag. Fold the binding over to right side, turn under a hem and top stitch below the previous seam.

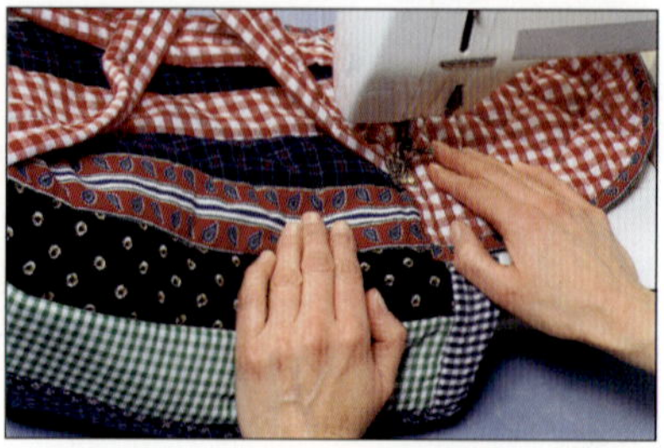

3

Bind the shaped edge of the flap with the gingham bias strip. Right sides facing, pin the flap to back of bag just below the casing. Stitch two rows, 1cm (½in) apart, close to the edge.

TO FINISH

Thread the rope through the casing and knot. Make a narrow fabric rouleau and sew to the flap. Sew on the toggle.

TOY BAG

Drawstring bags like this one make excellent storage space for all those tiny toys which most children seem to collect in large quantities. This bag has two rag dollies appliquéd on its pockets.

YOU WILL NEED

tracing paper and pencil
iron-on fusible bonding web
iron
red, green and cream fabric scraps
dressmaker's scissors
70cm x 115cm (27½in x 45in) striped cotton fabric
20cm x 90cm (8in x 36in) checked cotton fabric
sewing machine and matching thread
small amount of brown yarn
lace scraps
blue and red embroidery thread
crewel needle
dressmaker's pins
3m (3yd) cord

PREPARATION

Trace as many shapes as you need to make two dolls on to the fusible bonding web. Iron on to the fabric scraps and cut out. Cut out a rectangle 70cm x 100cm (27½in x 40in) in the striped fabric, and two pockets 20cm x 25cm (8in x 10in) in the checked fabric.

1

Assemble the fabric shapes and iron on to the pockets to make two dolls. Secure the pieces with machine zig zag. Sew lengths of yarn for hair and a scrap of lace on the dress hem. Sew blue french knots for eyes and sew a red smile.

2

Hem the long side of the striped fabric, fold in half and press. Hem the pocket tops, and press under the seam allowance on the other three sides. Pin the pockets to the front of the bag and top stitch in place.

3

Pin and stitch the bag along two sides. Fold over 10cm (4in) along the top edge and press.

4

Make two buttonholes each side of the seam, 15cm (6in) from the top edge. Stitch a line either side of the buttonholes. Cut the cord in half, thread through the buttonholes and knot.

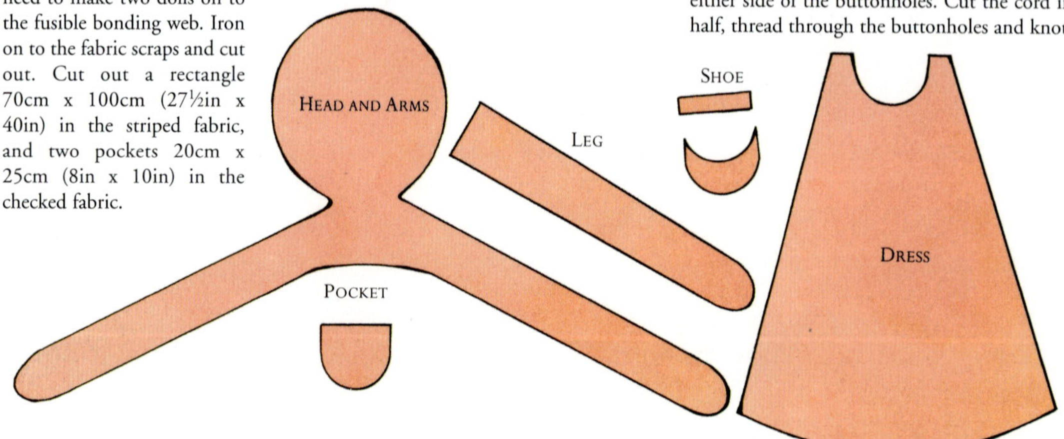

CHILD'S STRIP PATCHWORK WAISTCOAT

This waistcoat is made from patched strips. You can use long, narrow and seemingly useless pieces of fabric left over from previous projects. Fold the fabric like a concertina and cut into strips. Try to use strips that are somehow linked, either by colour tone or the size of the print.

YOU WILL NEED

commercial waistcoat pattern
assorted floral scraps
dressmaker's scissors
sewing machine and matching thread
iron
85cm x 90cm (34in x 36in) plain fabric
dressmaker's pins
needle
4 buttons

PREPARATION

Fabric amounts are given for a waistcoat to fit chest 64cm (26in). To make the patched piece, join five 6cm x 90cm (2½in x 36in) strips, taking a 5mm (¼in) seam allowance. Halve the patched piece and cut out two waistcoat fronts. Cut two backs, two fronts and two interfacings in plain cotton.

1

Right sides facing, machine the interfacings to the fronts and press the seams. Stitch the fronts to the back. Make up the lining and pin to the waistcoat, matching shoulder seams. Stitch round the outer edges leaving the side seams open. Trim the edges and clip.

2

Turn the waistcoat right side out and press. Pin the back to the fronts at the side seams and stitch, leaving a small gap. Clip and press open the seam allowances.

3

Make four evenly spaced buttonholes on the right front and sew four buttons to the left.

CHILD'S STRIP PATCHWORK SKIRT

This gathered skirt is made from pieced strips to match the child's waistcoat. The skirt is finished with a double hem band made from a floral and striped patchwork strip.

YOU WILL NEED

dressmaker's scissors

assorted scraps of floral and striped fabric

sewing machine and matching thread

40cm x 160cm (16in x 63in) plain fabric for lining

iron

needle

dressmaker's pins

elastic

PREPARATION

Fabric amounts are given for a skirt to fit waist 58cm (23in), with a back length of 50cm (20in). To make the patched piece, cut 32 strips 6cm x 40cm (2½in x 16in) from the floral and striped fabrics. Join together, taking a 5mm (¼in) seam allowance. Cut a striped and floral strip 6cm x 160cm (2½in x 63in) and join, long sides together, for the hem band. Right sides facing, join one edge of the hem band to the base of the skirt and the other to the lining fabric. Press and turn right sides out. For a waistband, cut a piece 12cm x 80cm (4¾in x 31½in).

1

Sew two rows of running stitch 5mm (¼in) and 1.5cm (½in) from the top of the skirt. Pull up the threads to gather the skirt to the size of the waistband.

2

Pin the waistband to the gathered edge and stitch. Fold over to the right side and pin. Top stitch along the waistband, just below the previous seam line, leaving a gap. Thread the elastic through the waistband and secure.

LOG CABIN THROW

The Log Cabin is a traditional patchwork design. While you can use any number of colours, choosing a limited combination is probably the best way to unify the whole design.

YOU WILL NEED

dressmaker's scissors

20cm x 90cm (8in x 36in) blue needlecord (fine-wale corduroy)

1m x 90cm (40in x 36in) red needlecord (fine-wale corduroy)

assortment of floral fabric scraps in red and blue

2m x 2.5m (2½yd x 3yd) plain blue fabric

dressmaker's pins

sewing machine and matching thread

iron

2m x 2.5m (2½yd x 3yd) red floral backing fabric

PREPARATION

The finished piece measures 1.8m x 2.3m (71in x 90½in) and is made from 12 blue pieced centres, six red pieced centres and 17 plain blue squares. It is edged with three borders. Cut out 12 blue and six red needlecord (fine-wale corduroy) 10cm (4in) squares. Cut the floral scraps, and some blue and red needlecord into strips 4cm (1½in) wide. Cut 17 plain blue 32cm (13in) squares. For the borders cut four red floral strips and four blue needlecord (fine-wale corduroy) strips 8cm (3in) wide. The pieced centres are worked from the middle out.

1

Sew a blue needlecord square to a red floral strip and trim even with the square. Sew a red floral string across the top edge of the pieced centre and trim even with the pieced centre. Sew a red floral strip to the left edge and trim.

2

To complete the centre, sew a fourth red floral strip to the lower edge, trim and press.

3

Continue to add strips round the centre. First add the blue floral strips, then the red floral strips and finally with the blue needlecord strips. Press and trim to 32cm (13in) square. Make up twelve blue centred squares and six red centred squares, alternating red and blue floral strips.

4

Sew a blue pieced centre to a plain blue square using the flag technique (see Basic Techniques). Repeat, until four blue pieced centres are separated by three plain blue squares. Make two more rows the same, then two rows with three red pieced centres separated by four plain blue squares. Join the rows so the colours alternate.

TO FINISH

Sew the borders to the patched piece (see Basic Techniques). Lay on top of the backing piece and, starting in the middle, tack (baste) through all the layers. Stitch round each pieced square to outline the quilt. Trim the backing to overlap the patchwork all round by 13cm (5in). Fold the backing over to the front of the throw to make an outer border. Turn under the raw edges and top stitch. Mitre the corners if wished (see Basic Techniques).

Cherry Basket Patchwork Cushion

The cherry basket used to decorate this striking cushion is a traditional patchwork design. Make it in plain contrasting colours, or in pretty prints for a completely different look.

You Will Need

paper and pencil
card (cardboard)
craft knife
scraps of red and white cotton fabric
dressmaker's scissors
38cm x 90cm (15in x 36in) cotton poplin
38cm (15in) square wadding (batting)
needle and tacking (basting) thread
dressmaker's pins
needle and matching thread
25cm (10in) square iron-on interfacing
iron
backing fabric
sewing machine and matching thread
square cushion pad

Preparation

Enlarge the triangle from the back of the book and cut out 18 card (cardboard) templates. Cut out 12 triangles in red fabric and six in white fabric, adding a 5mm (¼in) seam allowance. Cut out two 38cm (15in) squares in cotton poplin. Tack (baste) the wadding (batting) to the reverse of one square.

1

Pin and sew the triangles in pairs. Join eight triangles into a square, then join four more to the two top corners to make a large triangular shape. Follow the photographs for reference.

2

Pin the basket to the prepared poplin square, fold under the seam allowance and slip-stitch in place. Slip-stitch the two remaining triangles to make the base.

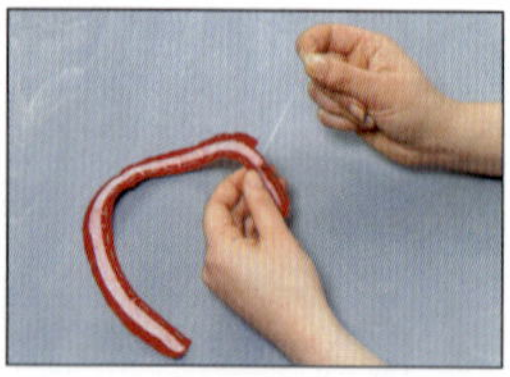

3

Draw a semi-circle on the interfacing with a 25cm (10in) base line and use this to cut out a handle 1cm (½in) wide. Iron on to a scrap of red fabric. Cut out, adding a 5mm (¼in) seam allowance, fold under the seam allowance and slip-stitch to the top of the basket.

To Finish

Work stab stitch round each triangle and the basket handle. Make a cushion cover (see Basic Techniques). Insert the cushion pad.

Hexagon Pin Cushion

Make this boldly patterned pin cushion from navy and white fabrics.

You Will Need

assorted plain and print scraps of navy fabric

tracing paper and pencil

card (cardboard)

craft knife

dressmaker's pins

needle and tacking (basting) thread

matching thread

wadding (batting)

Preparation

Enlarge and trace the hexagon on to paper and cut out 14 card (cardboard) templates. Cut out two plain navy patches, and four patches in three other navy fabrics, adding a 5mm (¼in) seam allowance. Pin and tack (baste) the patches to the card templates.

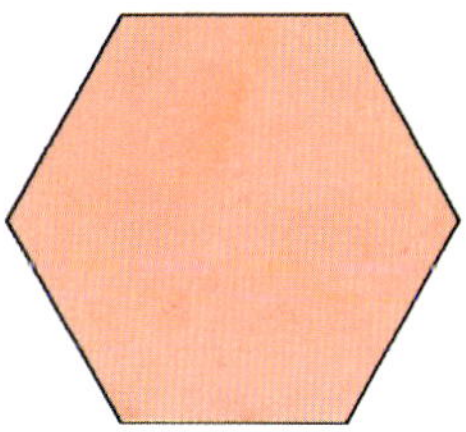

50%

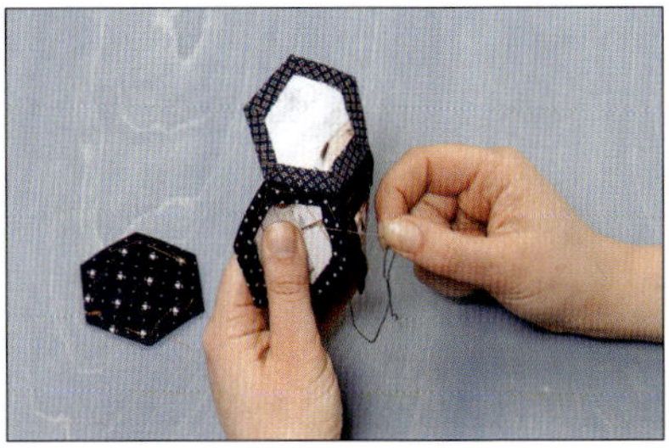

1

Join the hexagons into two flower shapes, with six patterned patches round a central navy patch. Oversew the piece neatly. Make a second flower shape the same way.

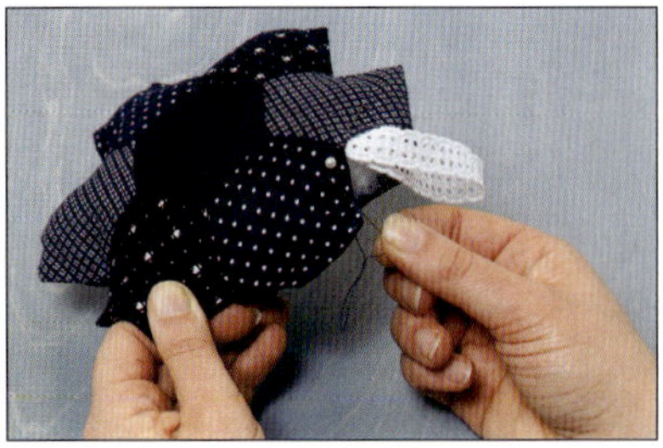

2

Wrong sides facing, pin and tack (baste) the two pieces together. Slip-stitch round the outside edge, leaving a small gap. Turn right side out. Fill with wadding (batting) and then slip-stitch the gap.

Crazy Patchwork Bootees

These pull-on quilted bootees have tops made from tiny pieces of crazy patchwork. Lined with gingham and secured at the top with elastic, they are a warm and comfortable gift for a baby.

You Will Need

paper and pencil

paper scissors

20cm x 90cm (8in x 36in) blue cotton denim

20cm x 90cm (8in x 36in) gingham fabric

dressmaker's scissors

scrap of wadding (batting)

assorted blue fabric scraps

dressmaker's pins

needle and tacking (basting) thread

sewing machine and matching thread

elastic

50cm (20in) bias binding

Preparation

Enlarge the pattern pieces from this page and from the back of the book. Cut out two tops, two soles and two front and side pieces in denim. Cut out two soles and four linings in gingham, and two soles in wadding (batting).

1

Cut small scraps of blue fabric and tack (baste) to the bootee tops, turning under the edges. Secure with machine zig zag stitch.

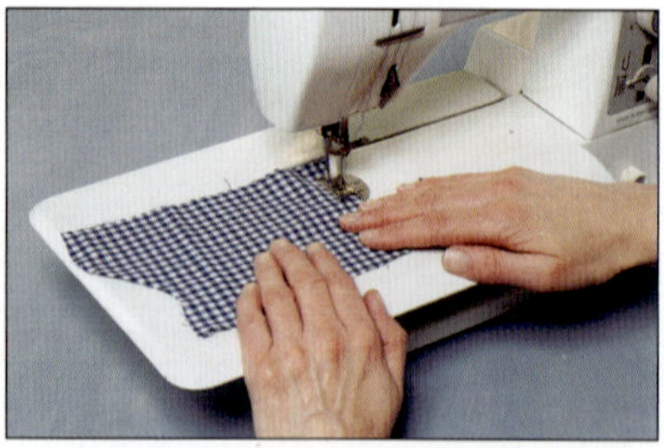

2

Stitch the lining pieces together along the two short edges.

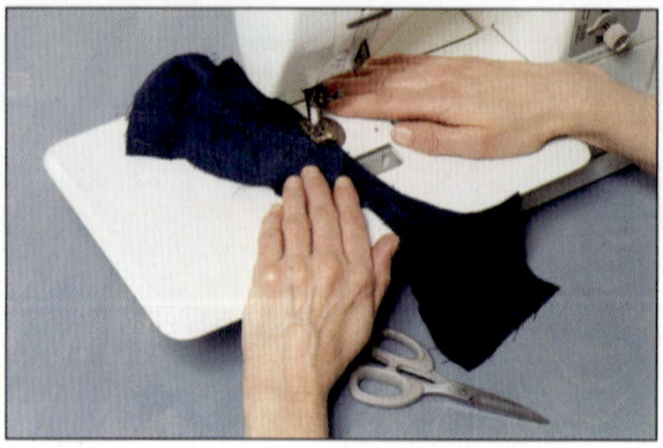

3

Right sides facing, insert the patchwork top into the denim front and side pieces. Pin the elastic along the top edge and stitch. Join the back seam. Right sides facing, attach the lining to the top edge, clip and turn through.

4

Sandwich the wadding (batting) soles between the denim and gingham soles. Tack through all the layers. Turn the bootees inside out, and pin and stitch the soles in place. Cover the seams with bias binding to neaten.

Front and Sides 50%

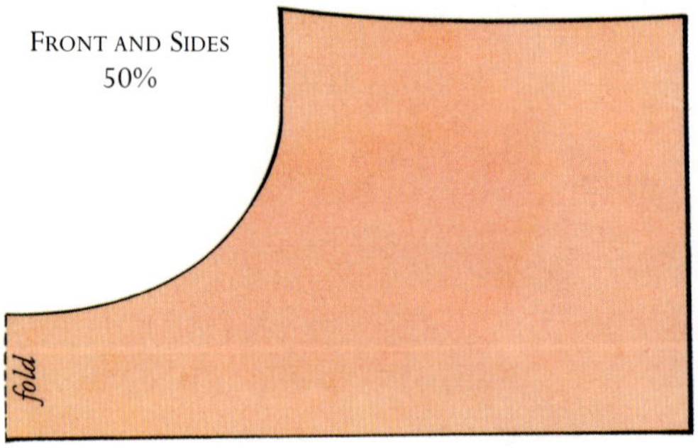

Lining 50%

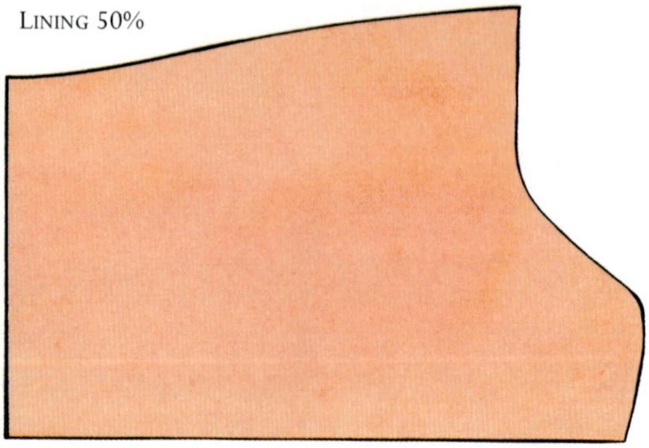

Baby's Appliqué Pillow

This little pillow is appliquéd with naïve bird and star motifs. The centre is surrounded by two borders, in gingham and striped fabric.

You Will Need

pencil and paper
iron-on interfacing
assorted fabric scraps
iron
dressmaker's scissors
36cm x 90cm (14in x 36in) calico
sewing machine and matching thread
blue and brown embroidery thread
crewel needle
small button (optional)
scraps of blue gingham
scraps of blue striped fabric
25cm (10in) square cushion pad
needle and matching thread

Preparation

Trace the motifs from the back of the book and transfer on to the interfacing. Iron to the fabric scraps and cut out. Cut out a 25cm (10in) square and a 36cm (14in) square in calico. Set the machine to zig zag and stitch the shapes on to the small calico square. Embellish with embroidery and sew on the button (optional). Cut four gingham strips 6cm x 25cm (2½in x 10in). Cut four striped strips 6cm x 36cm (2½in x 14in).

1

Right sides facing, make the gingham border, mitring the corners.

2

Pin and stitch the borders round the appliquéd square. Make up the striped border the same way and stitch round the first border. Clip the corners and press.

To Finish

Right sides facing, stitch the two calico squares together, leaving a small gap. Clip the corners and press. Turn right side out. Insert the pad and slip-stitch the gap.

Patchwork Cube

This soft baby's toy is a perfect project for a beginner to patchwork. Experiment with a different pattern for each side of the cube.

You Will Need

7cm x 90cm (2¾in x 36in) fabric strips, in five colours

dressmaker's scissors

dressmaker's pins

sewing machine and matching thread

wadding (batting)

needle and matching thread

Preparation

Cut each strip into thirteen 7cm (2¾in) squares. Following the illustrations, arrange the squares into six blocks, cutting some to make triangles. You can use a different patchwork design for each side of the cube.

1

Using the flag method (see Basic Techniques), pin and stitch the squares together to make six square blocks.

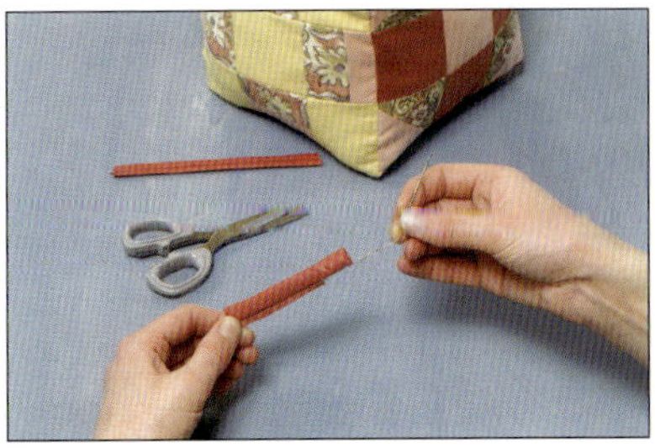

2

Right sides facing, pin and stitch four blocks to the central one. Join the top block to one side block. Stitch the sides in pairs, leaving a small gap on the last one to turn through. Fill with wadding (batting) and slip-stitch the gap. Make a small rouleau loop and stitch to one corner.

Patchwork Duffel Bag

This colourful duffel bag is made from a piece of curved block patchwork. The curved blocks bend in opposite directions when placed together for sewing.

You Will Need

50cm (20in) square turquoise cotton fabric
dressmaker's scissors
1m x 90cm (40in x 36in) black cotton fabric
1m x 90cm (40in x 36in) black lining fabric
paper and pencil
card (cardboard)
40cm (16in) square patterned cotton fabric
dressmaker's pins
sewing machine and matching thread
iron
80cm (32in) narrow piping cord
iron-on interfacing
60cm (24in) of 2cm (¾in) bias tape
needle and tacking (basting) thread
7 x 1cm (½in) brass rings
2m (2yd) thick cord

Preparation

The bag is made from 24 square blocks and measures 50cm (20in) deep by 75cm (30in). From the turquoise fabric, cut a top band 8cm x 80cm (3in x 32in). From the black cotton fabric, cut a circular base piece with a diameter of 30cm (12in), and bias strips for the piping. Cut the base to the same dimensions in the black lining fabric, then cut a lining measuring 55cm x 85cm (21½in x 34in).

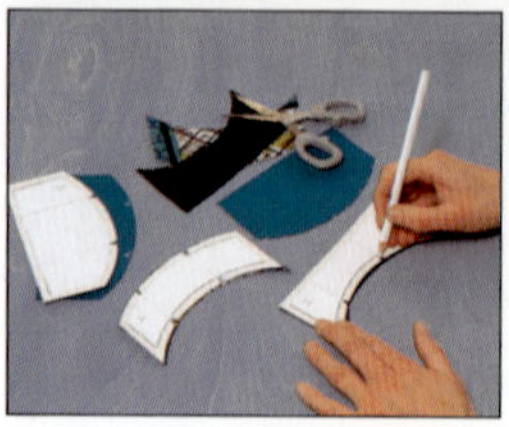

1

Trace the three templates from the back of the book on to card (cardboard). Cut out 24 pieces in each of the fabrics, using template 1 for the black, template 2 for the patterned fabric and template 3 for the turquoise fabric. Mark the notches and clip the curves (see Basic Techniques).

2

Working from the centre out, pin three different coloured pieces together between the notches to form a block. Repeat to make 24 blocks altogether. Stitch and press each block.

3

Lay out the blocks and arrange the design, alternating the curves as shown. Using the flag method (see Basic Techniques), sew into strips of four blocks. Sew the strips together to make one large patched piece, six blocks by four blocks.

To Finish

Tack (baste) the lining to the patchwork, wrong sides facing. Join the base to the bag and, using the narrow piping cord and the black bias strips, bind with piping (see Basic Techniques). Iron interfacing to the turquoise top band, turn under a small hem at top and bottom and pin to the bag. Insert six evenly spaced, doubled-over pieces of tape and rings round the band, and top stitch in place. Sew the last ring to the base. Thread the thick cord through the six rings and then tie it to the bottom ring.

CALICO BAG

The quilted base and pockets of this calico bag make it very strong, and so an ideal choice for travelling. When not in use, store bed linen in it for the spare room. The generous pockets can be filled with soap, towels and toothbrush to welcome your guest.

YOU WILL NEED

3m x 90cm (3yd x 36in) calico

50cm x 90cm (20in x 36in) cotton corduroy

1m (1yd) wadding (batting)

dressmaker's scissors

vanishing marker

dressmaker's pins

needle and tacking (basting) thread

sewing machine and matching thread

7 x 1cm (½in) eyelets (grommets)

2m (2yd) cotton rope

PREPARATION

For the base, cut a circle of calico, corduroy and wadding (batting) 43cm (17in) in diameter. For the pockets, measure the circumference of the circle and cut a piece of calico the length of the circumference by 45cm (18in). Fold this lengthwise round a strip of wadding (batting) and pin. For the bag, cut another piece of calico the length of the circumference by 60cm (24in). Cut five calico strips 8cm x 55cm (3in x 21½in), one 8cm x 65cm (3in x 26in) and one 5cm x 8cm (2in x 3in). Cut a wide bias strip to fit the circumference of the base.

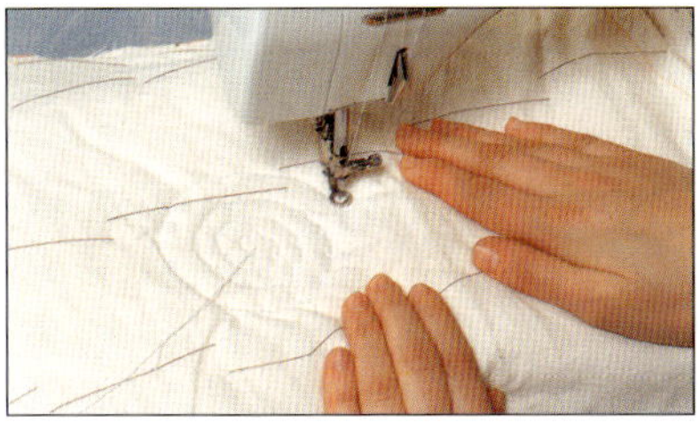

1

Place the wadding (batting) base circle between the corduroy and calico circles and tack (baste). Machine zig zag from the centre in a spiral. Tack the pocket piece, then zig zag lines up and down it. Remove the tacking threads.

2

Pin and stitch the bias calico strip to the base. Stitch the short strip of calico to the longest strip, fold over the small strip by 5cm (2in), tack and zig zag to make a square. Attach an eyelet (grommet).

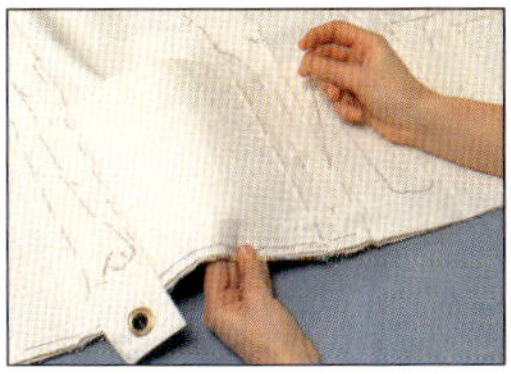

3

Pin the pocket piece and strips to the lower edge of the bag with the eyelet (grommet) positioned centrally, and hanging 4cm (1½in) below the lower edge. Top stitch the strips to the bag.

TO FINISH

Turn the top of the bag to the outside, first 1cm (½in), then 5cm (2in), and then another 5cm (2in). Press down and top stitch. Join the base to the bag and complete the binding. Attach pairs of eyelets (grommets) to the strips at the top of the bag, and thread with the rope.

San Blas Oven Mitts

Layers of brightly coloured cotton are used to make these attractive oven mitts. The bird shape is cut away layer by layer, and stitched by hand to reveal a different colour each time. The designs used by the San Blas Indians usually feature birds and animals.

You Will Need

dressmaker's paper
dressmaker's scissors
90cm x 45cm (36in x 18in) red cotton fabric
90cm x 45cm (36in x 18in) blue cotton fabric
90cm x 45cm (36in x 18in) white felt
vanishing marker
40cm x 23cm (16in x 9in) yellow cotton fabric
40cm x 23cm (16in x 9in) green cotton fabric
paper and pencil
dressmaker's pins
embroidery scissors
crewel needle
red, blue and green embroidery thread
iron
25cm x 2.5cm (10in x 1in) red bias binding

Preparation

Cut a pattern piece in dressmaker's paper 75cm x 18cm (30in x 7in), and round off the ends. Cut one in red cotton, one in blue cotton and one in white felt. Mark the pattern piece 20cm (8in) from one end and cut along the marked line for the mitt. Cut out two in red, yellow and green fabric, four in blue fabric and four in white felt.

1

Layer the pattern pieces in two stacks: blue, yellow, green, blue and red. Separate the bottom blue pieces. Pin the rest together. Enlarge and trace the bird motif from the back of the book twice, reversing it the second time.

2

Cut out one paper bird motif and place it on one mitt. Draw round it in pencil. Tack (baste) an inner line, 5mm (¼in) from the pencil line, to show where to cut.

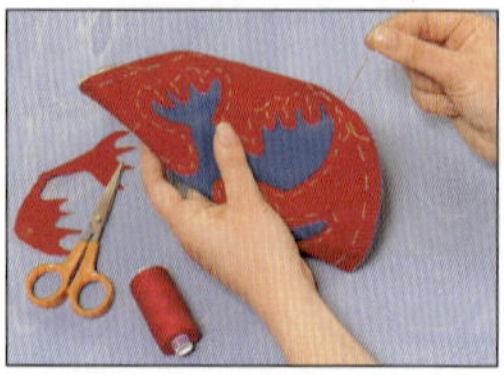

3

Cut away the red fabric inside the outline, leaving a small turning. Snip into the curves. Using red thread, turn under a small hem and slip-stitch through all layers.

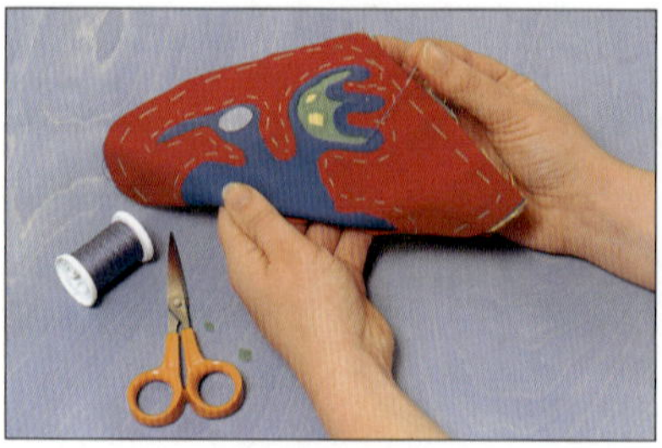

4

Draw the wings, head and tail on to the blue fabric. Cut away to reveal the green layer and hem in blue. Cut away to reveal the yellow wing details and hem in green thread. Remove the tacking stitches and press. Tack the reserved blue cotton piece to the last yellow piece as a lining. Bind the straight edge of the mitt with bias binding. Repeat for the second mitt, reversing the motif.

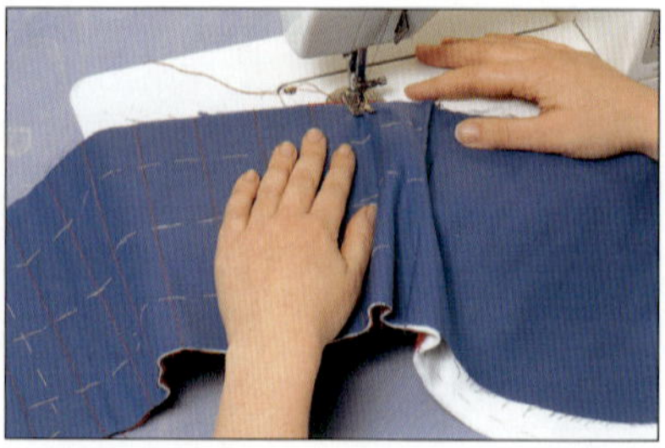

5

Tack pieces of cut felt to each end of the long felt strip. Lay this on the blue fabric with the extra felt next to the blue, and tack together. Mark a 4cm (1½in) grid along the length of the blue strip and machine quilt in red thread. Remove the tacking threads. Tack the red strip to the white felt. Lay the mitts with the blue lining facing the long red strip, tack and then sew close to the edge. Bind round the edges, then machine a bias binding loop to the join.

San Blas Cushion

This San Blas panel has been made up in brightly coloured cotton and sewn to a hessian (burlap) patch with a fringed border. The patch is then sewn on to a hessian cushion cover.

You Will Need

50cm x 90cm (20in x 36in) red cotton fabric
50cm x 90cm (20in x 36in) yellow cotton fabric
50cm x 90cm (20in x 36in) green cotton fabric
50cm x 90cm (20in x 36in) blue cotton fabric
dressmaker's scissors
paper and pencil
needle and tacking (basting) thread
crewel needle and yellow, blue, red, green and ecru embroidery thread
embroidery scissors
80cm x 90cm (32in x 36in) hessian (burlap)
dressmaker's pins
sewing machine and matching thread
40cm (16in) cushion pad

Preparation

Cut three red, two yellow, one green and one blue 20cm (8in) squares of fabric. Layer them red, yellow, green, red, yellow, blue, red, and tack (baste) together. Enlarge the motif and transfer to the fabric. Work the bird in San Blas appliqué (see San Blas Oven Mitts project). Machine a line 1cm (½in) from the edge of the patch and trim back. Cut out two pieces of hessian (burlap) 43cm (17in) square for the cover. Cut a hessian patch 28cm (11in) square.

1

Pin the bird motif on to the hessian (burlap) patch. Set the machine to zig zag and work satin stitch round the edge of the patch. With a pin draw the threads along all four sides to make the fringe. Make an envelope cushion cover to fit the pad (see Basic Techniques).

SAN BLAS DRAWSTRING BAG

Nine patches are sewn together to make the front panel for this colourful drawstring bag. The animal motifs include a butterfly, a peacock and a fish, and are taken from traditional South American designs.

YOU WILL NEED

45cm x 71cm (18in x 28in) red cotton fabric

sewing machine and red thread

25cm x 90cm (10in x 36in) red cotton fabric

25cm x 90cm (10in x 36in) yellow cotton fabric

25cm x 90cm (10in x 36in) blue cotton fabric

25cm x 90cm (10in x 36in) green cotton fabric

dressmaker's scissors

tracing paper and pencil

dressmaker's pins

crewel needle

red, yellow, blue and green embroidery thread

embroidery scissors

1m (1yd) thick cord

PREPARATION

To make the bag, fold over one of the long edges of the fabric by 5cm (2in), turn under a small hem and machine stitch. Cut the patchwork fabric into enough squares to make nine patches measuring 11cm (4½in) square. Layer the squares and tack (baste) together in stacks. Enlarge the motifs and transfer to the patches. Work the San Blas appliqué (see San Blas Oven Mitts project).

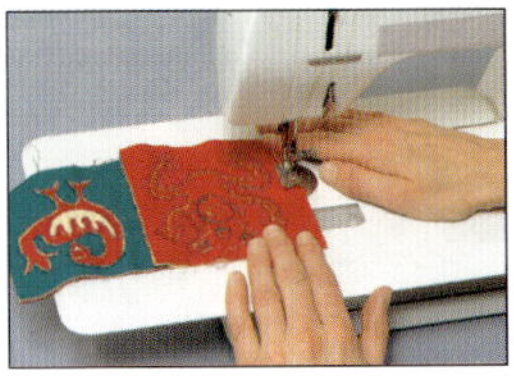

1

Join the patches in strips of three, then join the three strips to make a square.

TO FINISH

Pin the patchwork square to one side of the red fabric, parallel to the lower edge. Set the machine to zig zag and stitch the patchwork to the bag. Right sides facing, fold the bag in half and make up (see Basic Techniques). Thread the top channel with the cord and knot the ends.

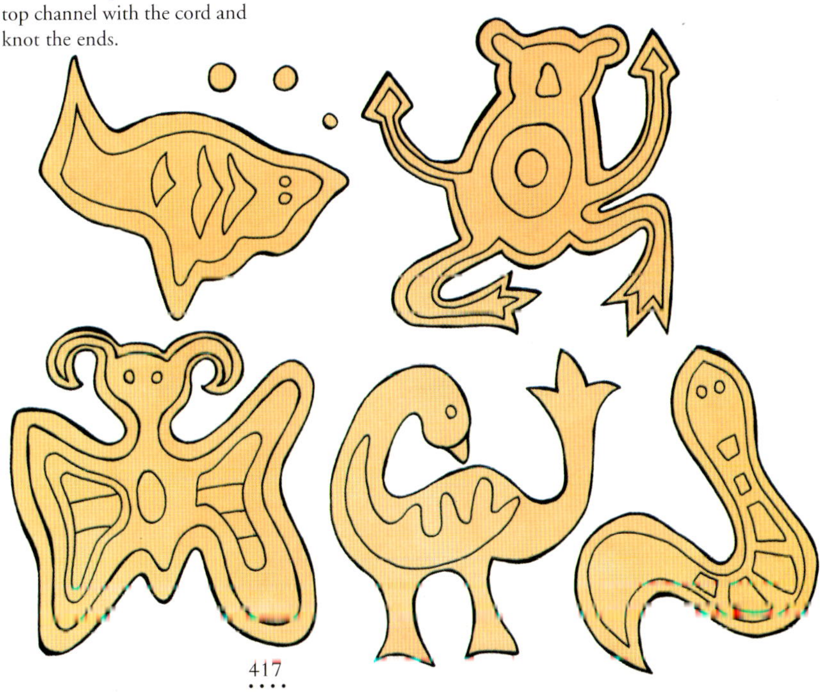

NOTEBOOK COVER

This notebook has been covered with a piece of Seminole patchwork. The paper is cut on the diagonal, sewn and patched to form diamonds. Cover an address book and diary to make a matching set.

YOU WILL NEED

notebook
card (cardboard)
selection of coloured papers
pencil
craft knife
paper scissors
sewing machine and matching thread
paper glue
paper varnish

PREPARATION

Open the notebook, lay it flat on a piece of card (cardboard) and draw round it. Using a ruler and craft knife, cut out the shape. Fold the card in half and press firmly along the fold line.

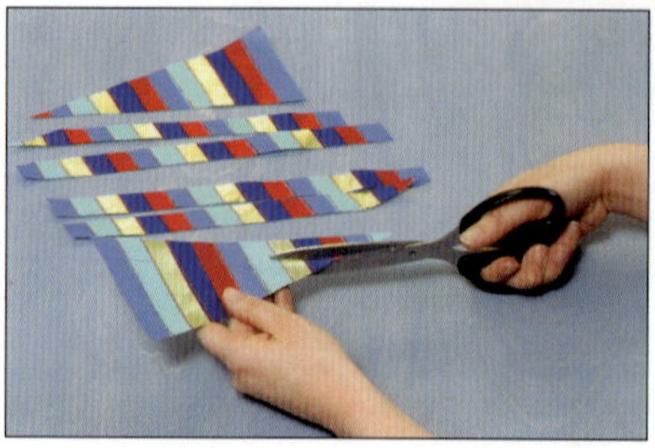

1

Measure the paper into strips 2cm (¾in) wide and cut out. Set the sewing machine to zig zag. Overlap the strips and stitch into one piece. Cut the piece into angled sections 2cm (¾in) wide, as shown.

2

Overlap the sections so that they are staggered to form vertical diamond shapes. Use up all the sections. Stitch together.

TO FINISH

Cut the patchwork into a rectangle and glue it to the piece of card (cardboard). Leave to dry and then trim to size. Varnish the cover and when dry, glue to the notebook.

PADDED COAT HANGER

Padded coat hangers are a practical way to keep clothes in good shape. Make this piece of Seminole patchwork from satin ribbons – the end result will be very colourful.

YOU WILL NEED

37cm (15in) wooden coat hanger

tape measure

scrap of wadding (batting)

dressmaker's scissors

needle and tacking (basting) thread

5cm x 50cm (2in x 20in) satin ribbon in three colours

sewing machine and matching thread

vanishing marker

scraps of ribbon

PREPARATION

Measure the coat hanger and cut a piece of wadding (batting) to fit. Wrap round the hanger and tack (baste) the long edges together.

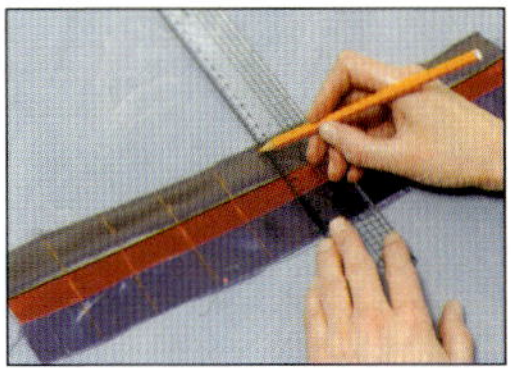

1

Machine the ribbons together. Mark across every 5cm (2in) and cut into strips.

2

Arrange the strips, offsetting them so that they are staggered. Reverse every other strip. Make two patches of equal length. Right sides facing, stitch them together round the edges, leaving a gap on the top edge.

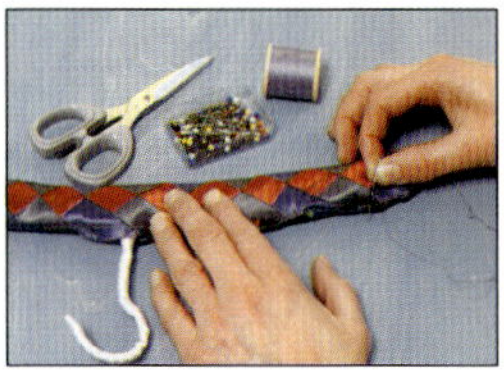

3

Turn right side out and cover the hanger. Turn under a hem on the raw edges and slipstitch.

TO FINISH

Wrap the metal hook with a length of ribbon and slipstitch in place. Decorate with contrasting ribbon.

GIFT TAGS

These gift tags are made from patchwork strips cut from plain coloured paper. Patterned gift wrapping paper could also be used in the same way to make an interesting piece of Seminole patchwork.

YOU WILL NEED

selection of coloured papers
paper scissors
sewing machine and matching thread
card (cardboard)
paper glue
paper varnish
hole punch
scraps of ribbon

DESIGN A PREPARATION

Cut two strips of paper in one colour 2cm (¾in) wide and one contrasting strip 1cm (½in) wide. Arrange the narrow strip between the wide ones. Overlap and machine zig zag stitch together. Next cut two strips 2cm (¾in) wide in two different colours, and one strip in a third colour 1cm (½in) wide. Arrange and stitch as before.

1
Cut the first patch into strips 1cm (½in) wide, and the second into strips 2cm (¾in) wide.

2
Arrange as shown, with one narrow strip placed between two wide ones, then stitch.

DESIGN B PREPARATION

Cut two strips of paper in two different colours 2cm (¾in) wide, and two strips in two more colours 1cm (½in) wide. Arrange the narrow strips between the wide ones. Overlap and machine zig zag stitch together. Next cut three strips of paper in different colours, one 3cm (1¼in), one 2cm (¾in) and one 1cm (½in) wide. Stitch the narrow strip between the two wide ones.

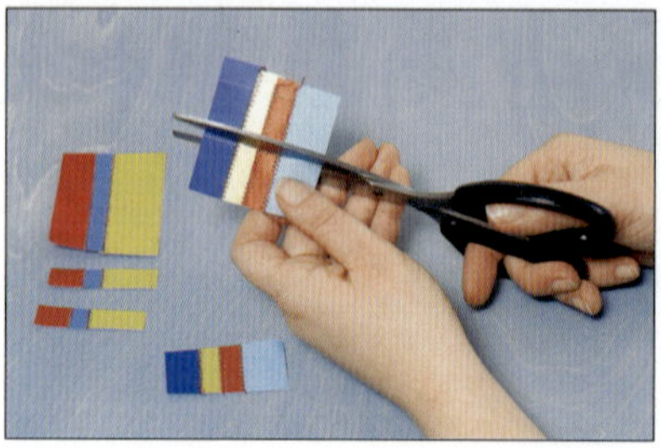

1
Cut one patch into strips 2cm (¾in) wide, and one into strips 1cm (½in) wide.

2
Arrange as shown, with two narrow strips placed between two wide ones, then stitch.

TO FINISH

Cut two pieces of card (cardboard) to size and glue on to the paper patches. Varnish and leave to dry. Punch a hole in one corner of each card and thread with ribbon.

SASHIKO QUILT

Sashiko quilting originated in Japan in the 18th century as protective clothing worn by firemen. The wadding (batting) is held between two layers of indigo fabric with white running stitches – the closer the stitches, the more durable the garment.

YOU WILL NEED

card (cardboard}
pencil
craft knife
2m x 90cm (2¼yd x 36in) assorted plain and print cotton fabrics
dressmaker's scissors
1.3m x 1.6m (52in x 64in) wadding (batting)
sewing machine and matching thread
iron
dressmaker's pins
1.3m x 1.6m (52in x 64in) cotton backing
vanishing marker
white quilting thread
crewel needle

PREPARATION

Make three card (cardboard) templates, one 11cm (4½in) square, one 5cm (2in) square and one 3cm (1¼in) square. Using the 11cm (4½in) template, cut the plain and print fabrics into 180 squares.

1

Using the two smaller card templates, draw three squares on each plain fabric square – two diagonal to the fabric square, and repeat the smallest square as a square on top of the smallest diagonal.

2

Lay the squares 12 across and 15 down. Stitch in horizontal rows using the flag method (see Basic Techniques). Press the seams in opposite directions. Stitch the strips together.

3

Sandwich the wadding (batting) between the patched piece and the cotton backing. Pin and tack (baste) the layers together (see Basic Techniques). Quilt along the marked lines in white thread using running stitch.

TO FINISH

Trim the wadding (batting) back to the finished edge and trim the backing to 2cm (¾in) from the edge. Turn the backing over to the top, mitre the corners and slip-stitch.

BOLSTER CUSHION

This small bolster cushion is made from calico and ribbed silk. A pattern of slashes is cut into the top silk fabric and neatly hemmed to the calico under-cover. This creates the interesting texture, which is complemented by fringing.

YOU WILL NEED

paper and pencil
70cm x 90cm (28in x 36in) calico
70cm x 90cm (28in x 36in) raw silk
dressmaker's scissors
vanishing marker
sharp scissors
iron
needle and tacking (basting) thread
sewing machine and matching thread
wadding (batting)

PREPARATION

Cut a paper template for the main piece. Cut out in both calico and silk. For the base, cut two in each fabric. To make the frayed fringe, cut two strips of calico, 5cm x 55cm (2in x 21½in).

TO FINISH

Right sides facing, stitch the short ends to make a tube, leaving a 10cm (4in) gap in the middle for turning. Tack (baste) the fringe strips each end of the tube. Stitch the base pieces to the tube. Turn the bolster right side out and fray the calico down to the seam line using a needle. Fill the bolster with wadding (batting) and slip-stitch the opening closed.

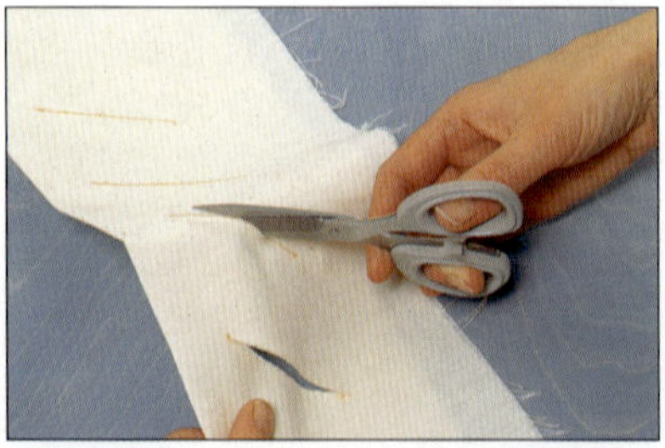

1

Transfer the slash line design to the calico with a vanishing marker and cut with sharp scissors.

2

Turn under a small hem on each of the slash lines and press on to the wrong side. Tack (baste) the calico to the silk round the almond shapes.

3

Slip-stitch round the almond shapes. Press flat on the wrong side.

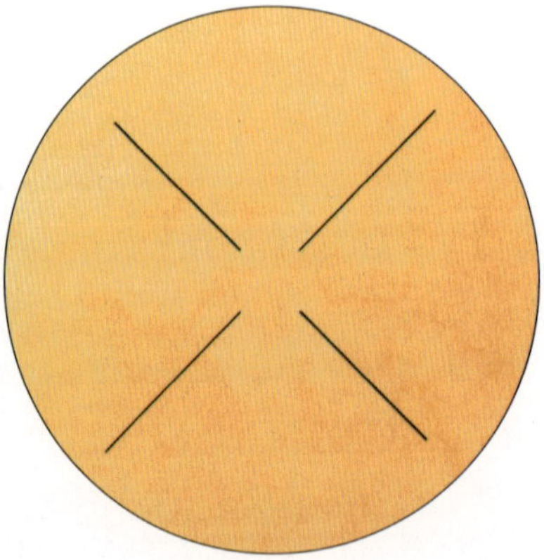

BASE
18cm (7in)

MAIN PIECE

BOOK COVER

Inlay appliqué is worked in silk to make this luxurious book cover. Rectangles are cut into the top layer and patches of brightly coloured silks are then fitted into the frame.

YOU WILL NEED

book

black silk scrap to fit the book, plus 5cm (2in)

vanishing marker

dressmaker's scissors

orange silk scrap, twice the size of the black silk

needle and tacking (basting) thread

sharp scissors

dressmaker's pins

matching thread

assorted silk scraps in bright colours

sewing machine

PREPARATION

Open the book, lay it flat on the black silk and draw round it. Cut out with a 2.5cm (1in) seam allowance. Cut another piece in orange silk. Halve the remaining piece of orange silk, lay the closed book on it, draw the outline and cut two pieces plus seam allowances.

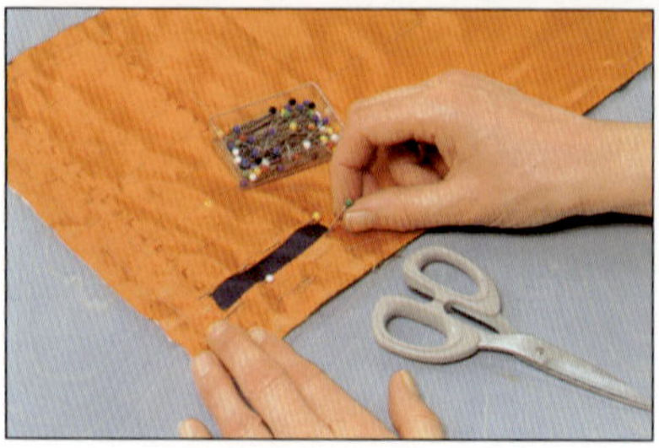

1

Tack (baste) the large piece of orange silk on top of the black silk. Mark a row of rectangles down the centre front half. Tack through the marked lines. One rectangle at a time, cut into the corners through the top layer. Turn under a hem round the rectangle, pin and stitch.

2

Cut several pieces of silk in assorted colours to fit the black rectangles. Centre and tack each piece in the centre of one black rectangle on the right side. Hem the inlay piece and push it behind the frame. Slip-stitch to the black silk.

TO FINISH

To make the cover pockets, turn under a hem on the long edge on each orange half piece. Machine stitch in place. Right sides facing, pin to the book cover and stitch. Fit the book sleeves into the pockets.

Slashed Silk Bag

This intriguing little bag is made from patches of slashed silks, sewn together inside out. This makes a design feature out of the seams and the ragged texture. The bag is fastened with a silk loop and a knotted silk button.

You Will Need

25cm x 90cm (10in x 36in) calico

dressmaker's scissors

iron

15cm x 90cm (6in x 36in) iron-on interfacing

scraps of silk in six contrasting colours

dressmaker's pins

sewing machine and matching thread

embroidery scissors

Preparation

Cut ten 12.5cm (5in) calico squares. Iron the interfacing to the squares and place them in pairs, interfacing sides together. Cover each one with six assorted silk squares cut to the same size and pin.

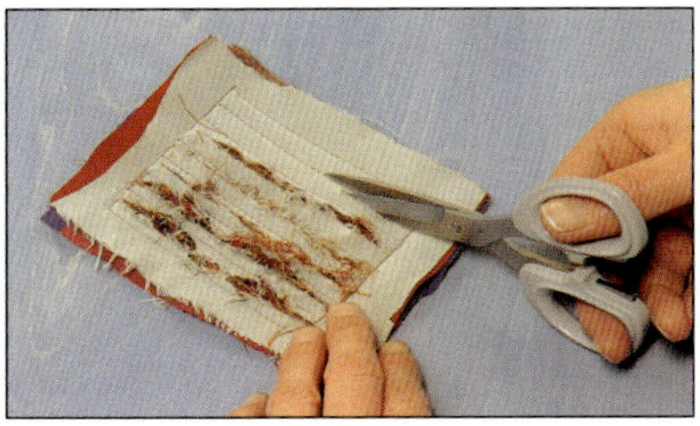

1

Stitch a line 1cm (½in) round the edges of each square then stitch lines, 1cm (½in) apart, within the square. Slice between the lines, cutting through all the colours except the last.

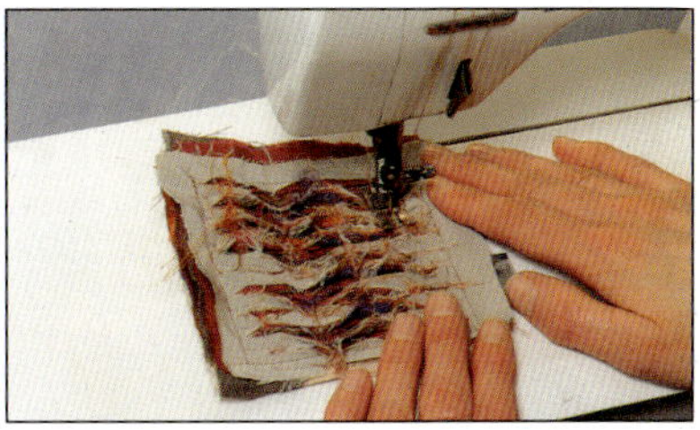

2

The layers of fabric will escape to the surface. Stitch a horizonal line across the vertical cuts in one direction, then work back in the other direction, 1cm (½in) apart. Cover the whole area in this way.

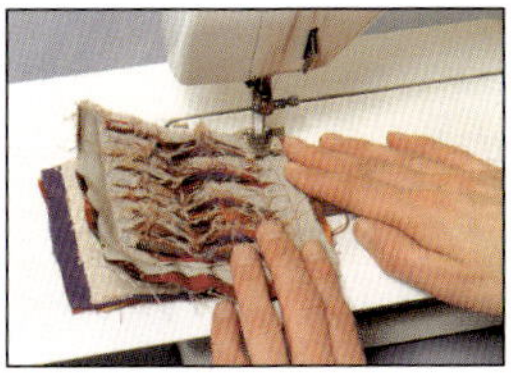

3

Place two finished squares together, calico sides facing, and stitch 1cm (½in) from the edge. Stitch another decorated patch to each side of the central square.

To Finish

Stitch the sides of the bag together. Sew a silk loop and a knotted button made from silk scraps to the top.

BABY BLANKET

This is another example of inlaid appliqué. Here the method is used to stitch a bird motif on to a baby's blanket. The motif is then decorated with brightly coloured embroidery threads.

YOU WILL NEED

wool blanket
dressmaker's scissors
paper and pencil
card (cardboard)
craft knife
scraps of coloured blanket fabric
dressmaker's pins
vanishing marker
needle and tacking (basting) thread
sharp scissors
sewing machine and contrasting thread
iron
assorted embroidery threads
crewel needle

PREPARATION

Cut the blanket to the required size for a cot (crib) or child's bed. Enlarge and trace the bird motif and cut templates in card (cardboard). Cut out the shapes in coloured fabric, adding a 2cm (¾in) seam allowance. Position the templates on the right side of the blanket and draw round. Tack (baste) carefully over the line.

1

Pin and tack the bird shapes to the wrong side of the blanket, on top of the tacked outline.

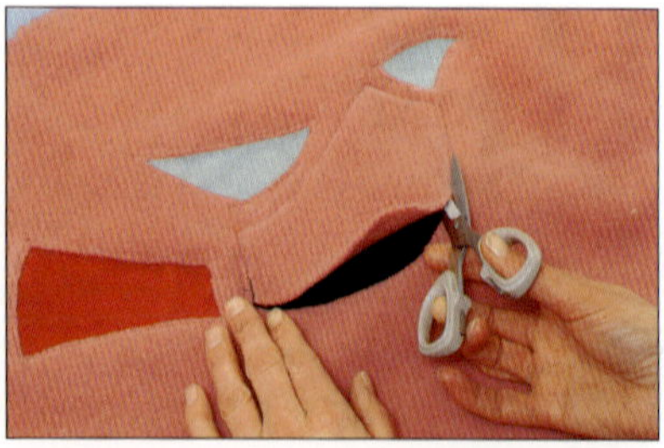

2

From the right side, carefully cut the fabric along the outline.

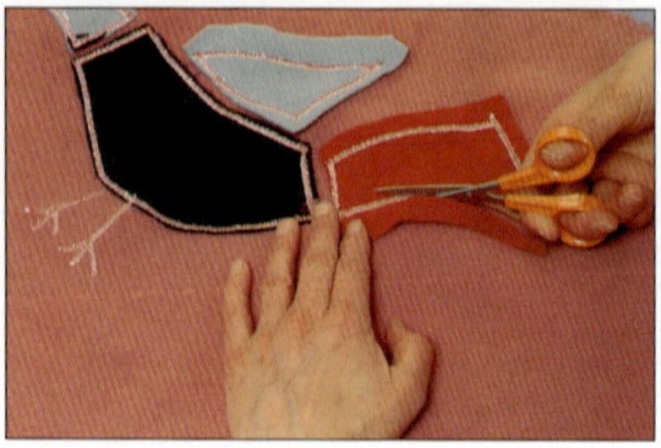

3

Set the machine to zig zag, pin a piece of paper to the wrong side of the appliqué pieces and work a wide satin stitch over the raw edges. Stitch the bird's legs, as shown. Trim away any excess fabric.

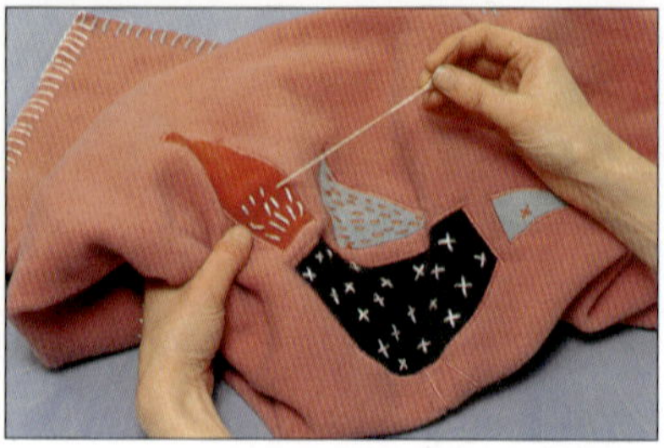

4

Press under a narrow hem all round the blanket and stitch with a wide blanket stitch in contrasting thread. Hand stitch details on to the bird using embroidery threads.

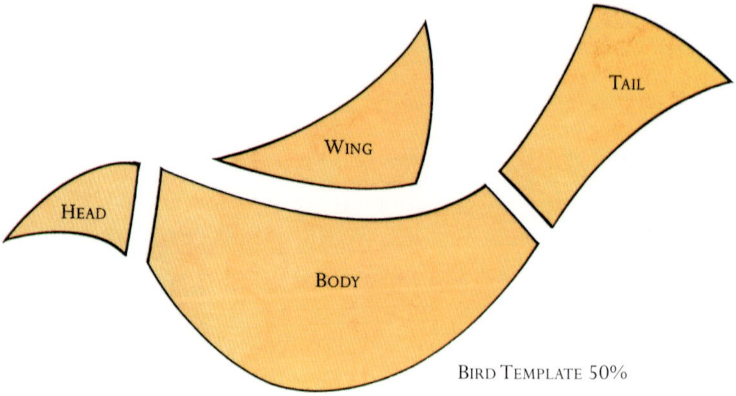

BIRD TEMPLATE 50%

Seminole Towel

A geometric patchwork piece, cut into narrow strips then stitched in rows, makes an attractive border for a bathroom towel.

You Will Need

12cm x 90cm (5in x 36in) cotton fabric in two colours

vanishing marker

dressmaker's scissors

iron

scrap of iron-on fusible bonding web

sewing machine and matching thread

20cm x 90cm (8in x 36in) backing fabric

dressmaker's pins

bath towel

Preparation

Cut both cotton fabrics into three strips 6cm x 40cm (2½in x 16in), and iron to the bonding web. Alternate the colours so that the strips overlap. Machine together with a zig zag stitch to make one piece of patchwork.

1

Cut the patchwork into strips 2cm (¾in) wide. Offset the strips on a piece of backing fabric as shown and iron on. Secure with a zig zag stitch.

2

Mark a horizontal line through the centre of the diamonds and cut into long strips.

3

Pin several strips to each end of the towel, running parallel to the edge. Machine in place.

QUILTED EGG COSY

This egg cosy is a tiny copy of a traditional Nepalese hat. It is quilted in cotton fabric with white thread and topped with a woollen tassel.

YOU WILL NEED

card (cardboard) and pencil
craft knife
dressmaker's scissors
18cm x 24cm (7in x 9½in) plain cotton fabric
18cm x 24cm (7in x 9½in) lining fabric, in contrasting colour
15cm x 20cm (6in x 8in) wadding (batting)
needle and tacking (basting) thread
vanishing marker
white quilting thread
crewel needle
embroidery scissors
sewing machine and matching thread
scraps of knitting wool

PREPARATION

Enlarge the template and cut out in card (cardboard). Cut out two pieces in both cotton and lining, adding a 1cm (½in) seam allowance all round. Cut out two pieces in wadding (batting), without any seam allowance, and sandwich each between the cotton and the lining. Tack (baste) the layers together (see Basic Techniques). Mark a geometric design, in freehand, on to both cotton shapes.

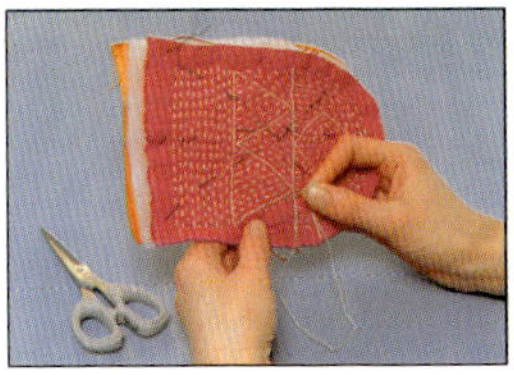

1

Work over the design in small, neat running stitches with quilting thread, filling the whole area. Make the second side the same.

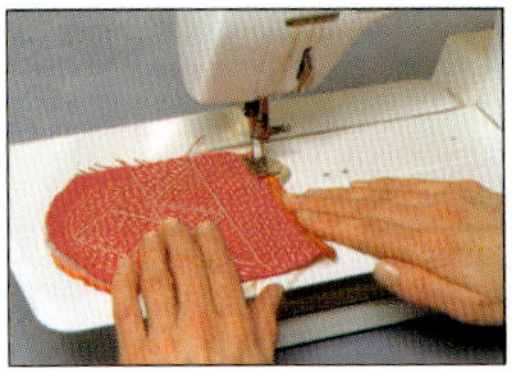

2

Trim the top fabric back to the wadding. Bind the lower edge with lining fabric and top-stitch. Right sides facing, stitch round the seam line.

3

Cut a piece of card (cardboard) 1cm x 2.5cm (½in x 1in) and wind lengths of knitting wool round it several times. The more you wind, the thicker the tassel.

50%

TO FINISH

Pull the wool carefully off the card (cardboard) and secure at the top with a short length of wool. Splice the wool through the other end of the loop, and trim. Bind the uncut strands together at the top. Stitch the tassel to the top of the finished egg cosy.

PA NDAU APPLIQUÉ FRAME

An elaborate maze design from the Hmong people of South East Asia, known as "crooked road" or "frog's legs". This normally complicated appliqué technique is simplified here.

YOU WILL NEED

dressmaker's scissors
45cm x 90cm (18in x 36in) black cotton fabric
30cm x 60cm (12in x 24in) white cotton fabric
45cm (18in) square graph paper
pencil
thick black pen
spray starch
iron
vanishing marker
dressmaker's pins
needle and matching thread
embroidery scissors
two mount board squares, 17.5cm (6¾in) square and 16.5cm (6½in) square
double-sided tape
fabric glue
brass curtain ring

PREPARATION

Cut the black fabric in half to make two pieces 45cm (18in) square, and the white fabric to make two pieces 30cm (12in) square.

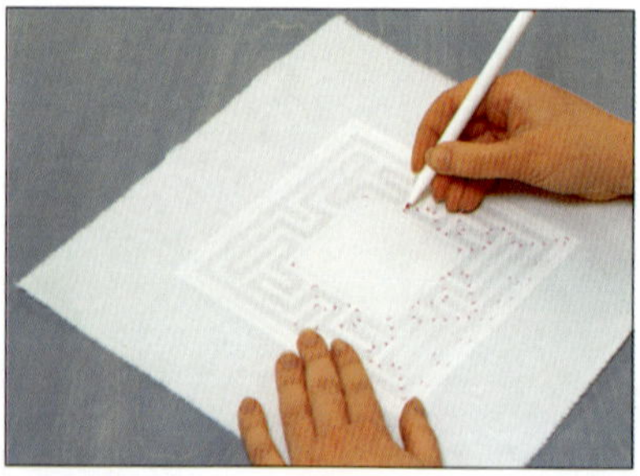

1

Trace the template from the back of the book on to graph paper and fill in the lines of the design with thick black pen. Spray both sides of one white square with starch and press. Lay the fabric on top of the graph paper and mark the corners of the design with the vanishing marker.

2

Place one square of black cotton between the two white squares with the marked one uppermost. Pin and tack (baste) around the inside and outside edges of the fabric frame. Tack (baste) crossways in the middle of each side. Cutting one section at a time, make a slit in the outside black line, always keeping the line central. Snip into the corners.

3

Using the point of the needle, fold under a tiny turning and slip-stitch a hem. Stitch closer together at the corners. Work the whole frame one quarter at a time. Use the corner marks as guidelines and keep referring back to the original design.

4

Pin a small hem on the outside and inside edges of the finished piece. Cut a 6cm (2½in) square in the centre of the large mount board. Lay the appliqué face down and cut into the corners of the window. Stretch the white fabric on to double-sided tape. Glue the black fabric to cover the small square. Place together and slip-stitch the sides. Sew a brass ring to the top.

WOOL HAT

This hat with a turn-back border is made from blanket fabric, and ties in a knot at the crown. The inlaid appliqué motifs which run round the border are whip stitched in a contrasting colour.

YOU WILL NEED

40cm x 90cm (16in x 36in) woollen blanket fabric

dressmaker's scissors

paper and pencil

card (cardboard)

craft knife

vanishing marker

scraps of woollen blanket fabric in two colours

60cm x 5cm (24in x 2in) iron-on interfacing

iron

needle and contrasting thread

sewing machine and matching thread

PREPARATION

Cut a piece of fabric 60cm x 40cm (24in x 16in). Turn under a double hem, 2cm (¾in) wide, and machine stitch. Cut two ties 23cm x 5cm (9in x 2in). Trace and cut templates out of card (cardboard).

1

Alternate the two templates along the hem, drawing round them. Cut out the shapes.

2

Draw the shapes on to the wool scraps, and cut out an equal number in each colour. Lay a cut motif into a corresponding shape and iron the interfacing over it. Work along the hem fusing the interfacing to the fabric as you go.

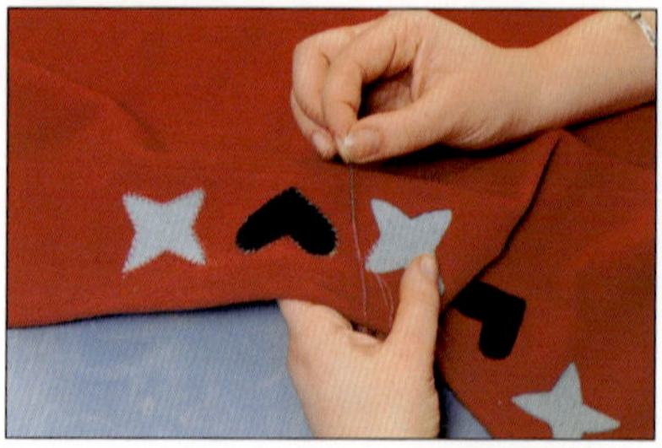

3

Right sides facing, whip stitch over the cut edges in a contrasting colour (see Basic Techniques). Fold the hat in half and machine the top and back seams.

4

To make the ties, press under both long and one short edge, fold in half lengthways and zig zag round the edges. Slip the raw ends into each top corner of the hat. Turn back the appliquéd border and slip-stitch to the hat. Stitch the ties to the top seam and tie in a knot.

Baby's Appliquéd Cardigan

Felt animal motifs reminiscent of mola work are appliquéd with tiny blanket stitches in a contrasting colour. Knit this patchwork cardigan, or buy one ready-made.

You Will Need

3 x 25 g (1 oz) balls random-dyed red yarn
1 x 25 g (1 oz) ball in two contrasting shades
4mm (No 8) knitting needles
white, red and navy felt
dressmaker's scissors
needle and tacking (basting) thread
paper and pencil
embroidery scissors
dressmaker's pins
white, red and navy embroidery thread
crewel needle

To fit: 50cm (20in) chest
Actual size: 58cm (23in)
Length: 29cm (11½in)
Sleeve length: 23cm (9in)

Preparation

Tension: worked in stocking stitch on 4mm (No 8) needles, 20 sts x 24 rows measures 10cm (4in). Knit the cardigan as follows.
Back: knit a piece 52 sts wide by 32cm (13in) long, with a 1cm (½in) border and divided into 16 patches, each 13 sts wide by 7cm (2¾in) deep.
Fronts: cast on 26 sts and work in patches, as back. Knit straight to 15cm (6in). Shape the neck by decreasing 9 sts on one edge over the remaining rows. Reverse the shapings for the other front.
Sleeves: cast on 39 sts and work a 2cm (¾in) border. The sleeves are divided into nine patches.
Press lightly. Sew the shoulder seams and set in the sleeves. Sew the side and sleeve seams.
Cut the felt into 10cm (4in) squares and layer red/white/red or navy/white/navy and tack (baste). Cut one stack for each front and each sleeve.

1

Trace the motifs from the back of the book on to paper and then transfer to felt. Cut out the felt shapes, cutting a wide base layer, and cut eyes and mouth from the top layer. Pin and tack (baste) the first shape to the cardigan. Working in layers, secure with small blanket stitches in contrasting coloured threads.

2

For the fastenings, cut four 2.5cm (1in) squares in white felt and fold in half to make triangles. Place the straight folded edge to the front edge of the cardigan and pin. Blanket stitch round two sides of the triangle in red.

3

For each tie, cut three 28cm (11in) lengths of embroidery thread. Sew the threads to the front, under the felt triangles. Plait the threads and tie together.

CHILD'S PATCHWORK SWEATER

This sweater is made of strips of different coloured squares knitted with simple motifs. The strips are then sewn together into blocks. The finished seams are laced in white and the border edged with pompons.

YOU WILL NEED

1 x 25 g (1 oz) ball yarn in six shades

4mm (No 8) knitting needles

pencil and squared paper

needle and matching thread

small amount of white yarn

crewel needle

70cm (28in) pompon tape

TO FIT: 61cm (24in) chest
ACTUAL SIZE: 68.5cm (27in)
LENGTH: 33cm (13in)
SLEEVE LENGTH: 23cm (9in)

PREPARATION

Tension: Worked in pattern on 4mm (No 8) needles, 24 sts x 26 rows measures 10cm (4in). To obtain the correct tension, change the needle size.

Draw the motifs from the back of the book on to squared paper. Each block is 26 stitches by 28 rows. For the back and front, knit three strips of three blocks. Shape the front neck half way up the last centre block.

1

For each sleeve, knit two strips of two blocks. Pin and sew the strips together from the wrong side.

2

Lace the work on the right side over the joined seams using white yarn. Then lace across from left to right to separate the coloured blocks.

3

Neaten the edges by knitting two rows round the neck edge and lower sleeve edges. Sew the pompon tape round the bottom edge.

APPLIQUÉ SUNFLOWER

Appliqué a shiny satin flower on to the bib of a child's dress or dungarees (overalls). This simple motif is stitched by hand.

YOU WILL NEED

paper and pencil
card (cardboard)
craft knife
scraps of iron-on interfacing
sharp scissors
iron
assorted satin scraps
dressmaker's pins
needle and matching thread

PREPARATION

Copy the templates on to card (cardboard) and cut out. Transfer each petal and the flower centre on to the interfacing. Cut out the shapes with a sharp pair of scissors.

FLOWER CENTRE AND PETAL

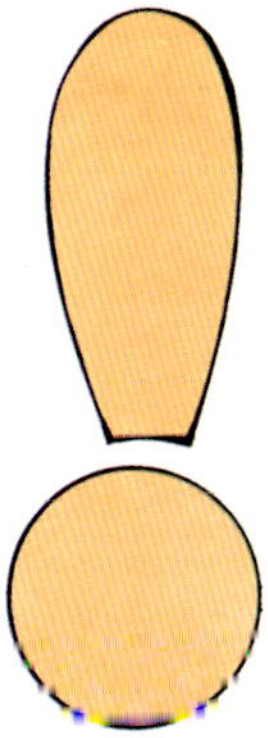

1

Iron the interfacing shapes to the back of the satin scraps. Cut out, adding a 5mm (¼in) seam allowance.

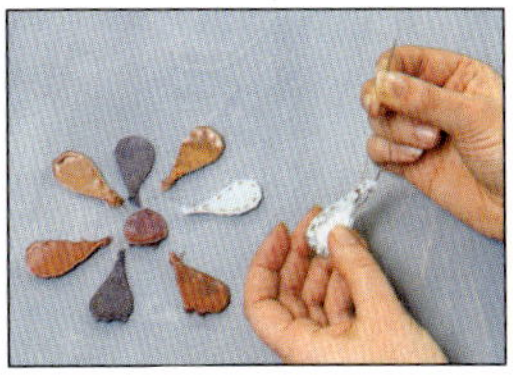

2

Turn under a hem on the raw edges, pin and tack (baste).

3

Position the motif on the garment. Pin and slip-stitch each section in place.

Hawaiian Appliqué Hanging

Patchwork and appliqué were taken to Hawaii by missionaries in the 19th century, but it was the Hawaiians themselves who developed this unique method of appliqué. The motifs are folded and cut in the same way as paper snowflakes.

You Will Need

1m x 90cm (40in x 36in) green cotton fabric
43cm (17in) square cream cotton fabric
dressmaker's scissors
spray starch
iron
30cm (12in) squared paper
pencil
paper scissors
vanishing marker
needle and matching thread
embroidery scissors
46cm (18in) square wadding (batting)
dressmaker's pins
embroidery hoop
quilting thread
crewel needle

Preparation

Cut the green cotton into two 43cm (17in) squares and a 10cm (4in) strip. Spray starch both sides of one green square and press. Cut three 10cm (4in) wide strips of fabric, fold the loops in half and stitch. Turn right side out. Enlarge the design from the back of the book.

1

Fold the paper into quarters and then fold again into a triangle. Trace the design on to the triangle. Draw the border round the edge following the shape of the snowflake. Cut along the lines and open out.

2

Trace round the template on to the green square using the vanishing marker and tack (baste) to the cream square, 5mm (¼in) from the outline of the motif and 5mm (¼in) from the outline of the border.

3

Cut the green fabric a little at a time to 3mm (⅛in) from the pencil line. Snip the curves.

4

Press on the wrong side. Neaten the edges, turning under a small hem. Slip-stitch in place.

5

Sandwich the wadding (batting) between the appliquéd square and the green cotton, securing the loops. Pin and tack.

To Finish

Stretch the appliqué on an embroidery hoop. Starting at the edge, hand quilt halos round the snowflake. Work parallel rows of tiny running stitches round the border. Trim the edges of the square. Cut two strips of green fabric 10cm x 38cm (4in x 15in), and two strips 10cm x 46cm (4in x 18in). Stitch to the edges as borders (see Basic Techniques).

PEG BAG

This peg bag is made from patchwork triangles placed in alternating colours to look like a windmill. Choose a contrasting piece of printed fabric to make up the bag.

YOU WILL NEED

40cm x 90cm (16in x 36in) printed cotton fabric

dressmaker's scissors

paper and pencil

card (cardboard)

craft knife

1m x 90cm (40in x 36in) green cotton fabric

50cm x 90cm (20in x 36in) yellow cotton fabric

dressmaker's pins

sewing machine and zipper foot

matching thread

1m x 90cm (40in x 36in) piping cord

37cm (15in) wooden coat hanger

PREPARATION

Enlarge the diagram from the back of the book on to paper and cut out two sides, one top and one back in printed fabric, adding a 1cm (½in) seam allowance. Enlarge the triangle motif and make a card (cardboard) template. Cut four triangles in green, and four in yellow, adding a 5mm (¼in) seam allowance. To make the piping, cut a 8cm x 65cm (3in x 26in) bias strip from yellow fabric (see Basic Techniques). Join it into a circle and press the seam open.

1

Join the triangles, alternating the colours as shown, to form a square patch. Clip and press the seams to one side.

2

Right sides facing, machine the patch to the side pieces. Press the seams open. Attach the top piece the same way, trim and press the seams flat towards the top.

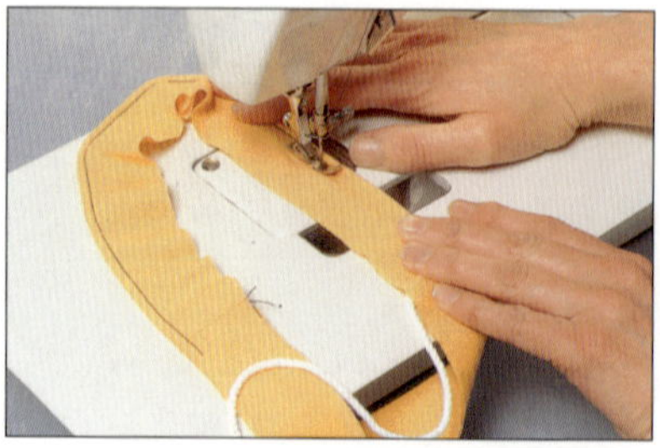

3

Fold the piping strip lengthways. Attach the zipper foot and stitch, enclosing the piping cord. Tack (baste) the piping strip to the opening, with the sewing line matching the seam. Stitch and clip the curved edge. Press under the piping seam allowance, trim and slip-stitch.

4

Right sides facing, match the front to the back, then stitch round the edge of the bag.

TO FINISH

Clip the corners, turn right side out and press flat. Push the hanger wire through the centre top seam.

MARSEILLE

PVC RUCKSACK

This rucksack is especially useful because the straps are in a luminous yellow. They will double up as safety strips on dark, winter evenings when your child is travelling home from school.

YOU WILL NEED

paper and pencil
card (cardboard)
craft knife
50cm x 90cm (20in x 36in) blue PVC
50cm x 90cm (20in x 36in) yellow PVC
10cm x 90cm (4in x 36in) red PVC
dressmaker's scissors
1m x 90cm (40in x 36in) lining fabric
dressmaker's pins
132cm (52in) of 4cm (1½in) black tape
sewing machine and matching thread
needle and tacking (basting) thread
7 large eyelets (grommets)
hammer
1m (1yd) nylon cord

PREPARATION

Enlarge the diagram and cut out the triangles, adding a 5mm (¼in) seam allowance. Follow the illustration for colour reference. Cut out a 66cm x 32.5cm (26in x 12¾in) rectangle in blue PVC for the bag. Cut out a 33cm x 14cm (13in x 5½in) rectangle in yellow PVC for the base. For the straps, cut two 7cm x 66cm (2½in x 26in) strips of yellow PVC. Cut out a bag piece and base in lining.

1

Pin and stitch the blue and yellow triangles together, following the diagram.

2

Add the red triangles, and then the large yellow triangles. Appliqué the patch to the blue PVC bag front.

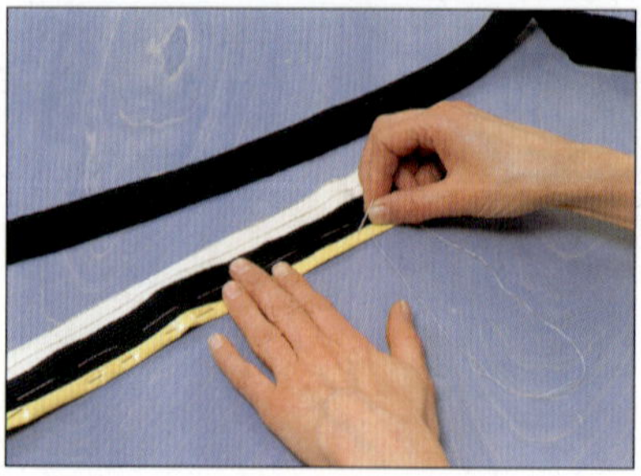

3

Cut the black tape in half and tack (baste) to the yellow PVC strips. Fold the PVC over the tape, leaving a 5mm (¼in) channel either side. Turn under a small hem, tack and top stitch in place. Pin the straps to the bag. Stitch the back seam, then pin and stitch the yellow base to the bag. Make up the lining, stitch along the top edge of the bag, leaving a gap. Pull through and slip-stitch the gap.

4

Attach the eyelets (grommets) 3cm (1¼in) from the outside top edge, spacing them evenly apart. Thread with the nylon cord and knot the ends.

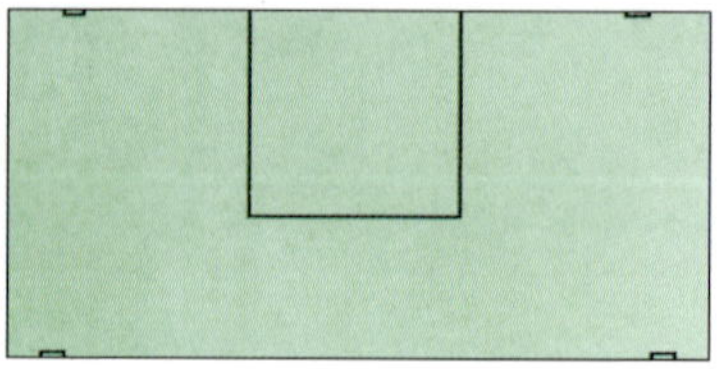

RUCKSACK PLAN 10%

PATCH DIAGRAM 50%

CHILD'S BERET

This PVC beret with a colourful daisy appliqué will brighten up a rainy day. Alternatively, buy a ready-made beret and sew the daisy motif on to it.

YOU WILL NEED

paper and pencil
paper scissors
tracing paper
dressmaker's scissors
10cm x 90cm (4in x 36in) iron-on interfacing
iron
assorted scraps of fabric
50cm x 90cm (20in x 36in) red PVC
50cm x 90cm (20in x 36in) polka dot cotton fabric
dressmaker's pins
embroidery thread
crewel needle
sewing machine and matching thread

25%

PREPARATION

Enlarge the templates and cut out in paper. Draw the daisy shapes on to tracing paper and transfer to the interfacing. Cut out the shapes, iron to the fabric scraps and cut out. Cut a circle in red PVC measuring 40cm (16in), and one in polka dot cotton for the lining. Cut a hat band, 5cm (2in) wide and 4cm (1¾in) larger than the head measurement, in both fabrics.

1

Position the daisy in the centre of the red PVC circle. Pin and blanket stitch in place, then add diagonal stitches on either side.

2

Join the short ends of the hat bands, trim and clip. Place the red PVC and the lining together, wrong sides facing, and pleat at the back of the beret. Pin the pleats, and adjust to the size of the bands.

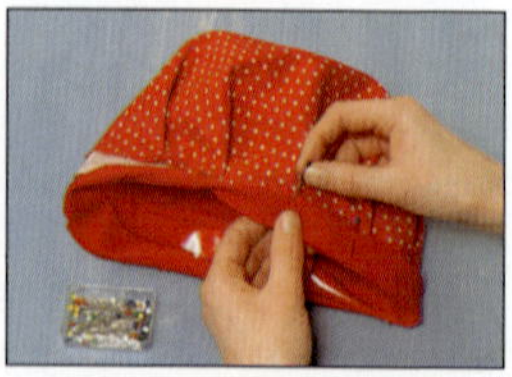

3

Stitch the PVC band to the pleated circle, then sew the second band to the first. Trim the seams and press flat. Fold the band to the wrong side and stitch.

SCOTTIE DOG T SHIRT

Decorate a plain T shirt with this Scottie dog motif. Alternatively, appliqué the motif on to a pair of dungarees (overalls).

YOU WILL NEED

iron
iron-on fusible bonding web
fabric scrap
paper and pencil
dressmaker's scissors
child's T shirt
needle and matching thread
13cm (5in) tartan ribbon
glass bead
embroidery thread

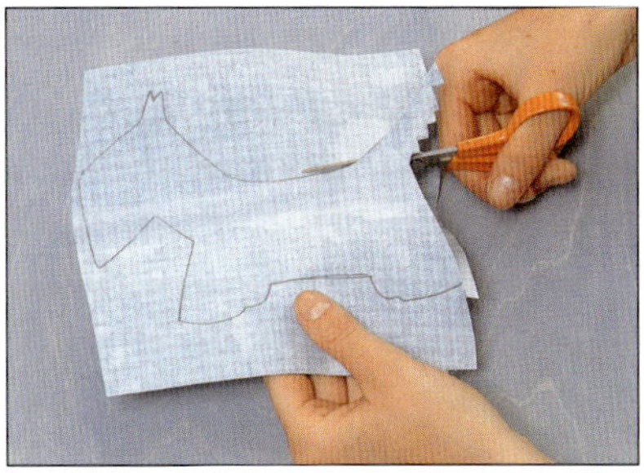

1
Iron the bonding web to the reverse of the fabric scrap. Enlarge the template and draw it on to the bonding web. Cut out the dog.

2
Peel off the backing, position the dog and iron in place. Slip-stitch to the T shirt.

3
Tie the ribbon into a bow and stitch to the dog's neck. Stitch on the bead for the eye, and work a few stitches for the mouth.

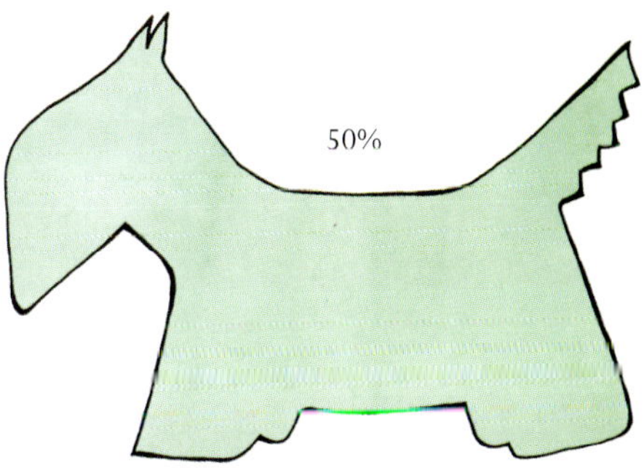

Beach Bag

This clever bag opens out flat to double up as a beach mat. Ten fabric fish and the sea are sandwiched between two sheets of clear plastic.

You Will Need

2m x 90cm (2¼yd x 36in) strong clear plastic

dressmaker's scissors

66cm square (26in) square blue satin fabric

paper and pencil

paper scissors

iron-on fusible bonding web

iron

assorted fabric scraps

marker pen

sewing machine and matching thread

1m (1yd) of 2cm (¾in) white tape

1m (1yd) of 2cm (¾in) red tape

3.5m (3¾yd) white bias binding

3m (3¼yd) thick cord

Preparation

Cut out two plastic circles, 90cm (36in) in diameter, and cut one satin circle with wavy sides, 60cm (24in) in diameter. Trace the fish motifs from the back of the book, varying the sizes, and cut out in paper.

1

Trace ten fish on to the bonding web. Cut out and iron on to the fabric scraps. Peel off the backing paper and iron the fish to the blue satin. Draw on the fins and eyes with the marker pen.

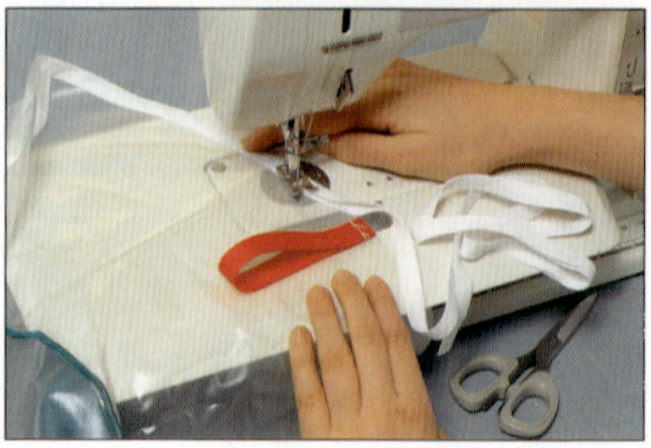

2

Sandwich the satin between the plastic circles and machine zig zag round the wavy outline. Cut each tape into six loops and pin round the edge. Bind the edge with bias binding. Thread the cord through the loops and knot the ends.

BEACH TOWEL

Old bath sheets or a length of towelling can be cut down to make an attractive beach towel when appliquéd with bold seaside motifs.

YOU WILL NEED

paper and pencil
paper scissors
assorted scraps of cotton fabric
iron
dressmaker's scissors
old towel or towelling fabric
sewing machine and matching thread
vanishing marker
dressmaker's pins

PREPARATION

Enlarge the seaside motifs from the back of the book and cut out in paper. Using a contrasting colour to the towel, cut two strips of fabric 1m x 7.5cm (1yd x 3in) for the binding. Turn the long edges under by 1cm (½in). Press.

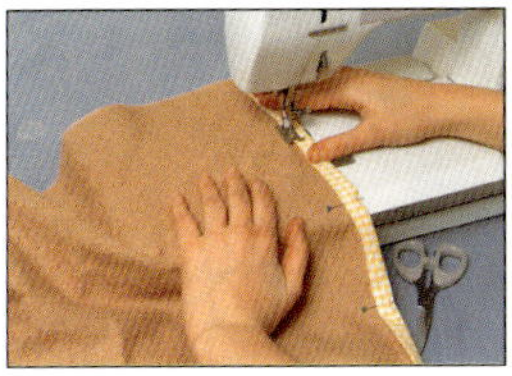

1

Pin and machine the binding to the ends of the towel or towelling fabric, enclosing the raw edges.

2

Pin the paper templates on to the fabric scraps and cut out the shapes.

3

Position and pin the motifs along one end of the towel. Overlap the bucket and spade motifs. Set the machine to zig zag and stitch in place.

Silk Christmas Cards

These Christmas trees are made from strips of checked silk sewn together and cut into triangles. This simple patchwork technique is very effective.

You Will Need

pencil and ruler
assorted scraps of checked silk fabric
dressmaker's scissors
sewing machine and contrasting thread
dressmaker's pins
fabric glue
card (cardboard)
paper scissors

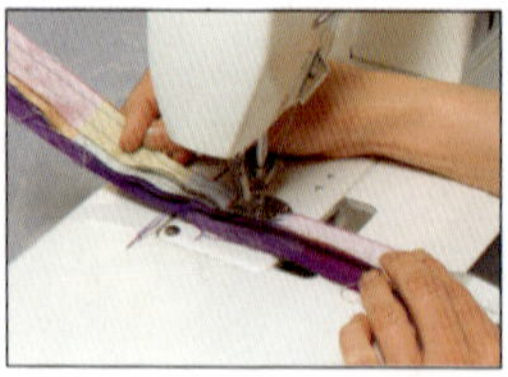

1

Cut the silk into strips 2.5cm x 36cm (1in x 14in). Overlap the strips and then stitch together lengthways using a contrasting thread.

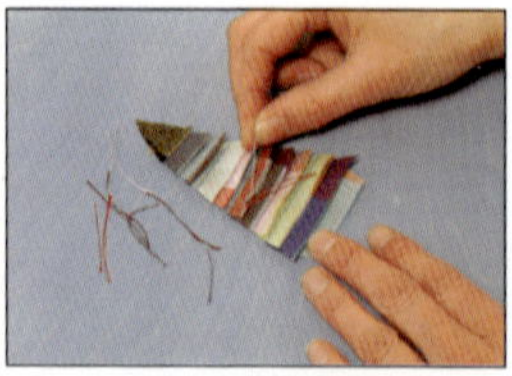

2

Cut the patchwork piece into triangular shapes. Using a pin, draw threads from the raw edges to fringe each layer.

3

Glue each triangle to a piece of silk backing fabric, then glue to a piece of card and cut out. Cut pieces of card (cardboard) and fold in half to make cards. Glue the trees on to the front of each card.

JAM JAR COVER

Appliqué this juicy strawberry on to a jam jar cover and embellish it with a few embroidery stitches. Make more covers and appliqué with a variety of fruits.

YOU WILL NEED

pencil

saucer

scraps of pink and green fabric

dressmaker's scissors

iron-on fusible bonding web

iron

tracing paper and pencil

embroidery thread

crewel needle

sewing machine and matching thread

40cm (16in) pink ribbon

PREPARATION

Draw round a saucer on to both the pink and green fabrics and cut out two circles. Iron the bonding web on to scraps of fabric. Trace the strawberry motif on to paper, transfer on to the bonding web and cut out. Peel off the backing, centre the motif on the green fabric and iron on.

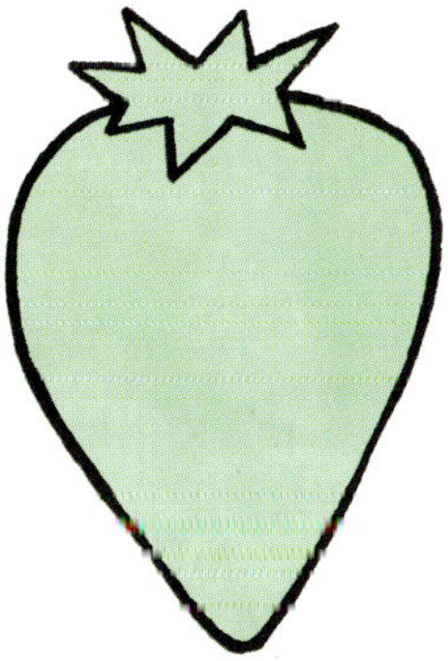

1

Outline the strawberry with colourful stitches. Embellish with cross stitches. Right sides facing, machine stitch the circles together, leaving a small gap.

2

Turn right side out. Sew running stitch round the edge. Attach the ribbon 5cm (2in) from the edge, place on a jam jar and tie in a bow.

TORAN HANGING

Designed to hang over a door, traditional torans can be found throughout India, adorning temple doorways. They are characterized by their use of brilliant colours and zany patterns as seen in this patchwork and appliqué toran.

YOU WILL NEED

paper and pencil
calico
dressmaker's scissors
wadding (batting)
assorted fabric scraps in silk, satin, velvet and cotton
embroidery scissors
embroidery hoop
assorted embroidery threads
crewel needle
beads, sequins and buttons
quilting thread
needle and tacking (basting) thread
sewing machine and thread
assorted bias binding, ribbon and tapes
curtain hooks

PREPARATION

Decide on the size and shape of your hanging and draw a plan dividing the area into patches. Cut out the shape in calico, adding a seam allowance. Cut the same shape in wadding without a seam allowance.

1

Cut fabric shapes freehand to form the design, then pin and tack (baste) to a fabric patch. Place in an embroidery hoop. Fill with wadding (batting) for a raised effect where necessary. Hand quilt round the shapes, stitching through all the layers. Embellish with beads, sequins and buttons.

2

Make a border from shaped patches of fabric, as shown. Right sides facing, pin along the top of the hanging. Machine stitch.

3

Fold back the border. Stitch rows of ribbon and tape along the edge of the hanging to cover the border. Pin bias binding or ribbon round the raw edges of the border. Stitch in place.

TO FINISH

Following your plan, stitch the patches together to make the toran. Sandwich the wadding (batting) between the patched piece and the calico backing, right sides out. Pin and tack (baste). Stitch a line round the outside edge. Bind any raw edges, using bias strip binding, ribbon or tape. Sew curtain hooks evenly spaced along the top edge.

LOVE AND LIVE HAPPY

1950s BISTRO PLACEMAT

This placemat has been appliquéd with a retro design of garden vegetables. This kitsch style is typical of kitchen design in the 1950s.

YOU WILL NEED

paper and pencil
paper scissors
dressmaker's pins
red, orange and yellow fabric scraps
dressmaker's scissors
20cm x 50cm (8in x 20in) green and red striped fabric
10cm x 27cm (4in x 10½in) yellow gingham fabric
needle and tacking (basting) thread
vanishing marker
green and brown embroidery thread
crewel needle
sewing machine and matching thread
iron
5cm x 36cm (2in x 14in) red cotton fabric
30cm x 36cm (12in x 14in) green gingham fabric
33cm x 42cm (13in x 16½in) single-sided quilted backing fabric

PREPARATION

Enlarge the motifs from the back of the book and cut out paper templates. Pin to the scraps and cut out, adding a 5mm (¼in) seam allowance. Cut two green and red striped fabric strips 5.5cm x 9cm (2¼ in x 3½in), and one 7cm x 36cm (2¾in x 14in).

1

Clip and turn under the seam allowances on the fabric motifs and tack (baste). Cut three 10cm x 9cm (4in x 3½in) rectangles from the yellow gingham fabric.

2

Tack one vegetable to each rectangle and slip-stitch in place. Mark details with a vanishing marker. Hand stitch with embroidery thread.

3

Right sides facing, stitch the two short striped strips between the appliquéd patches and press flat. Then stitch the red strip to the left edge and the long green and red striped strip to the right edge.

4

Right sides facing, stitch the green gingham to the red strip. Stitch one short end of the quilted fabric to the long striped strip. Tack the top to the backing. Trim the mat to 32cm x 42cm (13in x 16½in). Cut the remaining striped fabric into strips and bind the other three edges.

APPLIQUÉ FELT HAT

This hat is made from felted scraps of knitting. Cool colours which recede, like blues and greens, will look good for the base. In contrast, use hot colours like pink, orange and red for the motifs.

YOU WILL NEED

paper and pencil
paper scissors
dressmaker's scissors
assorted scraps of felted knitting
20cm x 90cm (8in x 36in) lining fabric
dressmaker's pins
sewing machine and matching thread
petersham
needle and tacking (basting) thread

PREPARATION

Enlarge the paper templates for the hat crown and band and cut out in paper. Cut the pieces out in both felted fabric and lining. Cut out enough felt squares in different colours to fit the band. Draw a design for the crown freehand and cut out in assorted colours of felt.

1

Pin the squares on to the band and zig zag stitch in place. Position your design on the crown and stitch the first layer.

2

Cut more shapes to decorate each square of the band. Appliqué the shapes in layers. Complete the crown design with a second layer of motifs.

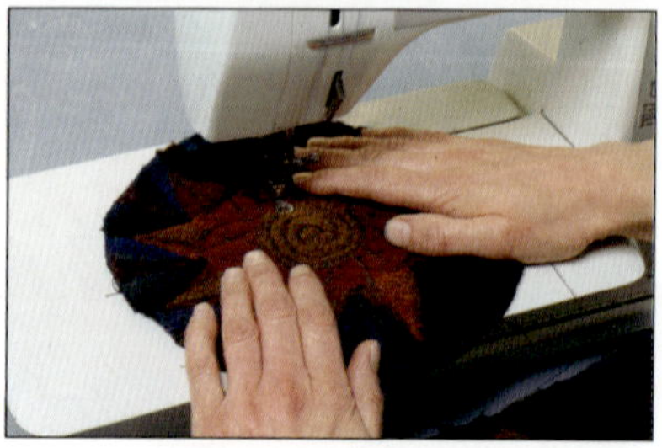

3

Machine embroider set stitches in geometric patterns all over both hat pieces.

TO FINISH

Join the short ends of the band to form a tube and stitch to the crown. Make up the lining and place inside the hat, wrong sides facing. Cut the petersham 3cm (1¼in) larger than your head measurement plus 1cm (½in) seam allowance. Join the short ends and tack (baste) to the lower end of the band. Fold into the hat and top stitch close to the lower edge.

CROWN
25%

HAT BAND
25%

BLACK AND WHITE APPLIQUÉ WAISTCOAT

Appliqué a black design on to plain calico to create this striking waistcoat. Draw the design freehand and stitch small sections at a time.

YOU WILL NEED

commercial waistcoat pattern

dressmaker's scissors

90cm x 150cm (36in x 60in) calico fabric

50cm x 90cm (20in x 36in) black cotton

vanishing marker

dressmaker's pins

sewing machine and black thread

sharp scissors

PREPARATION

Cut out the waistcoat fronts in both calico and black cotton. Cut the waistcoat back in calico only.

1

Draw a design freehand on to the wrong side of the two calico fronts. Use a vanishing marker.

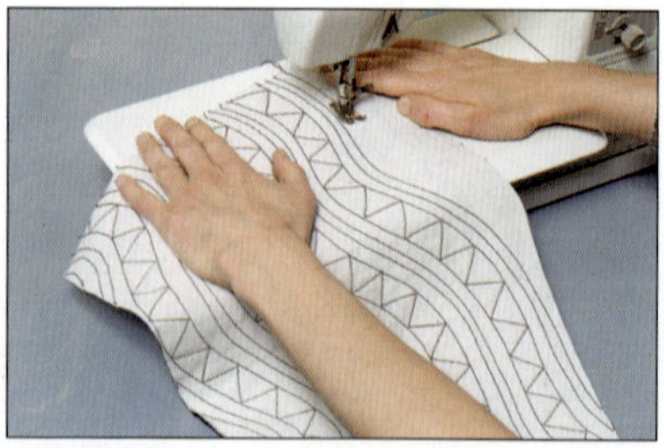

2

Pin the black fronts, right side uppermost, to the right side of the calico fronts. Machine stitch over the drawn lines in black thread.

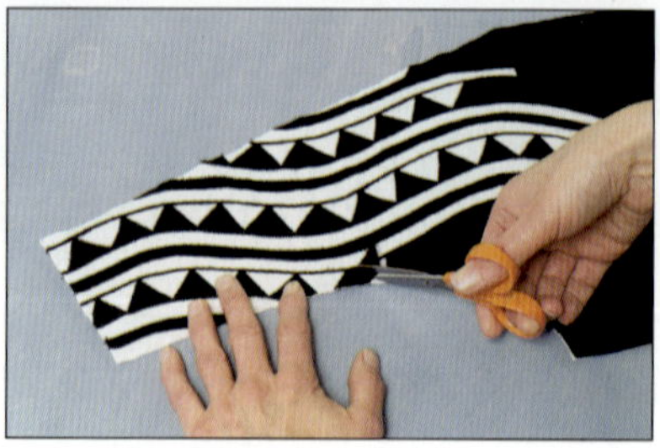

3

Right side facing and following the design, cut away a small section of the top black layer using sharp scissors. Cut close to the stitching line, to expose the calico below.

4

Carefully machine zig zag over all the raw black edges. Cut and machine until the whole piece has been worked.

TO FINISH

Make up the waistcoat, following the pattern instructions.

SATIN DUFFEL BAG

The checker board effect of this patchwork design is enhanced by using strong contrasting colours. The satin is backed with calico, but interfacing could be used instead.

YOU WILL NEED

50cm x 90cm (20in x 36in) calico

dressmaker's scissors

1m x 90cm (40in x 36in) black satin fabric

50cm x 90cm (20in x 36in) yellow satin fabric

needle and tacking (basting) thread

sewing machine and matching thread

50cm x 90cm (20in x 36in) cotton lining fabric

iron

dressmaker's pins

8 eyelets (grommets)

hammer

1.5m (1⅔yd) silk cord

PREPARATION

Cut out 36 5cm (2½in) calico squares. Tack (baste) half of the squares to the black satin, and half to the yellow satin. Cut 18 yellow and 18 black squares. Using the flag method (see Basic Techniques), stitch into strips of three, alternating black with yellow. Join the strips into one piece, 12 squares by three. Press the seams. Cut a round base 22cm (8½in) in diameter and back with calico cut to the same size. Cut out a rectangle the same size as the patchwork and a base in lining fabric.

1

Cut two strips of black satin 7cm x 38cm (2¾in x 15in). Press under a 1cm (½in) turning, pin and top stitch to either end of the patched piece. Stitch the short ends of the patched piece to form a tube.

2

Pin and stitch the base into the tube. Make up a lining in the same way. Right sides facing, pin the lining to the bag along the top edge. Stitch along the top edge of the bag, leaving a small gap. Clip, press and pull through. Close the gap and top stitch 5mm (¼in) from the top.

3

Attach seven equally spaced eyelets (grommets) round the top edge. Fold a satin square into three. Fold the ends in and stitch. Top stitch round the bottom of the bag and attach the remaining eyelets. Thread the cord through the eyelets and tie in a knot.

DIAMOND-IN-A-SQUARE SATIN PURSE

This opulent evening purse is made from a patched piece of richly coloured satin fabric. Follow the diagram at the back of the book for the arrangement of the patches.

YOU WILL NEED

paper and pencil
20cm x 90cm (8in x 36in) satin fabric, in four colours
dressmaker's scissors
iron-on interfacing
iron
dressmaker's pins
sewing machine and matching thread
20cm x 30cm (8in x 12in) lining fabric
50cm (20in) silk cord
gold bead, with a large hole

PREPARATION

Cut out the patchwork pieces, adding a 5mm (¼in) seam allowance. Cut two large 2.5cm (1in) squares in colour 1. Enlarge the triangle shape and make a paper template. Cut 16 triangles in both colours 2 and 3. Cut eight 4cm (1½in) squares in colour 4. Iron interfacing on to the back of all the patches. Following the diagram for reference, pin and stitch four triangles together then stitch a small square to each end. Make another piece the same. Pin and stitch four more triangles together to make a short strip, and repeat to make a second strip. Stitch either side of one large square. Cut a strip for the casing 32cm x 7cm (12½in x 3in) in colour 4 and a 11.5cm (4¼in) diameter circle for the base in colour 4.

1

Pin and stitch the two narrow patchwork strips either side of the wide one to make a square. Make another patch the same way. Right sides facing, stitch together.

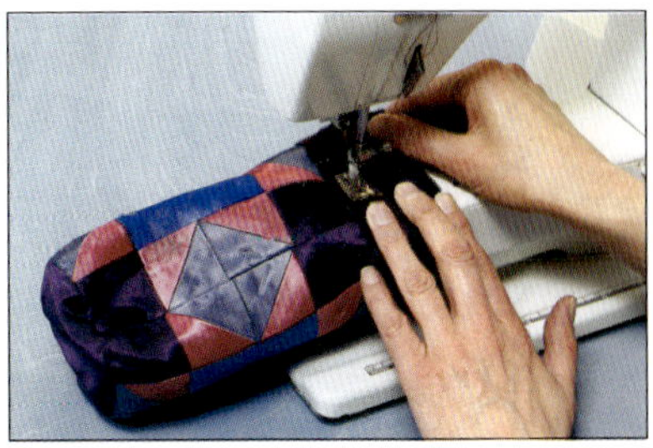

2

Stitch the casing strip to the top edge. Press the seams flat. Fold the piece in half and stitch the side seam. Stitch in the base, trim and clip. Make a lining to fit and insert. Top stitch two rows, 5mm (¼in) from the top edge and 5mm (¼in) apart, to form a channel. Thread the cord through the channel. Thread on the bead and knot. Fringe the ends of the cord.

PURPLE ZIG ZAG CUSHION

The basic triangle shape can be arranged in different patchwork formations to create various bold geometric patterns.

YOU WILL NEED

paper and pencil
card (cardboard)
1m x 90cm (40in x 36in) dark purple silk fabric
1m x 90cm (40in x 36in) pale purple silk fabric
dressmaker's scissors
dressmaker's pins
sewing machine and matching thread
iron
50cm x 90cm (20in x 36in) backing fabric

PREPARATION

Make card (cardboard) templates of the two triangle shapes. Cut out 21 large and six small triangles in both silk fabrics, adding a 5mm (¼in) seam allowance.

1

Arrange the large triangles in six rows to make the zig zag design. To square the ends, place a small half-triangle at the end of each row.

2

Right sides facing, pin and then stitch the triangles together in contrasting pairs. Press the seams. Stitch the pairs together in rows. Press.

3

Right sides facing, stitch the rows together to make a square. Press the seams.

4

This alternative shows the triangles arranged in a mountain design.

5

Another variation, with the triangles arranged in a diamond pattern.

TO FINISH

Right sides facing, join the patchwork pieces to the backing fabric to make an envelope cushion cover (see Basic Techniques).

50%

SNAKES AND LADDERS

This patchwork playmat doubles as a snakes and ladders board. It is constructed like a quilt, so you could make it large enough to cover a child's bed.

YOU WILL NEED

card (cardboard) and pencil
30cm x 90cm (12in x 36in) cotton fabric
dressmaker's scissors
scraps of coloured felt
vanishing marker
craft knife
sewing machine and matching thread
black embroidery thread
crewel needle
50cm x 90cm (20in x 36in) backing fabric
dressmaker's pins

PREPARATION

Make a 3cm (1¼in) square card (cardboard) template. Cut out 100 squares from the cotton fabric, adding a 5mm (¼in) seam allowance. Draw snakes, ladders and counters freehand on to the felt scraps and cut out.

TO FINISH

Cut the backing 3cm (1¼in) bigger than the mat all round. Wrong sides facing, pin to the mat. Bring the backing over to the front, mitre the corners and stitch the borders (see Basic Techniques).

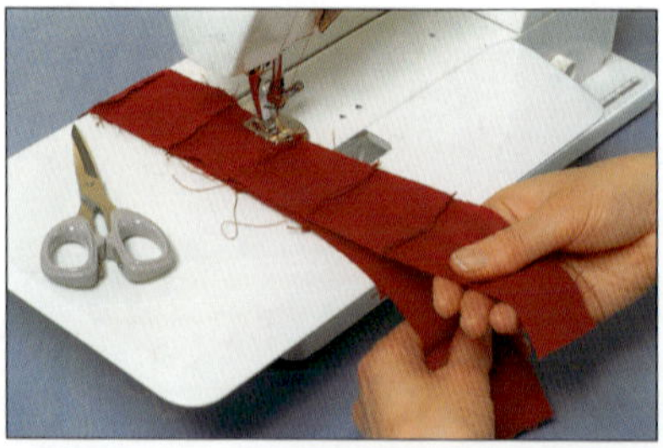

1

Stitch the squares together in strips of ten. Stitch all ten strips together to make a square.

2

Number the squares, using black embroidery stitches. Appliqué the snakes and ladders on to the mat.

CHILD'S BLANKET

Small children will love to snuggle up under this cosy blanket. It is appliquéd by hand with colourful circles decorated with buttons.

YOU WILL NEED

blanket fabric
dressmaker's scissors
tapestry wool
crewel needle
saucer
fabric marker
assorted scraps of coloured woollen or blanket fabric
large buttons

1

Cut the blanket to the size required, turn under a small hem and blanket stitch the edge in different colours (see Basic Techniques).

2

Draw round a saucer on to the scraps of fabric and cut out circles. Hand appliqué to the blanket in running stitch. Sew a button to the centre of each circle.

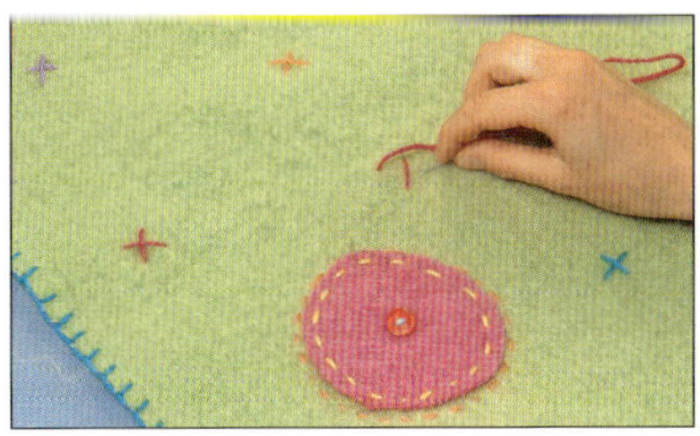

3

Work large cross stitches in a contrasting colour to fill the background fabric.

Shoe Bag

Choose an appropriate shoe to appliqué to this witty drawstring bag. A ballet shoe or gym shoe would also look good.

You Will Need

dressmaker's scissors

50cm x 90cm (20in x 36in) cotton fabric

sewing machine and matching thread

65cm x 7cm (26in x 2¾in) contrasting fabric

iron

paper and pencil

fabric marker

assorted fabric scraps

iron-on fusible bonding web

dressmaker's pins

scrap of narrow ribbon

50cm (20in) of 2.5cm (1in) wide ribbon

small button

Preparation

Cut the fabric to make a rectangle 45cm x 70cm (17¾in x 27½in). Fold 6.5cm (2½in) to the right side on one long edge, and machine stitch. Right sides facing, fold the rectangle in half and stitch round the base and sides of the bag. Turn right side out. Cut a contrasting strip 66cm x 7cm (26in x 2¾in) and press under a 5mm (¼in) hem on the long sides. Enlarge the template of the shoe motif, and trace on to the fabric scraps. Iron on to the bonding web and cut out.

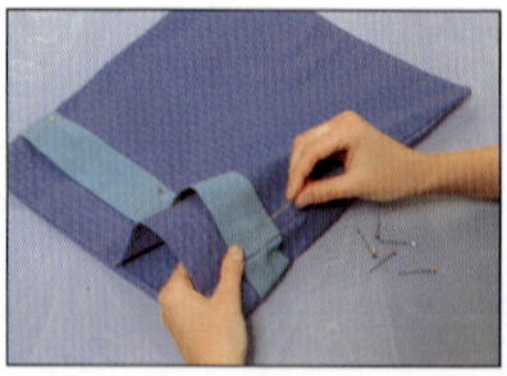

1

Starting at the seam, pin the contrasting strip to the right side of the bag, 5cm (2in) from the top. Top stitch the long edges by hand, leaving the short ends open.

2

Peel the backing off the bonding web and iron the shoe to the bag. Decorate the shoe with hand stitches and a small ribbon bow.

3

Thread the contrasting fabric channel with the wide ribbon. Fold under the raw ends of the ribbon, then join together by stitching the button through both ends.

50%

PATCHWORK TOY BAG

Stitch a piece of rainbow patchwork to make into a large toy bag. The colours run in diagonal lines to look like steps.

YOU WILL NEED

paper and pencil
card (cardboard)
craft knife
scraps of fabric, in six rainbow colours
iron-on interfacing
iron
sewing machine and matching thread
30cm (12in) wooden coat hanger
vanishing marker
red paint, optional

PREPARATION

Make a 10cm (4in) square template in card (cardboard) and cut 72 patches from the interfacing. Iron the interfacing to the fabric scraps and cut out, adding a 5mm (¼in) seam allowance. Arrange them in diagonal lines to form rainbow steps. Using the flag method (see Basic Techniques), join half of the squares into two blocks, each six by three. Press the seams flat. Make a large block, six squares by six, for the back of the bag.

1

Right sides facing, stitch the two small blocks together along half their length. Press the seam allowance along the opening. Tack (baste) and then top-stitch to neaten the right side.

2

Right sides facing, pin the two bag pieces together. Lay the coat hanger on the top edge and draw round it. Cut along the curved line.

TO FINISH

Stitch the two pieces together with a 1cm (½in) seam allowance. Clip the corners, press and turn through. Paint the coat hanger, if wished, and fit into the bag.

MOSAIC CUSHION

This patchwork technique mimics that of mosaic. Small pieces of fabric are sewn together by hand to create an all-over design.

YOU WILL NEED

paper and pencil
craft knife
dressmaker's pins
50cm x 90cm (20in x 36in) red cotton fabric
scraps of black, grey and white cotton fabric
dressmaker's scissors
needle and tacking (basting) thread
matching thread
embroidery scissors
sewing machine and matching thread
polyester wadding (batting)

1

Enlarge the design and make paper templates of all the shapes. Decide on a colour scheme and mark each shape.

2

Pin the paper templates to the back of the scraps of fabric and cut out, adding a 5mm (¼in) seam allowance.

3

Tack (baste) the fabric shapes to the paper templates.

4

Oversew the patches together, using neat whip stitches (see Basic Techniques). Follow the diagram for reference. Work on a small section at a time.

50%

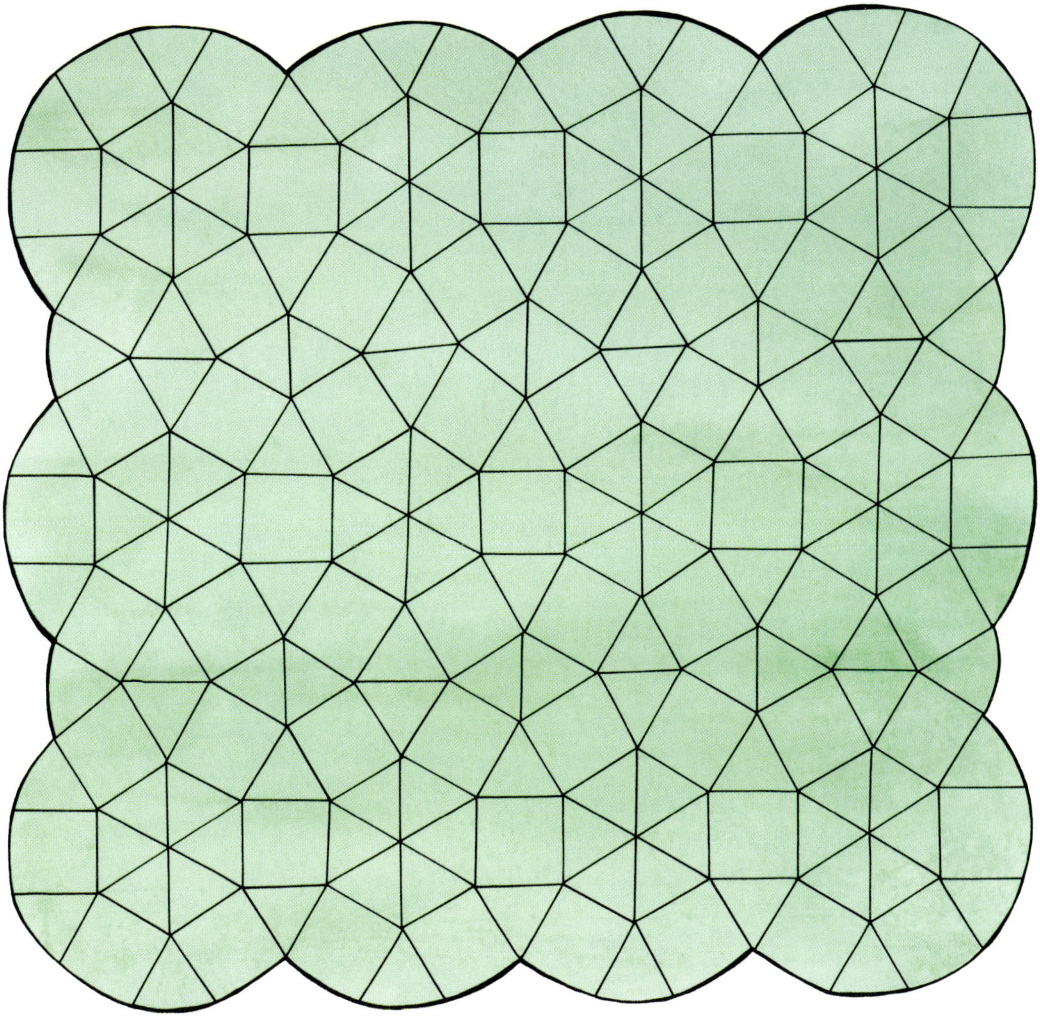

TO FINISH

Remove the tacking (basting) threads and paper templates, and press the seams flat. Cut the red cotton backing fabric to fit the patched piece and place together, right sides facing. Machine stitch round the edges, leaving a gap. Trim and clip the corners, turn right side out and fill with wadding (batting). Slip-stitch the gap closed.

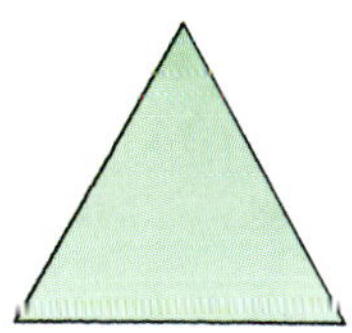

KITCHEN APRON

Make a bright apron with an unusual scalloped border and appliqué kitchen utensils on to it with colourful hand stitches.

YOU WILL NEED

paper and pencil
card (cardboard)
craft knife
fabric scraps
iron-on interfacing
iron
75cm x 90cm (30in x 36in) cotton fabric
dressmaker's scissors
75cm x 90cm (30in x 36in) contrasting cotton fabric
vanishing marker
embroidery thread
crewel needle
dressmaker's pins
sewing machine and matching thread
iron
1m (1yd) of 8cm (3in) wide ribbon

PREPARATION

Enlarge the knife, fork and spoon motifs and cut out in card (cardboard). Cut a semi-circle in thin card. Iron the interfacing to the reverse of the fabric scraps. Cut a front in cotton fabric, 60cm x 50cm (24in x 20in). Cut a backing piece in the contrasting fabric to match.

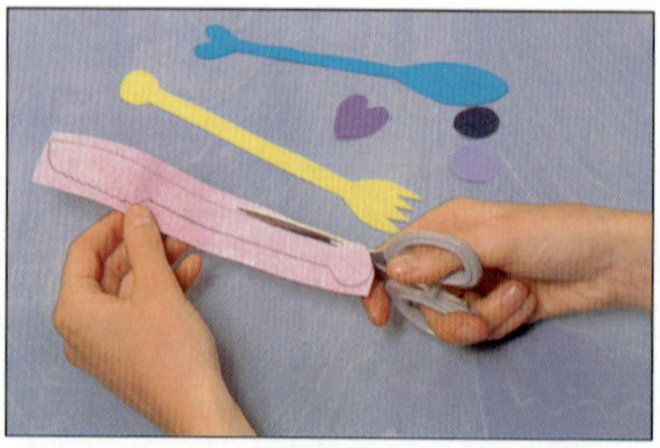

1

Draw round the templates on to the interfacing. Cut out in different colours.

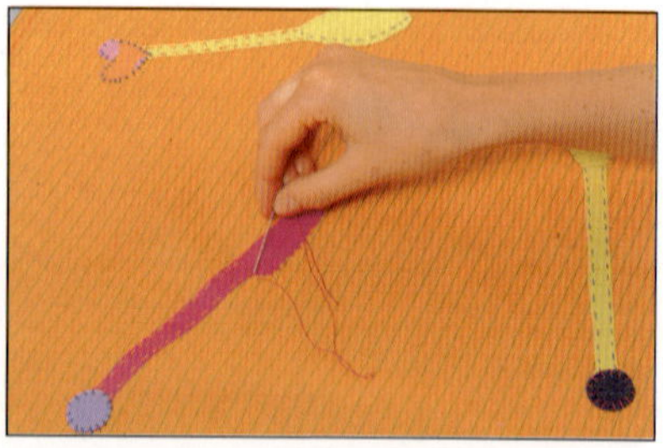

2

Appliqué the motifs to the apron front with large, colourful hand stitches.

3

Right sides facing, match the front to the backing and pin. Draw round the semi-circle along the reverse of the lower edge, to mark a scalloped line. Machine stitch round three sides, leaving the top open. Clip the corners and the scalloped edge.

4

Turn the apron right side out. Stitch a line of running stitches along the scalloped edge.

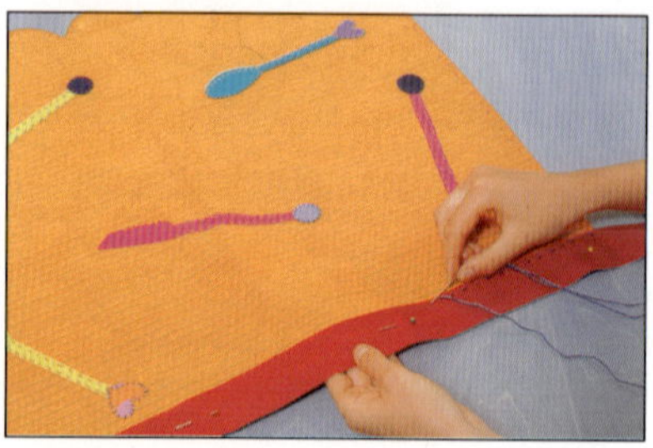

5

Fold under the open edge and press. Press the ribbon in half lengthways. Tack (baste) and top stitch round the top edge.

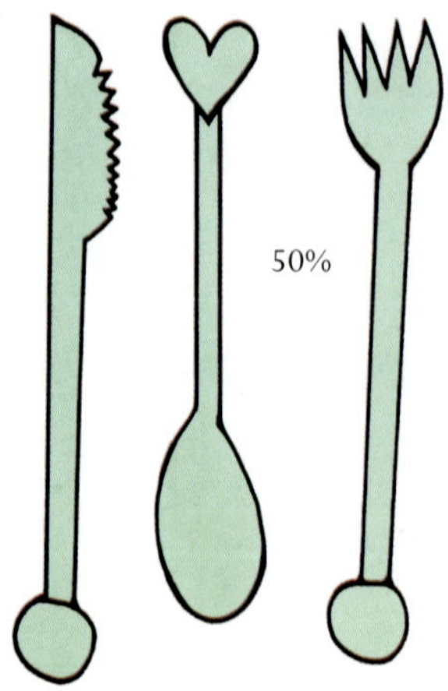

Appliqué Pillowslip

Appliqué these brightly coloured stars and hearts on to a ready-made pillowslip and decorate with simple stitches. This is an easy way to brighten up faded bedlinen.

You Will Need

paper and pencil
paper scissors
fabric marker
iron-on fusible bonding web
iron
assorted fabric scraps
dressmaker's scissors
pillowslip
assorted embroidery threads
crewel needle

1

Make paper templates of the heart and star motifs. Trace on to the bonding web. Iron the bonding web on to the reverse of the fabric scraps and cut out the motifs.

2

Peel off the backing paper and iron a motif to each corner of the pillowslip. Blanket stitch round the edge (see Basic Techniques) and decorate with embroidery stitches.

3

Sew a running stitch in a contrasting thread on both sides of the pillowcase.

WASH BAG

This little bathroom bag is made from washable fabric. It has a very unusual, asymmetrical patchwork design reminiscent of Art Deco.

YOU WILL NEED

paper and pencil
card (cardboard)
craft knife
dressmaker's scissors
30cm x 90cm (12in x 36in) white PVC
30cm x 90cm (12in x 36in) red PVC
30cm x 90cm (12in x 36in) blue PVC
dressmaker's pins
sewing machine and matching thread
71cm (28in) thick white cotton cord

PREPARATION

Enlarge the shapes and cut out in card (cardboard). Following the numbers on the plan, cut out the patches in PVC, adding a 5mm (¼in) seam allowance, as follows: cut numbers 1, 6, 13, 14 and 15 in white; 2, 3, 8, 10 and 12 in red; 4, 5, 7, 9 and 11 in blue. Cut a 38cm x 30cm (15in x 12in) lining in white PVC. Cut a blue PVC 18cm (7in) square for the back of the bag.

1

The patch is made in two halves. To stitch the first half, join blue 4 to red 2. Join blue 5 to red 3. Next, join 4/2 to white 6. Join 3/5 to white 6. Join the whole piece to white 1.

2

To stitch the second half, join blue 9 to red 10. Join 9/10 to white 14. Join red 10 to blue 11. Join 10/11 to white 13. Join blue 11 to red 12. Join blue 9 to red 8. Join 8/9 to white 15. Join blue 7 to red 8. Stitch the two patchs together.

TO FINISH

Right sides facing, stitch the patch to the blue back piece along one long seam. Stitch the lining to the top of the bag. Clip and trim the seam. Fold in half lengthways and stitch round the seams, leaving a small gap. Pull through then fold in the lining, leaving a 6cm (2½in) band at the top. Stitch two parallel lines 5mm (¼in) from the top edge, 1cm (½in) apart, for the channel. Thread the cord through the channel and knot the ends.

50%

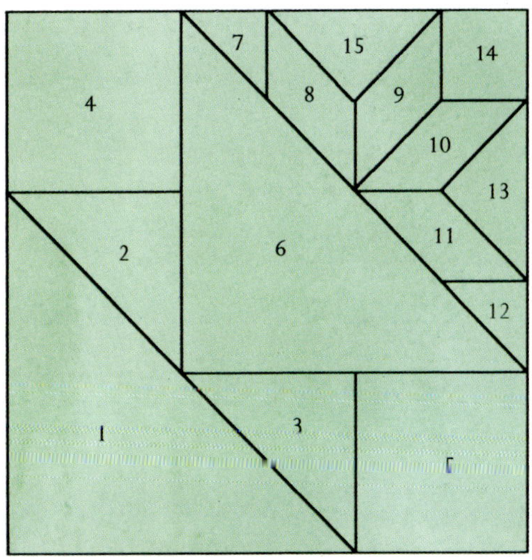

HOT WATER BOTTLE COVER

Strip patchwork is used for this jazzy cover, which is then quilted with a scroll and diamond pattern. The layers of padding will help to keep your hot water bottle warm on cold winter nights.

YOU WILL NEED

1m x 90cm (40in x 36in) white fabric

dressmaker's scissors

50cm x 90cm (20in x 36in) black fabric

sewing machine and matching thread

hot water bottle

vanishing marker

50cm x 90cm (20in x 36in) wadding (batting)

red thread

2m (2yd) of 2.5cm (1in) black bias binding

dressmaker's pins

iron

3 press studs (snap fasteners)

QUILTING DESIGNS 50%

PREPARATION

Cut the white fabric into four, and the black into six 50cm (19¾in) x 7.5cm (3in) strips. Join the strips lengthways in two sets of five, alternating the colours. Trace round a hot water bottle on to the patched pieces, add a 1cm (½in) seam allowance and cut out. Cut out two pieces the same from the white fabric for the lining. Trace and draw the quilting design on to the cover pieces.

1

Sandwich the wadding (batting) between the patched pieces and the lining, right sides facing out. Tack (baste) through all the layers. Stitch round the edge on both pieces. Stitch the quilting design in red.

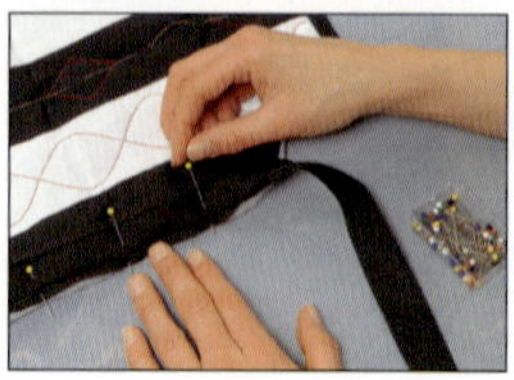

2

Bind the top edge with the bias binding. Pin another strip of bias binding round the side edges on the right side and stitch to the cover. Bind the second side. Place the two sides together, right sides facing, with the binding sandwiched between. Stitch round the seam line, leaving a 15cm (6in) opening at the top. Trim and press.

3

Turn right side out and slipstitch the opening. Attach the press studs (snap fasteners) to the top edge of the cover.

HEART BROOCH

This tiny appliqué heart made from scraps of fabric is embellished with gold thread. Mounted on a brooch back it makes a pretty badge, but it could also be appliquéd directly on to a pocket or the corner of a shirt collar.

YOU WILL NEED

paper and pencil
scrap of gold velvet or silk
sharp embroidery scissors
scraps of blue and grey woollen fabric
iron-on interfacing
iron
sewing machine and gold thread
scrap of cream organza
dressmaker's pins
brooch back

PREPARATION

Draw the heart shape, transfer it to the gold velvet or silk scrap and cut out. Cut a scrap of blue fabric 3cm x 4cm (1¼in x 1½in), and a scrap of grey fabric, 5cm x 4cm (2in x 1½in). Iron the grey fabric to the interfacing. Machine several lines of the gold thread in a square to make a frame.

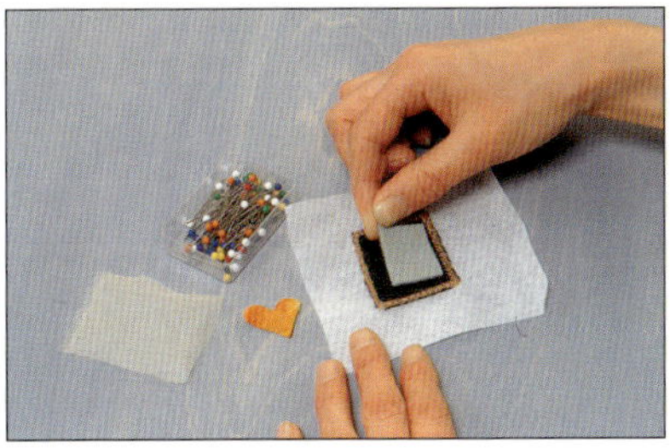

1

Place the blue fabric on to the frame, then the heart, and finally cover with a scrap of organza and pin. Machine stitch the organza to the backing close to the gold frame. Trim the organza back to the stitch line.

2

Pull the interfacing away from round the brooch. Sew the brooch back to the underside.

CHILD'S APRON

This painting apron is constructed from strips of fabric. It has a roomy pocket for pens and paintbrushes, trimmed with pompon tape. This apron is made in glazed cotton, but you could also use stain-resistant PVC fabric.

YOU WILL NEED

dressmaker's scissors
scraps of fabric
paper and pencil
50cm x 90cm (20in x 36in) red glazed cotton fabric
sewing machine and matching thread
iron
25cm (10in) pompon tape
dressmaker's pins
needle and tacking (basting) thread
1.5m (60in) of 2.5cm (1in) wide tape

PREPARATION

Cut five 6cm x 20cm (2½in x 8in) strips of assorted fabric for the pocket. Following the diagram, draw a basic apron shape on paper to fit a child and cut out in the fabric. Turn under a hem all round the apron and machine stitch.

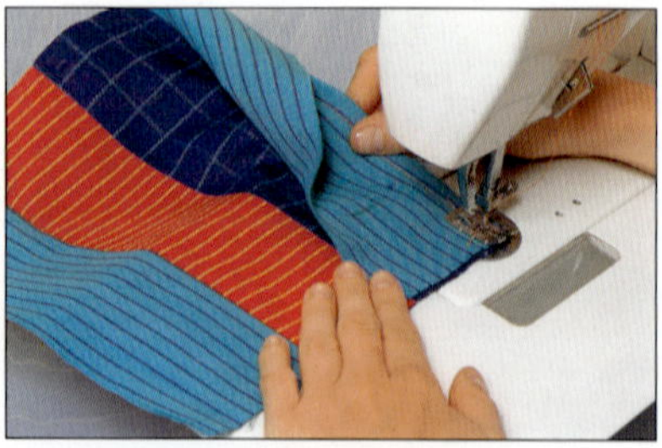

1

Stitch the strips together to make one piece. Cut a piece of cotton fabric to the same size. Right sides facing, pin and stitch the seams, leaving a small gap. Clip the corners, press and turn through.

BASIC APRON SHAPE

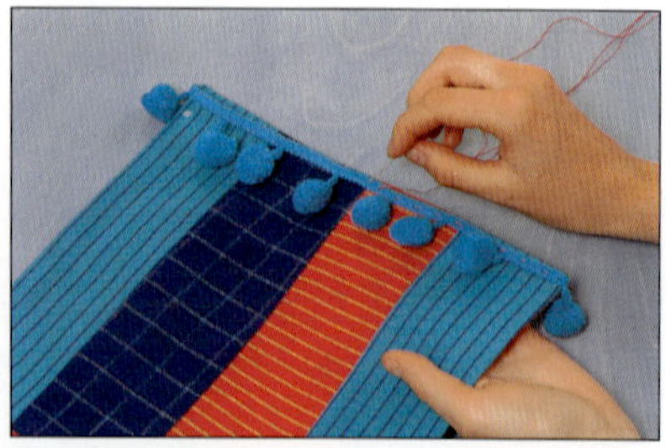

2

Slip-stitch the pompon tape to the top edge of the patched piece.

3

Tack (baste) the pocket to the apron and machine stitch.

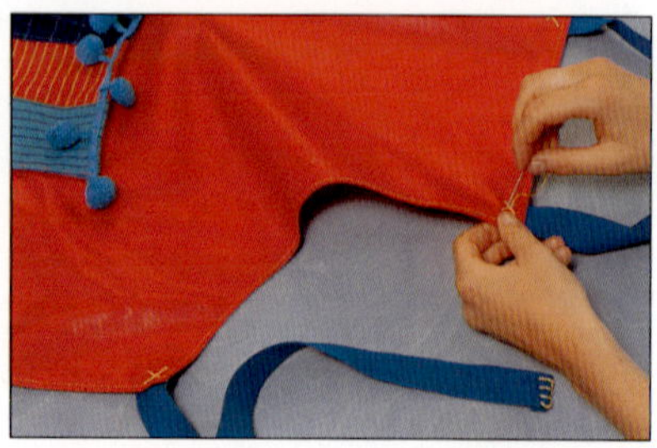

4

Cut a 61cm (24in) length of tape and sew to either side of the top edge. Cut the rest of tape in half and sew either side of the waist. Neaten the ends of the tape.

PVC BAG

This bag shows how unusual fabrics can create an effect completely different to traditional patchwork. Clip the curved seams to ensure a smooth fit.

YOU WILL NEED

paper and pencil

card (cardboard)

craft knife

dressmaker's scissors

1m (1yd) wadding (batting)

1m x 90cm (40in x 36in) blue PVC

50cm x 90cm (20in x 36in) red PVC

50cm x 90cm (20in x 36in) white PVC

dressmaker's pins

sewing machine and matching thread

iron

needle and tacking (basting) thread

knitting needle

PREPARATION

Enlarge the design from the back of the book and cut out two complete bag pieces in blue PVC for the lining and a wadding (batting) piece, adding a 1cm (½in) seam allowance. Cut out two of each patch shape in red and white PVC, adding 5mm (¼in) seam allowance. Cut a red and blue PVC base and a wadding base, adding a 1cm (½in) seam allowance. Cut two red handles 36cm x 10cm (14in x 4in).

1

Join patches, 1 and 3 to 2. Join 4 and 6 to 5. Join 7 and 9 to 8, and 10 and 12 to 11. Clip, and press the seams carefully under a piece of paper, using a cool iron. Join together to make two large squares, then join the squares together. Make two pieces the same. Clip and press the seams flat.

2

Place the two patched pieces and the red base on to the wadding (batting), and tack (baste) round the edges.

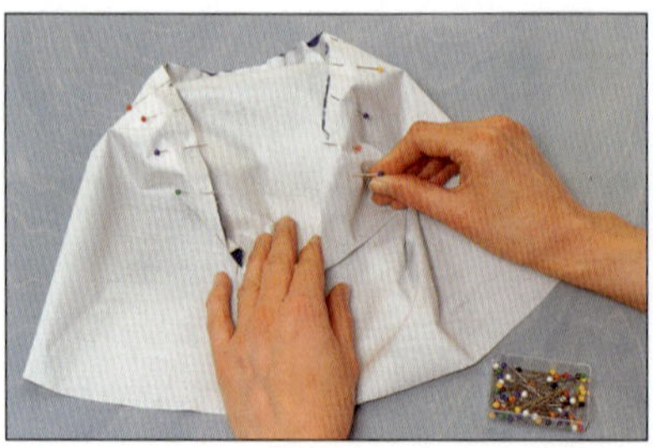

3

Make up the blue PVC lining.

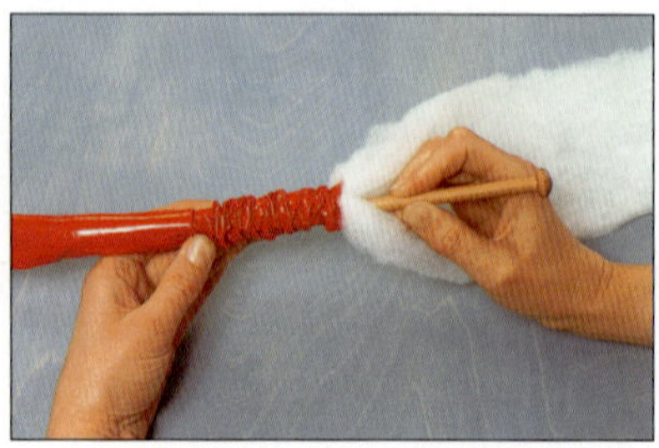

4

Stitch the red handle strips lengthways. Turn through and fill with wadding (batting), using a knitting needle. Pull through the wadding and trim off 2½cm (1in) at the ends.

TO FINISH

Stitch the side edges of the patched pieces to make a tube. Pin and stitch in the base. Trim and clip the seams. Pin the handles to the bag. Stitch the blue PVC lining to the top of the bag, securing the handles at the same time and leaving a 7.5cm (3in) gap. Pull the lining through and slip-stitch the gap. Press the bag under paper.

Hairslide (Barrette) p42

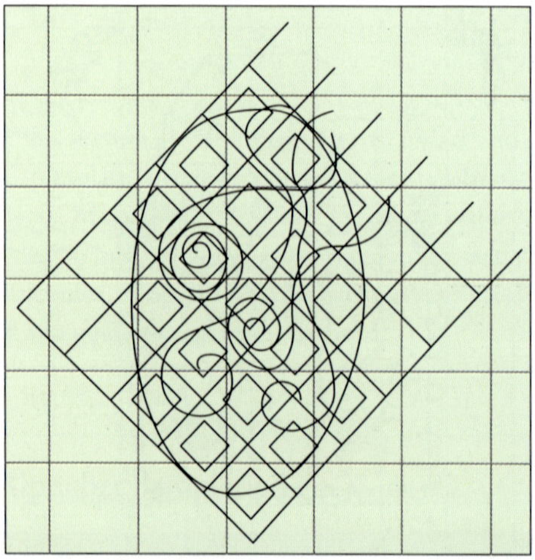

Embroidered Hat pp44–5

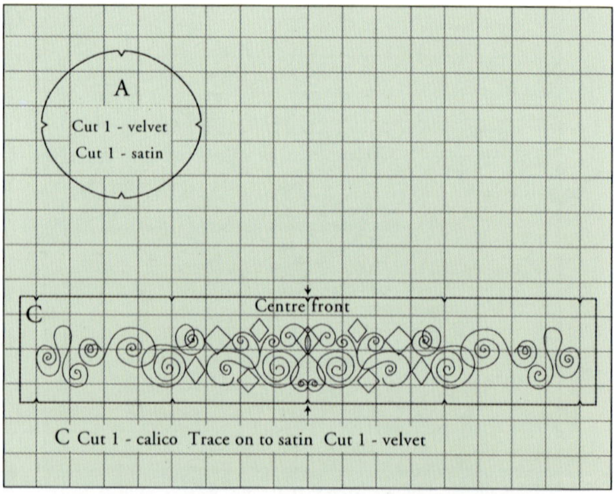

Picture Frame pp48–9

Drawstring Bag p43

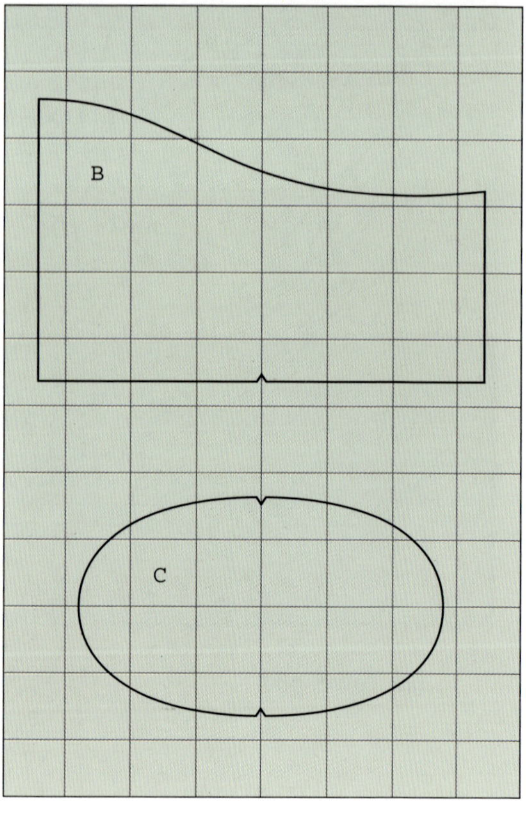

Embroidered Hat pp44–5 cont.

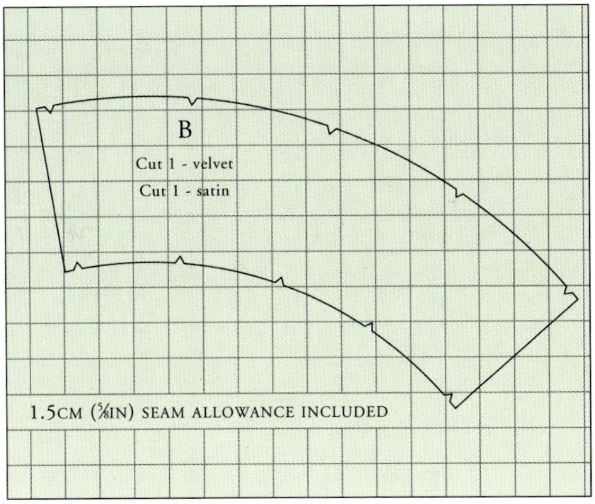

Placemat p46

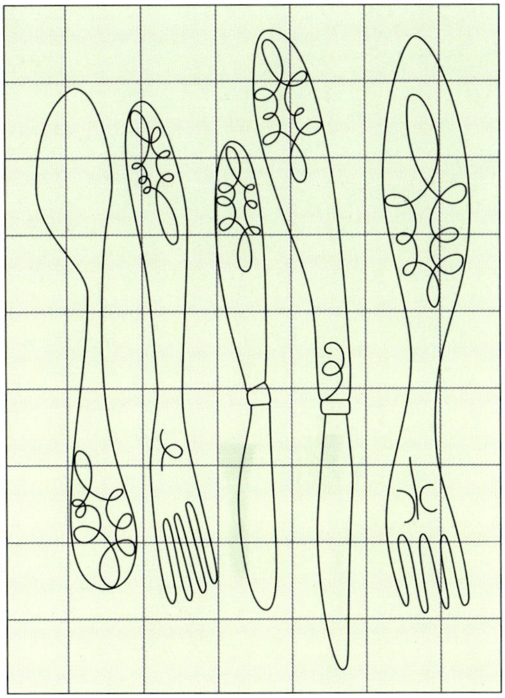

Drawstring Bag pp43 cont.

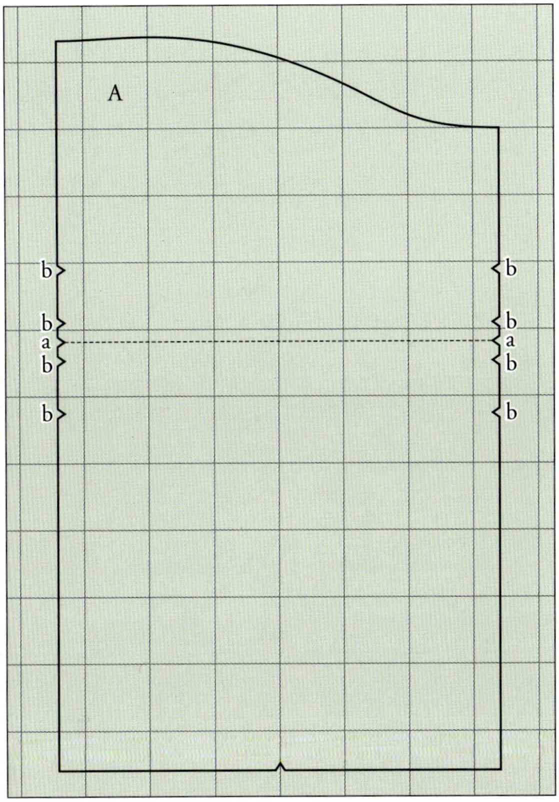

Cat Picture p47

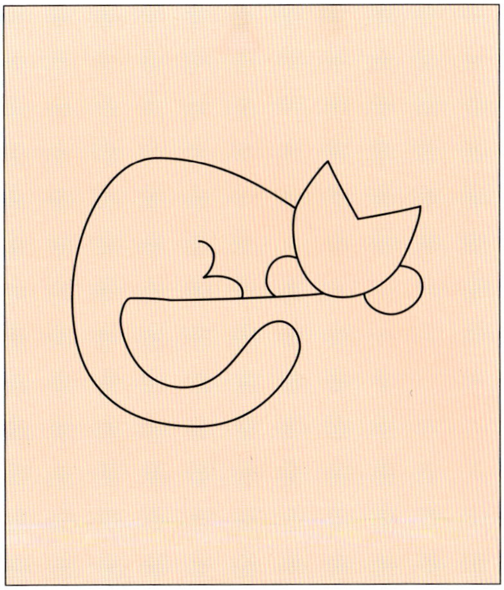

Fish Mobile pp50–1

Table Cloth pp52–3

Jewellery Box pp70–1

Lone-star Cushion (Pillow) p72

- Pale lilac
- Dark purple
- Indigo
- Light turquoise
- Crimson
- Dark turquoise
- Dark peach
- Orange
- Dark gold

Nine-star Cushion (Pillow) p73

- Pale lemon
- Light gold
- Pale pink
- Dark pink
- Dark gold
- Rust
- Burgundy
- Cream

Heart Picture p74

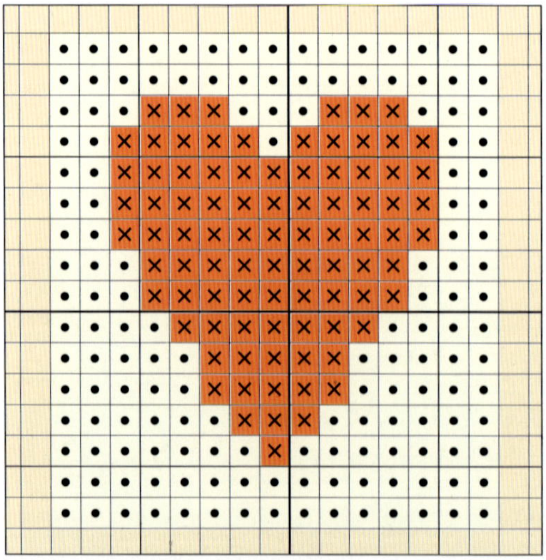

Circular Star p75

Cup and Saucer pp76

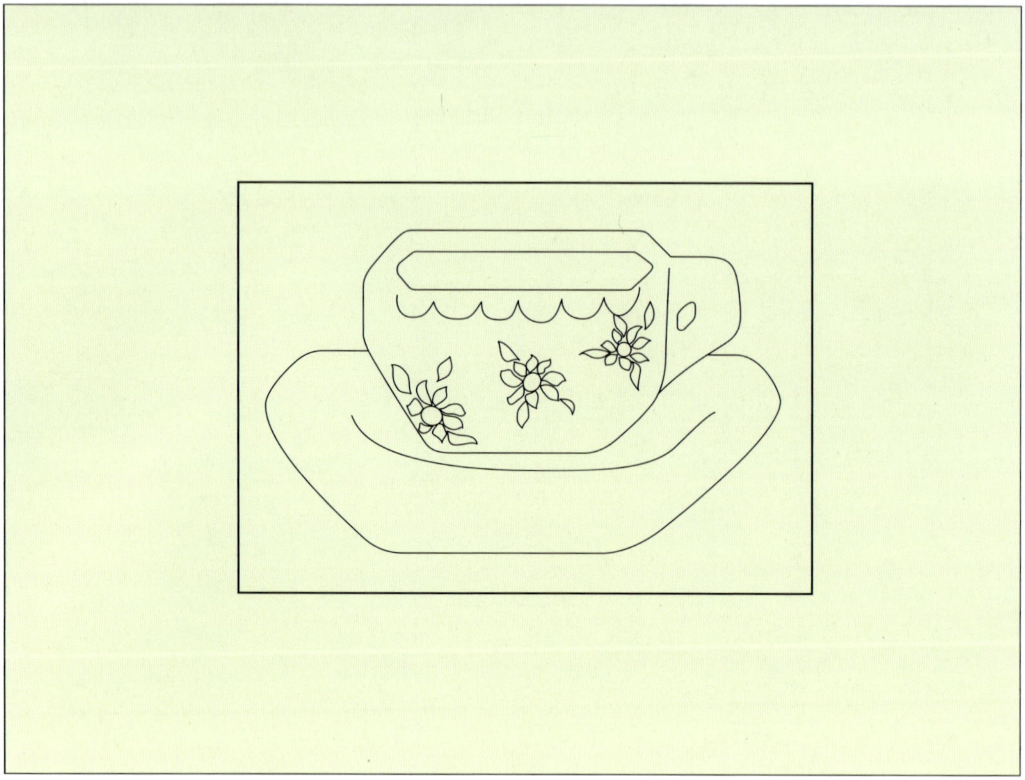

Sun Pincushion p77

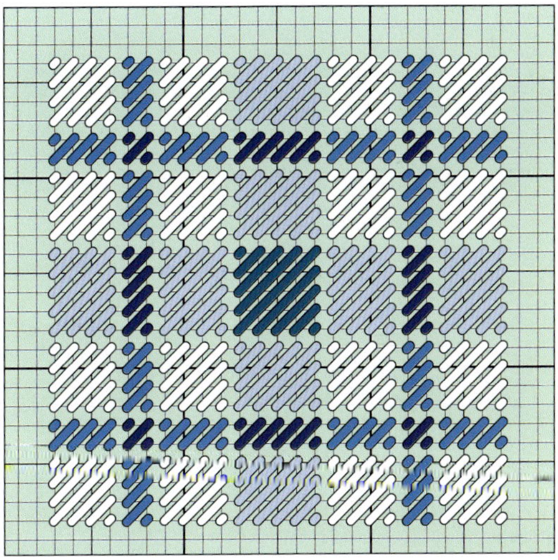

Brooch Cushion
(Pillow) pp78–9

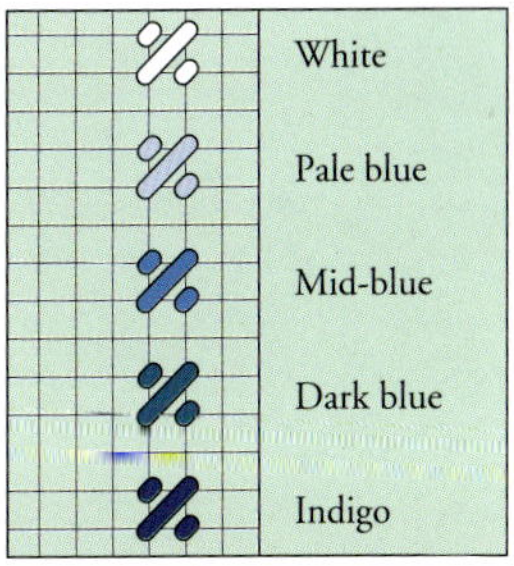

Needle Book pp80–1

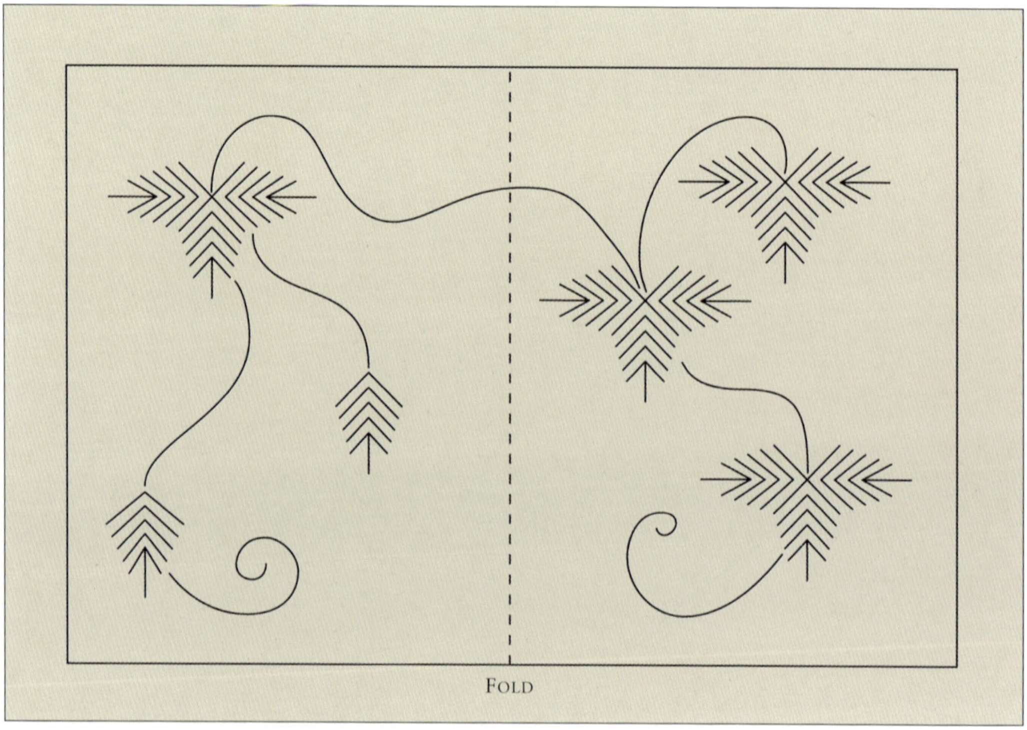

Scissor Case pp80–1

Baby Wrap pp104–5

×	Purple	△	Dark green	•	Beige	o	Turquoise	ı	Lilac

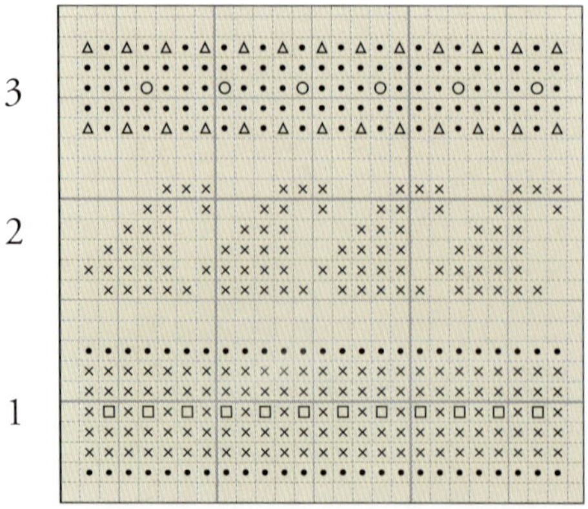

•	Light grey	×	Dark green
○	Cream	□	Brown
△	Beige		

Ski Hat p111

Purse Bag pp112–13

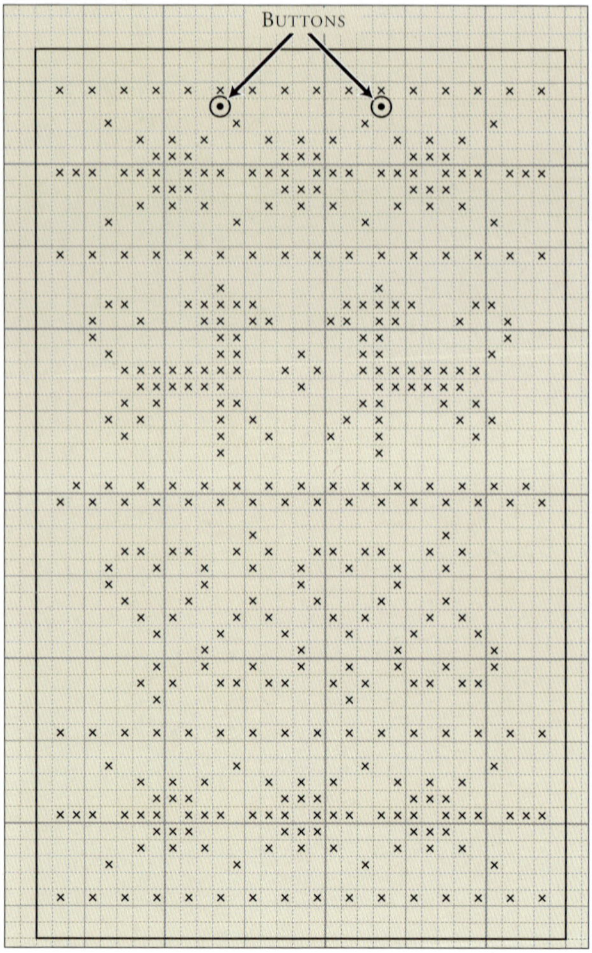

Alphabet Block pp192–3

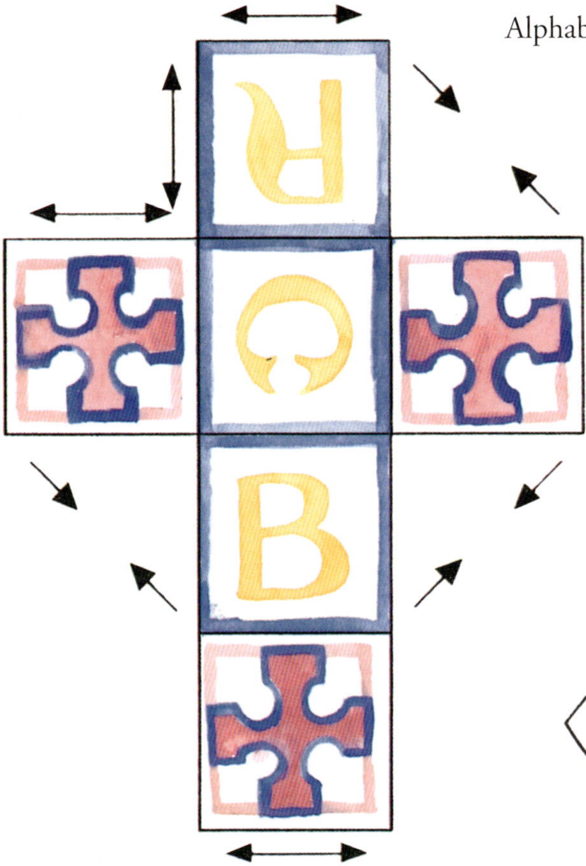

Blackwork Decorations pp212–13

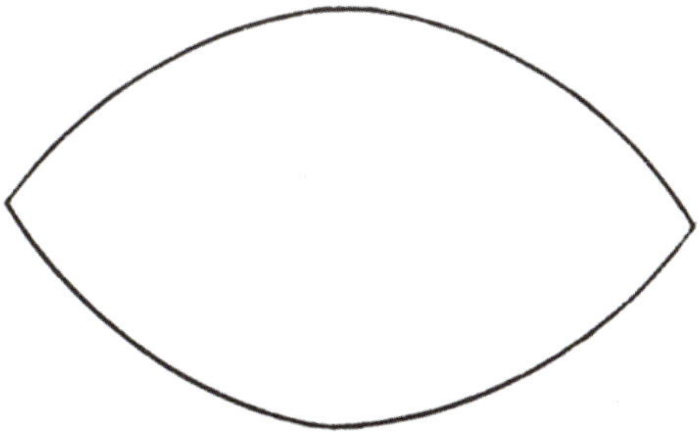

Nine-Star Picture p250

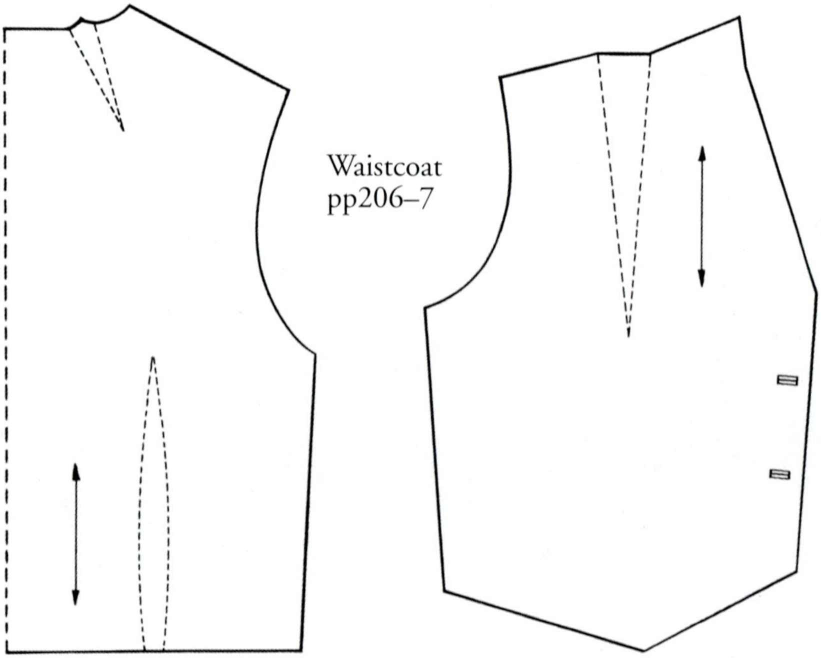

Waistcoat pp206–7

Tiebacks pp218–19

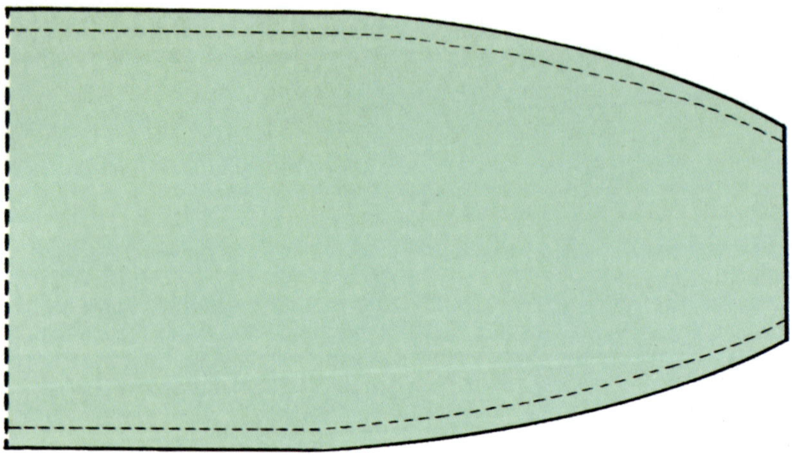

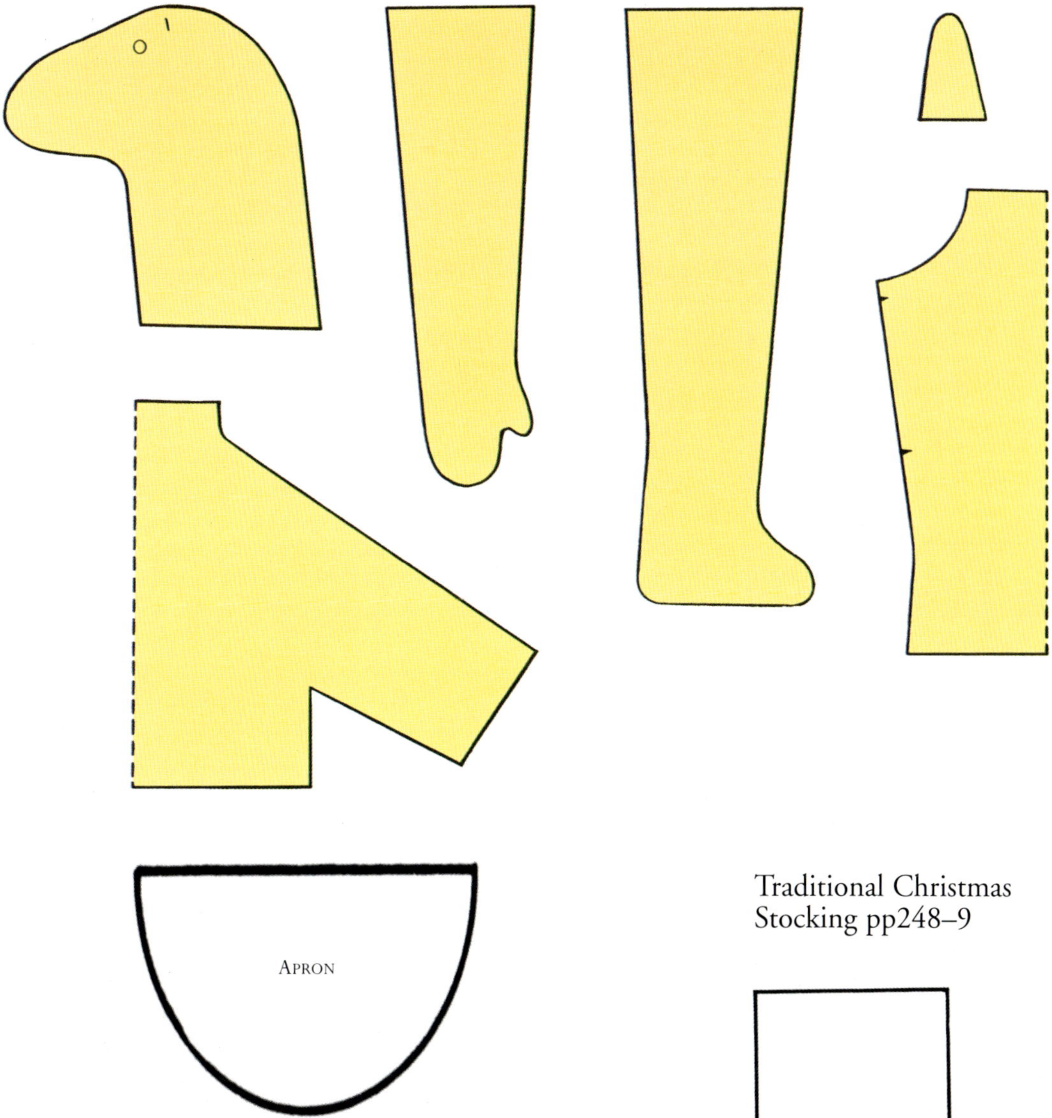

Party Horse pp264–5

Traditional Christmas Stocking pp248–9

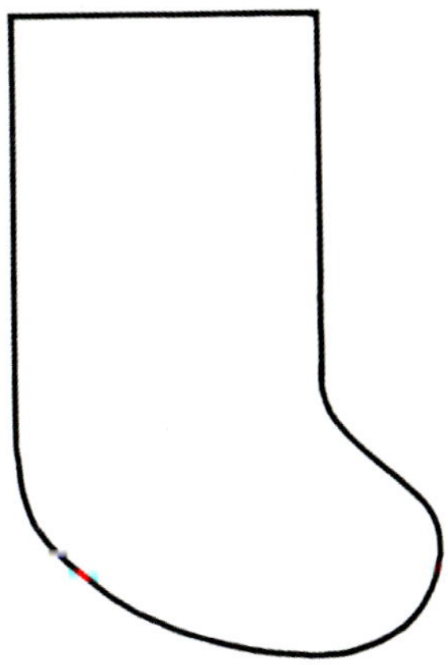

Embroidered Book pp290–1

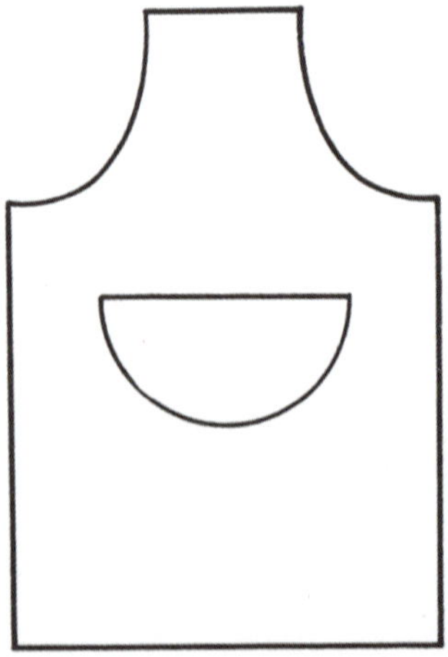

Garden Apron pp296–7

Child's Bag pp310–11

Child's Waistcoat p309

Nightdress Case pp358–9

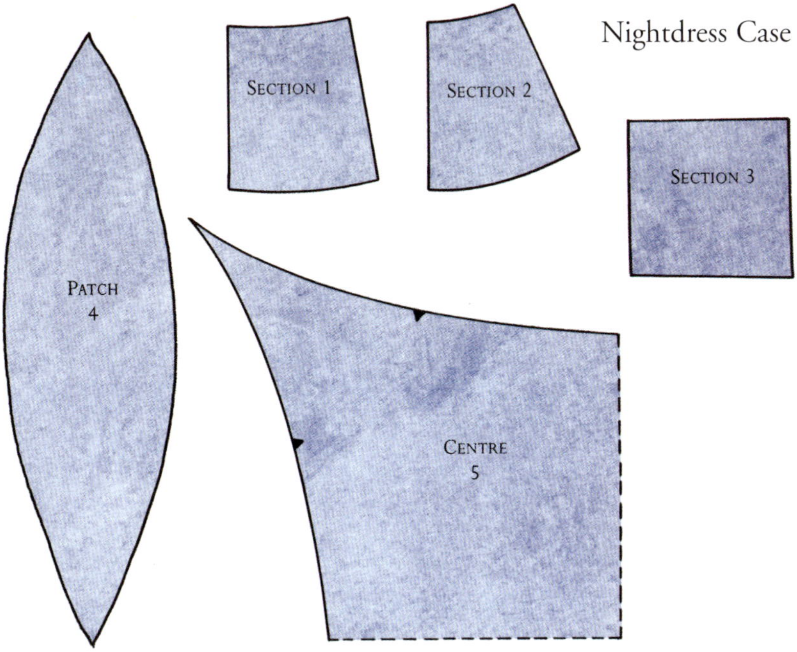

Medieval Quilt pp362–3

Medieval Quilt pp362–3 cont.

Quilted Hat pp368–9

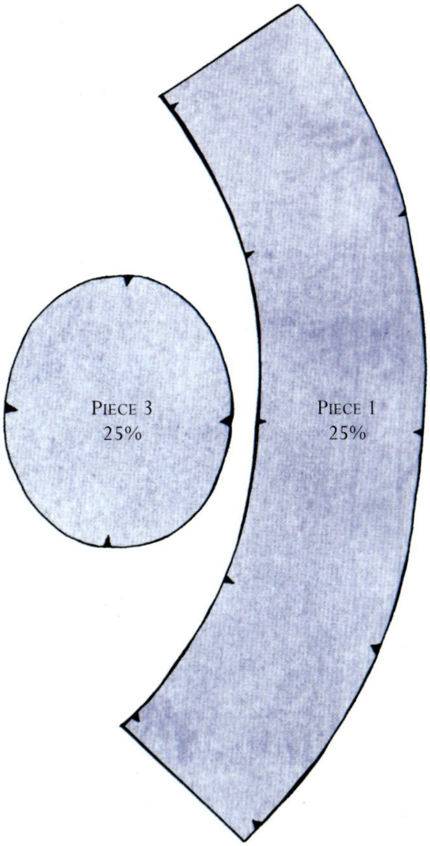

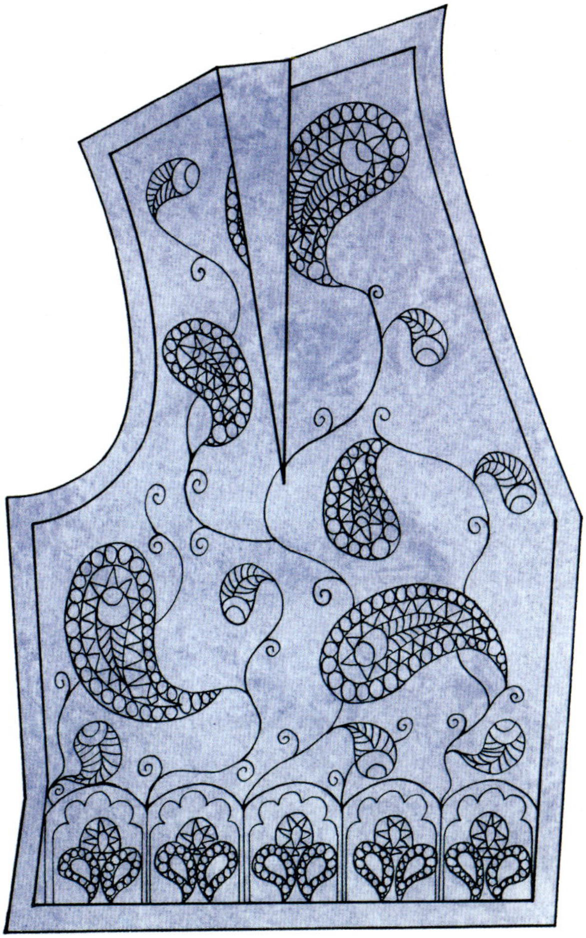

Quilted Waistcoat p364

Satin Handbag pp380–1

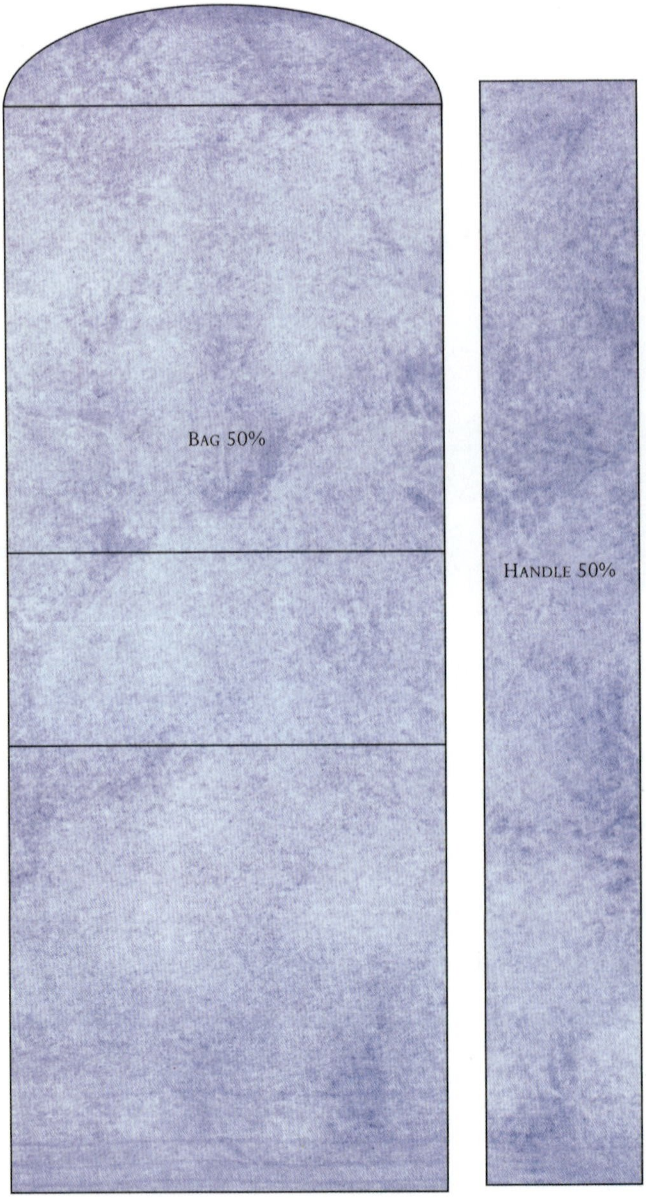

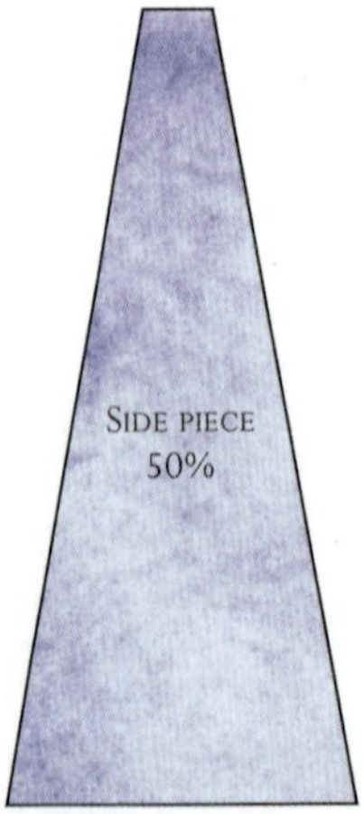

Quilted Hat pp368–9 cont.

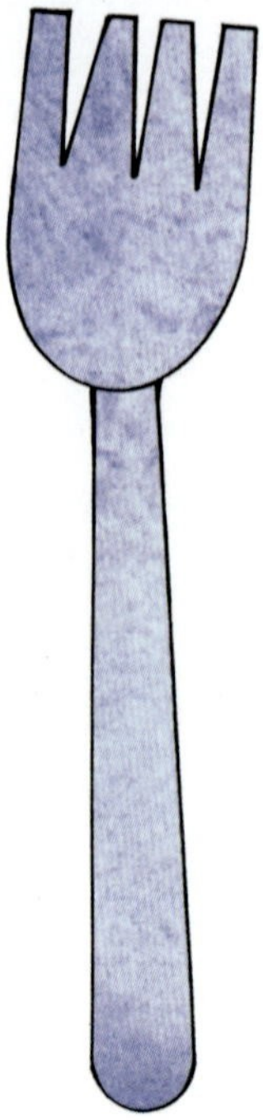

Broderie Perse Appliqué Napkins p375

Country Throw Motifs pp382–3

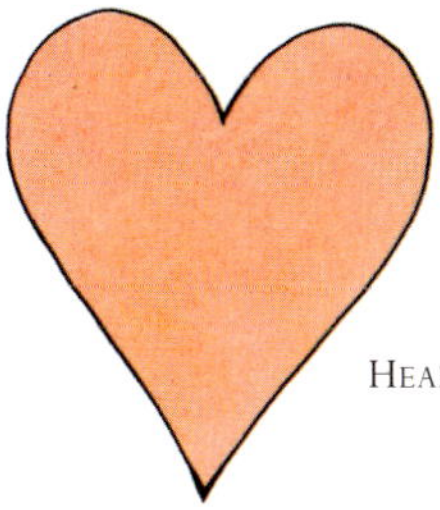

HEART

GRAPES

HAND

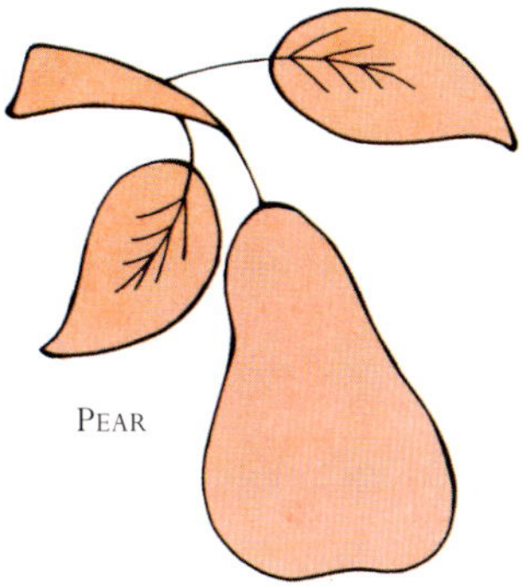

PEAR

BIRD 2

BIRD 1

FLOWER

STRAWBERRY

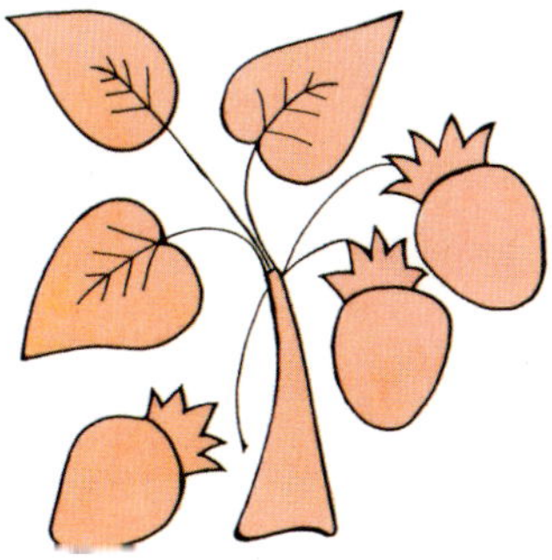

BIRD 3

Cherry Basket Patchwork Cushion p406

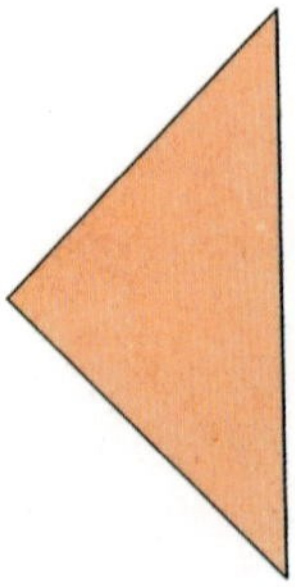

Crazy Patchwork Bootees pp408–9

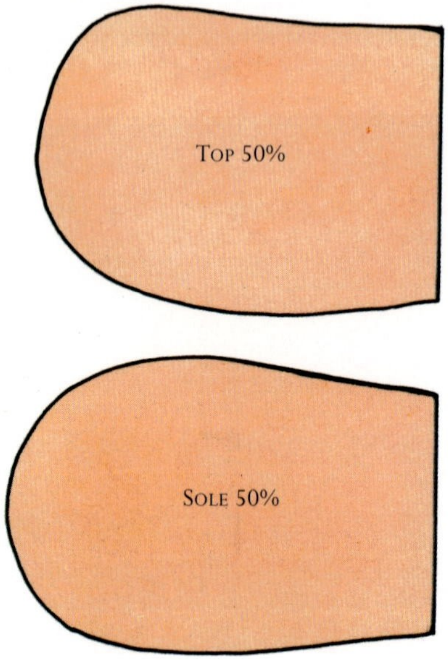

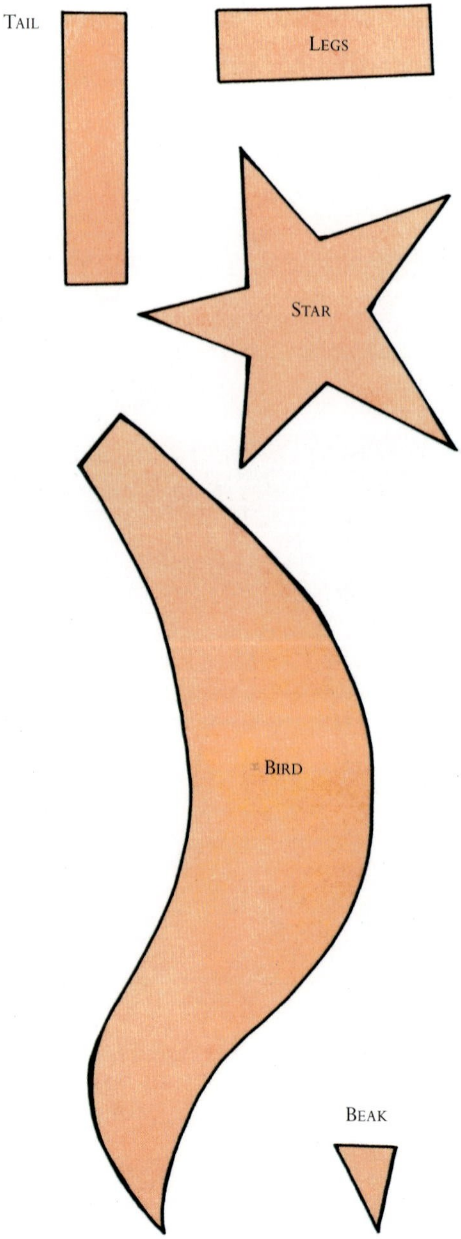

Baby's Appliqué Pillow p410

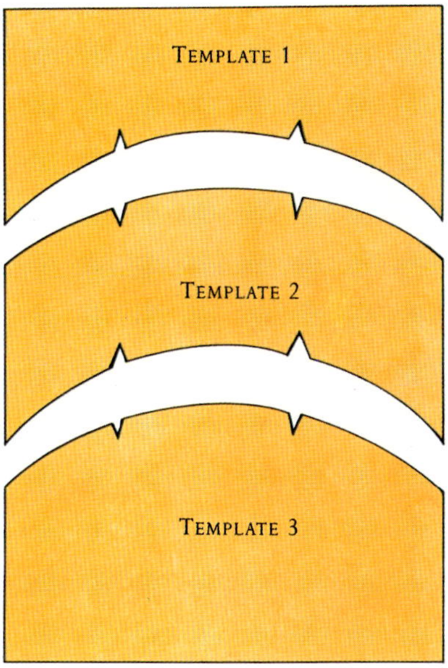

Patchwork Duffel Bag p412

San Blas Oven Mitts pp414–15

Baby's Appliquéd Cardigan pp436–7

Pa Ndau Appliqué Frame pp432–3

Hawaiian Appliqué Hanging pp440–1

Child's Patchwork Sweater p438

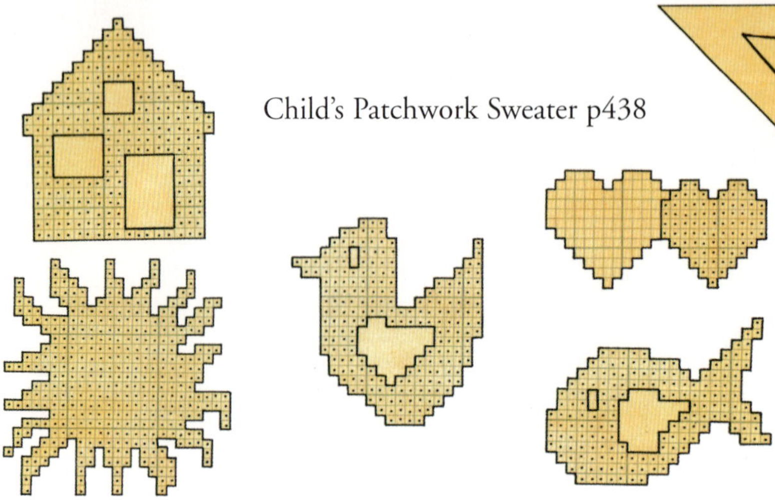

Peg Bag pp442–3

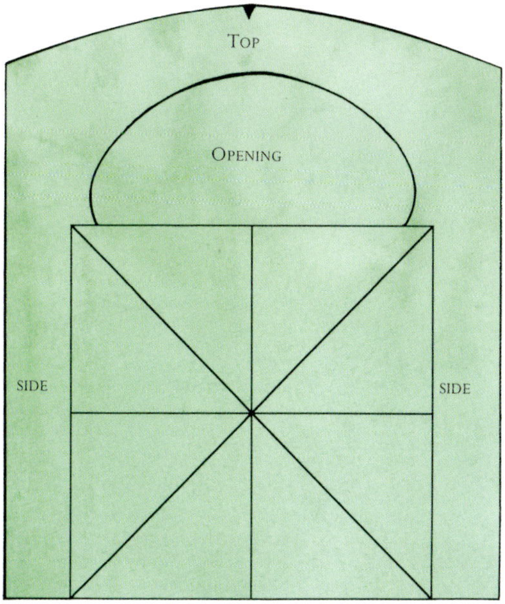

Beach Bag p448

FISH MOTIFS

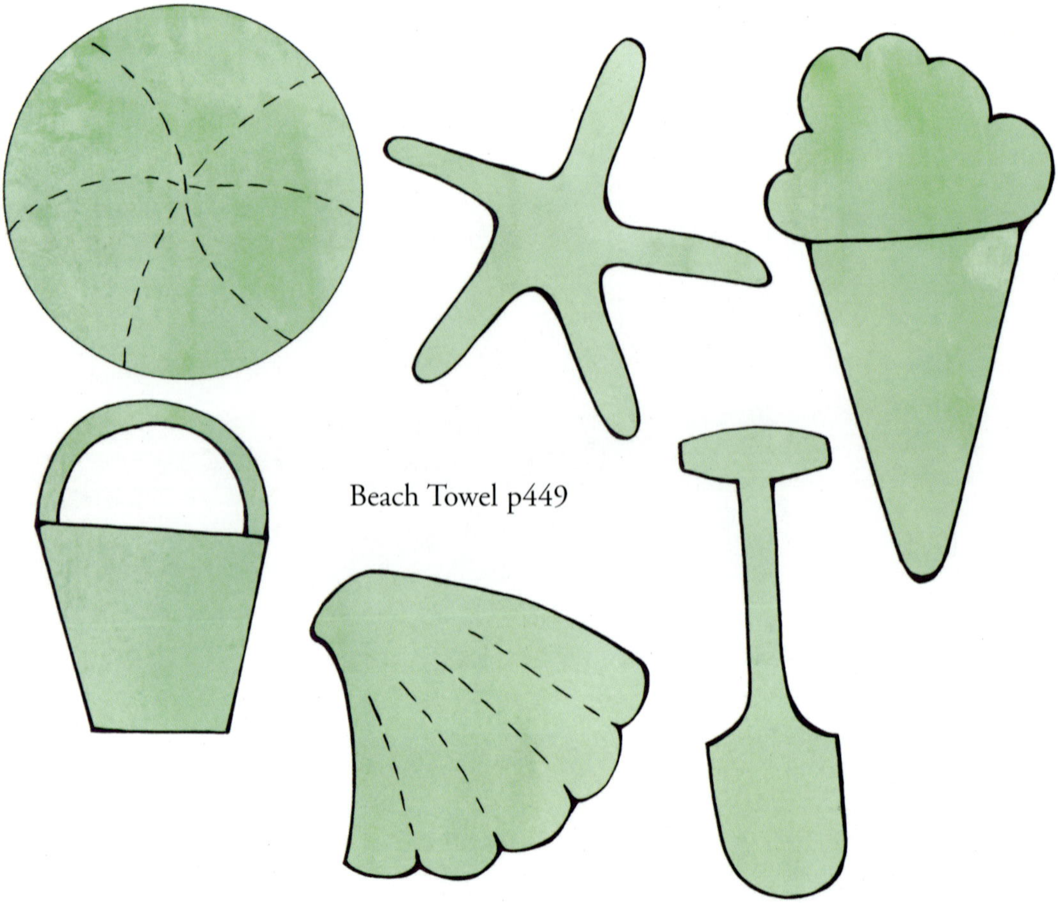

Beach Towel p449

1950s Bistro Placemat pp454–5

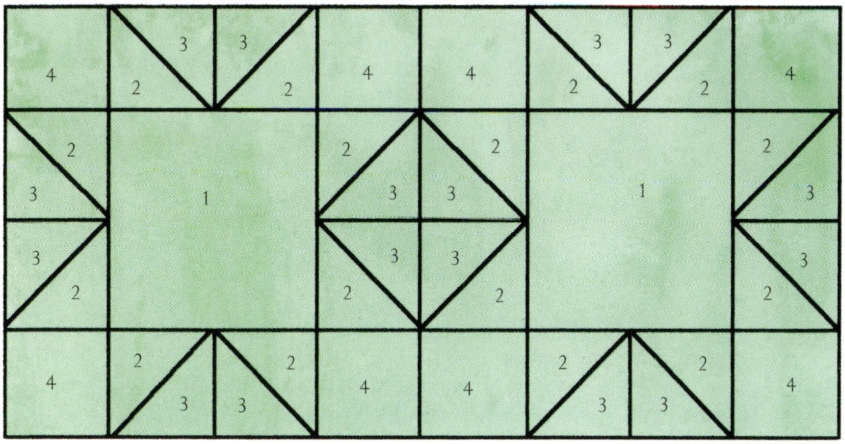

Diamond-in-a-square Satin Purse p461

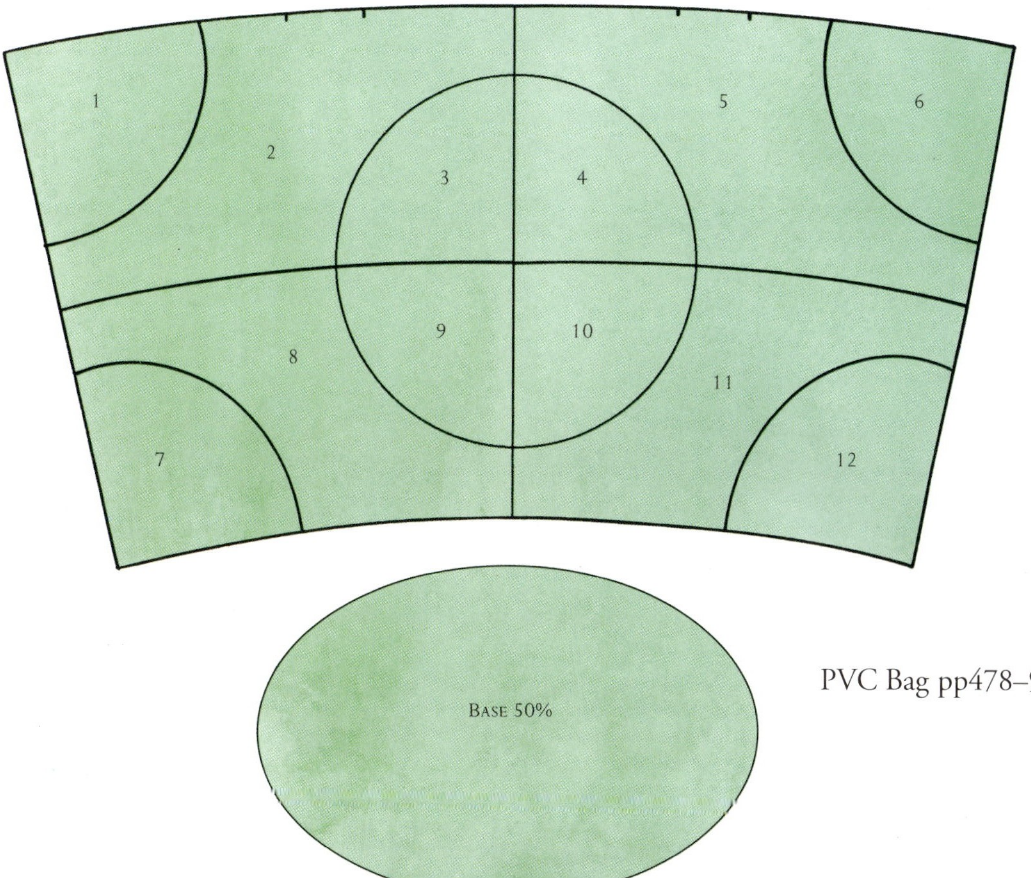

PVC Bag pp478–9

INDEX

SUPPLIERS

UNITED KINGDOM

Appleton Brothers
Thames Works
Church Street
London W4 2PE
Tel: 020 8994 0711
Tapestry and crewel yarns

Artisan Needlecrafts
Battlers Green Farm
Common Lane
Radlett
Hertfordshire WD7 8PH
Tel: 01923 853327
Easy grids and fabrics

C.M. Offrey & Son Ltd
Fir Tree Place
Church Road
Ashford
Middlesex TW15 2PH
Tel: 01784 247281
Ribbon

D.M.C. Creative World
Pullman Road
Wigston
Leicestershire LE18 2DY
Tel: 0116 2811040
Embroidery threads, fabrics, bands and canvas

Freudenberg Nonwovens LP
Vilene Retail
P.O. Box 3
Greetland
Halifax HX4 8NJ
Tel: 01422 313140
Quilting, fusible bonding and interfacing

Shaker
25 Harcourt Street
London W1H 1DT
Tel: 020 7724 7672
American homespun cloth

Strawberry Fayre Fabrics
Chagford
Devon TQ13 8EN
Tel: 01647 433250
Patchwork fabrics

The Craft Collection
Terry Mills
Westfield Road
Horley
Wakefield
West Yorkshire WF4 6HD
Tel: 01924 810812
Paterna Persian yarn

UNITED STATES

Aardvark Adventures
P.O. Box 2449
Livermore
CA 94551
Tel: (800) 388 2687
Fabrics, threads and trims

Bettekaril's Needlecrafts
P.O. Box 5008
Brandon
MS 39047
Tel: 601 992 3266
Cross stitch, crochet and knitting

Heartlands Crafts Discounters
Rte 6E, P.O. Box 65
Geneseo
IL 61254
Tel: (309) 944 6411
Threads, yarns and tools

Herrschers
Hoover Road
Stevens Point
WI 54481
Tel: (800) 441 0838
General tools and materials

Nancy's Notions
P.O. Box 683
Dept 32
Beaver Dam
WI 53916
Tel: (414) 887 0391
Sewing, quilting, beadwork, appliqué and embroidery

Yarnworks
519 Main Street
Grand Junction
CO 81501
Tel: (303) 243 5365
Knitting, crochet and dyeing

AUSTRALIA

Bargello
819 Glenferrie Road
Hawthorn
Vic 3122
Tel: (03) 9818 4853

Coats Patons Crafts Pty Ltd
89–91 Peters Avenue
Mulgrave
Vic 3170
Tel: (1800) 801 195

Craft Ideas
Shop 2065
Westfield Shopping Town
Indoorpilly
Queensland 4068
Tel: (07) 3378 4288

D.M.C. Needlecraft Pty Ltd
51–55 Carrington Road
Marrickville
NSW 2204
Tel: (02) 559 3088

Simply Stitches
153 Victoria Avenue
Chatswood
NSW 2067
Tel: (02) 412 4342